Evidence and Its Legal Aspects

Joseph D. Schloss
Golden West College

Charles E. Merrill Publishing Company
A Bell & Howell Company
Columbus, Ohio

This book is dedicated to my loving wife, Leah Rae. Without her support over the years I would not be where I am today, and this book would never have gotten off the dusty shelves of my mind. I also wish to thank my children, David, Danny, Dennis, and Jodi, for leaving Daddy alone when the "Restricted" sign was hanging on his typing room door.

KF
8934
.S34

Published by
Charles E. Merrill Publishing Company
A Bell & Howell Company
Columbus, Ohio 43216

139130

This book was set in Times Roman.
The Production Editor was Linda Johnstone.
The cover was designed by Will Chenoweth.

Copyright ©, 1976 by Bell & Howell Company. All rights reserved. No part of this book may be reproduced in any form, electronic or mechanical, including photocopy, recording, or any information storage and retrieval system, without permission in writing from the publisher.

International Standard Book Number: 0-675-08659-0
Library of Congress Catalog Card Number: 75-18432
1 2 3 4 5 6 7 8 9 10—83 82 81 80 79 78 77 76

Printed in the United States of America

PREFACE

The field of law enforcement has changed so rapidly in the past few years that police officers are finding it increasingly difficult to maintain the knowledge required of them as "squad-car lawyers." However, the officer who ventures into the field each day without the proper equipment and knowledge is only hampering his own effectiveness. Part of this necessary arsenal is knowledge of law and evidence, and it is this area upon which this book focuses.

In searching for a text for my own classes, I have found that some texts are too basic and yet not easily understandable for the law enforcement student/officer. Others, written in legal fashion, are also inappropriate. Therefore, in this book I have adapted material from the law student level to that of the law enforcement student/officer and have inserted many examples which should make the material easily comprehensible.

The field of evidence has changed so much in a short period of time that it has been extremely difficult for even teachers to stay abreast of the subject matter. I have therefore incorporated in this book all of the general rules being utilized throughout the United States and have included the new Federal Rules of Evidence, which went into effect on July 1, 1975.

If the instructor will utilize this text as it is intended—as a valuable aid to the classroom lecture—and couple the cases in each chapter into lecture material, this text can be an effective tool for the law enforcement student/officer.

PREFACE

There are nine chapters in this book dealing with the major rules of evidence with which the officer will be confronted. The student/officer is taught the basic rules for defining evidence so that he may properly perform his mission all the way to the rules for admitting or excluding it in court. Each of the chapters contains the new Federal Rules of Evidence, which are not included in any other text on this subject matter at this time. The chapters on search and seizure are explained to the student in a manner that anyone can understand, and important citations are given to the officer/student who has a need to do further research.

Included in the text are numerous examples dealing with each important concept. At the end of each chapter are found discussion questions to be used by the instructor in testing the knowledge of the student/officer. In addition, important cases which illustrate the rules learned in the chapter have been inserted at the end of the chapters for those instructors who have found the joy of teaching by the case method. I also hope that instructors using this book will insure that the student/officer master the terms contained in the glossary. This I see as another step toward total professionalization of the police officer.

I wish to thank Police Science Associates of Costa Mesa, California, for allowing me to use excerpts from my book on arrest, search, and seizure. This all-important section would not have been complete without their permission and help in compiling this material. I also wish to express my appreciation to the following for their helpful comments and criticisms: Glenn Clark, Chairman of Law Enforcement Technology, Columbus Technical Institute, Columbus, Ohio; Frederick P. Deutsch, Chairman of the Criminal Justice Department, Miramar Community College, San Diego, California; Robert B. Koverman, Director of Police, Englewood Police Department, Englewood, Ohio; and Henry Louwerens, Director of Law Enforcement Programs, Jackson Community College, Jackson, Michigan.

NOTE TO THE STUDENT

Each chapter of this book contains many examples of the various rules of evidence. The student should read the rules and the examples given and then write one or two additional examples based on his own understanding of the comparable rules being followed in the jurisdiction where he resides or works.

At the end of chapters the student will find sample cases. These cases have been selected to illustrate some of the key concepts covered in the chapters. The student should brief each case. A brief begins with the title of the case (e.g., Mapp v. Ohio) and the citation (367 U.S. 643). Next should come the FACTS; i.e., after reading the case the student should condense the important facts into one or two short paragraphs which cover the major points of law. The next portion of the brief should be the ISSUE. The issue is a question that the appeals court is being asked concerning a point of law. *Example:* Was the item of evidence seized relevant? The student must remember to state the issue in the form of a question concerning the law. After the issue has been clearly stated, the student should then write a CONCLUSION. After the student has read the ruling of the trial court on the point of law and the comments of the appellate court about the question, the student should come to his own conclusions about the rule of evidence and how it should be applied and write an answer to the question that he asked in the issue. An example of a brief follows.

NOTE TO THE STUDENT

CHIMEL v. CALIFORNIA
396 U.S. 752

FACTS: Law enforcement officers obtained a warrant of arrest for Mr. Chimel. They went to his home and found that he wasn't there, so they waited outside for Mr. Chimel to return. When he did, they entered the home and effected an arrest. They then made a search of the entire home for evidence of the burglary.

ISSUE: May police officers conduct a search of the entire premises on which an arrest was made?

CONCLUSION: The right of a police officer to conduct a search without a search warrant is limited. Normally, the officer is limited to making a search of the immediate area around the person arrested. This is more frequently referred to as a search within an arm's reach of the suspect. The officer is permitted to search into drawers or under items that are within the arm's reach of the suspect for the purpose of seeking out weapons that may be used against him or to aid the suspect in escaping or to search for items of evidence that the suspect may attempt to destroy.

CONTENTS

1 Nature and Kinds of Evidence — 1
  Definitions of Evidence   1
  Forms of Evidence   3
  Types of Evidence   4
  DISCUSSION QUESTIONS   6

2 Burden of Proof and Effect of Evidence — 7
  Burden of Proof   7
  Inferences   9
  Presumptions   9
  Summary   11
  DISCUSSION QUESTIONS   11
  CASES   12

3 Admission and Exclusion of Evidence — 43
  Ruling on Admissibility   43
  Timely Objection   44
  Specific Objection   44
  The General Objection   44
  Most Commonly Used Objections   45
  Valid Grounds for an Objection   46
  Prejudicial Error of a Judge in Overruling an
    Objection   46

Introduction of Evidence 47
Summary 48
DISCUSSION QUESTIONS 48
CASES 48

4 Relevancy 53
Materiality 54
Real Evidence 56
Scientific Tests or Experiments 59
Summary 61
DISCUSSION QUESTIONS 62
CASES 62

5 Witnesses 95
The Opinion Rule 96
Lay Person's Opinion 97
Expert Opinion 99
Form of Examination of Witnesses 101
Direct Examination 101
Cross-examination 102
Redirect Examination 104
Recross-examination 104
Questioning by the Judge 104
Impeachment and Rehabilitation of Witnesses 105
Privileges 109
Confessions 116
Admissibility of Confessions 117
Requirements of Miranda v. Arizona
Adequacy of Miranda Warnings 127
Waiver of Miranda Rights 128
Invocation of Miranda Rights 128
Use of Statements Taken in Violation of Miranda Rules 130
Recording of Statements 130
Confession Implicating Codefendant 132
Summary 132
DISCUSSION QUESTIONS 133
CASES 133

6 Search and Seizure 168
Search and/or Seizure with a Search Warrant 187
Search and/or Seizure Incident to Lawful Arrest 192
Search and/or Seizure with Consent 197
Search and/or Seizure in an Emergency 201
Summary 202
DISCUSSION QUESTIONS 202

CONTENTS

Searches   206
Seizure of Property   207
Arrest-Seizure of a Person   207
Factors of Probable Cause   208
Evaluating Evidence of Probable Cause   210
Sources of Probable Cause   210
Reasonableness of Search and/or Seizure   212
Stop-and-Frisk   221
Summary   224
Search Warrants   224
Lineups   235
Field Showups   241
Photographic Identification   242
CASES   245

7 Documentary Evidence   273

The Best Evidence Rule   273
The Parol Evidence Rule   275
Authentication of Official Records   275
Authentication of Private Writings   275
Summary   276
DISCUSSION QUESTIONS   277
CASES   277

8 Judicial Notice   281

Mandatory Judicial Notice   281
Optional Judicial Notice   283
Summary   285
DISCUSSION QUESTIONS   285
CASES   285

9 The Hearsay Rule and Its Exceptions   291

The General Hearsay Rule   291
Admission of Coconspirator Exception   295
Confession Exception   295
Dying Declaration Exception   296
Reported Testimony Exception   297
Official Records Exception   298
Past Recollection Exception   300
Res Gestae Exception   300
Family History Exception   303
Ancient Document Exception   304
Learned Treatise Exception   304
Affidavit Exception   304
Deposition Exception   304
Summary   305
DISCUSSION QUESTIONS   305
CASES   306

1

Nature and Kinds of Evidence

Over the years, there has been much confusion due to the legal jargon used by district attorneys and defense attorneys to categorize evidence into a specific type of evidence. This procedure should not be confusing if the student will remember that in a state having a restricted definition of evidence there are four broad headings defining evidence, four forms of evidence, and four types of evidence. Furthermore, the student should remember that in order for evidence to be admissible in court it must first fall within the definition in his state as evidence, that prior to its being admitted in court it must generally take one of the four forms, and that during the actual introduction into evidence at the trial it must take one of the four types.

Definitions of Evidence

Evidence has been given many definitions over the years for the police officer who has been in a quandry as to what it really is. In its simplest terms, evidence is nothing more than the means by which any fact under investigation may be either established or disproved. It is the material from which inferences may be drawn that serves as the basis of proof of either the truth or falsity of any fact that will be in issue in any case. Evidence also includes anything offered at the time of trial. It does not make any difference whether or not it is admissible (meaning, it shall be allowed into evidence). Therefore, evidence would include testimony given in the form of an opinion which is not admissible, or "hearsay" which is being testified to and which is barred by the Hearsay Rule.

Many states have now adopted the Uniform Rules of Evidence or have adopted their own evidence code. Under the definitions in these codes, the term *evidence* is more restrictive. *Example:* Under one state's evidence code, "evidence means testimony, writings, material objects, or other things presented to the senses that are offered to prove the existence or nonexistence of the fact." This definition clearly shows that presumptions and judicial notice are not evidence. However, as we shall see in later chapters, the state that adopted this very narrow interpretation of evidence utilizes presumptions and judicial notice as substitutes for evidence.

Testimony

In a state which has a narrow interpretation of evidence, the testimony which is being referred to as evidence includes only that testimony which is being given in front of a judicial body. The witness testifying has taken an oath, or affirmation to tell the truth. It is further required in most jurisdictions that the testimony be recorded and that the opportunity to cross-examine is afforded to the opposing party. This interpretation also includes testimony taken as a deposition, which is written testimony taken before a certified court reporter upon orders from the court. An oath is administered to the witness, and both attorneys and both parties are generally present.

Writings

Writings, as defined by the states using the restricted definition of evidence, include anything that has been reduced to a writing, as well as anything which has an image impregnated into it, either visual, or electronic, such as tape recordings, videotapes, motion pictures, photographs, computer printout sheets, and so forth. The student should be cautioned at this point not to be mislead by the Best Evidence Rule, which states that only the original document may be used in court. The Best Evidence Rule, as discussed in the chapter on documentary evidence (Chapter 7), applies to writings, and not to any other form of evidence. The student should have a clear knowledge of the Best Evidence Rule and remember that it only applies to documentary types of evidence, which in the states that have this very restricted definition of evidence would include anything defined as a writing.

Material Objects

Material objects are those things that a person can readily see and which have some evidentiary value, such as a bullet, knife, gun, billy club, blackjack, and other tangible devices.

Things Presented to the Senses

Things presented to the senses in the states following the restricted definition of evidence include anything presented to any of the senses (sight, sound, smell, taste, touch). *Example:* A police officer who is walking by a doorway smells something emanating from within, which in the officer's expert opinion is the odor of burning marijuana. The officer may now go to court and testify as to his senses as it is defined as evidence. The most common example is the officer who is on patrol and observes a crime being committed.

Forms of Evidence

The four forms of evidence are: (1) real evidence; (2) documentary evidence; (3) testimonial evidence; and (4) judicial notice.

Real Evidence

Real evidence generally consists of those items defined as material objects in our definition, including, but not limited to, bullets, knives, guns, jewelry, and television sets. These are tangible objects that are presented to the jury (trier of fact) for inspection. Most writers refer to real evidence as evidence of a type that "speaks for itself." Generally, real evidence is the most trustworthy of all of the types of evidence. Accordingly, under the rules of the majority of the states, the admissibility of real evidence is favored.

Even though real evidence is said to "speak for itself," the object or thing that is being shown or introduced for the jury to view will probably be of no value unless it is identified. The identification generally will have to be made by testimonial evidence. *Example:* A gun introduced into evidence will have relatively little value unless testimony is given to the fact, for example, that this was the one taken from the defendant's hand at the time of the shooting.

There are also many types of real evidence which will require the testimony of an expert witness in order for the jury to comprehend fully the value of the evidence in a particular case. *Example:* An expert's opinion will usually be needed to aid the jury in determining whether a bullet taken from the body of the deceased was fired from the gun that was found on the defendant's person at the time of his arrest. Specific problems dealing with the admissibility of real evidence will be discussed later in the chapter on admission and exclusion of evidence (Chapter 3).

Documentary Evidence

Documentary evidence is actually real evidence, but consists of writings rather than tangible objects. The writing is said to "speak for itself," especially as to the contents thereof. Also, as in the case of real evidence, even though the writing "speaks for itself" as to the contents, testimonial evidence will usually be required in order to properly authenticate the document. To properly authenticate a document, testimony is generally required so that the jury can properly determine if, in fact, it is the document in question and is what it purports to be.

There are numerous problems (including authentication and hearsay problems) involved in the admissibility of a document into evidence in a trial. At this point, the student must understand that a document is an item of real evidence and consists of a writing rather than a tangible object, such as a contract or a transcript from a trial, a ticket issued by a law enforcement officer, or a police report. If a document is not barred by another rule of evidence and is properly authenticated, it generally will be admissible into a trial.

Testimonial Evidence

Again referring to our definition of evidence, testimonial evidence is any oral testimony given in court by a witness or taken by deposition. This testimony may be found to be factual, or it may be opinion testimony. Under this form of evidence, there must be: (1) an oath; (2) a reporting or recording; (3) direct examination; and (4) the opportunity to cross-examine before a judicial body or quasi-judicial body authorized to receive testimony. Problems involving the admissibility of testimonial evidence will be discussed in chapters on hearsay (Chapter 9), witnesses (Chapter 5), and privileges (Chapter 5).

Judicial Notice

Judicial notice is a substitute for evidence and is the fourth form of evidence in most jurisdictions. The trial judge (trier of law) is entitled to take judicial notice of certain facts as a matter of his own knowledge, and in certain cases is required to take judicial notice of certain facts without the introduction of any evidence in the courtroom concerning the matters. *Example:* The judge may note that the abbreviation H_2O denotes water or that A.M. denotes morning hours, and P.M. evening hours.

There is considerable disagreement among the various jurisdictions as to whether matters judicially noticed are evidence at all. The majority view today is that if the court takes judicial notice of a matter it precludes any contrary evidence from being introduced. So, judicial notice amounts to a substitute for evidence on the fact noted. For further discussion, refer to the chapter on judicial notice (Chapter 8).

Types of Evidence

The four types of evidence are: (1) direct; (2) circumstantial; (3) cumulative; and (4) corroborative.

Direct Evidence

Direct evidence proves a fact in issue directly. That is to say, without any inferences or presumptions arising, direct evidence proves a point in and of itself. The jury is then presented with the evidence from which to make a determination of whether or not the evidence is, in fact, true. *Example:* In a robbery case, a witness testifies, "I saw the defendant rob the victim at the liquor store." This testimony establishes the fact that this witness claims to have seen the defendant robbing the victim, but is contingent upon whether or not the jury believes the witness' testimony.

Circumstantial Evidence

Circumstantial evidence is that evidence which only proves a fact indirectly. The jury must deduct using logical reasoning from the item that has been introduced, which is an inference as to what it is to prove. The jury is required to weigh all probability of matters other than just whether or not the witness is telling the truth. *Example:* A police officer on patrol at 1:00 A.M., driving by a liquor store, observes the defendant with his hand in his coat pocket, simulating a gun, and a clerk handing him a bag. Then, the defendant is seen by the officer to run from the liquor store and down the street, where he is apprehended by the officer. It is only circumstantial in nature that this particular person was seen holding his hand in his pocket simulating a gun. A reasonable inference must be drawn from this when it is presented to the jury as to whether or not (1) the defendant was in fact simulating a gun and robbing the defendant and (2) to a reasonable man the officer was correct in apprehending the person running down the street. It is also circumstantial in nature that he was then seen running down the street. The jury will have to draw an inference from his flight as to whether or not he was running from the scene of the crime or running for some other purpose.

Another example of circumstantial evidence was found a few years ago in a murder trial conducted in California. In this trial, even though neither the body nor any parts of it were ever found, the defendant was convicted of murder solely on circumstantial evidence. At the trial, evidence was introduced that the defendant had lied to many people about the whereabouts of his wife, and upon investigation, all of these stories were found to be false. It was further found that he had forged her signature and depleted her bank accounts. In addition, a partial dental plate was found in an incinerator and a pair of broken glasses was found on the floor near the incinerator. From these and other items of circumstantial evidence that were introduced, a reasonable man could draw an inference from the cumulative effect that, in fact, the victim might have been killed by the suspect. Not one of these circumstantial factors in and of itself would prove or disprove anything, but from the additive effect, reasonable inference could be deducted by the jury, thus substantiating the murder conviction.

Cumulative Evidence

Cumulative evidence is evidence which repeats that which has already been introduced into the record in the present trial. Because cumulative evidence does not add to nor deduct from evidence already introduced, the court may exclude it [see the chapter on relevancy (Chapter 4)]. If evidence is cumulative in effect, it generally has no evidentiary value.

Corroborative Evidence

Corroborative evidence generally has no direct bearing on the facts in issue, but tends to buttress other evidence that has already been introduced by substantiating it. *Example:* Two people standing together at an intersection observe one subject run out the front door of a bank and jump into a waiting automobile. Witness number one testifies in court that he saw a white, male American, 20–25 years of age, with red hair, jump into a 1969 white Chevrolet, license 123 ABC, and that the defendant is the person whom he saw. Witness number two then gives the same testimony, without adding or taking away from these factors. Witness number two's testimony will either be cumulative (because he is testifying to matters that have already been introduced) or corroborative. To be corroborative in nature, the district attorney would have to argue that the testimony bolsters witness number one's testimony and that it is being introduced as corroborative and not cumulative so as to lend more credence to witness number one's testimony by substantiating that he is telling the truth. Some courts, however, disfavor defining this evidence as corroborative, since witness number one's credibility has not been attacked. Therefore, in some jurisdictions, this evidence would be cumulative and excluded, unless on cross-examination witness number one's testimony was being discredited.

DISCUSSION QUESTIONS

1. Give a definition for the term *evidence*.
2. Discuss admissibility of evidence in your jurisdiction.
3. Define a writing.
4. What is meant by *material objectives*?
5. What are the most common types of real evidence with which a police officer is confronted?
6. Discuss each of the four forms of evidence.
7. What does the term *direct evidence* mean?
8. What is the major distinction between direct and circumstantial evidence?
9. What is cumulative evidence?
10. Distinguish cumulative evidence from corroborative evidence.

Burden of Proof and Effect of Evidence

Burden of Proof

The burden of proof (burden of persuasion) is nothing more than the end result of the evidence which has been introduced into any trial. It is the establishment of the necessary degree of belief in the minds of the jury as to all the facts that have been placed in issue at that specific trial. In its simplest terms, it is the cumulative effect which the evidence has on the jury. Each side, in either a civil or criminal case, must establish its burden of proof or it will have a judgment entered against itself.

There are two distinct concepts to be concerned with in talking about burden of proof. The first, and more important, is the party's obligation to produce the evidence required by law to prove the facts for its side of the case, or, in other words, the degree of proof necessary to convince the jury to return a favorable verdict for the party presenting evidence. The second is the party's obligation to go forward with the evidence. This means nothing more than the party's duty to introduce conflicting or new evidence to overcome evidence introduced by the opposing side. Failure to do so will result in an adverse verdict.

Each party bears the burden of persuasion on all essential elements of its cause of action (the corpus delicti — elements of the crime — must be proven by the prosecutor, and the defense must prove the defendant did not commit the crime, etc.). It is the obligation of the prosecution or the defense to establish, by legally admissible evidence, a degree of belief in the minds of the jury that its side should prevail. This does not mean that the burden will shift. The only effect of not meeting your burden of proof is that you will have an adverse verdict made against you.

In a criminal case, the prosecution is allotted the burden of proof as to the entire corpus delicti of the crime. The prosecution must establish each and every element of the corpus delicti in order to meet this burden of persuasion and then back up its claims with competent, legally admissible evidence to prove, in fact, that the crime was committed and that it was committed by the defendant. In a civil case, the rule is that the plaintiff who filed the action must be able to prove each and every element of a civil wrong that was committed against him, substantiating the claims with legally admissible evidence.

There are basically two degrees of proof required in all cases. In criminal cases, the prosecution (i.e., the people of the state, or the people) must establish the guilt of the defendant by proving *beyond a reasonable doubt* that the defendant committed the given crime. (This does not mean that guilt must be established *without any doubt*.) However, it must be noted that other factual issues in a criminal case, such as whether or not a confession was given voluntarily or whether or not a search was conducted lawfully, need only be proven *by a preponderance of the evidence*. In civil cases, a person need only prove *by a preponderance of the evidence* that he is entitled to a positive judgment.

In order to understand clearly the distinction between *beyond a reasonable doubt* and *by a preponderance of the evidence*, visualize a scale from 0 to 100. *A preponderance of evidence* would be somewhere over the 50 mark, and *beyond a reasonable doubt* would be between 95 and 100. This simply means that in order to win a judgment in a civil case, the party need prove to a lesser degree than in a criminal case that it is entitled to a positive judgment.

The burden of introducing evidence generally falls upon the party who bears the burden of persuasion as to each and every issue. Thus, in a criminal case, the prosecution has the burden of introducing all elements of the corpus delicti of the crime and then establishing that the defendant was the one who committed said crime. If the prosecution fails to do this, the trial judge may dismiss the action without the defense entering any items of evidence (this procedure is termed *directed verdict*, or *dismissal due to lack of evidence*). If the prosecution has satisfied this particular burden by using legally admissible evidence to introduce the elements of the crime, the burden of going forward is given to the defense in the case. The defense must now introduce conflicting evidence or evidence establishing that it has some defense in order to avoid having an adverse ruling made against it. *Example:* The prosecution introduces evidence to establish a burglary using the common law definition of burglary, i.e., that (1) an entry into a dwelling house of another was made, (2) the entry was committed at nighttime, (3) the house was occupied, (4) there was a break-in, (5) there existed the intent to commit a theft therein, (6) the defendant was observed leaving the house. Also suppose that all of the evidence proving each one of these elements was legally sufficient and admissible. At this point, the burden of proof shifts to the defense, which must, if it does not desire an adverse ruling, introduce conflicting evidence, such as an alibi (e.g., that the defendant was not there at the time), a defense of insanity in that the defendant lacked the capacity to commit the crime at that time, or other types of evidence which may be used to rebut or overcome that which has been introduced by the prosecution.

Inferences

An inference is a deduction of fact which is made by the jury from all of the evidence presented. In other words, it is the reasoning process by which the jury comes to a conclusion as to the value or weight of the evidence presented. The drawing of all inferences is largely a matter for the discretion of the jury in the particular case. The judge will make an initial determination to decide whether the evidence offered bears a significant relationship to the issue so that an inference could be drawn by the jury. Once a piece of evidence has been admitted by the judge, it is then usually up to the jury to decide what inferences, if any, can be drawn from that item of evidence. The only restriction on the jury's discretion in this area is that all inferences drawn must be logical and reasonable; that is, these inferences must be based on facts already presented in evidence at the trial. *Example:* A patrol officer receives a report of a silent alarm at a bank during business hours and, approaching the bank, sees a suspect run from the front door and proceed in an opposite direction down the street. The officer then pursues and stops the suspect. If this evidence were presented in court after the arrest of the suspect, it would be logical for the jury to draw an inference from the fact that the patrol officer had received a report of the robbery in progress at the given bank and had seen the defendant running from the bank. Assuming additional items of evidence had been introduced, it would be reasonable for the jury to draw an inference from this evidence that, in fact, if the officer was truthful, the defendant could be the robber in the case.

Presumptions

A presumption differs from an inference in that a presumption, is a deduction which the law requires to be made from a particular fact already introduced into evidence. A presumption, once introduced into evidence, has the effect of shifting the burden of going forward with that item of evidence.

There are two classifications of presumptions — conclusive presumptions and rebuttable presumptions — recognized throughout the United States.

Conclusive Presumptions

Conclusive presumptions are generally found in the rules of evidence; however, they are more substantive rules than evidentiary rules, because if a presumption is a true conclusive presumption, the law will permit no contradiction. Hence, the presumption cannot be rebutted by any contrary evidence, nor may its logic be disputed by any adverse evidence.

In most jurisdictions, the only conclusive presumption of concern to the law enforcement officer is that of the legitimacy of issue. *Example 1:*

Most statutes state that a child born to a married woman cohabiting with her spouse at the time of conception is conclusively presumed legitimate as long as the husband was not impotent at that time. The strong public policy of most jurisdictions favors the legitimacy of issue, which prevents any proof that a man who is cohabiting with his wife is not the father of her child. Even if a properly conducted blood test showed that it was biologically impossible for the husband to have fathered this child, this evidence would be inadmissible to dispute this presumption.

Example 2: A woman legally married becomes pregnant by another man while her husband is overseas. Her husband returns and finds his wife pregnant. The child is born, the husband has a blood test conducted by a medical doctor, refuses to support the child, and the state's attorney proceeds to prosecute him for nonsupport. The state's attorney introduces the fact that the man and woman are legally married and that the child is born to the woman while the husband, even though away temporarily, was still cohabiting with her. The husband now attempts to introduce, by way of expert testimony, the results of the blood test to prove that he could not be the father. An objection would then be made by the state's attorney and would be sustained by the judge, barring the introduction of the blood test evidence from this trial (due to the public policy factors favoring legitimacy of issue and the conclusive presumptions in existence). The end result of this presumption is to legitimate the issue born of two people who are married and cohabiting. Legitimacy of issue, being a strong presumption in our law, has been upheld many times by state supreme courts and by the U.S. Supreme Court under the conclusive presumption theory.

Rebuttable Presumptions

Rebuttable presumptions are called "true" presumptions, as they are the deductions which the law will require the jury to make from an item of evidence introduced until contrary evidence is also introduced.

One strong rebuttable presumption in the criminal field is that a person is presumed innocent until proven guilty. Thus, the defendant comes to trial with this rebuttable presumption already in effect, meaning that the prosecution must now go forward with its burden of producing evidence to show beyond a reasonable doubt that the defendant is guilty in this particular case. Another strong rebuttable presumption in most states is that a defendant is presumed sane at the time of trial. This presumption means that the defense has the burden of going forward with the evidence to prove that the defendant was not sane at the particular time of committing the crime.

Once a rebuttable presumption arises and contrary evidence has been introduced, it is then generally up to the jury as to what inferences to draw from the two conflicting points of evidence and to arrive at a conclusion.

Examples of the most commonly recognized rebuttable presumptions are: (1) persons who have gone through a valid wedding ceremony are legally married; (2) a person not heard from in seven years is dead;

(3) a person intends the normal consequences of his act; (4) official duties have been regularly performed; (5) a person is innocent until proven guilty; and (6) a person is sane at the time of commission of a crime. The student would be wise to check the local evidence code and rules of procedure to ascertain other rebuttable presumptions in effect in his jurisdiction.

A special rule applies in some criminal cases where an accused is on trial for a crime in which there is the element that he had knowledge of the particular substance which he possessed at the time of his arrest. A U.S. Supreme Court decision in 1965 (U.S. v. Gainey, 380 U.S. 63) held that if this knowledge was a required element of the corpus delicti, and as long as the defendant introduced substantial evidence that he did not have this knowledge, it would be an error for the judge to submit this case to the jury, or for the jury to find the defendant guilty solely based on a presumption that one having possession of a certain thing had the requisite degree of knowledge. *Example:* A burglary statute requires proof of specific intent (mental element) to enter and commit a theft inside a building. A defendant, while drunk, breaks into a jewelry store to go to sleep. The state must show the required intent.

Summary

In this chapter, we discussed burden of proof, degree of proof required *(beyond a reasonable doubt* and *preponderance),* inferences, and presumptions. Proof is defined as the end result of the evidence introduced. We learned which party substantiated its burden of proof by the verdict that is rendered in a specific case. Each party has the burden of persuasion on all essential issues of its case. It is the obligation of that party to establish, by legally sufficient evidence, a degree of belief in the minds of the jury that it should prevail. We also learned that the burden of going forward with the evidence falls on the party which has the burden of proof as to that specific issue; e.g., the prosecution must go forward and prove all elements of the crime.

An inference is a reasonable deduction of fact which is made by the jury from items of evidence that have been introduced into the trial. A conclusive presumpion is more of a statutory than an evidentiary creature. A conclusive presumption, once it comes into play, does not allow any contrary evidence to be introduced in the trial. A rebuttable presumption, however, is a deduction which the law requires to be made once evidence has been introduced but which allows the opposing side to come back and rebut or contradict that item of evidence.

DISCUSSION QUESTIONS

1. What is meant by the term *burden of proof?*
2. Distinguish the burden of proof from the obligation of the prosecutor in going forward with the evidence.
3. What is the degree of proof required in a criminal case?

4. Distinguish the degree of proof necessary in a criminal case with that necessary in a civil case.
5. What is the basic concept behind the rule on inferences?
6. How is an inference arrived at?
7. What is the major distinction between a rebuttable presumption and a conclusive presumption?
8. How do you overcome a rebuttable presumption?
9. Explain some of the most common rebuttable presumptions in your jurisdiction.
10. What conclusive presumptions apply in your jurisdiction?

GRIEGER v. VEGA
Supreme Court of Texas, 1954.
153 Tex. 486, 271 S.W.2d 85.

HICKMAN, CHIEF JUSTICE. This is a suit by respondent, Matilda Vega, against petitioner, Fred Grieger, for damages for the alleged wrongful killing of her son, Arthur Vega. Her petition alleged that petitioner "willfully and maliciously killed Arthur Vega by shooting him with a gun." The case was submitted to a jury on two special issues as follows:

"Special Issue No. 1: Do you find from a preponderance of the evidence that the action of Fred Grieger in shooting and killing the deceased Arthur Vega, was wrongful?

"Answer 'Yes' or 'No.'

... [The second issue related to the amount of damages.]

The first special issue was answered "No," and in accordance with the court's instruction the second issue was not answered. Upon the verdict, judgment was rendered that respondent take nothing. The case was reversed and remanded by the Court of Civil Appeals. 264 S.W.2d 498.

The charge defined the term "wrongful" as used in Special Issue No. 1 as follows:

"By the term 'wrongful,' as used in Special Issue No. 1, means the use by defendant of a greater degree of force than was reasonable and necessary under the circumstances then existing and that the defendant was not at the time acting in his own self-defense, as below explained...."

The evidence which came from respondent's own witnesses establishes these facts: Petitioner was a police officer in the city of Taylor. In the discharge of his duties he met the Vega brothers on a street in Taylor about eight o'clock at night. They were accompanied by Willie Olivarez. The Vega brothers were drunk and staggering. Petitioner requested Olivarez, who was not drunk, to take the Vega brothers off the street. Some words ensued, and then Arthur Vega attacked petitioner and threw him to the ground. Both he and his brother jumped upon petitioner and held him with his back to the ground. In that situation, petitioner called upon Olivarez for help, and Olivarez pulled one of the brothers off peititioner. Then petitioner was able to free himself from the other one, and got back on his feet. He then commanded the two brothers to sit down next to a wall. They squatted down with their backs to the wall while petitioner, with his pistol in his hand, held guard over them. Petitioner directed a passer-by to telephone the police department for help, but shortly thereafter both brothers arose and advanced toward petitioner, whereupon he killed both of them. . . .

Another point brought to the Court of Civil Appeals was that Special Issue No. 1 incorrectly placed upon respondent the burden of proving that in killing the deceased, petitioner was not acting in self-defense. That presents the most difficult question in the case. The sole right of respondent to recover damages is derived from the statute, Article 4671. That right did not exist at common law. The statute gives such a right when death "is caused by the wrongful act, neglect, carelessness, unskilfulness, or default of another". It will be observed that "wrongful act" is placed in the same category as the other grounds giving rise to a cause of action, from which it follows that the burden placed upon plaintiff to prove the death was caused by a "wrongful act" is the same as that for death by negligence or any of the other grounds named. So far as our investigation discloses, all authorities seem to agree that the burden is upon plaintiff to prove that the killing was wrongful. If he proves an intentional killing, and nothing more, he has met that burden, and if the defendant offers no evidence raising the issue of self-defense, the plaintiff is entitled to a judgment. This for the reason that an intentional killing unexplained is presumed to be wrongful. When, however, in the example just above mentioned, the defendant pleads self-defense in justification of the killing and offers evidence supporting that plea, the authorities are in conflict on the question of placing the burden of proof on the issue of self-defense. Some of the cases adopting the view that the burden rests upon the defendant to prove justification seem not to distinguish between burden of proof and necessity of going forward with the evidence. They proceed upon the theory that the burden of proof shifts during the trial of a case. In this jurisdiction it is held that the burden of proof never shifts from one party to the other at any time during the trial. . . .

When defendant's evidence raises an issue of justification, the presumption that the killing was wrongful is balanced, and the matter is set at large. The plaintiff can then no longer rely alone upon the presumption, but must prove the wrong by a preponderance of the evidence.

The above line of reasoning is not accepted in some jurisdictions, but we are referred to no case, and have discovered none, which would relieve the plaintiff of the burden of proof under the facts in this case.

"Where the plaintiff himself has put in evidence the incidents of an occurrence from which the jury within their province, might draw exculpatory inferences favorable to the defendant, it is error for the court to so instruct the jury as to convey a suggestion that the defendant must by an additional weight of evidence exonerate himself. . . ."

In establishing her case the respondent's witnesses testified to facts regarding the killing, from which facts the jury might well have based a finding of justification. Had the case been closed when she rested, this situation would have been presented: Petitioner intentionally killed respondent's son; such killing may have been wrongful, but, on the other hand, it may have been justified. The burden surely did not rest upon petitioner to prove that it was not wrongful, but was upon the respondent to prove that it was wrongful. . . .

UNITED STATES v. ENGLAND
United States Court of Appeals, Seventh Circuit, 1965.
347 F.2d 425.

GRANT, DISTRICT JUDGE. The indictment in this case charged William B. England and his son, William Bernard England, in one count with willfully attempting, during the period from about June 27, 1955, to the date of the indictment, November 27, 1962, to evade and defeat the payment of income taxes owed by the father for the years 1944, 1945, and 1946, "duly assessed" on February 4, 1955, by concealing and attempting to conceal the nature and extent of real estate owned by the father and by making false statements concerning the father's interest in certain real estate, in violation of Section 7201 of the Internal Revenue Code of 1954 and of Title 18, United States Code, Section 2.

After trial by jury, both appellants were found guilty. The father (William B. England, also known as William Benjamin England, and hereafter referred to as "England Senior") was sentenced to imprisonment for three years. The son (William Bernard England, also known as William B. England, Jr., and hereafter referred to as "England Junior") was placed on probation for a period of three years and sentenced to pay a fine in the sum of $4,000 and costs in the sum of $1,316.64. Each appellant filed a notice of appeal. The assignment of errors relied on therein allegedly arises out of instructions, rulings on evidence, and failure to grant defendants' motion for acquittal.

The evidence introduced at the trial consisted of (1) proof intended to show that valid assessments of income tax deficiencies, interest, and fraud penalties were made against England Senior on February 4, 1955, and (2) proof of various subsequent statements and acts of the appellants calculated to conceal from the Government the nature and extent of the property interests of England Senior, for the alleged purpose of preventing the Government from collecting the assessments.

As to the validity of the tax assessments, the Government introduced several pieces of documentary evidence. It was shown that England Senior was indicted on March 12, 1952, on two counts for willfully attempting to evade the federal income taxes owed by him for 1945 and 1946 by filing false and fraudulent income tax returns. This exhibit, consisting of the indictment, plea and sentence, was admitted in evidence only against England Senior. The same exhibit showed that England Senior on May 4, 1954, was permitted to withdraw his plea of not guilty and that he then entered a plea of guilty. On the same day, he was adjudged guilty and sentenced to pay a fine in the sum of $10,000. Furthermore, at the trial in this cause, England Senior (on direct examination by his own counsel) admitted that he was thus indicted in 1952 and that he pleaded guilty. The 1952 indictment alleged that England Senior reported taxes due of $644.90 for 1945 and of $559.89 for 1946, but that in fact the correct amounts of taxes were $8,303.22 for 1945 and $6,976.96 for 1946.

Having been adjudged guilty on May 4, 1954, as noted, England Senior thereafter signed certain waivers with respect to the assessment and collection of tax deficiencies, interest and penalties, in stated amounts, with reference to the years 1944, 1945, and 1946. Both waivers were on Internal Revenue Service Form 870, entitled "Waiver of Restrictions on Tax and Acceptance of Overassessment."

In addition to the waivers, the Government introduced in evidence two exhibits which were certificates showing that deficiencies, interest and penalties were in fact assessed against England Senior (jointly with his wife for the year 1944) on January 24, 1955, for the years 1944, 1945, and 1946.

The Government contended that the aforementioned exhibits showed the filing of false returns by England Senior and permitted an assessment after expiration of the three-year statute of limitations prescribed by Section 6501, Internal Revenue Code of 1954. Appellants, on the other hand, objected that the assessments were invalid because it was apparent of record that their filing in 1955 occurred long after the running of the statutory period. None of the exhibits were ever admitted in evidence against England Junior.

At the close of all the evidence, appellants requested instructions which would have permitted the jury to find the assessments valid or invalid as a matter of fact. These instructions, three in number, were refused by the trial court. The Government, on the contrary, requested an instruction that the assessments were valid as a matter of law, and the trial judge so charged the jury. The Government's instruction reads, in part, as follows:

"I now charge you as a matter of law that the assessments made against the defendant William B. England on February 5, 1955, in the amount of $9,849.78 as to the year 1944, and in the amount of $17,182.19 as to the years 1945 and 1946, have been valid obligations of the taxpayer to the United States Government since the dates on which the respective assessments were made until the date, November 27, 1962, on which the present indictment was returned and in the amounts, to the extent that all or any portion of these amounts have not been paid, which I have just enumerated."

Appellants have assigned the giving of the foregoing instruction as error. We are of the opinion that the giving of said instruction by the trial court, and taking from the jury the question of the validity of the assessments, constituted reversible error.

In reversing, we hold that, in the criminal prosecution of one charged with the commission of a felony, the defendant has an absolute right to a jury determination upon all essential elements of the offense. This right, emanating from the criminal defendant's constitutional right to trial by jury, is neither depleted nor diminished by what otherwise might be considered the conclusive or compelling nature of the evidence against him. This right is personal to the defendant, and, like his right to a jury trial, is one which he, and he alone, may waive; furthermore, in a situation wherein an understandingly tendered waiver is not forthcoming from the defendant, under no circumstances may the trial court usurp this right by ruling as a matter of law on an essential element of the crime charged.

There is no doubt that a valid assessment, and proof thereof, was an essential element of the case against appellants. Banks v. United States, 204 F.2d 666 (8th Cir. 1953), remanded on other grounds, 348 U.S. 905, 75 S.Ct. 311, 99 L.Ed. 710 (1955), reaffirmed, 223 F.2d 884 (8th Cir. 1955). That it was so, in fact, was admitted by the Government, as evidenced by the statement of the Government's attorney to the trial court that, "We have to show there was an assessment, a legal assessment." And, as an essential element of the felony charged, the Government shouldered the burden of proving its existence, as well as the other elements of the crime, beyond a reasonable doubt. As the court said in the Banks case, supra, 204 F.2d at 668:

"The court properly instructed the jury that the defendant is presumed to be innocent of the crimes alleged against him in the indictment, and that the burden was upon the government to prove him guilty beyond a reasonable doubt. That burden in this case, in which a violation of § 145(b) of the Internal Revenue Code, supra, is charged, required proof (1) *that a tax was due from defendant to the government for each of the years charged;* (2) that the defendant attempted to evade payment of that tax; and (3) that his attempt so to evade payment was willful."

Nor is there any doubt that the fact of a valid assessment was "in issue". This is so in spite of a contrary result reached in a recent case, quite similar to that before us here, Guy v. United States, 336 F.2d 595 (4th Cir. 1964). There, the defendants were charged with having a still set up in violation of law, working at an unregistered distillery, and possession of materials intended for illegal use in connection with such still. The evidence apparently showed that the still had been dismantled, and the question was raised by the defense whether the several disconnected parts in fact constituted a still. Inasmuch as the evidence on this point was uncontroverted, the trial court took the issue of the existence of a still—admittedly an essential element of the crime charged—from the jury and ruled upon it as a matter of law in favor of the Government. The Court of Appeals for the Fourth Circuit affirmed, stating that, while "issues of fact" must be left with the jury, there could be no such issues of fact "where credible testimony with respect to it is neither denied nor impeached." Id., at 597. In effect, the court ruled that a trial court could rule as a matter of law on an uncontroverted, essential element of a crime.

However, in our view, the holding in Guy ignores the traditional notion that a plea of not guilty by an accused to an indictment or information charging a criminal violation places "in issue" all essential averments contained therein. Once the defendant has entered a plea of not guilty, everything material to a finding of his guilt is "in controversy". Thus, under our system of jurisprudence, it is technically possible for a criminal defendant to enter a plea of not guilty, introduce little or no evidence in his own defense, and rely exclusively on his presumption of innocence and the possible inability of the prosecution to prove his guilt beyond a reasonable doubt. Thereupon, "guilt is determined by the jury, not the court."

"... (N)o fact, not even an undisputed fact, may be determined by the Judge. *The plea of not guilty puts all in issue, even the most patent truths.* In our federal system, the Trial Court may never instruct a verdict either in whole or in part."

Having thus established that the fact of a valid assessment of taxes was an essential element of the crime charged and that such fact was in issue in the trial below, we now pass to a brief review of the cases relevant to this inquiry.

Schwachter v. United States, 237 F.2d 640 (6th Cir. 1956), was a prosecution for selling a stolen automobile moving in interstate commerce, knowing the same to have been stolen. The trial judge, apparently of the opinion that the Government had proved that the automobile in question was in interstate commerce at the time it was sold, ruled as a matter of law as to the fact, the same being an essential element of the crime charged. Reversing on this issue, the court said:

"The rule is settled that in a criminal case the judge may not direct a verdict of guilty no matter how conclusive the evidence. It is necessary that the Government prove to the jury beyond a reasonable doubt every essential element of the offense charged. This includes the fact in this case that the car was a part of interstate commerce when the defendant sold it. The trail judge may not direct the jury to find a controverted material fact against the defendant. Konda v. United States, 7 Cir., 166 F. 91. . . .

"But the general rule is settled that the trial judge in a criminal case can not weigh the evidence or judge the credibility of the witnesses and take from the jury a controverted question of material fact, no matter how strongly he may be of the opinion that the evidence has established the fact beyond a reasonable doubt."

Prosecution for possession of non-taxpaid whiskey was involved in United States v. McKenzie, 301 F.2d 880. At the trial, the judge had ruled as a matter of law that the fact of possession existed, and stated that the only issue remaining was the identity of the persons who had such possession. Holding that it was necessary that the Government prove to the jury beyond a reasonable doubt every essential element of the offense charged, the Sixth Circuit reversed, saying:

". . . It was necessary in this case that the Government prove not only that appellant was driving the car, but also prove that the circumstances were such as to constitute possession by the appellant of the contents of the cardboard carton and that the carton contained non-taxpaid whiskey. Schwachter v. United States, 237 F.2d 640, C.A. 6th. No matter how conclusive the evidence may be in a criminal case on a controverted material fact, the trial judge cannot make the finding or withdraw the issue from the jury."

Brooks v. United States, 240 F.2d 905 was an appeal from a conviction of perjury. The trial court had instructed the jury correctly that an essential element of the offense charged was whether the special agent of the Internal Revenue Service who administered oaths to the defendants had authority to administer such oaths. However, the trial judge thereafter instructed the jury as a matter of law that the requisite authority existed. The defendants thereupon assigned the giving of this instruction as reversible error, to which the reviewing court replied:

"We agree for the all-sufficient reason that it deprived the jury of its function of determining whether or not, under the evidence and as exclusive judges of the facts and of the credibility of the witness, they believe beyond a reasonable doubt that Perry was an officer authorized to administer oaths in 1955 and thus violated appellants' constitutional right to a trial by jury as guaranteed by the Sixth Amendment. Heinous as the crime of perjury is under our law, it is entitled to no relaxation of the constitutional guaranty of the citizen in order to punish it."

In United States v. Manuszak, 234 F.2d 421 defendant was convicted for theft of goods from an interstate shipment of freight, for interstate transportation of stolen goods, and for conspiracy. At the trial, the court in effect instructed the jury as a matter of law that the "goods that were stolen were part of an interstate shipment", an essential ingredient of the offense. The Third Circuit Court of Appeals reversed on this issue, and said:

"The defense never agreed or stipulated that a theft had occurred. The presumption of innocence to which appellant was entitled demanded that all factual elements of the government's case be submitted to the jury. It is immaterial that the government's evidence as to the actual theft was uncontradicted. The acceptance of such evidence and the credibility of witnesses is for the jury, even though to the court the only possible reasonable result is the acceptance and belief of the government's evidence. A partial direction of the verdict occurs when the court determines an essential fact, and this denies the appellant trial by jury." (At 424–425).

Although the foregoing discussion is in no way an attempt to exhaust completely all that has been said in this line of cases, we turn our attention now to cases cited by the Government in this appeal. We do so for the reason that we acknowledge there to be a parallel line of cases to the contrary, albeit a "shorter" line and one less persuasive, we feel, than that here relied upon.

A case frequently cited reaching a contrary result, and one relied upon heavily by the Government here, is that of United States v. Jonikas, 197 F.2d 675 (7th Cir. 1952), cert. den. 344 U.S. 877, 73 S.Ct. 171, 97 L.Ed. 679 (1952). However, evaluation of the holding therein must be prefaced by a clear characterization of the significant distinction between *instructing as a matter of law* on an essential element of a criminal offense, on the one hand, and the prerogative of the trial judge to *comment upon the evidence*, on the other. With the latter, of course, we have no quarrel. That the trial judge may fairly comment upon the evidence was well-established at English common law in much earlier times, and this right of the trial judge has repeatedly been enunciated by the United States Supreme Court since the earliest days of this Republic.

With this distinction in mind, it is clearly apparent that the Jonikas case is distinguishable from the case at hand. Jonikas was a proceeding upon a motion for vacation of sentence under 28 U.S.C. § 2255, the petitioner therein having been convicted of passing counterfeit bills. The record disclosed that, at the trial, the court told the jury in its instructions that *in the opinion of the judge* he did not think there was "any great amount of question in the evidence" that the defendant "did pass these bills at the places indicated," so that "it narrows itself down pretty much in this case to the question of whether or not he knew these bills to be counterfeit." The court further told the jury:

"That they are counterfeit has been admitted and has been proved. *I do not think there is any doubt about that in the evidence . . . You can see that for yourself. . . . So you do not have to spend a great deal of time on that. . . .*"

The emphasized portion of this instruction makes it abundantly clear that, although the trial judge made known to the jury in very forceful terms what he thought the evidence to be, the issue in question was never actually taken from the jury and ruled upon as a matter of law. The mere fact that the jury did "not have to spend a great deal of time" on the question indicated that it could, at least, spend some time on it. And, this being true, it was technically possible for the jury to disregard the admonitions of the judge and decide upon the issue as it alone saw fit. Thus, left intact with the jury was what Mr. Justice Holmes once termed the "technical right" of the jury "to decide against the law and the facts," Horning v. District of Columbia, 254 U.S. 135, 138–139, 41 S.Ct. 53–54, 65 L.Ed. 185 (1920), a statement to which we here give our approval.

The distinction just drawn, between instructing upon a material fact and commenting upon the evidence, has not infrequently been stated by other courts. The Supreme Court said, in United States v. Murdock, 290 U.S. 389, 394, 54 S.Ct. 223, 225, 78 L.Ed. 381 (1933):

"A federal judge may analyze the evidence, comment upon it, and express his views with regard to the testimony of witnesses. He may advise the jury in respect of the facts, but the decision of issues of fact must be fairly left to the jury. . . ."

In Lovejoy v. United States, 128 U.S. 171, 173, 9 S.Ct. 57, 58, 32 L.Ed. 389 (1888), an earlier Court stated the general rule:

"It is established by repeated decisions that a court of the United States, in submitting a case to the jury, may at its discretion express its opinion upon the facts, and that such an opinion is not reviewable error, so long as no rule of law is incorrectly stated and all matters of fact are ultimately submitted to the determination of the jury. . . ."

Other pronouncements of this distinction are unnecessary and too numerous to set forth.

Aside from the Jonikas case, and for the same proposition, the Government has referred the court to Malone v. United States,

238 F.2d 851 (6th Cir. 1956), and Lyons v. United States, 325 F.2d 370 (9th Cir. 1963). And, as has been indicated, there are other cases to the same effect. To the degree that these cases rely upon Jonikas, we distinguish them for the same reason; and, to the degree they do not, we deem them improvident.

Surely the course we take here today is that which places the greater faith in the jury system. While it is not our purpose to recount the virtues of that system, we take special note of a case, very similar to the one at bar, decided by a predecessor of this court in which faith in the common law notion of the jury in a criminal prosecution was eloquently expressed. In Konda v. United States, 166 F.91 (7th Cir. 1908), defendant was convicted below of sending an obscene pamphlet through the mails in violation of law. One of the essential elements of the crime, which the Government had the burden of proving beyond a reasonable doubt, was that the material mailed was actually obscene. The trial court, however, ruled as a matter of law in favor of the prosecution on this issue and withdrew it from the jury's consideration. Reversing, this court said, and we quote at length:

"In our judgment, however, a defendant in a criminal case has the absolute right to require that the jury decide whether or not the evidence sustains each and every material allegation of the indictment. Material allegations are allegations of fact. And each, as much as any other, enters into a verdict of guilty. If the judge may decide that one or another material allegation is proven, he may decide that all are proven, and so direct a verdict of guilty. In a civil case, the judge may exercise the power of directing a verdict for the plaintiff when there is no conflict in the evidence and the only inference that can be drawn by reasonable minds as to the ultimate facts in issue favors the plaintiff. This power, we opine, grew out of the practical administration of the fundamental power to review, on a motion for a new trial, the findings of the jury. In the civil case above supposed, if the jury should return a verdict for the defendant, the judge would set it aside; and he would continue to set aside verdicts in that case until one should be returned that was in accord with the undisputed facts. So he cuts off the possibility of useless verdicts by directing in the first instance the jury to return the only verdict he will let stand. But in a criminal case, if the jury returns a verdict for the defendant, the judge, no matter how contrary to the evidence he may think the verdict is, cannot set it aside and order a new trial. Therefore, since the judge is without power to review and overturn a verdict of not guilty, there is no basis on which to claim the power to direct a verdict of guilty. *Our conclusion is that an accused person has the same right to have 12 laymen pronounce upon the truth or falsity of each material averment in the indictment, if the evidence against him is clear and uncontradicted, as he unquestionably would have if it were doubtful and conflicting. Inasmuch as jurors are rightly trusted, in close and difficult cases to maintain the peace and dignity of organized society, surely they may be relied on in the plain and simple ones."*

The holding in, and the language just quoted from, the Konda case might well be considered controlling of the issue now before the court. Not only has that case indicated the traditional and proper role of the jury in a criminal case in the federal courts, but implicit therein is the broader concept fundamental in our law that the rights of the criminal defendant are to be jealously guarded. We are not here concerned with the guilt or innocence of these appellants, and for that reason we have not attempted to weigh the evidence in the trial below with a view to possibly finding the error not prejudicial. Rather, we are presented here with a question going to the very heart of what we conceive to be fair and proper administration of criminal justice. "It is a fundamental precept of the administration of justice in the federal courts that the accused must not only be guilty of the offense of which he is charged and convicted, but that he be tried and convicted according to proper legal procedures and standards. In short, it is not enough that the accused be guilty; our system demands that he be found guilty in the right way." Wilson v. United States, 250 F.2d 312, 324–325 (9th Cir. 1958).

Having concluded that there was reversible error in the giving of Government's Requested Instruction No. 10, given in both the case against England Senior and that against England Junior below, it is unnecessary to discuss the remaining specifications of error. The judgments and sentences are therefore reversed and the cases are remanded to the District Court for new trials.

Reversed.

PEOPLE EX REL. JUHAN v. DISTRICT COURT FOR THE COUNTY OF JEFFERSON
Supreme Court of Colorado, 1968.
165 Colo. 253, 439 P.2d 741.

MOORE, CHIEF JUSTICE. The district attorney for the First Judicial District commenced this original proceeding to secure a determination of the constitutionality of an act of the legislature dealing with the defense of insanity in criminal cases. The facts giving rise to the controversy are as follows:

An information was filed in the district court of Jefferson county in which one Calvin Fulmer was accused of the crime of first degree murder. He entered a plea of not guilty by reason of insanity at the time of the alleged commission of the crime. A motion was filed by his attorney seeking entry of an order of court directing the prosecution to establish the sanity of the defendant to the satisfaction of the jury, beyond a reasonable doubt, notwithstanding the provision of C.R.S.1963, 39–8–1 as amended by Chapter 163, Session Laws of 1967, which purports to require a defendant who enters a plea of not guilty by reason of insanity to establish, by a preponderance of evidence, the fact of insanity. . . .

The trial court sustained the motion of counsel for Fullmer, holding that the above quoted statute violated the Constitution of the State of Colorado. Thereupon this original proceeding was commenced and we issued a rule to show cause as prayed for in the petition. The respondents have appeared, briefs have been filed, and oral arguments have been heard.

The answer and brief filed by respondents urge that the rule be discharged for three reasons as follows:

". . . We consider but one of the points relied on by counsel for Fulmer. Our determination of it disposes of the controversy. For reasons hereinafter stated we hold that the provisions of the statute which state: "The burden shall be on the defendant to prove by a preponderance of the evidence that he was insane at the time of the alleged commission of the crime," violates Article II, Section 25, of the Constitution of Colorado which provides: "No person shall be deprived of life, liberty, or property, without due process of law."

There are a number of fundamental principles of law applicable to criminal cases which have been so universally accepted and applied in this country as to have become component parts of our understanding of the term "due process of law." Among such basic concepts we find the doctrine that, at the outset of the trial, an accused person is presumed to be innocent of the offense charged against him; that the state must satisfy the jury of the guilt of the defendant beyond a reasonable doubt; and that if upon any material issue of fact essential to guilt the jury has a reasonable doubt, the defendant is entitled to the benefit of that reasonable doubt and a verdict of not guilty. Numerous cases decided by this court have imbedded these basic fundamentals in the main stream of the criminal law. . . .

In Carter v. People, 119 Colo. 342, 204 P.2d 147, this court said, *inter alia*:

". . . Upon the issue of insanity, if a reasonable doubt existed in the minds of the jury as to whether the defendant was, or was not, sane, he was entitled to a verdict of not guilty by reason of insanity."

In Becksted v. People, 133 Colo. 72, 292 P.2d 189, the question presented for determination was:

"In the prosecution of a charge of first degree murder in which the accused has entered a plea of not guilty by reason of insanity as well as that of not guilty, and where a separate trial is had upon the issue of insanity, is that to be conducted as a 'civil' action"?

The opinion disposes of the issue as follows:

"This question is answered in the negative. In a criminal case the defendant can assert as many defenses as can be supported by evidence. If affirmative defenses such as self defense or alibi are presented the issues thereon are tried as part of the criminal case, and if any such defense raises in the mind of a jury a reasonable doubt as to the defendant's guilt he should be acquitted. The defense of insanity stands upon the same footing. The fact that this issue has been separated from other questions for the purpose of trial does not make a civil case out of that which is tendered as a defense to an accusation of crime. . . .

The language of these cases has taken such form over a period of many years as to become part and parcel of our concept of constitutional "due process of law." As thus interpreted by the judiciary over the years the due process clause of the state constitution includes the doctrine that the state must prove guilt beyond a reasonable doubt, and that the accused cannot be required by legislative enactment to prove insanity or any other defense by a preponderance of the evidence. . . .

The recently enacted legislative act now considered presents to the court for the first time, under the due process clause of our constitution, the question of the power of the legislature to destroy all the numerous decisions of this court on this fundamental doctrine. The legislature has attempted to do by statute that which for almost one hundred years this court has held could not be done without violating fundamental principles of criminal justice. Thus "due process" of necessity becomes for the first time the basis of decision. Where stare decisis controls a situation "due process" is rarely the ground upon which decision rests. It is drawn into play, however, by a legislative act which fails to recognize constitutional limitations upon legislative power. . . .

The argument is made that in a criminal case, even though insanity is a full and complete defense, where that issue by statute must be tried separately no defendant can be found guilty, and for that reason "due process of law" does not require that this very material ingredient of guilt must be established beyond a reasonable doubt. By procedurally requiring a separate trial on this issue of mental capacity to commit any crime—which admittedly is a necessary ingredient of any offense—in some mystical way, it is argued that the material ingredient thus set apart for separate trial shall be governed by rules wholly inapplicable to all other necessary ingredients of the completed offense to be thereafter adjudicated; and this is urged notwithstanding the firmly established doctrine that as to every necessary ingredient of the total crime there must be proof beyond a reasonable doubt. In a substantial number of cases insanity is the only defense relied upon and as a practical matter the accused would be deprived of essential and time honored safeguards and would be required to establish his innocence by a preponderance of the evidence, if the statute is to be upheld.

The argument for such a result, in effect, seems to be that because on the separate trial of the sanity question perhaps only one-half the ingredients of total guilt will be determined, as to that half of total guilt the accused can be required to prove his innocence—lack of mental capacity—by a preponderance of the evidence. If the defendant fails to prove by a preponderance of evidence that this defense is well founded he has been, at least, fifty per cent convicted, notwithstanding that not one of countless Colorado decisions can be found which in any degree relieves the prosecutors from the burden of proving *every material element of every criminal charge* (100% of the total crime) by evidence sufficient to remove all reasonable doubt. All Colorado decisions from the beginning of territorial days to the present require application of the rule that total guilt must be established beyond a reasonable doubt. Mental capacity to commit a crime is a material part of total guilt for there can be no crime without the *mens rea*. . . .

In McNamara v. People, 24 Colo. 61, 48 P. 541, the issue arose out of a defense of alibi and the jury was instructed to the effect that the accused had the burden of establishing an alibi. In reversing the judgment this court said, *inter alia*:

". . . The court evidently misapprehended the nature of this defense, and, instead of treating it as a traverse of a fact that it was incumbent upon the prosecution to establish, to wit, the presence of defendant at the time and place of the occurrence, regarded it as an affirmative and independent defense, that the law imposed the burden of proving upon the accused. . . .

"This was clearly erroneous. In order to avail himself of the defense of alibi, it is not incumbent upon the accused to establish that he was not present at the commission of the crime, or that he was in some other place. If the evidence is sufficient to raise a reasonable doubt in the minds of the jury as to whether he was or was not present at the commission of the crime, he is entitled to an acquittal."

The opinion then quotes from Kent v. People, supra, with reference to this rule, as follows:

"The rule relating to the *res gestae*, which we have been considering, applies to all defenses which traverse the averments of the indictment and *go to the essence* of the guilt charged against the accused. . . . (Emphasis added.)

No distinction can be drawn between a defense of alibi and a defense of insanity. Each of them is a traverse of a necessary "averment of the indictment and go to the essence of the guilt charged against the accused." This point is made crystal clear by the opinion of this court in Becksted v. People, supra, written fifty-nine years after the opinion in *McNamara*, during all of which time there has been an uninterrupted, consistent, and very frequent adherence to the doctrine of *McNamara*. In Becksted v. People, supra, this court said:

". . . In a criminal case the defendant can assert as many defenses as can be supported by evidence. If affirmative defenses such as self defense or alibi are presented the issues thereon are tried as part of the criminal case, and if any such defense raises in the mind of a jury a reasonable doubt as to the defendant's guilt he should be acquitted. *The defense of insanity stands upon the same footing.* . . . (Emphasis added.)

In Van Straaten v. People, 26 Colo. 184, 56 P. 905, this court was concerned with a case in which the accused was charged with the crime of larceny and the court erroneously instructed in a manner to lead the jury to believe that "the guilt of the accused is a presumption which the law requires shall be made from the fact of his being found in possession. . . ." This court reversed and in treating the instruction said:

". . . It is also erroneous in imposing upon plaintiffs in error the burden of satisfying the jury that they came into possession of the property honestly. The law imposes no such burden upon a defendant in a criminal case. . . . If their explanation created a reasonable doubt in the minds of the jury as to that fact, it would be sufficient to rebut the presumption of guilt" (which might arise as an inference of fact from possession).

So in the case at bar if the evidence of insanity offered by the defendant created a reasonable doubt *as to that fact*, "it would be sufficient to rebut the presumption" of sanity which attends prior to plea raising the issue. . . .

In Shank v. People, 79 Colo. 576, 247 P. 559, this court held that on the question of insanity, if a reasonable doubt with regard thereto arose from the evidence, the defendant should be acquitted. An instruction which contained the following quoted language was approved as a correct statement of the law:

"It is not incumbent on the defendant, in order to entitle him to an acquittal on the ground of insanity, to prove to your satisfaction that he was insane when the act was committed. If upon the whole case you believe that the defendant was insane at that time, or if upon the whole case you have a reasonable doubt as to whether or not he was sane at that time, you should find him not guilty."

Shortly after the decision in the above case the 1927 Act was adopted which required the entry of a plea of not guilty by reason of insanity prior to trial, but as has already been conclusively established in the fore part of this opinion, no substantive rights were involved and only the "procedure" by which the issue is raised was changed. . . .

In conclusion, at long last, we return to Becksted v. People, supra, and emphasize the holding in that case that:

"... If affirmative defenses such as self defense or alibi are presented the issues thereon are tried as part of the criminal case, and if any such defense raises in the mind of a jury a reasonable doubt as to the defendant's guilt he should be acquitted. *The defense of insanity stands upon the same footing. The fact that this issue has been separated from other questions for the purpose of trial does not make a civil case of that which is tendered as a defense to an accusation of crime. . . ."* (Emphasis added).

That is exactly what the legislature tried to accomplish by the act under discussion in this case. It purported to do the very thing that was attempted by instruction in *Becksted*. It cannot be done either by instruction or by act of the legislature for the very simple reason that in this state our concept of due process of law prohibits it. In the instant case the trial court ruled properly.

The rule to show cause is discharged.

McWilliams and Kelley, JJ., dissent.

McWilliams, Justice (dissenting).

The majority hold that 1965 Perm.Supp., C.R.S.1963, 39-8-1, as amended by Chapter 163, Session Laws of 1967, is unconstitutional because it violates Article II, § 25 of the Colorado constitution. With this conclusion I am in very definite disagreement, as the statute in question in my view of the matter does not offend due process. . . .

At the outset it is well to examine rather carefully the precise nature of the proceeding which results from the entry of a plea of not guilty by reason of insanity. A plea of not guilty by reason of insanity is somewhat in the nature of a confession and avoidance in the sense that insofar as the plea itself is concerned, the defendant who elects to enter the plea seeks to avoid the consequences of his otherwise criminal actions by contending that he is insane and not accountable therefor. By this statement I do not mean to be understood as saying that a defendant cannot join a general plea of not guilty with a plea of not guilty by reason of insanity. He may, of course. What I am saying, however, is that the trial which is precipitated by a plea of not guilty by reason of insanity is not concerned with the defendant's guilt or innocence, as such, but is only concerned with his mental status, i. e., is the defendant insane? Furthermore, the statute set forth in 1965 Perm.Supp., C.R.S.1963, 38-9-3 provides that where the issue of insanity is raised in a criminal proceeding the matter should be determined in a trial which is completely separate and apart from the trial of the so-called main issue in the case, namely the guilt of the accused. And the fact that in a given case a defendant may be adjudged to be sane certainly does not mean that he is guilty of the crime with which he is charged. That is another issue to be separately litigated and determined.

Inasmuch, then, as the sanity trial is *not* one to determine the guilt of the accused, the so-called presumption of innocence, for example, I submit has no particular applicability. This is so inasmuch as the issue as to guilt, or not, is to be resolved in a separate and different proceeding where the presumption of innocence would of course come into play. Although at the outset of a trial to determine the guilt of the defendant there is a presumption of innocence, there never has been any presumption of innocence by reason of insanity. As a matter of fact, as concerns the issue of sanity, the presumption has always been to the contrary, namely that a defendant even though he has pled innocence by reason of insanity is nonetheless still presumed to be sane. This is the presumption which the majority in my opinion failed to properly recognize as playing an important role in the present controversy. And the reason for this presumption of sanity is the belief, which I indeed trust is correct, that the majority of people are sane.

Lest it be thought that Colorado is the only state to place on the defendant the burden of proving insanity, it should be pointed out that among the several states there presently is, and for a long time has been, a very pronounced split of authority as to whether the People have the burden of proving the accused's sanity or, conversely, the defendant has the burden of establishing his insanity. In Weihofen, Mental Disorder as a Criminal Defense 212–272 (1954) that learned author and authority indicates that the American courts are almost evenly divided on the question as to whether the People or the defendant has the burden of proof on the issue of insanity. Professor Weihofen lists those jurisdictions which either by statute or judicial decision have placed this burden of proof on the defendant as follows: Alabama, Arkansas, California, Delaware, Georgia, Iowa, Kentucky, Louisiana, Maine, Minnesota, Missouri, Montana, Nevada, New Jersey, North Carolina, Ohio, Oregon, Pennsylvania, Rhode Island, South Carolina, Texas, Virginia, Washington and West Virginia.

And, as indicated, the rule that the defendant has the burden of proving insanity when he elects to plead such a defense is most certainly not one of recent origin. By way of example, Oregon in 1864 enacted a statute providing that the defendant must prove insanity beyond a reasonable doubt if he would avoid responsibility for his acts. Indeed, that would appear to be the very rule of the famous *McNaghten* case, wherein it was stated:

"[T]he jurors ought to be told in all cases that every man is to be presumed to be sane, and to possess a sufficient degree of reason to be responsible for his crimes, until the *contrary be proved to their satisfaction*; and . . . to establish a defense on the ground of insanity, *it must be clearly proved that*, at the time of the committing of the act, the party accused was laboring under such a defect of reason, from disease of the mind, as not to know the nature and quality of the act he was doing. . . ." (Emphasis added.)

I recognize, however, that prior to 1967 in Colorado the burden of proof in a so-called insanity trial was admittedly placed on the prosecution. This rule was initially the result of judicial decision, and then later by statute. It is perhaps of historical interest to note that when this court by judicial decision adopted the rule that the People had the burden of proof in this regard it was not on any basis that "due process" required such a rule. On the contrary, it was simply on the basis that such rule was then believed to be "the better doctrine" and as of that time, at least, represented the so-called "weight of authority." See, for example, Pribble v. People, 49 Colo. 210, 112 P. 220. Initially, then, I contend that this court, or the General Assembly, could have gone "either way" on the question as to whether the People or the defendant had the burden of proof when the defendant pleads insanity. Such being the case, the fact that the court and then the General Assembly decided to place the burden on the People does not in my view of the matter mean that such determination is so engrafted onto due process that the rule could never thereafter be changed except by constitutional amendment.

Furthermore, my attention has not been directed to any reported decision from any jurisdiction where a statute of the type with which we are here concerned has been held to be violative of due process. And on the contrary there *are* decisions which hold that such statutes are *not* violative of "due process. . . ."

SOUTH v. UNITED STATES
United States Court of Appeals, Fifth Circuit, 1969.
412 F.2d 697.

DYER, CIRCUIT JUDGE. South appeals from a judgment of conviction entered on a jury verdict finding him guilty of using or causing others to use the facilities of interstate commerce for the promotion of an unlawful gambling activity in violation of 18 U.S.C.A. §§ 2 and 1952. He urges reversal on the grounds that there was insufficient evidence to support his conviction, that the District Court incorrectly charged the jury concerning specific intent, that the Government wrongly refused to stipulate that he was a professional gambler, and that he was prejudiced by the inflammatory remarks made by counsel for the Government during closing argument. We reverse.

On the night of May 27, 1963, one Bishop was sitting in the Brass Rail cocktail lounge in Tampa, Florida, having a few drinks and talking to Bob the bartender. Bob introduced

Bishop to South. Both had a keen interest in poker. South was a professional gambler who made his living by inducing suckers into a poker game in which South and other players working in concert with him would rig the game and split the amount lost by the sucker. Bishop, with the anodyne of a few drinks under his belt, believed that he was an unbeatable poker player. He was therefore a likely subject for South. Bishop, South, Bob and Kolsky, the owner of the Brass Rail, left the cocktail lounge and drove to a private home to play poker. Bob, South and Bishop played five card stud with South acting as banker. Bishop's euphoria was short lived. He began to lose and purchased more chips from South using blank checks which he thought were furnished by South. The checks were made out to cash and were drawn on the Security First National Bank of Lancaster, California. Bishop also gave one or more checks to Bob, but he remembered giving two particular checks, one for ninety-two dollars and one for three hundred dollars, to South. Bishop lost money in the game and Bob won money, but Bishop could not remember whether South won or lost. Three of the checks drawn by Bishop during the poker game, including the two given to South, were deposited in the International Bank of Tampa in an account maintained by Lillian Kolsky and endorsed by her but not by South. The checks were transmitted to the Security First National Bank through the usual clearing process. Two of the checks were returned because of insufficient funds in Bishop's account. When he became aware of this, Bishop called Bob at the Brass Rail and later Bishop went there and gave Bob cash for the checks. Bishop never talked with or saw South after the night of the game.

It was the Government's burden to prove that South had used or had caused another to use a facility of interstate commerce. This it failed to do. There is no direct evidence to support the conviction. South's name does not appear on either of the two checks purportedly given to him by Bishop, and his name does not appear on any of the bank records concerning the deposit and forwarding of the checks.

The Government's circumstantial case is no better. The Government proved that which South was eager to stipulate, i. e., that South was a professional gambler. In the process evidence was presented to the jury which was not probative of the charges in the indictment but which was prejudicial to South. For example, Government witnesses repeatedly described South as a cheat. While this may be true, it has nothing to do with the issue of South's guilt or innocence of the charges upon which he was tried.

The only evidence the Government was able to present was that Bishop gave South two checks for chips. There was no evidence that Bob split his winnings with South, and there was no evidence that South gave the checks to Lillian Kolsky for deposit in her account. The test in circumstantial evidence cases is whether or not the jury could conclude that the inferences to be reasonably drawn from the evidence are consistent with the guilt of the accused and inconsistent with "... every reasonable hypothesis of his innocence." Harper v. United States, 5 Cir. 1969, 405 F.2d 185; Montoya v. United States, 5 Cir. 1968, 402 F.2d 847; O'Connell v. United States, 5 Cir. 1968, 402 F.2d 760; Vick v. United States, 5 Cir. 1954, 216 F.2d 228. Applying the *Vick* standard, we hold that the jury could not have properly resolved every reasonable hypothesis of innocence against South.

Turning now to the trial judge's instruction on intent, the indictment charges that South used or caused another to use a facility of interstate commerce "... with the intent to promote, manage, establish, carry on and facilitate the promotion, management, establishment and carrying on of an unlawful activity...." The District Judge charged the jury on the element of intent as follows:

The acts which a defendant does may indicate a state of mind, that is, the intent to commit the offense charged. It is reasonable to infer that a person ordinarily knows and intends the natural and probable consequences of his act, *so unless the contrary appears from the evidence*, the jury may draw the inference that the accused intended all of the consequences which one standing in like circumstances, and possessing like knowledge should reasonably have expected to result from any acts knowingly done. (Emphasis supplied.)

Defense counsel objected to this instruction. We held an almost identical charge to be error in Mann v. United States, 5 Cir. 1963, 319 F.2d 404, in which we pointed out that:

> When the words, "So unless the contrary appears from the evidence" were introduced, the burden of proof was thereupon shifted from the prosecution to the defendant to prove lack of intent. If an inference from a fact or set of facts must be overcome with opposing evidence, then the inference becomes a presumption and places a burden on the accused to overcome that presumption. Such a burden is especially harmful when a person is required to overcome a presumption as to anything subjective, such as intent or wilfulness, and a barrier almost impossible to hurdle results.

The charge given here was erroneous.

This is the second time that South has been tried for the offenses charged in the case *sub judice*. We reversed the prior conviction. Having found that there was insufficient evidence to support the conviction, no good purpose would be served by ordering a third trial. See 28 U.S.C.A. § 2106. . . .

Reversed with directions to enter a judgment of acquittal.

LEARY v. UNITED STATES
Supreme Court of the United States, 1969.
395 U.S. 6, 89 S.Ct. 1532, 23 L.Ed.2d 57.
Noted, 48 Texas L.Rev. 493; 46 Denver L.J. 482; 19 DePaul L.Rev. 184.

MR. JUSTICE HARLAN delivered the opinion of the Court. This case presents constitutional questions arising out of the conviction of the petitioner, Dr. Timothy Leary, for violation of two federal statutes governing traffic in marijuana.

The circumstances surrounding petitioner's conviction were as follows. On December 20, 1965, petitioner left New York by automobile, intending a vacation trip to Yucatan, Mexico. He was accompanied by his daughter and son, both teenagers, and two other persons. On December 22, 1965, the party drove across the International Bridge between the United States and Mexico at Laredo, Texas. They stopped at the Mexican customs station and, after apparently being denied entry, drove back across the bridge. They halted at the American secondary inspection area, explained the situation to a customs inspector, and stated that they had nothing from Mexico to declare. The inspector asked them to alight, examined the interior of the car, and saw what appeared to be marijuana seeds on the floor. The inspector then received permission to search the car and passengers. Small amounts of marijuana were found on the car floor and in the glove compartment. A personal search of petitioner's daughter revealed a silver snuff box containing semi-refined marijuana and three partially smoked marijuana cigarettes.

Petitioner was indicted and tried before a jury in the Federal District Court for the Southern District of Texas, on three counts. First, it was alleged that he had knowingly smuggled marijuana into the United States, in violation of 21 U.S.C. § 176a. Second, it was charged that he had knowingly transported and facilitated the transportation and concealment of marijuana which had been illegally imported or brought into the United States, with knowledge that it had been illegally imported or brought in, all again in violation of § 176a. Third, it was alleged that petitioner was a transferee of marijuana and had knowingly transported, concealed, and facilitated the transportation and concealment of marijuana without having paid the transfer tax imposed by the Marijuana Tax Act, 26 U.S.C. § 4741 et seq., thereby violating 26 U.S.C. § 4744(a) (2).

After both sides had presented their evidence and the defense had moved for a judgment of acquittal, the District Court dismissed the first or smuggling count. The jury found petitioner guilty on the other two counts. He was tentatively sentenced to the maximum punishment, pending completion of a study and recommendations to be used by the District Court in fixing his final sentence. On appeal, the Court of Appeals for the Fifth Circuit affirmed. 383 F.2d 851 (1967). That court subsequently denied a petition for rehearing and rehearing *en banc.* 392 F.2d 220 (1968).

We granted certiorari, 392 U.S. 903, 88 S.Ct. 2058, 20 L.Ed.2d 1362 (1968), to consider two questions: (1) whether petitioner's conviction for failing to comply with the transfer tax provisions of the Marijuana Tax Act violated his Fifth Amendment privilege against self-incrimination; (2) whether petitioner was denied due process by the application of the part of 21 U.S.C. § 176a which provides that a defendant's possession of marijuana shall be deemed sufficient evidence that the marijuana was illegally imported or brought into the United States, and that the defendant knew of the illegal importation or bringing in, unless the defendant explains his possession to the satisfaction of the jury. For reasons which follow, we hold in favor of the petitioner on both issues and reverse the judgment of the Court of Appeals.

[The discussion of the first question is omitted]

II. Next, we consider whether, in the circumstances of this case, the application of the presumption contained in 21 U.S.C. § 176a denied petitioner due process of law.

A. Insofar as here relevant, § 176a imposes criminal punishment upon every person who:

"knowingly, with intent to defraud the United States, imports or brings into the United States marijuana contrary to law . . . , or receives, conceals, buys, sells, or in any manner facilitates the transportation, concealment, or sale of such marijuana after being imported or brought in, knowing the same to have been imported or brought into the United States contrary to law. . . ."

A subsequent paragraph establishes the presumption now under scrutiny:

"Whenever on trial for a violation of this subsection, the defendant is shown to have or to have had the marijuana in his possession, such possession shall be deemed sufficient evidence to authorize conviction unless the defendant explains his possession to the satisfaction of the jury."

The second count of the indictment charged petitioner with having violated the "transportation" and "concealment" provisions of § 176a. Petitioner admitted at trial that he had acquired marijuana in New York; had driven with it to Laredo, Texas; had continued across the bridge to the Mexican customs station; and then had returned to the United States. He further testified that he did not know where the marijuana he acquired had been grown.

In view of this testimony, the trial court instructed the jury that it might find petitioner guilty of violating § 176a on either of two alternative theories. Under the first or "South-North" theory, a conviction could have been based solely upon petitioner's own testimony that the marijuana had been brought back from Mexico into the United States and that with knowledge of that fact petitioner had continued to transport it. Under the second or "North-South" theory, the conviction would have depended partly upon petitioner's testimony that he had transported the marijuana from New York to Texas and partly upon the challenged presumption.

The Government contends that by giving testimony at trial which established all elements of the offense under the "South-North" theory, and by failing to object to the jury instructions on the ground now advanced, petitioner foreclosed himself from raising the point thereafter. We cannot agree. Even assuming that petitioner's testimony did supply all the evidence required for a valid conviction under the "South-North" theory, the jury nevertheless was told that it could alternatively convict with the aid of the presumption under the "North-South" theory. For all we know, the conviction did rest on that ground. It has long been settled that when a case is submitted to the jury on alternative theories the unconstitutionality of any of the theories requires that the conviction be set aside. See, *e.g.,* Stromberg v. California, 283 U.S. 359, 51 S.Ct. 532, 75 L.Ed. 1117 (1931).

It is true that petitioner did not object to the jury instructions on the basis of the presumption's alleged unconstitutionality. However, he did rely upon that ground in his previous motion for a directed verdict at the close of the prosecution's case and urged it again in his subsequent motion for a new trial. Both motions were denied. The Court of Appeals considered petitioner's constitutional argument on the merits, and rejected it. See 383 F.2d, at 868–870. In these circumstances, we conclude that the question is properly before us.

B. By what criteria is the constitutionality of the § 176a presumption to be judged?

Early decisions of this Court set forth a number of different standards by which to measure the validity of statutory presumptions. However, in Tot v. United States, 319 U.S. 463, 63 S. Ct. 1241, 87 L.Ed. 1519 (1943), the Court singled out one of these tests as controlling, and the *Tot* rule has been adhered to in the two subsequent cases in which the issue has been presented. The *Tot* Court had before it a federal statute which, as construed, made it a crime from one previously convicted of a crime of violence to receive any firearm or ammunition in an interstate transaction. The statute further provided that "the posession of a firearm or ammunition by any such person shall be presumptive evidence that such firearm or ammunition was shipped or transported or received, as the case may be, by such person in violation of this Act."

The Court, relying upon a prior decision in a civil case, held that the "controlling" test for determining the validity of a statutory presumption was "that there be a rational connection between the fact proved and the fact presumed." 319 U.S., at 467, 63 S.Ct., at 1245. The Court stated:

"Under our decisions a statutory presumption cannot be sustained if there be no rational connection between the fact proved and the ultimate fact presumed, if the inference of the one from proof of the other is arbitrary because of lack of connection between the two in common experience. This is not to say that a valid presumption may not be created upon a view of relation broader than that a jury might take in a specific case. But where the inference is so strained as not to have a reasonable relation to the circumstances of life as we know them it is not competent for the legislature to create it as a rule governing the procedure of courts." 319 U.S., at 467–468, 63 S. Ct., at 1245.

The *Tot* Court reduced to the status of a "corollary" another test which had some support in prior decisions: whether it was more convenient for the defendant or for the Government to supply proof of the ultimate fact which the presumption permitted to be inferred. The Court stated that "[t]he argument from convenience is admissible only where the inference is a permissible one...." 319 U.S., at 469, 63 S.Ct., at 1246. The Court rejected entirely another suggested test with some backing in the case law, according to which the presumption should be sustained if Congress might legitimately have made it a crime to commit the basic act from which the presumption allowed an inference to be drawn. The *Tot* Court stated simply that "for whatever reason" Congress had not chosen to make the basic act a crime. *Id.,* at 472, 63 S.Ct., at 1247.

Applying the "rational connection" test, the Court held the *Tot* presumption unconstitutional. The Court rejected the contention that because most States forbade intrastate acquisition of firearms without a record of the transaction or registration of ownership it could be inferred merely from possession that an acquisition which did not meet these requirements must have been interstate, noting the alternative possibilities of unlawful intrastate acquisition and interstate shipment prior to the beginning of state regulation. See *id.,* at 468, 63 S.Ct., at 1245.

The two subsequent cases in which this Court ruled upon the constitutionality of criminal statutory presumptions, United States v. Gainey, 380 U.S. 63, 85 S.Ct. 754, 13 L.Ed.2d 658 (1965), and United States v. Romano, 382 U.S. 136, 86 S.Ct. 279, 15 L.Ed.2d 210 (1965), involved companion sections of the Internal Revenue Code dealing with illegal stills. The presumption in *Gainey* was worded similarly to the one at issue here; it permitted a jury to infer from a defendant's presence at an illegal still that he was "carrying on" the business of a distiller "unless the defendant explains such presence to the satisfaction of the jury...." See 26 U.S.C. §§ 5601 (a) (4), 5601(b) (2).

We held that the *Gainey* presumption should be tested by the "rational connection" standard announced in *Tot.* We added:

"The process of making the determination of rationality is, by its nature, highly empirical, and in matters not within specialized judicial competence or completely commonplace, significant weight should be accorded the capacity of Congress to amass the stuff of actual experience and cull conclusions from it." 380 U.S., at 67, 85 S.Ct., at 757.

Applying these principles, we sustained the *Gainey* presumption, finding that it "did no more than 'accord to the evidence, if unexplained, its natural probative force.'" 380 U.S., at 71, 85 S.Ct., at 759.

The presumption under attack in United States v. Romano, *supra*, was identical to that in *Gainey* except that it authorized the jury to infer from the defendant's presence at an illegal still that he had possession, custody, or control of the still. See 26 U.S.C. §§ 5601(a) (1), 5601(b) (1). We held this presumption invalid. While stating that the result in *Gainey* was entirely justified because "[p]resence at an operating still is sufficient evidence to prove the charge of 'carrying on' because anyone present at the site is very probably connected with the illegal enterprise," 382 U.S., at 141, 86 S.Ct., at 282, we concluded:

"Presence is relevant and admissible evidence in a trial on a possession charge; but absent some showing of the defendant's function at the still, its connection with possession is too tenuous to permit a reasonable inference of guilt—'the inference of the one from proof of the other is arbitrary....'" Tot v. United States, 319 U.S. 463, 467, 63 S.Ct. 1241, 1245, 87 L.Ed. 1519. *Ibid.*

The upshot of *Tot, Gainey*, and *Romano* is, we think, that a criminal statutory presumption must be regarded as "irrational" or "arbitrary," and hence unconstitutional, unless it can at least be said with substantial assurance that the presumed fact is more likely than not to flow from the proved fact on which it is made to depend. And in the judicial assessment the congressional determination favoring the particular presumption must, of course, weigh heavily.

C. How does the § 176a presumption fare under these standards?

So far as here relevant, the presumption, quoted *supra*, at 1545, authorizes the jury to infer from a defendant's possession of marijuana two necessary elements of the crime: (1) that the marijuana was imported or brought into the United States illegally; and (2) that the defendant knew of the unlawful importation or bringing in. Petitioner argues that neither inference is valid, citing undisputed testimony at his trial to the effect that marijuana will grow anywhere in the United States, and that some actually is grown here. The Government contends, on the other hand, that both inferences are permissible. For reasons that follow, we hold unconstitutional that part of the presumption which relates to a defendant's knowledge of illegal importation. Consequently we do not reach the question of the validity of the "illegal importation" inference.

With regard to the "knowledge" presumption, we believe that *Tot* and *Romano* require that we take the statute at face value and ask whether it permits conviction upon insufficient proof of "knowledge," rather than inquire whether Congress might have made possession itself a crime. In order thus to determine the constitutionality of the "knowledge" inference, one must have direct or circumstantial data regarding the beliefs of marijuana users generally about the source of the drug they consume. Such information plainly is "not within specialized judicial competence or completely commonplace," United States v. Gainey, supra, 380 U.S., at 67, 85 S.Ct., at 757. Indeed, the presumption apparently was enacted to relieve the Government of the burden of having to adduce such evidence at every trial, and none was introduced by the prosecution at petitioner's trial. Since the determination of the presumption's constitutionality is "highly empirical," *ibid.*, it follows that we must canvass the available, *pertinent* data.

Of course, it must be kept in mind that "significant weight should be accorded the capacity of Congress to amass the stuff of actual experience and cull conclusions from it." *Ibid.* However, it quickly becomes apparent that the legislative record does not supply an adequate basis upon which to judge the soundness of the "knowledge" part of the presumption. We have therefore taken other materials into account as well, in an effort to sustain the presumption. In so doing, we have not confined ourselves to data available at the time the presumption was enacted in 1956, but have also considered more recent information, in order both to obtain a broader general background and to ascertain whether the intervening years have witnessed significant changes which might bear upon the presumption's validity.

As has been noted, we do not decide whether the presumption of illegal importation is itself constitutional. However, in view of the paucity of direct evidence as to the beliefs of marijuana smokers generally about the source of their marijuana, we have found it desirable to survey data concerning the proportion of domestically consumed marijuana which is of foreign origin, since in the absence of better information the proportion of marijuana actually imported surely is relevant in deciding whether marijuana possessors "know" that their marijuana is imported.

D. Since the importation question is a subsidiary one, we take it up first, beginning, of course, with the legislative history of § 176a. The House and Senate committee reports and the floor debates are relatively unhelpful. More informative are the records of extensive hearings before House and Senate committees. Near the outset of the Senate committee hearings the then Commissioner of Narcotics, Harry J. Anslinger, estimated that 90% of all marijuana seized by federal authorities had been smuggled from Mexico, and that "although there is considerable volunteer growth from old plantings in the Middle West . . . , [t]here is very little of the local land used because it just does not have the advantage of the long summer growing and [domestic marijuana] is not as potent as the Mexican drug." A number of officials responsible for enforcing the narcotics laws in various localities estimated that a similar proportion of the marijuana consumed in their areas was of Mexican origin.

On the other hand, written material inserted in the record of the Senate hearings included former testimony of an experienced federal customs agent before another Senate committee, to the effect that high-quality marijuana was being grown near the Texas cities of Laredo and Brownsville. A written report of the Ohio Attorney General recited that marijuana "may grow unnoticed along roadsides and vacant lots in many parts of the country," and a Philadelphia Police Academy bulletin stated that "Plenty of [marijuana] is found growing in this city."

Examination of periodicals and books published since the enactment of the presumption leaves no doubt that in more than a dozen intervening years there have been great changes in the amount and nature of marijuana used in this country. With respect to quantity, one readily available statistic is indicative: the amount of marijuana seized in this country by federal authorities has jumped from about 3,400 pounds in 1956 to about 61,400 pounds in 1967. With regard to nature of use, the 1955 hearing records and other reports portray marijuana smoking as at that time an activity almost exclusively of unemployed or menially employed members of racial minorities. Current periodicals and books, on the other hand, indicate that marijuana smoking has become common on many college campuses and among persons who have voluntarily "dropped out" of American society in protest against its values, and that marijuana smokers include a sizeable number of young professional persons.

Despite these undoubted changes, the materials which we have examined point quite strongly to the conclusion that most domestically consumed marijuana is still of foreign origin. During the six years 1962–1967, some 79% of all marijuana seized by federal authorities was seized in attempted smuggling at ports and borders. The Government informs us that a considerable part of the internally seized marijuana bore indications of foreign origin. While it is possible that these facts reflect only the deployment of federal narcotics forces, rather than the actual proportion of imported to domestic marijuana, almost all of the authorities which we have consulted confirm that the preponderance of domestically consumed marijuana is grown in Mexico.

Petitioner makes much of statistics showing the number of acres of domestic marijuana destroyed annually by state and federal authorities, pointing out that if harvested the destroyed acreage could in each year have accounted for all marijuana estimated to have been consumed in the United States, and that no one knows how many acres escape destruction. However, several factors weaken this argument from domestic growth. First, the number of acres annually destroyed declined by a factor of three between 1959 and 1967, while during the same period the consumption of marijuana, as measured by federal seizures, rose twenty-fold. Assuming constant diligence on the part of those charged with destruction, this would indicate that in 1967 a much smaller share of the market was domestically supplied than in 1959. Second, while the total number of acres annually destroyed has indeed been large enough to furnish all domestically consumed marijuana, the state-by-state breakdowns which are available for the years 1964–1967 reveal that in each of those years more than 95% of the destroyed acreage was in two midwestern states, Ilinois and Minnesota. The large, recurrent marijuana acreages discovered in those States can plausibly be ascribed to the "volunteer growth from old plantings in the Middle West" about which Commissioner Anslinger testified, while illicit cultivators of marijuana would be likely to choose States with sparser populations and more favorable climates. Third and last, reports of the Bureau of Narcotics and testimony of its agents indicate that in its far-reaching investigations the Bureau has never encountered a system for distributing sizeable quantities of domestically grown marijuana. In contrast, the Bureau has found evidence of many large-scale distribution systems with sources in Mexico.

E. The Government urges that once it is concluded that most domestically consumed marijuana comes from abroad—a conclusion which we think is warranted by the data just examined—we must uphold the "knowledge" part of the presumption in light of this Court's decision in Yee Hem v. United States, 268 U.S. 178, 45 S.Ct. 470, 69 L.Ed. 904 (1925). In that case, the Court sustained a presumption which was virtually identical to the one at issue here except that the forbidden substance was smoking opium rather than marijuana. With respect to the inference of knowledge from possession which was authorized by that presumption, the Court said:

"Legitimate possession [of opium], unless for medicinal use, is so highly improbable that to say to any person who obtains the outlawed commodity, 'since you are bound to know that it cannot be brought into this country at all, except under regulation for medicinal use, you must at your peril ascertain and be prepared to show the facts and circumstances which rebut, or tend to rebut, the natural inference of unlawful importation, or your knowledge of it,' is not such an unreasonable requirement as to cause it to fall outside the constitutional power of Congress." 268 U.S., at 184, 45 S.Ct., at 471.

The Government contends that Yee Hem requires us to read the § 176a presumption as intended to put every marijuana smoker on notice that he must be prepared to show that any marijuana in his possession was not illegally imported, and that since the possessor is the person most likely to know the marijuana's origin it is not unfair to require him to adduce evidence on that point. However, we consider that this approach, which closely resembles the test of comparative convenience in the production of evidence, was implicitly abandoned in Tot v. United States. As was noted previously, the Tot Court confronted a presumption which allowed a jury to infer from possession of a firearm that it was received in interstate commerce. Despite evidence that most States prohibited unregistered and unrecorded acquisition of firearms, the Court did not read the statute as notifying possessors that they must be prepared to show that they received their weapons in intrastate transactions, as Yee Hem would seem to dictate. Instead, while recognizing that "the defendants . . . knew better than anyone else whether they acquired the firearms or ammunition in intrastate commerce," 319 U.S., at 469, 63 S.Ct., at 1246, the Court held that because of the danger of overreaching it was incumbent upon the prosecution to demonstrate that the inference was permissible before the burden of coming forward could be placed upon the defendant. This was a matter which the Yee Hem Court either thought it unnecessary to consider or assumed when it described the inference as "natural."

F. We therefore must consider in detail whether the available evidence supports the conclusion that the "knowledge" part of the § 176a presumption is constitutional under the standard established in Tot and adhered to in Gainey and Romano—that is, whether it can be said with substantial assurance that one in possession of marijuana is more likely than not to know that his marijuana was illegally imported.

Even if we assume that the previously assembled data are sufficient to justify the inference of illegal importation, see supra, at 1552, it by no means follows that a majority of marijuana possessors "know" that their marijuana was illegally imported. Any such proposition would depend upon an intermediate premise: that most marijuana possessors are aware of the level of importation and have deduced that their own marijuana was grown abroad. This intermediate step might be thought justified by common sense if it were proved that little or no marijuana is grown in this country. Short of such a showing, not here present, we do not believe that the inference of knowledge can be sustained solely because of the assumed validity of the "importation" presumption.

Once it is established that a significant percentage of domestically consumed marijuana may not have been imported at all, then it can no longer be postulated, without proof, that possessors will be even roughly aware of the proportion actually imported. We conclude that in order to sustain the inference of knowledge we must find on the basis of the available materials that a majority of marijuana possessors either are cognizant of the apparently high rate of importation or otherwise have become aware that *their* marijuana was grown abroad.

We can imagine five ways in which a possessor might acquire such knowledge: (1) he might be aware of the proportion of domestically consumed marijuana which is smuggled from abroad and deduce that his was illegally imported; (2) he might have smuggled the marijuana himself; (3) he might have learned by indirect means that the marijuana consumed in his locality or furnished by his supplier was smuggled from abroad; (4) he might have specified foreign marijuana when making his "buy", or might have been told the source of the marijuana by his supplier; (5) he might be able to tell the source from the appearance, packaging, or taste of the marijuana itself.

We treat these five possibilities *seriatim*, in light of the available materials, beginning in each instance with the legislative record. We note at the outset that although we have been able to discover a good deal of relevant secondary evidence, we have found none of the best kind possible—testimony of marijuana users about their own beliefs as to origin, or studies based upon interviews in which users were asked about this matter. The committee hearings which preceded passage of § 176a included testimony by many marijuana smokers, but none was ever asked whether he knew the origin of the marijuana he smoked. It should also be kept in mind that the great preponderance of marijuana smokers are "occasional" rather than "regular" users of the drug, and that "occasional" smokers appear to be arrested disproportionately often, due to their inexpertness in taking precautions. "Occasional" users are likely to be less informed and less particular about the drug they smoke; hence, it is less probable that they will have learned its source in any of the above ways.

The first possibility is that a possessor may have known the proportion of imported to domestic marijuana and have deduced that his own marijuana was grown abroad. The legislative record is of no assistance in evaluating this possibility. Such indirect evidence as we have found points to the conclusion that while most marijuana users probably know that some marijuana comes from Mexico, it is also likely that the great majority either have no knowledge about the proportion which is imported or believe that the proportion is considerably lower than may actually be the case.

The second possibility is that a possessor may know the origin of his marijuana because he smuggled it into the United States himself. The legislative record is unhelpful in estimating the proportion of possessors who fall into this class. Other sources indicate that there are a considerable number of smokers who "smuggle their own," but that the great majority of possessors have obtained their marijuana from suppliers in this country.

The legislative record is also uninformative about the possibility that a possessor may have learned the source of his marijuana by indirect means. Other sources reveal that imported marijuana usually passes through a number of hands before reaching the consumer, and that the distribution system is kept secret. It would appear that relatively few consumers know the origin of their marijuana by indirect means.

The fourth possibility is that the possessor may have specified foreign marijuana when making his purchase or may have been told by his supplier that the marijuana was grown abroad. The legislative record is somewhat more helpful with respect to this possibility, for it does contain statements to the effect that Mexican marijuana is more potent than domestic and is consequently preferred by smokers. However, the legislative record also contains testimony by a customs agent that Texas marijuana is as "good" as that from Mexico. Most authorities state that Mexican marijuana generally does have greater intoxicating power than domestic marijuana, due to the higher temperatures and lower humidity usually encountered in Mexico. There are some indications that smokers are likely to prefer Mexican marijuana, but there is nothing to show that purchasers commonly specify Mexican marijuana when making a "buy." It appears that suppliers of marijuana occasionally volunteer the place of origin, but we have found no hint that this is usually done, and there are indications that if the information is not volunteered the buyer may be reluctant to ask, for fear of being thought an informer. We simply are unable to estimate with any accuracy, on the basis of these data, what proportion of marijuana possessors have learned the origin of their marijuana in this way. It is certainly not a majority; but whether it is a small minority or a large one we are unable to tell.

The fifth possibility is that a smoker may be able to tell the source of his marijuana from its appearance, packaging, or taste. As for appearance, it seems that there is only one species of marijuana, and that even experts are unable to tell by eye where a particular sample was grown. The Court of Appeals for the Ninth Circuit did find in Caudillo v. United States, 253 F.2d 513 (1958), on the basis of trial testimony, that "unmanicured" or "rough" marijuana—that is, marijuana containing some seeds and stems, as well as leaves—was much more likely to come from Mexico than from California; this was because the presence of seeds implied that the plant had been allowed to mature and evidence showed that California growers almost always harvested the plant before that stage. However, we have found nothing to indicate that this distinction holds good in other areas of the country, or that marijuana possessors are likely to realize its significance.

With respect to packaging, there is evidence that Mexican marijuana is commonly compressed into distinctive "bricks" and then wrapped in characteristically Mexican paper. Yet even if it is assumed that most Mexican marijuana bears such distinguishing marks when first brought into this country, there is no indication that they normally are still present when it reaches the consumer. The packaging method just mentioned apparently is intended to facilitate transportation of relatively large quantities of marijuana. A "brick" appears usually to contain about one kilogram of marijuana, and relatively few consumers sales will involve such a large amount, since a kilogram of marijuana will furnish some 3,300 marijuana cigarettes. Smokers appear usually to purchase marijuana by the "bag"—about one-fifth ounce; by the "can"—about one ounce; or by the pound. Hence, after importation "[t]he wholesalers will repackage the marijuana into smaller packages, . . . and they will do it in various ways." We infer that only a small percentage of smokers are likely to learn of the drug's origin from its packaging.

With respect to taste, the Senate hearing record contains the statement of a federal customs agent that "A good marijuana smoker can probably tell good marijuana from bad." As has been seen, there is a preponderance of opinion to the effect that Mexican marijuana is more potent than domestic. One authority states that purchasers of marijuana commonly sample the product before making a "buy." However, the agent quoted above also asserted that some "good" marijuana was grown in Texas. And the account of the sampling custom further states that tasting is merely a ritual since "[u]sually the intoxication will not differ much from one cigarette to another. . . ." Once again, we simply are unable to estimate what proportion of marijuana possessors are capable of "placing" the marijuana in their possession by its taste, much less what proportion actually have done so by the time they are arrested.

G. We conclude that the "knowledge" aspect of the § 176a presumption cannot be upheld without making serious incisions into the teachings of *Tot*, *Gainey*, and *Romano*. In the context of this part of the statute, those teachings require that it be determined with substantial assurance that at least a majority of marijuana possessors have learned of the foreign origin of their marijuana through one or more of the ways discussed above.

We find it impossible to make such a determination. As we have seen, the materials at our disposal leave us at large to estimate even roughly the proportion of marijuana possessors who have learned in one way or another the origin of their marijuana. It must also be recognized that a not inconsiderable proportion of domestically consumed marijuana appears to have been grown in this country, and that its possessors must be taken to have "known," if anything, that their marijuana was *not* illegally imported. In short, it would be no more than speculation were we to say that even as much as a majority of possessors "knew" the source of their marijuana.

Nor are these deficiencies in the foundation for the "knowledge" presumption overcome by paying, as we do, the utmost deference to the congressional determination that this presumption was warranted. For Congress, no less than we, is subject to constitutional requirements, and in this instance the legislative record falls even shorter of furnishing an adequate foundation for the "knowledge" presumption than do the more extensive materials we have examined.

We thus cannot escape the duty of setting aside petitioner's conviction under Count 2 of this indictment.

For the reasons stated in Part I of this opinion we reverse outright the judgment of conviction on Count 3 of the indictment. For the reasons stated in Part II, we reverse the judgment of conviction on Count 2 and remand the case to the Court of Appeals for further proceedings consistent with this opinion. We are constrained to add that nothing in what we hold today implies any constitutional disability in Congress to deal with the marijuana traffic by other means.

Reversed and remanded.

Mr. Chief Justice Warren joins Part II of the opinion of the Court. . . .

Mr. Justice Stewart, concurring.

I join Part II of the Court's opinion. . . .

Mr. Justice Black, concurring in the result.

I concur in the Court's outright reversal of the petitioner's conviction on Count 3 of the indictment for the reasons set out in Part I of the Court's opinion.

I also concur in reversal of the petitioner's conviction under Count 2 of the indictment, based on 21 U.S.C. § 176a. That section makes it a crime to import marijuana into the United States or to receive, conceal, or transport it, knowing it to have been imported contrary to law, and then goes on to provide that the mere possession of marijuana shall be "deemed sufficient evidence to authorize conviction unless the defendant explains his possession to the satisfaction of the jury." The trial court in this case charged the jury that proof that petitioner merely had possession of marijuana was sufficient to authorize a finding that he knew it had been imported or brought into the United States contrary to law. It is clear beyond doubt that the fact of possession alone is not enough to support an inference that the possessor knew it had been imported. Congress has no more constitutional power to tell a jury it can convict upon any such forced and baseless inference than it has power to tell juries they can convict a defendant of a crime without any evidence at all from which an inference of guilt could be drawn. See Thompson v. Louisville, 362 U.S. 199, 80 S.Ct. 624, 4 L.Ed.2d 654 (1960). Under our system of separation of powers, Congress is just as incompetent to instruct the judge and jury in an American court what evidence is enough for conviction as the courts are to tell the Congress what policies they must adopt in writing criminal laws. The congressional presumption, therefore, violates the constitutional right of a defendant to be tried by jury in a court set up in accordance with the commands of the Constitution. It clearly deprives a defendant of his right not to be convicted and punished for a crime without due process of law, that is a trial in federal cases before an independent judge, after an indictment by grand jury, with representation by counsel, an opportunity to summon witnesses in his behalf, and an opportunity to confront the witnesses against him. This right to a full-fledged trial in a court of law is guaranteed to every defendant in Article III of the Constitution, in the Sixth Amendment, and in the Fifth and Fourteenth Amendments' promises that no person shall be deprived of his life, liberty, or property without due process of law—that is, a trial according to the law of the land, both constitutional and statutory.

It is for these reasons, and not because I think the law is " 'irrational' or 'arbitrary,' and hence unconstitutional," *ante*, p. [317], that I would invalidate this presumption. I am firmly and profoundly opposed to construing "due process" as authorizing this Court to invalidate statutes on any such nebulous grounds. My quite different reasons for holding that the presumption does deny due process of law, that is the benefit of the "law of the land," have been fully set out in many opinions, including, for illustration, my concurring opinion in Tot v. United States, 319 U.S. 463, 473, 63 S.Ct. 1241, 87 L.Ed. 1519 (1943), and my dissenting opinion in United States v. Gainey, 380 U.S. 63, 74, 85 S.Ct. 754, 761, 13 L.Ed.2d 658 (1965).

UNITED STATES v. GAINEY
Supreme Court of the United States, 1965.
380 U.S. 63, 85 S.Ct. 754, 13 L.Ed.2d 658.
Noted, 33 Geo. Wash. L.Rev. 1137.

MR. JUSTICE STEWART delivered the opinion of the Court.

After a jury trial in the United States District Court for the Middle District of Georgia, respondent Jackie Gainey was convicted of violating 26 U.S.C. § 5601(a)(1) (possession, custody or control of a set up, unregistered still and distilling apparatus) and 26 U.S.C. § 5601(a)(4) (carrying on "the business of a distiller or rectifier without having given bond as required by law"). In the course of his instructions the trial judge informed the jury of two statutory provisions which authorize a jury to infer guilt of the substantive offenses from the fact of a defendant's unexplained presence at the site of an illegal still. The Court of Appeals for the Fifth Circuit reversed the convictions on the ground that these statutory inferences are unconstitutional, because it thought the connection between unexplained presence at an illegal still and the substantive offenses of "possession" and "carrying on" is insufficiently rational to satisfy the due process requirements formulated by this Court in Tot v. United States, 319 U.S. 463, 63 S.Ct. 1241, 87 L.Ed. 1519. We granted certiorari, sub nom. United States v. Barrett, to review the exercise of the grave power of annulling an Act of Congress. 375 U.S. 962, 84 S.Ct. 489, 11 L.Ed.2d 413.

If either statutory inference is valid, the judgment of the Court of Appeals must be reversed, because concurrent sentences were imposed by the District Court. Emspak v. United States, 349 U.S. 190, 195, 75 S.Ct. 687, 690, 99 L.Ed. 997; Sinclair v. United States, 279 U.S. 263, 299, 49 S.Ct. 268, 273, 73 L.Ed. 692 (1929). We find the inference authorized by § 5601(b)(2) constitutionally permissible, and therefore reverse the judgment without reaching the validity of § 5601(b)(1).

The legislative record shows that Congress enacted these provisions because of "the practical impossibility of proving . . . actual participation in the illegal activities except by inference drawn from [the defendant's] presence when the illegal acts were committed. . . ." The statutes were passed against a backdrop of varying formulations among the Circuits of the standards which should shape a trial judge's instructions to a jury in telling it what weight to accord the fact of a defendant's unexplained presence at an illegal still site. Long before 1958, the year the statutes were enacted, trial judges had been instructing juries that a defendant's presence at a still could be considered by them in determining whether the defendant had participated in carrying on the illegal operation. Barton v. United States, 267 F. 174, 175–176 (C.A.4th Cir.). Compare Wilson v. United States, 162 U.S. 613, 16 S.Ct. 895, 40 L.Ed. 1090. The Fourth Circuit had endorsed such a charge. Barton v. United States, supra. In the Third and Fifth Circuits the precedents were less clear. See Graceffo v. United States, 46 F.2d 852 (C.A.3d Cir.); Fowler v. United States, 234 F.2d 697, 699 (C.A.5th Cir.).

The variations among the courts of appeals concerned the reasonableness of inferring guilt of the substantive offense from the fact of unexplained presence at the site of the criminal enterprise. It is that question which Congress has now resolved in favor of the established practice of trial judges to include the inference in their charges. And it is the same question of reasonableness which the petitioner asks this Court to determine in passing on the constitutionality of § 5601(b)(2). . . .

But it is said that this statute is unconstitutional upon a different ground—that it impinges upon the trial judge's powers over the judicial proceeding. We cannot agree. Our Constitution places in the hands of the trial judge the responsibility for safeguarding the integrity of the jury trial, including the right to have a case withheld from the jury when the evidence is insufficient as a matter of law to support a conviction. The statute before us deprives the trial judge of none of his normal judicial powers. We do not interpret the provision in the statute that unexplained "presence . . . shall be deemed sufficient evidence to authorize conviction" as in any way invading the province of the judge's discretion. The language permits the judge to submit a case to the jury on the basis of the accused's presence alone, and to this extent it constitutes congressional recognition that the fact of presence does have probative worth in the determination of guilt. But where the only evidence is of presence the statute does not require the judge to submit the case to the jury, nor does it preclude the grant of a judgment notwithstanding the verdict. And the Court of Appeals may still review the trial judge's denial of motions for a directed verdict or for a judgment n. o. v.

The statute does not prevent the jury from being "properly instructed on the standards for reasonable doubt." Holland v. United States, 348 U.S. 121, 139, 75 S.Ct. 127, 139, 99 L.Ed. 150. In this case, the trial judge instructed the jury as follows:

"There is one other matter which I should mention. I charge you that the presence of defendants at a still, if proved, with or without flight therefrom, or attempted flight therefrom, if proved, would be a circumstance for you to consider along with all the other testimony in the case. Of course, the bare presence at a distillery and flight therefrom of an innocent man is not in and of itself enough to make him guilty. It is possible under the law for an innocent man to be present at a distillery, and it is possible for him to run when about to be apprehended, and such an innocent man ought never to be convicted, but presence at a distillery, if you think these men were present, is a circumstance to be considered along with all the other circumstances in the case in determining whether they were connected with the distillery or not. Did they have any equipment with them that was necessary at the distillery? What was the hour of day that they were there? Did the officers see them do anything? Did they make any statements?

"It is your duty to explore this case, analyze the evidence pro and con fairly. Presence at a still, together with other circumstances in the case, if they are sufficient in your opinion to exclude every reasonable conclusion except that they were there connected with the distillery, in an illegal manner, . . . carrying on the business as charged . . . , if you believe those things, would authorize you in finding the defendants guilty.

"And under a statute enacted by Congress a few years back, when a person is on trial for . . . carrying on the business of a distiller without giving bond as required by law, as charged in this case, and the defendant is shown to have been at the site of the place . . . where and at the time when the business of a distiller was engaged in or carried on without bond having been given, under the law such presence of the defendant shall be deemed sufficient evidence to authorize conviction, unless the defendant by the evidence in the case and by proven facts and circumstances explains such presence to the satisfaction of the jury.

"*Now this does not mean that the presence of the defendant at the site and place at the time referred to requires the jury to convict the defendant, if the defendant by the evidence in the case, facts and circumstances proved, fails to explain his presence to the satisfaction of the jury. It simply means that a jury may, if it sees fit, convict upon such evidence, as it shall be deemed in law sufficient to authorize a conviction, but does not require such a result.*"

The jury was thus specifically told that the statutory inference was not conclusive. "Presence" was one circumstance to be considered among many. Even if it found that the defendant had been present at the still, and that his presence remained unexplained, the jury could nonetheless acquit him if it found that the Government had not proved his guilt beyond a reasonable doubt. Holland v. United States, supra. In the absence of the statute, such an instruction to the jury would surely have been permissible. Cf. Wilson v. United States, supra. Furthermore, in the context of the instructions as a whole, we do not consider that the single phrase "unless the defendant by the evidence in the case and by proven facts and circumstances explains such presence to the satisfaction of the jury" can be fairly understood as a comment on the petitioner's failure to testify. Cf. Bruno v. United States, 308 U.S. 287, 60 S.Ct. 198, 84 L.Ed. 257. The judge's overall reference was carefully directed to the evidence as a whole, with neither allusion nor innuendo based on the defendant's decision to take the stand.

In McNamara v. Henkel, 226 U.S. 520, 525, 33 S.Ct. 146, 147, 57 L.Ed. 330, the Court approved a proceeding which did no more than "accord to the evidence, if unexplained, its natural probative force." That is all that Congress has done here. We cannot find that the law it enacted violates the Constitution.

Reversed.

MR. JUSTICE DOUGLAS, dissenting in part....

It would be possible to interpret the statute as compelling judges to give the following instruction to juries: "If you find that the defendant was present at the still, then the law requires you to assume that he was there carrying on the business of a distiller within the meaning of the statute; but you need not make this assumption if the defendant has given another explanation of his presence there and you are satisfied of the truth of that explanation." If the statute were read as compelling such an instruction. I would find it constitutionally intolerable, for the reasons so well stated by my Brother BLACK.

The Court, however, interprets the statute as merely allowing, not compelling, the jury to draw the inference of "carrying on" from the fact of "presence." The jury is left free to reject the inference if, in light of all the circumstances of the case, a reasonable doubt remains as to the defendant's guilt. That is the way the jury would normally function, apart from the statute. So, I have concluded that the statute, as construed, merely provides a rule of evidence and no more.

There are, to be sure, dangers inherent in any statutory presumption. Perhaps the jury will be overawed if it is told that some particular factual inference has been enshrined in an Act of Congress. Therefore the Court quite rightly suggests that the better practice would be to omit "any explicit reference to the statute itself in the charge." *Ante*, p. [334, n. 39]. Or perhaps the judge may feel that the statute restricts his power to withhold an insufficient case from the jury or to grant a judgment notwithstanding the verdict. The Court reassures the trial judge that the statute does not thus invade the province of his discretion. Nor is the function of the appellate courts in any way circumscribed. . . .

MR. JUSTICE BLACK, dissenting.

Respondent Gainey was tried and convicted of possession of an unregistered still and of carrying on the business of a distiller without having given bond in violation of a federal statute. Other provisions of the statute entitled "Presumptions," declare that presence at the site of such a distillery "shall be deemed sufficient evidence to authorize conviction, unless the defendant explains such presence to the satisfaction of the jury. . . ." At the trial federal and state officers testified, among other things, that they had seen Gainey at a still site. Gainey did not testify. The trial court, quite appropriately if the foregoing provisions are valid, instructed the jury that Gainey's unexplained presence at the still was "deemed in law sufficient" to convict. I think that the statutory provisions which authorize such a charge deprived Gainey (1) of his constitutional right to trial by jury, guaranteed him both in Art. III, § 2, and in the Sixth Amendment; (2) of due process of law guaranteed by the Fifth Amendment, which includes the right to be tried for a crime in a court according to the law of the land, without any interference with that court's judicial functions by the Congress; and (3) of his right guaranteed by the Fifth Amendment not to be compelled to be a witness against himself.

First of all, let me say that I am at a loss to understand the Court's puzzling statement that "where the only evidence is of presence the statute does not require the judge to submit the case to the jury, nor does it preclude the grant of a judgment notwithstanding the verdict." The provisions in question both say unqualifiedly that "presence of the defendant shall be deemed sufficient evidence to authorize conviction" unless the defendant explains his presence. The Court holds that this statutory command in § 5601(b) (2) is valid, but then for some reason adds that judges are free to ignore it or, after telling juries that they may rely on it, are free to set aside the verdicts of those juries which do. In other words, under the Court's holding the judge is left free to take the extraordinary course of following a valid statute or not, as he chooses. Judges are not usually given such unlimited discretion to disregard valid statutes. And as the Court indicates elsewhere in its opinion, it was to prevent judges from setting aside jury verdicts based on presence alone that Congress passed this statute in the first place. Besides being almost self-contradictory, it amounts to an emasculation of these statutory provisions, I think, to say that the judge was not required to tell the jury about them. But whether or not he was bound to do so, the fact is that here he did, and so this jury deliberated with the judge's solemn instruction that Congress had decided that proof of mere unexplained presence at a still was sufficient to convict Gainey of having illegally possessed it or carried on its business. Few jurors could have failed to believe that it was their duty to convict under this charge if presence was proved, and few judges could have failed to believe it was their duty to uphold such a conviction, even though all of them in a particular case might have felt that mere presence alone was not enough to show guilt.

It has always been recognized that the guaranty of trial by jury in criminal cases means that the jury is to be the factfinder. This is the only way in which a jury can perform its basic constitutional function of determining the guilt or innocence of a defendant. See, e. g., United States ex rel. Toth v. Quarles, 350 U.S. 11, 15–19, 76 S.Ct. 1, 4–6, 100 L.Ed. 8; Reid v. Covert, 354 U.S. 1, 5–10, 77 S.Ct. 1222, 1224–1227 (opinion announcing judgment). And of course this constitutionally established power of a jury to determine guilt or innocence of a defendant charged with crime cannot be taken away by Congress, directly or indirectly, in whole or in part. Obviously, a necessary part of this power, vested by the Constitution in juries (or in judges when juries are waived), is the exclusive right to decide whether evidence presented at trial is sufficient to convict. I think it flaunts the constitutional power of courts and juries for Congress to tell them what "shall be deemed sufficient evidence to authorize conviction." And if Congress could not thus directly encroach upon the judge's or jury's exclusive right to declare what evidence is sufficient to prove the facts necessary for conviction, it should not be allowed to do so merely by labeling its encroachment a "presumption." Neither Tot v. United States, 319 U.S. 463, 63 S.Ct. 1241, 87 L.Ed. 1519, relied on by the Court as supporting this presumption, nor any case cited in Tot approved such an encroachment on the power of judges or juries. In fact, so far as I can tell, the problem of whether Congress can so restrict the power of court and jury in a criminal case in a federal court has never been squarely presented to or considered by this Court, perhaps because challenges to presumptions have arisen in many crucially different contexts but nevertheless have generally failed to distinguish between presumptions used in different ways, treating them as if they are either all valid or all invalid, regardless of the rights on which their use may impinge. Because the Court also fails to differentiate among the different circumstances in which presumptions may be utilized and the different consequences which will follow, I feel it necessary to say a few words on that subject before considering specifically the validity of the use of these presumptions in the light of the circumstances and consequences of their use.

In its simplest form a presumption is an inference permitted or required by law of the existence of one fact, which is unknown or which cannot be proved, from another fact which has been proved. The fact presumed may be based on a very strong probability, a weak supposition or an arbitrary assumption. The burden on the party seeking to prove the fact may be slight, as in a civil suit, or very heavy—proof beyond a reasonable doubt—as in a criminal prosecution. This points up the fact that statutes creating presumptions cannot be treated as fungible, that is, as interchangeable for all uses and all purposes. The validity of each presumption must be determined in the light of the particular consequences that flow from its use. When matters of trifling moment are involved, presumptions may be more freely accepted, but when consequences of vital importance to litigants and to the administration of justice are at stake, a more careful scrutiny is necessary.

In judging the constitutionality of legislatively created presumptions this Court has evolved an initial criterion which applies alike to all kinds of presumptions: that before a presumption may be relied on, there must be a rational connection between the facts inferred and the facts which have been proved by competent evidence, that is, the facts proved must be evidence which is relevant, tending to prove (though not necessarily conclusively) the existence of the fact presumed. And courts have undoubtedly shown an inclination to be less strict about the logical strength of presumptive inferences they will permit in civil cases than about those which affect the trial of crimes. The stricter scrutiny in the latter situation follows from the fact that the burden of proof in a civil lawsuit is ordinarily merely a preponderance of the evidence, while in a criminal case where a man's life, liberty, or property is at stake, the prosecution must prove his guilt beyond a reasonable doubt. See Morrison v. People of State of California, 291 U.S. 82, 96–97, 54 S.Ct. 281, 287, 78 L.Ed. 664. The case of Bailey v. State of Alabama, 219 U.S. 219, 31 S.Ct. 145, 55 L.Ed. 191, is a good illustration of this principle. There Bailey was accused of violating an Alabama statute which made it a crime to fail to perform personal services after obtaining money by contracting to perform them, with an intent to defraud the employer. The statute also provided that refusal or failure to perform the services, or to refund money paid for them, without just cause, constituted "prima facie evidence" (i. e., gave rise to a presumption) of the intent to injure or defraud. This Court, after calling attention to prior cases dealing with the requirement of rationality, passed over the test of rationality and held the statute invalid on another ground. Looking beyond the rational-relationship doctrine the Court held that the use of this presumption by Alabama against a man accused of crime would amount to a violation of the Thirteenth Amendment to the Constitution, which forbids "involuntary servitude, except as a punishment for crime." In so deciding the Court made it crystal clear that rationality is only the first hurdle which a legislatively created presumption must clear—that a presumption, even if rational, cannot be used to convict a man of crime if the effect of using the presumption is to deprive the accused of a constitutional right. In Bailey the constitutional right was given by the Thirteenth Amendment. In the case before us the accused, in my judgment, has been denied his right to the kind of trial by jury guaranteed by Art. III, § 2, and the Sixth Amendment, as well as to due process of law and freedom from self-incrimination guaranteed by the Fifth Amendment. And of course the principle announced in the Bailey case was not limited to rights guaranteed by the Thirteenth Amendment. The Court said in Bailey:

"It is apparent that a constitutional prohibition cannot be transgressed indirectly by the creation of a statutory presumption any more than it can be violated by direct enactment. The power to create presumptions is not a means of escape from constitutional restrictions." 219 U.S., at 239, 31 S.Ct., at 151.

Thus the Court held that presumptions, while often valid (and some of which, I think, like the presumption of death based on long unexplained absence, may perhaps be even salutary in effect), must not be allowed to stand where they abridge or deny a specific constitutional guarantee. It is one thing to rely on a presumption to justify conditional administration of the estate of a person absent without explanation for seven years, see Cunnius v. Reading School District, 198 U.S. 458, 25 S.Ct. 721, 49 L.Ed. 1125; compare Scott v. McNeal, 154 U.S. 34, 14 S.Ct. 1108, 38 L.Ed. 896; it would be quite another to use the presumption of death from seven years' absence to convict a man of murder. I do not think it can be denied that use of the statutory presumptions in the case before us at the very least seriously impaired Gainey's constitutional right to have a jury weigh the facts of his case without any congressional interference through predetermination of what evidence would be sufficient to prove the facts necessary to convict in a particular case.

The Bailey case also emphatically answers the Court's insistence that this encroachment on Gainey's constitutional rights was justified or neutralized by the trial court's instruction that while evidence of unexplained presence was sufficient under the statute to convict, the jury nonetheless was not compelled to convict. This same kind of contention was made to this Court and rejected in Bailey where the Alabama Supreme Court had upheld that State's presumption on the ground that "with evidence before them, the jury are still left free to find the accused guilty or not guilty, according as they may be satisfied of his guilt or not, by the whole evidence." Bailey v. State, 161, Ala. 75, 78, 49 So. 886, 887. This Court answered that contention then, as I think it should now, saying:

"The point is that, in such a case, the jury may not accept that evidence as alone sufficient; for the jury may accept it, and they have the express warrant of the statute to accept it is as a basis for their verdict." 219 U.S., at 235, 31 S.Ct., at 149. (Emphasis in original.)

And the Court added that "The normal assumption is that the jury will follow the statute, and, acting in accordance with the authority it confers, will accept as sufficient what the statute expressly so describes." Id., at 237, 31 S.Ct., at 150.

Even if I could accept the doctrine that Congress after declaring that certain conduct shall be a crime has further power to tell judges and juries that certain evidence shall be sufficient to prove that conduct and convict a defendant, I could not agree that these statutory presumptions are constitutional. They declare mere presence at a still site without more to be sufficient evidence to convict of the crimes of carrying on a distillery business and possessing a still. While presence at a still is unquestionably a relevant circumstance to add to others to prove possession or operation of a still, I could not possibly agree that mere presence is sufficient in and of itself, without any supporting evidence, to permit a finding that, beyond a reasonable doubt, the person present carried on a distillery business or possessed a still or even added and abetted in committing those crimes. Indeed, with respect to the crime of possession, as the Court concedes, we held squarely to the contrary in Bozza v. United States, 330 U.S. 160, 67 S.Ct. 645, 91 L.Ed. 818, quite properly, I think. In setting aside the Bozza conviction for possession of a still, which had been based on mere presence at a still, this Court was acting in accordance with the historic principle that "independent trial judges and independent appellate judges have a most important place under our constitutional plan since they have power to set aside convictions." United States ex rel. Toth v. Quarles, 350 U.S. 11, 19, 76 S.Ct. 1, 6. This judicial responsibility to pass on the sufficiency of the evidence must be exercised in each case, no more to be controlled by a general congressional enactment than it could be by a special act directed to one case only. This protective function of the court is amply demonstrated in the case before us: while Gainey was originally indicted on four counts, the trial judge directed a verdict of acquittal on one and the Court of Appeals ordered acquittal on another.

It indeed is true, as the Court suggests, that it was to make convictions possible on no more evidence than presence that the presumption statute here under consideration was passed. Undoubtedly a presumption which can be used to produce convictions without the necessity of proving a crucial element of the crime charged—and a sometimes difficult-to-prove element at that—is a boon to prosecutors and an incongruous snare for defendants in a country that claims to require proof of guilt beyond a reasonable doubt. Quite accurately such a use of a presumption has been described as "First Aid to the District Attorney." Instead of supporting the constitutionality of such a use of statutory presumptions, however, I think this argument based on necessity and convenience points out its fatal defects. I suppose no one would deny that the Government's burden would also be made lighter if the defendant was not represented by counsel, compare Gideon v. Wainwright, 372 U.S. 335, 83 S.Ct. 792, 9 L.Ed.2d 799, or if the jury could receive and consider confessions extorted by torture, compare Brown v. State of Mississippi, 297 U.S. 278, 56 S.Ct. 461, 80 L.Ed. 682, or if evidence obtained from defendants through illegal searches and seizures could be used against them, compare Mapp v. Ohio, 367 U.S. 643, 81 S.Ct. 1684, 6 L.Ed.2d 1081, but this Court has not hesitated to strike down such encroachments on those constitutional rights. Yet here the Court sanctions a method less crude, but just as effective, to deny Gainey his constitutional right to a trial by jury.

I cannot subscribe to the idea that any one of the constitutional grants of power to Congress enumerated in Art. I, § 8, including the Necessary and Proper Clause, contains either an express or an implied power of Congress to instruct juries as to what evidence is sufficient to convict defendants in particular cases. Congress can undoubtedly create crimes, but it cannot constitutionally try them. The Constitution specifically prohibits bills of attainder. Congress can declare certain conduct a crime, unless barred by some constitutional provision, but it must, if true to our Constitution of divided powers and the Fifth Amendment's command that cases be tried according to due process of law, leave the trial of those crimes to the courts in which judges or juries can decide the facts on their own judgment without legislative constraint and judges can set aside convictions which they believe are not justified by the evidence. See Tot v. United States, 319 U.S. 463, 63 S.Ct. 1241, 1247 (concurring opinion). "[I]t is not within the province of a legislature to declare an individual guilty or presumptively guilty of a crime." McFarland v. American Sugar Refining Co., 241 U.S. 79, 86, 36 S.Ct. 498, 501, 60 L.Ed. 899. See Manley v. State of Georgia, 279 U.S. 1, 49 S.Ct. 215, 73 L.Ed. 575. Yet, viewed realistically, that is what the presumption which the Court today approves does in this case. I think that the presumption which should govern instead in criminal trials in the courts of this country is the time-honored presumption of innocence accorded to all criminal defendants until they are proved guilty by competent evidence.

Nor can a power of Congress to detract from the constitutional power of juries and judges to decide what facts are enough to convict be implied because of the power of Congress to make procedural rules or rules of evidence. See Ex parte Fisk, 113 U.S. 713, 720, 5 S.Ct. 724, 727, 28 L.Ed. 1117. It is not disputed that Congress has power to prescribe rules governing admissibility of evidence and purely procedural matters. The Congress unquestionably could declare the fact of presence to be admissible evidence, for certainly it is relevant when considered along with other circumstances. Yet this power to say what shall or shall not be admissible in no way empowers Congress to determine what facts, once admitted, suffice to prove guilt beyond a reasonable doubt. And I certainly cannot join the Court when it says:

"The process of making the determination of rationality is, by its nature, highly empirical, and in matters not within specialized judicial competence or completely commonplace, significant weight should be accorded the capacity of Congress to amass the stuff of actual experience and cull conclusions from it."

The implication of this statement is that somehow Congress is better qualified to decide what facts are sufficient to convict defendants than are courts and juries. I accept the proposition that Congress is the proper branch of our Government to decide legislative policies and enact general laws and that in so doing it must of necessity deal with facts to some extent. This is as the Constitution provides. But Congress is not authorized nor has it any special "expertise" with which I am familiar which entitles it to direct juries as to what conclusions they may or must draw from the unique facts of specific criminal cases tried in federal courts. Moreover, even were I to assume that Congress does have an expertise to assess facts in lawsuits which is superior to that of juries and judges, I still could not join the Court's opinion, for I think that the Founders of our Government decided for us that these are matters "within specialized"— and exclusive—"judicial competence." As this Court has said with reference to jury trial of facts:

"whether right or wrong, the premise underlying the constitutional method for determining guilt or innocence in federal courts is that laymen are better specialists to perform this task." United States ex rel. Toth v. Quarles, 350 U.S. 11, 18, 76 S.Ct. 1, 6.

Besides impairing Gainey's right to trial by jury according to due process safeguards, the statutes in this case I think violated Gainey's constitutional rights in still another way. These statutory presumptions must tend, when incorporated into an instruction, as they were here, to influence the jury to reach an inference which the trier of fact might not otherwise have thought justified, to push some jurors to convict who might not otherwise have done so. Cf. Pollock v. Williams, 322 U.S. 4, 15, 64 S.Ct. 792, 798, 88 L.Ed. 1095. The undoubted practical effect of letting guilt rest on unexplained presence alone is to force a defendant to come forward and testify, however much he may think doing so may jeopardize his chances of acquittal, since if he does not he almost certainly destroys those chances. This is compulsion, which I think runs counter to the Fifth Amendment's purpose to forbid convictions on compelled testimony. The compulsion here is of course more subtle and less cruel physically than compulsion by torture, but it is nonetheless compulsion and it is nonetheless effective. I am aware that this Court in Yee Hem v. United States, 268 U.S. 178, 185, 45 S.Ct. 470, 472, 69 L.Ed. 904, held that use of a presumptive squeeze like this one did not amount to a form of compulsion forbidden by the Fifth Amendment. The Court's reasoning was contained in a single paragraph, the central argument of which was that despite a presumption like this a defendant is left "entirely free to testify or not as he chooses." That argument, it seems to me, would also justify admitting in evidence a confession extorted by a policeman's pointing a gun at the head of an accused, on the theory that the man being threatened was entirely free to confess or not, as he chose. I think the holding in Yee Hem is completely out of harmony with the Fifth Amendment's prohibition against compulsory self-incrimination, and I would overrule it. See Feldman v. United States, 322 U.S. 487, 494, 64 S.Ct. 1082, 1085, 88 L.Ed. 1408 (dissenting opinion); compare Leyra v. Denno, 347 U.S. 556, 74 S.Ct. 716, 98 L.Ed. 948. See also State v. Lapointe, 81 N.H. 227, 123 A. 692, 31 A.L.R. 1212, quoted with approval in the opinion of the court below, 322 F.2d 292, 296 (C.A. 5th Cir.).

For all the foregoing reasons, I think that these two statutory presumptions by which Congress has tried to relieve the Government of its burden of proving a man guilty and to take away from courts and juries the function and duty of deciding guilt or innocence according to the evidence before them, unconstitutionally encroach on the functions of courts and deny persons accused of crime rights which our Constitution guarantees them. The most important and most crucial action the courts take in trying for crime is to resolve facts. This is a judicial, not a legislative, function. I think that in passing these two sections Congress stepped over its constitutionally limited bounds and encroached on the constitutional power of courts to try cases. I would therefore affirm the judgment of the court below and grant Gainey a new trial by judge and jury with all the protections accorded by the law of the land.

3

Admission and Exclusion of Evidence

Most people know that attorneys in court often make objections to the admissibility of certain types of evidence being introduced. Once an objection is raised and sustained by the trial judge, the evidence will then be excluded. However, if the objection is overruled, the evidence will be admissible into the trial.

One of the main purposes of an objection in a trial is to preserve the record for an appeal, should an appeal be needed. If an objection is not timely and specific, the attorney will not be able to appeal that particular issue.

Ruling on Admissibility

The trial judge has the sole responsibility of determining the admissibility of all items of evidence offered by either the defense or the prosecution. The judge determines whether or not the jury can even consider an item of evidence. However, the weight (value) of the evidence and inferences to be deducted from that evidence must be determined by the trier of fact. If no objection is made, the item of evidence will be received into evidence. Failure on the part of either counsel to object is deemed a waiver. Thus, the judge is not required to raise the objection on his own.

If either side in the trial introduces otherwise inadmissible evidence, it is deemed to have waived its right to object to its opponent's introducing legally inadmissible evidence as to the same issue. As stated in an Iowa court decision, "The defendant is entitled to fight fire with fire"; thus, the prosecutor may as well.

In order for an appellate court to reverse a verdict on an appeal due to evidence which has been erroneously admitted into the trial, the following four elements must be present: (1) a timely objection; (2) a specific objection; (3) that the grounds for the objection were valid; and (4) that the judge committed prejudicial error in overruling the objection.

Timely Objection

In order for an objection to be timely, it must be made before the evidence is received. *Example:* The prosecutor asks a law enforcement officer if he heard two parties conversing and, if so, what they said. The officer answers, yes, he did, and they said that the defendant was the guilty party. At this point, the defense attorney cannot make an objection because the evidence has already been received. In order for the objection to have been timely, the defense attorney must have made the objection before the officer had answered the question.

The proper way for the defense attorney to attack this evidence, now that it has been received, is to make a motion to strike. A motion to strike is, in effect, an objection that is made after the evidence has been received. If the judge sustains the motion, the evidence will then be stricken from the record and the jury admonished to disregard it in its deliberations.

In the course of a trial, it is the tendency of witnesses to respond immediately to questions put to them by either side. The police officer should be advised that if in fact he is answering questions posed by the defense attorney, a slight pause before answering the question is advisable to give the district attorney the opportunity to make an objection before the answer is in. It is a well-known fact that once objectionable items have been received, even though the judge may order them stricken from the record, members of the jury have heard the items and will be unable to totally disregard them when they go into deliberations.

Specific Objection

The courts usually require that an objection be specific, meaning that it states the specific and legally sufficient grounds as to why the evidence is not admissible. *Example 1:* Police officer *A* is asked by the prosecution if he heard John say anything before Mary jumped off the cliff. A specific objection would be that this question is not acceptable on the grounds that it is calling for hearsay and is barred by the Hearsay Rule. *Example 2:* The prosecutor has subpoenaed a priest to the stand and then asks the priest what the defendant told him in the confessional. A specific objection to this would be that the requested information is a privileged communication (since a statute protects the relationship, the witness need not answer) and therefore inadmissible.

The General Objection

In addition to the class of specific objections is the general objection, which states that the evidence being presented is "incompetent, irrelevant, and immaterial." The general objection can be made by either side.

ADMISSION AND EXCLUSION OF EVIDENCE

Recently, however, there has been great controversy in many jurisdictions as to whether or not the general objection constitutes a sufficient objection. By statute, most jurisdictions now hold that the general objection is invalid for purposes of preserving the record for appeal. However, there is some authority contra which holds that the general objection is sufficient if it is apparent to the court as to the real reason for that objection.

It should be noted that there is an exception to the general objection, called the "plain error" doctrine. This doctrine is applicable in all criminal cases and states basically that if the error in the admission or the exclusion of the evidence was so fundamental that it has tainted the entire proceedings and has deprived the accused of his constitutional right to a fair trial, the error is grounds for reversal on appeal, even though the accused failed to object at the time of the trial.

Most Commonly Used Objections

The following is a list of the most commonly used objections:

(1) The evidence is irrelevant, meaning that the evidence does not logically tend to prove or disprove any fact in issue in the case.
(2) The evidence is cumulative, meaning that the same evidence has been introduced prior to this evidence.
(3) The evidence is immaterial, meaning the same irrelevant evidence does not logically tend to prove or disprove a material fact in the case.
(4) The witness is incompetent, meaning that the witness is not qualified to testify.
(5) The evidence is hearsay, meaning that the witness is attempting to testify to matters that took place out of court and is not the person involved in that prior out-of-court declaration.
(6) The evidence is self-serving, meaning that it will aid the person who is testifying to it. (This objection is not generally allowed in the United States today.)
(7) The evidence is barred by the self incrimination rule provided by the Fifth Amendment of the U.S. Constitution, meaning that a person cannot be forced to give testimony which could incriminate him.
(8) The question is compound, meaning that more than one question is being asked of the witness.
(9) The question is leading or suggestive, meaning that the desired answer is in the question.
(10) The answer is privileged communication, meaning that a statutory privilege is in existence, such as that between husband and wife, attorney and client, priest and parishioner, etc.
(11) There has been improper impeachment of one's own witness. Generally, the side that calls a witness is barred from impeaching that witness.
(12) The question has already been asked and answered.
(13) The question is argumentative.

(14) The question or answer is assuming facts not in evidence.
(15) The question calls for conclusion on the part of the witness.
(16) The corpus delicti has not been established.
(17) No proper foundation has been laid.
(18) The evidence is barred by the Best Evidence Rule (rule that only the original document may be introduced into evidence).
(19) The question goes beyond the scope of direct examination.
(20) The question is unintelligible.
(21) The question calls for an opinion by a person who is a nonexpert on what is being asked.

The preceding list should be referred to frequently while going through the rest of the chapters of the book dealing with objections.

Valid Grounds for an Objection

Any attorney making an objection at a trial must state the valid grounds for that objection. The objection specifically stated must in fact be the legal grounds for the exclusion of that particular item of evidence. Even though the evidence could have been excluded on another ground, if the attorney makes the wrong objection and the evidence is excluded, no appellate court may overturn the exclusion on a ground different from that which the attorney originally stated. *Example*: The prosecution has a police officer on the witness stand who has a photostatic copy of an official police document. The prosecution introduces the document into the record, and the defense objects on the grounds that the document is barred from introduction by the Best Evidence Rule. This objection would not be valid, even though the document is an item of secondary evidence, i.e., a photostatic copy, because most jurisdictions allow secondary evidence if it is part of an official record. Therefore, if the trial judge overrules this objection, the attorney, if he did appeal on the basis of it being barred by the Best Evidence Rule, would not be entitled to have the appellate court reverse on those grounds, even though the proper objection should have been that no proper foundation had been laid.

Prejudicial Error of a Judge in Overruling an Objection

In order for the appellate court to reverse a verdict on the grounds that the trial judge committed an erroneous or prejudicial error in admitting or excluding evidence, it must be found that the error probably had a substantial influence on the jury and affected a substantial right (a right guaranteed by statute or the Constitution) of the party who had objected to the evidence. Because in a criminal case the appellate court is concerned with the constitutional safeguards and standards that have been established for the defendant in the case, it must be convinced beyond a reasonable doubt that illegal evidence has been admitted and could have, in fact, influenced the jurors in the specific case. In order for the appellate court to refuse to reverse a verdict, it must be convinced that the jurors would have convicted the accused regardless of any legally inadmissible evidence introduced and accepted in the specific trial.

Safeguards have also been established to protect the party who has had evidence erroneously excluded from introduction into the trial. In this case, the party must establish for the appellate court that there were no valid grounds for the objection, that the party had made an offer of proof, and that there was prejudicial error committed by the trial judge in sustaining the objection.

In order for an appellate court to justify the verdict, it would be necessary to find that the trial judge's erroneous exclusion of an item of evidence resulted in a miscarriage of justice. Evidence which was excluded, and the results of the judge's determination in excluding this evidence, were recorded in the trial transcript. If the evidence was legally inadmissible on any grounds, even though the attorney failed to object on the proper grounds, the appellate court would affirm the exclusion of that evidence. The reason for the reversal in the rule is that it is a strong policy of the law to attempt to affirm trial judgments if at all possible unless prejudice would result from their decision. The student can thus see that even if a general objection had been made, it would suffice if there were any grounds at all for the exclusion of this particular type of evidence.

The other requirement that must be brought before the appellate court is that the party had made an offer of proof. An offer of proof is generally made at the trial bench without the jurors or other witnesses hearing. When the attorney sees that evidence which he is offering is about to be excluded, he should ask the judge for a conference at the bench to make an offer of proof, at which time he will attempt to satisfy the judge by telling him how he is going to attempt to use this item of evidence and that it should be admissible and not excluded.

A peace officer needs to be aware of these procedural steps and safeguards so that he may be prepared to assist the prosecuting attorney in the presentation of the cases during the course of any trial. Many instances have been recorded in which the officer was totally unfamiliar with the rules of evidence. Thus, when offers of proof or objections were made at the trial, he was unable to assist the prosecuting attorney in getting the evidence admitted.

Introduction of Evidence

The basic steps that must be taken in the introduction of any evidence into a trial are that the item of evidence be (1) marked for identification by the court clerk, (2) shown to the opposing counsel, and (3) authenticated by a witness on the stand. After a witness has authenticated the evidence, the attorney offering it should make a formal motion that it be introduced into evidence. Then, if the evidence is objectionable, the opposing counsel should make an objection known to the court before the judge orders it admitted into the trial. *Example:* The defendant is on trial for rape. The prosecution is seeking to introduce into the trial the victim's ripped brassiere. The prosecutor takes the item of evidence to the court clerk, who attaches a tag marking it "People's No. 1." The prosecutor then should show the item of evidence to the defense attorney and, barring an objection, should take it to the witness and ask the witness if she knows what the item is and who it belongs to. Assuming that the victim answers that it is her brassiere that was ripped from her on the night in question, the prosecutor should then move that the court introduce it into evidence. If there is an objection to be made, it should be timely (made before the judge orders the item to be admitted) and, of course, specific.

Summary

In this chapter, we became familiar with the types of objections and now know that in the majority of jurisdictions, the general objection to materials on the grounds that they are "irrelevant, incompetent and immaterial" is not allowed. A majority of the jurisdictions require that a specific and timely objection be made. The student should be familiar with the requirements on the prosecuting attorney as to what is an offer of proof and what he can do to assist the prosecuting attorney in the presentation of this evidence in the court. We also learned the basic format for presentation of evidence to the court, i.e., the evidence is first marked for identification by the court clerk, then shown to the defense attorney, then authenticated by the witness, and then formally introduced into evidence barring objections or motions to suppress. For further reading, the student should refer to the chapter on witnesses (Chapter 5) and the form of examination of witnesses and remember that the court will have the same requirements as to objections being made to testimonial evidence as well as to physical forms of evidence.

DISCUSSION QUESTIONS

1. What is meant by the phrase *timely objection*?
2. What is meant by *a motion to strike*?
3. Distinguish the difference between a specific objection and the general objection.
4. Name as many of the most commonly used objections and their application to a criminal case as you can.
5. Discuss the basic steps for introducing evidence into a trial.

MEADE v. COMMONWEALTH
Court of Appeals of Kentucky, 1928.
225 Ky. 177, 7 S.W.2d 1052.

LOGAN, J. Newberry Meade, the appellant, on a Sunday morning in the summer of 1927, shot and killed Patrick H. Bates in Letcher county. He was charged with murder by indictment, and his trial before a jury resulted in a verdict of conviction. His punishment was fixed at 18 years' confinement in the penitentiary. . . .

The dying statement of Bates is as follows:

"As I passed down the road I saw three of them walking along. They had a bucket and basket. His little boy had the bucket and basket. In the bucket I could see something sloshing and I knew it was whiskey. I went back up home to see if I could catch up with them, because I knew they were going to Millstone or Kona one. The three of them went up the railroad and come back around and went up Millstone creek a little ways. I was just fixing to get on the train to go up to Kona and saw them pass along by Jesse Holbrooks'. I just started out after them and when I got in about twelve feet of him he turned and shot me, and I never spoke any to him. No one was with me. I was by myself. No one was with me; I was just aim to walk along with him and go on out there, and I made no arrest or said anything. He shot me one time in the hand and in the stomach. Neither of us spoke to each other. When he looked around and saw me, he said 'Don't you follow me any farther;' and just about that time he shot me, and I had no chance to get my gun. He had one of these overall jackets on his arm. When he shot me, he came toward me for about ten feet, and I backed and put my hand up to get my gun; he walked backwards, and told me if I didn't drop my hand he would shoot me again. Just as soon as he got in the bend he begin to run and I started after him, but I was afraid I was going to get sick from the shot, and he might shoot me again, so I turned around and come back. He had said he was going to kill me, but I didn't know it. During the time I was following him I didn't ever have my pistol out or make any attempt to injure Mr. Meade. At the time when he shot me we were both walking in the same direction, he was about ten steps ahead of me. I was walking faster than he was and when I was about to overtake him he turned and shot me.

"Realizing that I am not going to get well, I make this as my dieing declaration. . . ."

The question as to whether the dying declaration should have been admitted is not so easily disposed of. Before the dying declaration was read to the jury one of the attorneys representing appellant asked permission of the court to cross-examine the witness Judge Bentley, who was at the time testifying about the dying declaration. An objection was made to the admission of the dying declaration, which was overruled, and a proper exception was saved. After it was read appellant moved to strike it from the evidence and to withdraw it from the consideration of the jury. This motion was overruled and an exception taken. . . .

The court did not err in admitting the dying declaration, but there remains the question as to whether the court erred in admitting it as a whole without striking from it such parts as were incompetent. It is urged that parts of the statements are conclusions, and not facts. So far as that complaint is concerned, we may say in response to it that the statement is open to that criticism, but there is nothing in the conclusions expressed, which were very few, that was even slightly prejudicial. It is also urged that the statement is contradictory, and that it shows on its face that Bates did not understand it, or did not have mental capacity to know what he was doing at the time. The evidence is clear that Bates was in his right mind at the time he made the statement, and we do not find that the statement is contradictory in any material respect. It is contended that it contains matter which was not a part of the res gestae. There is such matter included in the statement, but in the main it is immaterial and could have had no effect on the mind of the jury, but there is one statement that may have been prejudicial. We refer to the statement: "He had said he was going to kill me, but I didn't know it." This was added to the evidence of another witness that appellant had used language in speaking of Bates which might be properly construed as a threat. The statement was incompetent under the authority announced in many opinions in this court. Caudill v. Com., 220 Ky. 191, 294 S.W. 1042; Mays v. Com., 200 Ky. 678, 255 S.W. 257.

But appellant is not in position to take advantage of this incompetent part of the dying declaration. The exceptions to the introduction of the statement went to it as a whole, and there was no objection or exception to any particular part of it. It is the general rule that, where objection is made and exception saved to the evidence as a whole, the party so objecting and excepting cannot avail himself of some isolated part of the evidence, if any part of it was competent. In the case of Ellis v. Com., 146 Ky. 715, 143 S.W. 425, the court announced this rule governing the question.

"It is very clear that, if this evidence of the witness was incompetent, no proper or available objection or exception was taken to it, as the motion at the conclusion of the evidence to exclude from the jury 'the testimony of Mrs. Sallie Spencer" was not sufficiently definite to call the attention of the court to the particular answers in her evidence that counsel desired to object to. By all the rules of practice with which we are familiar, when objection is made to the whole of the testimony of a witness, without specifying any particular part of it, the motion should be overruled, if any of it is competent. If it is desired to save an exception to incompetent evidence that can be available upon appeal, the exception should point out the particular evidence objected to. . . ."

Many cases are reversed because of the improper admission of dying declarations. In every instance where a dying declaration is to be introduced, the court, before there is any reference made to it in the presence of the jury, should hear the witnesses in regard thereto and determine as to its competency, and, if parts of it are competent and parts are incompetent, that which is incompetent should be eliminated. It is unfortunate when the court allows a witness to testify in the presence of the jury about the statements of the deceased when later it may be necessary to hold that the dying declaration cannot be admitted. The competency should be determined out of the presence of the jury. We find no grounds for reversing this case.

Judgment affirmed.

COMMONWEALTH v. WAKELIN
Supreme Judicial Court of Massachusetts, 1918.
230 Mass. 567, 120 N.E. 209.

Joseph Wakelin was convicted of manslaughter, and he excepts.

RUGG, C. J. . . . The defendant called a witness, who testified without objection that during a part of 1917 he occupied a cell in the Springfield jail with one Ducharme, who before the arrest of the defendant told the witness that he, Ducharme, killed Lauretta W. Wakelin (the person for whose killing the defendant was indicted); that Ducharme also showed the witness a newspaper account of the arrest of the defendant for the murder of Lauretta; and that Ducharme later made a confession in writing which the witness had submitted to Mr. Clark, the sheriff of Hampden county; and that Ducharme was dead, having been executed at the state prison. The defendant thereupon asked the witness to state the details respecting the locality and manner of killing Lauretta as told him by Ducharme, accompanying the question with offer of proof of testimony which, if Ducharme had himself been a witness would have been competent. This was excluded upon objection being made, the judge ruling that R.L. c. 175, § 66, did not apply to criminal cases, and, second, finding as matter of fact that the alleged statement was not made in good faith. . . .

The contention of the defendant in substance is that because the evidence as to the confession, although incompetent, had been admitted without objection, it thereupon became permissible for him as of right to introduce further evidence to the same effect likewise incompetent. Waiver of necessary formality of proof as to one piece of evidence does not open the door to all evidence of the same kind. Failure on the part of the district attorney to object to some incompetent evidence does not estop him from making objection to other like incompetent evidence. It is the law of this commonwealth that confessions by third persons out of court to the commission of the crime with which the defendant is charged, are inadmissible. Commonwealth v. Chabbock, 1 Mass. 144; Commonwealth v. Felch, 132 Mass. 22. . . .

The evidence as to the confession, having been admitted without objection, was entitled to its probative force. Hubbard v. Allyn, 200 Mass, 166, 171, 86 N.E. 356; Wood v. Blanchard, 212 Mass. 53, 55, 98 N.E. 616; Diaz v. United States, 223 U.S. 442, 450, 32 S.Ct. 250, 56 L.Ed 500, Ann.Cas. 1913C, 1138. It therefore was permissible for the commonwealth to introduce evidence to rebut its force by showing that Ducharme was in a distant part of the state on the day when the crime with which the defendant was charged was committed, and for several preceding and following days. The testimony as to the confession was not immaterial. It was pertinent, but incompetent, as evidence because of the means of proof. The confession having been offered by the defendant and having been admitted without objection and being material, it stood on the same footing as to contradiction as any other material evidence. It gained no added sanctity or security because, although incompetent, it had been admitted without objection. It is immaterial evidence alone, which can be contradicted only in the discretion of the presiding judge. Bennett v. Susser, 191 Mass. 329, and cases cited at 330, 77 N.E. 884.

All the other exceptions saved by the defendant have been examined carefully. But there is nothing in them which calls for comment. No error is disclosed.

Exceptions overruled.

CHICAGO CITY RY. v. CARROLL
Supreme Court of Illinois, 1903.
206 Ill. 318, 68 N.E. 1087.

Action by Robert Carroll against the Chicago City Railway Company. From a judgment in favor of plaintiff, affirmed by the Appellate Court, 102 Ill. App. 202, defendant appeals. . . .

RICKS, J. . . . It is also complained that appellee had closed his case, and appellant had offered its evidence, when appellee was allowed to recall his son John, and show by him the name or the inscription on the cars on appellant's line. This was not error. It is in the discretion of the trial court to allow evidence that has been overlooked or omitted, at any stage of the case; and unless that discretion has been abused, or injury is shown to have resulted from it, it cannot be said to be error. When this son of appellee was recalled, and allowed to testify relative to the name appearing on the cars, the court informed appellant that, if it so desired, he would hear evidence on its part in denial of what the evidence thus allowed tended to show, but appellant offered no such evidence.

When this witness retired from the stand, appellee announced that he rested his case. Appellant's attorney then said: "We desire to offer evidence, your honor, on the question of inspection of the cars, and so forth." The court replied: "Very well. I won't receive any evidence, except as to the ownership of this line, at this stage." Exception was taken, and it is now urged that, inasmuch as appellee was allowed to show the inscription on the cars, it tended to show ownership, and that appellant should have been allowed to show that it did inspect its cars; that, in the absence of proof of ownership, appellant was not required to prove anything; and that as there was no evidence, until the testimony of this son, of ownership, the court should have opened the case, and allowed proof upon the question of inspection.

It may first be said, there was evidence of ownership and operation of the car by appellant already in the record, and it would be a dangerous rule of practice to sustain error upon an assignment such as this. Appellant, in fact, offered no evidence upon the matter. No witness was put upon the stand. No question was asked. Nothing was done, except a mere conversation or talk had between counsel for appellant and the court. Such procedure as that does not amount to an offer of evidence, and the remarks of the court did not amount to a refusal to admit evidence. There can be no refusal to admit that which has not been offered, and counsel cannot, by engaging in a mere conversation with the court, although it may relate to the procedure, by merely stating what he desires to do, get a ruling from the court upon which he can predicate error. If appellant desired to make the contention it now makes, it should have at least put a witness upon the stand, and proceeded far enough that the question relative to the point it is now said it was desired to offer evidence upon was reached, and then put the question, and allow the court to rule upon it, and then offer what was expected to be proved by the witness, if he was not allowed to answer the question asked. It was not stated to the court that appellant did inspect the cars, or could prove that the cars had been regularly inspected or recently inspected, or that the inspection that was made was an examination of the trolley pole or its attachment; and to now hold that the case should be reversed upon the mere statement of counsel that he desired to offer evidence upon the question of the "inspection of the cars, and so forth," would, as we think, be setting a dangerous precedent, and one that would tend to irregularity in such matters. [Citations omitted.]

Affirmed.

4

Relevancy

One of the prime purposes of a trial is to determine the truth of the issues which are presented to the jury. However, the student must bear in mind that this does not mean that all evidence which could have a bearing on guilt or innocence will be admissible. Only that evidence which is relevant can be admissible into the court.

Relevancy, in its simplest form, means that the item of evidence which has been offered to prove a material issue has some probative value; i.e., that the evidence will logically tend to prove that for which it was offered. The new Federal Rules of Evidence define relevant evidence as "any evidence having any tendency to make the existence of any fact that is of consequence to the determination of the action more probable or less probable than it would be without the evidence."

The judge must make a logical determination based on common sense and experience whether the item of evidence being offered has any probative value; if it does, then it is relevant and should be admitted into the trial. A more concise definition is that if a reasonable man could draw a reasonable inference from the item of evidence and the fact that the defense or prosecution is attempting to prove with that item, then that item is, in fact, relevant.

The student should view the rule on relevancy as one of the first exclusionary rules in the law of evidence. Historically, we think of exclusionary rules only as to illegal searches and seizures or to certain privileges which may be in existence. However, as the student will learn, in order for any item of evidence to be admissible, it first must be relevant before any other problems concerning that specific item of evidence can be considered. In reviewing for any examination, or in reading any examination question, the student should first look for the relevancy of each item of evidence in the problem or investigation being studied.

Although in the majority of jurisdictions the terms *relevancy* and *materiality* are used interchangeably, evidence codes of many states make a distinction between the two. For academic purposes, the student should understand this distinction.

Materiality

Materiality simply relates to whether the item of evidence offered is in issue; i.e., will the item tend to prove or disprove part of the corpus delicti of the crime? The matters that are in issue in the trial are, of course, all elements of the crime which must be proven by the prosecution or disproven by the defense. *Example:* The defendant is on trial for a robbery in which he is alleged to have stolen $300 from the victim at gunpoint. The prosecutor has a witness on the stand and is seeking to introduce evidence that the defendant had committed a prior rape. The rape, of course, is not in issue in this specific trial; thus, the evidence is not material. Contrast this, however, with items of evidence that are being introduced to prove part of the corpus delicti, i.e., that the defendant had a gun on him at the time of his arrest and is on trial for robbery.

The student should check with his local jurisdiction to see if it makes a distinction between relevancy and materiality. The trend (as under the new Federal Rules of Evidence) is that there is no distinction between the two concepts; materiality is thought of as only a part of the test for relevancy.

If an item of evidence is in fact relevant, there are still provisions allowing the judge to exclude that relevant evidence if the probative danger outweighs the probative value, e.g., in situations where the evidence would: (1) cause undue prejudice to either party; (2) unfairly surprise either party; (3) consume too much time; or (4) tend to confuse the issues. *Example 1:* The defendant is on trial for a burglary, and the prosecution is attempting to introduce the fact that the defendant had been convicted of an earlier burglary. This item of evidence may be relevant, as it may tend to logically prove or disprove the fact that this defendant did burglarize the place in question. However, even though this item is relevant, the judge makes a determination based upon the timely and specific objection that this evidence has an inherent danger of raising a prejudice in the minds of the jury once it is introduced and thus should be excluded. The prosecutor might still have this evidence admitted. He must, however, first establish the corpus delicti of the present crime and then argue to the judge that the introduction of the item of evidence has a limited purpose, i.e., to establish the modus operandi, or common scheme and design, of the defendant. If the judge has any doubt as to the relevancy of the item in the criminal proceedings, the item must be excluded to protect the rights of the defendant. *Example 2:* The prosecutor calls a witness to the stand in a homicide case. The witness testifies that he saw the defendant kill the victim. Assuming that the defense attorney has not been afforded any rights of discovery, including the name and/or address of this specific witness, he could object on the grounds that it is unfair to surprise him at this time with this testimony. The testimony of this witness is relevant in that it will directly aid the jury in determining if the defendant killed this person. However, because it will unfairly surprise the defense, even though it is relevant, the judge may exclude that item of evidence.

Special problems are presented to the court when character evidence is being introduced. Character evidence is generally defined as evidence showing a particular human trait (e.g., violence, honesty, truthfulness). In other words, character evidence tends to show how a person normally would act, given a certain situation.

Whenever the judge is confronted with character evidence, it is very difficult to weigh the probative value of this evidence against all of the inherent probative dangers from the admissibility of the evidence. Determining whether character evidence will be admissible and, if so, what kind of evidence can be used to prove character will greatly depend upon the purpose for which the party is offering it. Is the item of evidence being offered to prove probable conduct? To prove a person's character? To prove a person's reputation in the community? To rehabilitate another witness or the defendant or to impeach another witness or himself?

In most jurisdictions where character evidence is admissible, there are three basic types of evidence that may be offered to prove character: (1) testimony by people who know a person as to their opinions of that person; (2) testimony by people who may or may not have known a person as to that person's reputation in the community; and (3) testimony as to specific acts of that person which will reflect on a trait of character involved. The type of evidence admissible will depend on the purpose for which it is being offered by the proponent.

In some cases, the court will allow the introduction of character evidence to prove that the person in question was likely to have acted in the particular way and from which the jury could draw inferences that the person did so act at the time of the crime. The court has wide discretion in judging this kind of evidence but allows it in very few cases. The court, however, usually allows this type of evidence in a criminal case to prove that other crimes have been committed by the accused. In this instance, the court will not accept information of prior crimes simply to show that the defendant has a propensity for committing crimes and thus committed the present crime. This type of evidence may also be admissible for other purposes, one of which is to prove identity. Prior crimes committed by the defendant may be admitted to establish the defendant's true identity, including his modus operandi.

Another example of an exception would be in the case when the prosecutor is offering a prior character trait to show a common scheme. *Example:* The defendant is charged with murder in which he sent poison candy through the mail. The prosecutor may offer evidence that the defendant had murdered one other victim by the same means and for the same motive, to collect insurance money. Some of the state courts have held this type of evidence admissible as a common scheme, because it tends to show malice and knowledge of means used to commit the crime charged in the present case.

Another exception is to allow this type of character evidence to prove the state of mind of the defendant. The state of mind, of course, could be his motive (his intent) to prove specific knowledge. *Example:* The defendant is being prosecuted for a burglary. Evidence of other burglaries by the defendant would be admissible to show that he had the intent to steal when he entered said building. A limitation on this exception, however, is that a prior crime must bear on the intent, and the present crime must also require a specific intent in order for this character trait to be introduced into evidence.

If the defendant now pleads insanity in this example, the people of the state will be entitled to introduce evidence of prior crimes of the defendant to refute the insanity claim. *Example:* The defendant had been convicted of a burglary shortly before the crime for which he is now on trial. The burglary conviction would be relevant to show that at the time of conviction the defendant was sane and could form the specific intent necessary.

If the prosecutor is attempting to show that the prior crimes reflect on the motive of the defendant, the defendant has to be given an opporunity to prove that he did not commit the prior crimes or to prove that he had no such motive at the time of commission of the prior crimes.

In any of the preceding cases, the court will require as a burden of proof that the prosecution establish that the defendant was guilty by a *substantial amount of evidence,* instead of *beyond a reasonable doubt.*

In any criminal prosecution, the accused, under the so-called mercy rule, is afforded the opportunity to introduce evidence of his good character to show that there is a likelihood that he did not commit the crime as charged. He may do so whether or not he takes the witness stand.

The modern rules have expanded the traditional view of the type of evidence the defendant may use and have allowed the use of any reputation or opinion evidence that the defendant's witnesses may give to the court as to the defendant's character. The traditional view was that witnesses could only testify as to the defendant's reputation in the community and not as to their personal opinions.

Even if the prosecution has not introduced a character trait to show common scheme, design, motive, or intent, it may rebut testimony given by character witnesses put on the stand by the defendant. The defendant is said to have "opened Pandora's box" when he takes the stand to testify or places his character in evidence through other witnesses, because the prosecution is entitled to go into the character of the defendant using the same type of evidence as the defendant has presented to the court.

A problem is presented when the procecutor attempts to introduce evidence of the defendant's prior crimes and the character witnesses of the defendant had no knowledge of this history of criminal conduct. The courts are split as to the introduction of this type of evidence, but the majority view is that the prosecutor cannot introduce this evidence independently if the witnesses had no knowledge of the prior criminal record of the defendant.

In certain types of cases, a particular trait of the victim will be admissible to prove conduct of the victim. For instance, there is much discussion at this time in some states concerning the introduction of the victim's past sexual conduct in a rape prosecution. In cases of rape or any other type of crime where the victim's consent is a defense, the victim's reputation may be admissible to show that the victim in fact did consent in the present case. *Example 1:* The defendant is on trial for forcible rape. He is permitted to show the woman's reputation for promiscuity in order to let the jury decide whether she consented to have sexual relations with him in the present case. *Example 2:* The defendant is on trial for murder and claims that he was defending himself. The defendant may introduce evidence of the victim's reputation for being a violent person to show that the victim was the aggressor in the present case or to show that the defendant's fear of the victim was reasonable.

If the defendant introduces the victim's character into evidence, the prosecutor always has the opportunity to rebut this by introducing evidence showing that the victim was of good character. Most jurisdictions would limit the prosecutor to introducing testimony as to the reputation of the victim in the community in question. However, the modern rules are more liberal and will allow opinion testimony by any witness who claims to have known the victim personally.

Real Evidence

Real evidence consists of tangible things that more or less speak for themselves, such as guns, bullets, shoes worn by a suspect, or the burglar's tools. The jury can perceive through its own senses this type of evidence and need not rely on a description of it from a witness or a police report.

The question of relevancy on any item of real evidence will depend on the background, or testimonial evidence, which links it with the crime. *Example:* In a prosecution for burglary, the prosecution is seeking to admit a crowbar left at the scene of the crime where a safe had been broken into. Testimony would have to be introduced to show that there was a burglary and that a crowbar had been found by the safe and was not there prior to the time the business was closed and that this was the crowbar that was so found.

All real evidence that is found, however, is not admissible. Even though the item of real evidence can be relevant, it is still subjected to the same limitations as any other form of evidence and, therefore, may be excluded.

In most criminal prosecutions, even though real items of evidence such as guns, bullets, or knives are admitted, the trial court generally excludes relevant evidence which would shock or inflame the jury, such as fetuses, severed fingers, severed ears, or any other type of item which would have a prejudicial effect. This decision to exclude or admit is a matter of discretion for the trial judge. Moreover, if the trial judge does admit such evidence, the appellate courts generally will sustain his decision, holding that it is within the judicial discretion of the trial judge whether or not the prejudicial dangers are outweighed by the probative effect.

The law enforcement officer is also involved with items of real evidence in the form of motion pictures, tape recordings, crime scene sketches, photographs of crime scenes, videotapes, and, at times X rays. Since all of these items are classified as real evidence, their admissibility will rest on the public policy which favors the utilization of reliable and scientific methods of reproducing the facts so that the jury can actually see what transpired.

The need for introducing these items, however, rests upon whether or not they can be properly authenticated, meaning that their reliability can be established as factually portraying what they show. The courts have long stated that the reason that these types of evidence need to be authenticated is to protect against the introduction of a different object from the one which the officer is testifying about and to insure that changes in the condition have not occurred since the taking of the photograph, X ray, etc. and its introduction into the court.

Different state courts require different degrees in types of authentication, depending on the type of evidence involved. When the police officer is seeking to introduce a photograph, the majority of courts simply require that a witness who is familiar with the object which the photograph portrays, or the person in the photograph, testify that the photograph actually represents this object or person. Other courts, however, require additional testimony, such as that from the person who actually took the picture, who must be able to testify to the camera angle, the speed of the shot, the lighting, the development process, and the care of the negative, in order to authenticate that it has not been retouched in any manner. However, this is the minority view in the United States today.

As with any other form of real evidence, the court has discretion to exclude photographic types of evidence, even though they have been authenticated and are relevant, if they would tend to prejudice the jury. *Example:* At a homicide, the officers take photographs of wounds showing that the victim has been disemboweled. The court determines upon viewing the pictures that they are gory and would inflame the passions of the jurors so that they could not fairly render a verdict in the case.

For some time, there have been divergent views whether or not it is relevant for jurors to view the scene of the crime. Because many different types of crime scenes cannot be brought into the court, the trial court may authorize the jury to go to the scene to see for themselves. This is a court proceeding. Thus, the jury, the judge, and all the defendants must be present at the viewing of the scene. The state courts are split as to whether or not the actual viewing of the scene by the jurors is in itself evidence. Some state courts rule that it is not evidence, but instead only an aid to the jury to help it understand the testimony being introduced. The majority view in the United States today, however, holds that the viewing by the jury is itself evidence and that the jury may render its verdict or finding based upon that view apart from any other testimonial evidence that is introduced into the trial.

Even though photographs, X rays, movie films, videotapes, etc. are relevant, there still will be constitutional limitations imposed upon their introduction into a criminal case. Thus, if there is a Fourth Amendment problem prohibiting the introduction of evidence that has been seized due to an unreasonable search or seizure, or due to wiretapping or eavesdropping, the evidence will be excluded even though it is relevant.

Scientific Tests or Experiments

Evidence of scientific tests or experiments is admissible if it is shown to be a reliable manner of ascertaining the truth, as to the facts. The admissibility of scientific experiments, however, is a question for the trial judge to decide, whether or not there are any probative dangers (prejudicial effect on the defendant, misleading of the jury, or undue time consumption).

In order for a scientific experiment to be admitted, it must be shown that the experiment was conducted under the same or similar conditions as those existing at the time of the facts in question. *Example:* In an attempt to introduce evidence to show that a given vehicle did not burn up due to a mechanical malfunction, experiments would have to be conducted on the same make and model of vehicle, under the same conditions that the actual car which had caught on fire was experiencing at the time of the actual fire.

Any experiment which is of a scientific nature must, of course, be conducted by an expert in that field. Such an expert must appear in court to testify as to how the test was conducted and as to the reliability of the test and the procedures involved. However, as scientific tests become better known throughout the country, the courts are taking additional notice as to the reliability of scientific tests such as radar, ballistics, fingerprint, blood-alcohol, breathalyzer, gas chromatograph, meaning that if the court takes judicial notice of one of these tests, evidence as to the reliability of the test need not be introduced into court.

There is no limit on the type of scientific experiments that may be offered in the courts today. As the student is well aware, we are increasing our knowledge in the scientific field day by day and are continually developing new devices to aid criminalists in the detection of the criminal. The following are examples of scientific evidence which have been admitted: firearms test to show to the jury patterns of powder and shot made upon an object at different distances; test of how fast a vehicle may be stopped once its brakes have been applied; test to show fatigue of metal which was alleged to have given way. From these examples, the student can see that the range of tests being accepted by the courts today is rather broad and not limited to the blood-alcohol test or the fingerprint test or the nihydrant process test.

Another type of evidence useful in the law enforcement field is the behavior of animals which have been specially trained for law enforcement purposes or of animals which have been trained to track. How the animal was trained, and the reliability of the animal in the same type of cases in the past must be established. *Example:* An officer finds an item of clothing left by a fleeing bank robber outside the bank and he turns it over to a canine officer, who has his animal trained for tracking purposes sniff it. The dog eventually leads the officer to an apartment house a block and a half away, where the officer executes an entry and makes an arrest. It would have to be established that the dog had, in fact, been trained for tracking, could, in fact, track, and had tracked in the past based upon sniffing an item of clothing in order for the courts to establish probable cause for the officer to have gone to the apartment house to have confronted the suspected criminal.

Scientific tests, of course, have been admitted for years in the law enforcement area in order to identify people. As long as it is relevant to establish that a party's identification is in issue, then scientific evidence to establish that would be admissible by the use of fingerprints, handwriting, hair samples, palm prints, voice prints, or other types of reliable scientific experiments. The use of voice prints to identify people, however, is still debatable. Some of the courts have been admitting the voice print evidence as being a scientific experiment which is highly reliable, but others are declining to introduce it because its reliability has not been established to their satisfaction.

Scientific tests that are utilized in an attempt to get the truth from a person are generally not admitted into evidence because they have not been scientifically proven reliable. The lie detector (polygraph) test is one of the scientific tests which has been under fire for many years. The general view is that results of a lie detector test are irrelevant and will not be admitted into evidence in either a civil or a criminal trial, the reason being that there are too many variables involved, especially the competence of the polygraph operator. There are a few recent cases, however, holding that the polygraph is scientifically reliable and that the results may be admitted under certain conditions. However, in a criminal case, mainly due to the Fifth Amendment privilege against self-incrimination, the results will not be admitted unless the defendant consents to the test and to its admissibility. Another similar test which the courts generally exclude is a test conducted in which the defendant was under the influence of a drug (commonly a truth serum) or hypnosis at the time that he made his statement. The courts generally will not admit this evidence due to its lack of scientific reliability.

Chemical tests to determine whether or not a person is under the influence of an alcoholic beverage are generally accepted in the United States, for the scientific reliability of these tests has been proven many times. It also has been proven that the variables of tolerance to alcohol does not detract from the reliability of the test.

There are various types of tests used to determine whether or not a person is under the influence of alcohol, including the blood-alcohol test, the breath test, and the urine test. The objection that is usually raised when one of these tests is sought to be introduced into evidence is that the test violates a person's privilege against self-incrimination under the

Fifth Amendment. The U.S. Supreme Court stated that it does not however violate a person's privilege if the person was in lawful custody at the time the sample was taken.

Blood-test evidence has been held admissible for the purpose of identifying a body even though it will only establish a possibility in a case, and may be a probability in others, depending on the several blood classifications that are involved. If the test is being introduced to show paternity, the courts are less inclined to introduce it than if it were for identification purposes. The majority of courts will exclude blood-test evidence where the test establishes the possibility that the suspect is the alleged father for fear that the jury would give too much weight to this evidence. Where the test results, however, exclude the possibility that this suspect could be the father of the child, many decisions now hold that the tests are conclusive on the issue and will not allow testimonial evidence to contradict it.

Summary

Relevancy is one of the first exclusionary rules in the law of evidence. In order for any item of evidence to be introduced at a trial, it is necessary that the item first be shown to be relevant to the issues at hand, relevancy meaning that the item logically tends to prove or disprove any material issue in the trial. The person seeking to introduce the evidence should consider any other rules of evidence which could bar its admission even though it may be relevant. A person should ask himself the following questions: (1) Will the item logically tend to prove or disprove any material issue in the case? (2) If so, is the item barred by any other rule of evidence? (3) Is the item highly prejudicial to the defendant in the case? (4) Is the introduction of the item cumulative in nature and thus subject to exclusions by the judge at his discretion? (5) Is presentation of the item too time consuming?

The police officer is often confronted with the character of the defendant in a trial in which the people are attempting to establish a modus operandi of the defendant. There are many problems involved in attempting to introduce the character of the defendant into evidence prior to the time that the defendant has placed his character in evidence. If the people are attempting to prove the modus operandi of a crime, past specific acts of the defendant are almost always admissible. However, if the people are attempting to show only that the defendant is a bad person, then the evidence will most always be excluded.

In most cases, evidence of the victim's character will not be admissible. There are exceptions to this rule. In sex crime cases, most jurisdictions generally allow the past sexual conduct of the victim to come into evidence at the trial. The reason for this rule is that some check is needed to make sure that the victim did not consent to the act. The feeling is that past sexual conduct may shed light as to whether or not the victim consented to the act which is now before the court. This rule, however, is currently being objected to in most jurisdictions on the grounds that it forces the victim to be placed on trial and to disclose past conduct. The objection is also raised that past sexual conduct by consent has nothing to do with being the victim of a sex crime.

The type of evidence which is admissible to prove the character of a person generally is introduced by testimony of witnesses who have heard in the community where the victim or the defendant resides as to their reputation in said community. The modern rules, however, are more liberal and allow opinion testimony by any witness who claims to have known the victim personally, or in the business community where the person whose character is in issue works.

DISCUSSION QUESTIONS

1. What is the basic meaning of *relevancy*?
2. Distinguish between relevancy and materiality.
3. Discuss the grounds under which relevant evidence may be excluded by the judge.
4. Distinguish the difference between character evidence and reputation evidence.
5. When is the character of a defendant in a criminal case placed in issue?
6. Discuss when the character of a victim is admissible in your jurisdiction.

STATE v. BALL
Supreme Court of Missouri, 1960.
339 S.W.2d 783.

BARRETT, COMMISSIONER. A jury has found William Arthur Ball guilty of robbery in the first degree; the jury also found prior felony convictions and, therefore, a mandatory sentence of life imprisonment was imposed. V.A.M.S. §§ 560.120, 560.135, 556.280.

The facts, briefly, as the jury could find them were that about 2:30 in the afternoon of October 15, 1958, two colored men, one of them tall and the other short, entered the Krekeler Jewelry Store at 1651 South 39th Street. The taller man spent ten or fifteen minutes selecting and buying a cigarette lighter, he also talked about buying and looked at watches and rings. As the taller man looked at jewelry and made his purchase the shorter man looked in the cases and moved about in the store. Later in the day, about 5:50, as John Krekeler was placing rings and watches in the safe preparatory to closing the store two men entered, one of them tall and the other short, and Krekeler immediately recognized them as the two men who had been in the store at 2:30, especially the taller man. He recognized the taller man's narrow-brimmed, tall hat, brown jacket, gray shirt and particularly a scar on his face. The shorter man started to walk behind the counter and as Krekeler intercepted him he "drew a long barreled blue .38 and stuck it in my face." Both men followed Krekeler, the shorter man with the gun in "his back," directing him to the watch repair department and finally into the rest room in the rear of the store. He was told not to turn around and stood facing the wall. He could hear jewelry being dumped into a bag and the "jingle" of the cash register. The two men left Krekeler in the rest room and after hearing the door slam he called the police. The two men had taken watches and rings of the stipulated value of $4,455.21 and $140 in cash from the register. Krekeler identified the appellant from pictures, and three weeks later, after his capture, in a hospital and upon the trial positively identified him as the taller of the two holdup men. . . .

Another of the appellant's sufficiently preserved claims in his motion for a new trial (V.A.M.S. § 547.030; Supreme Court Rule

27.20, V.A.M.R.) has to do with his arrest and the testimony of the two arresting officers. On November 4, 1958, about three weeks after the robbery, police officers in a squad car saw Ball walking on Easton Avenue. The officers stopped him, told him that they were officers and that he was under arrest. As officer Powell faced and searched Ball officer Ballard "holstered" his gun and attempted "to cuff" him. Ball shoved Powell over and ran down Easton Avenue, the officers ran after him, Powell being closest. Powell yelled, "Halt Ball, you're under arrest," and fired one shot high in the air but Ball continued running and Powell fired four more shots, two at his legs, one at his buttocks, and he finally fell from a bullet in his back. It is claimed that this evidence was not material or relevant, that it was too remote from the date of the robbery to indicate a consciousness of guilt and since it was of course prejudicial that he is entitled to a new trial. But unexplained flight and resisting arrest even thirty days after the supposed commission of a crime is a relevant circumstance (State v. Duncan, 336 Mo. 600, 611, 80 S.W.2d 147, 153), the remoteness of the flight goes to the weight of the evidence rather than to its admissibility. 20 Am.Jur., Sec. 293, p. 274.

When Ball was finally subdued and arrested the officers took from his person and impounded a brown felt hat, "a brownish" windbreaker type jacket, trousers, gray shirt and shoes — these were exhibits one and two. Ball admitted that they belonged to him although his evidence tended to show that he had purchased the jacket after October 15. In identifying Ball, in addition to the scar on his face, Krekeler was impressed with and remembered the brown ensemble, particularly the "tall brown hat." These items were of course relevant and admissible in evidence and there is no objection to them. State v. Johnson, Mo., 286 S.W.2d 787, 792. The appellant objects, however, in his motion for a new trial that a police officer was permitted to testify that $258.02 in currency and two pennies were taken from his person. It is said that the introduction of these exhibits was "immaterial and irrelevant, neither tended to prove nor disprove any of the issues involved in this case; that said money as seized at the time of the arrest was neither identified by Mr. Krekeler nor by any other person as the money which was allegedly stolen from the A. L. Krekeler & Sons Jewelry Company on the 15th day of October, 1958; that said evidence was considered by this jury to the prejudice of this defendant convincingly."

The circumstances in which this evidence was introduced were these: After the clothes were identified and introduced as exhibits one and two the prosecuting attorney inquired of officer Powell, "Did you also seize his personal effects?" Defense counsel immediately objected to any testimony relating to personal effects found on the defendant "at the time." The court overruled the objection and state's counsel inquired, "Well Officer, what personal effects were seized?" Defense counsel, evidently knowing and anticipating, objected "to any testimony relevant (sic) to any personal effects seized upon this Defendant at the time he was arrested by reason of the fact it is immaterial and irrelevant and tends to neither prove nor disprove any facts involved and ask that the jury be discharged and a mistrial be declared." The court overruled the objection and the officer said, "Ball's personal effects consisted of two hundred and fifty eight dollars and two cents in cash, with the denominations of the bill(s), two one hundred dollar bills, a twenty — two twenties, a ten, a five, three ones and two pennies. He had a ladies ring and a man's wristwatch. He had a *crusifixion* along with a small pen knife and a black leather wallet. Maybe one or two other personal articles." All of these items were then marked as exhibits, from three to nine, offered in evidence and described by the officer, exhibit three being the bills and pennies comprising the $258.02. According to the officer Mr. Krekeler was unable to identify any of these articles or the money as having come from the jewelry store robbery and there is no objection in the motion to any of the items other than the money and some of them were obviously not prejudicial, for example the keys, a small penknife and wallet.

Unlike the roll of dimes in State v. Hampton, Mo., 275 S.W.2d 356, the testimony as to the $258.02 was not offered in proof of the substantive fact of the crime. In that case the five-dollar roll of dimes wrapped in a roll of green paper was found on the defendant the same day of the burglary and while the fact was a circumstance admissible in evidence it was held not to constitute substantive evidence inconsistent with the hypothesis of the defendant's innocence of burglary. In State v. Gerberding, Mo., 272 S.W.2d 230, there was no timely or proper objection to the proof but $4,000 was taken in a robbery and the appellant had $920 in currency in his topcoat pocket when captured the day of the robbery. The proof of the money here was evidently on the theory that Ball did not have or was not likely to have such a sum of money on his person prior to the commission of the offense. 1 Wharton, Criminal Evidence, Sec. 204, p. 410. As to this the facts were that he had been out of the penitentiary about eight months and the inference the state would draw is that he had no visible means of support and no employment and could not possibly have $258.02 except from robberies. Of course, there was no such proof and Ball claimed that he had worked intermittently for a custodian or janitor of an apartment house and that he had won the $258.02 in a series of crap games at a named place. Not only was Krekeler unable to identify the money or any of the items on Ball's person as having come from the jewelry store so that in fact they were not admissible in evidence (annotation 3 A.L.R. 1213), the charge here was that Ball and his accomplice took jewelry of the value of $4,455.21 and $140 in cash from the cash register. There was no proof as to the denomination of the money in the cash register, it was simply a total of $140. Here nineteen days had elapsed, there was no proof that Ball had suddenly come into possession of the $258.02 (annotation 123 A.L.R. 119) and in all these circumstances "The mere possession of a quantity of money is in itself no indication that the possessor was the taker of money charged as taken, because in general all money of the same denomination and material is alike, and the hypothesis that the money found is the same as the money taken is too forced and extraordinary to be receivable." 1 Wigmore, Evidence, Sec. 154, p. 601. In the absence of proof or of a fair inference from the record that the money in Ball's possession at the time of his arrest came from or had some connection with the robbery and in the absence of a plain showing of his impecuniousness before the robbery and his sudden affluence (State v. Garrett, 285 Mo. 279, 226 S.W.4), the evidence was not in fact relevant and in the circumstances was obviously prejudicial for if it did not tend to prove the offense for which the appellant was on trial the jury may have inferred that he was guilty of another robbery.) State v. Bray, Mo.App., 278 S.W. 2d 49; People v. Orloff, 65 Cal.App.2d 614, 620–621, 151 P.2d 288; annotation 123 A.L.R. loc. cit. 132–134 and compare the facts and circumstances in State v. Garrett, supra. The admission of the evidence in the circumstances of this record infringed the right to a fair trial and for that reason the judgment is reversed and the cause remanded.

BULLARD v. UNITED STATES
United States Court of Appeals, Fifth Circuit, 1968.
395 F.2d 658.

TUTTLE, CIRCUIT JUDGE. This is an appeal from the conviction by a jury of Mabel L. Bullard of violating two sections of the Dyer Act, Title 18 U.S.C.A. Secs. 2312 and 2313. Appellant does not here contest the fact that the evidence adduced on her trial was sufficient for the jury to find her guilty beyond a reasonable doubt. Her principal complaint here is that the trial court committed prejudicial error in admitting testimony of a government witness, Pat Lynch, dealing with facts not related to, nor casting any light on, any of the issues of guilt or innocence of the appellant in the case being tried before the jury.

The appellant's defense in the district court was that she did not know that the two automobiles with which she was associated in company with her boy friend, Rochester, had been stolen. The government witness, Lynch, was permitted to testify as follows:

A. Well, I — at the time, I had been in the hospital, and I had been trying to sell my Camaro, and I didn't seem to have

any luck; and she came up to me and asked me had I ever thought of having it stolen or wrecked or burned. And at this point, I thought, you know, it was — well, she really wasn't being serious.
MR. BALL: I object, your honor, to this; this is irrelevant to this case, and it is highly prejudicial to this —
THE COURT: I will admit it for whatever light it might shed on the intent of this defendant insofar as she is charged in this indictment, and that is the restricted purpose it is admitted on. Go ahead.
A. And the conversation went on, and I wanted to know —
Q. I didn't hear that last statement?
A. The conversation went on, and I wanted to know how this could be done, and she said, "Well, you could just leave your car outside, let us know when your neighbors go to sleep or when you go to sleep, and by the next morning, your car will be across the State line."

There was no evidence as to when this conversation took place, that is to say it is not even shown that it happened before or after the transactions which were the basis of the present prosecution.

Appellant, of course, bases her complaint on the general proposition that a criminal defendant's prior difficulties with the law, specific prior criminal acts, or bad reputation, cannot be used by the Government to prove guilt of an unconnected crime, even though such facts might tend to prove a defendant's propensity to commit the crime for which he is on trial. Michelson v. United States, 335 U.S. 469, 69 S.Ct. 213, 93 L.Ed. 168.

The Government, on the other hand, claims that this testimony is admissible under the exception which permits the introduction of evidence of prior conduct or a prior offense which may throw light on either the intent of the accused or the accused's knowledge of essential facts in the present prosecution. Such exception, for instance, permits the introduction of testimony showing that a person being tried for knowingly passing counterfeit money has, on prior occasions, passed bills shown to be counterfeit, even though the instant prosecution does not involve the passing of the earlier bills. So, too, where an accused's conduct for which he is on trial is ambiguous in nature, that is where wrongful if done with an improper intent, but not criminal if done innocently, testimony of prior conduct by the accused may be shown to assist the jury in resolving the issue of intent. See Ehrlich v. United States (5th Cir.) 238 F.2d 481.

It is apparent that the trial court permitted the introduction of this testimony, clearly prejudicial to the appellant as to her general character, upon this theory of the law. However, as pointed out by this court in Helton v. United States (5th Cir.) 221 F.2d 338, the prior act of a damaging nature must truly illustrate something concerning the very issue before the trial court. Here, regardless of how anti-social this appellant was shown to be by testimony that she was willing to defraud an insurance company by staging a burning or theft of another automobile, this does *not* illustrate the issue of whether Miss Bullard knew or did not know that the two entirely different automobiles for whose illegal possession she was on trial had been stolen before being brought into the state of Alabama.

Naturally, a jury might well decide that a person about whom it was said that she was willing to participate in a fraud against an insurance company dealing with an automobile might be such a person as would, with guilty knowledge, take possession of the automobiles here in issue. This does not meet the test because the evidence did show only a propensity on the part of Miss Bullard to commit a fraud or possibly a crime and not that she actually knew that these particular automobiles had been stolen.

There is no doubt but that this testimony was extremely prejudicial. It was objected to by counsel for the appellant who thus preserved the matter for our review.

The judgment must be reversed and the case remanded for further proceedings in the trial court.

The judgment is reversed and the case remanded for further proceedings not inconsistent with this opinion.

JONES v. STATE
Court of Criminal Appeals of Texas, 1964.
376 S.W.2d 842.

WOODLEY, PRESIDING JUDGE. The indictment alleged that the appellant took money from the person and possession of D. M. Hause without his knowledge and without his consent, and with the intent to deprive him of its value and to appropriate it to her use and benefit. . . .

The state relied upon circumstantial evidence to show appellant's guilt of theft of money from the person and possession of D. M. Hause.

Hause testified that on December 13, 1962, the appellant came to his auto parts place of business around 3 P.M., while he was working on a generator; she grabbed C. V. Wells, who later became a partner in the business, and propositioned him for sexual intercourse. She had her hands all over him. He pushed her away. She then said she had to urinate and was shown an outside rest room. On the way she fell, or claimed to have fallen, and Hause, thinking she was drunk, tried to get her up. She raised up her dress and grabbed him.

Before he could drag her out she turned around and rubbed "her rear end" on him. She then said she had to use the telephone. He did not see her again until she was arrested on March 6, 1963.

Some five minutes after the appellant left, Hause reached for his handkerchief and discovered that the $150 or more he had in his billfold was gone, but the billfold was in his pocket and the checks were still in it. . . .

The state was permitted to prove that the appellant, on March 6, 1963, went to an automobile service shop or Transmission Shop in Austin during the noon hour and, after announcing that she wanted to use the bathroom, grabbed Mr. Grady, the proprietor, and propositioned him and he "pushed her back because she was drunk." She grabbed him again and then walked out. All of this time Mr. Grady was talking on the telephone. He discovered some 15 minutes later that the $125 he had in his billfold was gone. . . .

The state was also permitted to introduce evidence to the effect that the appellant, on or about December 31, 1962, went to the place of business of an Orthopedic Brace Company where the proprietor, Mr. Hess, was at work at his bench, put her hand on him like she was trying to keep from falling and acting "as if she was trying to solicit a street job," and as though she was drugged or doped. She then left suddenly and the brace maker soon found that his billfold, in which he had $20 or more, was gone. The billfold was later recovered, its contents other than the money was intact.

Appellant was identified by the witnesses as the person who came to each of the shops, propositioned the owner (each of whom was married and living with his wife), put her hand upon them, and left suddenly, her departure being soon followed by the discovery that the men's money had likewise departed.

The evidence regarding the conduct of the appellant and the loss of money from the billfold of Mr. Hess, the brace maker, and from the owner of the Transmission Shop was admitted over the objection that it was "irrelevant and immaterial, highly prejudicial. It is at a time different and subsequent to the date alleged in the indictment of December the 13th."

The evidence was offered and was admitted only for the purpose of showing identity, intent, motive, malice or common plan or scheme. It was so limited in the court's charge and the jury was instructed that such evidence could not be considered for any purpose unless they believed beyond a reasonable doubt that the defendant committed such other offenses.

The intent of the appellant in making physical contact with Mr. Hause was material and was uncertain. Proof that the money was taken as well as the intent of the appellant rested upon circumstances.

The two collateral offenses show more than a similarity in results. They show a common plan and systematic course of action. The peculiar way in which the other business men lost their money upon the same course of conduct by the appellant was a circumstance that was available to the state to prove the appellant's guilt of theft from the person of Hause. The evidence showed system, not merely systematic crime, and the court did not err in admitting it for the limited purposes stated. . . .

The evidence is sufficient to sustain the conviction and no error appears.

The judgment is affirmed.

STATE v. SPREIGL
Supreme Court of Minnesota, 1965.
272 Minn. 488, 139 N.W.2d 167. Noted, 51 Minn.L.Rev. 331.

OTIS, JUSTICE. Defendant has been found guilty of taking indecent liberties with his 11-year-old stepdaughter, Sandra, and appeals from the judgment of conviction and from an order denying his petition for a writ of coram nobis.

Sandra testified that on Sunday afternoon, May 6, 1962, defendant took her to the basement of an unfinished house adjacent to her home and committed on her what amounted to an unaccomplished act of sexual intercourse. Over the defendant's objection, Sandra disclosed that during the previous year, at intervals of 2, 3, or 4 weeks, defendant compelled her to indulge in acts of fellation with him in the bathroom of their home. In addition, the court permitted another stepdaughter, Pamela, then 10 years old, to testify that every week or two for an unspecified period of time the defendant forced her to commit similar acts of perversion. A stepson, Gerald, also 10, testified to one such offense committed by his stepfather in April 1962. Neither the children's mother nor defendant took the stand, and no testimony was introduced on his behalf except that of two school nurses who described the program on sex education for adolescent girls presented at the school which Sandra attended. Counsel for defendant requested an instruction that the jury disregard all evidence of defendant's prior misconduct except that for which he was being prosecuted, and moved that the evidence of other offenses be stricken. The motion was denied. The jury brought in a verdict of guilty on June 19, 1962. In February 1964 defendant petitioned for a writ of coram nobis based on affidavits submitted by a fellow employee and by defendant's mother which, in effect, attempted to establish an alibi.

Defendant assigns as error (1) the court's refusal to exclude the testimony of Sandra, Pamela, and Gerald concerning prior acts of fellation; (2) the failure of the court to give a cautionary instruction, sua sponte, with respect to the jury's consideration of the prior offenses; and (3) the court's refusal to grant the writ of coram nobis.

1. The basic issue is whether the unquestioned relevance of testimony that a defendant has committed other sex offenses, if true, gives it sufficient probative value to outweigh the patent unfairness which results to an innocent defendant who is confronted with charges against which he is not prepared to defend, which are inflammatory in the extreme, and which emanate from witnesses who are manifestly susceptible to influence and suggestion. We are of the opinion that under the circumstances of this case the challenged testimony should not have been received without prior notice of the state's intention to offer it. There must therefore be a new trial.

2. Subject to specific exceptions which have evolved in this country, our court has consistently adhered to the common-law rule excluding evidence connecting a defendant with other crimes, except for purposes of impeachment under Minn.St. 610.49 if he takes the stand on his own behalf.

In an early case dealing with the problem, we held that evidence of distinct and independent prior offenses was not admissible because it tried defendant for charges of which he had no notice and for which he was unprepared and which prejudiced him in the eyes of the jury. Subsequently, we enumerated various widely recognized exceptions to the general exclusionary rule where evidence of prior crimes was admissible to show motive, to negative mistake, to establish identity, or "where the previous offense is a part of a scheme or conspiracy incidental to or embraced in proof of the charge on trial." Some 10 years later we specifically referred to sex crimes as a class of prosecutions where the exclusionary rule had been liberally extended, and admitted evidence of prior acts of carnal knowledge with the same victim "on the theory of disclosing the relationship between the parties, opportunity and inclination to commit the act complained of, and as corroborative of the specific charge." Where the prior offense occurred with the same victim and was misconduct of the same or similar character, we stated that it gave rise to a strong inference the illicit relationship once created continued, and tended to characterize the conduct, inclination, and disposition of defendant toward the victim of the offense for which he was being prosecuted.

While this court by way of dictum in a prosecution for bribery listed sex crimes as a blanket exception to the exclusionary rule, our early cases uniformly excluded such evidence where the previous offense involved a victim other than the subject of the prosecution in question unless admissible under some other well-defined exception.

It was not until our decision in State v. DePauw, 246 Minn. 91, 74 N.W.2d 297, that we squarely passed on the admissibility of prior sex offenses involving third persons. There the charge was indecent assault against a 9-year-old girl. The trial court received evidence that defendant was guilty of similar misconduct against four other children between the ages of 8 and 9 years. All of the offenses occurred in the defendant's home; the victims were all children living in the immediate neighborhood; and all were playmates of defendant's son. We held that the prior offenses and the offense charged constituted a common plan, scheme, or pattern which brought them within the exception to the exclusionary rule. However, none of the prior victims was in any way related to defendant, and in each case the misconduct consisted of improperly fondling young children in the same manner as that charged in the principal proceedings. More recently, in State v. Arradondo, 260 Minn. 512, 110 N.W.2d 469, we held it proper in a carnal knowledge prosecution under the rule we adopted in the DePauw case to receive evidence that defendant had committed similar offenses against two other 16-year-old girls.

Unlike the DePauw and Arradondo cases, the prior misconduct here was of a somewhat different character from that with which defendant is now charged. However, both offenses involved sexually molesting small children, and we believe the similarity of behavior is sufficient to justify receiving the challenged evidence at the new trial.

3. A basic assumption implicit in decisions which permit a showing of prior sex offenses is that sex offenders have an established proclivity for recidivism. Nevertheless, courts have consistently refused to permit such evidence to show defendant's general propensity for crime although the distinction between inclination and disposition has been difficult to articulate in determining whether a common scheme or plan has been proved. In permitting evidence of prior offenses to be received as a part of a common plan or scheme, we have come perilously close to putting the defendant's character and record in issue notwithstanding his failure to take the witness stand, as in the instant case.

Where a defendant is charged with a particular offense, it has been argued that he should be prepared to defend against evidence of similar crimes involving the same victim. However unfair the result may be to an innocent defendant, where he has no notice of other charges it is even more unjust to confront him with evidence of equally repulsive and outrageous misconduct against third persons. We are not inclined to aggravate a situation which we already regard as potentially oppressive without promulgating appropriate safeguards.

A well-considered article on the admissibility of testimony of prior victims points out:

". . . At least it can be said that if the prosecuting witnesses did not know each other prior to trial; if their stories were recorded prior to communication between them; if they were subjected to thorough cross-examination and their stories stood up; then such evidence would be quite relevant and its relevancy would tend to increase with the number of witnesses who could testify to the *modus operandi*."

In other words, the opportunity for collusion and the probability of fabrication are less likely where unrelated, mature victims voluntarily come forward to testify to a defendant's previous sexual misconduct. The natural reluctance of such persons to disclose their identity entitles their testimony to considerable weight. In the instant case, on the other hand, all three of the alleged victims were small children, 10 and 11 years of age. They were brother and sisters, stepchildren of the defendant, living in the same household with their mother. Clearly, the opportunity for suggestion and for influencing their testimony was great. Under these circumstances, the court must exercise extreme caution in receiving such evidence and ordinarily should advise the jury of the limited purpose for which it is received. This danger of fabrication was not present in either the DePauw or Arradondo cases.

While, of course, failure to complain is not conclusively impeaching, the fact remains that in the instant case, so far as the record indicates, two of the children who claim to have been victims of repeated and shocking misconduct over an extended period of time made no complaint to their mother nor to anyone else until after the offense for which defendant is here charged, and the third child made no complaint at any time. This is something we cannot ignore in weighing the question of whether defendant should have a new trial.

4. Threaded through our precedents dealing with exceptions to the exclusionary rule is a note of concern, admonishing courts against depriving innocent persons of their constitutional right to a fair trial.

"... [I]t is not the rights of those alone who may be guilty of other offenses for whom the solicitude of the law is to be exercised, but it is more particularly for the innocent, oppressed with unfounded suspicions, who may find no other shield for his protection than an intelligent enforcement of his constitutional safeguards by the courts."

Where it is not clear to the court whether or not the evidence is admissible as an exception to the general exclusionary rule, "the accused is to be given the benefit of the doubt, and the evidence rejected." We have said, "The danger of it is that a jury may convict because, though guilt of the crime charged is not proved, it is satisfied to convict because of other crimes," and again:

"It is sometimes a close question whether the probative value of such evidence is outweighed by the risk that its admission will necessitate undue consumption of time, confuse the issues, surprise the defendant, or mislead and unduly prejudice the jury. . . ."

We have noted:

"In the adjudication of sexual offenses, particular caution must be exercised lest the law in pursuing the guilty deprive the innocent of their rightful protection."

Dean Wigmore has stated the problem succinctly in terms we have expressly approved (1 Wigmore, Evidence [3 ed.] §§ 193, 194):

"... That such former misconduct is relevant, *i. e.* has probative value to persuade us of the general trait or disposition, cannot be doubted. The assumption of its probative value is made throughout the judicial opinions on this subject. . . ."

"It may almost be said that it is because of this indubitable relevancy of such evidence that it is excluded. It is objectionable, not because it has no appreciable probative value, but because it has too much. The natural and inevitable tendency of the tribunal—whether judge or jury—is to give excessive weight to the vicious record of crime thus exhibited, and either to allow it to bear too strongly on the present charge, or to take the proof of it as justifying a condemnation irrespective of guilt of the present charge. Moreover, the use of alleged particular acts ranging over the entire period of the defendant's life makes it impossible for him to be prepared to refute the charge, any or all of which may be mere fabrications. . . .

"The reasons thus marshalled in various forms are reducible to three: (1) The overstrong tendency to believe the defendant guilty of the charge merely because he is a likely person to do such acts; (2) The tendency to condemn, not because he is believed guilty of the present charge, but because he has escaped unpunished from other offences; . . . (3) The injustice of attacking one necessarily unprepared to demonstrate that the attacking evidence is fabricated. . . ."

5. Although the responsibility for weighing the delicately balanced and conflicting considerations involved in receiving prior related misconduct is largely within the discretion of the trial court, we conclude that we have gone as far as we think proper in approving its admissibility. Because of the serious misgivings we have long entertained in this connection, we now hold that in the trial of this and future criminal cases where the state seeks to prove that an accused has been guilty of additional crimes and misconduct on other occasions, although such evidence is otherwise admissible under some exception to the general exclusionary rule, it shall not hereafter be received unless within a reaonable time before trial the state furnishes defendant in writing a statement of the offenses it intends to show he has committed, described with the particularity required of an indictment or information, subject, however, to the following exceptions: (a) Offenses which are part of the immediate episode for which defendant is being tried; (b) offenses for which defendant has previously been prosecuted; and (c) offenses

which are introduced to rebut defendant's evidence of good character.

6. Since there is to be a new trial, it is not necessary to consider assignment of error thereby rendered moot.

Reversed and new trial ordered.

PEOPLE v. VAN GAASBECK
Court of Appeals of New York, 1907.
189 N.Y. 408, 82 N.E. 718.

WILLARD BARTLETT, J. The defendant was indicted for the crime of murder in the second degree, and convicted of manslaughter in the first degree. The crime was charged to have been committed on the 4th day of December, 1905, at the town of Woodstock, in the county of Ulster. The victim of the alleged homicide was Oscar Harrison, a white person about 20 years of age at the time of his death. The defendant is a negro, who at that time was about 55 years old. Harrison was found dead in the dwelling of the defendant near Woodstock on the morning of December 5, 1905, under circumstances which left no doubt that his death had been caused by means of blows upon his head with a blunt instrument, probably a hammer which was lying in the same room. There was no direct evidence tending to show the commission of the crime by the defendant. Harrison, it appeared, had been in the habit from time to time of visiting the house where the defendant lived alone, and had occasionally spent the night there. He was last seen alive there in the company of the defendant, on the day before he was found dead. On the evening of that day the defendant, in an intoxicated condition, visited the post office and country store in Woodstock, and subsequently went to the residence of some colored people named Conine, where he spent the night sleeping in a chair by the fire. There appears to have been nothing unusual, however, in his conduct in this respect, as the testimony tends to show that he had frequently spent the night there in this manner on previous occasions.

In the morning one of the Conines suggested to the defendant that he should go over to his house and see what had happened there on the previous night, saying that he (Conine), on his way from Woodstock the evening before, had heard noises, groans, stamping on the floor, and heavy breathing proceeding from the defendant's dwelling. The defendant thereupon went to his own house, being accompanied by Conine, whom he requested to go with him. The defendant went ahead, pushed the door open, and found Harrison lying dead on the floor. He seems to have become agitated at the sight and asked Conine what he should do. Conine advised him to go to a neighbor's and telephone to Harrison's father, and the defendant acted upon this advice, and proceeded to the residence of a neighbor named Wolven, and said to him: "Will you telephone to John Harrison that Oscar is dead in my house. He has poisoned or killed himself in some way, I don't know how." The desired message was sent and shortly afterward the defendant disappeared from the immediate neighborhood and proceeded to West Saugerties, where he spent the night in the house of an acquaintance, whence he walked the next day to Purling, in Greene county, where he was arrested by a deputy sheriff of Ulster county, named Everett Rosa. The testimony of this officer tended more strongly than any other evidence in the case to connect the defendant with the commission of the crime. After narrating the circumstances of the arrest and saying that he told the defendant he would have to go back and answer for the body lying dead in his house, this witness testified as follows: "We came to Jennings' Hotel, and I said, 'Corn, you led me a merry chase.' Finally, he said, 'I didn't think I would get as far as I did.' I said, 'What did you lay the fellow out for in that way?' He said (dropping his head). 'I don't know.'" The defendant was sworn as a witness in his own behalf, and said in explanation of his flight that he was scared, but did not know what he was to do, and that when he left Woodstock he had no idea where he was going. He denied having killed Harrison, but did not controvert the truth of the statement which I have quoted from the testimony of the deputy sheriff who arrested him. He declared that the last that he ever saw of Harrison was on the afternoon before the discovery of the dead body, when he started for Woodstock, and that Harrison was outside of the house going towards the dwelling of the Conines. There was considerable evidence in the case tending to show that the relations between Harrison and the defendant had always been friendly, although one witness, who testified to having seen Harrison and the defendant engaged in conversation on the afternoon before the homicide, said that while he could not understand the words which they used "they were jangling quite sharp." . . .

The alleged errors upon which the Appellate Division has reversed the judgment of conviction arise upon exceptions to the exclusion of evidence which the defendant sought to obtain from two witnesses, Charles Merritt and Thomas B. Johnston. Merritt testified that he lived in Kingston; that he had known the defendant probably 25 or 30 years; that the defendant had worked for him on his farm, off and on, 3, 4, or 5 years; that whenever he wanted extra help he used to go and get the defendant; and that he was acquainted with his reputation and his character, so far as it related to whether or not he was of a quiet and peaceable disposition or otherwise. The witness was then asked: "What do you say his reputation is?" This question was objected to on the ground that there had been no foundation laid for the proof, and on the further ground that it was not the proper way to show character. The objection was sustained, and the defendant excepted. The other witness, Johnston, testified that he was a policeman in the city of Kingston, and had been such for about 19 years; that he had known the defendant 30 years; that he knew him when he was in the city, and knew his character "as to being a peaceable, quiet man." He was then asked: "What do you say of it?" This question was objected to, the objection was sustained, and an exception was taken in behalf of the defendant.

It will be observed that these exceptions present two entirely different questions. The ruling in respect to the evidence sought to be obtained from the witness Merritt was a ruling to the effect, first, that no sufficient foundation had been laid for the introduction of any proof whatever as to the character of the accused; and, secondly, that, even if the witness were qualified to speak on this subject, proof as to the general reputation of the defendant in regard to peaceableness and quiet was not admissible. By the second ruling in respect to the question put to the witness Johnston, the court held that it was not permissible for the defendant to give evidence tending to show that his character was that of a peaceable, quiet man, based upon the personal knowledge and observation of the witness. In our opinion the first ruling was erroneous, and justified and required a reversal of the judgment; but the second ruling was correct.

"It is not necessary to cite authorities," says the Supreme Court of the United States in Edgington v. U. S., 164 U.S. 361, 17 S.Ct. 72, 41 L.Ed. 467, "to show that in criminal prosecutions the accused will be allowed to call witnesses to show that his character was such as to make it unlikely that he would be guilty of the particular crime with which he is charged." The precise question here, however, relates to the nature of the testimony which such witnesses are permitted to give for this purpose. Must they be confined to a statement of their knowledge of the general reputation of the party whose conduct is under investigation, as seems to be contended by the learned counsel for the appellant; or may they go further, and testify as to his reputation in respect to the particular trait or traits involved in the issue? And, again, must they be confined to the general reputation of the person whose character is in question in respect to such traits; or may they testify to the existence or nonexistence of the particular traits involved basing their testimony upon their personal acquaintance with the party and their observation of his mode of life?

The fact sought to be established by evidence bearing upon the character of an accused person is the improbability that the defendant would commit the crime of which he is accused. The evidence being adduced for this purpose, it is manifestly proper, in order that it may be most useful in the guidance of the jury, that it should not be confined to the general good reputation of the defendant, but may be extended to his reputation in respect to the particular traits involved in the accusation. The common practice in this state seems to have been in accordance with this view. Thus, in the bill of exceptions in the celebrated murder case of Cancemi v. People, 16 N.Y. 501, a leading authority on the admissibility of evidence of good character in behalf of an accused person, it is stated that defendant's counsel on the trial of the case called 19 witnesses, all of whom testified to the general good character of the defendant for peace and quietness and for honesty and industry. This seems to be the rule generally throughout the Union. . . . If such good reputation is established, it is a fact to be considered by the jury, in connection with all the other facts in the case, in determining whether or not the defendant actually did commit the offense of which he is accused. The weight to be given to the evidence of good reputation is, of course, wholly a matter for the jury. The same doctrine is laid down in many other cases too numerous to cite.

It is often found stated in connection with the qualifying rule, which has been almost universally adopted in this country, to the effect that, while the community reputation as to particular traits is admissible upon the question of character, the personal knowledge and belief of the witness must be excluded. 3 Wigmore on Evidence, § 1980. Thus, in Hirschman v. People, 101 Ill. 568, where the defendant was tried on an indictment for manslaughter, it was held that he was properly permitted to give evidence of his general reputation in regard to peace and quiet, but that no error was committed in excluding all particular transactions in which he had been concerned tending to prove a quiet and peaceable disposition on the part of the accused. . . . When, therefore, a witness is called to prove the good character of the defendant, his testimony should not go beyond the reputation which the defendant sustains in the community as to the particular traits of character, the existence or nonexistence of which bear upon the probability or improbability that he would commit or refrain from committing the offense with which he is charged. State v. Pearce, 15 Nev. 188. The authorities which have been cited suffice to show that, while the defendant in the case at bar was entitled to give evidence of his general reputation as a man of quiet and peaceable disposition, he was not entitled to prove particular acts indicative of the fact that he possessed traits rendering it unlikely that he would assault his friend. . . .

In a few of the states, notably Iowa and Minnesota, the doctrine that the character of the defendant in a prosecution for homicide can be shown only by the evidence of his general good reputation, or his reputation in the community as a person of quiet and peaceable disposition, is rejected. The courts in those states go further, and hold that a defendant in such a case is entitled to show by the personal observation and knowledge of witnesses called in his behalf that he possesses those traits of character which would render it unlikely that he committed the offense with which he is charged. State v. Sterrett, 68 Iowa 76, 25 N.W. 936; State v. Lee, 22 Minn. 407, 21 Am. Rep. 769. . . . This view, however, is opposed to the prevailing rule in England as established in Reg. v. Rowton, 10 Cox's Crim. Cases, 25, 34, and, as we have seen, to the great weight of American authorities on the subject.

Prof. Wigmore, in his scholarly treatise on the Law of Evidence, argues strongly in favor of a rule admitting evidence of personal knowledge and belief concerning the character of an accused person as against the rule which restricts such evidence to the general reputation of the accused in respect to the moral traits at issue in the prosecution, declaring that, so far as practical policy and utility are concerned, there ought to be no hesitation between reputation and personal knowledge and belief. "A perusal of the records of state trials," he says, "will show how natural, straightforward, and useful was this method of asking after belief founded on personal experience and intimacy. Put any one of us on trial for a false charge, and ask him whether he would not rather invoke in his vindication, as Lord Kenyon said, 'the warm, affectionate testimony' of those few whose long intimacy and trust has made them ready to demonstrate their faith to the jury, than any amount of colorless assertions about reputation." 2 Wigmore on Evidence, § 1686.

The answer to this argument is found in overwhelming considerations of practical convenience. If a witness is to be permitted to testify to the character of an accused person, basing his testimony solely on his own knowledge and observation, he cannot logically be prohibited from stating the particular incidents affecting the defendant and the particular actions of the defendant which have led him to his favorable conclusion. In most instances it would be utterly impossible for the prosecution to ascertain whether occurrences narrated by the witness as constituting the foundation of his conclusion were or were not true. They might be utterly false, and yet incapable of disproof at the time of trial. Furthermore, even if evidence were accessible to controvert the specific statements of the witness in this respect, its admission would lead to the introduction into the case of innumerable collateral issues which could not be tried out without introducing the utmost complication and confusion into the trial, tending to distract the minds of the jurymen and befog the chief issue in litigation.

It is argued in behalf of the people that no foundation was laid for the proposed testimony by proof that the witnesses were acquainted with the reputation of the defendant. We cannot accede to this proposition as applicable to the witness Merritt. Indeed, he was allowed to state, without objection, that he was acquainted with the reputation of the defendant so far as it related to whether or not the defendant was of a quiet and peaceable disposition. The witness had known the defendant 25 or 30 years, and lived in Kingston, where the defendant had worked up to a period within 5 or 6 years before the trial. The learned county judge in his charge speaks of the house of the defendant, in which the homicide occurred, as being "some few miles distant" from Kingston. While the reputation which is receivable in evidence on the question of character must be confined to the place of residence of the person whose character is under consideration, or the neighborhood of such residence, and the time when such reputation existed must not be too remote, we think that it cannot be held as matter of law that upon the evidence in this record the witness Merritt was not qualified to testify as to the community reputation of the defendant as to peaceableness and quiet. . . . The time limit applicable to evidence of reputation is discussed by Beardsley, J., in Sleeper v. Van Middlesworth, 4 Denio, 431, where it was held to have been error to exclude evidence that four years before the trial the witness had already acquired a well-known character in the community where he resided. "No certain limit," said the court, "in point of duration, can be laid down for inquiries like this." . . .

The questions which have led to the reversal of the judgment in this case below, and the questions which seem almost certain to arise on the new trial, render it proper for us to suggest that a witness may be qualified to testify to the general reputation of a person as to particular traits of character, even though he may never have heard anybody say anything as to whether the person whose character is in question possesses such traits or not. In other words, the testimony of a person who has lived any considerable length of time in the same neighborhood as another to the fact that he has never heard anything against that other person in respect to his peaceableness or quiet behavior or honesty is competent evidence that his reputation is that of a person of pacific disposition and integrity. . . .

Three conclusions are involved in our review of this case: First, that upon a criminal prosecution evidence is receivable in behalf of the accused that he has enjoyed a good reputation in respect to the traits involved in the charge against him; second, that evidence is not receivable in his behalf as to the existence of such traits, when such evidence consists solely of the personal knowledge and observation of his conduct by witnesses, and not of their knowledge as to his reputation in such respects; and, third, that negative evidence is receivable to establish a good reputation. This statement may be of service as a guide to the solution of somewhat perplexing questions in this branch of the law of evidence which frequently arise upon criminal trials.

It follows, from what has been said, that the order of the Appellate Division, reversing the conviction of the defendant, must be affirmed.

COMMONWEALTH v. BECKER
Supreme Court of Pennsylvania, 1937.
326 Pa. 105, 191 A. 351.

DREW, JUSTICE. The defendant, John Becker, was indicted and tried for the murder of Kathryn Bracken who was employed by the Pittsburgh & Shawmut Railroad Company as a telegraph operator at the Shawmut signal tower in Brookville, Jefferson county. The jury returned a verdict of guilty of murder in the first degree and recommended the death penalty. From the judgment and sentence imposed, after refusal of defendant's motion for a new trial, this appeal was taken.

The record discloses a cruel and sordid crime. Some of the facts are of such a revolting nature that they do not bear repetition here; they may be found in the 945 pages of testimony. Suffice it to say that the body of the deceased was discovered lying in a shallow ditch at the bottom of a 25-foot embankment in the rear of the tower where Miss Bracken worked, some time between 9:30 and 10 o'clock on the night of April 10, 1936. It bore evidence of a brutal attack. There were five long scalp wounds, all two-sided or V-shaped, evidently inflicted by a blunt triangular weapon. Across the throat were three deep gashes, one of which had severed the jugular vein. The left wrist had been cut to the bone. Death was due to hemorrage from the throat and wrist wounds. It was clear that the motive for the attack was criminal assault. . . .

The Commonwealth relied for conviction principally upon the admissions of guilt in the statements made by the defendant, Joseph Becker's identification of him at the scene of the crime, and the testimony of a qualified pathologist that the blood of the deceased was type No. 1, that of the defendant type No. 2, and that he removed human blood stains of type No. 1 from defendant's trousers. The defense practically conceded that the deceased was murdered, and that it was murder of the first degree. Their evidence was restricted to proving that defendant was not the guilty party. . . .

We now pass to a consideration of assignments 22, 23, and 30 which complain primarily that the court permitted the district attorney, in cross-examination of some of defendant's character witnesses, to ask the following question: "Did you ever hear prior to April 10, 1936, that defendant had been accused of killing a man?" and allowed the witnesses to answer. The record reveals that these witnesses had been asked on direct examination whether defendant bore a reputation in his community of being a peaceful and law-abiding citizen, and had replied in the affirmative. Thereafter, before cross-examination, the question about to be put was stated at side-bar, the court asked defense counsel if there was any objection, and there was no answer.

The contention of the defense is that questions pertaining to specific offenses cannot be asked character witnesses as "rebuttal" of evidence of good reputation. This is perfectly true as a legal principle, but has no application to what was done in the instant case. The questions were asked by the Commonwealth on cross-examination, and not in rebuttal. If the witnesses had been called in rebuttal, they would have been offered to establish bad reputation, which, like good reputation, cannot be proved by evidence of particular acts. Commonwealth v. Jones, 280 Pa. 368, at page 370, 124 A. 486. The proper function of cross-examination in such a situation, the witness having qualified, is not to affirmatively establish the fact of bad reputation, but to break down the basis of the testimony of the witness as to good reputation. A distinction is drawn between cases where it is sought to prove particular acts of misconduct and those where the purpose of the examination is to test the accuracy of the testimony by showing either that the witness is not familiar with the reputation concerning which he has testified or that his standard of what constitutes good repute is unsound. An overwhelming majority of jurisdiction, including our own, recognize such a distinctiion. Commonwealth v. Thomas, 282 Pa. 20, 127 A. 427, 428; Commonwealth v. Jones, supra; State v. Rowell, 172 Iowa 208, 154 N.W. 488; Regina v. Wood, 5 Jur. 225; Wigmore on Evidence, 2d Ed. 1923 § 988; 71 A.L.R. 1505. The admission of testimony of good reputation is of doubtful value and often deceptive where there is not applied to it the acid test of cross-examination to prove the accuracy of the testimony, and the standard by which the witness measures reputation. See People v. Laudiero, 192 N.Y. 304, 85 N.E. 132.

This rule does not permit of the introduction of substantive evidence of the accused's previous conduct. Such testimony is admissible only to discredit the character witness. Where the record discloses that the actual purpose of such cross-examination was to show that defendant had committed a specific crime of which he is not now accused, and not to test the credibility of the character witness, it will be held improper if it tends to prejudice the accused. The problem in each case is to determine whether the inquiry at cross-examination is directed to the witnesses' hearing of the rumor, or is directed toward the substantive fact of the defendant's misconduct. So in Commonwealth v. Thomas, supra, and Commonwealth v. Jones, supra, it was held reversible error for the district attorney on cross-examination of defendant's character witnesses to ask whether they did not *know* that defendant was a married woman living in open adultery with the man she was charged with having killed. In the former case, we declared: "It is manifest from a reading of the record in the instant case that the questions propounded by the district attorney were not for the purpose of either testing the credibility of the witnesses, or the extent of their knowledge of the reputation of the accused. Such questions as were here propounded ought not to be allowed even for that purpose. Under certain circumstances, on cross-examination of a character witness, it may be proper to inquire whether the witness has ever *heard* persons in the neighborhood attribute to the defendant particular offenses, but it is never permissible for any purpose to interrogate the witness as to his *knowledge* of another specific crime laid at the defendant's door." (Italics added.) In the instant case, the questions were obviously directed, not at the witness' knowledge of the truth of the alleged rumor that defendant had killed a man but at whether or not they had heard he had done so. In Commonwealth v. Colandro, 231 Pa. 343, 80 A. 571, 576, we declared, inter alia: "A witness 'cannot be asked questions to elicit his knowledge of particular acts as distinguished from what he has heard.' . . . The inquiry must be limited to the general speech of the community on the subject." The statement in that case, 231 Pa. 343, at page 355, 80 A. 571, 575, "Had these questions been objected to, it would have been the duty of the court to have excluded them," referred to the fact that the questions asked on cross-examination were in the opinion of the court, not limited to the particular trait of character involved in the commission of the crime charged. See, also, Commonwealth v. Thomas, supra. Here, on the other hand, the issue was defendant's reputation as a peaceful and law-abiding citizen. And the questions put on cross-examination, now objected to, related directly to such traits. . . .

All the assignments of error are overruled, the judgment is affirmed, and the record remitted to the court below for the purpose of execution.

McKAY v. STATE
Court of Criminal Appeals of Texas, 1950.
235 S.W.2d 173.

BEAUCHAMP, JUDGE. Appellant was assessed a penalty of $50.00 by a jury on a charge of driving a motor vehicle on the streets of the City of Austin while intoxicated.

That he drove the vehicle on the streets at the time alleged is admitted. Appellant stoutly denied his intoxication, but did admit drinking four bottles of beer in the late afternoon and evening before his arrest. When taken to the City Hall by the police he signed a written permission for the officers to test his breath for alcohol by an instrument known as the Harger Drunkometer.

The officers who arrested him and observed him after his arrest gave ample evidence to sustain the jury's verdict independent of the complained of evidence in this case. We may not speculate, however, that they would have done so independent of the breath test—which is the real controversy in the appeal of the case before this Court. It, therefore, becomes important to discuss this issue which, in our view of the entire record, is the only question requiring consideration in this opinion.

Appellant's Bill of Exception No. 4 complains of the evidence of Dr. E. Beerstecher, a research biochemist at the University of Texas. This evidence is stated in the bill, a part of which reads as follows: " 'I am familiar with the instrument known as the Harger breath test; I have been studying that between ten and eleven months. I feel that the machine is extremely reliable. It shows how much alcohol is in a person's blood at the time the test was taken. Based on my experience and the tests run by the Medical Association, if a man has .270 of alcohol in his body by weight, I would say he was intoxicated. . . .' On cross-examination such witness further testified: "There is disagreement among scientists as to the accuracy of the (Harger) breath test. A chemical analysis of the blood itself shows what per cent or proportion of alcohol is in that blood sample. The theory of the (Harger) breath test is that the breath indicates a per cent of saturation in the blood; it is a calculated proportion. This breath test is used in a number of states. From my work with this machine for some ten to eleven months, observing the officers making the tests, and from my knowledge as an expert on alcohol, my opinion is that the (Harger) machine is very reliable. This test is not used in many other states. There, again, is a difference of opinion between the states, just as there is a dispute among the scientists about its accuracy.' "

The chief contention made by appellant, based on the foregoing bill, is found in his first proposition on page two of his brief, as follows: "It was error prejudicial to appellant for the trial court, over timely objections of appellant, to permit the State to introduce evidence of a Harger Drunkometer or alcoholometer or alcohol breath-test of appellant and the results purportedly shown thereby, because the State did not prove that such breath-test and its result is generally accepted by scientists as accurately establishing the alcoholic content of a subject's blood to show whether he was under the influence of intoxicating liquor and the extent of his intoxication."

As we interpret this contention there is no attack made on the manner in which the officers operated the machine in making the test. The objection is to the conclusion reached because Dr. Beerstecher, after qualifying as an expert witness, stated that there was a difference of opinion among scientists as to its accuracy. Neither do we find any controversy raised by the bill which contends that, if the machine be accurate and if the blood content actually contained .270 per cent by weight, the scientific conclusion stated by Dr. Beerstecher as to the intoxicated condition of accused is not supported by other scientists. There would probably be no ground for such contention.

The position that it is incumbent upon the State in the trial of the case to prove that the test is scientifically accepted may or may not be correct, depending upon the degree to which the fact is established by scientific research. This Court may recognize generally accepted scientific conclusions, even though there should be some who disagree with them. In all probability a scientist may be found who will disagree with practically every generally accepted scientific theory. We will take judicial knowledge of the scientific fact that the earth is round. At the same time, we know there are still individuals who claim to be scientists who have other theories, even to the extent of holding that instead of living on the outer surface of a globe we live within a globe, and that there are within it sun, moon, stars and all the heavenly bodies which we observe. We would have no trouble in disagreeing with such theory, but it does not destroy the fact that there are others who have a different view. The opinion of such others by no means bars the evidence of a scientific truth before a jury, nor would it preclude the courts from taking judicial knowledge of the truth of it.

Northwestern University, of Evanston, Illinois, has within the present year, 1950, published a work from which we quote: "The prosecution need no longer rely solely upon . . . objective symptoms. Scientific methods have been developed for determining the alcoholic concentration in the blood by the chemical analysis of body substances, i.e., blood, urine, breath, saliva, or spinal fluid. Such analyses will determine exactly the extent to which a suspect is 'under the influence of intoxicating liquor.' The evidence of the results of such chemical analyses may be used to supplement the evidence obtained from observation of the accused. Medical science, through years of research and experimentation, has established that *it is not the amount of alcohol consumed by a person that affects his driving ability but the amount of alcohol absorbed into his blood*, and thus circulated to the brain, that affects his nerves and, correspondingly, his mental and physical faculties."

We may remark, parenthetically that this scientific fact explains the reason why some people become intoxicated on less drink than others. Their system absorbs more alcohol from a given quantity of intoxicating liquor. It is the amount which goes into the blood and not the amount which the individual drinks which produces the intoxicated condition.

From this same work we quote further: "The most commonly used methods of determining a person's blood alcohol concentration is to chemically analyze the blood, urine, or breath. The amount of alcohol in the latter two substances directly parallels the amount of alcohol in the blood and, therefore, from the amount of alcohol excreted through the kidneys or lungs, the concentration of alcohol in the circulating blood can be determined accurately and scientifically."

It is further observed that the President's Highway Safety Conference, the American Medical Association's Committee on Street and Highway Accidents, the National Safety Council's Committee for Tests for Intoxication, and other national organizations have recommended the passage of laws by the states which will recognize the value of chemical analyses of the blood, urine, breath, or other bodily substances, and give rise to the presumption that if the test shows the accused to have .05 per cent or less by weight of alcohol that he is not under the influence of intoxicating liquor; that if he has in excess of that amount but less than .15 per cent, no presumption rests one way or the other; that where a test shows .15 per cent or more by weight of alcohol in his blood it shall be presumed that the defendant was under the influence of intoxicating liquor and that such evidence shall not be construed as limiting the introduction of other competent evidence bearing upon the question of his intoxication.

We are not holding, in the instant case, that the foregoing is established as a scientific fact. The publication is a worthy one from an authority which must be respected, and in all probability, may win such recognition from the courts of some states. The Legislature of Texas may pass such law, if within its constitutional powers, but the courts of Texas have no legislative duties or powers. At the same time, this proposal by such authorities is persuasive in supporting the evidence of Dr. Beerstecher, if that evidence needs to be supported, as to the effect of alcohol in the blood, but has no bearing on the accuracy of the instrument used. The brief and argument attack the entire evidence, but it is our view that the bill as taken goes only to the accuracy of the instrument.

We return, then, from a discussion of the question as presented by appellant in his brief to that which we believe to be a deciding view of the question here presented. Dr. Beerstecher testified that the instrument in question is accurate and he gave his reasons for it. He admitted that there are others who disagree with its accuracy. The objection to his testimony, therefore, goes to its weight and not to its admissibility. If it were the only evidence in the case it may be doubtful that the jury would have found appellant guilty. We are not called upon to say what our view would be if they had convicted on this evidence alone, because, as herein above stated, there is other evidence amply supporting the jury's verdict. Our conclusion is that this evidence is admissible, as presented to us in this record, for whatever it is worth, and it was not reversible error to overrule appellant's objection to it.

We have discussed only the overshadowing question in this case, but have given consideration to all others and find nothing requiring a reversal.

The judgment of the trial court is affirmed.

PRUITT v. STATE
Supreme Court of Tennessee, 1965.
216 Tenn. 686, 393 S.W.2d 747.

WHITE, JUSTICE. Plaintiff in error, David Clarence Pruitt, was tried and convicted for second degree murder growing out of an automobile accident in which two pedestrians were killed. He was sentenced to serve not more than twelve nor less than ten years in the State Penitentiary. . . .

These convictions arose out of an acciednt occurring on October 31, 1963, at about 7:45 P.M., on Wheeler Avenue in the City of Chattanooga. The plantiff in error's car and another car driven by Charley Smith were involved in a collision, in the process of which two children were killed as they walked along the side of the street. Plantiff in error immediately left the scene of the collision and drove to his home, not far up the street. The witness, Grady Smith, a passenger in the Smith vehicle, followed Pruitt and advised him, when he got out of the car at his home, that he had struck some children.

Pruitt testified that he then went into his house and drank half of a half pint of whiskey. About an hour later he was arrested and taken to Police Headquarters. The arresting officer and another officer who observed Pruitt at that time testified that in their opinion he was intoxicated.

At 9:20 P.M., at Police Headquarters, plaintiff in error was given a Breathalyzer test for intoxication. The test was administered by Police Officer Ingle. The results of the test showed .18 per cent alcohol in plaintiff in error's blood. By statute, T.C.A. § 59–1033 (1955), a concentration of at least .15 per cent alcohol by weight creates a rebuttable presumption of intoxication.

There are essentially two assignments of error:

(1) There is no competent evidence in the record that plaintiff in error Pruitt was intoxicated or had been drinking at the time of the accident; and (2) The evidence of the results of the Breathalyzer test was improperly admitted because the officer who performed the test was not competent as an expert to either administer the test or to testify as to its results, and, in addition, he did not follow the necessary precautions. . . .

Since the evidence of the Breathalyzer test goes to the sufficiency of the evidence of drunkenness at the time of the accident, we will consider whether the results of the test were properly admitted.

Of all the police service devices now in operation for testing intoxication, the Borkenstein Breathalyzer is perhaps the most recent, having been designed and developed in 1954. It operates on the principle that vapor alcohol from the lungs will oxidize in a solution of potassium dichromate and 50% sulfuric acid.

The solution then loses some of its original yellow color and the color change is recorded by a photoelectric cell in comparison with an identical yellow solution which has not been exposed to the alcohol.

First, the subject blows a certain volume of alveolar (deep lung) air into a cylinder-piston chamber, the cylinder measuring exactly 52.5 cubic centimeters. This volume of air, heated at about 40 to 55 degrees Centigrade, is bubbled through the test ampule of potassium dichromate and sulfuric acid. The test ampule should be at a temperature of about 65 degrees Centigrade (approximately 150 degrees Fahrenheit). From the degree of oxidation measured by the photoelectric cell, the weight of alveolar air alcohol that causes that much color change is measured.

This alveolar air alcohol percentage is then converted by a calibrated scale to indicate the blood alcohol content. The principle behind this conversion is the fact that the same amount of alcohol, by weight, found in 52.5 cc. of alveolar air is that to be found in 1/40 cc. of the subject's blood, a ratio of 1:2100. Also, this formula is based on the fact that in the average normal individual, the carbon dioxide (CO_2) content of alveolar air is 5.5 per cent.

The Breathalyzer is considered a reliable device for measuring intoxication. An extensive analysis of the accuracy of the Breathalyzer is reported by investigators in an article in 8 Journal of Forensic Sciences 149 (April 1963), cited in Gray, Attorney's Textbook of Medicine § 59.11(2) (Supp. 1963):

These investigators state that Breathalyzer readings taken on alcohol solutions of varying concentrations very closely approximate the calculated values. The standard error associated with a reading appears to increase slightly with an increase in alcohol concentration.

The authors feel that the data presented, indicating variability in Breathalyzer readings obtained under Police Department conditions by trained police operators, are within acceptable limits and compare favorably with the data found under experimental conditions.

However, the accuracy of this device does not relieve police investigators of the requirement that a competent expert operator perform the tests. Whatever the device used, this

Court has held that qualified experts must operate the machine, and they, or someone else qualified, must interpret these test results in evidence before a trial court. Fortune v. State, 197 Tenn. 691, 277 S.W.2d 381 (1954).

Requirements for an expert to qualify in testifying to the results of scientific tests are very flexible. The trial judge has discretion in admitting expert testimony, at least as to the qualifications of the expert. Fortune v. State, supra; McElroy v. State, 146 Tenn. 442, 242 S.W. 883 (1922); 7 Wigmore, Evidence § 1926 (3d ed. 1940). But this does not mean that this Court must accept without question the discretion of the trial judge, especially where no foundation or predicate has been laid for qualification of the expert.

The State is required to show that the measuring device is scientifically acceptable and accurate for the purpose for which it is used, and that the witness who presents the test results is qualified to interpret them. It is reversible error for the State to fail to qualify a witness as an expert on the operation and results of intoxication tests with scientific devices. Fortune v. State, supra; Lopez v. State, 154 Tex.Cr.R. 227, 225 S.W.2d 852 (1949). If such testimony is admitted without proper predicate and qualification, it can be shown on cross-examination that such witness is not qualified, and it is then proper to strike his testimony. If the witness were properly qualified in advance, cross-examination would only test his credibility as an expert.

We must then determine whether the portion of the record concerning the evidence presented by the State witness Ingle showed sufficient qualifications for him to testify.

A reading of cases listed in an annotation in 77 A.L.R.2d 971 (1961) indicates there is no settled formula for determining proper qualifications for an operator of an intoxication testing device. The cases vary from one that holds two days' training sufficient to qualify a witness, Omohundro v. Arlington County, 194 Va. 773, 75 S.E.2d 496 (1953), and to our own decision in the Fortune case, and the case of Hill v. State, 158 Tex.Cr.R. 313, 256 S.W.2d 93 (1953), which have held that a witness who operated the device should be able to understand the mathematical formula for converting alveolar air alcohol content to blood alcohol content.

In People v. Morgan, 236 N.Y.S.2d 1014 (Misc. 1962), a witness who was "not [a] medical doctor, pathologist, biologist, hematologist, physiologist, biochemist or toxicologist," but who had six months' training as a practical nurse and "on-the-job training" under a police lab director in urine analysis was held not a competent expert to testify as to transposition or interpolation from urine alcohol content to blood alcohol content.

In State v. Gregoire, 88 R.I. 401, 148 A.2d 751 (1959), a witness who had received only three hours instruction in the operation of an "alcometer" was held not competent to testify as to results of the machine he operated even though an expert research chemist and designer of the scientific instruments stated that a man of ordinary intelligence could operate it. A trained qualified person was held especially necessary "when a new device is presented for the consideration of the courts." However, the result in this case was specifically rejected in the cases of State v. Roberts, 102 N.H. 414, 158 A.2d 458 (1960), and City of Wichita v. Showalter, 185 Kan. 181, 341 P.2d 1001 (1959)—at least as concerns the alcometer.

Furthermore, in State v. Bailey, 184 Kan. 704, 339 P.2d 45 (1959), it was held not to be necessary that the witness who testifies as to the results be the one who also operated the machine; however, the witness must have been properly qualified as an expert, at least to some extent, and the test must have been carried out under his supervision and control.

Robert L. Donigan, in his book, Chemical Tests and the Law (1957), introduces his chapter on the qualifications of persons preparing and presenting chemical test evidence with this statement:

In litigation, procedures involved in conducting chemical tests to determine alcoholic influence may be divided into five principal steps: (1) the taking of a specimen of body fluid or breath from the subject person, (2) the chemical analysis of the specimen to determine its alcoholic content, (3) the translation of this result to blood alcohol concentration, (4) the presentation of all this evidence in court from the witness stand, and (5) interpretation of the result of the test from the witness stand in the courtroom....

... For personnel who will qualify for steps (3) and (5), the police administrator will require someone who is more than just a competent technician qualified to operate a breathalyzer or drunkometer. He must be an expert in the field of chemical tests generally.

There is a practical limitation on the facilities of police administration to provide trained toxicologists or pathologists with extensive educational backgrounds. Such training is not required. We do not say that an expert in the general broad field of chemical tests is a necessity here. It is not beyond practical limits, however, to provide expert technicians with an understanding of the theoretical and operative functions of a single device for testing intoxication. He must at least be able to understand why a breath test can be translated into a certain percentage of alcohol in the blood.

To trust to the procedure of simply following instructions and getting a correct reading without any understanding of the theory that makes the reading accurate would be to approve pure hearsay evidence of intoxication. Fortune v. State, supra.

It is our conclusion, then, that even though the person who operates the testing device may be shown to know adequately the steps in handling the machine, he must further have knowledge of the reasons for such operation and the scientific principle that reflects the results as an accurate reading of blood alcohol content.

With the rapid increase in automobile traffic in recent years, and consequently the proportional increase in cases involving drunk driving, police departments usually have one of these technicians with a background in alcohol testing....

Police Officer Ingle was not shown to have been qualified to present adequately the results of the Breathalyzer test. He had about one week's training from two superior police officers in how to operate the machine, but there is nothing in the record to indicate his knowledge of the theory behind the machine and the principle of conversion from alveolar air alcohol content to blood alcohol content.

The State concedes in its brief that Ingle was not shown to have the type of background that this Court requires for such technicians under the authority of Fortune v. State, supra. Nevertheless, the State insists that since Fortune did not involve a Breathalyzer, that Fortune is distinguishable from the case at bar.

The case is perhaps distinguishable in that the mechanics of operating the machine were somewhat different from those in the present case. However, the principle of conversion of lung air alcohol content to blood alcohol content is the same in both cases, and in both cases there is no proof of a knowledge of this principle or the chemical process involved on the part of the police officer.

There is also undisputed proof that Officer Ingle did not conduct the test properly and thus did not take precautions against the possibility of inaccurate results. It is a recognized requirement by experts in the operation of a Breathalyzer that before beginning the test, the operator must observe the person tested for a least fifteen (15) minutes before that person blows into the instrument. Borkenstein & Smith, "The Breathalyzer and its Application", 2 Medicine, Science, and the Law 13 (1961); Turner, "Chemical Tests for Intoxication — Prosecution Viewpoint", 1 Trauma, No. 3, p. 19 (Oct. 1959); State v. Baker, 56 Wash.2d 846, 355 P.2d 806 (1960).

The purpose of this waiting period is to make sure that the person tested has no foreign matter in his mouth, that he doesn't hiccough, vomit, belch, smoke, or take another drink — all of which could produce a false reading. Also, this period is used to keep the subject quiet, as violent physical activity may produce an abnormally high carbon dioxide content which would make the reading inaccurate. Turner, supra. If there is suspected recent drinking or foreign matter in the mouth, a duplicate sample of breath should be taken in another 15 minutes for comparison with the first test. Borkenstein & Smith, supra.

Officer Ingle tested a plaintiff in error almost immediately after he was called in to administer the test. He had plaintiff in error under observation for a period of only about six minutes. We think that six minutes observation was not adequate for this defendant where the authority is unanimous—even from the developer of the device himself — that a subject must be kept under observation for at least fifteen minutes. Every precaution should have been taken to produce an accurate result, especially because of the seriousness of the crime with which plaintiff in error was charged.

For these reasons we are compelled to hold that the evidence of the Breathalyzer test results was improperly admitted and should have been stricken from the record. . . .

The conviction for second degree murder is reversed and remanded for further proceedings consistent with this opinion.

STATE v. ROWLAND
Supreme Court of North Carolina, 1965.
263 N.C. 353, 139 S.E.2d 661.

At the November Term 1959, defendant was convicted upon a bill of indictment charging that on September 23, 1959, with the use of a dangerous weapon, *a large club or blunt instrument,* he feloniously took from the person of Maggie Hunt three hundred dollars. Thereafter the sentence imposed was vacated because defendant had not been represented by counsel, and defendant was tried *de novo* at the April Term 1964.

The State's evidence tends to establish these facts: Between 3:00 and 4:00 p.m. on September 23, 1959, Maggie Hunt, a seventy-six-year-old woman, was alone at her home. In a moneybag tied around her waist under her clothes, she had two one-hundred dollar bills and some fives and tens, "a little over three hundred dollars in all." That afternoon, as he had done regularly since January, when he was shot in the right hand and lost a finger, defendant came to the door of her home with a jar and a paper bag to beg for food. Into the jar Mrs. Hunt put milk she had just churned and into the bag, food. She handed both to him from the door. She then went to her front porch and sat down for ten or fifteen minutes. Hearing a racket in a back room she went inside to investigate. Until she came to in the hospital, where she remained for two weeks, the last thing Mrs. Hunt remembers is standing with her back to the kitchen door. About sundown her daughter-in-law found her sitting, with her head down, in a chair on the front porch. She was unconscious and bleeding from her nose and from a wound in the back of her head. It required eight stitches to close the wound. Her money was gone. There was blood on the floor in the room next to the kitchen.

Deputy Sheriff Thompson came to the house shortly after dark. In the backyard, in soft dirt, he found distinctive tracks. "One side of the foot had a few little ridges on it, the rest of the shoe was worn slick and there were two round holes in the track in the bottom of each shoe. The side of one of the shoes had some tread on it and the other side slick. The other shoe was worn slick. The tracks led from the back of Maggie's home into the corn field." Deputy Sheriff Thompson went home and got the bloodhound which he had acquired from prison authorities four years previously and which he described as follows:

"At that time the bloodhound was a pretty old dog. He was a thoroughbred. He had been trained to tracking the human scents and human bodies. I had been using him for years myself for the purpose of tracking human scents. I have used him to track a lot of people. I would say seventy-five or a hundred. The dog was reliable in tracking human scent. . . . (T)hat is all he would ever run, that was human scent. . . . (he) had been trained by the State and prison camp."

According to Deputy Thompson, the dog had the ability to discriminate between different human scents. He put the dog on the tracks at the edge of the yard. With reference to succeeding events he testified:

"I trailed him on down through the cornfield, hit a sandy spot in the cornfield and this same set of tracks, with holes in the bottom of the shoes, and walked this sandy strip, crossed a streak of woods into a pasture, went through the pasture, and went under a barbed wire fence into a highway, crossed the highway to the left-hand shoulder, went to the right down the highway about two hundred yards, crossed the highway back in front of Wesley Carter's wife's home, where she lives, went up in the yard, and the dog went up the front steps. I knocked on the door and Wesley's wife said, 'come in.' I pushed the door open. She was sitting across the room to the left of the door. Frank Rowland was sitting on a long sofa. The dog went into the house with me. . . .

"When I walked in I noticed Rowland, he pulled his hand out of his left pocket and slipped it down under him, to the side. I went to him, got him up and searched him, and where he was sitting, where he put his hand, I found two one-hundred dollar bills and eighteen or nineteen other dollars, there was five, ten and ones. In the right-hand pocket he had one fifty cents and three quarters and I believe a nickel or dime in the right-hand pocket."

Wesley Carter's wife, Earline, disclaimed any knowledge of the money. Defendant said it was not his, and he could not explain where he got it. Defendant was wearing a new pair of shoes—not the ones which made the tracks the dog had followed. The day before, defendant, wearing old tennis shoes, had told Deputy Thompson that he needed some shoes and clothes and asked him for work. When questioned about the new shoes, defendant told the deputy that he had bought them late that afternoon in Rowland and had put his old ones in a trash can at Annie Washington's place. There the officer found a pair of rubber boots, cut off at the ankles, which he had seen defendant wearing. About 9:00 p.m. defendant was arrested and charged with robbing Maggie Hunt with the use of a dangerous weapon. The next morning the deputy went to Wesley Carter's home, where defendant lived and which is about five hundred yards from Mrs. Hunt's place. He testified:

"I went in a room in Wesley Carter's home and this pair of shoes that I was trailing, tennis shoes I call them, was sitting under Rowland's bed, had two round holes in the soles, and some ridges on the right shoe. I compared them with tracks I had followed the day before. They compared exactly the same. I talked with Rowland and he said that was his shoes."

Wesley Carter and his wife lived in homes about one mile apart. Wesley permitted defendant to live in his home because he "did not have any place to stay . . . and he didn't have anything to pay with." When the deputy put his dog on the tracks at the edge of the field, the dog went straight from the Hunt home to the home of Earline Carter without ever going near Wesley Carter's home. The record does not disclose the distance from the Hunt home to Earline Carter's house, but it took the dog between thirty-five and forty minutes to lead the deputy there.

Defendant did not testify. He put on four witnesses, the testimony of two of whom tended to establish an alibi, placing him at the time in question at Annie Washington's place, where defendant told the officer, he had purchased a pint of liquor. Earline Carter, testifying as a witness for defendant, said that he came to her house fifteen or twenty minutes ahead of Deputy Thompson; that she had been away from home between 1:00 and 4:30 p. m. and her house was locked during that time; that the deputy found defendant "sitting on the money" at her house; that the money was not hers; that nobody but defendant had come to her house after she got home that evening; and that she knew defendant had no money of his own. (Of this money $223.00 was returned to Maggie Hunt.)

The jury returned a verdict of guilty as charged. From the sentence imposed defendant appeals. . . .

SHARP, JUSTICE. Defendant's appeal presents two questions: (1) Was defendant's motion for nonsuit properly overruled? (2) Did the court err in admitting evidence of the action of the dog, with which, according to the State's evidence, the deputy sheriff tracked defendant?

Even if the bloodhound evidence were eliminated, the remaining evidence was, taken in the light most favorable to the State, sufficient to establish these facts: Three hundred dollars (two one-hundred dollar bills and others of smaller denomination) was taken from the person of Maggie Hunt while she was unconscious from a blow. An unseen assailant had inflicted the blow within minutes after Mrs. Hunt had heard a noise inside of the house and while she was investigating it. Defendant had been on the premises fifteen minutes previously, begging food. He had been penniless the day before and had been wearing the tennis shoes with holes in them. The afternoon Mrs. Hunt's money was taken, defendant purchased, among other things, shoes and whiskey. That night, when the deputy entered the room where defendant was, defendant attempted to conceal between the cushions and the coverlet of the sofa on which he was seated two one-hundred dollar bills and eighteen or nineteen dollars in smaller bills. The only statement he made was that the money was not his. . . .

Defendant next contends that he is entitled to a new trial because the bloodhound evidence was both incompetent and prejudicial.

In State v. McLeod, 196 N.C. 542, 146 S.E. 409, a case in which bloodhound evidence was held incompetent and prejudicial because the action of the dogs afforded no reasonble inference of identity of the prisoner as the guilty party, Stacy, C. J., said:

"It is fully recognized in this jurisdiction that the action of bloodhounds may be received in evidence when it is properly shown: (1) That they are of pure blood, and of a stock characterized by acuteness of scent and power of discrimination; (2) that they possess these qualities, and have been accustomed and trained to pursue the human track; (3) that they have been found by experience reliable in such pursuit; (4) and that in the particular case they were put on the trail of the guilty party (who) . . . was pursued and followed under such circumstances and in such way as to afford substantial assurance, or permit a reasonable inference, of identification." Id. at 545, 146 S.E. at 411.

Defendant argues that the State did not lay a proper foundation for the bloodhound evidence in that it failed to establish either that Deputy Thompson's dog was of pure blood or that, at the end of the trial, the dog identified defendant with reasonable certainty — requisites (1) and (4) as set out above in McLeod.

With reference to the first requisite, the deputy described his dog as "a bloodhound" and "a thoroughbred." "The terms *thoroughbred, full-blood,* and *pure-bred* are generally used in this country as practically synonymous." 3 Dictionary of American English 1861 (1942 ed.). In State v. Wiggins, 171 N.C. 813, 89 S.E. 58, identification of the defendant by "bloodhounds brought from Tennessee" was admitted. In State v. Yearwood, 178 N.C. 813, 101 S.E. 513, the admission of evidence of identification by a dog described only as "an English bloodhound" was approved. In practice, if the dog has been identified as a bloodhound, it has been the conduct of the hound and other attendant circumstances, rather than the dog's family tree, which have determined the admissibility of his evidence.

We find no North Carolina cases, and defendant has cited us to none, in which bloodhound evidence has been excluded for a deficiency in the proof of the bloodhound's pedigree *if* he is shown to be naturally capable of following the human scent, *i. e.,* that he is a bloodhound, *and if* the evidence is corroborative of other evidence tending to show defendant's guilt. See Annot., Evidence of trailing by dogs, 94 A.L.R. 413, 419. In State v. Yearwood, supra, 178 N.C. at 818, 101 S.E. at 516, Walker, J., said: "The dog which trailed this defendant proved his own reliability." So, also, it seems to us, did the deputy's dog. The performance of this "pretty old" dog without any papers puts him in a class with the young horse which was the subject of many a chapel talk to his boys by famed old schoolmaster William Robert ("Old Sawney") Webb at the Webb School in Bellbuckle, Tennessee. His story was that when a young horse of obscure lineage (no registration papers) won the derby in a record-breaking burst of speed, horse fanciers began scouring the country for his sire, dam, and siblings. This young stallion, according to "Old Sawney," had "pedigreed his ancestors," and that was all that the school-master demanded of his boys. By his performance, the old dog in this case pedigreed himself, at least. This record leaves little doubt that the shoe prints which he had followed from Maggie's to Earline's belonged to defendant.

It is true that the evidence is silent as to what the dog did when he and the deputy arrived at Earline Carter's. She said that the officer tied the dog outside and never brought him into the house. The deputy said that the dog went in with him, but counsel for neither the State nor defendant inquired into the dog's actions inside the house. They, as we, probably considered the dog's conduct at the end of the trial immaterial when, there, the deputy found defendant sitting on a cache of money, which included two one-hundred dollar bills. Such a circumstance ordinarily would satisfy the fourth requisite given above in McLeod. See State v. Norman, 153 N.C. 591, 595, 68 S.E. 917, 918. We conclude that the bloodhound evidence is not incompetent for failure to comply with McLeod. If, however, defendant had been found at the end of the trail without the hundred-dollar bills, the evidence would undoubtedly be incompetent. The law of probability makes it as certain as anything in life can be that the bills belonged to Maggie Hunt; under these facts it made no difference whether the dog bayed defendant.

The feat of the dog in following defendant's tracks from Maggie Hunt's to Earline's furnished, in itself, no relevant evidence, under the facts of this case, that defendant was the robber, i.e., no relevant evidence linking defendant with the *corpus delicti*. It is irrelevant that defendant's tracks led from Maggie's house, for he had been there earlier to beg, a lawful mission. That defendant was present at Earline's house *at the time the dog arrived there* was clearly a coincidence. Since, *coincidentally*, defendant happened to be at Maggie's with the money, we think the admission of the evidence, if error, was not prejudicial error. It explained the deputy's timely arrival and is equivalent to the testimony we frequently hear from officers that "in consequence of a telephone call from *X*" they went to a designated spot, where they found a certain item or person. Such evidence does not itself tend to link a defendant with the *corpus delicti,* but it does relate to other evidence so tending. . . .

In the trial we find No error.

BOECHE v. STATE
Supreme Court of Nebraska, 1949.
151 Neb. 368, 37 N.W.2d 593.

MESSMORE, JUSTICE. Eileen Boeche, hereinafter referred to as defendant, was charged with the crime of uttering and publishing two bank checks as true and genuine when in fact they were false or forged instruments. She was convicted and sentenced to serve a term in the Nebraska Reformatory for Women. She prosecutes error to review the record of her conviction. . . .

Jack Knudtson testified that he is a criminal investigator for the Nebraska Safety Patrol, had worked in that capacity for a year prior to the time of trial, and had been connected with the patrol for eight years; that he is known as a polygraph operator, and is engaged in the process of setting up a criminal laboratory for the state; that a polygraph machine, commonly referred to as a lie detector, is one that makes many recordings, such as the increase and decrease of blood pressure. It is also a galvanometer that records the increase and decrease of perspiration, and also a munograph that records respiration and inhalation and expiration of breath. He described the machine and the manner in which it makes the recordings, and testified that the defendant voluntarily submitted to certain tests. The defendant then offered the witness to testify to and prove the results of the tests so made which would show a normal reaction to all the questions propounded with reference to the commission of the offenses charged, and indicate that the defendant was not guilty of such offenses. Objection was made to the competency of such evidence and was sustained, we believe properly so for the reasons hereinafter given.

This brings us to the assignment of error where the trial court refused to admit evidence of the results of tests made on the defendant by the use of a polygraph, commonly known and referred to as a lie detector, to which the defendant voluntarily submitted.

We have heretofore set forth the qualifications and study made by the officer in charge of giving of tests on the polygraph in behalf of the Nebraska Safety Patrol.

In the following reported cases the courts have generally rejected such tests on the ground that their reliability has not yet been fully established.

In People v. Forte, 279 N.Y. 204, 18 N.E.2d 31, 119 A.L.R. 1198, in speaking of a polygraph or lie detector, the court said that the court may not take judicial notice that such an instrument is or is not effective for examining the truth, and, until the fact be demonstrated by qualified experts, it cannot be said, as a matter of law, that the trial court erred in denying the motion to reopen a case to have the defendant submit to an examination by the polygraph.

Cogent reasons in support of this attitude readily suggest themselves. In the first place, the vital function of cross-examination would be impaired. The operator, appearing as a witness to report and interpret the results of the test, might be questioned as to his qualifications, experience, his methods, and on similar matters, and that is about all. But the machine itself — conceding the comparatively high percentage record as to accuracy and reliability claimed for it — escapes all cross-examination. There is no persuasive analogy here with such tests as fingerprinting which have a strictly physical basis, clearly demonstrable. It is not contended that the lie detector measures or weighs the important psychological factors. Many innocent but highly sensitive persons would undoubtedly show unfavorable physical reactions, while many guilty persons, of hardened or less sensitive spirit, would register no physical indication of falsification. This the trained operators of course understand, and proceed upon the basis of a large percentage of error. But it seems quite too subtle a task of evaluation to impose upon an untrained jury. See State v. Lowry, 163 Kan. 622, 185 P.2d 147. See, also, annotations in 139 A.L.R. 1174, 34 A.L.R. 147, 86 A.L.R. 616, 119 A.L.R. 1200; Frye v. United States, 54 App.D.C. 46, 293 F. 1013, 34 A.L.R. 145; State v. Bohner, 210 Wis. 651, 246 N.W. 314, 86 A.L.R. 611; State v. Cole, 354 Mo. 181, 188 S.W.2d 43, 189 S.W.2d 541.

It is apparent from the foregoing authorities that the scientific principle involved in the use of such polygraph has not yet gone beyond the experimental and reached the demonstrable stage, and that it has not yet received general scientific acceptance. The experimenting psychologists themselves admit that a wholly accurate test is yet to be perfected.

We conclude the trial court did not err in rejecting this evidence. . . .

[On other grounds] reversed and remanded.

CHAPPELL, JUSTICE, concurring. . . . In People v. Kenny, 167 Misc. 51, 3 N.Y.S.2d 348, which People v. Forte, supra, did not overrule in principle, defendant prior to trial was subjected to a lie detector test at Fordham University under a modern triple-test machine similar to that at bar, designed for accurately testing human emotional reactions by graphically recording the increase or decrease of blood pressure, perspiration, and respiration of the subject while under examination.

In his defense, defendant offered the testimony as to the findings of the witness who asked the questions and operated the machine. Such witness was head of the Department of Psychology of the Graduate School of Fordham University, held a degree of doctor of physics from Georgetown University and one in philosophy from the Gregorian University. For seven years he was a professor of physiology at the Medical School of Georgetown University and had done extensive research work and private study in Europe, especially at the University of Vienna. His claim for scientific accuracy and reliability of the apparatus and tests resulting therefrom was based upon a study which covered more than 6,000 individual tests in which his findings were subsequently affirmed. He expressed the firm conviction, based upon evidence and investigations, that the tests, when properly employed upon those actually charged with crime, would prove 100 percent efficient and accurate in the detection of deception.

The state conceded the scientific value and practical utility of the apparatus and technique, but objected to evidence of its findings upon the grounds, among others, that the scientific principle involved in its use had not yet gone beyond the experimental and reached the demonstrable stage, and had not yet received general scientific acceptance. . . . The objection was overruled, and the court directed that the testimony should be received to be evaluated by the jury. . . .

I agree that in the case at bar no sufficient foundation was laid to qualify the operator of the machine as an expert and that likewise no sufficient foundation was laid for admission of the exhibits demonstrating the recorded results of the tests to which defendant voluntarily submitted upon request of county and state officials, who, as an inducement therefor, promised her a release if the tests showed, as they concededly did, that she was telling the truth when denying her guilt.

However, I am convinced that if such a foundation were laid, as was done in People v. Kenny, supra, then the testimony of the operator and the results obtained by the tests would be admissible in criminal cases, such as that at bar, wherein defendant had voluntarily submitted to the tests. That complicated and difficult questions may arise therefrom in the trial of cases should be no reason for the exclusion of such evidence. Modern court procedures must embrace recognized modern conditions of mechanics, psychology, sociology, medicine, or other sciences, philosophy, and history. The failure to do so will only serve to question the ability of courts to efficiently administer justice. . . .

COMMONWEALTH v. MUSSOLINE
Supreme Court of Pennsylvania, 1968.
429 Pa. 464, 240 A.2d 549.

ROBERTS, JUSTICE. Appellant, Anthony Mussoline, was tried before a judge and jury and convicted of malicious mischief in connection with the dynamiting of a scrap yard owned by one Salvatore Gaudiano. Relying entirely on circumstantial evidence to prove Mussoline's guilt, the Commonwealth was permitted to establish, inter alia, that three small droplets of blood found 60 feet from the scene of the explosion were of the same type, "A", as that of appellant. It is uncontradicted that type A is the second most common blood type, appearing in approximately 30% of all human beings. Appellant has advanced several reasons for the inadmissibility of this evidence, including the argument that it was legally irrelevant to the issue of whether appellant was present at the scene of the crime.

In order to place the blood type evidence in its proper perspective, we shall review the Commonwealth's case in some detail. Three witnesses testified that early on the morning of February 10, 1965, at about 2:30 A.M., they heard a loud explosion in the area of Gaudiano's scrap yard. No one, however, saw anybody at the scene of the blast at that time. An expert witness testified as to the cause of the explosion and its origin. He concluded that dynamite had been placed under a davenport in the scrap yard office. In order to link appellant to this dynamite, testimony was introduced to show that Anthony Mussoline and his brother Barney were engaged in the business of strip mining (appellant apparently pursued this business as a side line, for his main occupation was that of police officer), that this business made use of high explosives, and that Barney had purchased some dynamite, in the name of the business only, about three weeks before the scrap yard explosion. No attempt was made to link the dynamite actually used in the blast with that purchased by appellant's brother.

The Commonwealth next sought to show motive. Salvatore Gaudiano, owner of the demolished yard, testified that on the day before the explosion he and appellant had inadvertently met in a local garage, whereupon a conversation ensued concerning a debt owed Gaudiano by appellant. No harsh words were exchanged, nor were any blows struck by either man. Gaudiano did tell Mussoline, however, that if appellant did not pay the money by the end of the week he (Gaudiano) would have Mussoline arrested. Gaudiano concluded his testimony by stating that the debt has since been paid, that he and Mussoline are still friends, and that they continue to do business with each other.

With the exception of the evidence recited above (evidence tending to show only that appellant had some possible motive for the crime, and that he had access to dynamite), the balance of the Commonwealth's case consisted entirely of an attempt to place Mussoline at the scene of the crime by the use of blood-type evidence. Viewing this evidence in a light most favorable to the Commonwealth, it appears that in 1960 Mussoline entered the Hazleton State General Hospital for surgery, pursuant to which his blood was then typed as Landsteiner A, Moss 2, Rh positive. The blood spots found near the scene of the crime were also of this type. A nurse at the Hazleton Hospital testified that on the morning of the crime, at approximately 3:15 A.M., Mussoline came to the accident ward with a two inch long laceration on the inside of his right forearm. He explained to the nurse that he had sustained the injury about two hours before (well prior to the time of the explosion) when he slipped on some ice in his driveway while putting his car into the garage. According to Mussoline, he cut his arm on a piece of jagged concrete. When asked why he had waited so long before coming to the hospital, appellant told the nurse that he first believed the wound to be minor, and only after his wife urged him to obtain treatment did he finally come to the accident ward. The story told by the nurse was in all material aspects corroborated by a police officer who had interviewed appellant the following day while investigating the case. In addition to the nurse the Commonwealth called to the stand the doctor who actually treated Mussoline's wound. He stated that the bleeding had substantially stopped by the time he saw the wound, and that it was probably caused by a sharp object such as a piece of glass. On cross examination, however, the doctor admitted that the cut could also have been caused by a piece of jagged concrete. Finally, a police detective related that he had conducted an investigation of the blast area which indicated that no one knew of or saw anyone injured on the night of the crime.

We think it clear that under our own case law, as well as that of other jurisdictions, mere proof that a criminal defendant shares a blood type with that of samples found near the crime scene is legally irrelevant to show that the defendant was in fact present at the scene of the crime without *some additional*, independent evidence *tending* to show either (1) that the man who committed the crime did lose blood in the process or (2) that the defendant was present at the scene. In short, blood-type evidence such as this can only be used to *corroborate* other evidence of the defendant's whereabouts at the crucial time.

Pennsylvania's leading case in this area, Commonwealth v. Statti, 166 Pa.Super. 577, 73 A.2d 688 (1950), presents a classic example of how blood-type evidence may be used to corroborate other testimony. In *Statti*, defendant was indicted for rape. Not only did the prosecutrix positively identify Statti as her assailant, but she also told of how she bit his finger during their struggle. In charging the jury, the trial judge carefully warned that "if there is blood of the same type as the blood of the defendant found about the person and garments of Mrs. Savicky [the prosecutrix], you are not to conclude in the same fashion that that means it was of necessity the defendant's blood. *It is merely a circumstance given to you in corroboration of the testimony of Mrs. Savicky.*" 166 Pa.Super. at 585, n. 5, 73 A.2d at 692, n. 5. (Emphasis supplied.) Similar language appears in the body of the Superior Court opinion itself at page 584, 73 A.2d at 692, where it is said: "Evidence of the result of these tests . . . was properly admitted as a circumstance bearing on the identification of the defendant, in corroboration of the testimony of the prosecuting witness that he was her assailant."

By comparison, the Commonwealth's evidence in the present case offers no corroboration whatsoever. Even the other bits of circumstantial evidence presented go only to *motive* and *ability* to commit the crime. This evidence in no manner indicates that Mussoline was in fact near the scrap yard on the night of the explosion. Any inference of *that* fact must come solely from the blood spots and appellant's lacerated arm. Since mere guess and conjecture would have to underpin such an inference, the evidence of blood-type cannot be deemed legally relevant to this case.

A study of cases from other jurisdictions also support the conclusion that a mere similarity between a defendant's blood and blood samples found at the crime scene, or, as is frequently the case in rape prosecutions, a similarity between the blood type of the victim and blood samples found on defendant, his car, or his clothing, is not relevant evidence of defendant's presence at the scene unless supported by something else. In Shanks v. State, 185 Md. 437, 45 A.2d 85, 163 A.L.R. 931 (1945) evidence that the accused's coat had blood stains whose type matched that of his alleged rape victim was held competent evidence *after* defendant had explained the blood stains as being the result of a fight with a third party whose blood turned out to be a different type than that found on the coat. Thus, the evidence was used to impeach the defendant's testimony rather than to place him at the scene of the crime. There was also, in *Shanks,* eyewitness identification by the prosecutrix.

In State v. Alexander, 7 N.J. 585, 83 A.2d 441, cert. denied, 343 U.S. 908, 72 S.Ct. 638, 96 L.Ed. 1326 (1951), the defendant in a murder case admitted presence at the scene, but claimed self defense. Thus, the prosecution was permitted to introduce evidence that the defendant's blood type matched blood found on the handle of the murder knife as support for its theory that defendant had become enraged when the decedent cut defendant's hand with the knife. Other cases where blood-type evidence has been used to corroborate separate testimony include State v. Tipton, 57 N.M. 681, 262 P.2d 378 (1953), a rape case in which the blood-type identity between samples found in defendant's car and prosecutrix's own blood was used to substantiate the victim's eyewitness identification, and Davis v. State, 189 Md. 640, 57 A.2d 289 (1948), a murder prosecution wherein the blood-type evidence was used in conjunction with the fact that defendant had stolen decedent's car and was apprehended in it. Cf. State v. Thomas, 79 Ariz. 158, 285 P.2d 612 (1954), cert. denied, 350 U.S. 950, 76 S.Ct. 326, 100 L.Ed. 828 (1956).

Baney v. People, 130 Colo. 318, 275 P.2d 195 (1954) presents an excellent example of the irrelevancy of uncorroborated blood-type evidence to place a defendant at the crime scene. In this case the prosecution's evidence consisted of the following: (1) testimony by a bartender that he had seen decedent with defendant on the night of the rape (victim died after the assault and the charge was increased to murder); (2) testimony of a deputy sheriff and a doctor to whom decedent had recited her entire ordeal; (3) similarity of blood type between decedent's blood and that found in defendant's car. At trial the blood-type evidence was allowed because it corroborated the story allegedly told to the sheriff and the doctor by the decedent. However, on appeal, the Supreme Court of Colorado held the sheriff's and the doctor's testimony to be hearsay. Without this vital link in the prosecution's case, the court held that the conviction could not stand on the uncorroborated blood-type evidence and the bartender's testimony. It said at 130 Colo. 327, 275 P.2d 199: "There is absolutely nothing in this record to indicate that the Type 'O' blood found in the car came from the body of Miss Gall."

We are of course sensitive to the oft-quoted doctrine that evidence to be relevant need not be so probative as to support an entire case by itself. However, we are also aware of many areas in the law where certain types of evidence are deemed not legally relevant unless they can be supported by additional testimony. Thus, for example, where drunken driving is an issue one may not introduce evidence tending to show that a driver had been drinking unless this evidence is coupled with testimony on the issue of how much alcohol in fact was in the bloodstream and how much it would take for an individual of that size to become intoxicated. Wentworth v. Doliner, 399 Pa. 356, 160 A.2d 562 (1960); Fisher v. Dye, 386 Pa. 141, 125 A.2d 472 (1956). Also, it has been firmly established that "[w]henever the condition of a particular place or thing at a certain time is in question, evidence of its condition at a prior or subsequent time is inadmissible, unless there is accompanying proof that it had not changed in the meantime." Murray v. Siegal, 413 Pa. 23, 29, 195 A.2d 790, 793 (1963).

The reason behind such rules is clear. Although evidence of a man's drinking, for example, may be in one sense "relevant" to the issue of whether he was able to operate his car safely — relevant because it does indeed make the likelihood of his drunken driving greater than that likelihood would be without such evidence, nevertheless, the law presumes this evidence legally irrelevant without some additional corroboration. This is so because the inquiry into truth is only slightly advanced by such evidence, if advanced at all, while the attendant prejudice spawned by the testimony rises markedly. Such, we believe, is the case when a jury is permitted to hear expert testimony on blood typing which is really nothing more, in the present case, than proof that somebody bled near the scene of the crime and that this defendant, along with 30 percent of the entire population, might have been such person. There has not been presented here one shred of evidence that the person responsible for dynamiting Gaudiano's yard actually lost blood during the process. Nor has the Commonwealth been able to offer any additional evidence, direct or circumstantial, that Mussoline was anywhere near the scene of the crime on the night in question.

We are therefore convinced that the lower court erred in refusing to sustain defendant's objections to the admission of the blood test evidence on the ground of irrelevancy. However, even with the presence of this blood-type evidence, we are also convinced that the Commonwealth's case falls woefully short of establishing guilt beyond a reasonable doubt. Having shown merely a weak motive, access to dynamite, and the possibility that Mussoline, along with 30 percent of the entire population, was among the group of people who might have shed blood at the scrap yard, this case presents a clear example of insufficient evidence.

The order of the Superior Court affirming the court below is reversed, the judgment of the Court of Quarter Sessions of Luzerne County is vacated, appellant's motion in arrest of judgment is granted, and he is hereby discharged from custody.

PEOPLE v. COLLINS
Supreme Court of California, 1968.
68 Cal.2d 319, 66 Cal.Rptr. 497, 438 P.2d 33, noted 48 Ore.L.Rev. 281 (1969).

SULLIVAN, JUSTICE. We deal here with the novel question whether evidence of mathematical probability has been properly introduced and used by the prosecution in a criminal case. While we discern no inherent incompatibility between the disciplines of law and mathematics and intend no general disapproval or disparagement of the latter as an auxiliary in the fact-finding processes of the former, we cannot uphold the technique employed in the instant case. As we explain in detail infra, the testimony as to mathematical probability infected the case with fatal error and distorted the jury's traditional role of determining guilt or innocence according to long-settled rules. Mathematics, a veritable sorcerer in our computerized society, while assisting the trier of fact in the search for truth, must not cast a spell over him. We conclude that on the record before us defendant should not have had his guilt determined by the odds and that he is entitled to a new trial. We reverse the judgment.

A jury found defendant Malcolm Ricardo Collins and his wife defendant Janet Louise Collins guilty of second degree robbery (Pen. Code, §§ 211, 211a, 1157). Malcolm appeals from the judgment of conviction. Janet has not appealed.

On June 18, 1964, about 11:30 a.m. Mrs. Juanita Brooks, who had been shopping, was walking home along an alley in the San Pedro area of the City of Los Angeles. She was pulling behind her a wicker basket carryall containing groceries and had her purse on top of the packages. She was using a cane. As she stooped down to pick up an empty carton, she was suddenly pushed to the ground by a person whom she neither saw nor heard approach. She was stunned by the fall and felt some pain. She managed to look up and saw a young woman running from the scene. According to Mrs. Brooks the latter appeared to weigh about 145 pounds, was wearing "something dark," and had hair "between a dark blond and a light blond," but lighter than the color of defendant Janet Collins' hair as it appeared at trial. Immediately after the incident, Mrs. Brooks discovered that her purse, containing between $35 and $40, was missing.

About the same time as the robbery, John Bass, who lived on the street at the end of the alley, was in front of his house watering his lawn. His attention was attracted by "a lot of crying and screaming" coming from the alley. As he looked in that direction, he saw a woman run out of the alley and enter a yellow automobile parked across the street from him. He was unable to give the make of the car. The car started off immediately and pulled wide around another parked vehicle so that in the narrow street it passed within six feet of Bass. The latter then saw that it was being driven by a male Negro, wearing a mustache and beard. At the trial Bass identified defendant as the driver of the yellow automobile. However, an attempt was made to impeach his identification by his admission that at the preliminary hearing he testified to an uncertain identification at the police lineup shortly after the attack on Mrs. Brooks, when defendant was beardless.

In his testimony Bass described the woman who ran from the alley as a Caucasian, slightly over five feet tall, of ordinary build, with her hair in a dark blond ponytail, and wearing dark clothing. He further testified that her ponytail was "just like" one which Janet had in a police photograph taken on June 22, 1964.

On the day of the robbery, Janet was employed as a housemaid in San Pedro. Her employer testified that she had arrived for work at 8:50 a.m. and that defendant had picked her up in a light yellow car about 11:30 a.m. On that day, according to the witness, Janet was wearing her hair in a blonde ponytail but lighter in color than it appeared at trial.

There was evidence from which it could be inferred that defendants had ample time to drive from Janet's place of employment and participate in the robbery. Defendants testified, however, that they went directly from her employer's house to the home of friends, where they remained for several hours.

In the morning of June 22, Los Angeles Police Officer Kinsey, saw a yellow Lincoln automobile with an off-white top in front of the house. He talked with defendants. Janet, whose hair appeared to be a dark blonde, was wearing it in a ponytail. Malcolm did not have a beard. The officer explained to them that he was investigating a robbery specifying the time and place; that the victim had been knocked down and her purse snatched; and that the person responsible was female Caucasian with blonde hair in a ponytail who had left the scene in a yellow car driven by a male Negro. He requested that defendants accompany him to the police station at San Pedro and they did so. There, in response to police inquiries as to defendants' activities at the time of the robbery, Janet stated, according to Officer Kinsey, that her husband had picked her up at her place of employment at 1 p. m. and that they had then visited at the home of friends in Los Angeles. Malcolm confirmed this. Defendants were detained for an hour or two, were photographed but not booked, and were eventually released and driven home by the police. . . .

Officer Kinsey interrogated defendants separately on June 23 while they were in custody and testified to their statements over defense counsel's objections based on the decision in *Escobedo* and our first decision in *Dorado*. According to the officer, Malcolm stated that he sometimes wore a beard but that he did not wear a beard on June 18 (the day of the robbery), having shaved it off on June 2 1964. . . .

At the seven-day trial the prosecution experienced some difficulty in establishing the identities of the perpetrators of the crime. The victim could not identify Janet and had never seen defendant. The identification by the witness Bass, who observed the girl run out of the alley and get into the automobile was incomplete as to Janet and may have been weakened as to defendant. There was also evidence, introduced by the defense, that Janet had worn light-colored clothing on the day in question, but both the victim and Bass testified that the girl they observed had worn dark clothing.

In an apparent attempt to bolster the identifications, the prosecutor called an instructor of mathematics at a state college. Through this witness he sought to establish that, assuming that the robbery was committed by a Caucasian woman with a blond ponytail who left the scene accompanied by a Negro with a beard and mustache, there was an overwhelming probability that the crime was committted by any couple answering such distinctive characteristics. The witness testified, in substance, to the "product rule," which states that the probability of the joint occurrence of a number of *mutually independent* events is equal to the product of the individual probabilities that each of the events will occur. *Without presenting any statistical evidence whatsoever in support of the probabilities for the factors selected,* the prosecutor then proceeded to have the witness *assume* probability factors for the various characteristics which he deemed to be shared by the guilty couple and all other couples answering to such distinctive characteristics.

Applying the product rule to his own factors the prosecutor arrived at a probability that there was but one chance in 12 million that any couple possessed the distinctive characteristics of the defendants. Accordingly, under this theory, it was to be inferred that there could be but one chance in 12 million that defendants were innocent and that another equally distinctive couple actually committed the robbery. Expanding on what he had thus purported to suggest as a hypothesis, the prosecutor offered the completely unfounded and improper testimonial assertion that in his opinion, the factors he had assigned were "conservative estimates" and that in reality "the chances of anyone else besides these defendants being there . . . having every similarity, . . . is somewhat like one in a billion."

Objections were timely made to the mathematician's testimony on the grounds that it was immaterial, and it invaded to province of the jury, and that it was based on unfounded assumptions. The objections were "temporarily overruled" and the evidence admitted subject to a motion to strike. When that motion was made at the conclusion of the direct examination, the court denied it, stating that the testimony had been received only for the "purpose of illustrating the mathematical probabilities of various matters, the possibilities for them occurring or re-occurring."

Both defendants took the stand in their own behalf. They denied any knowledge of or participation in the crime and stated that after Malcolm called for Janet at her employer's house they went directly to a friend's house in Los Angeles where they remained for some time. According to this testimony defendants were not near the scene of the robbery when it occurred. Defendants' friend testified to a visit by them "in the middle of June" although she could not recall the precise date. Janet further testified that certain inducements were held out to her during the July 9 interrogation on condition that she confess her participation.

Defendant makes two basic contentions before us: First, . . . and second, that the introduction of evidence pertaining to the mathematical theory of probability and the use of the same by the prosecution during the trial was error prejudicial to defendant. We consider the latter claim first.

As we shall explain, the prosecution's introduction and use of mathematical probability statistics injected two fundamental prejudicial errors into the case: (1) The testimony itself lacked an adequate foundation both in evidence and in statistical theory; and (2) the testimony and the manner in which the prosecution used it distracted the jury from its proper and requisite function of weighing the evidence on the issue of guilt, encouraged the jurors to rely upon an engaging but logically irrelevant expert demonstration, foreclosed the possibility of an effective defense by an attorney apparently unschooled in mathematical refinements, and placed the jurors and defense counsel at a disadvantage in sifting relevant fact from inapplicable theory.

We initially consider the defects in the testimony itself. As we have indicated, the specific technique presented through the mathematician's testimony and advanced by the prosecutor to measure the probabilities in question suffered from two basic and pervasive defects—an inadequate evidentiary foundation and an inadequate proof of statistical independence. First, as to the foundation requirement, we find the record devoid of any evidence relating to any of the six individual probability factors used by the prosecutor and ascribed by him to the six characteristics as we have set them out in footnote 10, *ante*. To put it another way, the prosecution produced no evidence whatsoever showing, or from which it could be in any way inferred, that only one out of every ten cars which might have been at the scene of the robbery was partly yellow, that only one out of every four men who might have been there wore a mustache, that only one out of every ten girls who might have been there wore a ponytail, or that any of the other individual probability factors listed were even roughly accurate.

The bare, inescapable fact is that the prosecution made no attempt to offer any such evidence. Instead, through leading questions having perfunctorily elicited from the witness the response that the latter could not assign a probability factor for the characteristics involved, the prosecutor himself suggested what the various probabilities should be and these became the basis of the witness' testimony (see fn. 10, ante). It is a curious circumstance of this adventure in proof that the prosecutor not only made his own assertions of these factors in the hope that they were "conservative" but also in later argument to the jury invited the jurors to substitute their "estimates" should they wish to do so. We can hardly conceive of a more fatal gap in the prosecution's scheme of proof. A foundation for the admissibility of the witness' testimony was never even attempted to be laid, let alone established. His testimony was neither made to rest on his own testimonial knowledge nor presented by proper hypothetical questions based upon valid data in the record. (See generally: 2 Wigmore on Evidence (3d ed. 1940) §§ 478, 650–652, 657, 659, 672–684; Witkin, Cal. Evidence (2d ed. 1966) § 771; McCormick on Evidence pp. 19–20; Evidence: Admission of Mathematical Probability Statistics Held Erroneous for Want of Demonstration of Validity (1967) Duke L.J. 665, 675–678, citing People v. Risley (1915) 214 N.Y. 75, 85, 108 N.E. 200; State v. Sneed (1966) 76 N.M. 349, 414 P.2d 858.) In the *Sneed* case, the court reversed a conviction based on probabilistic evidence, stating: "We hold that mathematical odds are not admissible as evidence to identify a defendant in a criminal proceeding *so long as the odds are based on estimates, the validity of which have [sic] not been demonstrated.*" (Italics added.) (414 P. 2d at p. 862.)

But, as we have indicated, there was another glaring defect in the prosecution's technique, namely an inadequate proof of the statistical independence of the six factors. No proof was presented that the characteristics selected were mutually independent, even though the witness himself acknowledged that such condition was essential to the proper application of the "product rule" or "multiplication rule." (See Note, supra, Duke L.J. 665, 669–670, fn. 25.) To the extent that the traits or characteristics were not mutually independent (e.g. Negroes with beards and men with mustaches obviously represent overlapping categories), the "product rule" would inevitably yield a wholly erroneous and exaggerated result even if all of the individual components had been determined with precision. (Siegel, Nonparametric Statistics for the Behavioral Sciences (1956) 19; see generally Harmon, Modern Factor Analysis (1960).)

In the instant case, therefore, because of the aforementioned two defects—the inadequate evidentiary foundation and the inadequate proof of statistical independence—the technique employed by the prosecutor could only lead to wild conjecture without demonstrated relevancy to the issues presented. It acquired no redeeming quality from the prosecutor's statement that it was being used only "for illustrative purposes" since, as we shall point out, the prosecutor's subsequent utilization of the mathematical testimony was not confined within such limits.

We now turn to the second fundamental error caused by the probability testimony. Quite apart from our foregoing objections to the specific technique employed by the prosecution to estimate the probability in question, we think that the entire enterprise upon which the prosecution embarked, and which was directed to the objective of measuring the likelihood of a random couple possessing the characteristics allegedly distinguishing the robbers, was gravely misguided. At best, it might yield an estimate as to how infrequently bearded Negroes drive yellow cars in the company of blonde females with ponytails.

The prosecution's approach, however, could furnish the jury with absolutely no guidance on the crucial issue: *Of the admittedly few such couples, which one, if any, was guilty of committing this robbery?* Probability theory necessarily remains silent on that question, since no mathematical equation can prove beyond a reasonable doubt (1) that the guilty couple *in fact* possessed the characteristics described by the People's witnesses, or even (2) that only *one* couple possessing those distinctive characteristics could be found in the entire Los Angeles area.

As to the first inherent failing we observe that the prosecution's theory of probability rested on the assumption that the witnesses called by the People had conclusively established that the guilty couple possessed the precise characteristics relied upon by the prosecution. But no mathematical formula could ever establish beyond a reasonable doubt that the prosecution's witnesses correctly observed and accurately described the distinctive features which were employed to link defendants to the crime. (See 2 Wigmore on Evidence (3d ed. 1940) § 478.) Conceivably, for example, the guilty couple might have included a light-skinned Negress with bleached hair rather than a Caucasian blonde; or the driver of the car might have been wearing a false beard as a disguise; or the prosecution's witnesses might simply have been unreliable.

The foregoing risks of error permeate the prosecution's circumstantial case. Traditionally, the jury weighs such risks in evaluating the credibility and probative value of trial testimony, but the likelihood of human error or of falsification obviously cannot be quantified; that likelihood must therefore be excluded from any effort to assign a *number* to the probability of guilt or innocence. Confronted with an equation which purports to yield a numerical index of probable guilt, few juries could resist the temptation to accord disproportionate weight to that index; only an exceptional juror, and indeed only a defense attorney schooled in mathematics, could successfully keep in mind the facts that the probability computed by the prosecution can represent, *at best*, the likelihood that a random couple would share the characteristics testified to by the People's witnesses—*not necessarily the characteristics of the actually guilty couple*.

As to the second inherent failing in the prosecution's approach, even assuming that the first failing could be discounted, the most a mathematical computation could *ever* yield would be a measure of the probability that a random couple would possess the distinctive features in question. In the present case, for example, the prosecution attempted to compute the probability that a random couple would include a bearded Negro, a blonde girl with a ponytail, and a partly yellow car; the prosecution urged that this probability was no more than one in 12 million. Even accepting this conclusion as arithmetically accurate, however, one still could not conclude that the Collinses were probably *the* guilty couple. On the contrary, as we explain in the Appendix, the prosecution's figures actually imply a likelihood of over 40 percent that the Collinses could be "duplicated" by at least *one other couple who might equally have committed the San Pedro robbery*. Urging that the Collinses be convicted on the basis of evidence which logically establishes no more than this seems as indefensible as arguing for the conviction of X on the ground that a witness saw either X or X's twin commit the crime.

Again, few defense attorneys, and certainly few jurors, could be expected to comprehend this basic flaw in the prosecution's analysis. Conceivably even the prosecutor erroneously believed that his equation established a high probability that *no* other bearded Negro in the Los Angeles area drove a yellow car accompanied by a ponytailed blonde. In any event, although his technique could demonstrate no such thing, he solemnly told the jury that he had supplied mathematical proof of guilt.

Sensing the novelty of that notion, the prosecutor told the jurors that the traditional idea of proof beyond a reasonable doubt represented "the most hackneyed, stereotyped, trite, misunderstood concept in criminal law." He sought to reconcile the jury to the risk that, under his "new math" approach to criminal jurisprudence, "on some rare occasion . . . an innocent person may be convicted." "Without taking that risk," the prosecution continued, "life would be intolerable . . . because . . . there would be immunity for the Collinses, for people who chose not to be employed to go down and push old ladies down and take their money and be immune because how could we ever be sure they are the ones who did it?"

In essence this argument of the prosecutor was calculated to persuade the jury to convict defendants whether or not they were convinced of their guilt to a moral certainty and beyond a reasonable doubt. (Pen.Code, § 1096.) Undoubtedly the jurors were unduly impressed by the mystique of the mathematical demonstration but were unable to assess its relevancy or value. Although we make no appraisal of the proper applications of mathematical techniques in the proof of facts (see People v. Jordan (1955) 45 Cal.2d 697, 707, 290 P.2d 484; People v. Trujillo (1948) 32 Cal.2d 105, 109, 194 P.2d 681;

in a slightly differing context see Whitus v. State of Georgia (1967) 385 U.S. 545, 552, fn. 2,87 S.Ct. 643, 17 L.Ed.2d 599; Finkelstein, The Application of Statistical Decision Theory to the Jury Discrimination Cases (1966) 80 Harv.L.Rev. 338, 338–340), we have strong feelings that such applications, particularly in a criminal case, must be critically examined in view of the substantial unfairness to a defendant which may result from ill conceived techniques with which the trier of fact is not technically equipped to cope. (See State v. Sneed, supra, 414 P.2d 858; Note, supra, Duke L.J. 665.) We feel that the technique employed in the case before us falls into the latter category.

We conclude that the court erred in admitting over defendant's objection the evidence pertaining to the mathematical theory of probability and in denying defendant's motion to strike such evidence. The case was apparently a close one. The jury began its deliberations at 2:46 p.m. on November 24, 1964, and retired for the night at 7:46 p.m.; the parties stipulated that a juror could be excused for illness and that a verdict could be reached by the remaining 11 jurors; the jury resumed deliberations the next morning at 8:40 a.m. and returned verdicts at 11:58 a.m. after five ballots had been taken. In the light of the closeness of the case, which as we have said was a circumstantial one, there is a reasonable likelihood that the result would have been more favorable to defendant if the prosecution had not urged the jury to render a probabilistic verdict. In any event, we think that under the circumstances the "trial by mathematics" so distorted the role of the jury and so disadvantaged counsel for the defense, as to constitute in itself a miscarriage of justice. After an examination of the entire cause, including the evidence, we are of the opinion that it is reasonably probable that a result more favorable to defendant would have been reached in the absence of the above error. (People v. Watson (1956) 46 Cal.2d 818, 836; 299 P.2d 243.) The judgment against defendant must therefore be reversed.

5

Witnesses

In order for a witness' testimony to be introduced into evidence, the witness must be adjudged competent (qualified to testify). The weight that will be given to a witness' testimony is always up to the jury; however, his competency is always a question of law that is to be decided by the judge. Most jurisdictions follow the federal rule which states: "Except as otherwise provided by law, all persons are competent as witnesses." The modern rule differs from the older rule, which held that there were several grounds upon which a person could be disqualified from giving his testimony: (1) prior conviction of a felony crime; (2) infancy; (3) bias; (4) insanity; (5) marriage to a party in the action; and (6) lack of belief in God. The modern rules have done away with most of these disqualifications and generally only require that the witness have a capacity to perceive and be able to recollect what he perceived and to know and understand his duty to tell the truth and be able to express himself to the jury.

The new Federal Rules go even further and hold that a witness may only be disqualified if he lacks personal knowledge. Inability of a witness to express himself clearly or to clearly show to the jury that he understands his duty to tell the truth may only be considered by the jury as to determine the weight which it shall apply to his testimony, and not as to its admissibility.

There is much confusion among law enforcement officers as to how old a child must be before he may be competent to testify in a court of law. The general rule is that a child of any age may be permitted to testify as long as the judge is satisfied that the child is a competent witness.

There are some states, however, that have statutes which raise a presumption that children over a certain age are competent, while the competency of children under that age must be determined by the trial court. In these jurisdictions, just because there is a presumption of competency at a certain age does not mean that anyone under that age may not testify. The police officer must become familiar with the age requirements in his jurisdiction. If he has a child of "tender years" as a victim or a witness to the crime, he should include in his investigation report to the prosecuting attorney the qualifications, if any, to show why this child should be allowed to testify in court. *Example:* A child of five years of age is called to the witness stand to testify against a suspected child molester. The district attorney should inquire of the child what happens to the child if he tells a lie, and then the child responds with an answer, such as, "My mother or my daddy spanks me or they send me to bed without supper," clearly showing that he has a duty to tell the truth. Another common approach is to ask the child if he goes to church or Sunday school. If so, does he know what God says or what the Sunday school teacher tells him will happen if he tells a lie. The typical response is that God doesn't like people to tell lies, and so on. The next question that would be put to the child would be to determine the child's ability to perceive, to recollect, and to now tell the court what he has perceived and what he now remembers about that perception. If he has satisfied the trial judge, the child, regardless of his age, will be allowed to testify in the trial.

A law enforcement officer is frequently confronted with a victim of a crime or a witness of a crime who is mentally ill. The officer should not immediately seek to close his case out because he does not have a competent witness. The general rule is that mental incapacity in and of itself does not disqualify a person from being a witness. Before he can be disqualified, the mental condition of an individual must be such that his ability to perceive, to recollect, and to testify are impaired. If they are not, that person is just as competent a witness as any other person.

Under old law, there were other categories of people that were normally considered incompetent to testify, such as those who did not believe in God or those who were convicted felons. Under modern law, the person who does not believe in God is still a competent witness. He will affirm to the truth. The jury or judge may not exclude this person from testifying or tend to give his testimony less weight merely because of his beliefs. A person who has been convicted of a prior felony crime is still a competent witness if he meets all other requirements. However, as we shall see, his prior conviction may be the basis for impeaching him as a witness (discrediting his testimony).

The Opinion Rule

An opinion is merely an inference which has been drawn by a person, either a lay person or an expert, from facts which he has observed. The general rule is that an opinion or conclusion of the witness is not admissible. As with any other rule of evidence, however, there are always exceptions, and there are many to the lay person's opinion rule as well as to the rules concerning an expert's opinion.

Lay Person's Opinion

A lay person may not testify as to an opinion or conclusion except where he has personal knowledge of the facts in issue and has made a personal observation of the facts, and unless no other type of evidence can be obtained from his observation. In order for a lay person's opinion to be admissible, the judge first must be convinced that the witness personally observed that which he is about to testify or render an opinion on, that the matter is one which any other normal person could and would normally have formed an opinion on, and that the giving of this opinion is the best way of letting the jury hear the evidence and determine for itself the weight that should be applied.

The new Federal Rules of Evidence only permit a lay person to express his opinion where the judge finds that the opinions are rationally based on the perception of the witness and are very helpful to the clear understanding of his testimony or as to determination of any fact in issue. There are five common examples on which a lay person is almost always allowed to give an opinion in court: (1) identity of another; (2) dimensions; (3) value of his property; (4) handwriting of another; and (5) mental or physical condition of another.

Identity of Another

The lay person is able to form an opinion as to the identity of any other person. Usually, this is the only adequate way of proving identification in the courtroom. *Example:* A victim of a robbery is testifying in a trial and states that the defendant looks like the man that robbed him. Or, the victim states, "I heard the robber say, 'Get your hands up,' and his (the defendant's) voice sounds like that of the robber."

Dimensions

A lay person may testify concerning any measurement or dimension which will aid the jury in the case. *Example 1:* A witness is standing at an intersection and sees a vehicle coming down a residential street at what he estimates to be 60 miles an hour. The vehicle crashes into another car at the intersection. This lay person will be able to testify if any other lay person having the same general background as this witness could have formed an opinion based upon what he had perceived, i.e., the car was speeding, and that it was going 60 miles an hour. *Example 2:* A lay person testifies that a car was approximately 15 feet away from him at the time it crashed into another vehicle. If any normal person could have formed this opinion, then this person is able to testify to it in the courtroom. Of course, the attorneys will attempt to have this witness indicate the distance in the courtroom so that the jury can perceive whether or not he in fact is fairly accurate.

Value of His Property

A lay person who has been the victim of a theft is permitted to testify to the reasonable value of a piece of his property which was stolen. The police officer should interrogate any victim of the property crime where the value will be in issue in the trial as to a reasonable market value, based on the condition of the item on the date that it was stolen. The courts are not interested in the new cost of the item, nor are they interested in the replacement cost of the item or how much money the victim wants from the insurance company.

Handwriting of Another

A general rule of evidence allows any lay person to give his opinion as to the handwriting of another person as long as it is shown that the witness is acquainted with the person whose handwriting he is now testifying to and has seen that person write, or simply sign his name, on more than one occasion. It is not necessary to have an expert testify as to the handwriting if another person has viewed the writing of another enough times so that he may form an opinion as to whether the questioned document was signed by that other person. *Example:* A secretary is called to the witness stand, is shown a check, and is asked if she recognizes the signature on the check. She states that she recognizes it and that it is that of the defendant, who is her boss. It is established that she has been working for this man for one year and has seen him sign his signature on hundreds of occasions. Thus, she is qualified to testify as to the identity of the defendant from the handwriting that she has been shown.

Mental or Physical Condition of Another

The old adage that only a doctor may testify as to the mental or physical condition of another has no foundation in the laws or rules of evidence. Any lay person may give an opinion as to the physical or the mental condition of another person as long as another reasonable lay person observing the same set of facts could have formed an opinion of that other's mental or physical condition. *Example:* A law enforcement officer arrested a person for being drunk in public. Even though that law enforcement officer may qualify as an expert, in most cases he is testifying as a lay person that he observed certain physical characteristics of the defendant, i.e., a staggering walk, bloodshot and watery eyes, and slurred speech. From these observations, he formed the opinion that the person was in fact drunk. The officer, of course, is allowed to testify to that drunken condition in a court of law. A lay person would also be permitted to testify as to pain being experienced by another person, or as to the age of another person, as long as he reasonably formed an opinion from his own observations.

In attempting to admit a lay person's opinion as to the mental condition of another, most courts require that the lay person testifying be a close relative or close acquaintance of the person whose condition is now in issue. *Example:* The defendant, being tried for murder of a small child in a neighborhood where he resided, seeks to introduce testimony of the people who lived on either side of his house. It is established that these people have lived there for a period of time and that they have observed the defendant on many occasions acting irrationally, in their opinion. They would be permitted to testify as to their observations and then as to their opinions, which they formed based on these observations of the mental condition of the defendant in the case.

Expert Opinion

A person testifying as an expert in a court of law is not testifying to aid either side in the case, but is introduced as an aid to the jury. Thus, he should be an impartial witness in any trial. Before a person may testify as an expert, it must be established that he is qualified as an expert in the field in which he is now attempting to give an opinion. The person must be prepared to testify that he has some special knowledge or skill due to his experience or his education in a specific field. *Example:* The prosecutor is seeking to introduce into evidence the results of a blood-alcohol test and calls the criminalist to the stand to testify. The criminalist, after he has stated his name, occupation, and employer, is asked to state his educational experience. He answers that he holds a bachelor's degree from the University of Wisconsin with a major in chemistry and a master's degree from the University of Illinois with a major in chemistry, that he studied while in the universities under certain professors and performed blood/alcohol analyses under their direct supervision and control, that since the time of his graduation he has performed 250 similar tests, and that upon being checked by his supervisor or by his university professors he was found to be accurate in his findings. He then may be asked how he performed the tests and must be able to recite the procedures used to come up with his opinion, as well as show himself knowledgeable in all treatises in his field of expertise.

A law enforcement officer is frequently called upon to testify as an expert as to the modus operandi of a criminal. The officer should be prepared to establish that he has acquired certain skills or expertise in determining modus operandi due to investigating techniques, special schools, basic police academies, and other types of study courses, as well as on-the-job experience.

An expert will not be permitted to testify as to any fact from which a reasonable man could draw an inference without expert help. *Example:* A criminalist is attempting to testify as an expert that a container which was found in the car of the defendant had an odor like that of an alcoholic beverage. Any common reasonable man, i.e., a member of the jury, could have, if given that container, formed the same opinion. Thus, the criminalist would not be allowed to testify to this fact, as it is beyond the realm on which an expert may give his opinion. He could, however, give his opinion as a lay person. If possible, the container should be used in evidence and passed around to the jury so that it may form its own opinion.

Assume for the sake of argument that in the year 2000 children are trained in school to read fingerprints and that fingerprints are a common method of identification in the business community. The defendant is now on trial and a police fingerprint expert is called and presents a photograph of a fingerprint lifted from a crime scene, as well as a comparison print of the card of the defendant. He then attempts to show the jury the similarities. With the prior training and knowledge of the reasonable man in the year 2000, this fingerprint man would not be allowed to testify as an expert. All that would be needed would be to show the fingerprint to the jury members, who could form an opinion themselves, as could any other reasonable man in the same or similar circumstances.

There is a big difference between the weight given an opinion of a lay person and that of an expert. The jury must weigh a lay person's opinion with the other evidence introduced in the trial. On the other hand, when the jury is considering an expert's opinion, it need not give this opinion any weight at all in its deliberations, simply because the expert is testifying as an aid to the jury. If the jury desires to disregard his testimony entirely, they may do so without any explanation.

The opposing side may cross-examine and impeach an expert witness on the same grounds as any other witness, as well as on the following additional grounds: (1) a showing that the so-called expert lacks expert qualifications. By introducing independent evidence, or by cross-examining the expert, the opposing counsel may show that the expert lacks the qualifications that he claimed on direct examination; (2) prior inconsistent opinions in the same case. The general rule, however, is that the judge will allow prior inconsistent opinions from the same case, but not those given in another case; (3) remuneration received by the expert. The general rule is that the opposing counsel may cross-examine as to any monies or expenses which have been or are being paid the expert witness by either side in the case. This testimony is allowed so that the jury may determine whether it thinks that the money received by the expert tends to bias him in his opinion in the present case; and (4) a showing of contrary views of other experts who have written textbooks or knowledgeable treatises. The counsel attempting to cross-examine or impeach the expert witness may properly refer to any textbooks or treatises on which the expert witness claims to have relied in forming his own opinion. The cross-examiner, of course, would want to rely on these books to show that they really do not support the expert witness and the opinion which he has formed in the present case.

The new Federal Rules and many states permit cross-examination of any expert witness as to contrary views which have been expressed in any scientific textbook or treatise, whether or not the expert claims to have relied upon or even read them. In a jurisdiction, such as the federal courts or any state which would allow this type of evidence, a hearsay problem is confronted. The Federal Rules of Evidence provide that a text or treatise is admissible as an exception to the hearsay rule, whereas in other courts the general rule is that it is admissible solely to impeach the expert and not as substantive evidence. Thus, texts and treatises are not barred by the hearsay rule.

Form of Examination of Witnesses

The new Federal Rules of Evidence state that the court shall exercise reasonable control over the mode and order of interrogating witnesses and presenting evidence so as to: (1) make the interrogation and presentation effective for the ascertainment of the truth; (2) avoid needless consumption of time; and (3) protect witnesses from harrassment or undue embarrassment. A general rule in most jurisdictions is that the judge will control the order and mode of interrogating witnesses. A judge, being the unbiased person in the case, is there to facilitate the orderly introduction of evidence and to protect all parties in the action.

Most jurisdictions now allow a witness to be excluded from the courtroom upon motion of either party. Upon the motion being made, the judge, in his discretion, may overrule the motion. Usually, he will sustain the motion and order a witness excluded from the courtroom to insure that that witness' testimony is not tainted by that of another witness who precedes him in the trial. In addition, the new Federal Rules of Evidence state that the judge must, on request of either side, order all witnesses excluded so that they may not hear the testimony of other witnesses, with the limitation that any party to the action (chief investigator for the prosecution, defendant, and chief investigator for the defense) who is also to be a witness may not be excluded from the courtroom.

Direct Examination

Under direct examination (direct exam), a witness must first be sworn to tell the truth or must affirm that he will tell the truth. After the witness takes the stand and identifies himself for the record, the attorneys then proceed to question him on direct exam. The direct exam is conducted by the party who has called the witness to the stand. *Example:* A police officer testifying as to an arrest that he made would first be examined directly by the district attorney. During the direct examination, the examiner is generally limited as to the type of questions he may ask of the witness. Who, what, where, when, and how questions are perfectly permissible.

Frequently the witness being examined directly is asked a question which calls for a narrative answer, such as, "Now, officer, will you tell the court what happened from the first moment that you saw the defendant?" This type of narrative question is not permitted in the majority of courts in the United States, because it is too difficult for the judge to determine whether certain parts of the testimony will be objectionable before the witness has uttered them. The law enforcement officer, however, favors a narrative question because it allows him to get into evidence otherwise objectionable material. Therefore, the officer should continue to answer the narrative question unless the defense counsel objects to it and the objection is sustained.

On direct examination, the officer many times is confronted with a question which calls for him to form a conclusion. Generally, an answer to a question which calls for an opinion or a conclusion is not allowed. *Example 1:* "Did the victim see the defendant prior to the time he was shot?" This question calls for the witness not to testify as to something on which he has personal knowledge, but to form an opinion or to give a conclusion based upon the investigation that he has conducted. Thus, if an objection is made, the question will not be allowed. *Example 2:* "Why did the defendant commit the act?" This question, as well, calls for the witness to form a conclusion as to the state of mind of the defendant when he committed a certain act and would be objected to and excluded from evidence during the trial.

One of the most frequent types of objections made by a defense attorney during a criminal prosecution is that a question which has been asked has already been answered and is in the record. The prosecutor, or perhaps the defense attorney, is trying to bolster items of information which have already been introduced into the trial by continuing to ask a repetitive type of question so that these items will be impressed upon the jury. As we have learned, however, if the question has already been asked and answered, it is cumulative evidence, and may be excluded at the discretion of the judge.

Another type of question that is not allowed on direct examination is the leading question. A leading question is one which leads the witness to a desired answer or suggests a fact to the witness which has not yet been introduced into evidence. The general rule is that leading questions are not allowed on direct examination. *Example:* "Is it not true that the defendant was drunk?" This question obviously shows the witness the answer desired by the examiner, i.e., "Yes, he was drunk," which is a purely suggestive answer which carries with it implications of facts not admitted into evidence.

On direct examination, leading questions are permitted to set the stage for the witness' testimony where the witness is being asked questions prior to his testimony as to his background. *Example:* Questions by the prosecutor: "Is it not true that you are a police officer? Is it not true, officer, that you have been through a police-training academy?" A leading question would also be allowed during direct examination when the examiner is attempting to refresh the recollection of the witness. In addition, whenever the witness is confused, hostile, or a child of tender years, the court, in its discretion, will usually allow leading questions on direct examination.

Cross-examination

After a witness has been fully examined directly by the side that calls him, the opposing counsel is given the right to cross-examine the witness. The purpose of cross-examination (cross-exam) is to test the credibility and accuracy of the testimony of the witness. The right to cross-examine witnesses in a criminal prosecution is constitutionally protected, and if cross-examination were denied to a defendant, there would be automatic reversal on appeal for that defendant.

Contra the rules on direct examination, leading questions are always permitted during cross-examination. In addition to leading questions, the cross-examiner may use any type of question which would have been proper on direct examination as an aid in testing the accuracy of the testimony of the witness.

There are many types of questions, however, which are not permitted on cross-examination, such as, a compound question, which requires only one answer to more than one question (*Example:* "Did your wife and your child see you at home?") or an argumentative question (*Example:* "You did it, didn't you?") A question which assumes facts not yet in evidence is also not permitted. *Example:* In a robbery case, the question "What did the defendant then do?" is asked prior to anyone identifying the defendant as the robber. The most frequently used improper questions are the questions which call for a conclusion on the part of the witness ("Did the defendant commit the robbery?") or an opinion which he is not qualified to give *(Example:* A police officer testifying in a narcotics case is asked on cross-examination what tests were used to determine the contents of the suspected package, and the officer is not a criminalist, nor does he have any special knowledge or training in criminalistics). Another form of question which is frowned upon on direct examination as well as on cross-examination is a question which has already been asked and answered. However, because more repetition is usually allowed on cross-examination, cumulative evidence will come in more frequently than on direct exam.

There are divergent views in the United States as to the scope of the cross-examination. The federal view, which is not generally accepted at this time, allows a witness to be cross-examined on all relevant matters whether or not they were covered on direct examination. The only limitation is that the trial court may, in its discretionary powers, limit the examination. Thus, the Federal Rules follow the old common law rule that once a witness is called by either side, inquiry may be made of that witness on any matter that is relevant to the case. The procedure followed in most jurisdictions, however, restricts cross-examination to matters that have already been introduced in direct examination. *Example:* The prosecution calls a police officer to the stand and asks one question only: "Were you on duty the night of July 7, 1974?" The officer responds, "Yes." On cross-examination, the defense attorney asks the officer what he observed that night. This latter question would be permissible, as it is within the scope of the direct exam. The prosecution has placed him on duty, and now it is permissible to inquire of him what occurred when he was on duty that night. However, a question upon cross-examination about what occurred on any other night would exceed the scope of the direct examination and would be objected to and excluded from evidence. As the student has seen, however, under the more liberal federal rules, the question as to any other night would be perfectly permissible as long as it was relevant to the issue in the present case.

Redirect Examination

After a witness has been examined directly and cross-examined, then the party who called him to the stand may take him on redirect examination. The rules governing redirect examination are the same as those governing direct exam. Moreover, the person who initially called the witness to the stand cannot on redirect exam ask questions which were covered on direct exam, even though they were not considered on cross exam, nor may he ask a question which he merely forgot to ask during the direct examination. The court has been given broad latitude in this matter, however, and may in its discretion allow the examiner to reopen the direct exam and go into new material.

The rule in the minority of courts, including the federal courts, which follows the common law rule of cross-examination that any matter may be inquired into on cross-examination, also allows on redirect exam any matter to be inquired into, regardless of whether it has previously been inquired into or merely forgotten by the examiner. Thus, the cross-examiner is not limited to only questioning concerning facts brought out during direct examination.

Recross-examination

After redirect examination, at the discretion of the judge, recross-examination of the witness may be allowed to the defense attorney. The purpose of recross-examination is to overcome the opposing attorney's attempts to rehabilitate a witness or to rebut evidence which is damaging to the defense. Some jurisdictions allow recross-examination as a matter of right under the evidence code (state rules concerning evidence). Other jurisdictions, including the federal courts, state that it is discretionary with the trial judge whether recross-examination is permitted.

Questioning by the Judge

On many occasions, the judge conducts the entire examination of the witness. The trial judge who does this obviously is seeking to bring out what he deems relevent evidence so that the jury may consider it in their deliberations. A major problem creating prejudice to one side can occur where the judge himself calls a party to be a witness and interrogates that party as any other witness in the case. The judge may use any type of question he desires as long as he conducts a fair examination and does not intimidate the witness in any manner. Either party still has the right to object to either the form or manner of the examination of the witness and, of course, has the right to cross-examine the witness regardless on which side he is testifying. The court has the inherent power as well to call expert witnesses which it deems necessary to overcome conflicting testimony by experts already called by the parties in the action. Remember that an expert's opinion need not be considered by the jury in its deliberations. Therefore, a witness being called as an aid to the jury may have his testimony totally disregarded by the jury when they deliberate.

Impeachment and Rehabilitation of Witnesses

There is often much confusion between the terms *impeachment* and *rehabilitation*. *Impeachment* merely means that a witness' statement(s) has been discredited. *Rehabilitation* means that the discrediting information has been overcome and that the credibility of the witness' statement has been reestablished (rehabilitated) in the eyes of the jury.

A general rule on impeachment is that a party may not impeach its own witness. The reasoning behind this rule, which has been with us since early common law times, is that a party that calls a witness in fact vouches for the credibility of that witness, and thus is bound by his testimony. However, under this general rule, a party may impeach its own witness in the following five situations: (1) when the witness is one whom the law requires the party to call to the stand; (2) when the witness is an adverse party in the action of a spouse, partner, or employee of that party; (3) when the witness shows hostility while on the stand; (4) when the witness is biased; and (5) when the party calling the witness is truly surprised by that witness' testimony (e.g., when the witness makes a statement which is inconsistent with a previous statement).

Under the new Federal Rules, and in the majority of jurisdictions, this common law rule against impeaching one's own witness has been abolished, and either party may impeach any witness it calls either on direct or redirect examination. The other side, of course, has the fundamental right of impeaching the witness, since the witness' credibility is always an issue in cross-examination (and recross-examination).

The mere fact that contradictory evidence has been introduced into a trial does not mean that a previous witness' testimony must be stricken or disregarded by the jury. The jury still may consider all testimony which has not been stricken from the record when it goes into deliberations. Thus, impeachment simply raises a doubt in the mind of the jury as to the credibility of the witness.

The different methods of impeaching a witness generally fall within one of two categories: (1) attacking the credibility of the witness, such as proving that the witness has been previously convicted of a crime or does not have the capability of perceiving impressions to which he has testified (*Example:* A witness testifies to seeing a robbery committed 30 feet away and he is totally blind); and (2) introducing contradictory evidence. A witness' testimony *may* be impeached by providing contrary evidence which overwhelms the jury, meaning that the jury in fact now believes the rebuttal witness to have completely discredited the prior witness' testimony.

Just because contrary evidence has been introduced does not mean that the credibility of the prior witness is in doubt. It merely means that the rebuttal evidence has more substantive weight than that evidence which was previously introduced.

There are generally four broad categories which contain the grounds on which a witness' testimony may be impeached: (1) showing of conviction of a crime; (2) misconduct which did not result in conviction; (3) poor reputation for truthfulness; and (4) lack of perceptory ability and inconsistent statements.

Prior Conviction of a Crime

When a witness takes the stand, he has placed his character for honesty in issue and may be impeached by any evidence that shows his character is such that he may now perjure himself. One type of evidence which might be introduced for impeachment on this ground is prior conviction of a crime. In early common law, evidence that a person had been convicted of any felony or misdemeanor which showed that he was dishonest would be allowed into evidence to show that this person was now incompetent to testify in any trial. There are many divergent views in the United States as to what crimes constitute grounds for impeachment here. Some states hold that any felony can be introduced to impeach a witness regardless of the crime involved, while other states hold that the conviction of any crime, be it felony or misdemeanor, may be introduced to impeach the witness. The better, and more generally accepted, view in the United States today is that the crime of which the witness has been convicted must be one which would discredit the veracity or credibility of the witness. The new Federal Rules allow a witness to be impeached upon a showing of a conviction of any felony or any other crime involving dishonesty or any false statements.

If a witness has been called to testify and either side has information that he was convicted of a crime which is grounds for impeachment in the state within which he is testifying, that side may either ask the witness about the prior crime or introduce a certified copy of the record of conviction without any prior questioning of that witness. If the witness is first confronted with the question of whether he has ever been convicted of a crime and he denies conviction of a crime, the party seeking to impeach him must then introduce proof that the witness is in fact the person who was convicted and that his name is not just similar to that of the person who was convicted. Once it has been shown that the witness has suffered a conviction, the details of the conviction may not be inquired into in the present case.

The new Federal Rules hold that if the witness has received a full pardon, then that conviction may not be used against him for impeachment purposes. However, most states still rule that the conviction may be shown for impeachment purposes even though the witness has received this pardon. It is generally immaterial how old the conviction is.

The modern view, however, allows the trial judge to exercise his discretionary powers in deciding to exclude testimony about convictions whenever the probative value of such information is outweighed by the danger of unfair prejudice in that specific trial. Thus, under this view, the judge may choose to exclude convictions which are deemed to be too remote in time or because of changed circumstances (rehabilitation of the witness) or because of the nature of the offense. The general rule on the use of juvenile convictions holds that they are not admissible for impeachment purposes. However, under the new Federal Rules, the judge in a criminal case, has the discretion to admit such evidence.

Misconduct

The side seeking to impeach a witness may desire to show acts of misconduct on the part of the witness which did not result in a felony conviction. While the old common law rule would permit this type of question, the majority opinion in the United States today is that the misconduct of the witness may only be shown if it clearly illustrates his lack of truthfulness and would not result in any confusion or undue risk of prejudice in the case.

Poor Reputation for Truthfulness

The most frequently used ground for impeachment is that a witness has a poor reputation for truthfulness. Seeing that in a trial his credibility is always in issue, impeachment on this ground is permissible in most jurisdictions. It has already been pointed out that a person who takes the witness stand has placed his reputation for truthfulness in issue in that case. Thus, the opposing side may have other witnesses testify as to his reputation for truthfulness and veracity in the community where he lives. Some jurisdictions will now also allow evidence of his reputation in the community in which he works. The older view was that a witness who was asked, for impeachment purposes, about the reputation of a prior witness in the case could only give his opinion based upon what he had heard and not upon personal knowledge. However, the more modern view is to allow a witness to give his opinion as to the truthfulness of a preceding witness based on his own personal opinion of that previous witness.

 The counsel on cross-examination may also be able to prove that a prior witness had an adverse interest in the case. *Example:* An expert witness is called to testify and it is brought out on cross-examination that he is being paid for his testimony in the case. This does not mean that his testimony will be stricken from the records, but it does mean that the jury will be allowed to weigh the fact that he was paid to come and testify when it determines whether or not the witness was, in fact, truthful in this specific case.

 Say that in a criminal prosecution a witness testifying for the prosecution is asked during cross-examination whether charges against him have been dismissed or whether there have been any promises or leniency granted him due to his testimony in this case. The inferences that may be deducted from this question if it were true, by the jury, are useful in determining the truthfulness of that witness.

 If a witness whose testimony is being attacked is related to one of the parties in the action, it certainly can be inferred that he may be biased in that party's favor. Thus, it may be permissible for the jury to know about this relationship. A general rule holds, however, that a person cannot be impeached merely because he is related to a party in the action, since one cannot pick his relatives as he may his friends. But, by showing a person as a close friend or business associate to the party in the action for whom he has testified, it is a proper inference by the jury that this person will be biased in the case.

Lack of Perceptory Ability

The law enforcement officer should be particularly observant of any grounds for impeachment due to the perceptory ability of people he interviews prior to the trial. Information that a potential witness shows a lack of memory as to factors which another reasonable man would normally recollect should be included in the investigation report to the district attorney. Other perceptory problems of a witness (e.g., the witness wears a hearing aid or glasses) should also be pointed out to the prosecuting attorney, since it is perfectly permissible to impeach a witness by showing lack of knowledge or perceptory ability on the part of any witness by either side of the action.

Inconsistent Statements

Another method of discrediting the testimony of a witness is to show that he has made a prior inconsistent statement regarding the matter to which he has just testified. The modern rules hold that prior to the introduction of an inconsistent statement, the witness must be given an opportunity to explain or deny the inconsistent statement which he previously made. He need not be shown the writing, if the prior inconsistent statement was in fact in writing, nor need the contents be disclosed to him, although it will be necessary to show the writing to the opposing attorney upon request. The attorney seeking to impeach the witness who has made a prior inconsistent statement need only ask him if he has at any time made any written or contrary statement to the fact to which he has just testified, and, if so, the reason for the inconsistency.

The old common law view requires that the witness always be asked about a prior inconsistent statement before the inconsistent statement may be introduced into the trial. In a jurisdiction following the common law view, the person conducting the cross-examination must: (1) ask the witness if he made the statement; (2) disclose the substance of the statement; (3) give the time and place of the statement, and the person to whom it was made; and (4) if the statement was in writing, show the witness a copy of the writing itself. The penalty for not fulfilling these four requirements would be that the inconsistent statement could not be received into evidence.

If the witness admitted making the prior inconsistent statement, the majority of courts would not allow the statement itself to be admissible. If, on the other hand, the witness denied making the statement or claimed a lapse of memory, then the preceding four foundational requirements have been met and the counsel may put the statement into evidence during his case in chief.

There is disagreement as to the effect of an inconsistent statement once it is admitted into evidence. The more modern view holds that the inconsistent statement can be admitted as substantive proof of all matters contained therein, whereas the common law view, and still the majority view in the United States, holds that the prior inconsistent statement is hearsay and therefore cannot be used as proof of the facts contained therein unless there is an exception to the hearsay rule which would admit it. In jurisdictions following the common law view, an inconsistent statement, then, may only be used for impeachment purposes, and the jury must be given a limiting instruction so that it does not consider the statement as substantive proof.

Rehabilitation of Witnesses

Once a cross-examiner has attempted to impeach a witness, the party that placed that witness on the stand will be allowed on redirect examination to attempt to rehabilitate that witness. As we have seen, to rehabilitate a witness means to restore the credibility of that witness. Rehabilitation of a witness will not be allowed merely because contradictory evidence has been introduced into the trial. It must appear to the judge that the credibility of the witness has been attacked. If the credibility of the witness has not been attacked, there will be nothing to rehabilitate, and any attempt to introduce evidence of rehabilitation will be excluded. *Example 1:* A witness testifies on direct examination that she was with the defendant at the time of the alleged crime in another location. On cross-examination, it is brought out that the witness is the girl friend of the defendant. Thus, her credibility is in issue by a showing of bias. On redirect examination, it would then be proper to question her as to how long ago she had dated the defendant, and whether or not she still was his girl friend, or whether they were merely casual acquaintances. *Example 2:* A witness has testified for the prosecution. On cross-examination, it is brought out that the witness has a poor reputation in the community for being truthful. The prosecutor may then introduce other character witnesses to testify to the good reputation of the witness. Under the new Federal Rules, cross-examination of impeachment witnesses will be permitted to show specific instances of honest conduct by the witness whose truth or veracity is in doubt. An exception may be found, however, where the attempt to impeach the witness has been by a showing of a past criminal conviction. The general rule in the majority of courts holds that no explanation may be offered in evidence of the circumstances surrounding a conviction, nor may evidence of the witness' good character be introduced into evidence.

Privileges

A privilege is a statutory rule which permits a witness to refrain from giving testimony which he otherwise would be compelled to give or allows the defendant to prevent a witness from testifying against him in order to protect a specific relationship or interest. A privilege will keep out competent, relevant testimony because of the strong public policy that there is a relationship existing which needs to be protected. Because a privilege will exclude relevant evidence, the courts construe privileged areas very narrowly. In fact, the majority of states have specific statutes which provide that no privilege will be recognized except those that are set forth in their statutes. The student should refer to his state's rules on evidence to ascertain exactly which privileges are in existence in his own jurisdiction.

A privilege is said to be personal in nature in that it may only be used by the holder of the privilege, meaning the person whose interest or relationship the statute seeks to protect, such as a husband-wife, doctor-patient, or client-attorney relationship. Thus, the holder of the privilege is the only person who may now raise that privilege in court. But, if he is not present at the time of the hearing in court, then any party may bring to the court's attention that the testimony about to be introduced is subject to a privilege. The court will then generally exclude the testimony. When the privilege is held by a third-party witness (a party not in the case at present), it is up to the testifying witness himself to claim that privilege, as no one else will do it for him.

Most privileges will survive the death of the holder of the privilege, meaning that the privilege may be asserted after death by the person in charge of the estate of the deceased. There are exceptions to this. For instance, confidential communications between husband and wife will terminate in most states when one of the parties to the marriage dies.

In order for a person to claim a privilege, it is necessary that he prove that a communication which is privileged was made in confidence. *Example:* A man goes to his home and makes a statement to his wife that he has just committed a crime. In order for the husband-wife privilege to be asserted in court, it must be shown that he made this communication to her in confidence, relying on the marital privilege. Many states, however, today have a presumption that any communication made during a privileged relationship has been made in confidence and will be excluded if the privilege is asserted.

If a privilege is asserted, the majority of courts in the United States recognize that no inferences can be drawn from the fact that a witness claimed this privilege, either prior to or during the trial. Thus, the counsels and the judge are prohibited from making any comments or arguments to the jury based on the fact that the person refused to testify due to asserting a privilege.

A privilege may be waived if it is not raised by an appropriate and timely objection when the testimony is first offered into evidence. The objection must be specific, for the general objection as to it being incompetent, irrelevant, and immaterial will not suffice.

Any person who holds a privilege may waive such privilege by consent, either in a contract or by voluntary testimony by the holder of the privilege during the trial, or by a voluntary disclosure of the majority of the privileged communication to a third person.

There are many views in the United States as to whether an eavesdropper to a privileged communication can testify to what he overheard. One view holds that the eavesdropper can testify to what he overheard whether or not his overhearing was due to the carelessness of the privileged parties. The more modern view is that the holder of the privilege still may assert that privilege as long as he did not make a voluntary disclosure to a third party. Under this latter view, the eavesdropper would not be permitted to testify. *Example:* A husband is making a confidential communication to his wife. Unbeknownest to them, a person standing outside the closed door overhears the conversation. Under the old view, the eavesdropper could testify, whereas under the modern view, as long as it was not reasonable for the husband and wife to anticipate the eavesdropper's presence, the eavesdropper would be prohibited from testifying.

Husband-Wife Privilege

The husband-wife privilege, which has been in existence for many years, is based upon a strong public policy to have marital harmony in the home and not allow one spouse to come to court and testify against the other. There are really two different types of exclusionary rules to be concerned with under this privilege: (1) a rule prohibiting one spouse from testifying against or for the other party and (2) the husband-wife privilege prohibiting either spouse from revealing confidential communications made during the marriage. It is necessary under both of these situations to prove that there was and is a valid marriage in existence between the parties.

Spouses Testifying For or Against. In early common law, both husband and wife were disqualified and held to be incompetent witnesses. Thus, they could not testify for or against the other spouse in either a criminal or civil trial, the reason being that if one spouse was permitted to testify for the other, he/she would obviously be biased or would perjure himself/herself, and to allow one to testify against the other would disrupt the marital harmony in the home. The modern rule which has been adopted in a majority of states rejects the common law rule as far as allowing a spouse to testify for the other spouse in either civil or criminal cases as long as the party is an otherwise competent witness. A common law rule is still generally used, however, in prohibiting testimony by either spouse to be utilized against the other in a criminal trial.

The modern rule today is that the privilege may be asserted to prevent the husband and wife from testifying in the present case and also to exclude any previous testimony given in any other proceeding.

There are divergent views today on who may assert the husband-wife privilege. Some courts hold that the privilege belongs to the defendant spouse, in which case the witness spouse may be forced to testify if the defendant spouse fails to object. The general rule, however, is that the privilege belongs to both husband and wife, and even if the defendant spouse consents, the witness spouse may still refuse to testify against the defendant spouse. The minority view, on the other hand, is that the privilege is held by the witness spouse, and if the witness spouse desires to testify even though the defendant spouse objects, the testimony will be introduced under the rationale that if one spouse wants to testify against the other, there is not much of a marriage left to protect.

The husband-wife privilege may only be asserted during the time of the marriage and thus terminates upon divorce or annulment, in which events each party can be compelled to testify against the other. Quite often a problem arises when a person marries the prosecution's star witness prior to the commencement of the action in order to bar that person's testimony at the trial. In this case, there are some jurisdictions that will still assert the husband-wife privilege and will not allow one married spouse to testify against the other. However, the more modern view is that if the marriage took place after the commencement of the proceedings, the privilege does not exist, and the one spouse can be forced to testify against the other.

There are certain circumstances where the husband-wife privilege is held not to exist due to acts of the spouses themselves, such as when (1) one spouse commits a crime against the other spouse or against the property of the other spouse; (2) one spouse commits a crime against the children of either one of the spouses; or (3) one spouse violates certain types of penal statutes (e.g., the Mann Act concerning the transport of a female across a state line for immoral purposes or the importation of aliens for purposes of prostitution).

Spouses Divulging Confidential Communications. The common law rule prohibiting husband-wife testifying as to a confidential communication is still followed in the majority of jurisdictions in the United States. The common law rule states that neither spouse can be examined as to any confidential communication made by either husband or wife during the marriage without the consent of the other party to the communication. The rule requires that a communication be made between the two parties, that no third party is present, and that the subject matter is such that the spouse who is making the communication would most likely desire that it be kept secret. As previously stated, most jurisdictions have a presumption which states that a communication made during the time of a marriage is presumed to have been intended as confidential. If a person objects to this claim of privilege, he then would have the burden of proof to show that the communication was in fact not confidential or privileged.

Frequently, a problem arises in which a husband or wife makes observations of the other spouse which they desire to introduce into trial. The general rule is that there is no husband-wife privilege as to one spouse's observations of the other spouse concerning physical and mental conditions or actions of any conduct of the other spouse, since there is no communication involved. Some of these jurisdictions, however, hold that an act on the part of the husband or wife is a communication and is thus privileged. *Example:* A wife observes her husband come home late one night and unload 20 large television consoles into the garage and cover them with a tarpaulin. Some jurisdictions would hold that this observation is a communication and privileged, while an equal number hold the opposite.

This confidential communication privilege may be asserted in any action either civil or criminal and the privilege does not terminate when the marriage is dissolved or by death of either party.

Attorney-Client Privilege

The holder of the attorney-client privilege is the client. This privilege allows the client to keep his attorney from disclosing any confidential communications that he made relating to the rendering of his services as an attorney. This privilege is usually recognized in all types of proceedings, both civil or criminal. In a minority of states, however, its use is limited to criminal trials.

Before the attorney-client privilege can be asserted, it must be shown that the person was a client of the attorney, and that the communication had to do with a professional consultation with or a seeking of professional advice or opinion from the attorney. It also must be shown that the communication was made to a member of the bar, or to his secretary or law clerk for communication to him. However, there are some jurisdictions that hold that as long as the client reasonably felt that he was talking to a lawyer, even though it turns out that he was not, the communication will be privileged.

Frequently, an enforcement officer encounters the situation in which a client turns over to his attorney items of real evidence, such as books, records, or papers, and the attorney says that a privilege exists which denies law enforcement officers access to these items. In this area, the courts have held that items given by a client to his attorney will be privileged only if they are intended to provide information to the attorney. When the attorney is merely acting as a custodian, or holder, of the item, there is no privilege to assert. On the other hand, the courts have consistently ruled that real evidence (such as the suspected gun or knife utilized in a crime or books) which has been turned over to the attorney is not a communication, and thus is not protected by this privilege. The attorney may be forced to turn over such evidence.

Due to strong public policy, the attorney-client privilege is held not to apply where a communication has been made to the attorney concerning a proposed crime about to be committed or to be committed in the future by the client. There is no privilege in existence as to a communication made from a client to an attorney which enables that client to commit a crime or a fraud. *Example:* A man who intends to set up a narcotics smuggling ring goes to an attorney seeking his advice on how to protect himself from getting caught and on how to insure his release if he does get caught. As no crime has yet been committed, no privilege exists, and the attorney would be forced to testify concerning this communication.

Doctor-Patient Privilege

The doctor-patient privilege, not in existence during common law time, is a modern-day, statutory-type privilege based upon the public policy that encourages a patient to fully disclose to his physician all factors so that the physician may properly treat him. The holder of the privilege is the patient, whether or not he is a party in the present action. The holder himself may refuse to disclose, and may prevent the doctor from disclosing, any information that was acquired by the doctor in confidence from him.

The doctor may be compelled to testify if the patient has waived the privilege. Also, the doctor may assert the doctor-patient privilege if the patient is not present.

The majority of states only permit use of the doctor-patient privilege in civil cases. Thus, if a doctor's testimony is necessary in a criminal proceeding, there is no privilege in existence, and he may be forced to testify.

In order for the privilege to be asserted in the proper case it must be established that the doctor consulted was licensed to practice. Again, as in the attorney-client privilege, some states still hold that the doctor-patient privilege applies as long as the patient reasonably thought the person to whom he was making this communication was a licensed physician. It also must be established that the subject matter which was disclosed by the patient is normally needed for treating a medical matter.

Many jurisdictions today are also creating psychotherapist, psychiatrist, psychologist, or social worker privileges under the doctor-patient privilege. The same rules as discussed here will apply in jurisdictions having these privileges.

Priest-Penitent Privilege

The priest-penitent privilege was not a common law privilege, but instead is a modern-day statutory privilege utilized in the majority of jurisdictions and under the Federal Rules of Evidence. A person who has made a confidential communication to a clergyman (not just a priest) may prevent that clergyman from disclosing any confidential communication he has made as long as the clergyman was consulted in his professional capacity as spiritual advisor.

This privilege may be asserted by either the preacher or the penitent in either a civil or criminal case. The student should consult the statute in his jurisdiction, as there are still a few states which only limit this privilege to the contents of a confession made to a priest. However, regardless of the rule in existence, communications are the only things that are privileged under the priest-penitent statutes. Any observation made by the preacher is not privileged, and he may be forced to testify to it.

Governmental Official Privilege

The governmental official privilege was in existence under the common law, but has been expanded greatly during modern times. If the disclosure of any information is forbidden by any state or federal law, the privilege is absolute and no court may force disclosure. The federal, state, county, or city government has a privilege to refuse to disclose official information and to prevent any other persons from disclosing this information if they can show that the disclosure is against the public interest.

The privilege applies generally to state secrets, meaning information which, if disclosed, would be detrimental to the national defense or international relations of the United States. Any confidential or official information which would relate to the internal affairs of the federal, state, city, or county government may be privileged if the judge determines that the public interest would only be protected in preserving the confidentiality of the material or source of information in this specific case. *Example:* If it appears that disclosure of reports of police agencies, personnel reports, grand jury proceedings, etc., would undermine the public safety or would cause embarrassment, such information may be excluded from evidence in court.

The trial judge is given a wide latitude in deciding whether or not there is a state secret in the present case, in which instance the privilege would apply. The judge will generally hold what is called an *in camera* (off-the-record) hearing in order to determine whether or not there is a privilege in existence. At this type of hearing, only the governmental official and his attorney will appear in the judges chambers, and no record will be made of the hearing.

If the judge determines that he does not believe a state secret is in existence or is necessary to protect, and the government still maintains that there is a privilege, the judge may either strike the testimony, declare a mistrial, or dismiss the prosecution.

Identification of Police Informers

Today, the police officer is recognized as having a privilege to refuse to disclose the identity of any informant who gave him information which led to the arrest and prosecution of a defendant. Again, the court will hold an *in camera* hearing as to whether or not by invoking the officer's privilege the constitutional rights of the defendant will be impaired. The judge will determine in this hearing attended by the prosecutor, the police officer, and the judge if the informant was a material witness to the crime. If he was, his identity must be disclosed or the charges dismissed. If there is any question as to whether the informant was a material witness (i.e., witnessed the crime), the judge must resolve the problem in the defendant's favor. Thus, the defendant need only establish a reasonable probability that the informant may have evidence which could in fact exonerate him from the crime.

The most common example, however, is where the informant was not a witness to the crime, but only gave to the police information upon which they based their investigation, which in turn provided them with probable cause to either arrest the defendant or search his property. In this case, the failure of the police to identify the informant does not interfere with any constitutional right of the defendant, and the privilege may be asserted. As long as the trial judge is satisfied as to the reliability of the informant, the defendant will not be allowed to attack the legality of the arrest or the search on the grounds that the police refused to identify the informant for him.

Newsman Privilege

The privilege of a newsman is another statutory privilege which was not recognized at common law. In fact, it is currently recognized only in a few states under the new Federal Rules. In those jurisdictions that recognize this privilege, the privilege applies to a publisher, editor, or reporter, and states that they may not be compelled to disclose the source of any information which they publish.

Some jurisdictions hold that a newsman does not have a privilege, but only holds a right not to be adjudged in contempt of court should he refuse to divulge his source. This right, however, may be revoked at any time in the interest of justice.

The United States Supreme Court held in Branzburg v. Hayes, at 408 U.S. 665, that in the absence of a statutory protection, a newsman has no privilege to withhold the sources of his news stories, at least in a criminal prosecution. The Court further stated that the free-press claim is outweighed by the public interest in enforcement of its laws.

Privilege against Self-incrimination

The United States Constitution in the Fifth Amendment states that "no person shall be compelled in any criminal case to be a witness against himself." This Fifth Amendment restriction against self-incrimination is applicable to federal court and state court proceedings through the due process clause of the Fourteenth Amendment, as the United States Supreme Court held in Malloy v. Hogan in 378 U.S. 1. This privilege may be utilized either by the accused in a criminal proceeding or by any witness called to testify.

Confessions

A confession is a statement by a person accused of a crime to the effect that he is guilty of the crime. It is a declaration of the defendant's intentional participation in the criminal act and must implicate the defendant on each and every element of the crime involved. An admission, by contrast, is merely an acknowledgement of some fact or circumstance which only tends to prove guilt. Whether a statement is an admission or a confession depends upon a careful analysis of that statement. For the most part, the legal requirements for taking and preserving an admission parallel those for taking and preserving a confession. Where the laws differ, these differences will be noted.

Admissibility of Confessions

Requirements of Due Process

Under the due process clause of the United States Constitution, in order for a confession to be admissible, it must be voluntary; it must be knowingly made, and the accused must exercise "mental freedom" in deciding to confess.

There are several reasons why coerced confessions are not allowed into evidence: (1) Coerced confessions are frequently untrustworthy. If a suspect is subjected to sufficient pressure, he may confess merely because he fears a possible conviction less than he fears the consequences of a continued refusal to confess. Under such circumstances, a confession is merely another way of saying "uncle." (2) There is a social policy that the police must obey the law while enforcing the law and that life and liberty can be as much endangered from illegal methods used to convict those thought to be criminals as from the acts of the criminals themselves. Denying law enforcement agencies any benefit from the coercion of confessions is thought to be a deterrent for such police practices. (3) Where evidence has been obtained in a fundamentally unfair manner and in flagrant violation of the rights of an accused, the courts feel that their own integrity is compromised if they allow confessions so obtained into evidence.

In determining whether a confession is voluntarily given, the "totality of the circumstances" surrounding the giving of the confession will be examined very carefully. While the voluntariness of the confession will be determined from the facts of each case, the following factors are generally relevant:

Physical Setting of the Interview. Clearly, if the suspect were to be interrogated in a dungeon, surrounded by instruments of torture, few courts would claim that his confession was voluntary. Less extreme circumstances may cause the court to come to the same conclusion. If, for example, the accused is held incommunicado, placed in handcuffs, set before bright lights, and surrounded with officers in a padded cell, the court might well find that the setting was "inherently coercive."

Again, the effect of each of the preceding factors would have to be carefully weighed. For example, the mere fact that a defendant is held incommunicado is not in itself sufficient to render a confession inadmissible. If, however, he is confronted with a threat of contained incommunicado detention, and is induced by the promise of communication or access to his family if he confesses, the court would likely find the confession involuntary. Again, each factor will be scrutinized in light of the "totality of the circumstances."

Physical Abuse. It goes without saying that if a suspect confesses as a result of beatings or torture, his confession is involuntary. Likewise, if a suspect's will to resist is weakened by denial of food, elimination, or sleep, any confession will be considered inadmissible.

Threats. Not only actual abuse of a suspect, but also threats of abuse render a confession inadmissible. In the same category are threats to a suspect to expect heavier punishment or certain conviction unless he confesses. Any threat, in fact, which causes a suspect to confess to avoid the consequences threatened rather than because he wishes to confess of his own free will will render any confession inadmissible.

The threatened harm need not be directed toward the suspect himself. If officers threaten to arrest a relative or wife of the suspect, or to hold that person in custody unless the suspect confesses, any confession so obtained is involuntary. In one Supreme Court case, a woman was told that her children would be cut off welfare unless she confessed. The confession was held not to be "the product of a rational intellect and a free will."

Promises. If a suspect confesses because of a direct or implied promise made by a person who appeared to have official authority, his confession is not considered to be voluntary. For example, if the suspect confesses in response to a promise by an officer that the officer would "do whatever he could" for the suspect, or that the suspect would be set free or receive a lighter sentence, the confession would be inadmissible. On the other hand, a statement to the suspect that it would "probably be a good thing if he got what he had on his mind off his chest" is construed as relating only to the defendant's personal relief rather than any benefit he might receive in the court of law. Likewise, statements by officers to the effect that they have the "goods" on the suspect and that "he might just as well come clean" are not considered to imply that the defendant will benefit if he confessed. In addition, the fact that the suspect hopes to gain some advantage, such as a lighter sentence, by confessing does not affect the admissibility of the confession as long as this hope was not induced by people in apparent authority.

Confronting the Defendant with Evidence. There is no impropriety in confronting the defendant with evidence against him, particularly in advising the defendant of the existence of a confession by a codefendant, provided that the evidence was obtained legally and that the defendant's will is not otherwise overborne. If, however, the evidence is particularly grisly, such as a corpse or skeleton, confining or threatening to leave a timid or superstitious defendant in a room with the evidence might well be held to be coercive tactics.

Confronting the Defendant with Untrue Evidence. It is not improper for law enforcement officers to tell a suspect that they have evidence against him which they do not in fact possess in hopes of making him believe that continued denials are futile. These representations must not, however, be of such a nature as to cause an innocent suspect to confess. For example, it has been held proper to falsely inform a suspect that his fingerprints were found at the scene of the crime or on the getaway car, or that he was seen at the scene of the crime, or for an officer to pick a number out of the air and comment to the defendant that, "It is our understanding that you got $240 from the robbery."

Prolonged Questioning. The mere fact that a defendant is questioned over a long period of time does not in itself render a confession inadmissible. Cases which have held that lengthy interrogations rendered a confession involuntary have also involved additional factors, such as the preceding. In one Supreme Court case, for example, the suspect was continuously questioned for 36 hours and was therefore denied sleep and rest. In another case, an epileptic woman was confined with drunks and psychopaths and repeatedly questioned for several days. Thus, while it is proper to engage in lengthy interrogation of the suspect, the interrogation should not be calculated to physically weaken the suspect or overbear his will to resist demands to confess.

Miranda Warnings. Even though the Miranda warnings may not be required in a given situation, the fact that the warnings are given anyway can be used as evidence that the suspect's statements were voluntarily given.

If improper methods are used to induce a suspect to confess, every subsequent confession is involuntary and inadmissible unless it clearly appears that the improper tactics did not influence the suspect, so that his confession was free and voluntary. The prosecution must demonstrate that effects of the improper influence were so diminished that there is no causal connection between them and the subsequent confession.

Mental or Physical Condition of the Suspect

If for any reason the suspect lacks the mental capacity to understand what he is saying and what he did, his confession is inadmissible. Particular problems are discussed below.

Suspect under the Influence of Drugs. If law enforcement officers administer "truth serums" to obtain a confession, the confession is inadmissible. If, however, the defendant is intoxicated by means of drugs he administered to himself or is suffering from withdrawal symptoms, his confession will be admissible, providing the confession is otherwise free and voluntary and the defendant knows and understands what he is saying.

When police have reason to believe that a suspect is under the influence of some drug, they should note this fact in their report and carefully observe the suspect's behavior, noting especially whether his answers are rational and responsive and whether he appears to be alert or in a stuporous condition.

Suspect under the Influence of Alcohol. The rules relating to a suspect under the influence of drugs are equally applicable to alcohol.

The Insane Suspect. If the suspect lacks the mental capacity to understand what he is doing, his confession is inadmissible. On the other hand, the fact that the suspect is of below average intelligence or has less than average emotional stability does not affect the admissibility of his confession. Again, law enforcement officers should make careful note of the behavior of the suspect with an eye toward rebutting a possible claim of incapacity. Where it is suspected that such a claim may be made, an investigation of the suspect's background should be made.

The Youthful Suspect. A minor has the capacity to make a voluntary confession if he has the capacity to know what he is saying. The court will consider such factors as his age, intelligence, education, and experience in evaluating whether the minor has the ability to make a voluntary confession. Furthermore, the minor is competent to confess irrespective of the desire of his parents. The age of the suspect will, however, be taken into account in considering whether other possibly coercive elements had the effect of rendering the confession involuntary.

Statement Taken after an Illegal Search

As was mentioned before, when a suspect confesses because of confrontation with illegally seized evidence, the confession is inadmissible. The confession is deemed the "fruit of the poisonous tree," or an exploitation of the illegal search. Where one suspect is induced to confess because he is confronted with another's confession, which in turn was induced by confrontation with illegally seized evidence, both confessions are inadmissible.

Illegal Arrest or Detention

When a suspect confesses after an illegal arrest or while being illegally detained, the confession is not always inadmissible. The prosecution may be able to prove that the confession was nonetheless voluntary. The very fact of an illegal arrest is, however, a significant factor and renders it difficult to prove that the suspect's statement was the product of his own choice and not that of illegal restraint.

Delay in Arraignment

Under California law, statements taken from a defendant after the time when he should have been arraigned are not necessarily inadmissible, although this delay in arraignment is a factor in determining whether the statement was voluntary.

Confessions Taken from Those Charged with a Crime

After a suspect has been formally charged with a crime in an information or indictment, he has the right to have counsel present at any time he is being questioned. It does not matter that a confession is voluntary. Officers should contact counsel and not rely solely on a waiver of Miranda rights.

The right to the presence of counsel at such an interrogation may not be evaded by means of undercover police agents whose function is to engage the unsuspecting suspect in conversation and later report incriminating statements at trial. (However, it should be noted that it is proper to obtain confessions from a suspect by means of undercover informants before he is formally charged in an information or indictment).

Requirements of Miranda v. Arizona

Even if all of the preceding requirements are met, however, the admissibility of a confession is not assured. In certain cases, the requirements laid down in Miranda v. Arizona, 384 U.S. 436 (1966), must also be complied with. The purpose of this discussion is to provide some guidelines concerning when the requirements of Miranda apply and what is necessary to comply with those requirements. It should be noted that this section is intended to define the present limits of the law and indicate when the advisement of Miranda warnings is absolutely necessary. Good police practice, however, is to give such warnings in any doubtful situation.

Custodial Questioning

If a suspect is in custody, Miranda warnings must be given. A suspect is in custody if he is physically deprived of his freedom of action in any significant way or is led to believe, as a reasonable person, that he could not leave freely. Whether a suspect is in custody can only be determined from a careful evaluation of all of the circumstances surrounding the questioning.

Clearly, if a defendant is under arrest, he is in custody. The defendant may, however, be considered to be in custody without a formal arrest. The following factors are important in determining whether or not a suspect is "in custody." This is not to say that any of these factors, standing alone, would lead a court to conclude that a suspect is or is not in custody.

Physical Restraint. If a suspect is in handcuffs, or being held by an officer, or in any other way physically prevented from leaving, it is likely he will be held to be in custody.

Statements of Officers. If a suspect is told by an officer that he is not under arrest and is free to leave at any time, this is a strong indication that the defendant is not in custody. If, on the other hand, the suspect is told that he is under arrest and is not free to leave, it is likely that he will be held to be in custody.

Place of Interrogation. While the place where a suspect is interrogated is important in determining whether he is in custody, it is not a conclusive factor. In general, though, if a suspect is questioned in jail or at a police station, the courts are much more likely to find that the suspect was in custody than if the interrogation had taken place in the familiar atmosphere of the suspect's home or on the street. It must be emphasized that these rules are not absolute.

In one case, the defendant was found not to have been in custody when he came to a police station voluntarily to secure the release of a vehicle which was found to be a stolen car. In another case, the defendant was held not to be in custody when he told the officer that he was a witness to a fight resulting in the victim's death, and the officer, not suspecting the defendant of any crime, asked him to come down and tell his story. Of course, if a defendant had been "booked" prior to his being questioned at the jail or the police station, it would indicate that he was in custody. Important factors are whether the surroundings are familiar to the suspect and whether the suspect is isolated from the outside world.

Recently, it has been held that the restraint which accompanies a stop for issuing a traffic citation does not amount to custody. If, on the other hand, the traffic stop leads to discovery of evidence of another, more serious offense, the continued detention of the suspect might well be considered "custodial" rather than the "insignificant, transitory" restraint incident to the issuance of a traffic citation.

Persons Present at Interrogation. If a suspect is questioned in the presence of members of his family or other friendly and familiar people, the questioning is less likely to be considered custodial. If, on the other hand, the defendant is led into a room and surrounded by policemen, it is more likely the court will find the defendant to be in custody because the suspect will not likely feel free to leave. Again, the suspect's reasonable conclusions concerning whether he is free to leave determines whether he is in custody, not the officers' intention to hold him or let him go.

Probable Cause to Arrest. Some cases seem to indicate that when an officer has probable cause to arrest, questioning of the suspect is custodial. *Narcotic officers' note:* If a defendant makes a statement to an undercover agent or informer, including an agent or informer "wired for sound," the statement will generally be considered not to have been made while the defendant was in custody because the suspect would not know he was speaking to an officer of the law. This result applies even where there is probable cause to arrest the suspect. Merely because there is probable cause to arrest does not mean that the suspect does not feel free to leave. The necessity of carrying on investigations even after enough evidence to arrest has been gathered justifies this rule.

Unrelated Charges. A defendant in custody on any charge is in custody even as to questioning concerning unrelated crimes. For example, if the suspect is in custody on a murder charge, he would not be considered "out of custody" for the purposes of questioning on a burglary charge.

Other Factors. The possible fact situations and combinations of factors which might lead a court to conclude that a given suspect is or is not in custody are potentially endless. The preceding factors listed are by no means exhaustive. Other relevant factors include the demeanor of the officers, the length of the questioning, whether the suspect had initially called the police, whether or not the suspect is arrested after the interview, and so forth. Again, all of the factors in a situation must be considered in determining whether or not the suspect was in custody.

Practical Tip. If Miranda warnings are not given prior to questioning, officers should carefully record in their reports any factors which would tend to indicate that a defendant was not in custody.

Investigatory Questioning

The court in Miranda stressed that Miranda ". . . is not intended to hamper the traditional function of police officers in investigating crime." If the questioning of a citizen can be characterized as "merely investigatory," it is unnecessary that the citizen be given Miranda warnings. The following situations are typical.

General On-the-scene Questioning. The court in Miranda stressed that "general on-the-scene questioning as to facts surrounding a crime or other general questioning of citizens in the fact-finding process is not affected by our holding." If officers arrive at the scene of the crime, and in attempting to ascertain what has occurred question someone at the scene, this will generally be considered "investigatory questioning" rather than "custodial interrogation." *Example:* An officer is confronted with three wounded persons covered with blood. The officer also sees blood on the living room floor. One of the persons points in the direction of the defendant and says, "He beat me." The officer asks the defendant, "What happened?" and the defendant says he has been shot by his wife. The officer later goes to defendant again and asks him "to tell (him) what happened." The defendant then makes an incriminating statement. In this case, the court would say something like:

> It was his duty as an officer to investigate, and he started his investigation, a general inquiry, with the routine question, "What happened?" At this time, the defendant was not under arrest; there is not the slightest evidence in the record that he was in custody or deprived of his freedom of action. At this point, the deputy was accusing no one; nor was he, through his single inquiry, "What happened?" carrying out a process of interrogations in an attempt to elicit incriminating statements from the defendant. The sole purpose of his question was to find out what had occurred; it is a justifiable type of routine inquiry designed to determine what actually happened, as a means of commencing an investigation. . . .

Statements Taken during Stop-and-frisk. If officers have properly stopped a suspect, they may question him for a short period to determine whether or not a crime has been committed without giving him Miranda warnings. Likewise, if the officers are conducting a lawful pat-down search, questions asked in order to determine whether or not a crime has been committed need not be preceded by Miranda warnings. *Example:* Officers, conducting a lawful pat-down search, find a knife and then feel a bulge in the defendant's shirt pocket. The officer asks, "Is this stuff?" The defendant replies, "Yes, I guess it is." This statement will be held admissible since it was part of the investigatory process undertaken for the purpose of determining whether the defendant had committed any crime. The court will also note the "momentary detention and questioning."

Corroborating or Disproving Information from Informants. Officers may usually question a suspect to corroborate an informant's information, where necessary to obtain probable cause to arrest without giving Miranda warnings. The questioning is usually considered "investigatory" at this stage. *Example:* The police question defendant following a child's accusation that the defendant had molested him. The defendant is not arrested for a day and a half after the conversations with the police. The court will hold that there was only a general investigatory questioning which did not require a warning:

> At the time the first two statements were elicited, all that the officers had was the story of the child and his identification. Considering the fertile imagination of children and the comparative unreliability of their recollection, it would be straining the situation to say that the investigatory stage had ceased and the process had become accusatory. . . . True, if a crime had been committed, there was at the time no suspect but appellant, but this does not mean that the officers were accusing him.

Interrogation

Even though a suspect is in custody, unless the officers interrogate him, Miranda warnings are not required. Just what constitutes interrogation is not entirely clear. Some cases suggest that any questioning of the suspect amounts to interrogation, while other cases suggest that something more than mere questioning is necessary.

Some cases indicate that mere statements by the police to which the defendant responds, as opposed to questioning which elicits answers, does not constitute interrogation. *Example:* An officer tells the defendant that the victim would like to know where his motorcycle is and would like to have it back. The court will hold that this did not amount to interrogation and that the defendant merely replied to a statement by the officer. Great care must be exercised in this regard. In one case, the suspect was confronted with a statement of an accomplice which required an explanation. The court held that this constituted a form of interrogation. As a practical matter, whenever officers intend to interview a suspect in custody concerning criminal activity in which they suspect he may be involved, Miranda warnings should be given.

As the following examples make clear, not all methods of obtaining evidence and information from a suspect amount to interrogation.

Routine Questioning. Asking a suspect for "routine information" having nothing to do with the circumstances of the crime does not amount to interrogation within the meaning of Miranda.

Conduct of the Suspect. Miranda warnings are unnecessary if officers are merely requesting a defendant to engage in some conduct, rather than to provide them with information.

Handwriting Exemplars. If officers merely request a sample of a suspect's handwriting so that it can be compared to other samples, this is not considered interrogation. The suspect is not being asked to provide any information, but merely to engage in conduct. Miranda therefore does not apply.

Lineups. A suspect need not, and should not, be given Miranda warnings prior to being asked to participate in a lineup.

Fingerprints. Like obtaining handwriting exemplars, requesting fingerprints does not require prior Miranda warnings.

Sobriety Tests. Miranda warnings are unnecessary whether the evidence of a suspect's drunkenness consists of the officer's observations of his performance in a field sobriety test, blood tests, breathalyzer test, or other tests of intoxication.

Voice Identification. A suspect need not be given Miranda rights prior to being required to repeat phrases so that his voice may be identified.

Nalline Tests. Like tests for blood alcohol, tests for narcotics do not require Miranda warnings.

Other Conduct of the Suspect. Again, if what the officers desire from a defendant is conduct and not statements, Miranda is inapplicable. For example, if the defendant is asked to try on a coat found at the scene of a homicide to see if it fits, or is asked to tie up a bundle of clothing with a knot to see if the knot is similar to an unusual knot in a cord around the victim's neck, Miranda warnings are unnecessary.

Volunteered Statements

The court in Miranda stressed that "volunteered statements of any kind are not barred by the Fifth Amendment and their admissibility is not affected by our holding today." A statement is "volunteered" when it is made by the suspect on his own initiative without solicitation, encouragement, or interrogation by an officer. For example, if a man walks into a police station and begins to confess to a crime, the officer need not stop him and administer Miranda warnings. Likewise, if a suspect is placed under lawful arrest and blurts out incriminating statements, Miranda warnings are unnecessary.

In cases where the suspect is volunteering the statement, officers should limit their questions to neutral inquiries intended to clarify the suspect's remarks. *Example:* If a man comes into a police station and says, "I killed her," and proceeds to relate the details of a homicide, officers could properly ask, "Whom did you kill?"

Officers should not attempt to obtain additional information from the suspect by means of such questions. For example, it would be improper for officers to ask, in the preceding case, whether the man meant to kill the woman, or premeditated the killing. A good technique is to allow a person volunteering a statement to say all he has to say. These statements will clearly be admissible. Officers should make notes of ambiguities or vague portions of the statement and ask neutral questions intended only to clarify the statement at the end.

Conversation Initiated by the Suspect

The situation in which a suspect volunteers statements should be contrasted to a situation in which a suspect initiates a conversation. If a suspect initiates a conversation, he is inviting questions and comments from the officer. If he is volunteering a statement, he may not be inviting questions or comments. Therefore, if a suspect initiates a conversation, the permissible scope of the officer's questions or comments is expanded. While the officer should not attempt to "grill" the suspect, he need not confine himself to neutral clarifying inquiries, but may engage the suspect in conversation.

When a suspect initiates the conversation, no Miranda warnings are required. Thus, for example, if a suspect is in jail and asks to speak to the arresting officer, statements made during a conversation with that officer are admissible despite the lack of Miranda warnings.

In order for this exception to apply, the conversation must truly be initiated by the defendant. If it appears that pressure was brought to bear on the defendant to initiate a conversation, either at the time or perhaps earlier, this exception will be inapplicable. In such situations, it is likely that the suspect would waive his rights anyway. Cautious practice indicates advising a suspect of his rights in such situations, especially since advising a suspect of his rights affords greater leeway to the officer in questioning the suspect.

Giving the Suspect a Chance to Explain

Under certain circumstances, it may be proper to allow a person under arrest to clear himself by providing an explanation of his activities. It would seem that this exception may properly be applied after Miranda, at least in those situations where the police do not have an air-tight case, i.e., where there is some reasonable expectation that the defendant may have a nonincriminating explanation of the evidence against him. In such a case, both the defendant and the police benefit from the explanation. The defendant may go free and the police may catch the guilty party at the earliest possible time. It seems clear, however, that where this exception is used to circumvent Miranda in situations where the police are really seeking a confession and have no expectation of any real explanation, the statements will be inadmissible. This exception, however, may not be used to render admissible every interrogation simply because it commences with some phrase such as, "Can you explain...."

"Lifesaving" Questions

Where at least one of the primary purposes of the questioning is to save a life (as in a kidnap case when the victim may still be alive), the courts have justified questioning which would otherwise require a warning and waiver of rights. In such a case, the interest in saving the life justifies the officers in not impeding their rescue efforts by informing the defendant of his Miranda rights.

The Interrogator

If the interrogation is conducted by one who is not a law enforcement officer, the fact that Miranda warnings are not given will not render the statements inadmissible. For example, if private guards interrogate a suspect that is detained while awaiting arrival of police, Miranda warnings are unnecessary. If however, officers in any way use someone who is not an officer to interrogate a suspect in custody, the interrogator will be considered an agent of the police, and the lack of Miranda warnings will render the suspect's statements inadmissible.

Adequacy of Miranda Warnings

When Miranda warnings are required, the following admonition and waiver, or an approved form closely paralleling it, should be given:

(1) You have a right to remain silent.
(2) Anything you say can and will be used against you in a court of law.
(3) You have the right to consult a lawyer before we talk to you and to have him with you while we talk to you.
(4) If you cannot afford to hire a lawyer, one will be appointed to represent you before any questioning, free of charge.
(5) Do you understand each of the rights explained to you?
(6) Do you want to talk about this case or not?
(7) Do you want a lawyer or not?

The law enforcement officer does not have to advise as to matters other than those stated in these warnings.

That a suspect is a hardened criminal or a lawyer who unquestionably knows his Miranda rights is no excuse for not giving him his Miranda rights. If such warnings are required, but not read, the suspect's statements will be inadmissible.

If a suspect contends at trial that he was not given adequate Miranda warnings, the officer may not merely testify that he "advised the defendant of his Miranda rights." Rather, the officer must state what rights he advised the suspect of and whether the suspect indicated he understood those rights and that he wished to waive them. Complete records of what was said by the officers and the suspect should be kept.

Repetition of Miranda Warnings for Subsequent Interrogation

Once a suspect has waived his Miranda rights and undergone one interrogation, need he be readvised of his Miranda rights upon a subsequent interrogation? The better practice is to repeat Miranda warnings prior to each interrogation. However, the cases presented indicate that one warning is sufficient to cover subsequent interrogations which are not too far removed in time and in which there are no significant intervening circumstances or changes of circumstances which would require a new admonition. Note, however, that a warning of Miranda rights prior to interrogation does not suffice to establish a waiver of the right to counsel at a subsequent lineup.

Waiver of Miranda Rights

The prosecution must establish that the suspect was advised of his Miranda rights and waived those rights voluntarily, knowingly, and intelligently. The best evidence that a suspect understands and wishes to waive his rights is that he expressly so indicates. The preceding sample admonition, therefore, includes questions to the suspect concerning whether he understands his rights and whether he wishes to waive them. In proper cases, however, circumstantial evidence that a suspect understands and wishes to waive his rights may be sufficient.

The waiver and statements do not have to be set down in writing and signed by the suspect. It is, of course, advisable that the suspect's statements be recorded.

Voluntariness of the Waiver

The factors considered before on the issue of whether a statement is voluntarily made are equally relevant to a determination of whether a suspect voluntarily waived his Miranda rights. If the court finds the suspect did not voluntarily waive his rights, the waiver is ineffective.

Invocation of Miranda Rights

Whether the conduct of a specific suspect indicates that he wishes to exercise his Miranda rights and remain silent or obtain an attorney is a question of fact to be decided on the basis of all of the circumstances of the case. Certain guidelines can, however, be given. The mere fact that a suspect refuses to give a written statement, insisting that his statement be oral, does not constitute an invocation of rights. A suspect's refusal to sign a waiver form is strong evidence that the suspect has invoked his rights. However, evidence that his reluctance pertains only to the *signing,* but not the waiver, may be sufficient to make the statement admissible. *Example:* A suspect has expressly stated orally that he is willing to talk to the police after being advised of his rights. This might be sufficient. Officers should ask the suspect whether he wishes voluntarily to waive his rights despite the fact that he is unwilling to sign a waiver form. The suspect's reply should be carefully noted.

A suspect's refusal to answer specific questions need not mean that he is invoking his rights and thus precluding questions on other matters. The cautious procedure would be to ask the suspect if he still wishes to talk about the case without an attorney.

A suspect's expressed intention to obtain the services of an attorney after interrogation does not amount to an invocation of his right to counsel during interrogation.

Officers may question the suspect to determine whether an ambiguous statement indicates a request for counsel.

Invocation of Rights and Instant Interrogation

As the court in Miranda said:

Once warnings have been given, the subsequent procedure is clear. If the individual indicates in any manner, at any time prior to or during questioning, that he wishes to remain silent, the interrogation must cease. At this point he has shown that he intends to exercise his Fifth Amendment privilege. . . . If the individual states that he wants an attorney, the interrogation must cease until an attorney is present. At that time, the individual must have an opportunity to confer with the attorney and to have him present during any subsequent questioning. If the individual cannot obtain an attorney and he indicates that he wants one before speaking to police, they must respect his decision to remain silent.

The mere fact that an individual has requested an attorney does not obligate officers to provide one, or even to attempt to provide one. However, officers may not interrogate the individual in the absence of his attorney.

Invocation of Rights and Subsequent Interrogation

One California Supreme Court case may be interpreted to hold that where a suspect refuses to waive his Miranda rights but where the police nevertheless attempt again to solicit a waiver is "interrogation," and any statement the suspect gives is inadmissible. However, court of appeal cases have held that merely readvising the suspect of his rights without "compulsion, simple or otherwise," is not improper. The question is still unsettled.

Where, however, a suspect is originally arrested on one charge, which he refuses to discuss, and the police then learn that he may be involved in a completely separate offense, and where the initial arrest was not a subterfuge for holding the defendant with respect to the separate offense, and in the absence of coercive police tactics, the police may readvise the suspect of his Miranda rights and ask him whether he wishes to discuss the separate offense.

Change of Mind by the Suspect

If a suspect who has invoked his Miranda rights later decides, on his own initiative, without any prompting, coercion, or other undue influence by officers to change his mind and talk to the officers, there is nothing improper in officers' interrogating the suspect to the same extent as if he had initially waived his Miranda rights.

In order to insure against a later contention by the defendant that he did not intend to change his mind and waive his Miranda rights, or that he had forgotten his rights, or like contentions, both frivolous and meritorious, it is advisable for officers to readvise the suspect of his Miranda rights and allow him to expressly waive those rights.

Use of Statements Taken in Violation of Miranda Rules

The mere fact that a statement is taken in violation of Miranda does not mean that it is not usable for any purpose. The U. S. Supreme Court recently held that a statement taken in violation of Miranda may be used for "impeachment purposes," to prove that a witness is lying by introducing previous inconsistent statements. Also, statements taken in violation of Miranda may be used by the Adult Authority to terminate parole. Likewise, such statements may be used in probation revocation proceedings.

Recording of Statements

The complete and accurate recordation of the content of a suspect's confession as well as the circumstances surrounding the taking of his confession is of utmost necessity in admitting recorded statements into evidence. First, and most obviously, a confession sketchily or inaccurately recorded is of little use to the prosecution. Secondly, however the statement is recorded, officers will have to "authenticate" the evidence, i.e., to establish that the evidence is genuine and accurate. Finally, the prosecution has the burden of establishing that the confession was made freely and voluntarily, without coercion, threats, or undue pressure, and without promises of reward, immunity from punishment, or leniency, real or apparent, by those in apparent authority. While in most situations it is sufficient for the officer to merely testify that the confession was free and voluntary, if his testimony is challenged by contrary evidence, the officer will have to testify with particularity concerning the circumstances of the taking of the confession. It is, therefore, essential that officers include in their reports the circumstances of the taking of the confession and all evidence, including the demeanor of the suspect, to establish that the confession was freely and voluntarily given.

Methods of Recording

Written Statements. If a suspect's confession is reduced to writing and the suspect signs the confession, this document is admissible in evidence once the prosecution proves that the confession was voluntary. It does not matter that the confession was not transcribed in the defendant's own words, and it does not matter whether the confession is written in narrative form or is a transcript of a question-and-answer session.

Oral Statements. When the officers hear a suspect confess, they may testify concerning the content of his confession in court. No hearsay problem is presented because of a special exception for admissions and confessions. When an officer relies solely on his memory, he is "wide open" to cross-examination concerning the accuracy of his memory.

The best policy in preserving a defendant's oral statement is, of course, to ask the suspect to sign a report of the statement. The fact that he refuses to do so does not, however, make the confession inadmissible. It does, however, create evidentiary hurdles to getting the writing into evidence. Several methods of authentication are possible, and peace officers should be alert to the possibility of establishing a foundation for any or all of these methods.

Adoptive Admission. Written evidence of the confession may be admissible if the defendant read the statement and by his words or other conduct expressed his belief in its truth. This belief may be expressed either by positive statements or by gestures. Officers should carefully note a suspect's conduct with a view toward establishing the admissibility of the evidence and the suspect's statement as an adoptive admission.

Business Record — Official Record Exception. Written reports of the defendant's confession may be admissible as a business record. To be so admissible, officers must establish that (1) the officer wrote the report as part of his duty; (2) the writing was made soon after the confession or the contents of the confession are fresh in the officer's mind; (3) a qualified witness can testify to the identity of the writing and the mode of its preparation; and (4) the circumstances of the making of the writing indicate its trustworthiness.

Past Recollection Recorded. Sometimes an officer will record a suspect's statement but is unable to remember the statement at the trial. Written memoranda of the officer's recollection of the defendant's statement will be admissible in evidence if the officer can testify that (1) he has insufficient present recollection to enable him to testify fully and accurately concerning the defendant's confession; (2) the memorandum of the confession was made when the confession was fresh in the officer's memory; (3) the writing was made by the officer testifying or under his direction or by some other person for the purpose of recording the witness' statement at the time it was made; (4) the officer testifies that the report was a true statement of the confession; and (5) the writing is authenticated.

Present Memory Refreshed. The officer may, of course, testify concerning his recollection of what a defendant said. He may refer to his report of what the defendant said in order to refresh his memory. If he does so, he must produce the report at the hearing at the request of the defendant and should be prepared for cross-examination concerning the report. Production of the report is only excused if the officer no longer has the report and the report cannot reasonably be procured by any available means, including the use of the court's process.

Confessions Made through an Interpreter. A suspect's confession should be recorded in the language in which it was given. A translation made by an interpreter at the time the confession was given is not admissible, although an interpreter can translate the confession at the time of trial.

The interpreter may, in any case, testify as to his recollection of what the suspect said.

Sound Motion Pictures. Taking a defendant's confession by means of a sound motion picture is an excellent method of preserving a confession. Projecting a film at a trial and allowing a jury to watch the confession come out of the defendant's own mouth is much more effective and dramatic than introducing a piece of paper. If this method is used, officers should be prepared to testify both to the accuracy of the picture and to the voluntariness of the confession.

Confession Implicating Codefendant

If the defendant has given a valid confession implicating a codefendant, the confession is admissible against himself but inadmissible against his codefendant. In a joint trial, however, it would be impossible for the jury to ignore the effect of the confession insofar as it implicates the codefendant. In such a situation, the prosecution can either delete all reference in the confession to the codefendant, whether direct or indirect, or if this cannot effectively be done, can request a severance of trial. If neither of these alternatives is followed, the confession is inadmissible.

Courts have been fairly strict concerning what statements might indirectly implicate a codefendant. One case held that references to a car used in a robbery which belonged to the codefendant were improperly admitted because incriminating reference to the codefendant were inevitable.

It would seem good police practice, when taking a confession which implicates a codefendant, to also take a confession deleting any references, direct or indirect to the codefendant. Once a confession is set in cold type, effective editing may be impossible. The best time to do such editing is at the time the statement is given.

Summary

A witness' competency under the modern view is generally not in issue unless it is attacked by one of the parties to the action. Competency is generally concerned with the age, mental capacity, and the perceptory ability of the witness and his knowledge of a duty to tell the truth.

The opinion rule is concerned with a lay person's opinions or an expert's opinions. A lay person generally is permitted to give his opinion on the identity, physical and mental conditions of another, value of property which he owns, and dimensions and handwriting of another with whom he is closely acquainted. It need only be shown that any other reasonable man in the same or similar circumstances as the witness could have or would have formed an opinion concerning what the lay person is now testifying to. An expert, however, must be shown to have a special expertise in a certain area which will aid the jury in arriving at the truth of the matter in issue. If a lay person gives an opinion in the trial, it must be weighed by the jury, whereas, if an expert gives an opinion, the jury may totally disregard that opinion in its deliberations.

In presenting evidence at a trial, a party first takes a witness on direct examination in the form of narrative questions; questions calling for conclusions, questions which have been asked and answered, and leading questions are generally not permitted. The opposing counsel then is given the right to cross-examine the witness and generally may ask any type of question that is relevant in his examination. Under one view, the cross-examiner is limited to examining on matters brought out on direct exam, yet, under the more modern view, the cross-examiner is not limited and may bring up any relevant matter from the witness. After cross-examination is completed, the party who called the witness then has the opportunity to take the witness on redirect examination. Then, the opposing party has the right to recross-examine the same witness.

To impeach a witness merely means to attack that witness' credibility by showing a prior conviction of a crime, misconduct which has not resulted in a conviction, poor reputation for truthfulness in the community, hostility or bias, lack of perceptory ability, or by showing a prior inconsistent act or statement on the part of the witness. Once a witness has been impeached, the party who called him to the stand then has the opportunity to rehabilitate that witness by explaining the deficiency which was brought out in the impeaching evidence.

DISCUSSION QUESTIONS

1. What are the qualifications for being a witness in your jurisdiction?
2. Discuss the most common grounds for the discrediting of a witness in your jurisdiction.
3. Discuss the general competency rules as to persons with a diminished mental capacity and children of tender years.
4. What is the rule on opinions?
5. Discuss and distinguish between a lay person's opinion and an expert's opinion.
6. Of what may a lay person generally give an opinion in your jurisdiction?
7. Discuss the criteria for qualifying a person as an expert witness.
8. Distinguish between direct examination and cross-examination.
9. What is really meant by the phrase *impeachment of a witness*?

FARLEY v. COLLINS
Supreme Court of Florida, 1962.
146 So.2d 366.

THORNAL, JUSTICE. By a petition for a writ of certiorari we are requested to review a decision of the District Court of Appeal, Third District, which has been certified by that court as passing upon a question of great public interest. Collins v. Farley, Fla. App., 137 So. 2d 31; Art. V, Section 4(2), Florida Constitution, F.S.A.

We must determine whether an automobile collision constitutes a "transaction" within the contemplation of Section 90.05, Florida Statutes, F.S.A., otherwise known as "The Dead Man's Statute."

The factual situation is delineated in detail in the cited decision of the Court of Appeal which has been submitted for review. Farley, while driving a motorcycle, collided with an automobile then being driven by one, Dann, who was deceased at the time of the trial. Farley instituted an action for damages allegedly resulting from the collision. The action was brought against Collins as administrator of the estate of Dann. The trial judge permitted Farley to testify as to the movements of his motorcycle immediately prior to the collision. He also testified as to the movements of his motorcycle and the Dann automobile during the occurrence of the collision. The detailed testimony was set out in the opinion of the Court of Appeal in Collins v. Farley, supra. The administrator objected to the testimony on the ground that it related to a "transaction" between the plaintiff and a party deceased at the time of the trial. The trial judge overruled the objection and allowed the testimony. The Court of Appeal, Collins v. Farley, supra, reversed this ruling with a holding that the collision between Farley's motorcycle and the automobile of the decedent constituted a "transaction" between the two so that the testimony was inadmissible under Section 90.05, Florida Statutes, F.S.A. It is this decision which has been submitted for review.

The petitioner Farley contends that the fortuitous occurrence of a collision does not constitute a "transaction" within the meaning of the cited statute.

The respondent insists that the language of the statute is sufficiently broad to comprehend every type of occurrence between a testifying party and a deceased adversary. . . .

The pertinent part of Section 90.05, Florida Statutes, F.S.A., is as follows:

". . . no party . . . shall be examined as a witness in regard to any transaction or communication between such witness and a person at the time of such examination deceased. . . ."

At common law, no party or person interested in the results of litigation was permitted to testify. The interest of the witness was an absolute disqualification which precluded him from giving testimony. 58 Am.Jur., Witnesses, Section 169, page 120. In 1843 the disqualification of interested persons was removed in England by statute. 6 and 7 Vict. c. 85. In 1851 the disqualification of parties was removed by statute in England. 14 and 15, Vict. c. 99. Since then these disqualifying elements have been removed by statute in practically all of the states. The Florida statute, Section 90.05, supra, was enacted as chapter 1983, Laws of Florida, 1874. Its statutory predecessor in this country was enacted originally by the State of New York, and is now cited as Section 347, New York Civil Practice Act. To the extent, therefore, that the Florida statute and the New York statute are in harmony we would look to the New York decisions as a guide to our own conclusion. Adams v. Board of Trustees of the Internal Improvement Fund, 37 Fla. 266, 20 So. 266.

Although, admittedly, Section 90.05, supra, is in derogation of the common law, nevertheless to the extent that it removes the disqualification of a witness because of interest, it should be construed liberally for the reason that it is remedial in nature. 58 Am.Jur. Witnesses, Section 169, page 120; Texas v. Chiles, 21 Wall. (U.S.) 488, 22 Law Ed. 650; Nolan v. Moore, 81 Fla. 600, 88 So. 601. The objective of statutes which eliminate disqualifications is to expand the opportunities for making available previously excluded evidence. It has generally been concluded that the exclusion of the testimony of a party merely because of interest will more likely result in wide-spread injustices than would a rule permitting the testimony subject to traditional tests of credibility. On the other hand, the exception to the rule of admissibility which is comprehended by exclusions under the Dead Man's Statute is to be strictly construed. The restriction against admitting the testimony of an interested party in a cause against the representatives of a deceased adversary is a limitation on the remedial aspects of the statute which permits interested parties to testify. Hence, the language of the Dead Man proviso should be strictly construed and limited to its narrowest application. By applying this rule we reduce to a minimum the restrictions on the broader remedial statute. Day v. Stickle, Fla.App., 113 So.2d 559, 80 A.L.R. 2d 1291, cert. den. 115 So.2d 414; Harper v. Johnson, Tex.1961, 345 S.W.2d 277; Jones on Evidence (5th Ed.) Vol. 3, Section 774, page 1440; Wigmore on Evidence (3rd Ed. 1940), Section 578.

With a view to the rules of statutory construction and the historical background of the subject statute, we return to our consideration of the prime question which is whether the word "transaction" as used in the exception contained in the Florida Statutes, should be construed broadly to include an automobile collision.

This Court has recognized that the so-called Dead Man's Statute may in proper cases be applied to tort actions. In some of those cases a broad definition of the word "transaction" has been cited. Embrey v. Southern Gas and Electric Corp., Fla., 63 So.2d 258; Herring v. Eiland, Fla., 81 So.2d 645. However, as emphasized by the certificate of the Court of Appeal certifying the instant case to us, this Court has never been confronted squarely with the problem which challenges our present considerations.

Herring v. Eiland, supra, involved a suit by the guardian of an incompetent passenger against the driver of a vehicle in which the passenger was injured as a result of a collision. The trial court considered upon motion for a summary judgment the deposition of the defendant driver regarding the activities of the parties shortly preceding the accident, as well as his own actions and the speed and movement of his automobile immediately before the accident. On appeal this Court held that the occurrence of the accident allegedly resulting from the negligence of the driver was not such a "transaction" between the driver and his incompetent guest that would bar the testimony of the driver in defense of the claim asserted against him.

In Day v. Stickle, supra, a passenger in one automobile brought suit against a personal representative of the driver of another automobile involved in a collision resulting in injury to the passenger. The Court of Appeal which has certified the instant problem to us held that the injured passenger could testify regarding the circumstances of the collision. The Court correctly recognized the rule of strict construction applicable to the Dead Man's Statute. It held in summary that the collision between the automobile in which the injured plaintiff was a passenger and the automobile driven by the deceased whose estate was being sued did not constitute a "transaction" between the two.

Admittedly, there is a difference of view among the courts as to whether an automobile collision constitutes a "transaction" between the drivers of the two vehicles involved. Some courts adhere to the position that such a collision is a "transaction" and that the testimony of a surviving driver is inadmissible in an action against the estate of his adversary. In re Mueller's Estate, 166 Neb. 376, 89 N.W.2d 137; Countrymen v. Sullivan, 344 Ill.App. 371, 100 N.E.2d 799; Zeigler v. Moore, 75 Nev. 91, 335 P.2d 425. On the other hand, a number of courts have adopted the contrary view by limiting the Dead Man's Statute to its most restrictive interpretation. These courts construe the word "transaction" as requiring something in the nature of a negotiation or a course of conduct or a mutuality of responsibility resulting from the voluntary conduct of opposing parties. In this view a "transaction" results when one enters upon a course of conduct after a knowing exchange of reciprocal acts or conversations. We have the opinion that the latter view is the better view and should govern the instant case. In addition to the decisions which we shall cite, we are supported by the leading authorities on the rules of evidence. Jones on Evidence, Vol. 3, Section 774; Wigmore on Evidence (3rd Ed. 1940) Section 578. Recently, in Harper v. Johnson, Tex.1961, 345 S.W.2d 277, the Supreme Court of Texas, when confronted by a statute very similar to ours, held that a "transaction" involves a mutuality or concert of action. It does not include the circumstances "surrounding an involuntary and fortuitous collision between two motor vehicles driven by two complete strangers." To apply the statute to such a situation, said the Texas court, would be to extend the language of the Dead Man's Statute beyond the bounds of the rule of strict construction applicable to it. The court then directly held, as do we here, that the survivor of an automobile collision may testify as to his observations and may describe the physical situation and the movements of the vehicles prior to and at the time of the accident.

While the foregoing conclusion has not been reached without some difficulty, it appears to us to provide a rule more nearly consistent with the legislative intent as announced by the subject statute. It is also consistent with the policy of the law to make available all relevant evidence in its quest for the truth in any particular factual situation. The credibility of the testifying survivor who is under oath may certainly be evaluated by the jury and tested by cross-examination. In the ultimate, we agree with those courts which have taken the position that the exclusion of such testimony will work greater injustices by preventing recovery on legitimate claims as against the view that admissibility might result in the establishment of fraudulent claims against decedents' estates. The view which we have above announced is also supported by Knoepfle v. Suko, N.D., 108 N.W.2d 456; Rankin v. Morgan, 193 Ark. 751, 102 S.W.2d 552; Krause v. Emmons, 6 Boyce 104, 29 Del. 104, 97 A. 238. In other decisions, although there was a slight difference in the language of the statute, we are of the opinion that the difference is not of controlling materiality and the result was the same as that reached by us here. Shaneybrook v. Blizzard, 209 Md. 304, 121 A.2d 218; Seligman v. Orth, 205 Wis. 199, 236 N.W. 115; McCarthy v. Woolston, 210 App. Div. 152, 205 N.Y.S. 507; Turbot v. Repp, 247 Iowa 69, 72 N.W.2d 565.

We, therefore, hold that the collision in the instant case did not constitute a "transaction or communication between" the surviving driver of the motorcycle and the deceased driver of the automobile. The testimony of the surviving driver of the motorcycle which was permitted in evidence by the trial judge, was not inadmissible under Section 90.05, Florida Statutes, F.S.A. The trial judge, therefore, ruled correctly in allowing the testimony. By the decision certified to us for review the District Court of Appeal committed error in reversing the trial court on this ruling.

The writ of certiorari having been issued, judgment of the Court of Appeal is quashed to the extent considered by the foregoing opinion and the cause is remanded to the Court of Appeal for further proceedings consistent herewith.

It is so ordered.

PEOPLE v. McCAUGHAN
Supreme Court of California, 1957.
49 Cal.2d 409, 317 P.2d 974, noted, 32 S.Cal.L.Rev. 65.

TRAYNOR, JUSTICE. A jury found defendant guilty of involuntary manslaughter (Pen.Code, § 192, subd. 2), and the court denied her motion for a new trial. Judgment was suspended, and defendant was admitted to probation for a term of three years on the condition that she serve one year in a county detention facility. Defendant appeals.

Defendant was a psychiatric technician at the state hospital in Modesto in charge of a ward of fifty mental patients. One of the patients in defendant's ward was Grace Belill, a 71 year old woman suffering from involutional psychosis, a mental condition that commonly causes a patient to refuse to eat. On October 12, 1955, a doctor at the hospital noted in Miss Belill's record that if necessary she was to be spoon fed. On October 14, 1955, at the noon meal, Miss Belill was not eating, and defendant spoon fed her. During the feeding the patient collapsed and shortly thereafter died. The cause of death was asphyxiation from the aspiration of stomach contents.

The gravamen of the charge against defendant is that she used improper methods and excessive force in spoon feeding the decedent. The People sought to prove that defendant's conduct constituted either criminal negligence or a misdemeanor and that the misdemeanor consisted of a violation of either section 242 (battery) or section 361 (treatment of insane persons) of the Penal Code. The jury was given instructions appropriate to each of the People's theories, including an instruction in the statutory language of section 361, and returned a general verdict of guilty. . . .

Defendant contends that the court erred in qualifying as competent witnesses several mental patients in the state hospital at Modesto. All of these patients were in the ward over which defendant had supervision, and some of them had histories of insane delusions relating to food and to persecution by hospital personnel. Much of the evidence most damaging to defendant is in the testimony of these patients. We deem it unnecessary to discuss the witnesses individually, for their testimonial qualifications may be changed at the time of a new trial and would have to be reexamined at that time. Our review of the record, however, indicates the desirability of our reviewing the rules governing the qualifications of an insane person as a witness.

Section 1321 of the Penal Code provides, with exceptions with which we are not here concerned, that the rule for determining the competency of witnesses in civil actions apply also to criminal actions. Section 1880 of the Code of Civil Procedure provides: "The following persons cannot be witnesses: 1. Those who are of unsound mind at the time of their production for examination. . . ." This section, however, does not impose an absolute disqualification on insane persons. As was said in People v. Tyree, 21 Cal.App. 701, 706, 132 P. 784, 787, "The statute does not undertake to prescribe or define the amount or degree of mental unsoundness that must exist in order to disqualify the witness, but the reason for the existence of such a statute should be invoked, and we interpret that reason to require that the witness should have some apprehension of the obligation of the oath, and that he shall be capable of giving a fairly correct account of the things he has seen or heard, and this test should be made with special reference to the field of inquiry and character of the subject on which the witness is to give testimony."

The question to be determined is whether the proposed witness's mental derangement or defect is such that he was deprived of the ability to perceive the event about which he is to testify or is deprived of the ability to recollect and communicate with reference thereto. People v. Ives, 17 Cal.2d 459, 476, 110 P.2d 408; People v. Harrison, 18 Cal.App. 288, 294, 123 P. 200; see Wigmore on Evidence, 3rd ed., vol. 2, §§ 493–495, pp. 586–587. It bears emphasis that the witness's competency depends upon his *ability* to perceive, recollect, and communicate. (See Wigmore on Evidence, supra, § 478, p. 519.) Whether he did perceive accurately, does recollect, and is communicating accurately and truthfully are questions of credibility to be resolved by the trier of fact.

The language of section 1880 is addressed to the time at which a witness is produced for examination, and there is language in several cases suggesting that insanity at the time of the event witnessed is not a matter for consideration in the determination whether or not a proposed witness is competent to testify. . . . The rule is to the contrary. It is apparent from the requirement that the witness have the ability to give a substantially accurate account of the event witnessed (People v. Tyree, supra, 21 Cal.App, at pages 706–708, 132 P. at pages 786–787 and cases there cited; People v. Ives, supra, 17 Cal.2d at page 476, 110 P.2d at page 417) that he must have had the ability to perceive the event with a substantial degree of accuracy. Moreover, section 1879 of the Code of Civil Procedure requires as a general testimonial qualification the ability to perceive the event about which testimony is to be given. See, also, Wigmore on Evidence, supra, §§ 492–493, p. 586; Bradburn v. Peacock, 135 Cal.App. 2d 161, 164, 286 P.2d 972, construing Code Civ.Proc. § 1880(2); Code Civ.Proc. § 1845. It follows that if the proposed witness was suffering from some insane delusion or other mental defect that deprived him of the ability to perceive the event about which it is proposed that he testify, he is incompetent to testify about that event. Any implication to the contrary in the foregoing cases is disapproved.

It is universally recognized that the competency of a witness is to be determined by the trial court in the exercise of its judicial discretion. People v. Ives, supra, 17 Cal.2d at page 476. 110 P.2d at page 417; People v. Harrison, supra, 18 Cal.App. at page 295, 123 P. at page 295; see McCormick on Evidence, p. 123. Manifestly, however, sound discretion demands the exercise of great caution in qualifying as competent a witness who has a history of insane delusions relating to the very subject of inquiry in a case in which the question is not simply whether or not an act was done but, rather, the manner in which it was done and in which testimony as to details may mean the difference between conviction and acquittal. . . .

The orders denying a new trial and admitting defendant to probation are reversed. [For errors in the charge.]

STATE v. THORP
Supreme Court of North Carolina, 1875.
72 N.C. 186.

READE, J. The prisoner was charged with drowning her child in a river. A witness saw her going towards the river with a child in her arms. The witness said he knew the prisoner and identified her, he knew the child also, but he was one hundred yards off and was not sure who the child in her arms was. He was then asked if he recognized the child as the deceased? Which question was objected to by the prisoner and ruled out by the Court: for what reason we cannot conceive, as it was clearly competent. Possibly it was ruled out as being a leading question. The Solicitor then asked, "Is it your best impression that the child she had in her arms, was her son Robert Thorp?" The witness said it was. This question was objected to but was admitted. If the former question was leading, this was more so, but there is a more substantial objection to it.

It is true that in very many cases a witness may give "his impressions" or his "opinions" as to facts. Indeed memory is so treacherous, knowledge so imperfect, and even the senses so deceptive, that we can seldom give to positive assertions any other interpretation than that they are the impressions or opinions of the witness. Do you know when a certain act was done? I do. When was it? I think it was in January. Where was it? It was in Raleigh. At what place in Raleigh? I think it was at the hotel, it may have been at the capitol. Who did it? Mr. A. Was it not Mr. B? It was one or the other and my best impression is that it was Mr. A. All that would be proper, because the witness is speaking of facts within his knowledge and as he understands them. So if in this case the witness had been asked "Did you know the deceased child? Yes. Did you see it in the person's arms? Yes. Did you recognize it as the deceased? Yes, I think it was, that is my best impression." All that would have been proper. But we think the case presented to us will bear the interpretation that the witness said, "I saw the prisoner have a child in her arms. I was so far off that I could not tell what child it was, but I knew that she had a child of her own, and I suppose she would not have been carrying any other child than her own, therefore I think it was her own child. That is my best impression." And this was clearly improper. This was but his *inference* from what he saw and knew. And we suppose that any bystander in the Court who heard the trial might have been called up and he would have testified that his "best impression" was that it was her child, from the evidence. A witness must speak of facts within his knowledge. He knew that the prisoner had a child of her own, and he knew that she had a child in her arms, and these facts it was proper for him to state, but he could not go further and say, "from these facts which I know I infer that the child was her own, I am not sure but that is my best impression." This may not have been the sense in which he intended to be understood, but we think it will bear that construction. And in favor of life we so construe it. He certainly did not mean to say that he recognized the child as the child of the prisoner, and yet he knew her child very well. Why did he not recognize the child as he did the prisoner? Evidently because at that distance he could not recognize one child from another in the arms of the prisoner. It was probably but little more distinct than a bundle and he just took it to be her child because she had it in her arms. Probably this was all he meant by his "best impression." And it was error to allow it.

COMMONWEALTH v. CAVALIER
Supreme Court of Pennsylvania, 1925.
284 Pa. 311, 131 A. 229.

SCHAFFER, J. Counsel for appellant, prosecuting this appeal from a conviction of murder of the first degree, call to our attention the fact that at the time of the commission of the crime their client was a boy not quite 6 months past the age of 14 years, and contend that he was not mentally responsible for his crime; also that the record discloses trial errors, which should cause us to set the verdict aside. The killing was cold-blooded, premeditated, and atrocious, as the confession of the defendant discloses. Telling of its circumstances, he said:

"I was sitting out on the back porch when I first thought about killing my grandmother; she was out in the yard. I then went upstairs and got the 22 calibre rifle out of her room; also some cartridges. I then went downstairs and sat down in a rocking chair until she came in and went upstairs, then I followed her up about five minutes later. The door of her room was open and she was standing at the foot of the bed, sort of sideways. She did not see me, as I didn't make any noise going up the stairs. I was standing in the room next to hers in the doorway when I shot her the first time; I aimed for her head; she fell over on the floor. I stood there for a few minutes, then I walked into her room and fired another shot into her body as she was lying on the floor. I then searched her clothes and found her pocketbook in the pocket of her dress. I took the money out and threw the pocketbook in the closet of the room. I put the rifle back in the corner where she always kept it, went downstairs, locking the door of her room when I left it, putting the key in a little bowl on the shelf in the room next to hers. I put some toilet paper in her mouth as she was lying on the floor because she was moaning. She was taking off her shoes when I shot her. After I went downstairs I cut the screen in the kitchen window. After cutting the screen I shook the blood off my right hand onto the wall near the door, then I washed my hands and went out on the porch and sat down until my grandfather came home. I told him that grandmother went away. I left the house about half past 4 and went to my mother's home on First street and had supper and then went to the movies and after the movies went home and went to bed. Before going to bed I put the money in a pillow under the mattress." . . .

The defense attempted to be made for appellant is that he was mentally incompetent and insane at the time of the killing. To meet this defense the commonwealth called, among other witnesses, Dr. Albert P. Knight, who, in answer to a hypothetical question, gave it as his professional opinion that the defendant knew the nature and quality of his act, and could distinguish between right and wrong. It is urged that this doctor was not competent to express an opinion. The witness was a practicing physician, a graduate of the University of Pennsylvania, and at the time of the trial had been engaged in the practice of his profession for some 4 or 5 years. He was at no time connected with an institution having for its main purpose the treatment of mental diseases and had not seen very many cases of insanity. He had as a part of his medical education studied the subject of insanity, and would appear to have at least the general knowledge of the subject that the ordinary medical practitioner has.

The question of the competency of a witness to testify as an expert is usually for the discretion of the trial court. (Wharton's Criminal Law [11th Ed. 1912] vol. 1, p. 108, note; Delaware & Chesapeake Steam Towboat Co. v. Starrs, 69 Pa. 36, 41; Stevenson v. Ebervale Coal Co., 203 Pa. 316, 331, 52 A. 201), and we are not convinced that there was an abuse of discretion in receiving the testimony. "It is not necessary that one should be a professed psychiatrist or alienist, in order that his expert opinion may be received. A physician and surgeon who has come in contact with a number of cases of insanity in his general practice may express an opinion as to the sanity of the defendant." Trickett's Criminal Law (1908) vol. 2, p. 721. "A general family practitioner may be received to give an opinion, whatever may be its weight, as to whatever comes within the range of such practice." Wharton's Criminal Evidence (10th Ed. 1912) vol. 1, p. 841. It would be an impracticable thing to lay down a hard and fast rule as to how much experience a practicing physician must have had with insane persons to qualify him to speak as an expert. We think the determination of this question is wisely left with the trial judge, who has the witness before him, and is better competent than we are to judge of his capacity to express an opinion. 22 Corpus Juris, p. 526. The weight to be given his opinion is, of course, for the jury.

Challenge is made in the third assignment of error of the ruling of the court against the admissibility of the opinion of Carrie Walker, a witness called by the defense as to the sanity or mental condition of appellant. This witness was the matron of the House of Detention, where defendant was kept following the commission of the crime, and she had observed him daily during that period. She testified to certain facts concerning his conduct; that he would whistle, but never in tune; that he fought constantly with the other children in the Detention House, including those who were younger than himself; that, if she said anything to him, he would not disobey, but would walk upstairs and would not eat; that he did not show any remorse for his act; that he made faces at himself constantly in the mirror and made faces at her; that he told her he saw a ghost, which turned out to be a white garment in a closet. The court excluded her testimony as to the mental condition of the defendant, on the ground that the facts to which she testified were not sufficient upon which to base an opinion as to the mental condition of the defendant; that none of them nor all of them together indicated insanity.

While the cases in this jurisdiction may not be in accord on the question of the admissibility of the opinion of a nonexpert witness as to insanity or mental condition (see Wigmore on Evidence [2d Ed.] vol. 4, p. 138), and there are cases like Taylor v. Commonwealth, 109 Pa. 262, where it is said, at page 270, that the evidence of such witnesses is receivable after they have testified to acts and conversations which they deem sufficient to found an opinion upon, and that it is for the jury to decide whether the acts and conversations justified the conclusions, nevertheless we think the wise and proper rule is that such opinion testimony should not be received unless in the opinion of the trial judge the facts testified to were sufficient upon which to base an opinion. "But, when a [lay] witness is offered to express the opinion that the prisoner was sane or insane, he must state facts observed by him, that, in the judgment of the court, tend to justify the opinion which he is about to express. Having done this, he may say whether, in his opinion, the defendant was conscious of his purposes, but until he does it, his opinion is properly excluded." Trickett's Criminal Law, vol. 2, p. 724; Underhill's Criminal Evidence (3d Ed.) § 264; Commonweath v. Wireback, 190 Pa. 138, 145, 42 A. 542, 70 Am.St.Rep. 625; Commonwealth v. Marion, 232 Pa. 413, 423, 81 A. 423; Commonwealth v. Henderson, 242 Pa. 372, 378, 89 A. 567. The facts testified to by this witness did not, to the trial judge, and do not to us, indicate insanity in the defendant, but rather the actions of a bad boy; therefore the court properly excluded the opinion testimony of this witness. The ruling of the court as to another witness Robert Walker, husband of the preceding one, who testified to having observed the same acts of the defendant which were testified to by the wife, was proper for the reasons given in disposing of the contention relative to his wife's testimony.

We think, possibly, that much of the confusion in the cases may be ascribed to the failure to distinguish between different situations obtaining when witnesses are called to testify, on the one hand, that they have noticed nothing which leads them to believe that a person was of unsound mind, and, on the other, that in their opinion a person was insane. A lay witness, who has had contact with one whose mental state is the subject of inquiry, may testify, after stating his opportunities for observation, but without first stating all the facts justifying his conclusion, that he has observed nothing in the conduct or speech of the individual which would lead to the opinion that he is not of normal mind. Commonwealth v. Wireback, 190 Pa. 138, 145, 42 A. 542, 70 Am.St.Rep. 625. It is one thing to have lay witnesses thus testify and quite a different situation to have them give an opinion, after the recital of facts coming into their observation, that a person was insane. Commonwealth v. Marion, 232 Pa. 413, 81 A. 423; Commonwealth v. Henderson, 242 Pa. 372, 89 A. 567. In the latter case, if the facts testified to would not warrant the conclusion of insanity, it would be irrational to permit the witness to pronounce the conclusion. The jury, having the facts before them indicating no insanity, could not, except perversely, come to the conclusion that the given individual was insane. . . .

The judgment is affirmed, and the record is remitted to the court below for the purpose of execution.

JENKINS v. UNITED STATES
United States Court of Appeals, District of Columbia Circuit, 1962.
307 F.2d 637.

BAZELON, CIRCUIT JUDGE. Appellant relied solely upon the defense of insanity in a jury trial which culminated in his conviction for housebreaking with intent to commit an assault, assault with intent to rape, and assault with a dangerous weapon. He alleges that the

District Court erred in . . . (2) excluding diagnostic opinions of two defense psychiatrists on the ground that their opinions were without "proper basis." . . .

I. *The Facts* The record discloses the following pertinent information. After indictment, appellant was committed to the District General Hospital for a mental examination on September 4, 1959, to determine his competency to stand trial and his condition at the time of the alleged offense. Appellant was given a series of psychological tests on October 20 and 22, 1959, by staff psychologists under the supervision of the Chief Psychologist, Dr. Bernard I. Levy. Appellant scored 63, high moron, on the I.Q. section of the tests. He was also interviewed three or four times by Dr. Richard Schaengold, Assistant Chief Psychiatrist. Appellant's test performance and his "dullness and inability to relate correctly" led Dr. Schaengold to consider and reject the possibility of undifferentiated psychosis in favor of a diagnosis of mental defect: a basic, unchanging deficiency in brain function. His findings were confirmed by Dr. Mary V. McIndoo, District General's Chief Psychiatrist, on the basis of interviews on November 23, 24 and 25, and a review of appellant's history and test results. By letter of November 25, 1959, signed by Dr. Schaengold and countersigned by Dr. McIndoo, the District Court was advised that appellant was "suffering from an organic brain defect resulting in mental deficiency and impaired judgment. He is, therefore, psychotic, incompetent, and incapable of participating in his own defense." Appellant was adjudicated incompetent to stand trial on the basis of this report and was committed to "Saint Elizabeths Hospital until he is mentally competent to stand trial persuant to Title 24, Section 301, District of Columbia Code, 1951 Edition, as amended August 9, 1955."

At St. Elizabeths, Dr. Lawrence Tirnauer, a staff psychologist, administered another battery of psychological tests on February 25 and March 2, 1960, in which appellant scored 74 on the I.Q. section. Dr. Tirnauer concluded that appellant was suffering from schizophrenia. Thereafter Dr. David J. Owens of St. Elizabeths interviewed appellant several times, "probably [for] fifteen or twenty minutes," and saw him at a staff conference on October 3, 1960. Dr. Owens found no evidence of mental disease or defect. He classified appellant as "a borderline intelligence." Dr. William G. Cushard, another psychiatrist at St. Elizabeths, who saw appellant at the staff conference, reviewed the test reports and agreed with Dr. Owens' findings. Dr. Margaret Ives, Chief Psychologist at St. Elizabeths, was also present at the staff conference. Subsequently, she reviewed Dr. Tirnauer's test results and appellant's past history and administered one part of a six-part Szondi profile test. She agreed with Dr. Tirnauer that appellant "had a mental illness by name of schizophrenia."

Ten days later, the Acting Superintendent of the Hospital notified the District Court that "it has been determined that he [appellant] is, at this time, mentally competent to stand trial and to consult with counsel and assist properly in his own defense. He is not suffering from mental disease. . . . Although he is not suffering from mental deficiency, he has only borderline intelligence." Upon appellant's objection to this report, the court conducted a hearing on November 4, 1960, wherein appellant was found competent and ordered to stand trial.

In preparation for their testimony at trial, Drs. McIndoo and Schaengold noted the later and different diagnosis and the apparent change in appellant's I.Q. reported by the St. Elizabeths psychologists. They requested Dr. Levy of their staff to re-test appellant in order to reconsider their diagnoses that he was mentally defective on June 10, 1959, the date of the alleged offenses. This time appellant scored 90 on the I.Q. test, an improvement inconsistent with mental defect. In reporting this result, Dr. Levy, who had previously been unable to make a diagnosis, concluded that upon review of all test data appellant "is psychotic and schizophrenic." Considering this report in the light of the hospital record and "reports" from St. Elizabeths, Drs. McIndoo and Schaengold revised their previous diagnoses without seeing appellant again. Dr. McIndoo concluded that appellant was schizophrenic, and Dr. Schaengold diagnosed his condition as undifferentiated psychosis.

II. *Admissibility of the Psychiatrists' Opinions* The trial court, *sua sponte*, excluded the revised diagnoses of Drs. McIndoo and

Schaengold and instructed the jury to disregard testimony of the three defense psychologists that appellant had a mental disease when he committed the crimes charged.

We discuss first the exclusion of Dr. Schaengold's testimony. After questioning him at great length about the basis of his revised opinion, the court ruled: "All I will allow is that in his opinion on June 10, 1959 [the date of the alleged offenses], the defendant was mentally defective"; it excluded Dr. Schaengold's later diagnosis of mental illness because "there isn't any testimony here that is based on any proper evidence that he was suffering from a mental disease. I am not going to allow it on the basis of a report of a psychologist." The court gave no further explanation.

The Government suggests that the ruling rests on the familiar principle that an expert witness' knowledge of "basic facts" must be adequate to support his conclusion. It urges that the later psychological reports could not provide Dr. Schaengold with such information, "absent a personal re-examination of appellant," since thirteen months had elapsed between his personal examination of appellant and his revised diagnosis. The proposition seems to be that a psychiatric witness may not rely on psychological test reports unless he has considered them in conjunction with a contemporaneous personal examination. We are aware of no authority for such a rigid and artificial stricture.

Dr. Schaengold, whose expert qualifications were unquestioned, testified that he could arrive at a valid diagnosis on the basis of an earlier examination and later test reports. The court must be deemed to have rejected this statement. We find no basis for such action. We think it clear that Dr. Schaengold's ability to make the revised diagnosis without conducting a personal re-examination presents a question for the consideration of the jury, under appropriate instructions, in assessing the weight of his testimony and not a question for the court upon which it may rest exclusion of the diagnosis as a matter of law.

It is at least as likely, however, that the court predicated its ruling on cases which bar an expert's opinion based upon facts not in evidence unless it is derived solely from his own observations. But we agree with the leading commentators that the better reasoned authorities admit opinion testimony based, in part, upon reports of others which are not in evidence but which the expert customarily relies upon in the practice of his profession. The Wisconsin Supreme Court has forcefully stated the policy underlying the application of this rule to medical testimony:

"In order to say that a physician, who has actually used the result of . . . tests in a diagnosis . . . may not testify what that diagnosis was, the court must deliberately shut its eyes to a source of information which is relied on by mankind generally in matters that involve the health and may involve the life of their families and of themselves—a source of information that is essential that the court should posses in order that it may do justice between these parties litigant.

"This court . . . will not close the doors of the courts to the light which is given by a diagnosis which all the rest of the world accepts and acts upon, even if the diagnosis is in part based upon facts which are not established by the sworn testimony in the case to be true" [Sundquist v. Madison Ry., 197 Wis. 83, 221 N.W. 392, 393 (1928).]

The record in this case confirms the well-known practice of psychiatrists of relying upon psychologists' reports in aid of diagnosis. And it shows that Dr. Schaengold's changed diagnosis did not rest solely on the later test reports which were not in evidence when he testified, but also upon his own earlier examination. This diagnosis was "the type of clinical opinion he is accustomed to form and to rely upon in the practice of his profession. . . . Though [his] conclusions were not mathematically demonstrable certainties, neither were they mere conjectures, suspicions or hunches." Blunt v. United States, 100 U.S. App.D.C. 266, 275, 244 F.2d 355, 364 (1957).

It follows from the foregoing that the court's *sua sponte* exclusion of Dr. Schaengold's testimony concerning his changed diagnosis was error. Since the exclusion was clearly prejudicial, the conviction must be reversed for a new trial.

STATE v. PERKINS
Supreme Court of Appeals of West Virginia, 1947.
130 W.Va. 708, 45 S.E.2d 17.

Katherine Perkins was convicted of murder in the second degree and she brings error.

KENNA, J. Katherine Perkins was indicted by a grand jury of Wayne County for the murder of her husband, P. P. Perkins. She pleaded not guilty, was tried and convicted of murder of the second degree, and sentenced to imprisonment for a term of five to eighteen years. She brings the case here by writ of error.

On the evening of September 1, 1944, defendant, while riding in the automobile of a friend on Monroe Avenue in the City of Huntington, observed her husband in his automobile embracing a woman. At the request of defendant, the automobile was stopped, and defendant then went to the vehicle in which her husband and his companion were seated, and there engaged in a fight with the woman. The husband interfered in the struggle, enjoined defendant not to hurt his companion, and finally hit and kicked defendant several times. The defendant reentered her friend's automobile and returned to her home in the Town of Ceredo.

About ten o'clock p.m. of the same day, the husband returned to his home, and, according to defendant's testimony, he was angry and inclined to be violent. The quarrel between defendant and her husband was renewed and ended by the husband striking and kicking the defendant. After committing the second assault on defendant, the husband left his home and did not return until about midnight. . . .

On the morning of September 2, 1944, defendant prepared breakfast for a boarder, herself and her family. She and her daughter-in-law ate breakfast together, after which defendant went to the business section of the town for the purpose of paying a grocery bill. . . .

Defendant returned to her home, went to an upstairs bedroom, and began combing her hair. While doing so her husband came to the door; severely criticized defendant on her conduct in fighting the night before; said in substance that he was not further interested as he was leaving and started toward defendant, saying, "I will break your God damned neck."

The record is not clear as to what took place after the threat had been made by the husband. Defendant does not admit shooting her husband, but it is a reasonable inference, well supported by the facts, that she shot the deceased three times. One bullet entered his right shoulder, one about the middle of his right thigh, and another at the ninth dorsal vertebra. All bullets entered from the back. It is also a reasonable inference that defendant shot herself in the forehead, a pistol having been found near her body in the upstairs hall, and she was bleeding from a gunshot wound in her head. . . .

Defendant testified in her own behalf. At the commencement of her re-direct examination, her counsel asked one question, which she did not answer. At that time the judge of the trial court commenced to cross-examine defendant in the presence of the jury and asked, without permission, forty-one questions. It would unduly prolong this opinion to quote all the questions asked by the judge and answered by defendant. Such questions related to the ownership of the revolver, and also how the revolver came to be on the second floor when the room of the owner thereof was on the first floor. The cross-examination also elicited the fact that defendant had made the roomer's bed on the morning of the shooting; that deceased was shot three times in the back; and that defendant also suffered a gunshot wound.

After developing these two subjects, the judge of the trial court then asked defendant the following questions:

"Q. Mrs. Perkins, you have told the jury you had a blackout up there on the evening when you found your husband with this woman and you don't remember anything except what your husband did to you, is that right?"

"A. That is right, exactly right.

"Q. You remember everything that happened from then on until this shooting?

"A. Yes, sir.

"Q. You remember your husband standing with a flashlight in his hand and his gun in his hand?

"A. Yes, sir.
"Q. You remember that?
"A. Yes, sir.
"Q. Then you testified to the jury that you had a blackout from that time on, is that right?
"A. Yes, sir.
"Q. You don't know what happened?
"A. I don't remember anything that happened until late that evening in the hospital.
"Q. When that blackout struck you where were you standing?
"A. In the doorway.
"Q. Room No. 2?
"A. Yes, sir.
"Q. Where was he?
"A. In the hall.
"Q. Facing each other?
"A. Yes.
"Q. And you don't know how that gun which has been exhibited in evidence got there in the hallway and found there after you were shot?
"A. I don't remember ever having that gun in my hands.
"Q. You didn't have a blackout except on those two occasions, is that right?
"A. I don't understand what you mean.
"Q. You told the jury your mind was a blank at the time of the trouble with this woman, now you tell the jury your mind was a blank from the time your husband was standing there in the hall and you were in the room facing him.
"A. I guess I was so mad, I don't know anything else."

Thereupon defendant objected to the questions asked by the trial judge and rested her case. . . .

In this case the demeanor of the trial judge is not portrayed by the record, nor is it shown whether the questions were brusque or otherwise. But it suffices to say that the trial judge in this case conducted a vigorous, searching and sustained cross-examination of the defendant. Upon consideration of any single question, we could not say that there was prejudice. But upon consideration of the forty-one questions asked defendant by the trial judge, the conclusion is inescapable that the trial judge by such cross-examination of defendant in the manner here shown intimated to the jury his opinion upon the facts in issue.

We cannot say to what extent the minds of the jurors who tried defendant were influenced by the cross-examination conducted by the trial judge, but we must assume that if the trial judge indicated to the jury his belief in her guilt, such belief influenced the jury in arriving at its verdict.

We do not intend to say that a trial judge should not ask questions during the progress of a criminal trial at proper times and in a proper manner. Clarifying questions are necessary, but we see no occasion for the trial judge to take over the duties of a prosecuting officer.

In accordance with the foregoing we reverse the judgment of the Circuit Court of Wayne County, set aside the verdict, and award the defendant a new trial. . . .

STATE v. HORNE
Supreme Court of North Carolina, 1916.
171 N.C. 787, 83 S.E. 433.

Appeal from Superior Court, New Hanover County; Rountree, Judge.

Melvin Horne was convicted of murder in the first degree, and he appeals.

BROWN, J. The prisoner was convicted of the murder of D. L. T. Capps, and sentenced to death. On the trial the court of its own motion called as an expert witness one Dr. Stovall. The witness, after examination, was found by the court to be an expert. The question presented is whether or not a judge is at liberty of his own motion to call expert witnesses who are not desired either by the state or by the defendant. This is a matter within the sound discretion of the trial judge. He has the right to call to the witness stand and examine any witness who may be able to shed light upon the controversy. He should exercise this right with care, and should so conduct the examination as not to prejudice either party.

It has been the immemorial custom for the trial judge to examine witnesses who are tendered by either side whenever he sees fit to do so, and the calling of a witness on his own motion differs from this practice in degree and not in kind. This practice, in the case of ordinary witnesses, has been approved in some instances. Clark v. Com., 90 Va. 360, 18 S.E. 440; Hill v. Com., 88 Va. 633, 14 S.E. 330, 29 Am.St.Rep. 744; O'Connor v. Ice Co., 121 N.Y. 662, 24 N.E. 1092; 57 L.R.A. 875, note. This practice is especially allowable in the matter of expert witnesses who were originally regarded as amici curiae and were called generally by the court. 3 Chamberlayne on Evidence, §§ 2376, 2552.

The prisoner excepts to the following charge:

"The state relies to a considerable extent upon the testimony of Dr. Stovall, who, it appears, from the witness stand, was selected by the court to make an investigation of this defendant, and to take the stand and testify before you impartially as to his opinion upon the matter. The state calls your attention to the fact that Dr. Stowall gave an admirably lucid account of what he conceived to be, and his opinion of, the mental condition of the defendant."

The general tone of this commendation of the witness is much warmer and stronger than is consistent with that moderation and reserve of expression which is enjoined upon a trial judge. Powell v. Railroad, 68 N.C. 395; Withers v. Lane, 144 N.C. 184, 56 S.E. 855. While the learned judge had the right to call the expert witness to the stand, he had no right to throw into the jury box the weight of his own good opinion of the witness. It was well calculated to weigh heavily against the prisoner.

New trial.

UNITED STATES v. RICCARDI
United States Court of Appeals, Third Circuit, 1949.
174 F.2d 883.
Writ of Certiorari Denied 1949, see 337 U.S. 941, 69 S.Ct. 1519, 93 L.Ed. 1746.

KALODNER, CIRCUIT JUDGE. The defendant was indicted under 18 U.S.C. (1940 ed.) Sections 415 and 417 in four counts charging him with wilfully, unlawfully and feloniously having transported or having caused to be transported in interstate commerce certain chattels of the value of $5,000 or more. The first and third counts were dismissed, and the defendant was convicted on the second and fourth counts, from which conviction he appeals.

We are not here primarily concerned with the particular fraudulent representations which the defendant made. Rather we are called upon to decide the propriety of the method utilized at the trial to prove what chattels the defendant obtained and transported, and their value. In short, the principal question is whether the witnesses who testified to these essentials were properly permitted to refresh their memory. In addition, the defendant also asserts error in the acceptance of evidence relating to the transactions between the defendant and the complaining witness, but which was not necessarily a part of the indictment.

The chattels involved are numerous items of bric-a-brac, linens, silverware, and other household articles of quality and distinction. They were the property of Doris Farid es Sultaneh, and were kept in her home at Morristown, New Jersey, from which the defendant is alleged to have transported them to Arizona in a truck and station wagon. The defendant did not deny receiving some of the lady's chattels, but did deny both the quantity and quality alleged. Moreover, it does not appear open to doubt that the truck made but one trip, and the station wagon three, carrying the goods in controversy.

To prove the specific chattels involved, the government relied on the testimony of Doris Farid; to prove their value, it relied on the testimony of an expert, one Leo Berlow.

Farid testified that as the chattels were being moved from the house, she made longhand notes, and that later she copied these notes on her typewriter. Only one of the original notes was produced, and became part of the evidence of the case, a search by Farid having failed to disclose the others. The government sought to have Farid testify with respect to the chattels by using the typewritten notes for the purpose of refreshing her recollection.

Although the defendant's objection was overruled, the government, on the next day of the trial, submitted to Farid lists of chattels taken out of a copy of the indictment, but from which had been deleted such information as dates and values. With the aid of these lists, the witness testified that her recollection was refreshed and that she presently recognized and could identify each item. She was then permitted to read the lists aloud, and testified that she knew that the items were loaded on the truck or station wagon, as the case was. The lists were neither offered nor received in evidence.

The expert, Berlow, testified that he had visited Doris Farid's home on numerous occasions in his professional capacity as dealer in antiques, bric-a-brac, etc.; that he was very familiar with the furnishings therein, having examined the household for the purpose of buying items from Farid or selling them for her on commission. He was shown the same lists which Farid had used to refresh her recollection, and with their aid testified that he could recall the items individually, with some exceptions; that he remembered them to the extent that he could not only describe the items, but in many instances could state where in the house he had seen them; and that he could give an opinion as to their value. This he was permitted to do.

In denying the acceptability of the evidence related, the defendant rests primarily on Putnam v. United States, 1896, 162 U.S. 687, 16 S.Ct. 923, 40 L.Ed. 1118, and refers to this Court's decision in Delaney v. United States, 3 Cir., 1935, 77 F.2d 916. It is his position that the lists should not have been used because they were not made by the witnesses at or shortly after the time of the transaction while the facts were fresh in memory. It is further contended that the witnesses were not hostile to the government, and what Farid did, in fact, was to read off the lists as proof of the actual articles loaded on the vehicles.

The government, on the other hand, asserts that the witnesses gave their independent recollection, which is admissible, albeit refreshed, because it is the recollection and not the writing which is the evidence. It goes further, and urges that where the witness has an independent recollection, anything may be used to stimulate and revitalize that recollection without regard to source or origin.

Refreshing the recollecion of a witness is not an uncommon trial practice, but as a theory of evidentiary law its content and application are far from clear. The large collection of cases found in 125 A.L.R. 19–250 illusstrates the point. An analysis as good and trustworthy as presently exists appears in Chapter XXVIII, 3 Wigmore on Evidence (3rd ed. 1940). Professor Wigmore separated, broadly, what he called "past recollection recorded" from "present recollection revived", attributing much of the confusion in the cases to a failure to make this distinction and to the use of the phrase "refreshing the recollection" for both classes of testimony. The primary difference between the two classifications is the ability of the witness to testify from present knowledge: where the witness' memory is revived, and he presently recollects the facts and swears to them, he is obviously in a different position from the witness who cannot directly state the facts from present memory and who must ask the court to accept a writing for the truth of its contents because he is willing to swear, for one reason or another, that its contents are true.

Recognition of the basic difference between the two categories of evidence referred to is explicit in the federal cases, although in some the distinction is obscured by the lack of necessity for it. . . .

The difference between present recollection revived and past recollection recorded has a demonstrable effect upon the method of proof. In the instance of past recollection recorded, the witness, by hypothesis, has no present recollection of the matter contained in the writing. Whether the record is directly admitted into evidence, or indirectly by the permissive parroting of the witness, it is nevertheless a substitute for his memory and is offered for the truth of its contents. It assumes a distinct significance as an independent probative force, and is therefore ordinarily required to meet certain standards. These requirements are the more understandable in consideration of the fact that the court is at once desirous of determining whether the writing may be safely received as a substitute for the witness' memory and for the truth of the matter therein asserted, and of affording to the trier of fact information upon which it can form a reliable judgment as to its worth for the purposes offered.

In the case of present recollection revived, the witness, by hypothesis, relates his present recollection, and under oath and subject to cross-examination asserts that it is true; his capacities for memory and perception may be attacked and tested; his determination to tell the truth investigated and revealed; protestations of lack of memory, which escape criticism and indeed constitute a refuge in the situation of past recollection recorded, merely undermine the probative worth of his testimony. It is in recognition of these factors that we find:

"The law of contemporary writing or entry qualifying it as primary evidence has no application. The primary evidence here is not the writing. It was not introduced in evidence. It was not offered. The primary evidence is the oral statement of the hostile witness. It is not so important when the statement was made or by whom if it serves the purpose to refresh the mind and unfold the truth." Hoffman v. United States, 9 Cir., 1937, 87 F.2d 410, 411.

"When a party uses an earlier statement of his own witness to refresh the witness' memory, the only evidence recognized as such is the testimony so refreshed.... Anything may in fact revive a memory: a song, a scent, a photograph, and allusion, even a past statement known to be false. When a witness declares that any of these has evoked a memory, the opposite party may show, either that it has not evoked what appears to the witness as a memory, or that, although, it may so appear to him, the memory is a phantom and not a reliable record of its content. When the evoking stimulus is not itself an account of the relevant occasion, no question of its truth can arise; but when it is an account of that occasion, its falsity, if raised by the opposing party, will become a relevant issue if the witness has declared that the evoked memory accords with it...." United States v. Rappy, 2 Cir., 1947, 157 F.2d 964, 967–968, certiorari denied 329 U.S. 806, 67 S.Ct. 501, 91 L.Ed. 688....

Since the purpose of the writing is to activate the memory of the witness, there is always the possibility, if not probability, that the writing will exert a strong influence upon the direction of the memory, that is, the nearer the writing to the truth, the lesser the deviation of the witness' memory from the truth. But this is not a binding reason for insistence upon establishing the reliability of the writing previous to permitting the witness to state whether his memory is refreshed. The reception of a witness' testimony does not depend upon whether it is true; truth is a matter for the trier of fact unless, of course, the evidence is so improbable that reasonable men would not differ upon it. When the witness testifies that he has a present recollection, that is the evidence in the case, and not the writing which stimulates it. If his recollection agrees with the writing, it is pointless to require proof of the accuracy of the writing, for such proof can only amount to corroborative evidence. The testimony is received for what it is worth. New York & Colorado Mining Syndicate v. Fraser, 1889, 130 U.S. 611, 620, 8 S.Ct. 665, 32 L.Ed. 1031. And the testimony should be received if it is capable of a reasonably satisfactory evaluation. Undoubtedly, the nature of the writing which the witness says is effective to stimulate his memory plays a part in that evaluation, and the dangers from deficiencies in the witness' testimonial qualifications are not less susceptible of evaluation by the trier of fact than in the case of past perception recorded; indeed, they are more readily subject to test for the witness, as already noted, asserts a present memory and cannot gain protection from a denial of the very memory which he claims to have.

Of course, the categories, present recollection revived and past recollection recorded, are clearest in their extremes, but they are, in practice, converging rather than parallel lines; the difference is frequently one of degree. Moreover, it is in complication thereof that a cooperative witness, yielding to suggestion, deceives himself, that a hostile witness seizes an opportunity, or that a writing is used to convey an improper suggestion. Circumstances, or the nature of the testimony, may belie an assertion of present memory; more often the credibility of the witness generally, and the cross-examiner's attack upon the reliability of his memory, will decide the claim to an independent recollection.

Properly, the burden to ascertain the state of affairs, as near as may be, devolves upon the trial judge, who should in the first instance satisfy himself as to whether the witness testifies upon a record or from his own recollection. It is upon this satisfaction that the reception of the evidence depends, for if it appear to the court that the witness is wholly dependent for the fact upon the memorandum he holds in his hand, the memorandum acquires a significance which, as stated, brings into operation certain guiding rules. Similarly, the trial judge must determine whether the device of refreshing recollection is merely a subterfuge to improperly suggest to the witness the testimony expected of him. It is axiomatic, particularly with respect to the reception of evidence, that much depends upon the discretion of the trial judge. . . .

In the instant case, the learned trial judge determined that both Farid and the expert, Berlow, testified from present recollection. On the record, we cannot say that it was plainly not so. Both witnesses stated that they knew the chattels and could identify them. Farid, who testified that she was present and helped to pack them, said she could remember which were transported; Berlow said he could give an opinion of their value. On a number of occasions the trial judge investigated the foundations of their claim to present recollection and satisfied himself as to its bona fides. The case is, therefore, distinguishable from Jewett v. United States, supra, wherein it was held that the witness had no independent recollection, and from Delaney v. United States, supra, where the Court concluded that the witness did no more than read from a photostatic copy. While the defendant asserts that neither Farid nor Berlow did more, the trial judge immediately recognized that the items of property involved were so numerous that in the ordinary course of events no one would be expected to recite them without having learned a list by rote memory. On the other hand, the items were such that a person familiar with them reasonably could be expected to recognize them and tell what he knows. Under these circumstances, the District Judge might well have permitted the government, in lieu of the procedure followed, to ask Farid leading questions, directing her attention to specific items, and asking her whether she knew what happened to them. This is especially true of Berlow, who did not purport to have any knowledge of the movement of the articles. Clearly, it would have been pointless to ask him to give the value of every article he had ever seen in Farid's home. The same result could have been achieved legitimately without the use of the lists by orally directing his attention to any specific article previously identified by Farid and asking him whether he had seen it, presently remembered it, and could give an opinion as to its value. By the use of lists, nothing more or different was accomplished.

Moreover, we think the procedure followed lay within the discretion of the trial court, and that no prejudicial error ensued. The evidence was capable of a reasonably satisfactory evaluation and was receivable for what it was worth. In the long run, the primary issue of the case was that of credibility, and it is sufficient that the jury had as sound a basis for weighing the testimony as it would in any other instance. The defense had at its disposal the customary opportunities and all the necessary material to test the witness' recollection and other testimonial qualifications, including the single original long-hand list which Farid located, the typewritten lists which she said were made at the time of the events involved, and the lists the prosecution used. It might very well have put Farid through severe cross-examination with respect to each chattel she identified on direct examination, but chose instead to attack the reliability of her memory by other means.

Accordingly, it is our conclusion that the learned trial judge did not abuse his discretion, either in determining that the witnesses testified from present recollection, or in permitting the use of the lists described herein. . . .

For the reasons stated, the judgment of the District Court will be affirmed.

GALE v. STATE
Supreme Court of Georgia, 1910.
135 Ga. 351, 69 S.E. 537.

LUMPKIN, J. Prince Gale was convicted of the murder of Calvin Brown, and, upon recommendation of the jury, was sentenced to life imprisonment. He moved for a new trial, which was refused, and he excepted.

Pending the cross-examination of a witness

for the state, she collapsed physically and had to be taken from the courtroom. Just before she was removed from the stand, she did not answer several questions of the cross-examining attorney. This, however, was apparently the result of her condition, rather than of contumaciousness. The presiding judge endeavored to compel her to answer, but she seemed to be unable to do so. The judge had a physician called, who examined the condition of the witness and reported that she would be unable to testify further that day. This was about the middle of the afternoon, and the court took a recess until next morning. On the reconvening of court next day the witness was not present. The testimony of the physician and other evidence was heard, from which the presiding judge became satisfied that the witness was still unable to testify, and that it was entirely uncertain whether she would be able to do so. The judge then caused the jury to retire from the courtroom and stated to counsel for defendant, in the hearing of the latter, that a mistrial would be granted, if the defendant desired it. Defendant's counsel stated that a mistrial was not desired, and the case proceeded; the judge allowing the evidence of the witness, so far as given, to stand and refusing to rule it out. A number of the grounds of the motion for a new trial arise out of this incident, an account of which appears in a note appended by the judge to the motion.

Undoubtedly the right of cross-examination is a valuable right, and, if it be improperly denied, a reversal must result. There is authority in England to the effect that if a witness dies, or becomes incapable of being further examined, at any stage of his examination, the evidence given before he became incapable is good; but it has been said that in this country the rule is different, where there has been no opportunity for cross-examination. Clark's Crim.Proc. 549; Stephen's Dig.Ev. (Beer's Ed) 434; Rex. v. Doolin, 1 Jebb.Cr. Cas. 123; 8 Enc.Pl. & Pr. 99. In 2 Wigmore on Evidence, § 1390, p. 1742, it is said: "Where the witness' death or lasting illness would not have intervened to prevent cross-examination but for the voluntary act of the witness himself or the party offering him — as, by a postponement or other interruption brought about immediately after the direct examination — it seems clear that the direct testimony must be struck out. Upon the same principle, the same result should follow where the illness is but temporary and the offering party might have reproduced the witness for cross-examination before the end of the trial. But, where the death or illness prevents cross-examination under such circumstances that no responsibility of any sort can be attributed to either the witness or his party, it seems a harsh measure to strike out all that has been obtained on direct examination. Nevertheless, principle requires in strictness nothing less. The true solution would be to avoid any inflexible rule, and to leave it to the trial judge to admit the direct examination so far as the loss of cross-examination can be shown to him to be not in that instance a material loss. Courts differ in their treatment of this difficult situation, except that, by general concession, a cross-examination begun but unfinished suffices if its purposes have been substantially accomplished. Where, however, the failure to obtain cross-examination is in any sense attributable to the cross-examiner's own consent or fault, the lack of cross-examination is, of course, no objection—according to the general principle (ante, section 1371) that an opportunity, though waived, suffices." This is quoted somewhat at length on account of the clearness with which the author has stated his views, and also because of the collection of authorities in the note, among them being Randall v. Atkinson, 30 Ont. 242; Scott v. McCann, 76 Md. 47, 24 Atl. 536; Fuller v. Rice, 4 Gray (Mass.) 343; Lewis v. Insurance Co., 10 Gray (Mass.) 508, 511; People v. Kindra, 102 Mich. 147, 151, 60 N. W. 458. See, also, 1 Gr.Ev. (16th Ed.) §§ 163c, 163d, p. 280.

In People v. Cole, 43 N.Y. 508, where, on a trial for larceny, the wife of the prosecutor, having given material evidence, on behalf of the people on her direct examination, immediately went into convulsions before the prisoner had an opportunity to cross-examine her, and so remained until the close of the trial, it was held to be error to permit her evidence to go to the jury. This case is often cited. From the report of facts it appears that counsel for the defendant called for the production of the witness in court for examination, moved that her evidence be stricken out, asking a postponement of the trial until she should recover, and asked that the prisoner be discharged. Each of these motions was overruled.

In Sturm v. Atlantic Mut. Ins. Co. 63 N.Y. 77, the same court said: "It may be taken as the rule that where a party is deprived of the benefit of the cross-examination of a witness, by the act of the opposite party, or by the refusal to testify or other misconduct of the witness, or by any means other than the act of God, the act of the party himself or some cause to which he assented the testimony given on the examination in chief may not be read." See, also, Bradley v. Mirick, 91 N.Y. 293; Hewlett v. Wood, 67 N.Y. 394. We will not stop to discuss the difference between common-law and equity practice.

It is clear that, while the right of cross-examination is not to be violated, yet it may be waived expressly, or by conduct of the party entitled to it; and that (in the language of Prof. Wigmore), if "the failure to obtain cross-examination is in any sense attributable to the cross-examiner's own consent or fault, the lack of cross-examination is of course no objection."

When the witness collapsed during the progress of the cross-examination, there was no error in having her removed from the stand and examined by a physician and suspending the trial until the next day, upon hearing his testimony in regard to her condition. When court reconvened next day, there was no error in hearing evidence touching her condition, she not being present; nor, under the evidence adduced, can we say that the court did not decide properly that she was unable to return to the courtroom and testify, and that it was uncertain when she would be able to do so. She was the principal witness for the state, being an eyewitness to the commission of the homicide. The court was thus, in the expressive language of a distinguished American, confronted with a condition, not a theory. It was impracticable to suspend the case indefinitely. No motion for a postponement was made by counsel for the defendant, as was done in People v. Cole, supra. Counsel for the accused asked that the entire previously given evidence of the witness should be ruled out, and that a verdict be directed finding the accused not guilty; the witness being the only one introduced by the state in chief. The presiding judge recognized the right of cross-examination, and did not desire to cut off such right or to force accused to proceed with the trial under such circumstances. What appeared to him to be the only practicable method of accomplishing that result was to declare a mistrial, if the defendant desired it. This would have resulted in starting the trial afresh at a later date. If the state could not then have produced the witness, the consequences of the inability would have fallen upon it. If it did produce her, she would have been subject to cross-examination. But this was not what the defendant desired. His counsel asked for no postponement, and announced that he did not want a mistrial. What he evidently wanted was for the case to terminate, when it was impossible to cross-examine the witness, to have the main evidence for the state ruled out, and for an acquittal to result because of the illness of the witness.

The severity of punishment for felonies which was inflicted in England at one time (when they were generally punishable by death) begat in practice certain technical loopholes for escape for criminals, in no way affecting the merits of the case. This has, to some extent at least, passed away, save where rules of procedure have been crystallized by constitutional provisions, or legislative enactments, or by the decisions of courts of last resort. But we think that neither in England nor in America have the decisions on the subject of interruption of an examination by sickness or death carried the rule to the extent contended for in this case. Every person accused of crime is entitled to a fair and impartial trial, according to the rules of law. But an accused person is not entitled to be set free, regardless of his guilt or innocence, because of a providential interference with the cross-examination of the state's principal witness, and the unwillingness of the defendant to accept a reasonable method of securing a complete cross-examination.

When, through his counsel, the accused announced that he did not want a mistrial, which appeared from the evidence to be the only method by which the witness could be again produced and examined, we think that he waived the right, or at least that his conduct was such as to obstruct the possibility of its exercise. Under the circumstances, the court did not err in refusing to strike the evidence which had been given by the witness for the state and to direct a verdict for the accused.

3. After the trial proceeded, with the evidence of the witness remaining in, the judge correctly ruled that it was for the jury to determine the weight to be given to it. The case was not one for the exclusion of a witness as incompetent to testify.

4. The case made by the evidence for the state was one of murder. It tended to show that the accused, on account of an insult offered to his mother, went to the house of Calvin Brown, called him out, and shot him to death. The defense was that the accused sought to settle the dispute, made no assault, and had no intention to kill Brown; that the latter saw who it was, stepped back into the house and obtained his gun, advanced on the accused and was seeking to kill him, when the latter shot in self-defense. The killing was murder or justifiable homicide. Voluntary manslaughter was not involved, and there was no error in failing to charge in regard of it. . . .

Judgment affirmed. All the Justices concur.

TUCKER v. UNITED STATES
United States Court of Appeals, Eighth Circuit, 1925.
5 F.2d 818.

Before KENYON, Circuit Judge, and TRIEBER and PHILLIPS, District Judges.

PHILLIPS, DISTRICT JUDGE. Dudley R. Tucker, William L. Tucker, and Howard A. Tucker, hereinafter called defendants, were charged by indictment with the violation of section 215 of the Penal Code (25 Stat. 873 [Comp.St. § 10385]). The indictment contained five counts. The first count charged that the defendants, having devised a scheme and artifice to defraud certain persons named in that count, on the 15th day of September, 1920, for the purpose of executing such scheme and artifice to defraud, caused to be placed in the United States post office at Oklahoma City, Okl., for mailing and delivery by the post office establishment of the United States, a certain newspaper, to wit, the Daily Oklahoman, which contained an advertisement, prepared by the defendants and printed in said newspaper at the special instance and request of the defendants, in words and figures following to wit:

"Very attractive proposition open to responsible man who can invest $2,000 cash; pays $60 per week and all expenses; handling road picture shows; playing in Oklahoma towns. Investment guaranteed. Tucker Bros. Amusement Co., 310½ W. Main St., Dreamland Theatre. Phone M 1192 or M 5620."

The first count further alleged in detail the scheme and artifice to defraud and the means and methods by which the defendants intended to carry out the same. . . .

[The other counts in the indictment set forth other similar advertisements alleged to have been inserted by the defendants. The defendants were convicted and assign error on the ground] that the trial court erred in requiring the defendant Dudley R. Tucker to answer on cross-examination whether he had inserted or caused to be inserted, in the Daily Oklahoman, the advertisements alleged in the several counts of the indictment.

The crimes charged are made up of two principal elements: (1) A scheme or artifice devised or intended to be devised to defraud; (2) causing an advertisement to be placed in the post office to be sent or delivered by the post office establishment of the United States, for the purpose of executing such scheme or artifice, or attempting so to do. Robins v. U.S. (C.C.A. 8) 262 F. 126; Bowers v. U.S. (C.C.A. 9) 244 F. 641, 157 C.C.A. 89; U.S. v. Young, 232 U.S. 155, 34 S.Ct. 303, 58 L.Ed. 548. . . .

Dudley Tucker was called as a witness in behalf of the defendants. He testified to the plan he had worked out for operating road motion picture shows, and to what he stated to prospective employees, and to his good faith in the matter. He at no time in any way mentioned or referred to the advertisements or the insertion of the same in the newspaper. He made no reference to the statements concerning the advertisements testified to by the persons who called upon him in response to advertisements. In short, his direct testimony went wholly to a refutation of the first element of the offenses charged, namely, the scheme to defraud, and at no time went to the question of using the post office in furtherance of any such scheme.

On cross-examination he was asked if he inserted or caused the insertion of the advertisements charged in the first four counts of the indictment. Objection was interposed to the effect that such questions were outside the scope of the direct examination, were therefore improper cross-examination, and in effect made Dudley Tucker the government's witness, and compelled him to be a witness against himself.

The privilege against self-incrimination was first recognized by the common-law courts in England about the middle of the seventeenth century.

By the Act of March 16, 1878, 20 Stat. 30 (Comp.St. § 1465), Congress provided that "the person so charged shall, at his own request, but not otherwise, be a competent witness. And his failure to make such request shall not create any presumption against him." What is the effect of the defendant availing himself of this statute and testifying in his own behalf upon the privilege guaranteed to him by the Fifth Amendment? All courts recognize that he subjects himself to cross-examination. So far as we have been able to determine no court or legal writer has suggested that after the accused has testified in his own behalf he can be called as a witness against himself by the prosecution. If the accused testifies in his own behalf, manifestly his testimony should be subjected to the same tests for determining its truthfulness as that of any other witness. The primary purpose of cross-examination in the federal courts is to test the truth of the testimony adduced by the direct examination and to clarify or explain the same. It is not to prove independent facts in the case of the cross-examining party.

If there is good reason why a defendant should not be compelled to be a witness against himself, there ought to be equally good reason why, if he has testified voluntarily upon one issue, he should not be compelled to testify against his will concerning matters wholly unrelated to that issue, which would not be within the scope of proper cross-examination if he were an ordinary witness.

We conclude that, when a defendant in a criminal case voluntarily becomes a witness in his own behalf, he subjects himself to cross-examination and impeachment to the same extent as any other witness in the same situation, but he does not subject himself to cross-examination and impeachment to any greater extent. Harrold v. Territory of Oklahoma (C.C.A. 8) 169 F. 47, 94 C.C.A. 415, 17 Ann. Cas. 868; Paquin v. U.S. (C.C.A. 8) 251 F. 579, 163 C.C.A. 573; Fitzpatrick v. U.S., 178 U.S. 304, 315, 316, 20 S.Ct. 944, 44 L.Ed. 1078; Sawyer v. U.S., 202 U.S. 150, 165, 26 S.Ct. 575, 50 L.Ed. 972, 6 Ann. Cas. 269.

To sustain the ruling of the learned trial judge, counsel for the government cite and rely upon the following cases: Quintana v. State 29 Tex.App. 401, 16 S.W. 258, 25 Am.St.Rep. 730; People v. Bussey, 82 Mich. 49, 46 N.W. 97; State v. Ober, 52 N.H. 459, 13 Am. Rep. 88; Commonwealth v. Nichols, 114 Mass. 285, 19 Am.Rep. 346; Andrews v. Frye, 104 Mass. 234; Commonwealth v. Lannan, 13 Allen (Mass.) 563; Commonwealth v. Mullen, 97 Mass. 545. The above cases generally recognize the rule that the defendant who offers himself as a witness in his own behalf subjects himself to cross-examination the same as any other witness, but hold that the cross-examination may include any question pertinent to the issues. We find, however, that is the rule regulating the scope of cross-examination of an ordinary witness in those jurisdictions. . . .

From the foregoing it will be seen that the courts of Texas, Michigan, Massachusetts, and New Hampshire open a much broader field to the cross-examiner than do the national courts.

The rule fixing the limitation upon the cross-examination of a witness generally in the national courts, is stated in Heard v. U.S. (C.C.A.) 255 F. 829, at page 833, 167 C.C.A. 157, 161, as follows:

"The rule on this subject in the national courts is that the party in whose behalf a witness is called has the right to restrict his cross-examination to the subjects of his direct examination, and a violation of this right is reversible error. If the cross-examiner would inquire of the witness concerning matters not opened on direct examination, he must call him in his own behalf. Philadelphia & Trenton Railway Co. v. Stimpson, 39 U.S. (14 Pet.) 448, 460, 10 L.Ed. 535; Houghton v. Jones, 1 Wall. 702, 706, 17 L.Ed. 503; Resurrection Gold Mining Co. v. Fortune Gold Mining Co., 129 Fed. 668, 674, 64 C.C.A 180, and cases there cited; Illinois Central Railway Co. v. Nelson, 212 Fed. 69, 74, 128 C.C.A. 525; Harrold v. Territory of Oklahoma, 169 Fed. 47, 52, 94 C.C.A. 415, 17 Ann.Cas. 868." ...

The questions asked the witness Dudley Tucker on cross-examination were clearly outside the scope of his direct testimony. They had reference to the second element of the offenses charged, while his direct examination was limited to a refutation of the first element. The questions on cross-examination did not in any way test the truth of the direct examination; they did not seek to explain or modify the same; they were asked for the sole purpose of proving an independent element in the government's case. In eliciting the answers to the questions propounded to Dudley Tucker with reference to the insertion of the advertisements, the government made Dudley Tucker its witness, and compelled him over seasonable and proper objection to be a witness against himself, in violation of the Fifth Amendment to the Constitution. There is no higher nor more important duty resting upon the courts than to see that the citizen is fully afforded the rights and immunities guaranteed to him by the Constitution.

For the reasons above stated, the cause is reversed, with instructions to grant the defendants a new trial; and it is so ordered.

SMITH v. ILLINOIS
Supreme Court of the United States, 1968.
390 U.S. 129, 88 S.Ct. 748, 19 L.Ed.2d 956.

Opinion of the Court by Mr. Justice STEWART, announced by Mr. Justice FORTAS.

In Pointer v. State of Texas, 380 U.S. 400, 403, 85 S.Ct. 1065, 1068, 13 L.Ed.2d 923, this Court held that the Sixth Amendment right of an accused to confront the witnesses against him is a "fundamental right . . . made obligatory on the States by the Fourteenth Amendment." The question presented in this case is whether Illinois denied that right to the petitioner, Fleming Smith. He was convicted in a criminal court of Cook County, Illinois, upon a charge of illegal sale of narcotics, and his conviction was affirmed on appeal. We granted certiorari to consider his constitutional claim.

At the trial the principal witness against the petitioner was a man who identified himself on direct examination as "James Jordan." This witness testified that he had purchased a bag of heroin from the petitioner in a restaurant with marked money provided by two Chicago police officers. The officers corroborated part of this testimony but only this witness and the petitioner testifed to the crucial events inside the restaurant, and the petitioner's version of those events was entirely different. The only real question at the trial, therefore, was the relative credibility of the petitioner and this prosecution witness.

On cross-examination this witness was asked whether "James Jordan" was his real name. He admitted, over the prosecutor's objection, that it was not. He was then asked what his correct name was, and the court sustained the prosecutor's objection to the question. Later the witness was asked where he lived, and again the court sustained the prosecutor's objection to the question.

As the Court said in *Pointer*, "It cannot seriously be doubted at this late date that the right of cross-examination is included in the right of an accused in a criminal case to confront the witnesses against him." 380 U.S., at 404, 85 S.Ct., at 1068. Even more recently we have repeated that "[a] denial of cross examination without waiver . . . would be constitutional error of the first magnitude and no amount of showing of want of prejudice would cure it." Brookhart v. Janis, 384 U.S. 1, 3, 86 S.Ct. 1245, 1246, 16 L.Ed.2d 314.

In the present case there was not, to be sure, a complete denial of all right of cross-examination. But the petitioner was denied the right to ask the principal prosecution witness either his name or where he lived, although the witness admitted that the name he had first given was false. Yet when the credibility of a witness is in issue, the very starting point in "exposing falsehood and bringing out the truth" through cross-examination must necessarily be to ask the witness who he is and where he lives. The witness' name and address open countless avenues of in-court examination and out-of-court investigation. To forbid this most rudimentary inquiry at the threshold is effectively to emasculate the right of cross-examination itself.

In Alford v. United States, 282 U.S. 687, 51 S.Ct. 218, 75 L.Ed. 624, this Court almost 40 years ago unanimously reversed a federal conviction because the trial judge had sustained objections to questions by the defense seeking to elicit the "place of residence" of a prosecution witness over the insistence of defense counsel that "the jury was entitled to know 'who the witness is, where he lives and what his business is.'" 282 U.S., at 688–689, 51 S.Ct., at 218. What the Court said in reversing that conviction is fully applicable here:

"It is the essence of a fair trial that reasonable latitude be given the cross-examiner, even though he is unable to state to the court what facts a reasonable cross-examination might develop. Prejudice ensues from a denial of the opportunity to place the witness in his proper setting and put the weight of his testimony and his credibility to a test, without which the jury cannot fairly appraise them. . . . To say that prejudice can be established only by showing that the cross-examination, if pursued, would necessarily have brought out facts tending to discredit the testimony in chief, is to deny a substantial right and withdraw one of the safeguards essential to a fair trial. . . .

". . . The question, 'Where do you live?' was not only an appropriate preliminary to the cross-examination of the witness, but on its face, without any such declaration of purpose as was made by counsel here, was an essential step in identifying the witness with his environment, to which cross-examination may always be directed. . . .

"The extent of cross-examination with respect to an appropriate subject of inquiry is within the sound discretion of the trial court. It may exercise a reasonable judgment in determining when the subject is exhausted. . . .

But no obligation is imposed on the court, such as that suggested below, to protect a witness from being discredited on cross-examination, short of an attempted invasion of his constitutional protection from self incrimination, properly invoked. There is a duty to protect him from questions which go beyond the bounds of proper cross-examination merely to harass, annoy or humiliate him. . . . But no such case is presented here. . . ." 282 U.S., at 692–694, 51 S.Ct., at 219–220.

In Pointer v. State of Texas, supra, the Court made clear that "the right of an accused to be confronted with the witnesses against him must be determined by the same standards whether the right is denied in a federal or state proceeding. . . ." 380 U.S., at 407–408, 85 S.Ct., at 1070. In this state case we follow the standard of *Alford* and hold that the petitioner was deprived of a right guaranteed to him under the Sixth and Fourteenth Amendments of the Constitution.

Reversed.

MR. JUSTICE WHITE, with whom MR. JUSTICE MARSHALL, joins, concurring.

In Alford v. United States, 282 U.S. 687, 694, 51 S.Ct. 218, 220, 75 L.Ed. 624 (1931), the Court recognized that questions which tend merely to harass, annoy, or humiliate a witness may go beyond the bounds of proper cross-examination. I would place in the same category those inquiries which tend to endanger the personal safety of the witness. But in these situations, if the question asked is one that is normally permissible, the State or the witness should at the very least come forward with some showing of why the witness must be excused from answering the question. The trial judge can then ascertain the interest of the defendant in the answer and exercise an informed discretion in making his ruling. Here the State gave no reasons justifying the refusal to answer a quite usual and proper question. For this reason I join the Court's judgment and its opinion which, as I understand it, is not inconsistent with these views. I should note in addition that although petitioner and his attorney may have known the witness in the past, it is not at all clear that either of them had ever known the witness' real name or knew where he lived at the time of the trial.

STATE v. ROBBINS
Supreme Court of Washington, 1950.
35 Wash.2d 389, 213 P.2d 310.

HAMLEY, JUSTICE. At his trial upon a charge of grand larceny involving the theft of an automobile, defendant sought to exclude the adverse testimony of his former wife. . . . He was convicted, and judgment and sentence were entered. He has appealed. . . .

The state called twenty-two witnesses to prove the crime charged. Their combined testimony tended to show that appellant, James J. Robbins, alias James Driscoll, had stolen a 1942 Pontiac automobile belonging to Merle D. Cohn; had altered the motor number to correspond to that of another Pontiac automobile, owned by Ralph Alberthal, which had been totally wrecked; and had obtained a transfer of the title of the wrecked Pontiac to himself, under the name of James Driscoll, and subsequently from James Driscoll to Jimmie J. Robbins. One of these witnesses, an employee of the state department of licenses, produced an application for a certificate of title for a Pontiac automobile, in which Ralph Alberthal was listed as the former owner and the motor number of the Alberthal automobile was given. This application was signed "James Driscoll, By (wife) Mrs. June Driscoll."

The state then called appellant's former wife, Mrs. Geraldine Milne, to testify regarding this application. Over the objection of appellant, Mrs. Milne testified that she married appellant in November, 1946 (she misspoke in giving the year as 1946—the record shows that the marriage license was issued on November 23, 1945); that she divorced him in June, 1948; that, in August, 1946, while appellant waited in the automobile for her, she went to an office in the County-City building, in Seattle, and applied for license plates and a certificate of title for a Pontiac automobile (identifying the application, which had been introduced in evidence, as the one she had filed); that she signed the application "James Driscoll, By (wife) Mrs. June Driscoll"; that Driscoll was not her real name, but was her father's name; that at this time she and "James Driscoll" did not live at the address given in the application; and that she did not know whether "James Driscoll" had ever acquired title to the automobile from Ralph Alberthal, named in the application as the former owner.

Whether this testimony was admissible depends upon the effect to be given to Rem.Rev. Stat. § 1214, paragraph 1, reading as follows: "A husband shall not be examined for or against his wife without the consent of the wife, nor a wife for or against her husband without the consent of the husband. But this exception shall not apply to a civil action or proceeding by one against the other, nor to a criminal action or proceeding for a crime committed by one against the other."

The testimony in question consists of a number of separate statements. Several of these can be dismissed from consideration, for the reason that they did not impart information which came to the witness by reason of any communication from her husband, but were facts at all times within her own knowledge. Of this kind was the testimony regarding the date of marriage and divorce; that "Driscoll" was not the true name of the witness; and that at the time of the transaction she and "James Driscoll" did not live at the address given in the application. The statement that the witness did not know whether Driscoll had acquired title to the automobile from Alberthal did not convey any information except her own lack of knowledge.

This leaves for consideration the admissibility of the statement that, while appellant waited in the automobile for her, the witness went to an office in the County-City building in Seattle and applied for license plates and a certificate of title for a Pontiac automobile, signing "James Driscoll, By (wife) Mrs. June Driscoll."

The statement that appellant was waiting outside in an automobile was testimony as to an act of the other spouse, as distinguished from testimony as to an oral or written communication. The privilege established by the statute does not ordinarily extend to testimony regarding the *acts* of the other spouse. Wigmore on Evidence, 3d Ed., vol. VIII, § 2337. For example, in a prosecution for the crime of rape, a divorced wife was permitted to testify that, on a certain occasion, she discovered her then husband in the act of sexual intercourse with her daughter, the complaining witness. State v. Snyder, 84 Wash. 485, 147 P. 38. Likewise, in a murder prosecution, a wife was permitted to testify that she discovered her husband dumping some object into a hole in which the deceased's body was found. Smith v. State, 198 Ind. 156, 152 N.E. 803.

However, there are circumstances under which testimony as to an act of the other spouse is clearly protected by the statutory privilege. Where the act is one which would not have been done by one spouse in the presence of, or with the knowledge of, the other but for the confidence between them by reason of the marital relation, testimony as to such act is inadmissible. See the very recent case of Menefee v. Commonwealth, 189 Va. 900, 55 S.E.2d 9, where the cases and authorities are discussed at length. The rule is stated as follows in 70 C.J., Witnesses, p. 388, § 520: "The term 'communication,' within the meaning of the privileged communication rule, as to husband and wife should be given a liberal construction and is not confined to mere audible communications or conversations between the spouses, but embraces all facts which have come to his or her knowledge or under his or her observation in consequence or by reason of the confidence of the marital relation, and which but for the confidence growing out of it would not have been known. It includes knowledge communicated by an act, which would not have been done by one spouse in the presence of, or within the sight of, the other, but for the confidence between them by reason of the marital relation. . . ."

It would at first be supposed that appellant's act of waiting in an automobile in sight of all on a public thoroughfare, was not an act done in reliance upon the confidence established by the marital relation. He was apparently willing to be seen by the public, including acquaintances who might be passing by. The reason he was not afraid of being seen by the general public, however, was that it was unlikely that this would result in connecting appellant with the transaction then taking place inside the building. But his wife knew why he was waiting there, and was accordingly in a position to disclose appellant's connection with the transaction then in progress. It is obvious that he would not have waited in the automobile had he not relied upon the confidence between them by reason of the marital relation. The testimony of the witness as to appellant's act of waiting was accordingly inadmissible.

We reach a different conclusion with respect to the witness' testimony that she applied for license plates and a certificate of title. Disassociated from her further testimony that her husband was waiting outside in the car, her statement that she made this application was testimony concerning the witness' own act. It was not testimony as to a communication between husband and wife.

If the witness had testified that she was authorized by her husband to file the application, that would have been testimony as to a communication. But she did not do so. It is true that the application, which had already been placed in evidence by another witness, was signed "James Driscoll, By (wife) Mrs. June Driscoll," and that Mrs. Milne testified that she signed in that manner. From this the jury was undoubtedly expected to conclude, and may well have concluded, that Mrs. Milne was in fact authorized by her husband. But this would be a conclusion based upon an inference—not upon the witness' direct testimony. She did not testify as to the truth of any representation contained in the application.

We are not willing to extend the rule of privileged marital communications to the point where it is necessary to hold testimony as to a witness' own acts inadmissible if the jury might infer therefrom a communication between husband and wife.

We conclude that the trial court erred in admitting Mrs. Milne's testimony relative to appellant's act of waiting in the automobile. The remainder of her testimony was properly received. . . .

The judgment is reversed, with instruction to grant appellant a new trial.

ROBINSON, HILL, and MALLERY, JJ., concur.
SIMPSON, C. J., dissents.

CLARK v. STATE
Court of Criminal Appeals of Texas, 1953.
159 Tex.Crim. 187, 261 S.W.2d 339, noted, 32 Texas L.Rev.615.

MORRISON, JUDGE. The offense is murder; the punishment, death.

The deceased secured a divorce from appellant on March 25, 1952. That night she was killed, as she lay at home in her bed, as the result of a gunshot wound. From the mattress on her bed, as well as from the bed of her daughter, were recovered bullets which were shown by a firearms expert to have been fired by a .38 special revolver having Colt characteristics. Appellant was shown to have purchased a Colt .38 Detective Special some ten months prior to the homicide. . . .

Marjorie Bartz, a telephone operator in the City of San Angelo, testified that at 2:49 in the morning of March 26, 1952, while on duty, she received a call from the Golden Spur Hotel; that at first she thought the person placing the call was a Mr. Cox and so made out the slip; but that she then recognized appellant's voice, scratched out the word "Cox" and wrote "Clark." She stated that appellant told her he wanted to speak to his lawyer, Jimmy Martin in Dallas, and that she placed the call to him at telephone number Victor 1942 in that city and made a record thereof, which record was admitted in evidence. Miss Bartz testified that, contrary to company rules, she listened to the entire conversation that ensued, and that it went as follows:

The appellant: "Hello, Jimmy, I went to the extremes."

The voice in Dallas: "What did you do?"

The appellant: "I just went to the extremes."

The voice in Dallas: "You got to tell me what you did before I can help."

The appellant: "Well, I killed her."

The voice in Dallas: "Who did you kill; the driver?"

The appellant: "No, I killed her."

The voice in Dallas: "Did you get rid of the weapon?"

The appellant: "No, I still got the weapon."

The voice in Dallas: "Get rid of the weapon and sit tight and don't talk to anyone, and I will fly down in the morning."

It was stipulated that the Dallas telephone number of appellant's attorney was Victor 1942. . . .

Proposition (1b) is predicated upon the contention that the court erred in admitting the testimony of the telephone operator, because the conversation related was a privileged communication between appellant and his attorney.

As a predicate to a discussion of this question, we note that the telephone operator heard this conversation through an act of eavesdropping.

In 20 Am.Jur., p. 361, we find the following:

"Evidence procured by eavesdropping, if otherwise relevant to the issue, is not to be excluded because of the manner in which it was obtained or procured. . . ."

This Court has recently, in Schwartz v. State, supra, affirmed by the Supreme Court of the United States on December 15, 1952, 73 S.Ct. 232, authorized the introduction of evidence secured by means of a mechanical interception of a telephone conversation.

We now discuss the question of the privileged nature of the conversation. Wigmore on Evidence (Third Edition), Section 2326, reads as follows:

"The law provides subjective freedom for the client by assuring him of exemption from its processes of disclosure against himself or the attorney or their agents of communication. This much, but not a whit more, is necessary for the maintenance of the privilege. Since the means of preserving secrecy of communication are entirely in the client's hands, and since the privilege is a derogation from the general testimonial duty and should be strictly construed, it would be improper to extend its prohibition to third persons who obtain knowledge of the communications."

The precise question here presented does not appear to have been passed upon in this or other jurisdictions.

In Hoy v. Morris, 13 Gray 519, 79 Mass. 519, a conversation between a client and his attorney was overheard by Aldrich, who was in the adjoining room. The Court therein said:

"Aldrich was not an attorney, not in any way connected with Mr. Todd; and certainly in no situation where he was either necessary or useful to the parties to enable them to understand each other. On the contrary, he was a mere bystander, and casually overheard conversation not addressed to him nor intended for his ear, but which the client and attorney meant to have respected as private and confidential. Mr. Todd could not lawfully have revealed it. But, in consequence of a want of proper precaution, the communications between him and his client were overheard by a mere stranger. As the latter stood in no relation of confidence to either of the parties, he was clearly not within the rule of exemption from giving testimony; and he might therefore, when summoned as a witness, be compelled to testify as to what he overheard, so far as it was pertinent to the subject matter of inquiry upon the trial. . . ."

In Walker v. State, 19 Tex.App. 176, we find the following:

"Mrs. Bridges was not incompetent or disqualified because she was present and heard the confessions made by defendant, even assuming that the relation of attorney and client subsisted in fact between him and Culberson."

The above holding is in conformity with our statute, Article 713, Code Cr.Proc.

"All other persons, except those enumerated in articles 708 and 714, whatever may be the relationship between the defendant and witness, are competent to testify, except that an attorney at law shall not disclose a communication made to him by his client during the existence of that relationship, nor disclose any other fact which came to the knowledge of such attorney by reason of such relationship". . . . .

We hold that the trial court properly admitted the evidence of the telephone operator. . . .

Finding no reversible error, the judgment of the trial court is affirmed.

On Appellant's Motion for Rehearing

WOODLEY, JUDGE. We are favored with masterful briefs and arguments in support of appellant's motion for rehearing, including amicus curiae brief by an eminent and able Texas lawyer addressed to the question of privileged communications between attorney and client. . . .

As to the testimony of the telephone operator regarding the conversation between appellant and Mr. Martin, the conversation is set forth in full in our original opinion. Our holding as to the admissibility of the testimony of the operator is not to be considered as authority except in comparable fact situations. . . .

It is in the interest of public justice that the client be able to make a full disclosure to his attorney of all facts that are material to his defense or that go to substantiate his claim. The purpose of the privilege is to encourage such disclosure of the facts. But the interests of public justice further require that no shield such as the protection afforded to communications between attorney and client shall be interposed to protect a person who takes counsel on how he can safely commit a crime.

We think this latter rule must extend to one who, having committed a crime, seeks or takes counsel as to how he shall escape arrest and punishment, such as advice regarding the destruction or disposition of the murder weapon or of the body following a murder.

One who knowing that an offense has been committed conceals the offender or aids him to evade arrest or trial becomes an accessory. The fact that the aider may be a member of the bar and the attorney for the offender will not prevent his becoming an accessory.

Art. 77, P.C. defining an accessory contains the exception "One who aids an offender in making or preparing his defense at law" is not an accessory.

The conversation as testified to by the telephone operator is not within the exception found in Art. 77, P.C. When the Dallas voice advised appellant to "get rid of the weapon" (which advice the evidence shows was followed) such aid cannot be said to constitute aid "in making or preparing his defense at law." It was aid to the perpetrator of the crime "in order that he may evade an arrest or trial."

Is such a conversation privileged as a communication between attorney and client?

If the adviser had been called to testify as to the conversation, would it not have been more appropriate for him to claim his privilege against self-incrimination rather than that the communication was privileged because it was between attorney and client?

Appellant, when he conversed with Mr. Martin, was not under arrest nor was he charged with a crime. He had just inflicted mortal wounds on his former wife and apparently had shot her daughter. Mr. Martin had acted as his attorney in the divorce suit which had been tried that day and had secured a satisfactory property settlement. Appellant called him and told him that he had gone to extremes and had killed "her", not "the driver". Mr. Martin appeared to understand these references and told appellant to get rid of "the weapon".

We are unwilling to subscribe to the theory that such counsel and advice should be privileged because of the attorney-client relationship which existed between the parties in the divorce suit. We think, on the other hand, that the conversation was admissible as not within the realm of legitimate professional counsel and employment.

The rule of public policy which calls for the privileged character of the communication between attorney and client, we think, demands that the rule be confined to the legitimate course of professional employment. It cannot consistent with the high purpose and policy supporting the rule be here applied.

The murder weapon was not found. The evidence indicates that appellant disposed of it as advised in the telephone conversation. Such advice or counsel was not such as merits protection because given by an attorney. It was not in the legitimate course of professional employment in making or preparing a defense at law.

Nothing is found in the record to indicate that appellant sought any advice from Mr. Martin other than that given in the conversation testified to by the telephone operator. We are not therefore dealing with a situation where the accused sought legitimate advice from his attorney in preparing his legal defense. . . .

Appellant's motion for rehearing is overruled.

CITY AND COUNTY OF SAN FRANCISCO v. SUPERIOR COURT
Supreme Court of California, 1951.
37 Cal.2d 227, 231 P.2d 26, 25 A.L.R.2d 1418.

TRAYNOR, JUSTICE. James Hession brought an action for personal injuries against the City and County of San Francisco and the Western Pacific Railroad Company. He alleged that he suffered brain concussion, nerve root damage, and nervous shock. At the request of Hession's attorneys, Dr. Joseph Catton, a physician specializing in nervous and mental diseases, twice gave Hession a neurological and psychiatric examination. In his deposition Dr. Catton testified that there was no physician-patient relationship between him and Hession; that he did not advise or treat Hession; that the sole purpose of the examination was to aid Hession's attorneys in the preparation of a lawsuit for Hession; and that he was the agent of the attorneys. He refused to answer questions regarding Hession's condition on the grounds that the information sought was privileged under subdivisions 2 and 4 of Section 1881 of the Code of Civil Procedure and that the questions called for "the use of faculties of a physician, neurologist, and psychiatrist and for an opinion based thereon, which opinion is a portion of my property which I do not wish to be deprived of without due compensation and arrangement having been made in relation thereto." Hession's counsel also claimed that the information was privileged.

Petitioner, the City and County of San Francisco, seeks a writ of mandamus to compel respondent court to order Dr. Catton to answer the questions.

The Physician-Patient Privilege

Dr. Catton testified that "there was no physician-patient relationship in the sense that I was examining him for the purpose of giving him advice or treatment, . . . nor did I at any time give him any such advice or treatment; so that there wasn't that usual physician-patient relationship." He also filed an affidavit in which he averred that he "has not at any time prescribed for or treated the said James Hession as a patient or otherwise." Under such circumstances there is no physician-patient privilege under subdivision 4 of section 1881 of the Code of Civil Procedure. That privilege cannot be invoked when no treatment is contemplated or given. "The confidence that is protected is only that which is given to a professional physician during a consultation with a view to curative treatment; for it is that relation only which the law desires to facilitate." 8 Wigmore, Evidence, 3d ed. 1940, § 2382, p. 817; In re Baird's Estate, 173 Cal. 617, 623–624, 160 P. 1078. [Additional citation omitted.]

Even if there had been a physician-patient relationship, the privilege would be waived under section 1881(4) by Hession's bringing the action for personal injuries. Phillips v. Powell, 210 Cal. 39, 42, 290 P. 441; Ballard v. Pacific Greyhound Lines, 28 Cal.2d 357, 360, 170 P.2d 465; see also Moreno v. New Guadalupe Mining Co., 35 Cal.App. 744, 754–755, 170 P. 1088.

Relying on Webb v. Francis J. Lewald Coal Co., 214 Cal. 182, 4 P.2d 532, 77 A.L.R. 675, respondent and Hession, the real party in interest, contend that since the privilege set forth in section 1881(4) is phrased in the language "prescribe *or act* for the patient" and the personal-injury-litigant exception is phrased in the language "prescribed for or treated said person" the exception to the privilege in the case of personal-injury litigants is not so broad as the privilege. (Italics added.) They conclude that the privilege exists here because Dr. Catton "acted" for Hession when he examined him and delivered to his counsel a written report of his findings, but that the exception cannot apply because Dr. Catton did not prescribe for or treat Hession. The Webb case clearly supports this conclusion, but a re-examination of that case compels the conclusion that this ground of the decision must be disapproved.

The whole purpose of the privilege is to preclude the humiliation of the patient that might follow disclosure of his ailments. When the patient himself discloses those ailments by bringing an action in which they are in issue, there is no longer any reason for the privilege. The patient-litigant exception precludes one who has placed in issue his physical condition from invoking the privilege on the ground that disclosure of his condition would cause him humiliation. He cannot have his cake and eat it too.

The view taken in the Webb case defeats the purpose of the statute by seizing upon the phrase "act for the patient" and giving it a meaning that cannot reasonably be attributed to the Legislature. The statute reads: "A licensed *physician or surgeon* can not, without the consent of his patient, be examined in a civil action, as to any information acquired in attending the patient, which was necessary to enable him to *prescribe or act* for the patient." (Italics added.) "Prescribe" is the correlative of "physician"; a physician prescribes for a patient. "Act" is the correlative of "surgeon"; a surgeon acts for a patient. A Missouri statute makes this clear by providing ". . . which information was necessary to enable him to prescribe for such patient as a physician, or do any act for him as a surgeon". Mo.R.S.1949, § 491.060(5). The California statute embodies the same meaning by using the nouns physician or surgeon in the disjunctive and the verb applicable to each—prescribe or act—likewise in the disjunctive. Even if "act" were construed as relative to a physician as well as to a surgeon, the privilege could still not be extended to personal-injury litigants that the statute excepts. The statute refers to "information acquired in *attending* the patient". (Italics added.) A physician attends a patient to treat, prescribe for, or act for him to prevent, palliate, or cure an ailment. If the person examined is not a patient there is no physician-patient relationship and therefore no physician-patient privilege.

Even if there is a physician-patient relationship, it is settled that the privilege given by the statute is that of the patient, not that of the physician, and that if the patient does not claim the privilege, it is waived. Hirschberg v. Southern Pacific Co., 180 Cal. 774, 777, 183 P. 141; Lissak v. Crocker Estate Co., 119 Cal. 442, 445, 51 P. 688; Wheelock v. Godfrey, 100 Cal. 578, 587, 35 P. 317; San Francisco Credit Clearing House v. MacDonald, 18 Cal.App. 212, 219, 122 P. 964; see 20 Calif. L.Rev. 302, 311; 8 Wigmore, supra, § 2386,

p. 828. The view taken in the Webb case, however, would enable the physician to defeat the purpose by claiming the privilege even though the patient does not. The plaintiff in that case, the only one who could assert the privilege, did not do so; it was the physician who asserted it. "Respondent's counsel, however, remained silent and expressly stated to the court that they would take no part in this phase of the proceeding." Webb v. Francis J. Lewald Coal Co., supra, 214 Cal. at page 185, 4 P.2d at page 533.

The Contention That Dr. Catton Need Not Testify If He Is Not Paid More Than The Ordinary Witness Fee

Doctor Catton asserted a privilege personal to himself, a privilege not to testify to knowledge and opinions that were the result of his special learning without payment of more than the ordinary witness fee. Petitioner asks him to testify, not by reason of his expertness in a special field, but because of his knowledge of specific facts as to Hession's condition, facts pertinent to an issue to be tried. He is like any other witness with knowledge of such facts; it is immaterial that he discovered them by reason of his special training. In testifying as a witness he would simply be imparting information relevant to the issue, as he would had he been a witness to the accident in which Hession was injured. "[A] physician who has acquired knowledge of a patient or of specific facts in connection with a patient may be called upon to testify to those facts without any compensation other than the ordinary witness receives for attendance upon court." McClenahan v. Keyes, 188 Cal. 574, 583, 206 P. 454, 458. [Additional citations omitted.]

Although Dr. Catton can invoke no privilege of his own and there was no physician-patient privilege in this case, we have concluded that Dr. Catton was an intermediate agent for communication between Hession and his attorneys and that Hession may therefore invoke the attorney-client privilege under section 1881, subdivision (2) of the Code of Civil Procedure. That subdivision reads: "An attorney, can not, without the consent of his client, be examined as to any communication made by the client to him, or his advice given thereon in the course of professional employment; nor can an attorney's secretary, stenographer, or clerk be examined, without the consent of his employer, concerning any fact the knowledge of which has been acquired in such capacity." See also, Bus. & Prof. Code, § 6068(e). This privilege is strictly construed, since it suppresses relevant facts that may be necessary for a just decision. Satterlee v. Bliss, 36 Cal. 489, 508; Samish v. Superior Court, 28 Cal.App.2d 685, 695, 83 P.2d 305; see 27 Cal.Jur. 44, 51; 58 Am.Jur., Witnesses, § 464, p. 261. It cannot be invoked unless the client intended the communication to be confidential, . . . and only communications made to an attorney in the course of professional employment are privileged. [Citations omitted.]

The privilege is given on grounds of public policy in the belief that the benefits derived therefrom justify the risk that unjust decisions may sometimes result from the suppression of relevant evidence. Adequate legal representation in the ascertainment and enforcement of rights or the prosecution or defense of litigation compels a full disclosure of the facts by the client to his attorney. "Unless he makes known to the lawyer all the facts, the advice which follows will be useless, if not misleading; the lawsuit will be conducted along improper lines, the trial will be full of surprises, much useless litigation may result. Thirdly, unless the client knows that his lawyer cannot be compelled to reveal what is told him, the client will suppress what he thinks to be unfavorable facts." Morgan, Foreword, Am.-Law.Inst.Code of Evidence, pp. 25–26. Given the privilege, a client may make such a disclosure without fear that his attorney may be forced to reveal the information confided to him. "[T]he absence of the privilege would convert the attorney habitually and inevitably into a mere informer for the benefit of the opponent." 8 Wigmore, supra, § 2380a, p. 813.

The privilege embraces not only oral or written statements but actions, signs, or other means of communicating information by a client to his attorney. Ex parte McDonough, 170 Cal. 230, 234, 149 P. 566; L.R.A.1916C, 593; see 58 Am.Jur., Witnesses, § 486, p. 272. "[A]lmost any act, done by the client in the sight of the attorney and during the consultation, may conceivably be done by the client as the subject of a communication, and the only question will be whether, in the circumstances of the case, it was intended to be done as such. The client, supposedly, may make a specimen of his handwriting for the attorney's information, or may exhibit an identifying scar, or may show a secret token. If any of these acts are done as part of a communication to the attorney, and if further the communication is intended to be confidential . . . , the privilege comes into play." 8 Wigmore, supra, § 2306, p. 590.

Petitioner contends that under the express terms of section 1881(2) it is only the attorney and the attorney's secretary, stenographer, or clerk who cannot be examined, and that since Dr. Catton was not engaged in any of these capacities he cannot withhold the information requested.

The statute specifically extends the client's privilege to preclude examination of the attorney's secretary, stenographer, or clerk regarding information of communications between attorney and client acquired in such capacities, to rule out the possibility of their coming within the general rule that the privilege does not preclude the examination of a third person who overhears or otherwise has knowledge of communications between a client and his attorney. Sharon v. Sharon, 79 Cal. 633, 677, 22 P. 2. [Additional citations omitted.]

It does not follow, however, that intermediate agents of communication between attorney and client fall within that general rule. Had Hession himself described his condition to his attorneys there could be no doubt that the communication would be privileged and that neither the attorney nor Hession could be compelled to reveal it, even though a client is not listed in section 1881(2) among those who cannot be examined. Verdelli v. Gray's Harbor, etc., Co., 115 Cal. 517, 47 P. 364, 778; Birmingham Railway & Electric Co. v. Wildman, 119 Ala. 547, 24 So. 548, 549–550; State v. White, 19 Kan. 445, 446–447; Hemenway v. Smith, 28 Vt. 701, 707; see, 8 Wigmore, supra, § 2324, p. 628. It is no less the client's communication to the attorney when it is given by the client to an agent for transmission to the attorney, and it is immaterial whether the agent is the agent of the attorney, the client, or both. "(T)he client's freedom of communication requires a liberty of employing other means than his own personal action. The privilege of confidence would be a vain one unless its exercise could be thus delegated. A communication, then, by *any form of agency* employed or set in motion by the client is within the privilege.

"This of course includes communications through an *interpreter*, and also communications *through a messenger* or any other *agent of transmission*, as well as communications *originating with the client's agent* and made to the attorney. It follows, too, that the communications of the *attorney's agent* to the attorney are within the privilege, because the attorney's agent is also the client's sub-agent and is acting as such for the client." 8 Wigmore, supra, § 2317, pp. 616–617. [Additional citations omitted.]

Thus, when communication by a client to his attorney regarding his physical or mental condition requires the assistance of a physician to interpret the client's condition to the attorney, the client may submit to an examination by the physician without fear that the latter will be compelled to reveal the information disclosed. Webb v. Francis J. Lewald Coal Co., 214 Cal. 182, 186–187, 4 P.2d 532, 77 A.L.R. 675; see 5 So.Cal.L.Rev. 446. In Arnold v. City of Maryville, 110 Mo.App. 254, 85 S.W. 107, 108, and McMillen v. Industrial Comm. of Ohio, Ohio App., 37 N.E.2d 632, on which petitioner relies, it was held, as we hold in the present case, that there was no physician-patient privilege. In neither case, however, was the attorney-client privilege invoked or considered.

It is contended that the purpose of the patient-litigant exception in subdivision 4 of section 1881 would be defeated if the attorney-client privilege in subdivision 2 can be invoked to prevent a physician from divulging the results of his examination of a person for the purpose of aiding his attorneys in the preparation of an action for personal injuries. The two subdivisions relate to two separate and distinct privileges. Since there was no physician-patient relationship, there was no physician-patient privilege to waive; the whole of subdivision 4 including the exception was therefore inapplicable. It does not follow that if there is no physician-patient privilege there can be no attorney-client privilege. The patient-litigant exception applies only to the physician-patient privilege in subdivision 4 and there is no corresponding client-litigant exception in subdivision 2. Had Dr. Catton treated Hession before being asked to serve as an intermediate agent between Hession and his attorneys, the patient-litigant exception would apply and Dr. Catton would then have been like any other witness with knowledge of facts pertinent to an issue to be tried. The exception could not be defeated by asking the physician to reveal his knowledge of the facts to the attorneys, for a litigant cannot silence a witness by having him reveal his knowledge to the litigant's attorney. See Hickman v. Taylor, 329 U.S. 495, 506–509, 67 S.Ct. 385, 91 L.Ed. 451; 8 Wigmore, supra, §§ 2317–2318, pp. 615–618; 58 Am.Jur., Witnesses, § 498, pp. 279–280. Similarly, if Dr. Catton should now treat Hession, any information acquired in the course of that treatment would not be privileged, although the results of his previous examinations and his reports to Hession's attorneys would be.

The alternative writ of mandamus is discharged, and the petition for the peremptory writ is denied.

GIBSON, C. J., and SHENK, EDMONDS, CARTER, SCHAUER and SPENCE, JJ., concur.

UNITED STATES v. REYNOLDS
Supreme Court of the United States, 1953.
345 U.S. 1, 73 S.Ct. 528, 97 L.Ed. 727.

MR. CHIEF JUSTICE VINSON delivered the opinion of the Court.

These suits under the Tort Claims Act arise from the death of three civilians in the crash of a B-29 aircraft at Waycross, Georgia on October 6, 1948. Because an important question of the Government's privilege to resist discovery is involved, we granted certiorari. 343 U.S. 918, 72 S.Ct. 678, 96 L.Ed. 1332.

The aircraft had taken flight for the purpose of testing secret electronic equipment, with four civilian observers aboard. While aloft, fire broke out in one of the bomber's engines. Six of the nine crew members, and three of the four civilian observers were killed in the crash.

The widows of the three deceased civilian observers brought consolidated suits against the United States. In the pretrial stages the plaintiffs moved, under Rule 34 of the Federal Rules of Civil Procedure, for production of the Air Force's official accident investigation report and the statements of the three surviving crew members, taken in connection with the official investigation. The Government moved to quash the motion, claiming that these matters were privileged against disclosure pursuant to Air Force regulations promulgated under R.S. § 161. The District Judge sustained plaintiffs' motion, holding that good cause for production had been shown. The claim of privilege under R.S. § 161 was rejected on the premise that the Tort Claims Act, in making the Government liable "in the same manner" as a private individual had waived any privilege based upon executive control over governmental documents.

Shortly after this decision, the District Court received a letter from the Secretary of the Air Force, stating that "it has been determined that it would not be in the public interest to furnish this report...." The court allowed a rehearing on its earlier order, and at the rehearing the Secretary of the Air Force filed a formal "Claim of Privilege." This document repeated the prior claim based generally on R.S. § 161, and then stated that the Government further objected to production of the documents "for the reason that the aircraft in question, together with personnel on board, were engaged in a highly secret mission of the Air Force." An affidavit of the Judge Advocate General, United States Air Force, was also filed with the court, which asserted that the demanded material could not be furnished "without seriously hampering national security, flying safety and the development of highly technical and secret military equipment." The same affidavit offered to produce the three surviving crew members, without cost, for examination by the plaintiffs.

The witnesses would be allowed to refresh their memories from any statement made by them to the Air Force, and authorized to testify as to all matters except those of a "classified nature."

The District Court ordered the Government to produce the documents in order that the court might determine whether they contained privileged matter. The Government declined, so the court entered an order, under Rule 37(b) (2) (i), that the facts on the issue of negligence would be taken as established is plaintiffs' favor. After a hearing to determine damages, final judgment was entered for the plaintiffs. The Court of Appeals affirmed, both as to the showing of good cause for production of the documents, and as to the ultimate disposition of the case as a consequence of the Government's refusal to produce the documents.

We have had broad propositions pressed upon us for decision. On behalf of the Government it has been urged that the executive department heads have power to withhold any documents in their custody from judicial view if they deem it to be in the public interest. Respondents have asserted that the executive's power to withhold documents was waived by the Tort Claims Act. Both positions have constitutional overtones which we find it unnecessary to pass upon, there being a narrower ground for decision. Touhy V. Ragen, 1951, 340 U.S. 462, 71 S.Ct. 416, 95 L.Ed. 417; Rescue Army V. Municipal Court of Los Angeles, 1947, 331 U.S. 549, 574–585, 67 S.Ct. 1409, 1422–1427, 91 L.Ed. 1666.

The Tort Claims Act expressly makes the Federal Rules of Civil Procedure applicable to suits against the United States. The judgment in this case imposed liability upon the Government by operation of Rule 37, for refusal to produce documents under Rule 34. Since Rule 34 compels production only of matters "not privileged," the essential question is whether there was a valid claim of privilege under the Rule. We hold that there was, and that, therefore, the judgment below subjected the United States to liability on terms to which Congress did not consent by the Tort Claims Act.

We think it should be clear that the term "not privileged" as used in Rule 34, refers to "privileges" as that term is understood in the law of evidence. When the Secretary of the Air Force lodged his formal "Claim of Privilege," he attempted therein to invoke the privilege against revealing military secrets, a privilege which is well established in the law of evidence. The existence of the privilege is conceded by the court below, and, indeed, by the most outspoken critics of governmental claims to privilege.

Judicial experience with the privilege which protects military and state secrets has been limited in this country. English experience has been more extensive, but still relatively slight compared with other evidentiary privileges. Nevertheless, the principles which control the application of the privilege emerge quite clearly from the available precedents. The privilege belongs to the Government and must be asserted by it; it can neither be claimed nor waived by a private party. It is not to be lightly invoked. There must be a formal claim of privilege, lodged by the head of the department which has control over the matter, after actual personal consideration by that officer. The court itself must determine whether the circumstances are appropriate for the claim of privilege, and yet do so without forcing a disclosure of the very thing the privilege is designed to protect. The latter requirement is the only one which presents real difficulty. As to it, we find it helpful to draw upon judicial experience in dealing with an analogous privilege, the privilege against self-incrimination.

The privilege against self-incrimination presented the courts with a similar sort of problem. Too much judicial inquiry into the claim of privilege would force disclosure of the thing the privilege was meant to protect, while a complete abandonment of judicial control would lead to intolerable abuses. Indeed, in the earlier stages of judicial experience with the problem, both extremes were advocated, some saying that the bare assertion by the witness must be taken as conclusive, and others saying that the witness should be required to reveal the matter behind his claim of privilege to the judge for verification. Neither extreme prevailed, and a sound formula of compromise was developed. This formula received authoritative expression in this country as early as the Burr trial. There are differences in phraseology, but in substance it is agreed that the court must be satisfied from all the evidence and circumstances, and "from the implications of the question, in the setting in which it is asked, that a responsive answer to the question or an explanation of why it cannot be answered might be dangerous because injurious exposure could result." Hoffman v. United States, 1951, 341 U.S. 479, 486–487, 71 S. Ct. 814, 818, 95 L.Ed. 1118. If the court is so satisfied, the claim of the privilege will be accepted without requiring further disclosure.

Regardless of how it is articulated, some like formula of compromise must be applied here. Judicial control over the evidence in a case cannot be abdicated to the caprice of executive officers. Yet we will not go so far as to say that the court may automatically require a complete disclosure to the judge before the claim of privilege will be accepted in any case. It may be possible to satisfy the court, from all the circumstances of the case, that there is a reasonable danger that compulsion of the evidence will expose military matters which, in the interest of national security, should not be divulged. When this is the case, occasion for the privilege is appropriate, and the court should not jeopardize the security which the privilege is meant to protect by insisting upon an examination of the evidence, even by the judge alone, in chambers.

In the instant case we cannot escape judicial notice that this is a time of vigorous preparation for national defense. Experience in the past war has made it common knowledge that air power is one of the most potent weapons in our scheme of defense, and that newly developing electronic devices have greatly enhanced the effective use of air power. It is equally apparent that these electronic devices must be kept secret if their full military advantage is to be exploited in the national interests. On the record before the trial court it appeared that this accident occurred to a military plane which had gone aloft to test secret electronic equipment. Certainly there was a reasonable danger that the accident investigation report would contain references to the secret electronic equipment which was the primary concern of the mission.

Of course, even with this information before him, the trial judge was in no position to decide that the report was privileged until there had been a formal claim of privilege. Thus it was entirely proper to rule initially that petitioner had shown probable cause for discovery of the documents. Thereafter, when the formal claim of privilege was filed by the Secretary of the Air Force, under circumstances indicating a reasonable possibility that military secrets were involved, there was certainly sufficient showing of privilege to cut off further demand for the document on the showing of necessity for its compulsion that had then been made.

In each case, the showing of necessity which is made will determine how far the court should probe in satisfying itself that the occasion for invoking the privilege is appropriate. Where there is a strong showing of necessity, the claim of privilege should not be lightly accepted, but even the most compelling necessity cannot overcome the claim of privilege if the court is ultimately satisfied that military secrets are at stake. A *fortiori,* where necessity is dubious, a formal claim of privilege, made under the circumstances of this case, will have to prevail. Here, necessity was greatly minimized by an available alternative, which might have given respondents the evidence to make out their case without forcing a showdown on the claim of privilege. By their failure to pursue that alternative, respondents have posed the privilege question for decision with the formal claim of privilege set against a dubious showing of necessity.

There is nothing to suggest that the electronic equipment, in this case, had any causal connection with the accident. Therefore, it should be possible for respondents to adduce the essential facts as to causation without resort to material touching upon military secrets. Respondents were given a reasonable opportunity to do just that, when petitioner formally offered to make the surviving crew members available for examination. We think that offer should have been accepted.

Respondents have cited us to those cases in the criminal field, where it has been held that the Government can invoke its evidentiary privileges only at the price of letting the defendant go free. The rationale of the criminal cases is that, since the Government which prosecutes an accused also has the duty to see that justice is done, it is unconscionable to allow it to undertake prosecution and then invoke its governmental privileges to deprive the accused of anything which might be material to his defense. Such rationale has no application in a civil forum where the Government is not the moving party, but is a defendant only on terms to which it has consented.

The decision of the Court of Appeals is reversed and the case will be remanded to the District Court for further proceedings consistent with the views expressed in this opinion. Reversed and remanded.

MR. JUSTICE BLACK, MR. JUSTICE FRANKFURTER, and MR. JUSTICE JACKSON dissent substantially for the reasons set forth in the opinion of Judge Maris below. 192 F.2d 987.

MURPHY v. WATERFRONT COMMISSION OF NEW YORK HARBOR

Supreme Court of the United States, 1964.
378 U.S. 52, 84 S.Ct. 1594, 12 L.Ed.2d 678, motion den. 379 U.S. 898, 85 S.Ct. 183, 13 L.Ed.2d 174. Noted, 41 N.Dak.L.Rev. 208.

MR. JUSTICE GOLDBERG delivered the opinion of the Court.

We have held today that the Fifth Amendment privilege against self-incrimination must be deemed fully applicable to the States through the Fourteenth Amendment. Malloy v. Hogan, 378 U.S. 1, 84 S.Ct. 1489. This case presents a related issue: whether one jurisdiction with our federal structure may compel a witness, whom it has immunized from prosecution under its laws, to give testimony which might then be used to convict him of a crime against another such jurisdiction.

Petitioners were subpoenaed to testify at a hearing conducted by the Waterfront Commission of New York Harbor concerning a work stoppage at the Hoboken, New Jersey, piers. After refusing to respond to certain questions about the stoppage on the ground that the answers might tend to incriminate them, petitioners were granted immunity from prosecution under the laws of New Jersey and New York. Notwithstanding this grant of immunity, they still refused to respond to the questions on the ground that the answers might tend to incriminate them under *federal* law, to which the grant of immunity did not purport to extend. Petitioners were thereupon held in civil and criminal contempt of court. The New Jersey Supreme Court reversed the criminal contempt conviction on procedural grounds but, relying on this Court's decisions in Knapp v. Schweitzer, 357 U.S. 371, 78 S.Ct. 1302, 2 L.Ed.2d 1393; Feldman v. United States, 322 U.S. 487, 64 S.Ct. 1082, 88 L.Ed. 1408; and United States v. Murdock, 284 U.S. 141, 52 S.Ct. 63, 76 L.Ed. 210, affirmed the civil contempt judgments on the merits. The court held that a State may constitutionally compel a witness to give testimony which might be used in a federal prosecution against him. 39 N.J. 436, 452–458, 189 A.2d 36, 46–49.

Since a grant of immunity is valid only if it is coextensive with the scope of the privilege against self-incrimination, Counselman v. Hitchcock, 142 U.S. 547, 12 S.Ct. 195, 35 L.Ed. 1110, we must now decide the fundamental constitutional question of whether, absent an immunity provision, one jurisdiction in our federal structure may compel a witness to give testimony which might incriminate him under the laws of another jurisdiction. The answer to this question must depend, of course, on whether such an application of the privilege promotes or defeats its policies and purposes.

I. THE POLICIES OF THE PRIVILEGE

The privilege against self-incrimination "registers an important advance in the development of our liberty — 'one of the great landmarks in man's struggle to make himself civilized.'" Ullmann v. United States, 350 U.S. 422, 426, 76 S.Ct. 497, 500, 100 L.Ed. 511. It reflects many of our fundamental values and most noble aspirations: our unwillingness to subject those suspected of crime to the cruel trilemma of self-accusation, perjury or contempt; our preference for an accusatorial rather than an inquisitorial system of criminal justice; our fear that self-incriminating statements will be elicited by inhumane treatment and abuses; our sense of fair play which dictates "a fair state-individual balance by requiring the government to leave the individual alone until good cause is shown for disturbing him and by requiring the government in its contest with the individual to shoulder the entire load," 8 Wigmore, Evidence (McNaughton rev., 1961), 317; our respect for the inviolability of the human personality and of the right of each individual "to a private enclave where he may lead a private life," United States v. Grunewald, 2 Cir., 233 F.2d 556, 581–582 (Frank J., dissenting), rev'd 353 U.S. 391, 77 S.Ct. 963, 1 L.Ed.2d 931; our distrust of self-deprecatory statements; and our realization that the privilege, while sometimes "a shelter to the guilty," is often "a protection to the innocent." Quinn v. United States, 349 U.S. 155, 162, 75 S.Ct. 668, 673, 99 L.Ed. 964.

Most, if not all, of these policies and purposes are defeated when a witness "can be whipsawed into incriminating himself under both state and federal law even though" the constitutional privilege against self-incrimination is applicable to each. Cf. Knapp v. Schweitzer, 357 U.S. 371, 385, 78 S.Ct. 1302, 1310 (dissenting opinion of MR. JUSTICE BLACK). This has become especially true in our age of "cooperative federalism," where the Federal and State Governments are waging a united front against many types of criminal activity.

Respondent contends, however, that we should adhere to the "established rule" that the constitutional privilege against self-incrimination does not protect a witness in one jurisdiction against being compelled to give testimony which could be used to convict him in another jurisdiction. This "rule" has three decisional facets: United States v. Murdock, 284 U.S. 141, 52 S.Ct. 63, held that the Federal Government could compel a witness to give testimony which might incriminate him under state law; Knapp v. Schweitzer, 357 U.S. 371, 78 S.Ct. 1302, held that a State could compel a witness to give testimony which might incriminate him under federal law; and Feldman v. United States, 322 U.S. 487, 64 S.Ct. 1082, held that testimony thus compelled by a State could be introduced into evidence in the federal courts.

Our decision today in Malloy v. Hogan, supra, necessitates a reconsideration of this rule. Our review of the pertinent cases in this Court and of their English antecedents reveals that Murdock did not adequately consider the relevant authorities and has been significantly weakened by subsequent decisions of this Court, and, further, that the legal premises underlying Feldman and Knapp have since been rejected.

II. THE EARLY ENGLISH AND AMERICAN CASES

A. *The English Cases Before the Adoption of the Constitution* In 1749 the Court of Exchequer decided East India Co. v. Campbell, 1 Ves. sen. 246, 27 Eng.Rep. 1010. The defendant in that case refused to "discover" certain information in a proceeding in an English court on the ground that it might subject him to punishment in the courts of India. The court unanimously held that the privilege against self-incrimination protected a witness in an English court from being compelled to give testimony which could be used to convict him in the courts of another jurisdiction. . . .

In the following year, this rule was applied in a case involving separate systems of courts and law located within the same geographic area. The defendant in Brownsword v. Edwards, 2 Ves. sen. 243, 28 Eng.Rep. 157, refused to "discover, whether she was lawfully married" to a certain individual, on the ground that if she admitted to the marriage she would be confessing to an act which, although legal under the common law, would render her "liable to prosecution in ecclesiastical court." . . .

B. *The Saline Bank Case* It was against this background of English case law that this Court in 1828 decided United States v. Saline Bank of Virginia, 1 Pet. 100, 7 L.Ed. 69. The Government, seeking to recover certain bank deposits, brought suit in the District Court against the bank and a number of its stockholders. The defendants resisted discovery of "any matters, whereby they may impeach or accuse themselves of any offense or crime, or be liable by the laws of the commonwealth of

Virginia, to penalties and grievous fines. . . ." Id., 1 Pet., at 102. The unanimous opinion of the Court, delivered by Chief Justice Marshall, reads as follows:

"This is a bill in equity for a discovery and relief. The defendants set up a plea in bar, alleging that the discovery would subject them to penalties under the statute of Virginia.

"The Court below decided in favour of the validity of the plea, and dismissed the bill.

"It is apparent that in every step of the suit, the facts required to be discovered in support of this suit would expose the parties to danger. The rule clearly is, that a party is not bound to make any discovery which would expose him to penalties, and this case falls within it.

"The decree of the Court below is therefore affirmed." Id., 1 Pet., at 104.

This case squarely holds that the privilege against self-incrimination protects a witness in a federal court from being compelled to give testimony which could be used against him in a state court. . . .

IV. CONCLUSIONS

In light of the history, policies and purposes of the privilege against self-incrimination, we now accept as correct the construction given the privilege by the English courts and by Chief Justice Marshall and Justice Holmes. See United States v. Saline Bank of Virginia, supra; Ballmann v. Fagin, [200 U.S. 186, 26 S.Ct. 212, 50 L.Ed. 433]. We reject—as unsupported by history or policy—the deviation from that construction only recently adopted by this Court in United States v. Murdock, supra, and Feldman v. United States, supra. We hold that the constitutional privilege against self-incrimination protects a state witness against incrimination under federal as well as state law and a federal witness against incrimination under state as well as federal law.

We must now decide what effect this holding has on existing state immunity legislation. In Counselman v. Hitchcock, 142 U.S. 547, 12 S.Ct. 195, this Court considered a federal statute which provided that no "evidence obtained from a party or witness by means of a judicial proceeding . . . shall be given in evidence, or in any manner used against him . . . in any court of the United States. . . ." Id., 142 U.S., at 560, 12 S.Ct., at 197. Notwithstanding this statute, appellant, claiming his privilege against self-incrimination, refused to answer certain questions before a federal grand jury. The Court said "that legislation cannot abridge a constitutional privilege, and that it cannot replace or supply one, at least unless it is so broad as to have the same extent in scope and effect." Id., 142 U.S., at 585, 12 S.Ct., at 206. Applying this principle to the facts of that case, the Court upheld appellant's refusal to answer on the ground that the statute:

"could not, and would not, prevent the use of his testimony to search out other testimony to be used in evidence against him or his property, in a criminal proceeding in such court. . . ." id., 142 U.S., at 564, 12 S.Ct., at 198,

that it:

"could not prevent the obtaining and the use of witnesses and evidence which should be attributable directly to the testimony he might give under compulsion, and on which he might be convicted, when otherwise, and if he had refused to answer, he could not possibly have been convicted. . . ." ibid.,

and that it:

"affords no protection against that use of compelled testimony which consists in gaining therefrom a knowledge of the details of a crime, and of sources of information which may supply other means of convicting the witness or party." Id., 142 U.S., at 586, 12 S.Ct., at 206.

Applying the holding of that case to our holdings today that the privilege against self-incrimination protects a state witness against federal prosecution, supra, at 1608–1609, and that "the same standards must determine whether [a witness'] silence in either a federal or state proceeding is justified," Malloy v. Hogan, 378 U.S., at 11, 84 S.Ct., at 1495, we hold the constitutional rule to be that a state witness may not be compelled to give testimony which may be incriminating under federal law unless the compelled testimony and its fruits cannot be used in any manner by federal officials in connection with a criminal prosecution against him. We conclude, moreover, that in order to implement this constitutional rule and accommodate the interests of the State and Federal Governments in investigating and prosecuting crime, the Federal Government must be prohibited from making any such use of compelled testimony and its fruits. This exclusionary rule, while permitting the States to secure information necessary for effective law enforcement, leaves the witness and the Federal Government in substantially the same position as if the witness had claimed his privilege in the absence of a state grant of immunity.

It follows that petitioners here may now be compelled to answer the questions propounded to them. At the time they refused to answer, however, petitioners had a reasonable fear, based on this Court's decision in Feldman v. United Staes, supra, that the federal authorities might use the answers against them in connection with a federal prosecution. We have now overruled Feldman and held that the Federal Government may make no such use of the answers. Fairness dictates that petitioners should now be afforded an opportunity, in light of this development, to answer the questions. Cf. Raley v. Ohio, 360 U.S. 423, 79 S.Ct. 1257, 3 L.Ed.2d 1344. Accordingly, the judgment of the New Jersey courts ordering petitioners to answer the questions may remain undisturbed. But the judgment of contempt is vacated and the cause remanded to the New Jersey Supreme Court for proceedings not inconsistent with this opinion.

It is so ordered.

Judgment sustained in part and vacated in part and cause remanded with directions.

MR. JUSTICE BLACK concurs. . . .

MR. JUSTICE WHITE, with whom MR. JUSTICE STEWART joins, concurring. . . .

The Constitution does not require that immunity go so far as to protect against all prosecutions to which the testimony relates, including prosecutions of another government, whether or not there is any causal connection between the disclosure and the prosecution or evidence offered at trial. In my view it is possible for a federal prosecution to be based on untainted evidence after a grant of federal immunity in exchange for testimony in a federal criminal investigation. Likewise it is possible that information gathered by a state government which has an important but wholly separate purpose in conducting the investigation and no interest in any federal prosecution will not in any manner be used in subsequent federal proceedings, at least "while this Court sits" to review invalid convictions. Panhandle Oil Co. v. State of Miss. ex rel. Knox, 277 U.S. 218, at 223, 48 S.Ct. 451, at 453, 72 L.Ed. 857 (Holmes, J., dissenting). It is precisely this possibility of a prosecution based on untainted evidence that we must recognize. For if it is meaningful to say that the Federal Government may not use compelled testimony to convict a witness of a federal crime, then, of course, the Constitution permits the State to compel such testimony.

"The real evil aimed at by the Fifth Amendment's flat prohibition against the compulsion of self-incriminatory testimony was that thought to inhere in using a man's compelled testimony to punish him." Feldman v. United States, 322 U.S. 487, 500, 64 S.Ct. 1082, 1088, (Black, J., dissenting). I believe the State may compel testimony incriminating under federal law, but the Federal Government may not use such testimony or its fruits in a federal criminal proceeding. Immunity must be as broad as, but not harmfully and wastefully broader than, the privilege against self-incrimination.

MR. JUSTICE HARLAN, whom MR. JUSTICE CLARK joins, concurring in the judgment. . . .

ELLIS v. UNITED STATES
United States Court of Appeals, District of Columbia Circuit, 1969.
135 U.S.App.D.C. 35, 416 F.2d 791. Noted, 15 Howard L.J. 686.

LEVENTHAL, CIRCUIT JUDGE. These appellants were convicted of arson and of carrying a dangerous weapon. They seek reversal on the ground that the trial judge erred in compelling the testimony of one Izzard who had been their companion in crime.

The prosecution called Izzard to testify at trial, whereupon the trial judge advised the witness of his privilege against self-incrimination, and asked him if he wished to take the stand. The witness responded in the negative. The prosecuting attorney asked that counsel be appointed to advise the witness. Counsel was appointed; he consulted the witness, and reviewed the transcript of the grand jury proceedings at which the witness had already testified, and he advised the witness to claim his privilege.

Thereafter a long colloquy ensued among court and counsel. The prosecutor urged that the witness should be compelled to testify based on his prior waiver of the privilege at the grand jury proceedings. He argued that there could be no prejudice if the witness merely reiterated what he had already said for the record, and that the standard for waiver under the Supreme Court decisions was that there had to be an actual, realistic possibility of harm.

Government counsel also urged that the defendants had no standing to object to the ruling on the claim of privilege of a witness, and that there could be no prejudice to the witness, if the court erroneously compelled the testimony, in view of Murphy v. Waterfront Comm'n, 378 U.S. 52, 84 S.Ct. 1594, 12 L.Ed.2d 678 (1964), and other Supreme Court decisions. In opposition counsel for witness Izzard contended that there was some doubt in Izzard's mind as to whether he was being charged or under investigation, etc. at the time he testified before the grand jury, and thus he had not waived his privilege there, and that in any event he had not been given immunity and thus could reclaim the privilege at the subsequent proceeding.

The trial judge rejected outright the Government's contention that the waiver of privilege before the grand jury carried through to a subsequent proceeding, and subscribed to the rule announced in other circuits, even though there was no binding precedent from this court. He concluded, however, that there was no reason not to compel the testimony, since, under his reading of Murphy v. Waterfront Comm'n, *supra,* the witness would be protected from its subsequent use against him.

On appeal Government counsel invoke the doctrine that a party may not appeal because of the court's alleged error in overruling the claim of privilege of a witness who is not a party. We hold that while this doctrine has vitality, it does not bar review of the action complained of here. For convenience we defer development of this ruling upholding appellants' standing to Part B of this opinion, since it will involve consideration of the material presented in Part A.

As to the merits, we hold (in Part A) that the trial judge erred when he required the witness to testify on the ground that the witness was protected against prejudice by virtue of Murphy v. Waterfront Comm'n. We further hold (in Part C) that there was validity in the prosecutor's contention that the claim of privilege asserted at trial should be overruled in view of the witness's voluntary testimony before the grand jury, and that the judge erred in rejecting this contention, and accordingly affirm since we see no valid basis for Izzard's disavowal of his waiver before the grand jury.

A. *The trial judge's ruling compelling the witness to testify was based on an approach beyond his judicial authority*

1. As to the merits, we begin by saying we agree with the assumption of the trial judge that a witness compelled by a judge to testify over a claim of privilege will be protected under the doctrine of Murphy v. Waterfront Comm'n, 378 U.S. 52, 84 S.Ct. 1594 (1964). While the matter is not free from doubt, the thrust of Murphy and other recent Supreme Court decisions serves to protect the witness.

Appellant Murphy had been held in civil contempt for his refusal to answer questions before a state investigating commission. Murphy argued that the immunity conferred by the state immunity statute was not coextensive with his privilege, since the answers might incriminate him under federal law and lead to federal prosecution. All the Justices agreed that the threat of prosecution by a coordinate sovereign whittled away at the policy underlying the privilege and concurred in holding, on different doctrinal grounds, that federal officials would not be permitted to use the testimony or initiate prosecution based on the disclosure or its fruits.

In *Murphy* the order to testify was preceded by a grant of immunity pursuant to statute. What of a case where there is compulsion by a judge in the absence of an immunity statute, by an order that erroneously overrules the witness's claim of privilege? We think the witness is protected by the approach and principle underlying *Murphy. See also* Garrity v. New Jersey, 385 U.S. 493, 500, 87 S.Ct. 616, 17

L.Ed.2d 562 (1967); Lawn v. United States, 355 U.S. 339, 78 S.Ct. 311, 2 L.Ed.2d 321 (1958), both the majority opinion of Justice Whittaker (p. 355, 78 S.Ct. 311) and Justice Harlan's dissent (p. 363, 78 S.Ct. 311); and Adams v. Maryland, 347 U.S. 179, 181, 74 S.Ct. 442 (1954). The Wigmore text also expresses the view that such a court ruling protects the witness.

2. A trial judge cannot reject a witness's claim of privilege merely on the ground that the ruling cannot hurt the witness because it will establish an immunity from subsequent prosecution.

We are not here concerned with a case where a judge has made a mistake in applying legal rules, like a case where he erroneously rules that a witness has waived his privilege. In the case before us the judge did not purport to deny that the witness had correctly presented a claim of privilege. He merely asserted that the witness would nevertheless be protected, by *Murphy*, against prosecution based on his testimony.

The ruling was made by an able and conscientious trial judge. We are confident it was made in good faith, and can even discern how the judge may have come to a mis-reading of *Murphy*. Nevertheless, his ruling was in the nature of a circular, self-fulfilling prophecy that in substance can only be viewed as a grant of immunity. That ruling was outside the scope of judicial authority.

This is an area that has been considered by Congress and where it has acted with care and particularity, limiting the power to grant immunity—in the presence of a valid claim of privilege—to a limited group of federal officials. We need not consider what would be the legal situation in the absence of such a statute. With that statute on the books, the power to grant immunity is plainly outside the judicial province. . . .

B. *Appellants have standing to object to the judge's usurpation of prerogative*

We do not entertain this appeal merely to review an erroneous ruling on a claim of testimonial privilege. Here there was a usurpation of a prerogative that Congress has withheld from the courts.

We must look to the substance and not the form of the ruling. What appears to be a mere ruling on a claim of privilege is, "in reality and effect," an action tantamount to exchanging immunity for the witness's testimony. If the trial court had been ruling that the witness erred in presenting a claim of privilege the question would simply be whether the judge was correct. But by "resolving [the issue] in terms of the Murphy case," the trial court agreed that the witness was quite right in raising the claim of privilege, that he would be deprived of protection to which he was entitled if he testified without asserting the claim of privilege. And then the court in effect asserted the authority of the judiciary to compel testimony simply because the witness would be protected in the future by virtue of the court's compulsion.

The propriety of such an action by a judge raises serious questions concerning the power of courts and the limitations on their proper role in the administration of justice. The issue raised by the District Court's ruling goes to the distribution of power among the three coordinate branches of Government. This is the kind of issue that is so fundamental that appellate courts are constrained to consider and grant extraordinary writs, if necessary, in order to obviate the extra-judicial encroachment. The appellate function embraces a correction in the particular case and deterrence against future repetition.

The need for a stern restraint on judges to stay within the judicial province is a proper basis for extraordinary appellate consideration—in some cases, as already noted by mandamus; and in the case before us by recognizing a limited exception to a general rule on standing to raise questons. . . .

Ordinarily a defendant does not have standing to complain of an erroneous ruling on the scope of the privilege of a witness. That principle most recently announced by this court in *Long*, is not modified by our opinion today. But a defendant does have standing, we hold, to complain that his conviction was obtained in a case where the trial judge went outside his judicial province to grant immunity to a witness. We sustain his standing on the basis of the principle recognized in such cases as Barrows v. Jackson, 346 U.S. 249, 73 S.Ct. 1031, 97 L.Ed. 1586 (1953), and Griswold v. Connecticut, 381 U.S. 479, 85 S.Ct. 1678, 14 L.Ed.2d 510 (1965). *See also*, Berger v.

New York, 388 U.S. 41, 55, 104, 87 S.Ct. 1873, 18 L.Ed.2d 1040 (1967).

In Burrows v. Jackson, the Supreme Court recognized that the principle disclaiming standing to raise the rights of third persons who were non-parties was subject to important exceptions, stating (346 U.S. at 257, 73 S.Ct. at 1035):

Under the peculiar circumstances of this case, we believe the reasons which underlie our rule denying standing to raise another's rights, which is only a rule of practice, are outweighed by the need to protect the fundamental rights which would be denied by permitting . . . the action to be maintained. . . .

In . . . unique situations which have arisen in the past, broad constitutional policy has led the Court to proceed without regard to its usual rule.

On this point *Barrows* is in good standing.

In the case before us that principle leads to according standing to present the constitutional issues—focused as they are in the paramount need for adherence to limitations of judicial power—when presented through the only meaningful channel available. Although the "peculiar circumstances" of *Barrows* are different on the facts the essential principle is the same. *Barrows* is not distinguishable simply because the questions presented here could have been raised by Izzard had he chosen to risk contempt and appeal from the resulting order. We must focus on realities, not formalities. *Cf.* Mills v. Alabama, 384 U.S. 214, 217, 86 S.Ct. 1434, 16 L.Ed.2d 484 (1966). The reality is that the self-fulfilling nature of the District Court's ruling effectively eliminated Izzard from the action below. It would be unrealistic to project that an appeal could or might have been lodged by a witness who was wronged, since the ruling gives him de facto protection and resistance would expose him to possible punishment for contempt, at a minimum, and to the risk of antagonizing the prosecutor. As in *Barrows* the issue on this appeal would likely be effectively foreclosed from review if we do not "proceed without regard to [the] usual rule."

We repeat that this opinion does not modify the rule of *Long* for the broad areas of issues, where what is involved is an alleged error on an evidentiary question, or in definition whether the witness properly raised a claim to protection. But in this case, where the trial judge did not disagree with the witness's claim of right to protection, but proceeded by an action that was tantamount to granting immunity, we conclude that a defendant adversely affected in fact has standing to bring such departure from the judicial province to the appellate court for review and correction.

C. *The privilege against self-incrimination cannot be claimed at trial by a witness who has voluntarily testified, before the grand jury which returned the indictment, without invoking the privilege*

In our view a witness who voluntarily testifies before a grand jury without invoking the privilege against self-incrimination, of which he has been advised, waives the privilege and may not thereafter claim it when he is called to testify as a witness at the trial on the indictment returned by the grand jury, where the witness is not the defendant, or under indictment.

While the prevailing rule is that a waiver of Fifth Amendment privilege at one proceeding does not carry through to another proceeding, there appears to be no controlling authority in this circuit. We think that rule unsound, at least for the circumstance before us, and decline to adopt it.

Although numerous policies have been advanced to explain and support the privilege against self-incrimination, the paramount interest that is protected is the right to remain silent rather than make disclosures that may in fact lead to prosecution. When prosecution is barred for some reason, no privilege exists. Witnesses are compelled to speak when jeopardy has attached, the statute of limitations has run, a pardon has been granted, or adequate immunity conferred. The rationale for these holdings is that the witness's disclosure cannot prejudice him since he is no longer subject to prosecution.

Once a witness has voluntarily spoken out, we do not see how his protected interest is jeopardized by testifying in a subsequent proceeding, provided he is not required to disclose matters of substance which are unknown to the Government. We see "no real danger of legal detriment" arising out of a second disclosure. *Compare* Rogers v. United States, 340 U.S. 367 at 373, 71 S.Ct. 438, 95 L.Ed. 744. In short we agree with Professor McCormick's criticism of the prevailing rule:

A mechanical rule has been placed upon the application of [the] doctrine of waiver. . . . Consequently, a witness . . . who freely testifies before the Grand Jury . . . when called as a witness at the trial . . . may claim the privilege. . . . The rule . . . protects chiefly the person accused of crime, and gives very little protection to the witness. If he has already given material evidence of his own guilt, such evidence, in the form of a transcript of his testimony, or of a signed affidavit, can readily be proved against him if he is tried for the crime. The present testimony [i.e. second disclosure] will not add to his hazard except as additional facts or details are brought out.

The rule we think sound is like the rule put forward in the Restatement and the proposed Uniform Rules of Evidence.

The community's interest in law enforcement is a fundamental basic concern of our country, for freedom and security are intertwined. That interest cannot be used to justify trampling on the Constitution. The need for "intelligent and effective law enforcement" is, however, rightly taken into account in defining the scope of constitutional protections. Those protections are not to be extended by "mechanical rules" that serve no meaningful freedom, but interfere with and hamper sound law enforcement.

It would impede sound law enforcement if an implicated but cooperating witness can decide, after he has made disclosure to the grand jury, that he will refuse to testify at trial. The Government may have structured its case around this witness, and be unable at a late hour, often after jeopardy has attached, to recast an investigation. Leads that might have been explored in the past, with expenditure of much money and time, and were put aside with this witness's cooperation, may now be lost beyond retrieval. The witness may have obtained an effective immunity for himself, especially if the investigation ripened just before the expiration of the statute of limitations, and then be able to balk all prosecution. And even a cooperative witness may be made vulnerable, by a doctrine that gives him choice, to the threats and blandishments of the defendant. There are doubtless other considerations of like import, but these suffice to establish the interest of law enforcement.

What of the other side of the coin? Is there a Fifth Amendment policy that would be furthered by restricting a witness's waiver before the grand jury so as to give him a mint-new privilege at trial? We can discern none. As Professor McCormick notes, such restriction "gives very little protection to the witness" once he has already disclosed incriminating facts. Although it has been suggested that the privilege protects a privacy interest, reflection makes it clear that this is not the crucial interest, for it does not survive to protect the privilege once the fear of prosecution is gone, as in case of granted immunity. . . .

The privilege of course remains as to matters that would subject the witness to a "real danger" of further crimination, and that the witness need not demonstrate that danger "in the sense in which a claim is usually . . . demonstrated in court." Hoffman v. United States, supra, 341 U.S. at 486, 71 S.Ct. at 818. The witness is not required to run the risk if the answers may have a tendency to incriminate. Malloy v. Hogan, supra at 12, 84 S.Ct. 1489. . . .

It may be that in some situations the passage of time, and change in purpose of an investigation, may open up new real dangers. The question must be faced realistically, however, and not mechanically. In the case before us involving a grand jury presentation and then a trial without unusual delay, this danger does not have substance. . . .

To the extent that defense counsel's cross examination might probe matters of substance as yet unrevealed, the witness must retain his privilege, and the Government runs the risk of a mistrial or reversal, since the defendant cannot be deprived of his Sixth Amendment right to confrontation. The Government is not being exposed to an unreasonable burden, since it can control the scope of cross examination by its presentation on direct.

But it does assume some risk in presenting a nonrecalcitrant witness if he can successfully assert his privilege in response to probing that lies within the latitude to which a defendant is entitled on cross examination of a witness.

A realistic approach to the privilege, and possibility of "real danger," does present more problems to counsel and courts than a mechanical rule. Simple solutions cannot always be found in a complex society. The call of the law lies, however, in a diligent effort to give just weight to the various interests of individuals and their society, and to harmonize them with maximum attention to reality.

We now turn to In re Neff, 206 F.2d 149 (3d Cir. 1953). . . . The court in discussing the waiver question relied on the "settled" rule that "a person who has waived his privilege of silence in one trial or proceeding is not estopped to assert it as to the same matter in a subsequent trial or proceeding." 206 F.2d at 152. . . .

However sound the result in *Neff* on its facts, we decline to adopt its broad language as controlling for all circumstances. We think the better rule is to hold that the waiver carries through unless there is new material, or possibly new conditions, that may give rise to further incrimination. To the extent that the *Neff* court apprehended prejudice from the mere fact of repetition of the earlier testimony we reject its holding.

We hold that where a non-indicted witness has waived his Fifth Amendment privilege by testifying before a grand jury voluntarily and with knowledge of his privilege, his waiver extends to a subsequent trial based on an indictment returned by the grand jury that heard his testimony. We repeat, for emphasis, that our holding does not apply when the witness is himself accused or under indictment. We also hold that the witness is entitled to counsel, either his own or court appointed, and may object to any question that would require disclosure of new matter of substance.

In our view this approach accommodates both the policies underlying the Fifth Amendment's privilege and the interest of obtaining full disclosure whenever possible in criminal trials.

D. *Disposition of the case before us*

Our disposition is shaped by the scope of appellants' standing, *cf.* Smuck v. Hobson, supra, which is limited to the propriety of the trial judge's granting immunity to Izzard. While we disagree with the theory of the District Court, reversal does not follow since his ruling is sustainable on other grounds, which we have set forth in Part C.

As there noted we hold that a witness's voluntary testimony before a grand jury is a waiver for purposes of trial. This still leaves room for consideration of whether under the facts of any particular case the witness's pretrial statement constitutes a waiver.

If the trial judge had considered the question and ruled there was a waiver, the defendant would not have standing to attack the ruling, even if erroneous, as a ground of reversal. In this case the trial judge did not make a ruling but we feel the record before us is clear enough to indicate that the interest of justice does not justify a remand. The transcript shows (Tr. 42–44) that Izzard expressly stated to the grand jury that he had consulted a lawyer prior to going before the grand jury; that he wished to cooperate with the Government though he understood he did not have to; that this cooperation was voluntary, and that he knew anything he said could be used against him. Izzard's counsel at trial pointed out that before the grand jury Izzard said he did not think he was presently charged for the offense. We think this of no significance. Izzard subsequently and expressly testified to the grand jury that he did understand, and his attorney had explained that anything he said could be used against him; and understanding that it was his wish to tell what he knew about the case.

The judgment is affirmed.

SCHMERBER v. CALIFORNIA
Supreme Court of the United States, 1966.
384 U.S. 757, 86 S.Ct. 1826, 16 L.Ed.2d 908. Noted, 35 Fordham L.Rev. 131 (1966).

MR. JUSTICE BRENNAN delivered the opinion of the Court.

Petitioner was convicted in Los Angeles Municipal Court of the criminal offense of driving an automobile while under the influence of intoxicating liquor. He had been arrested at a hospital while receiving treatment for injuries suffered in an accident involving the automobile that he had apparently been driving. At the direction of a police officer, a blood sample was then withdrawn from petitioner's body by a physician at the hospital. The chemical analysis of this sample revealed a percent by weight of alcohol in his blood at the time of the offense which indicated intoxication, and the report of this analysis was admitted in evidence at the trial. Petitioner objected to receipt of this evidence of the analysis on the ground that the blood had been withdrawn despite his refusal, on the advice of his counsel, to consent to the test. He contended that in that circumstance the withdrawal of the blood and the admission of the analysis in evidence denied him due process of law under the Fourteenth Amendment, as well as specific guarantees of the Bill of Rights secured against the States by that Amendment; his privilege against self-incrimination under the Fifth Amendment; his right to counsel under the Sixth Amendment; and his right not to be subjected to unreasonable searches and seizures in violation of the Fourth Amendment. The Appellate Department of the California Superior Court rejected these contentions and affirmed the conviction. In view of constitutional decisions since we last considered these issues in Breithaupt v. Abram, 352 U.S. 432, 77 S.Ct. 408, 1 L.Ed.2d 448—see Escobedo v. State of Illinois, 378 U.S. 478, 84 S.Ct. 1758, 12 L.Ed.2d 977; Malloy v. Hogan, 378 U.S. 1, 84 S.Ct. 1489, 12 L.Ed.2d 653, and Mapp v. State of Ohio, 367 U.S. 643, 81 S.Ct. 1684, 6 L.Ed.2d 1081—we granted certiorari. 382 U.S. 971, 86 S.Ct. 542, 15 L.Ed.2d 464. We affirm.

I. *The Due Process Clause Claim* *Breithaupt* was also a case in which police officers caused blood to be withdrawn from the driver of an automobile involved in an accident, and in which there was ample justification for the officer's conclusion that the driver was under the influence of alcohol. There, as here, the extraction was made by a physician in a simple, medically acceptable manner in a hospital environment. There, however, the driver was unconscious at the time the blood was withdrawn and hence had no opportunity to object to the procedure. We affirmed the conviction there resulting from the use of the test in evidence, holding that under such circumstances the withdrawal did not offend "that 'sense of justice' of which we spoke in Rochin v. [People of] California, 1952, 342 U.S. 165, 72 S.Ct. 205, 96 L.Ed. 183." 352 U.S., at 435, 77 S.Ct. at 410. *Breithaupt* thus requires the rejection of petitioner's due process argument, and nothing in the circumstances of this case or in supervening events persuades us that this aspect of *Breithaupt* should be overruled.

II. *The Privilege against Self-incrimination Claim* *Breithaupt* summarily rejected an argument that the withdrawal of blood and the admission of the analysis report involved in that state case violated the Fifth Amendment privilege of any person not to "be compelled in any criminal case to be a witness against himself," citing Twining v. State of New Jersey, 211 U.S. 78, 29 S.Ct. 14, 53 L.Ed. 97. But that case, holding that the protections of the Fourteenth Amendment do not embrace this Fifth Amendment privilege, has been succeeded by Malloy v. Hogan, 378 U.S. 1, 8, 84 S.Ct. 1489, 1493, 12 L.Ed.2d 653. We there held that "[t]he Fourteenth Amendment secures against state invasion the same privilege that the Fifth Amendment guarantees against federal infringement—the right of a person to remain silent unless he chooses to speak in the unfettered exercise of his own will, and to suffer no penalty . . . for such silence." We therefore must now decide whether the withdrawal of the blood and admission in evidence of the analysis involved in this case violated petitioner's privilege. We hold that the privilege protects an accused only from being compelled to testify against himself, or otherwise provide the State with evidence of a testimonial or communicative nature, and that the withdrawal of blood and use of the analysis in question in this case did not involve compulsion to these ends.

It could not be denied that in requiring petitioner to submit to the withdrawal and chemical analysis of his blood the State compelled him to submit to an attempt to discover evidence that might be used to prosecute him for a criminal offense. He submitted only after the police officer rejected his objection and directed the physician to proceed. The officer's direction to the physician to administer the test over petitioner's objection constituted compulsion for the purposes of the privilege. The critical question, then, is whether petitioner was thus compelled "to be a witness against himself."

If the scope of the privilege coincided with the complex of values it helps to protect, we might be obliged to conclude that the privilege was violated. In Miranda v. Arizona, 384 U.S. 436, at 460, 86 S.Ct. 1602 at 1620, 16 L.Ed.2d 694 at 715, the Court said of the interests protected by the privilege: "All these policies point to one overriding thought: the constitutional foundation underlying the privilege is the respect a government—state or federal—must accord to the dignity and integrity of its citizens. To maintain a 'fair state-individual balance,' to require the government 'to shoulder the entire load,' . . . to respect the inviolability of the human personality, our accusatory system of criminal justice demands that the government seeking to punish an individual produce the evidence against him by its own independent labors, rather than by the cruel, simple expedient of compelling it from his own mouth." The withdrawal of blood necessarily involves puncturing the skin for extraction, and the percent by weight of alcohol in that blood, as established by chemical analysis, is evidence of criminal guilt. Compelled submission fails on one view to respect the "inviolability of the human personality." Moreover, since it enables the State to rely on evidence forced from the accused, the compulsion violates at least one meaning of the requirement that the State procure the evidence against an accused "by its own independent labors."

As the passage in *Miranda* implicitly recognizes, however, the privilege has never been given the full scope which the values it helps to protect suggest. History and a long line of authorities in lower courts have consistently limited its protection to situations in which the State seeks to submerge those values by obtaining the evidence against an accused through "the cruel, simple expedient of compelling it from his own mouth. . . . In sum, the privilege is fulfilled only when the person is guaranteed the right 'to remain silent unless he chooses to speak in the unfettered exercise of his own will.' " Ibid. The leading case in this Court is Holt v. United States, 218 U.S. 245, 31 S.Ct. 2, 54 L.Ed. 1021. There the question was whether evidence was admissible that the accused, prior to trial and over his protest, put on a blouse that fitted him. It was contended that compelling the accused to submit to the demand that he model the blouse violated the privilege. Mr. Justice Holmes, speaking for the Court, rejected the argument as "based upon an extravagant extension of the 5th Amendment," and went on to say: "[T]he prohibition of compelling a man in a criminal court to be a witness against himself is a prohibition of the use of physical or moral compulsion to extort communications from him, not an exclusion of his body as evidence when it may be material. The objection in principle would forbid a jury to look at a prisoner and compare his features with a photograph in proof." 218 U.S., at 252–253, 31 S.Ct., at 6.

It is clear that the protection of the privilege reaches an accused's communications, whatever form they might take, and the compulsion of responses which are also communications, for example, compliance with a subpoena to produce one's papers. Boyd v. United States, 116 U.S. 616, 6 S.Ct. 524, 29 L.Ed. 746. On the other hand, both federal and state courts have usually held that it offers no protection against compulsion to submit to fingerprinting, photographing, or measurements, to write or speak for identification, to appear in court, to stand, to assume a stance, to walk, or to make a particular gesture. The distinction which has emerged, often expressed in different ways, is that the privilege is a bar against compelling "communications" or "testimony," but that compulsion which makes a suspect or accused the source of "real or physical evidence" does not violate it.

Although we agree that this distinction is a helpful framework for analysis, we are not to be understood to agree with past applications in all instances. There will be many cases in which such a distinction is not readily drawn. Some tests seemingly directed to obtain "physical evidence," for example, lie detector tests measuring changes in body function during interrogation, may actually be directed to eliciting responses which are essentially testimonial. To compel a person to submit to testing in which an effort will be made to determine his guilt or innocence on the basis of physiological responses, whether willed or not, is to evoke the spirit and history of the Fifth Amendment. Such situations call to mind the principle that the protection of the privilege "is as broad as the mischief against which it seeks to guard." Counselman v. Hitchcock, 142 U.S. 547, 562, 12 S.Ct. 195, 198.

In the present case, however, no such problem of application is presented. Not even a shadow of testimonial compulsion upon or enforced communication by the accused was involved either in the extraction or in the chemical analysis. Petitioner's testimonial capacities were in no way implicated; indeed, his participation, except as a donor, was irrelevant to the results of the test, which depend on chemical analysis and on that alone. Since the blood test evidence, although an incriminating product of compulsion, was neither petitioner's testimony nor evidence relating to some communicative act or writing by the petitioner, it was not inadmissible on privilege grounds.

III. *The Right to Counsel Claim* This conclusion also answers petitioner's claim that in compelling him to submit to the test in face of the fact that his objection was made on the advice of counsel, he was denied his Sixth Amendment right to the assistance of counsel. Since petitioner was not entitled to assert the privilege, he has no greater right because counsel erroneously advised him that he could assert it. His claim is strictly limited to the failure of the police to respect his wish, reinforced by counsel's advice, to be left inviolate. No issue of counsel's ability to assist petitioner in respect of any rights he did possess is presented. The limited claim thus made must be rejected. . . .

Affirmed.

MR. JUSTICE HARLAN, whom MR. JUSTICE STEWART joins, concurring. . . .

MR. CHIEF JUSTICE WARREN, dissenting. . . .

MR. JUSTICE BLACK, with whom MR. JUSTICE DOUGLAS joins, dissenting. . . .

In the first place it seems to me that the compulsory extraction of petitioner's blood for analysis so that the person who analyzed it could give evidence to convict him had both a "testimonial" and a "communicative nature." The sole purpose of this project which proved to be successful was to obtain "testimony" from some person to prove that petitioner had alcohol in his blood at the time he was arrested. And the purpose of the project was certainly "communicative" in that the analysis of the blood was to supply information to enable a witness to communicate to the court and jury that petitioner was more or less drunk.

I think it unfortunate that the Court rests so heavily for its very restrictive reading of the Fifth Amendment's privilege against self-incrimination on the words "testimonial" and "communicative." These words are not models of clarity and precision as the Court's rather labored explication shows. Nor can the Court, so far as I know, find precedence in the former opinions of this Court for using these particular words to limit the scope of the Fifth Amendment's protection. There is a scholarly precedent, however, in the late Professor Wigmore's learned treatise on evidence. He used "testimonial" which, according to the latest edition of his treatise revised by McNaughton means "communicative" (8 Wigmore, Evidence § 2263 (McNaughton rev. 1961), p. 378), as a key word in his vigorous and extensive campaign designed to keep the privilege against self-incrimination "within limits the strictest possible." 8 Wigmore, Evidence § 2251 (3d ed. 1940), p. 318. Though my admiration for Professor Wigmore's scholarship is great, I regret to see the word be used to narrow the Fifth Amendment's protection play such a major part in any of this Court's opinions.

I am happy that the Court itself refuses to follow Professor Wigmore's implication that the Fifth Amendment goes no further than to bar the use of forced self-incriminating statements coming from a "person's own lips." It concedes, as it must so long as Boyd v. United States, 116 U.S. 616, 6 S.Ct. 524, 29 L.Ed. 746, stands, that the Fifth Amendment bars a State from compelling a person to produce papers he has that might tend to incriminate him. It is a strange hierachy of values that allows the State to extract a human being's blood to convict him of a crime because of the blood's content but proscribes compelled production of his lifeless papers. Certainly there could be few papers that would have any more "testimonial" value to convict a man of drunken driving than would an analysis of the alcoholic content of a human being's blood introduced in evidence at a trial for driving while under the influence of alcohol. In such a situation blood, of course, is not oral testimony given by an accused but it can certainly "communicate" to a court and jury the fact of guilt. . . .

The refined, subtle reasoning and balancing process used here to narrow the scope of the Bill of Rights' safeguard against self-incrimination provides a handy instrument for further narrowing of that constitutional protection, as well as others, in the future. Believing with the Framers that these constitutional safeguards broadly construed by independent tribunals of justice provide our best hope for keeping our people free from governmental oppression, I deeply regret the Court's holding. . . .

Mr. Justice Douglas, dissenting. . . .

Mr. Justice Fortas, dissenting.

I would reverse. In my view, petitioner's privilege against self-incrimination applies. I would add that, under the Due Process Clause, the State, in its role as prosecutor, has no right to extract blood from an accused or anyone else, over his protest. As prosecutor, the State has no right to commit any kind of violence upon the person, or to utilize the results of such a tort, and the extraction of blood, over protest, is an act of violence. Cf. Chief Justice Warren's dissenting opinion in Breithaupt v. Abram, 352 U.S. 432, 440, 77 S.Ct. 408, 412, 1 L.Ed.2d 448.

BEECHER v. ALABAMA
Supreme Court of the United States, 1967.
389 U.S. 35, 88 S.Ct. 189, 19 L.Ed.2d 35.

Per Curiam. On the morning of June 15, 1964, the petitioner, a Negro convict in a state prison, escaped from a road gang in Camp Scottsboro, Alabama. On June 16, a woman's lifeless body was found not more than a mile from the prison camp. The next day, the petitioner was captured in Tennessee; he was then returned to Jackson County, Alabama, where he was indicted, tried, and convicted on a charge of first degree murder. The jury fixed his punishment at death. After the Supreme Court of Alabama affirmed his conviction, he filed this petition for certiorari, contending that a coerced confession was used as evidence at his trial, in violation of the Due Process Clause of the Fourteenth Amendment.

The uncontradicted facts of record are these. Tennessee police officers saw the petitioner as he fled into an open field and fired a bullet into his right leg. He fell, and the local Chief of Police pressed a loaded gun to his face while another officer pointed a rifle against the side of his head. The Police Chief asked him whether he had raped and killed a white woman. When he said he had not, the Chief called him a liar and said, "If you don't tell the truth I am going to kill you." The other officer then fired his rifle next to the petitioner's ear, and the petitioner immediately confessed. Later the same day he received an injection to ease the pain in his leg. He signed something the Chief of Police described as "extradition papers" after the officers told him that "it would be best . . . to sign the papers before the gang of people came there and killed" him. He was then taken by ambulance from Tennessee to Kilby Prison in Montgomery, Alabama. By June 22, the petitioner's right leg, which was later amputated, had become so swollen and his wound so painful that he required an injection of morphine every four hours. Less than an hour after one of these injections, two Alabama investigators visited him in the prison hospital. The medical assistant in charge told the petitioner to "cooperate" and, in the petitioner's presence, he asked the investigators to inform him if the petitioner did not "tell them what they wanted to know." The medical assistant then left the petitioner alone with the State's investigators. In the course of a 90-minute "conversation," the investigators prepared two detailed statements similar to the confession the petitioner had given five days earlier at gunpoint in Tennessee. Still in a "kind of slumber" from his last morphine injection, feverish, and in intense pain, the petitioner signed the written confessions thus prepared for him.

These confessions were admitted in evidence over the petitioner's objection. Although there is some dispute as to precisely what occurred in the petitioner's room at the prison hospital, we need not resolve this evidentiary conflict, for even if we accept as accurate the State's version of what transpired there, the uncontradicted facts set forth above lead to the inescapable conclusion that the petitioner's confessions were involuntary. See Davis v. State of North Carolina, 384 U.S. 737, 741–742, 86 S.Ct. 1761, 1764–1765, 16 L.Ed.2d 895.

The petitioner, already wounded by the police, was ordered at gunpoint to speak his guilt or be killed. From that time until he was directed five days later to tell Alabama investigators "what they wanted to know," there was "no break in the stream of events". Clewis v. State of Texas, 386 U.S. 707, 710, 87 S.Ct. 1338, 1340, 18 L.Ed. 2d 423. For he was then still in plain, under the influence of drugs, and at the complete mercy of the prison hospital authorities. Compare Reck v. Pate, 367 U.S. 433, 81, S.Ct. 1541, 6 L.Ed.2d 948.

The State says that the facts in this case differ in some respects from those in previous cases where we have held confessions to be involuntary. But constitutional inquiry into issue of voluntariness "requires more than a mere color-matching of cases," Reck v. Pate, 367 U.S. 433, 442, 81 S.Ct. 1541, 1547, 6 L.Ed.2d 948. A realistic appraisal of the circumstances of *this* case compels the conclusion that this petitioner's confessions were the product of gross coercion. Under the Due Process Clause of the Fourteenth Amendment, no conviction tainted by a confession so obtained can stand.

The motion for leave to proceed *in forma pauperis* and the petition for certiorari are granted and the judgment is reversed.

Reversed.

MR. JUSTICE BLACK concurs in the judgment of the Court reversing the conviction in this case but does so exclusively on the ground that the confession of the petitioner was taken from him in violation of the Self-Incrimination Clause of the Fifth Amendment to the Constitution of the United States, which Amendment was made applicable to the States by the Fourteenth Amendment. Malloy v. Hogan, 378 U.S. 1, 84 S.Ct. 1489, 12 L.Ed.2d 653 (1964).

MR. JUSTICE BRENNAN, whom THE CHIEF JUSTICE and MR. JUSTICE DOUGLAS join.

I concur in the judgment of reversal. This confession was taken after our decision in Malloy v. Hogan, 378 U.S. 1, 84 S.Ct. 1489, 12 L.Ed.2d 653. Under the test of admissibility stated in *Malloy,* the facts plainly compel the Court's conclusion that the petitioner's confession was inadmissible because involuntary. We said in *Malloy,* at 7, 84 S.Ct. at 1493:

"... the admissibility of a confession in a state criminal prosecution is tested by the same standard applied in federal prosecutions since 1897, when, in Bram v. United States, 168 U.S. 532, 18 S.Ct. 183, 42 L.Ed. 568, the Court held that '[i]n criminal trials, in the courts of the United States, wherever a question arises whether a confession is incompetent because not voluntary, the issue is controlled by that portion of the Fifth Amendment to the Constitution of the United States commanding that no person "shall be compelled in any criminal case to be a witness against himself."' Id., 168 U.S. at 542, 18 S.Ct. at 187. Under this test, the constitutional inquiry is not whether the conduct of state officers in obtaining the confession was shocking, but whether the confession was 'free and voluntary: that is, [it] must not be extracted by any sort of threats or violence, nor obtained by any direct or implied promises, however slight, nor by the exertion of any improper influence....' Id., 168 U.S. at 542–543, 18 S.Ct. at 186–187; see also Hardy v. United States, 186 U.S. 224, 229, 22 S.Ct. 889, 891, 46 L.Ed. 1137; Ziang Sung Wan v. United States, 226 U.S. 1, 14, 45 S.Ct. 1, 3, 69 L.Ed. 131; Smith v. United States, 348 U.S. 147, 150, 75 S.Ct. 194, 196, 99 L.Ed. 192."

SIMS v. GEORGIA
Supreme Court of the United States, 1967.
385 U.S. 538, 87 S.Ct. 639, 17 L.Ed.2d 593.

MR. JUSTICE CLARK delivered the opinion of the Court.

Petitioner, a Negro, has been convicted of raping a white woman and has been given the death penalty. He raises five federal questions for consideration by this Court, among which is that his Fourteenth Amendment rights to a fair trial were violated by the state trial judge's failure to determine the voluntariness of his alleged confession prior to its admission into evidence before the jury, as required by the rule in Jackson v. Denno, 378 U.S. 368, 84 S.Ct. 1774, 12 L.Ed.2d 908 (1964). The Supreme Court of Georgia ruled that *Jackson* was not applicable and affirmed petitioner's conviction, Sims v. State, 221 Ga. 190, 144 S.Ed.2d 103. We granted certiorari limited to the five questions, 384 U.S. 998, 86 S.Ct. 1953, 16 L.Ed.2d 1013. We have determined that petitioner's case is controlled by *Jackson,* supra, and therefore we do not reach any of the other issues raised.

I. The record indicates that on April 13, 1963, a 29-year-old white woman was driving home alone in her automobile when petitioner drove up behind her in his car, forced her off the road into a ditch, took the woman from her car into nearby woods and forcibly raped her. When he returned to his car, he could not start the engine so he left the scene on foot. Some four hours later he was apprehended by some Negro workers who had been alerted to be on the watch for him. He told these Negroes that he had attacked a white woman. They then turned petitioner over to their employer who delivered him to two state patrolmen. He was then taken to the office of Doctor Jackson who had previously examined the victim. Petitioner's clothing was removed in order to test it for blood stains. Petitioner testified that while he was in Doctor Jackson's office he was knocked down, kicked over the right eye and pulled around the floor by his private parts. He was taken to a hospital owned by Doctor Jackson, which was adjacent to his office, where four stitches were taken in his forehead. Thereafter the patrolmen took petitioner to Waycross, Georgia, some 30 miles distant, where he was placed in the county jail. During that evening, he saw a deputy sheriff whom he had known for some 13 years and who was on duty on the same floor of the jail where petitioner was incarcerated. He agreed to make a statement and was taken to an interview room where, in the presence of the sheriff, the deputy sheriff and two police officers, he signed a written confession. Two days later he was arraigned.

Prior to trial petitioner filed a motion to suppress the confession as being the result of coercion. A hearing was held before the court out of the presence of the jury. The sheriff and the deputy sheriff testified to the circumstances surrounding the taking and signing of the confession. Petitioner testified as to the abuse he had received while in Doctor Jackson's office. He testified that he "felt pretty rough for about two or three weeks [after the incident], more on my private than I did on my face" and that he "was paining a right smart." There was no contradictory testimony taken. The court denied the motion to suppress without opinion or findings and the confession was admitted into evidence at petitioner's trial.

At the trial, Doctor Jackson was a witness for the State. On cross-examination he denied that he had knocked petitioner down while the latter was in his office, or that he had kicked him in the forehead but made no mention of the other abuse about which petitioner testified. The doctor stated that petitioner was not abused in his presence but he refused to say whether the patrolmen present abused petitioner as he was not in the office at all times while the petitioner was there with the patrolmen. In this state of the record petitioner's testimony in this regard was left uncontradicted.

II. There is no actual ruling or finding in the record showing that the trial judge determined the voluntariness of the confession. Although he admitted it into evidence, it appears that he was only following a long-standing state practice that the "State having made out a prima facie case that the alleged confession was freely and voluntarily made, it was a question for the jury to determine on conflicting evidence whether the alleged confession was freely and voluntarily made." Downs v. State, 208 Ga. 619, 621, 68 S.E.2d 568, 570. Defense counsel called the court's attention to the Jackson v. Denno ruling of this Court and stated that he did not "know whether the procedure being followed at this time satisfies the rule decided by the Supreme Court on June 22nd, 1964, that the Court must make judicial determination whether the statement was made voluntarily before it is read to the jury." In his charge to the jury the judge directed that it was for the jury to determine whether the confession was actually made or not and to disregard it if not made freely and voluntarily.

III. On appeal to the Supreme Court of Georgia, it was held proper for the trial judge to have left the question of the voluntariness of the confession to the jurors with instructions that they should disregard it if they should determine that it was not, in fact, voluntarily made. Indeed, that court specifically found that the "related facts made a prima facie showing that the statement was freely and voluntarily made and admissible in evidence." 221 Ga., at 198, 144 S.E.2d, at 110. It therefore seems clear from the opinion of the highest court of Georgia that it has applied its own rule rather than having followed the rule set down in *Jackson* for the procedural determination of the voluntariness of a confession. This conclusion is buttressed by the fact that the court below also found that the "Georgia rule presents the question to the jury without giving them the judgment of the judge." Id., at 200, 144 S.E.2d, at 111. This is the exact procedural device which is proscribed by the rule in *Jackson.*

IV. The Supreme Court of Georgia reasoned, however, that *Jackson* was not applicable because of the safeguards that Georgia's laws erect around the use of confessions. It pointed out that under Georgia law, before a confession may be admitted it must be corroborated and a showing made that it was freely and voluntarily given. In addition, the trial judge has the power to set aside the verdict of the jury and grant a new trial if, in his opinion, the jury was in error. The court concluded that the rule in *Jackson* is satisfied by Georgia law and that "It would be difficult to find a more complete satisfaction of the requirement of Jackson than Georgia provides." Id., at 201, 144 S.E.2d, at 111. The court also felt that if this not be true, in any event, "the unsound implications of Jackson should not be extended one iota to make it cover cases not explicitly covered by it such as this case where there was no evidence to make any issue of voluntariness. Without an issue there is nothing to try." Ibid. We cannot agree. There was a definite, clear-cut issue here. Petitioner testified that Doctor Jackson physically abused him while he was in his office and that he was suffering from that abuse when he made the statement, thereby rendering such confession involuntary and the result of coercion. The doctor admitted that he saw petitioner on the floor of his office; that he helped him disrobe and that he knew that petitioner required hospital treatment because of the laceration over his eye but he denied that petitioner was actually abused in his presence. He was unable to state, however, that the state patrolmen did not commit the alleged offenses against petitioner's person because he was not in the room during the entire time in which the petitioner and the patrolmen were there. In fact, the doctor was quite evasive in his testimony and none of the officers present during the incident were produced as witnesses. Petitioner's claim of mistreatment, therefore, went uncontradicted as to the officers and was in conflict with the testimony of the physician. Under *Jackson,* it was for the trial judge to first decide these conflicts and discrepancies. This he failed to do.

Furthermore, Georgia's highest court, in finding that its rule satisfied the requirements of Jackson, overlooked the fact that the same safeguards offered by the Georgia practice were present in the procedures of New York in *Jackson* and were rejected by this Court. A constitutional rule was laid down in that case that a jury is not to hear a confession unless and until the trial judge has determined that it was freely and voluntarily given. The rule allows the jury, if it so chooses, to give absolutely no weight to the confession in determining the guilt or innocence of the defendant but it is not for the jury to make the primary determination of voluntariness. Although the judge need not make formal findings of fact or write an opinion, his conclusion that the confession is voluntary must appear from the record with unmistakable clarity. Here there has been absolutely no ruling issue and it is therefore impossible to know whether the judge thought the confession voluntary or if the jury considered it as such in its determination of guilt. *Jackson,* having been decided June 22, 1964, was binding on the courts of Georgia in this case, it having been tried October 7, 1964. Such rule is, as we have said, a constitutional rule binding upon the States and, under the Supremacy Clause of Article VI of the Constitution, it must be obeyed.

The judgment, is, therefore, reversed and cause is remanded for a hearing as provided by Jackson v. Denno, supra, 378 U.S. at 393–396, 84 S.Ct. at 1789–1791. It is so ordered.

Reversed and remanded.

Mr. Justice Black dissents for the reasons stated in his dissent in Jackson v. Denno, 378 U.S., at 401, 84 S.Ct. at 1793.

HARRIS v. NEW YORK
Supreme Court of the United States, 1971.
— U.S. — , 91 S.Ct. 643, 28 L.Ed.2d 1.

MR. CHIEF JUSTICE BURGER delivered the opinion of the Court.

We granted the writ in this case to consider petitioner's claim that a statement made by him to police under circumstances rendering it inadmissible to establish the prosecution's case in chief under Miranda v. Arizona, 384 U.S. 436, 88 S.Ct. 1602, 16 L.Ed.2d 694 (1966), may not be used to impeach his credibility.

The State of New York charged petitioner in a two-count indictment with twice selling heroin to an undercover police officer. At a subsequent jury trial the officer was the State's chief witness, and he testified as to details of the two sales. A second officer verified collateral details of the sales, and a third offered testimony about the chemical analysis of the heroin.

Petitioner took the stand in his own defense. He admitted knowing the undercover police officer but denied a sale on January 4. He admitted making a sale of contents of a glassine bag to the officer on January 6 but claimed it was baking powder and part of a scheme to defraud the purchaser.

On cross-examination petitioner was asked seriatim whether he had made specified statements to the police immediately following his arrest on January 7—statements that partially contradicted petitioner's direct testimony at trial. In response to the cross-examination, petitioner testified that he could not remember virtually any of the questions or answers recited by the prosecutor. At request of petitioner's counsel the written statement from which the prosecutor had read questions and answers in his impeaching process was placed in the record for possible use on appeal; the statement was not shown to the jury.

The trial judge instructed the jury that the statements attributed to petitioner by the prosecution could be considered only in passing on petitioner's credibility and not as evidence of guilt. In closing summations both counsel argued the substance of the impeaching statements. The jury then found petitioner guilty of the second count of the indictment. The New York Court of Appeals affirmed in a *per curiam* opinion, 25 N.Y.2d 175, 303 N.Y.S.2d 71, 250 N.E.2d 349 (1969).

At trial the prosecution made no effort in its case in chief to use the statements allegedly made by petitioner, conceding that they were inadmissible under Miranda v. Arizona, 384 U.S. 436, 86 S.Ct. 1602, 16 L.Ed.2d 694 (1966). The transcript of the interrogation used in the impeachment, but not given to the jury, shows that no warning of a right to appointed counsel was given before questions were put to petitioner when he was taken into custody. Petitioner makes no claim that the statements made to the police were coerced or involuntary.

Some comments in the *Miranda* opinion can indeed be read as indicating a bar to use of an uncounseled statement for any purpose, but discussion of that issue was not at all necessary to the Court's holding and cannot be regarded as controlling. *Miranda* barred the prosecution from making its case with statements of an accused made while in custody prior to having or effectively waiving counsel. It does not follow from *Miranda* that evidence inadmissible against an accused in the prosecution's case in chief is barred for all purposes, provided of course that the trustworthiness of the evidence satisfies legal standards.

In Walder v. United States, 347 U.S. 62, 74 S.Ct. 354, 98 L.Ed. 503 (1954), the Court permitted physical evidence, inadmissible in the case in chief, to be used for impeachment purposes.

"It is one thing to say that the Government cannot make an affirmative use of evidence unlawfully obtained. It is quite another to say that the defendant can turn the illegal method by which evidence in the Government's possession was obtained to his own advantage, and provide himself with a shield against contradiction of his untruths. Such an extension of the *Weeks* doctrine [Weeks v. United States, 232 U.S. 383, 34 S.Ct. 341, 58 L.Ed. 652] would be a perversion of the Fourth Amendment.

"... [T]here is hardly justification for letting the defendant affirmatively resort to perjurious testimony in reliance on the Government's disability to challenge his credibility." 347 U.S., at 65, 74 S.Ct. at 356.

It is true that Walder was impeached as to collateral matters included in his direct examination, whereas petitioner here was impeached as to testimony bearing more directly on the crimes charged. We are not persuaded that there is a difference in principle that warrants a result different from that reached by the Court in *Walder*. The conflict between petitioner's testimony in his own behalf concerning the events of January 7 contrasted sharply with what he told the police shortly after his arrest. The impeachment process here undoubtedly provided valuable aid to the jury in assessing petitioner's credibility, and the benefits of this process should not be lost, in our view, because of the speculative possibility that impermissible police conduct will be encouraged thereby. Assuming that the exclusionary rule has a deterrent effect on proscribed police conduct, sufficient deterrence flows when the evidence in question is made unavailable to the prosecution in its case in chief.

Every criminal defendant is privileged to testify in his own defense, or to refuse to do so. But that privilege cannot be construed to include the right to commit perjury. See United States v. Knox, 396 U.S. 77, 90 S.Ct. 363, 24 L.Ed.2d 275 (1969); cf. Dennis v. United States, 384 U.S. 855, 86 S.Ct. 1840, 16 L.Ed.2d 973 (1966). Having voluntarily taken the stand, petitioner was under an obligation to speak truthfully and accurately, and the prosecution here did no more than utilize the traditional truth-testing devices of the adversary process. Had inconsistent statements been made by the accused to some third person, it could hardly be contended that the conflict could not be laid before the jury by way of cross-examination and impeachment.

The shield provided by *Miranda* cannot be perverted into a license to use perjury by way of a defense, free from the risk of confrontation with prior inconsistent utterances. We hold, therefore, that petitioner's credibility was appropriately impeached by use of his earlier conflicting statements.

Affirmed.

MR. JUSTICE BLACK dissents.

MR. JUSTICE BRENNAN, with whom MR. JUSTICE DOUGLAS and MR. JUSTICE MARSHALL, join, dissenting. . . .

6

Search and Seizure

One of the most complex problems confronting any law enforcement officer today involves the seizure of evidence and/or the taking of statements from persons suspected of a crime. Officers must be familiar with the U.S. Supreme Court decisions and of the state supreme court and courts of appeal decisions in their respective jurisdictions in order to function adequately in this area.

The U.S. Constitution in the Fourth Amendment provides that, "the right of the people to be secure in their persons, houses, papers, and effects, against unreasonable searches and seizures, shall not be violated, and no Warrants shall issue, but upon probable cause, supported by oath or affirmation, and particularly describing the place to be searched, and the person or things to be seized." Most of the state constitutions contain this same, or a very similar, provision. The student should be familiar with the section of his state's constitution which parallels the Fourth Amendment of the Constitution.

The modern thinking of the U.S. Supreme Court is that the Fourth Amendment applies not only to federal courts and federal officers, but also to state courts. The Fourth Amendment of the U.S. Constitution is incorporated through the Fourteenth Amendment (Mapp v. Ohio, 367 U.S. 643) due process of law and equal protection clause, thus making it applicable to all state courts and their actions.

For many years, the U.S. Supreme Court stated that the Fourth Amendment of the Constitution applied only to federal officers. From this thinking was derived what became known as the "silver platter" doctrine (Byers v. U.S., 273 U.S. 28). Under this doctrine, which is no longer valid, federal officers, being hampered by the restrictions placed on them by the Fourth Amendment, would inform local law enforcement officers of factors which would not justify a search by the federal agents. The local officers would then make the search and give the evidence to the federal officers on a "silver platter." This evidence would then be admissible in the federal courts. This doctrine was overturned by the U.S. Supreme Court in 1960 in the Elkins v. U.S. (364 U.S. 206) case. In its decision, the Court held that *all* unreasonable searches were barred by the Fourth Amendment. Thus, the "silver platter" doctrine was placed in its grave.

The student should acquaint himself with the rules in his jurisdiction as to who has standing (i.e., the person whose interest was violated) to raise the issue of an illegal search and/or seizure. Under the Federal Rules, only a person having some interest in the premises searched or in the items seized therefrom can raise the issue of an illegal search and/or seizure. However, in other jurisdictions, the courts have held that any person against whom an item of evidence is being offered which has been seized illegally may raise the issue of the illegal search and/or seizure.

In determining the issue of an illegal search and/or seizure, it is necessary to know what will be excluded by the court. The item which has been seized illegally, if it is being used as evidence of the crime charged, cannot be used as part of the prosecution's case against the defendant, nor may it be used in rebuttal or to show that the person committed the crime that has been charged. The modern rule is that the illegally seized item, however, may be utilized to impeach the defendant's testimony if he chooses to take the witness stand and testifies in his own defense. The limitation imposed, however, is that the item which has been seized illegally may only be used to impeach testimony given by the accused which is inconsistent with that item.

Not only the illegally seized item, but also the "fruits" of the unlawful search will be excluded (under the "fruits of the poisonous tree" theory, Nardone v. U.S., 308 U.S. 338 and Silverthorne Lumber Company v. U.S., 251 U.S. 385). *Example:* A police officer makes an illegal entry and seizure of an address book from a bookie establishment. The address book leads him to another place, where he seizes gambling paraphernalia. In this case, everything seized, because of the illegal entry and the first illegal seizure of the book, will be excluded from any trial court (Wong Sun v. U.S., 371 U.S. 471).

In order for evidence to be admissible in a court of law, it must be seized in conformance with the requirements of the Fourth Amendment of the U.S. Constitution. There are four ways to make a lawful search or seizure under the Fourth Amendment: (1) with a search warrant; (2) incident to a lawful arrest; (3) with consent; (4) in an emergency.

The Fourth Amendment prohibits only unreasonable searches and seizures. Thus, a search which is authorized by a search warrant meets the requirements of the second clause of the Fourth Amendment and qualifies as a reasonable search. The evidence obtained as the result of a search warrant will be admissible in any trial.

Search, and/or Seizure with a Search Warrant

A search warrant is a written order from the court in the name of the people of the state, signed by a magistrate and directed to a peace officer commanding that peace officer to search for personal property and to bring it before that magistrate. Historically, there have been four component parts of every search warrant: (1) the affidavit; (2) the search warrant; (3) the receipt for property seized; and (4) the return of that property to the court.

The Affidavit

The heart of the search warrant is the sworn affidavit generally made by a peace officer. It must contain the probable cause which will make the search valid. If it falls short of establishing probable cause, the warrant will not issue or will later be declared invalid in court. If the affidavit does not establish probable cause, any search or seizure of contraband and/or other items of evidence which result therefrom will be held to be illegal and in violation of the Fourth Amendment of the U.S. Constitution. The evidence and/or contraband will either be ordered to be returned to the person or suppressed after being declared inadmissible to any judicial proceedings, thereby jeopardizing any criminal prosecution of the defendant in that particular case.

Probable Cause. The most important part of the affidavit is that probable cause must be established and laid before the magistrate who is reviewing the affidavit and being asked to issue the search warrant (Carroll v. U.S., 267 U.S. 132). Probable cause means that the facts in possession of the officer at the time he is seeking the search warrant would lead any other reasonable man to a conclusion that it is highly probable that there are certain items of evidence and/or contraband to be found at the premises described in the affidavit. The degree of probable cause that is necessary is generally the same as that which would justify an officer to make an arrest for a felony without a warrant. Probable cause has been defined in some cases to be "such a state of facts as would lead a man of ordinary intelligence to believe and conscientiously entertain a strong suspicion of the guilt of the accused or that legitimate objects of a search are present on a specified premise." The exception to this rule, however, is when the officer has received information from an informant who is untested. If the magistrate has a personal opportunity to question this untested informant and observe his demeanor and concludes that he is credible, then his information will substantiate the affidavit for a search warrant.

A general rule is that the affidavit setting out the probable cause must be based on competent evidence. However, note here that hearsay is considered competent in an affidavit for a search warrant. The officer must substantiate in his probable cause that, in fact, if the judge allows a search to be made, the evidence or contraband sought to be seized is probably located at the premises where the search is being authorized.

When the affidavit is being based solely upon the personal knowledge of the investigating officer, there are generally no problems with probable cause. However, when the officer is using informants to gather the information, then the affidavit must comply with decisions laid down by the U.S. Supreme Court in determining the sufficiency of the information received. There is a two-pronged test which the U.S. Supreme Court laid down in Aguilar v. Texas (378 U.S. 108), the first being personal, specific knowledge of the informant. The Court requires that the affidavit alleges the informant's statement in language that is factual rather than conclusionary and establishes that the informant spoke with personal knowledge of the matters which are contained in the affidavit. *Example:* The informant states to the affiant (person that swears to an affidavit) that he was present when the suspect stated that he had concealed on the premises two kilos of marijuana. In this instance, the Court does not require personal knowledge in the matter (that the informant personally observed the suspect conceal the marijuana), but only that the informant was personally present and heard certain words or read certain things which can be directly connected with the suspect or the person in charge of the premises to be searched.

The second requirement laid down in the Aguilar test is that the person giving the information be a reliable informant. A reliable informant is a person who has in the past proven his reliability by giving to law enforcement officials information which has always been substantiated. This does not mean that the information given has always been proven to be correct, but only that it was given and was substantiated one way or the other by the law enforcement officer who received that information. The Court requires that in order for the magistrate issuing the search warrant to determine the reliability of the informant, the law enforcement officer present to that magistrate all factors to prove or disprove the reliability of that informant. *Example:* A person has given a law enforcement officer information on five separate occasions. The officer on three of those occasions checked out the information and made arrests based upon the information received from that informant, all resulting in convictions. On the other two occasions, the law enforcement officer checked out the information and found that it was false. The officer must allege all five incidents to the magistrate in the affidavit, telling him the results of the occasions when he received the information, thus allowing the magistrate to make an independent decision whether the information being given on this specific occasion by the informant is reliable or not. If a law enforcement officer should allege in an affidavit merely that the informant is reliable, the subsequent warrant, if it is issued, and items seized, would be quashed by the court, as this does not meet the standards set down by the U.S. Supreme Court to establish the reliability of an informant (see Spinelli v. U.S., 393 U.S. 410 and Draper v. U.S., 358 U.S. 307).

Information received from a citizen informant generally needs little corroboration compared to that received from a criminal informant, which will need to be corroborated in most instances. A citizen informant is defined as one who is not connected in criminal activity, but who is making information known to him available to the police officer out of his civic responsibility. If a citizen should call and give information to a police officer which appears to be truthful on its face, the officer need only substantiate it to a small degree in order to obtain a search warrant based on that information, as long as he clearly lays out the information received and the source of the information to the magistrate. On the other hand, if the information is received from a person who is suspected of or involved in any way in criminal activity, the police officer will have to use the test in establishing in the affidavit that he is a reliable informant.

Description of the Place to Be Searched. The constitutional standards require that before any search warrant may be issued the affidavit and the warrant must contain a specific description of the premises to be searched. As a general rule of thumb, the law enforcement officer should give not only the street address of the premises to be searched, but should also include a verbal description of the premises so that if the street number were stricken from the affidavit or the search warrant, the premises could still be located by any other reasonable, prudent man. The law enforcement officer should be especially careful in describing an apartment or an office in a large building or building complex, being sure to include all detached or attached storage facilities, garages and/or out buildings in the warrant. *Example:* 111 West First Street, Cucamonga, California: a one-story, white, stucco-constructed family residence with a gray, asphalt, shingled roof, having a wishing well on the east side of the house, made of red brick, said house being the third house, north, on the west side of First Street, from the intersection of First and Main, the front door of the house facing east with a driveway running along the north side of the house and a detached, two-car garage on the west side of the premises.

Description of the Person to Be Searched. Again, if a specific person is to be searched under the authority of the warrant, his description must be laid down so that the magistrate or any other reasonable man will know with specificity who that person is and what he looks like. This means that the officer must not only have the date of birth, exact height, weight, color of hair and eyes of the person to be searched, but also must give as much information as possible to the magistrate to aid him in deciding whether the specificity requirement has been met.

Generally, a law enforcement officer will not know too much about the person that he is seeking to search under the authority of the warrant. Thus, he must rely on information from informants or other sources and must be sure to establish from whom he received this information. If an officer has no physical descriptions of the person to be searched, he may simply tell the magistrate in the affidavit that he desires to search a person known only as "Sam," who is a white, male, in his thirties, and who generally answers the door at the residence where the officer is seeking to conduct the search.

Description of the Property or Thing to Be Seized. Again, the U.S. Supreme Court requires that in an affidavit for a search warrant the officer must, with specificity, describe the property or thing to be seized. *Example of insufficient description:* One General Electric steam-spray, dry iron taken in a burglary. This description is clearly insufficient, because the one General Electric, steam-spray, dry iron mentioned is not identifiable from the other millions that had been manufactured and sold by the General Electric Corporation. Thus, in order to substantiate a search warrant based on this item of evidence only, there would have to be a serial number which is particular to this specific iron, not to any other iron, or some other mark of identification which is identifiable as to any other reasonable man. *Example of sufficient description:* One 38-caliber, Smith and Wesson revolver, bearing serial number 12345.

There are only certain categories of property which can be the lawful objects of a search warrant. They are (1) stolen or embezzled property; (2) property or thing used to commit a felony; (3) property in possession of a person who intends to use that property as a means to commit a felony; and (4) property or things which have some probative value to show that a crime has been committed or that a person has committed a crime.

Historically, the right of the government to search and seize property was dependent upon the claim that the government had a "superior interest" in the property to be seized. This "superior interest" covered contraband property, such as narcotics, counterfeit money, or other items which had been declared illegal or were "fruits" of a crime. The person who had possession of the contraband had no valid claim to it because it did not belong to him, was an instrumentality of a crime (object used to commit a crime) or fell under the Mere Evidence Rule. Objects which were merely evidence could not be seized because the government had no superior right to these items. Today, under the Federal Rules of Criminal Procedure, the rule still stands that items that are merely evidence cannot be seized. However, since most items which are mere evidence are also instrumentalities of a crime, seizure of such items would be permitted by these same rules. [*Note:* The U.S. Supreme Court recently overruled the Mere Evidence Rule, holding that the primary purpose of the Fourth Amendment is to protect privacy, not property. Hence, any kind of evidence is subject to a lawful search and seizure (Katz v. U.S., 389 U.S. 347 and Kaiser v. New York, 394 U.S. 280).]

Anonymity. There are additional inherent requirements in the affidavit for a search warrant. For instance, any time an informant is listed in an affidavit as a reliable, confidential informant or as a citizen informant whose name must remain anonymous, the affidavit must contain the reasons why the identity of the informant must remain confidential. *Example:* "John Doe, informant, whose identity must remain confidential due to the fact that he fears for his safety and/or the safety of his family and property if it is learned who he is. The informant has heard the suspects in this case repeatedly state that they would kill any person whom they found informing on them."

Nighttime Searches. In some jurisdictions, if the law enforcement agency is seeking to conduct a nighttime search under the statutes of that state, a separate paragraph as to why the search must be conducted at nighttime must be contained in the affidavit to allow the magistrate to decide whether or not the search should be made. (There are many definitions of nighttime in the United States. Some statutes hold that nighttime is between sundown and sunrise, others that it is between 10:00 P.M. and 6:00 A.M. The student should check the statutes in his jurisdiction.) *Example:* The affiant desires to conduct a search during the hours of nighttime on the described premises because the crime was just committed, during the hours of nighttime, and it is felt that if the search is not conducted immediately, items of evidence and/or instrumentalities of the crime will be concealed to the people of the state.

"Knock and Announce" and "No-knock" Clauses. It is also best to include a separate clause in the affidavit if a "no-knock" search warrant is desired. The right of the people to be protected against unreasonable searches and seizures implies that they shall be free from agents entering their homes without knocking and announcing. Most jurisdictions now have what are commonly referred to as "knock and announce" sections in their criminal statutes. An officer who enters the premises either to execute a warrant to make an arrest or to execute a search warrant without complying with the "knock and announce" requirements will have made an unlawful entry, and any subsequent arrest made or items of evidence seized will be suppressed from the court.

Most statutes require that an officer knock loudly on the front door and announce his authority and purpose for demanding entry to the premises. If it is felt that by knocking and announcing the suspect will escape, that items of evidence will be concealed, lost, or destroyed, that the officers will be placed in a dangerous situation, or that someone else's life will be jeopardized, information to that effect should be included in the affidavit or search warrant. Some jurisdictions now hold that an independent magistrate may not determine in advance that an officer may be excused from knocking and announcing for any of these reasons. The courts following this modern trend state that the situation be assessed only after the officer arrives at the scene, not beforehand in a judge's chambers.

The Search Warrant

A search warrant is a written order from a magistrate to a peace officer to go to a specifically described place and to conduct a search of those premises and/or any specifically described persons thereon or certain described property which is listed with specificity on the face of the search warrant. The warrant will also contain an order from the magistrate that the search be conducted forthwith and the property immediately returned to the magistrate who issued the warrant.

The Receipt for Property Seized

The receipt for property seized must be filled out and left at the place where the property was seized. The receipt will generally contain a list of all items of evidence that were found at those specific premises, based on the authority of the search warrant. The receipt will then either be signed by a person in charge of the premises to the effect that he acknowledges receiving a copy of it, or it will be posted in a conspicuous place on the premises if no one is present.

The Return of Property Seized

The receipt must be attached to the return, a statement made out by the officer executing the warrant which contains a sworn declaration that all items of evidence that were seized under the authority of the search warrant are listed hereon and have been returned to the magistrate who issued the search warrant.

Some jurisdictions are now authorizing telephonic search warrants. In those jurisdictions, the student should consult with the prosecuting attorneys in his area to insure the procedures necessary under the laws. Telephonic search warrants have not been authorized by the U.S. Supreme Court, nor has there been any case taken before the U.S. Supreme Court on the legality of this type of warrant.

Search and/or Seizure Incident to Lawful Arrest

Probable Cause

The second instance in which an officer may make a search under the Fourth Amendment of the Constitution is when that search is incident to a lawful arrest (Chimel v. California, 395 U.S. 752). In order for this search to be lawful, it is necessary that the officer establish that he had probable cause to effect the arrest. Thus, the officer must have complied with his local statutes in making the arrest and determining if any crime had been committed. Most jurisdictions have statutes allowing an officer to make an arrest whenever he has reasonable cause to believe that the person to be arrested has committed a public offense in his presence. There are three basic elements under this type of statute: (1) *reasonable cause*, which is interchangeable with the term *probable cause*; (2) *a public offense*, which generally includes any misdemeanor or felony; (3) *in his presence*, which is liberally construed by the courts. Use of any of the officer's senses to acquire probable cause will satisfy the requirement that the crime was committed within that officer's presence. For instance, an officer who acquires information from another law enforcement officer and makes an arrest based upon that information is making an arrest of a crime committed within his presence. An officer who is walking down a corridor of an apartment complex and smells an odor of fresh burning marijuana has a crime being committed in his presence as well.

An officer generally can also make an arrest of a person who has committed a felony, although not in the presence of the officer. The third situation in which an officer is usually permitted to make an arrest is when he has probable cause to believe that the person to be arrested has committed a felony crime, whether or not a felony crime has in fact been committed.

Reasonableness of the Search

When an officer has made an arrest lawfully under the statutes of the jurisdiction which employs him, he may be permitted to make a reasonable search and/or seizure incident to that arrest. The sole determining factor before the court where an arrest has been made and a search and/or seizure incident thereto is the reasonableness of the search conducted by the law enforcement officer. The question here is the manner in which the search and/or seizure were conducted. This is as vital a part of the inquiry as whether they were justified at all, for the Fourth Amendment proceeds as much as by limitations upon the scope of governmental action as by the initiation of it.

Evidence may not be introduced which was discovered by means of a search and/or seizure which was not reasonably related in scope to the item being sought there or the place being searched. In this area, there is a big distinction between a search made incident to an arrest in a house and a search made incident to a arrest in an automobile. The Fourth Amendment would protect the home more than the automobile. Thus, there is more latitude on the part of the officer in the search of an automobile than there would be of a person's residence, and what may be an unreasonable search of a house may be reasonable in the case of a motor vehicle.

The general rules limiting searches conducted incident to arrest are that a search must be limited to the premises where the arrest is made, be contemporaneous, not remote, with the arrest, have a definite object, be reasonable in scope, and be reasonably related to the arrest.

The law enforcement officer should be particularly attuned to the problem of justifying the reasonableness of a search. If he is making a search of a person, is it reasonable for him to subject that person to a complete body search, including the body cavities, clothing, and/or other effects? For instance, if heroin was found in the body cavity and the arrest was made for being under the influence of alcoholic beverages, the court will be presented with the problem, of determining the reasonableness. Of course, a reasonable man would not be able to justify a search of the body cavity looking for alcoholic beverages. Basically, any search conducted by a law enforcement officer must be reasonably related to the offense for which the person was arrested. This means that the officer must look for the means or instrumentalities by which the crime has been committed.

A defendant's conduct, or the officer's observations of contraband in plain sight, however, may justify an arrest on grounds different from those for which the officer originally detained the defendant. In such cases, the search may be sustained as incident to arrest of the subsequent committed offense observed by the officer. *Example:* A full search is authorized on a defendant who is being booked into a jail on a drunk driving charge. If incident to that arrest and booking, the officer finds narcotics on the person, an additional charge and subsequent further search may be made of the person.

It is also required that there be a specific object for which the law enforcement officer is searching. An officer cannot conduct a general exploratory search. He must be searching with a specific object in mind. *Example 1:* A person is arrested for driving under the influence and the officer is conducting a search of the person and/or vehicle with a specific object in mind, i.e., alcoholic beverages or narcotics, to prove that the person was driving under the influence. *Example 2:* An officer has made an arrest of a suspect for armed robbery. He is conducting a search for a specific object, i.e., the fruits of the crime or weapons or instrumentalities used in committing the offense.

In the search for evidence of one crime (with one specific object in mind) yields evidence of another crime, the admissibility of this subsequent evidence will depend on the extent and the intensity of the search conducted by the law enforcement officer. If the search is conducted in places unlikely to harbor the evidence which the officer was originally seeking, it may be unlawful. The officer must be careful always to conduct a search reasonable in scope and manner so that it will be upheld in a court of law.

Contemporaneity

To be lawful, a search must be contemporaneous or substantially contemporaneous with the arrest. A contemporaneous search may precede the arrest if there was probable cause to arrest at the outset of the search. Further, a search made at the time of the arrest is generally considered contemporaneous as long as it is reasonably related to the arrest. Also, a search which is made when the person is being booked into jail is generally considered contemporaneous in time. However, if the arrest was unlawful, the search and any fruits thereof would also be unlawful. The student should check local statutes and case law in his jurisdiction, because some jurisdictions now hold that all searches made based upon a traffic arrest or a traffic warrant arrest other than for driving under the influence of alcohol or narcotics or for those cases covered by felony sections may not be made until such time as the person is formally booked into jail. This does not mean that in these jurisdictions a pat-down frisk for weapons may not be made in the field, but only that the officer cannot conduct a full booking search until after the person has been given a reasonable opportunity to post bail.

Under the Terry v. Ohio (392 U.S. 1) decision, an officer is allowed to make a pat-down search of the outer clothing of a person whom he has probable cause to detain for questioning prior to an arrest. This pat-down search shall be conducted only of the outer clothing and only when the officer fears for his safety or has probable cause to believe that a serious crime is about to occur. If the officer, during the conduct of his pat-down search of the outer clothing, feels what reasonably can be testified to as a weapon, he may then enter that specific pocket and extract that object only, and no other.

Usually when an officer is involved in the search of a person, he has made an arrest of that person for driving under the influence of alcohol or drugs. The officer should remember that any blood, breath, or urine samples taken from the person would constitute a search, and that the person would be protected under the incident-to-arrest exception of the Fourth Amendment. The officer would be allowed, only after making a lawful arrest, to extract these specimens. As long as they were taken in a medically approved manner, they would be admissible in court.

Search of Motor Vehicles

As a general rule, a search of a motor vehicle without a warrant will only be upheld when it is incident to a lawful arrest, contemporaneous therewith, limited in scope, and has a definite object. If the defendant was in a motor vehicle and officers had probable cause to affect the arrest, a search of the car prior to the formal arrest would be acceptable and would be admissible in court.

Automobiles generally fall within the emergency exception to the Fourth Amendment as well. Because the mobility of the automobile makes a search warrant that can be executed in time impractical, the courts generally sustain any search of a motor vehicle which was remote in time and place from the arrest, provided there was reasonable cause to believe the car would contain articles that the officers could legally seize. When the element of mobility or the emergency is lacking, probable cause to believe the car contains evidence would not justify a warrantless search not incident to an arrest. The exception to this is when the remoteness has been caused by the suspect and not by the law enforcement agency. *Example:* A burglary suspect flees in an automobile and is pursued by law enforcement officers. He abandons the vehicle and runs, but is arrested two or three hours later. The officers would then still have the right to return to the vehicle and make a search of that vehicle under the emergency exception to the Fourth Amendment.

If an officer has temporarily detained a motor vehicle, any search of that vehicle must be conducted based only upon probable cause to detain the occupant. There must be a lawful detention for a reasonable length of time, and any entry into that vehicle during this detention must even be a limited one and related to the purpose for which the person is being detained.

At the time an arrest is made, the driver and the motor vehicle may be searched for evidence related to the offense. An officer who stops a car for speeding, and charges and arrests the driver, certainly has no right to search the motor vehicle, since there would be no evidence in the car which could be admissible in court pertaining to the arrest for speeding. On the other hand, if the officer has made an arrest of the driver of a motor vehicle for being under the influence, a search of the vehicle certainly would be authorized to find the substance for which the person is suspected of being under the influence. A search, in this instance, is also considered to be reasonably related to the crime for which the person has been arrested.

Although an officer may always search a vehicle and the occupants of the vehicle at the time and place of the arrest, a problem of contemporaneity arises when the defendant is removed from the scene of arrest and the car is to be searched later at the police station. The U. S. Supreme Court has indicated that any separation of the defendant and the vehicle automatically prohibits a later search because the search would not be contemporaneous to the arrest in time or place. However, the supreme courts of some states have recently held that once a defendant has been removed from the scene and the car taken to the station, there may be certain circumstances which make it reasonable to continue the search of that vehicle at the station. *Example:* One officer makes an arrest in a neighborhood where a hostile crowd is gathering and threatening to do bodily harm to another officer. He removes the suspect and the vehicle to the police station and there conducts a search of the vehicle. It appears from recent decisions that this search would be reasonable and not barred by the contemporaneous rule due to the actions of the hostile crowd at the scene. However, in any case where it is reasonable for a law enforcement officer to acquire a search warrant for the vehicle, a search warrant would be required by the courts. Thus, when the officer attempts to delay a search or impound a vehicle to search it later, he still must substantiate the search by one of the exceptions to the Fourth Amendment of the U.S. Constitution.

Search in a Dwelling Place

The general rule is that no search of any house may be conducted without a search warrant except as incident to a lawful arrest. In the landmark decision of Chimel v. California (395 U.S. 752), the scope of a search without a warrant inside a dwelling house is limited to the person of the suspect and to the surrounding area within his immediate reach and control. The objects of the search are limited to the need to seize weapons which could be used against the arresting officer or to effect an escape and the need of the law enforcement officer to prevent the hiding or destruction of evidence.

An exception to the findings in this case, however, occurs when the officer in making his lawful arrest observes objects in plain view. These items, even though some distance from the officer, may be seized. They are not protected by the Fourth Amendment, as no search is being made. Another exception is when the suspect moves about inside the house of his own free will. *Example:* A woman arrested informs the officer that she wishes to put on some other clothing before going to jail. The officer may properly search the dressing area where she will be changing for any offensive weapons or items of contraband that she may attempt to secrete or destroy. There is another exception when an officer has reasonable cause to believe that there may be other suspects inside the dwelling. The officer may then enter other rooms looking for the other suspects and may properly seize other items of evidence which are in plain view.

Search and/or Seizure with Consent

A search and/or seizure by a law enforcement officer may be justified even though unrelated to an arrest if the officer has acquired a valid consent from a person authorized to give consent to search the premises in which the evidence is found.

In order for the court to determine the validity of any consent search, the first question asked will depend upon whether the suspect was a pedestrian, a motorist, or the occupant of a dwelling. If the person is a pedestrian or a motorist, the police officer must have probable cause to detain that person before he may request the consent to search the person or his vehicle. If the person is inside a dwelling, the officer must establish a lawful entry into the premises, usually gained by consent and permission to make the search. The burden of proof in either set of circumstances is upon the people of the state.

A consent search, even though accepted by the courts, is looked at very cautiously. It is very easy for a defendant in a criminal case where evidence has been seized based upon the consent search to overcome the evidence presented by the people that the consent was, in fact, given freely and voluntarily. Any physical or psychological pressure exerted upon the person who gives the consent will justify the defendant in quashing the consent and thus any items of evidence that were seized (Bumper v. North Carolina, 391 U.S. 543 and Lewis v. U.S., 385 U.S. 206). Physical coercion, needless to say, warrants no discussion, as it has been banned by the courts for years. Any officer who uses his physical powers to obtain a consent or subsequent confession is aware that all of the evidence will be quashed in court. Psychological coercion, however, may be exerted by an officer merely because he is present and talking to a person while wearing his gun and uniform. *Example:* An officer in full uniform goes to the door of a house, confronts the occupant, and asks to search the home. The person says, "Sure, go ahead," and later testifies in court that the only reason the consent was given was that he felt it was his duty to yield to the authority of an officer in uniform — that he felt psychologically compelled to give this person permission to search the home even though he did not desire to do so. This testimony raises doubt that the initial consent was given freely and voluntarily, and thus the court should hold that the defendant had quashed any items seized as a result of that search. *Example:* A defendant in custody is psychologically pressured by law enforcement officers to give a consent to search his vehicle or his home when the officers tell him that they are thinking of arresting a loved one of his unless he cooperates with them fully. The person gives them consent, and items of evidence are found. The defendant need only go to court and relate to the court the details concerning his granting of the consent. The court would quash any items of evidence found, holding the consent invalid. Therefore, an officer must first be concerned with acquiring a free and voluntary consent given without any psychological or physical coercion of the suspect in the case.

Warning of Constitutional Rights

The U.S. Supreme Court in a recent case (Schneckeloth v. Bustamonte, 36 L.Ed. 854) clearly indicated that a law enforcement officer is not required to give a suspect who is being asked to consent to a search any constitutional warnings. However, the Court indicated that the fact that warning was not given may be used to show that the consent was not freely and voluntarily given. The Court also indicated that information that a warning was given could be introduced into evidence to prove that the consent was free and voluntary.

If an officer is to give a warning to a person, the warning should include the following: (1) "You have the constitutional right to consult with an attorney prior to the time you grant or deny me permission to conduct the search of the premises or your person"; and (2) "If you refuse to give me consent to search your person or your premises, I will be required to obtain a search warrant prior to the time I conduct this search." Most jursidictions also inform the officer that he should, as a matter of practicality, give a full Miranda warning, as follows:

(1) You have the absolute right to remain silent.
(2) Anything you say can and will be used as evidence against you in court.
(3) You have the right to consult with an attorney, to be represented by an attorney, and to have an attorney present before any questions are asked.
(4) If you cannot afford an attorney, one will be appointed by the court, free of charge, to represent you before any questioning, if you desire.

These four statements constitute the Miranda warning.

After the warning and in order to secure a waiver, the following questions should be asked and an affirmative reply secured to each:

(1) Do you understand the rights I have just explained to you?
(2) With these rights in mind, are you willing to talk to me about the charges against you?

Right to Give Consent

Another major problem which confronts an officer attempting to get a valid consent is who may give this consent. The general rule is that any person who is in lawful possession and custody of the property the officer is seeking to search and or seize has the right to consent to a search. In giving this consent, the person gives up his Fourth Amendment rights requiring a search warrant. If the defendant is present and is the person in charge of the premises the officer is seeking to search, and he gives his free and voluntary consent, any evidence found will be admissible in court. A problem most frequently occurs when the defendant is absent, a joint occupant of the house gives the consent, and items of evidence are found (292 F.2d 460 and Fraser v. Cupp, 394 U.S. 731). If the joint occupant had exclusive possession and control of the premises at the time and of the contents therein, it is to be determined by the court whether that person had a property interest in the item seized. The federal rule is that only a person having the proprietary interest in the property may give the consent to search for that property, whereas some state courts have a broader rule which holds that any person against whom the evidence is being used would have standing to object to the introduction of that evidence thus, meaning that more than one person may have to give consent in order for it to be upheld by the court (Goldstein v. U.S., 316 U.S. 114). To determine whether or not the person giving the consent has the authority to do so, the law enforcement officer must be familiar with rules on apparent, expressed, or implied authority. Apparent authority means that a reasonable man placed in the same or similar circumstances as the law enforcement officer at the time would reasonably believe that the person from whom he is getting the consent has the apparent authority to grant that consent. Express authority, on the other hand, means that the authority has been granted by the defendant in the case to the person who now is giving the consent to the law enforcement officer. Implied authority occurs when the person giving the consent has been given the right to give that consent due to the circumstances under which he is in charge of or in possession of the property which the law enforcement officers seek to search. *Example:* A man lends his car to a woman. The police stop the car and ask the woman for consent to search. It is implied that the woman may give the consent, as she was given the vehicle.

A police officer should be very cautious when seeking a consent from a landlord or from a motel manager or hotel clerk, as these persons generally have no authority, apparent, express, or implied, to grant consent to search any rooms that have been rented or leased out to another person, even though they may have a clause in the rental agreement stating that they may do so (Stoner v. California, 376 U.S. 473).

The law enforcement officer is frequently confronted with the situation in which he desires to search the room occupied by a child and asks the parent for consent to search that room. The parent generally has the authority to grant the officer permission to search the child's room. However, some courts have held that if the parent has given the child exclusive control and possession over the room, then only the child may give that consent, even though he may be under the age of majority. *Example:* A child has placed a padlock on the door of his room and his parents have respected his privacy and not entered that room for some time. The law enforcement officer now gets permission to search from the parent. Knowing these facts, the search would be subsequently suppressed in some jurisdictions. If the child has not exercised exclusive possession and control over the room, e.g., has not placed a lock on the door, has not paid rent on said room, etc., then the parent has the authority to grant consent to the law enforcement officer to search the child's room. Another problem confronting the law enforcement officer is when the child has reached the age of majority but is still residing in the parents' home. In this circumstance, the officer should be guided by general rules of search and seizure governing cotenants in order to determine whether the parent's consent would be valid in that jurisdiction.

Scope of the Consent

Once a person has granted a free and voluntary consent to the law enforcement officer to conduct a search, it must be determined that the officer did not exceed the scope of the permission that was given. *Example 1:* An officer asks for and receives consent to search the bedroom of a home. The officer has no authority to search the rest of the home without expressed consent given by the person in charge of the rest of the house. *Example 2:* A law enforcement officer is granted consent to search a house but does not find the items of evidence he is looking for. On the way out he decides to search a car which is registered to the person who occupies the home and is parked in front of the premises. The search of this car would not be justified by the consent to search the house. A subsequent consent, a search warrant, or another exception to the Fourth Amendment would be necessary.

Once the law enforcement officer has been given a valid consent to search a place, that consent may be withdrawn by the person who gave the consent at any time prior to the seizure of items of evidence. *Example:* A free and voluntary consent is given by a man to search his home, but prior to the time the officers find any contraband, the man repudiates the consent and asks the officers to leave. The officers continue to search and find narcotics concealed in a bedroom dresser drawer. The narcotics would be suppressed in court, as the consent had been withdrawn prior to the time the evidence was found. If the officer is confronted with this situation, and consent is withdrawn, he may use the consent as one aspect of his probable cause and place it in an affidavit for a search warrant along with the rest of his probable cause.

Parolees

A parolee is a prisoner at large allowed outside the prison walls by authority of the Board of Parole. He is considered to have given his consent to any search of his person or premises by his parole officer once he is released from prison. The law enforcement officer is restricted in making a search of a parolee. Based upon his parole status, a search may only be justified if the officer is acting upon the authority of the parole officer and is seeking evidence of a parole violation, or if the search is incident to an arrest or performed in an emergency situation. *Example:* A peace officer knows that a man under investigation is on parole. The officer, trying to incriminate the man on a burglary, proceeds to his residence and conducts a search without a search warrant, not incident to an arrest, and not in an emergency situation. He finds items of evidence that indicate that the parolee has been involved in burglary. The modern rule would exclude these items of evidence since the officer cannot exercise the authority of the parole officer in conducting the search. In this situation, the officer should lay all factors in his possession before the parole officer to aid that parole officer in determining whether or not he thinks there is probable cause to believe that the person is violating his parole. If he does believe that there is probable cause, the parole officer may then exercise the right to search, or he may authorize the police officer to exercise that right for him.

Another problem connected with a parolee search occurs when there is a cotenant of the parolee present. The courts have held that a cotenant (a wife or mistress or other persons living with the parolee) may not claim his Fourth Amendment right unless the parolee could have claimed that right at that particular time. An officer should also be cautious concerning the "knock and announce" requirements as laid down in the specific state statutes, since he must first make a lawful entry into the parolee's dwelling before making any search, as in the case of any other citizen.

Certain states, as a condition of probation, are now putting probationers on the street under the condition that they consent to search and/or seizure at any time or any place of their person, home, or vehicle by any law enforcement officer. However, the states that are now allowing this type of search and seizure clause hold that before the officer may stop and search a probationer who has signed this condition, he must have probable cause to believe that the probationer is violating a specific part of his conditions and terms of probation. Either that, or the officer must be investigating the specific crime for which the person was placed on probation. Thus, a random stop of a person on probation with no probable cause other than the search and seizure clause and the finding of evidence on that person will be suppressed in court as if the search had been conducted on any other citizen.

Search and/or Seizure in an Emergency

The law recognizes that there will be certain emergency circumstances which may justify a search or entry or seizure without a warrant (Schmerber v. California, 384 U.S. 757 and 330 F.2d 543). Although a search made based upon an emergency may be justified without probable cause to arrest and without evidence of consent, it still must be reasonable under the circumstances of the emergency.

The courts have stated in various cases throughout the country that "necessity often justifies an action which would otherwise constitute a trespass, or where the act is prompted by a motive of preserving life or property and reasonably appears to the actor to be necessary for that purpose." *Example 1:* An officer who is pursuing a fleeing felony suspect has the right to pursue that suspect and enter any places that the person enters to search for that suspect without the necessity of a search warrant. *Example 2:* A description of an automobile has been broadcast. The occupant of the car is being sought for an armed robbery. The car is found by an officer, abandoned shortly after the commission of the crime. Here, the officer is justified under the emergency circumstances to execute a search of the vehicle for evidence of the crime and/or for the suspect.

The courts have long recognized the emergency circumstance in which police officers are seeking contraband and are threatened with the imminent destruction, concealment, or removal of that contraband should they wait for a search warrant. Thus, they may exercise the emergency exception, conduct the search, and seize the property without a search warrant in their possession.

As a general rule, under any emergency situation, the search must still be reasonably related to the emergency which justified the officer in searching. If officers were pursuing a fleeing felon into a dwelling, they could not rummage through chests of drawers, medicine chests, or other small places where it would be impossible for the suspect to be found hiding. Some state courts, however, have upheld the search of a dwelling where the officers were looking for identification of a fleeing suspect so that they would know who he was and therefore be better able to apprehend him.

As previously discussed in this chapter, most automobile searches that are conducted by law enforcement officers are justified under the rationale of the emergency exception to the Fourth Amendment, that being that a car is a vehicle of high mobility, and if a search is not made immediately upon the situation confronting the law enforcement officer, the value of any items of evidence or contraband may be lost forever.

Summary

In order to be a valid search, the Fourth Amendment of the U.S. Constitution requires that a search be made with a search warrant. However, there are certain circumstances in which the courts have allowed searches to be conducted and seizures made without a search warrant, such as incident to a lawful arrest, with consent, or in an emergency situation. It is vitally important for the law enforcement officer and student to become familiar with all of the state court decisions in their particular jurisdiction and to update themselves constantly in this field, as the laws are changing daily, and a textbook may only cover general propositions of law, certainly not all specific laws in every jurisdiction in the country.

DISCUSSION QUESTIONS

1. Discuss the Fourth Amendment of the U.S. Constitution and the search and seizure amendment to the constitution of your state.
2. What is meant by the phrase *fruits of the poisonous tree?*

3. What are the four ways to make a lawful search and/or seizure?
4. Name and identify the component parts to a search warrant.
5. Discuss the major contents of the affidavit for a search warrant.
6. What does *probable cause* really mean?
7. Distinguish between a reliable informant and an unreliable informant.
8. Discuss the various types of items that may lawfully be the subject of a search warrant.
9. Define the knock and announce requirements under your state's criminal statutes.
10. Discuss the permissible scope of a search incident to a lawful arrest in a house and/or in an automobile.

Supplement to Chapter 6:

Search and Seizure

Most of us value privacy. Yet, many times there is no choice except to invade the privacy of an individual. A murderer has to be jailed. If there are good reasons for believing important evidence of guilt is in his house, a suspect's right of privacy may have to bow to the people's need to search. The rules we shall examine attempt to trace when privacy must give way to the government's need to intrude, and also when the rights of privacy are permitted to stand. This process basically involves weighing the police officer's reasons and balancing them against the degree of intrusion. When the officer has enough reason to arrest a person or to make a search, we say he has probable cause (reasonable cause).

People often speak of probable cause as if it were a mathematical amount, which it is not. The courts themselves have said that there is no exact formula for the determination of reasonableness. They say that each case must be decided on its own facts and circumstances and on the total atmosphere of the case.

We must keep in mind that it is impossible to determine probable cause by some scientific test. Rather, evidence must be presented in a court where a judge evaluates the case and makes a ruling. Judges have varying views and attitudes and it is difficult to predict whether a given piece of evidence will be valid when presented to a judge.

The lessons for a police officer are apparent. He must be careful about evaluating his probable cause. He can best achieve a favorable judicial

---

*This supplement is adapted from *Handbook of Arrest, Search and Seizure*, Police Science Associates, Costa Mesa, California.

ruling on the validity of his arrest or search by familiarizing himself with the rules so as to build the strongest possible case.

Searches

The basis for all search and seizure rules is the Fourth Amendment, which provides that the "right of the people to be secure in their persons, houses, papers, and effects, against unreasonable searches and seizures, shall not be violated. . . ." The Fourth Amendment governs the actions of peace officers in enforcing the laws of the state.

One of the first questions about any search or seizure problem is, Was there a search? If there was no search, it usually follows that there was no issue of reasonableness. If the officer's conduct did constitute a search, then we inquire into whether it was reasonable or not under the circumstances. A search is an act by a law enforcement officer in which he pries into hidden places for that which is concealed. A search is a looking for or seeking out—in other words, an exploratory investigation.

When an officer sees something in plain sight from a public place, there is no search. The courts have held that objects which are in "plain view" are not searched for. Thus, if a suspect drops a marijuana cigarette to the ground and flees on sight of the officer, there is no search.

The law permits a police officer to go to a great many places without invading privacy. He can walk or ride on the public streets, he can call at homes to seek interviews with suspects and witnesses, he can go into common garages and hallways of multiunit dwellings (if they are not otherwise closed to the public), he can go in driveways and look around private homes and see what is to be seen from the street or walkways or driveways to the home. He may not look into trash cans or go into an enclosed backyard, but he can look through the windows into a house, unless he has to climb up to some out-of-the-way perch so that the occupant would have an expectation of privacy. An officer can look through the window of a car and he can use a flashlight to improve his view.

The test is not merely whether the officer sees an object in plain view. The officer must also have a right to be in a position to have the view. This is where the doctrine of privacy comes into play. The courts say that the officer cannot unreasonably invade the privacy of someone and then claim that what he seized was taken legitimately because it was in plain view. If he illegally breaks into a house and sees something in plain view, it cannot be used.

Some aspects of what constitutes a search are as follows:

Public Restrooms

The California Supreme Court has restricted police observations of public restrooms for a number of years. Clandestine surveillance of restroom facilities has generally been disapproved of by the court. Recently, there have been legislative enactments prohibiting observations by peace officers through one-way mirrors into restrooms. The California Supreme

Court has recently also ruled that even though the doors have been removed from the cubicles in a restroom, a police officer may not surveil the area inside the cubicle without a search warrant.

Open Fields

Even though the U.S. Supreme Court has said that the Fourth Amendment protection does not extend to open fields, cases are now holding, and if a person has done anything to exhibit or harbor a reasonable expectation of privacy, even in a farm field, the Fourth Amendment must be complied with, and a search warrant must be obtained for consent, or a search must be made incidental to an arrest or in an emergency situation.

Garages

At one time, garages were treated as open fields, but now more constitutional protection is accorded to them. They are entitled to the same privacy as a home. If the garage is common to several apartments, however, there may be a different rule, since the tenant could not insist on the same degree of privacy.

Minor Civil Trespasses

The fact that a minor civil trespass is committed will not necessarily defeat a subsequent search or arrest. Without committing an unlawful search, officers have been permitted to walk onto someone's property and to look through a window. If the area is closed off from public access, the view could be held to be illegally obtained. The test posed by the courts is whether there is a reasonable expectation of privacy. If the window or area around the home is sufficiently insulated from public access, it may be an illegal search to invade that area.

Seizure of Property

A seizure, as reflected in the Fourth Amendment, is the forcible dispossession of someone's property. Not everything that comes into plain sight may be seized. In general, an officer can only take contraband, stolen property, evidence, things used to commit the crime (instrumentalities), or abandoned property.

Arrest-Seizure of a Person

An arrest is a taking of a person into custody so that he may answer for commission of a crime. It is a seizure of the person within the meaning of the Fourth Amendment that subjects him to the will and control of the arresting officer.

An officer may arrest for a misdemeanor whenever he has reasonable cause to believe that the person has committed a public offense in his presence. An arrest for a felony may be made if there is reasonable cause to believe a person has committed a felony. A police officer cannot make an arrest for a misdemeanor not committed in his presence. *Presence* is liberally construed to include what is apparent to the officer's senses, including his sight, hearing, smell, and taste. The officer can enlarge his senses by using a telephone, an electronic device, or a telescope. A policeman who did not see the offense, i.e., it was not committed in his presence, can assist a citizen who saw it in making the arrest. For a felony an arrest can be made on probable cause.

The courts tell us in a general way that probable cause is such a state of facts as would lead a man of ordinary care and prudence to believe and conscientiously entertain an honest and strong suspicion that the person is guilty of a crime. It has also been defined as having more evidence for than against. It is said to incline the mind to believe but to leave some room for doubt. The test is not whether the evidence is enough to convict, but only whether the person should stand trial.

Factors of Probable Cause

Turning now to the specific kinds of evidence a peace officer will rely on in making an arrest, we note several standard categories of evidence or factors.

Resemblance of Suspect

Where police have adequate information that a person fits the description of a felon, an arrest will be justified.

Adequate Description of Vehicle

Instead of having a description of a suspect who committed a robbery or other felony, the police may have a description of a car that left the scene of the crime. The officer may be entitled to stop the car to question, or even under some circumstances, to arrest, the occupants.

Criminal Record

The fact that a suspect has a criminal record will not alone provide reasonable cause for arrest. However, the criminal record is a factor that may be taken into consideration. The fact or nature of the felony record may relate to what presents itself to the police. Officers may see a convicted felon in possession of a weapon, or they may see a person with a known narcotics record attempt to dispose of what appears to be narcotics.

Furtive Conduct

The conduct of a suspect when he has contact with the police often adds to reasonable cause. While there is a whole range of related conduct, including flight and an attempt to escape, evasiveness, admissions, and confessions, we consider here efforts to secrete or destroy items at the approach of the police. If an officer is sure that a suspect is concealing, swallowing, or destroying contraband, an arrest may be made. Several state courts have recently cautioned us, however, that an innocent gesture can often be mistaken for a guilty movement. The courts hold that the officer needs to have specific knowledge relating the suspect to evidence of crime.

Evasiveness

When a person attempts to mislead the police or gives an inherently unreasonable explanation, his false statements may reflect a consciousness of guilt, a factor that may be used for probable cause.

Narcotic Usage

An officer may see a variety of indications of narcotics usage, e.g., needle marks, constricted pupils, paraphernalia, slurred speech, difficulty in balancing. If the officer can reasonably conclude that the person is under the influence of a narcotic, an arrest for possession may be proper. However, a number of the factors, taken alone, may be insufficient. Marks or dilated pupils by themselves may not be enough.

Admissions

If a suspect makes admissions, they can be used to justify his arrest.

High Crime Area

Frequently mentioned to support probable cause is a suspect's presence in or about a high crime area. Although this alone will not justify arrest, it may be given some consideration in conjunction with other factors. The U.S. Supreme Court has repeatedly emphasized in recent years that a high crime area cannot convert innocent circumstances into probable cause.

Recent Neighborhood Crime

Analogous to the preceding section is a suspect's presence and conduct near the scene of recent criminal activity. While this alone is insufficient, it is often considered with other circumstances. The type of crime is relevant. More latitude would be allowed in the investigation of a reported homicide than in an arrest for a lesser crime.

Reputation of Premises

The fact that a person is on premises where officers have reason to believe there is criminal activity will not, alone, justify either his arrest or search. However, this fact may be considered with others.

Flight

While flight is not of itself grounds for an arrest, an officer may investigate the reason for the flight.

Unusual Hour

The hour of the night is often relied on as a factor justifying police intervention, particularly in connection with unusual conduct by suspects, e.g., squatting in a parked car, stopping at an intersection for a long time, or being in a closed service station. However, we have to keep in mind that innocent people are often abroad at night.

Presence of Other Known Felons

The fact that a suspect is with a known felon is not enough to warrant his arrest, but it too may weigh against a suspect in the probable cause equation.

Evaluating Evidence of Probable Cause

Facts Known to Officer

To justify an arrest, an officer can use only evidence that he knows at the time the arrest is made. Hence, we have the familiar rule that a search cannot be justified by the evidence it turns up.

Independence of Guilt or Innocence

Since we are only concerned with an officer's purity of mind when he makes the arrest or search, it follows too that it makes no difference whether the evidence he gets is or is not accurate, so long as he reasonably thought it was. Thus, if he arrests the wrong person by mistake in good faith and with an adequate description, the arrest will not be illegal. This is why the lawfulness of an arrest is a question independent of guilt or innocence.

Illegal Evidence

In building probable cause, the officer must exclude any illegally obtained evidence or the products of it.

Officer's Training and Experience

What appears to be innocent conduct may, in the eyes of an experienced officer, warrant an investigation or even an arrest. An officer, because of his specialized knowledge, may be able to tell that objects are auspicious, as with packaging of contraband. There are limits to this rule, and essentially innocent conduct cannot be made culpable.

Officer's Senses

A policeman can rely on his sensory perceptions—what he sees, hears, smells, feels, and touches in building probable cause to arrest.

Sources of Probable Cause

An officer can rely not only on what he himself sees, but also can build probable cause with what others tell him. Hearsay can be used.

Police Broadcasts

Police can make arrests based on information coming from official sources. Examples would be a police teletype informing officers of an outstanding warrant, the telegraphic warrant itself, or a telephone call or police radio broadcast. However, the prosecution must show that the officer who initiated the request for the arrest had probable cause. Also, the arresting officer should know the facts necessary for arrest, if possible.

Informers

It is common for police to receive information about criminal activity from persons in all walks of life. Whether or not an arrest can be made depends on the situation, as follows:

Reliable Informers. It is well established that information from a reliable informer may constitute reasonable grounds to make an arrest and search without a warrant. However, there are two conditions that must be met. First, the information from an informer must include some of the underlying circumstances about which he reports. In other words, he must have personal knowledge of that which he relates as distinguished from repeating hearsay. Second, there must be some indication that the informer is reliable. For example, an officer may know that a person has given information in the past that has led to arrest or conviction.

Anonymous or Untested Informers. An informer who is anonymous or untested cannot ordinarily give information that will authorize an arrest, unless his information is corroborated. However, the identity and apparent good character and reputation of the informer or the trustworthiness of the statement itself may justify reliance on it.

Corroboration. If an informer is anonymous or untested, and no arrest can be made on the basis of what he has said, it is still possible to investigate the information and to corroborate it. If it is adequately corroborated, then an arrest will be proper. By *corroboration* is meant additional evidence of a different character that will strengthen and confirm what the informer said.

Citizen Informers. A citizen informer is a person who is free of taint—who is not himself involved in criminal activity. His statements need not be corroborated and are usually considered reliable per se. Obviously, it is helpful to learn something about the person giving information. If he is the principal of a school, or a clergyman, for example, that will be helpful in establishing the reliability of his information.

Identity of Informers. Police are often under pressure to preserve the confidentiality of an informer's identity. However, the identity of a material witness on the issue of guilt must be disclosed. A material witness is an eyewitness or a participant in the crime or a person who could give evidence on the issue of guilt which might result in the defendant's exoneration.

If an informer only supplied information for probable cause, it may be possible to keep his identity confidential. The trouble with this is that the defendant only has to show a reasonable possibility that the informer would be a material witness on the issue of guilt. These rules make it difficult to keep the identity of the informer a secret.

Production of Informers. The prosecution does not have to produce the informer for the trial, but it does have to accumulate information about him. The police should make such inquiries and arrangements as are reasonably necessary to enable the prosecution and defense to locate him.

Reasonableness of Search and/or Seizure

Let us assume that a search within the meaning of the Fourth Amendment has been conducted. The issue now is, Was the search reasonable? The general rule is that a search warrant is needed to make a search. In recent years, the courts have placed increasing pressure on police to obtain search warrants, in effect narrowing the situations where searches can be made without them. We turn now to examine the situations where a search can be made without a warrant. There are several bases for the right to search (or preconditions that must exist before a search may be made). We will also examine the limitations of the right to search.

Search Incident to Arrest

Knowing what information it takes to make an arrest, we now focus on what an officer may do when he makes a valid felony arrest.

Search of a Person. When an arrest is made, it is reasonable for the arresting officer to search the person arrested for weapons. It is also reasonable for the officer to search for and seize any evidence on the arrestee's person to prevent its concealment or destruction. This scope of search can extend to the area into which an arrestee might reach to grab a weapon or evidentiary items. (Searches of the person in traffic arrests are discussed subsequently in connection with motor vehicles.)

Search of a Person Arrested in a Dwelling Place. Once an arrestee has been placed in custody and handcuffed, and a search made of him and the area within arm's length, there will ordinarily be no danger of destruction of evidence, and the danger of assault by the arrestee should be minimized. The justification for a wider search without a warrant will therefore disappear. Thus, when an officer wants to search other rooms or drawers or closets for evidence, he needs a warrant.

Exceptions. If an officer sees a weapon or contraband beyond the reach of the arrestee, but in plain view, he may seize it. If the arrestee places an item out of his reach to prevent its seizure, it may be seized. If the arrestee or other person in charge of the premises consents to a wider search, it would be proper. Police may also make a cursory search of other rooms for confederates if there is a reasonable basis to believe confederates are involved. If there is an emergency situation, for example involving hot pursuit, or someone hurt and/or sick, the failure to secure a warrant may be excused.

Limitations on the Right to Search.

Arrest as Pretext to Search. Generally speaking, when an officer has probable cause to arrest, the arrest will not be considered a pretext for a proper search. When the search goes beyond proper bounds, the courts have sometimes said that the arrest was a pretext to search, and is therefore illegal.

Definite Object.   Apart from the broad search of the person permitted with respect to booking-type arrests, a search incident to the arrest must be to obtain evidence of the offense which the officers reasonably believe was committed. In other words, the search must be reasonably related to the arrest.

Exploratory Search.   A search must be reasonable in scope. If it becomes excessive, it is said to be exploratory. Thus, where a whole house is searched incident to an arrest, the search will be exploratory if there is no warrant. This is another facet of the rule that the search has to have a definite object.

Search with Consent

A person who consents to a search has waived his Fourth Amendment right to be free from search without a warrant. Therefore, a search based on a valid consent is lawful, even where there is no other justification for the search, if in fact all of the following factors may be found:

(1)   Consent is made with knowledge of the right not to consent to it;
(2)   Consent is voluntarily given, meaning freely given without duress or coercion;
(3)   The consent is clear and explicit.

If the police officer thus secures a valid consent, he does not need a warrant to search, nor does he need probable cause. Consent is its own justification for an intrusion into the privacy of an individual.

Even though the courts have stated that no exact form of words will be necessary to give consent, expressions such as "Go ahead," "Come on in," "Go ahead and look," "Do what you want," have been held by the courts to be sufficient. In fact, consent need not even be expressed in words. A gesture of invitation may be sufficient. However, care should be exercised if a mere gesture or invitation is given, since if the gesture has any innocent connotations, the courts will construe it in its innocent connotation rather than in the way the officer desires it to have meant a consent freely given.

Consent of Others.   Third persons in control of a defendant's property may consent to its being searched. A variety of situations are listed as follows:

Husbands or Wives.   A valid consent can be given by a husband or wife.

Mistresses.   A mistress or common law wife can also give a valid consent to a search of a defendant's property.

Parents.   A father or mother with whom a son or daughter is living may consent to a search of his or her bedroom in the parent's home.

One sibling, however, is not allowed to give a valid consent to a search of another sibling's bedroom.

Other Occupiers. A person in control, or in joint control of premises, can give a valid consent, at least as to those things under his control or jointly controlled. However, an objecting joint occupant's refusal to consent cannot be overridden by the consent of the other joint tenant.

Innkeepers and Guests. A hotel clerk or manager cannot consent to a search of a defendant's room. A different rule may obtain where the tenancy has expired.

Landlords and Tenants. A landlord may not, absent an emergency, consent to a search of the premises of his tenant. Where the tenant abandons the premises or has been evicted, the landlord's consent is valid. The owner can consent to police entry to deal with a trespasser.

Private Belongings. The consent of a third party may not be sufficient in some instances if the purpose is to search property that is exclusively that of the defendant.

Advice of Rights. The U.S. Supreme Court has held that it is not necessary to have advised a person from whom the officer is seeking a consent that he has a right to refuse to give that consent and that, if in fact he does refuse, the officer must leave the premises or secure a search warrant before he goes ahead with the search. The U.S. Supreme Court, however, stated that the fact that no warning was given to the defendant may be used in an attempt to show that the consent was not voluntary. It further held that if the officer gave a warning, this information could be introduced by the prosecution to show that the consent was given voluntarily.

Scope of the Search. The scope of a search must not go beyond that authorized by the consenting party. *Examples:* Consent to a pat search, i.e., a cursory search of the outer clothing, does not authorize a search of pockets. Consent to search a car is not consent to search a jacket or a closed container in the car. Consent to enter a house to look for a man does not infer a right to search the house and its closet for a crowbar.

The courts have clearly indicated that if a person who has freely and voluntarily given his consent withdraws said consent at any time, even though the officers are getting close to what they feel is the item that they have been searching for, the officers must then stop and secure a search warrant. A withdrawal of consent may indicate the consent was involuntary. It may also make a search after the withdrawal invalid.

Search and/or Seizure of Abandoned Property

A search and/or seizure of abandoned property is lawful. This rule permits the search of a suitcase in a vacated hotel room. However, a seizure will not be lawful if the abandonment was a response to unlawful police activity. Thus, if police illegally break into a house and the suspect, on seeing them, drops contraband and runs, its seizure does not become lawful because he "abandoned" it.

Search and/or Seizure in Emergencies

One of the characteristics of police work is that an officer may be presented at any moment with an emergency situation. With respect to search and/or seizure, this may mean that an officer will be permitted to act without a warrant or to make an intrusion on privacy that would not otherwise be justified.

Hot Pursuit and Other Emergencies. The pursuit of a suspected armed felon will permit a warrantless entry of a house he has just entered. If he abandons a vehicle, the search of it may be justified.

Entry into a home may be justified when screams for help are heard from inside, or when a bombing had just been committed, or when police had information that a helpless child might be violently assaulted inside.

To Render Aid. Even when no crime is involved, officers may be permitted to force entry in order to render aid. For example, entry may be proper where an officer hears moaning inside, or where he searches premises to discover what kind of poison an occupant has taken.

Stop-and-Frisk

Even if a police officer does not have enough information to make an arrest, he may have enough to warrant investigation and to make a lesser intrusion on privacy than that involved in arrest.

Detention. The most common temporary situation is when an officer confronts a person on the street because of some suspicious circumstances. The officer may be able to detain and question the person (an intrusion less than arrest), but he has to show a reasonable basis to warrant the intrusion. He does not however have to show enough evidence to warrant an arrest.

Pat Search. A situation may be such that an officer will want to know whether the person detained has a weapon. To learn this, he makes a pat search and runs his hands over the outer clothing. Such action is a search within the meaning of the Fourth Amendment. This search cannot automatically be made whenever a person is detained. There must be some facts to show that the person is armed or that the officer's safety is endangered, although the officer need not be absolutely certain that the individual is armed. When made, the pat search must be confined to an attempt to locate weapons.

Search of Inner Clothing. If a pat search discloses an object which feels like a weapon, then it would be reasonable for an officer to reach into the inner clothing and recover it. However, if the officer extracts something which could not in any reasonable man's mind have been a weapon or felt like a weapon, it will be held to be illegal and suppressed by the court. However, if the officer merely pulls out what felt like a weapon and it in fact has the consistency of being a weapon and other innocent items are attached thereto, they may be admitted in the evidence. The courts, however, will look with a jaundiced eye upon any innocent-type items that were extracted by the law enforcement officer which in no way could have felt like a weapon.

Motor Vehicles

The rules for stopping motor vehicles are essentially those for arrest and stop-and-frisk, with a somewhat different mask. A car, as well as a person, can be stopped on less information than it takes to arrest. However, there must be some cause to stop the car. Police cannot just stop cars indiscriminately, although safety checks have been upheld. A traffic or equipment violation will justify stopping a vehicle.

After a traffic stop, the officer may ask the occupants of the vehicle to get out. The driver may be asked for his registration. The situation may be such that a radio check of the person's record would be proper, or that the person could be asked to step back to the police car, or even, in a rare case, be taken to the police station.

The right to stop a car does not automatically carry with it a right to search the vehicle. Ordinarily, there will be no right to search unless the car is stopped for more than questioning.

Search of Vehicle Incident to Arrest. A traffic violation will not ordinarily justify a search of the car since any search in the car would not yield any evidence reasonably related to the offense. A search of a car, however, may always be made incident to a felony arrest. Such a search may at least encompass an area the arm's length of the person arrested and the area under his seat.

An officer with probable cause to believe that a vehicle itself contains contraband may often have the right to search it without a warrant, even where it is not incident to arrest. Such a search may be made when it is not practicable to secure a warrant because the vehicle can be quickly moved out of the locality or jurisdiction. This standard differs from that applied to a home, when probable cause to believe seizable evidence is inside a dwelling house alone furnishes no justification for a search without a warrant.

Search of Person Incident to Vehicle Stop. When a person is detained for a minor traffic citation, there will ordinarily be no occasion for a search of his person. As in any stop-and-frisk situation, however, if additional facts show justification for a pat search, it may be made.

Search of Person Incident to Traffic Arrest. If a person is placed in custody for a minor traffic offense instead of being given a traffic citation, he may be searched for weapons on a limited basis. However, as in any stop-and-frisk situation, if the officer has a basis to fear for his safety above and beyond a minor traffic violation, a weapons pat search may be justified, even if the person is not put into custody. If a person is to be booked into a jail, a generalized search of the person may be permitted in the field. A strip search may be made at booking.

Search of Vehicle Based on Information Acquired after Stop. It is not uncommon, following a stop of a vehicle for a minor traffic violation, for the behavior of the driver or other occupants to cause the officer to believe that a more serious crime is being committed in his presence. For example, if the driver fails to produce a license or registration and gives conflicting stories as to ownership, the officer may reasonably believe the car is stolen; or the officer may see contraband in the vehicle; or the driver may be intoxicated; or the driver may make some effort to conceal or destroy contraband. Some of the factors are listed and appraised as follows.

Nervousness is of little materiality in all but unusual cases, as it is a natural response to the stress situation presented. The fact that it is night does not, without more information, transform an innocent gesture into a guilty one. The fact that the driver alights and walks back to the police car could easily be caused by a variety of wholly innocent motives. A failure to stop the car is one of the more persuasive circumstances that will justify further action, but even here, a delay could be reasonable, caused by road conditions, speed, or other traffic. The most reliable circumstance that will justify a search is still the sight of contraband inside the vehicle.

A California court has recently warned that reliance on furtive conduct has on occasion been unjustified. The most troublesome cases seem to be those where the driver makes some gesture or movement. Some specific knowledge on the part of the officer is needed to show that the suspect's action really shows criminal activity.

Impound Search. Generally speaking, it is required that a search be contemporaneous (close in time and space) to the arrest. What happens, however, if the car is impounded and searched a day or two later at a police garage?

A search may be permissible under several circumstances: (1) when a car itself is held as evidence of a crime; (2) when a search is a continuation of the one in the field; (3) when a car is subjected to further scientific examination; (4) when a car is searched at the station or garage instead of in the field. However, an inventory search, except of items in plain view, is no longer a valid basis for search, in some states. The prosecution may also have the burden of explaining the necessity of taking the vehicle into custody.

Dwelling Houses

The law places some of its strongest protections around a home. The general rule is that a search warrant is needed unless there is an exception. These exceptions involve a pressing emergency, where entry is needed to render aid, or when there is consent to entry. If an officer enters to arrest, he will have only a limited power to search. Officers cannot use trickery to gain entry if they have no probable cause, and a demand for entry will not result in a valid consent. Police cannot make any spy holes. In the past, cases have sustained warrantless entry to make an arrest or to capture a fugitive. The U.S. Supreme Court, however, has questioned the assumption that warrantless entry of a person's home at night to arrest him on probable cause is per se legitimate. However, the Court did not resolve the issue, although it called it a grave constitutional question and spoke critically of the practice.

Forcible Entry. Whether or not an officer secures a warrant, he is not entitled to force entry into a home even if he has probable cause to arrest or believe contraband is there. The usual rule is that a police officer must first identify himself, demand admittance, and explain the purpose for which admittance is required. If admittance is refused, then forcible entry is proper.

The officer's announcement is insufficient if made in a voice too weak to be heard, or if it is made simultaneous to entry, for the occupant has been given no reasonable opportunity to grant or refuse admittance.

Definition of Entry. The rule covers unannounced entries that would be considered a "breaking" in common law burglary. What of opening a screen door, or using a passkey, or opening a closed but unlocked door, or entering through an open door? Under present law, it is best to comply with the announcement rules in all of these cases. It would also be unwise to attempt to gain entry by trickery to avoid the announcement rule. If there is a valid consent to entry, unsecured by trickery, then there is no need to make any announcement.

A forcible entry to make an arrest is not proper unless it is reasonably believed the person is within the structure. A search warrant, however, may be authorized to search premises when no one is there.

Exceptions to the Announcement Rule. There are important exceptions to the requirements that a police officer announce himself. He need not do so when he acts on a reasonable and good faith belief that compliance would increase his peril, frustrate an arrest, or permit the destruction of evidence. Confrontation with an armed and dangerous suspect will also excuse compliance. If the police have information that the defendant is planning to destroy the evidence, that will justify a forced or unannounced entry. However, the fact that the case involves narcotics will not alone excuse a failure to make an announcement. There may also be situations where unannounced entry is justified by the need to render aid.

The cases say that mere silence in response to knocking is insufficient to justify a forced entry. The police have to reasonably believe the person inside is intentionally not responding. Some court decisions do not allow forced entry even then when only a few seconds have elapsed.

The officer's belief that a felony is being committed inside does not alone justify entry by force, but if the occupants are engaging in a criminal act, explaining the purpose of the police visit may not be necessary.

A failure to comply with these rules will render the evidence seized inadmissible.

Border Searches

Entry into the United States from a foreign country authorizes a search of the broadest possible character by customs agents. There is no question of probable cause under state law. Searches of body cavities and other highly personal places have been permitted by federal courts where there was real suspicion. A customs search need not be made exactly at the border, but may be made at some substantial distance within the country, as long as officers have valid probable cause.

Searches by Private Individuals

The Fourth Amendment is not applicable to searches by private individuals. Evidence secured illegally by a police officer will be found inadmissible, whereas the same evidence secured by a private citizen in the same manner will be allowed into court. However, if the private citizen acts as a state agent, then the evidence will be excluded.

Searches by Police Officers Acting as Private Citizens

A police officer will sometimes wear the hat of a private citizen. This situation may occur when he is off duty. In some cases, his activities have been said to show that he was acting as a private citizen. However, it has also been said that an off-duty police officer retains the right to arrest as a police officer.

Another time a police officer is considered to be a private citizen is when he leaves the boundary of the jurisdiction by which he is employed. He will retain his police powers even then if he is engaged in fresh pursuit; if he is acting on an offense committed in his jurisdiction; if there is probable cause to think it was; or if an offense is committed in his presence and there is a danger to person or property or of escape. He can also act as a police officer outside of his area with the consent of the local police chief or sheriff.

If the policeman is not able to use his police powers, his actions will be tested as if he were a private citizen. One difference is that a private citizen has no right to make a search incident to the private citizen arrest, except to take from the person arrested all offensive weapons.

Parolees

Actions against a parolee often do not involve an arrest or warrant since the parolee is in constructive custody. He is merely transferred from constructive to physical custody, when we would say he is arrested. As an old case put it, he is in a prison without bars. Today, a parolee is still not regarded by the law as an entirely free man, and it has generally been agreed that the parolee's person and premises may be searched by his parole officer on less than full probable cause. The Supreme Court has recently said, though, that diminution of Fourth Amendment protection for parolees can only be justified to the extent of the legitimate demands of the operation of the parole process.

In effecting entry to a parolee's premises, officers must comply with the announcement rules of their own state's criminal code unless there is some basis for noncompliance. Neither can police use the parole agent as a tool by which to make a search when they have ample time to get a search warrant. The parole agent, however, can solicit police help.

Parolees, persons on probation, and individuals on outpatient status from prison may be required by their parole or other agreement to submit to police searches.

"Fruits of the Poisonous Tree"

Fruits of the poisonous tree is a picturesque label for a group of legal problems that deal with the consequences of an illegal act by an officer. On the one hand, the rule is that an illegality's direct consequence will result in exclusion of the evidence. If we illegally arrest a man, the narcotic we find in his pocket will be excluded. *Examples:* Photostats are said to be as much the product of the illegal search as the original papers that have been seized. A consent to search obtained after an illegal arrest or entry, is ordinarily invalid. A search warrant is invalid if it is obtained upon information secured in an unlawful search and seizure. Admissions made by a defendant upon being confronted with the fruits of an illegal search are not usable. On the other hand, there are occasional instances where, in spite of an unlawful arrest or search made by a police officer, it may be possible to use evidence that subsequently is obtained. *Example 1:* A defendant illegally arrested is taken to a hospital for a blood test. He asks for a cigarette and is told he cannot smoke. He takes a marijuana cigarette from his shirt pocket. The officer's seizure of it is said not to be a product of the illegal arrest. *Example 2:* Police officers illegally enter an apartment. Ten minutes later, a defendant flees through an open window. The evidence of his flight was not obtained by exploiting the illegality of entry. *Example 3:* The police obtain a defendant's telephone number by illegally arresting someone else, but they already knew the defendant's whereabouts. It will be held that there is not a sufficiently direct connection to require exclusion of the evidence. *Example 4:* A defendant flees from an illegal arrest. Six months later, he kills a police officer who tries to question him. The prosecution may tell about the illegal arrest to show defendant's state of mind.

It remains true, however, that all direct products of an illegal act will be held to be illegal. Not only the tree will be poisoned, but also the fruits of the tree. The "taint" may be "purged" and the evidence admitted when other factors enter the picture. The defendant may commit some volunteered act so that it can be said that the police did not exploit what they did illegally. Or the police may have independent information or sources so that the evidence would have been secured anyway. Or the circumstances that link the illegal act to the evidence may be so many and varied that there is said to be "attenuation"; that is, we can look at the chain of events and feel that the connection is too weak to require exclusion. In fact, there may even be situations where a defendant is trying to show some minor police misstep to immunize his later unrelated conduct.

Stop-and-Frisk

The Fourth Amendment prohibits unreasonable searches and seizures. The courts have held that when individuals are "stopped" for investigation by a peace officer, a "seizure" of the person has occurred within the meaning of the Fourth Amendment. As a result, there must be a reasonable basis for the seizure. The Fourth Amendment attempts to strike a balance between the individual's right of privacy and the legitimate need of law enforcement to conduct without the necessity of making an arrest. The law of stop-and-frisk is designed to strike that balance.

The Stop

An officer may stop a citizen for investigation whenever such a course is necessary to the discharge of the officer's duty. There are no hard and fast rules as to when the stopping is necessary. Three requirements, however, must be met:

(1) There must be a rational suspicion by an officer that some activity out of the ordinary is or has been taking place. An officer has no right to stop a person who is merely walking down the street or engaging in some other innocent activity.

(2) There must be some factor to connect the person under suspicion with the unusual activity. The mere fact that there has been a report of a burglary will not justify an officer in stopping every person within ten miles of the burglary.

(3) There must be some suggestion that the activity is related to a crime. Generally speaking, an officer should be able to explain what crime he suspects, as distinguished from a vague suspicion.

The courts have held the following factors to be significant in determining whether an officer properly stops an individual. It should not be assumed that any of these factors standing alone necessarily justifies stopping an individual. For example, a person may not be stopped merely because he is present in a high crime area. This fact, though, taken with other facts, may justify the detention.

(1) There has been report of recent crime in the area. The kind of crime reported, as well as how recently it was reported, will be relevant.

(2) It is nighttime. Generally speaking, the courts allow more latitude in detention at night than during the day.

(3) The place is known as an area of frequent and current crimes, such as sales of narcotics.
(4) There is information that criminal activity was scheduled to take place of the type consistent with what the suspects are seen doing.
(5) There is knowledge that the suspect was previously convicted of the suspected crime.
(6) The suspect is driving a car in an erratic or suspicious fashion.
(7) The suspect is sitting in a parked car at an unusual time and place.
(8) The suspect gives cause to believe that he is violating motor vehicle laws.
(9) The suspect acts in an unusual manner at the approach of an officer.

The courts have stressed (Terry v. Ohio, 392 U.S. 1) that in justifying the particular detention a police officer must be able to point to specific facts, clearly expressed which, when taken together with rational inferences from those facts, reasonably warrant the intrusion. The courts apply an objective standard. An officer's inarticulate hunches and subjective good faith are not enough to justify the detention. It is therefore important that in writing his reports the law enforcement officer include all the factors which justified the detention of the suspect. These factors may be based on his observations or expertise, information received from other sources, other circumstantial factors previously mentioned, or a combination of all of these.

Once a person has been lawfully stopped, he may be detained for as long as is reasonably necessary to accomplish the purpose for the stop. If, for example, an officer stops a vehicle for equipment failure, he could detain the vehicle long enough to issue a citation. If in the absence of other evidence indicating the possible commission of other crimes—he detains the vehicle for a longer period—no evidence obtained during this period is admissible in court. On the other hand, if further suspicious facts are brought to the officer's attention during a period of lawful detention, this will justify detaining the person until the further facts can be investigated. For example, when an automobile is stopped for equipment failure and the driver is unable to produce evidence of ownership of the vehicle, it is proper for the officer to detain the driver until registration of the vehicle can be established.

If necessary in the reasonable investigation of a crime, a person may be detained so that the victim of a crime may confront him (officers should be careful that this confrontation complies with applicable constitutional requirements pertaining to the conduct of in-the-field identification).

The Frisk

A frisk is a cursory search of the outer clothing of the person stopped. Just as a stop is a seizure within the meaning of the Fourth Amendment, a frisk is a search within the meaning of the Fourth Amendment. As in the case of a stop, there must be a reasonable basis for a frisk. The basis for any frisk is to prevent danger to the officer from an unexpected assault, but there must be some evidence that an officer reasonably believes he is confronting a person who has an instrumentality on his person capable of inflicting injury. Thus, the courts have held that an officer must be able to point to particular facts from which he reasonably believed in the light of his experience that the person he was dealing with was armed and dangerous.

It should be stressed that an officer need not be absolutely certain that a person is armed. If an officer errs in this respect, it should be on the side of caution. Nonetheless, he may not indiscriminately frisk every person he stops, and should be able to point to particular facts which gave rise to concern that the person was armed and dangerous.

When considering making a frisk, the following factors are among those which should be taken into consideration:

(1) The nature of the suspected crime and whether it involved a weapon;
(2) Whether it is day or night. The courts allow more latitude at night;
(3) Knowledge of the record or reputation of the person stopped;
(4) The number of officers making the stop;
(5) The number of suspects stopped;
(6) The demeanor of the suspect;
(7) Whether the suspect's clothes bulge in such a manner as to suggest the presence of weapons;
(8) Whether the suspect's companion is found to be armed;
(9) Whether the suspect makes a furtive movement as if he were reaching for a weapon.

Not all of these factors will in themselves justify a frisk. Merely because an officer has made a stop at nighttime, or in a high crime area, for example, will not justify a frisk. If, on the other hand, the individual has been stopped pursuant to a report of an armed robbery, for example, a frisk will almost always be justified.

The courts have stressed that in determining whether an officer acted reasonably under the circumstances, weight will be given not to his suspicion or "hunch," but "to the specific reasonable inferences which he is entitled to draw from the facts in light of his experience." Again, it should be stressed that the officer's report should reflect the specific facts and inferences which justified the frisk.

The purpose of the frisk is to discover guns, knives, clubs, or other hidden instruments that might be used to assault the officer. The scope of the search for weapons should be the minimum necessary to discover the weapons and should be initially confined to a superficial pat search for weapons. An officer should not ask a suspect to empty his pockets or pull up his sweater, for example, since a pat search would suffice.

An officer may conduct a cursory search, not only of the person's outer clothing, but also of any area from which the person might easily procure weapons, if the officer reasonably suspects that a weapon is located there. For instance, although an officer may have the right to pat-search a suspect's outer clothing, he may not reach inside the clothing of the suspect or search further unless he has reason to believe that the pat search has disclosed the presence of a weapon. The officer must feel some object which a prudent man could believe is an object usable as an instrument of assault. Absent this, the officer may not remove any object out of the suspect's pocket or demand that the suspect empty his pockets. Thus, if the officer feels a hard object resembling a knife or a gun, he may remove the object from the suspect's pocket. If, on the other hand, the officer feels a soft bulge in the suspect's pocket, he may not take further action unless he reasonably believes that the object is likely to be a weapon and is able to explain the reason for his belief.

Once the suspect has removed the object from his pocket, if the officer is satisfied that it is not a weapon, he may not search the contents or the otherwise lawfully possessed object further. For example, if the officer discovers that the hard object in the suspect's pocket is a cigarette box rather than a weapon, he has no right to open the package to search for contraband.

Summary

The courts have held that it is permissible for a peace officer to detain a person for investigation without probable cause to arrest. However, the officer must have reasonable grounds based on specific facts which he can clearly express to the court, telling it why the detention was necessary in the interest of prevention of crime or detection of a criminal act. The officer should bear in mind that if he has probable cause, based on specific facts, to believe that the person he is detaining is armed or dangerous, he may make the person submit to a superficial frisk. If the officer then feels an object which reports to be a weapon, he may remove that object from the person's clothing or possession. If the officer does not have probable cause to frisk the person, then the removal of any object from that person's possession will be unreasonable, and an illegal search procedure. If the officer conducts a search and goes beyond the pat search for discovery of weapons, the search, though valid at the start, will be held unreasonable in scope. If the stop, the frisk, or the scope of the search are unreasonable, then the evidence obtained by the officer, as a result of his actions, will not be admitted in court.

Search Warrants

This section attempts to convey the basic information a police officer should know about search warrants so that he will understand what the district attorney needs to prepare adequate search warrant papers. As the courts continue increasingly to require the use of search warrants, law enforcement agencies must be informed of the legal rules for the preparation and execution of warrants. An officer's working knowledge of the law applicable to search warrants substantially assists the district attorney in preparing the warrant and accompanying affidavit, and thereby improves the efficiency of the warrant procedure. No attempt has been made here to answer every question relating to search warrants; the effort is to give the essentials.

A search warrant is an important legal tool for a police officer. With it, he can do many things he cannot do without it. For example:

(1) With a search warrant, a police officer is not confined to making a search incident to an arrest. With one, he can search at a different time or place, and even if there is no arrest at all.

(2) Without a search warrant, a police officer with probable cause to believe seizable evidence is inside a dwelling house cannot search for it if the dwelling is unoccupied; with a warrant, he can.

(3) If a dwelling is occupied, but there is no arrest or consent, without a warrant, it may not be searched even if there is probable cause to believe it contains seizable evidence. Armed with a warrant, an officer can search.

(4) If an arrest is made on the street in front of a person's house, a search of the house would not be incidental to an arrest. A warrant will authorize the search of the house.

(5) If an arrest is made inside a house, the scope of the search will be limited by Chimel v. California, 395 U.S. 752. A warrant will permit a wider search.

The courts have said that in doubtful or marginal cases, evidence procured by a search warrant may be admitted, while such a search made without a warrant might fail. There are four essential documents involved in serving search warrants (the search warrant, the affidavit, the receipt and the return), and we will consider them in turn.

The Search Warrant

Search-warrant law, and what the warrant should contain, are founded on the Fourth Amendment to the U.S. Constitution, which says, in part, "... no warrants shall issue, but upon probable cause, supported by oath or affirmation, and particularly describing the place to be searched, and the persons or things to be seized." Thus, one of the main rules with respect to search warrants is that the place to be searched be clearly specified and the things to be seized be specifically described. The law condemns general warrants which impose little or no restriction on the area to be searched or what can be taken.

The search warrant itself is a written order issued by a judge directing a police officer to go to a particular place and to search for designated items. The first step in obtaining a search warrant is to prepare the form of the warrant as prescribed by the penal code of the given jurisdiction. It is important that the same detailed description of the place to be searched and the things to be seized appear both in the warrant and in the affidavit which accompanies the warrant. Once the form of the warrant is prepared, the same description can be used again for the affidavit.

It cannot be urged too strongly that the warrant and the affidavit be prepared with care. They should be reviewed, or prepared, by a deputy district attorney before they are presented to a judge.

Form of the Search Warrant. Most penal codes require the warrant to be in substantially the following form:

In the Municipal Court of _____ Judicial District
County of _____,
State of _____

or

In the Superior Court of the State of _____
In and for the County of _____

SEARCH WARRANT

The people of the State of _____:

To: Any sheriff, constable, marshal, policeman or any other peace officer in the County of _____, State of _____.

Proof, by affidavit, having been made this day before me by _____ that there is probable and reasonable cause for the issuance of the Search Warrant in accordance with Section _____ of the Penal Code.

You are therefore commanded to make immediate search in the daytime — at any time of the day or night, good cause being shown therefore, of the premises located and described as: _____
_____
_____
_____
_____

and the vehicle(s) described as: _____
_____
_____

and the person(s) of _____
_____
_____

for the following personal property, to-wit: _____
_____
_____
_____

_____
_____
_____
_____

and if you find the same or any part thereof, to bring it forthwith before me at the Municipal Court of _____ Judicial District or Superior Court of the State of _____, for the County of _____, or to any other court in which the offense(s) in respect to which the property or things taken is triable, or retain such property in your custody, subject to the order of the Court pursuant to Section _____ of the Penal Code.

Given under my hand this _____ day of _____, 19 _____.

_____
Judge of the Municipal Court
Judge of the Superior Court

Place to Be Searched.

Houses. A good starting point in describing a house or apartment to be searched is to give the address. Most warrant forms provide a space for an address. To fail to give the "North" or "South" prefix may be fatal to the warrant's validity. Another way of describing the premises is as follows: ". . . the one-story dwelling house on North Broadway which is the second house north of Pico Boulevard on the east side of North Broadway." It is also helpful in pinning down the exact premises to name the occupant.

Multi-residence Dwellings. Where there is more than one residence in a building, the part of the building to be searched should be designated. Usually, this can be done by giving the apartment number or room number. If the search is to be limited to a specific room, the affidavit should say so and designate it. It would be helpful for an officer to personally visit the location. Be particularly wary of relying on an informer's description of the place to be searched, as there could be a large possibility of error.

Garages. If an officer desires to search the garage or other outbuildings connected with the premises, it is best to specifically recite that in the affidavit and warrant. Example: ". . . a one-story dwelling house, including all rooms, attics, basements, and other parts therein, the surrounding grounds and any garage, storage rooms and outbuildings of any kind, attached or unattached, located thereon."

Vehicles. The description of a car should be as complete as is reasonably possible. *Example:* ". . . a 1970 Chevrolet sedan, brown in color, with primer spots on the left front fender, bearing a 1971 Ohio license plate of 123 HBD." Something less may suffice if closer surveillance would be detected and evidence destroyed. Also, remember that a warrant may not be necessary to search a car because of its mobility. After a car is impounded and stored, a search of it may require a warrant under some conditions.

Things to Be Seized. Generally, a warrant can direct the seizure of contraband, stolen property, or evidence of instrumentalities of crime. What is to be seized must be set out with reasonable particularity, as required by the Fourth Amendment. The purpose is to make sure that a warrant will not be used to seize something other than what is described in it. If the description is too general, then the warrant will be invalid. If the description is sufficiently definite so that any officer executing the warrant would know what to seize, then the description will probably be legally adequate.

Narcotics. ". . . heroin, a narcotic, and derivatives of same, and narcotic paraphernalia, consisting in part of and including, but not limited to: hypodermic syringes, hypodermic needles, eyedroppers, spoons, cotton, milk sugar, scales and other weighing devices, balloons, condoms, paper bundles, gelatin capsules, measuring devices, containers of various types commonly associated with storage of narcotics." An officer may want to include the seizure of articles that could prove the identity of the possessors of the narcotics and paraphernalia. *Example:* ". . . and articles of personal property tending to establish the identity of persons in control of premises, vehicles, storage areas, or containers, where narcotics are found, consisting in part of and including, but not limited to, utility-company receipts, rent receipts, canceled mail envelopes, and keys."

Bookmaking. ". . . papers, books, records, pencils, pens, racing information, sporting publications, bet registrations, radio, telephone, clock, and all other bookmaking property and paraphernalia used or capable of being used for the purpose of recording or registering bets upon race horses." Do not say only, "bookmaking and pool-selling paraphernalia."

Stolen Property, Deadly Weapons, Business Machines, and Appliances. It is not enough to refer generally to "stolen property" or "stolen merchandise." A list should be secured from the victim or a crime report made specifying each item if possible and detailing a description of it. A lesser description may suffice if a better one cannot be secured, but it would be helpful to relate the explanation in the full affidavit. Brand names, identifying marks and features, and especially serial numbers are important.

Nighttime Search. The courts have held that entry and search of a dwelling house at night requires more careful attention. The magistrate must affirmatively authorize a nighttime search on the face of the warrant. Failure to obtain judicial authorization for search at night may invalidate the warrant. Nighttime searches are those which occur between 10:00 P.M. and 7:00 A.M., and in some states, between sundown and sunrise.

The Affidavit

As stated earlier, the Fourth Amendment requires that ". . . no warrant shall issue but upon probable cause." The affidavit accompanying the warrant is a statement of the probable cause to believe that the things to be seized will be found at the place described in the warrant. The following is an example of an affidavit:

In the Municipal Court of _____ Judicial District
        County of _____,
        State of _____

or

In the Superior Court of the State of _____
    In and for the County of _____

State of _____)   AFFIDAVIT IN SUPPORT
) ss OF SEARCH WARRANT
County of _____)

Personally appeared before me this _____ day of _____, 19 ____, _____, who, on oath, makes complaint, and deposes and says:

That __ he has, and there is just, probable and reasonable cause to believe, and that he does believe that there is now on the premises located at: _____
_____
_____

and in vehicle(s) described as: _____
_____

and on the person(s) of _____
_____

the following personal property, to-wit: _____
_____
_____

Your affiant says that there is probable and reasonable cause to believe and that he does believe that the said property constitutes:
_____
_____

Your affiant says that the facts in support of the issuance of the Search Warrant are as follows: that your affiant is a _____ and has been so employed for _____;

That your affiant, while acting in said capacity, has received the following information: _____

NIGHTTIME SERVICE

Your affiant states that in his experience in investigation of _____

has shown that _____

continues day and night; it is therefore important that the aforementioned personal property be seized as soon as possible, otherwise your affiant fears that it will become non-existent through _____

hence for this reason and because of the other facts and circumstances heretofore stated, your affiant requests that this Warrant contain a direction that it may be served at any time of the day or night, good cause appearing therefore.

Your affiant has reasonable cause to believe that grounds for the issuance of a Search Warrant exist, as set forth in Section _____ of the Penal Code, based upon the aforementioned facts and circumstances.

Your affiant prays that a Search Warrant be issued, based upon the above facts, for the seizure of said property, or any part thereof—in the daytime—at any time of the day or night, good cause being shown therefore, and that the same be brought before this Magistrate or retained subject to the order of the court, or of any other court in which the offense(s) in respect to which the property or things taken, is triable, pursuant to Section _____ of the Penal Code.

Subscribed and sworn to before me this _____ day of _____, 19 _____.

_____
Judge of the Municipal Court
Judge of the Superior Court

Sources of Probable Cause. Probable cause may be developed in a number of ways. It may come to an officer from reliable informants, untested informants, citizen informants, through official channels, or from the officer's own investigation or expertise. A police officer's affidavit does not have to be based on what he has personally seen or heard. It can be information he receives from others.

Reliability of Informer. Information from a single reliable informer can be a sufficient basis for an arrest or search if the affidavit sets forth evidence that the informer is reliable. For example, he may have given information in the past that led to arrests and convictions.

Personal Knowledge of Informer. There is an additional requirement which must be fulfilled before a reliable informer's evidence can be the basis for a search warrant. The informant must have personal knowledge of the facts he recites, as distinct from repeating hearsay. Some of the underlying circumstances about the information must be spelled out. For example, it is not enough to recite that a reliable informer said there were narcotics in a house. The statement must include something to indicate how the informer concluded the evidence was where he claimed it was.

An informer's personal knowledge is not always, "I saw. . . ." It can include information that he has accumulated in various ways. It is also possible to infer that the informer did personally see the object of the search from the detail of his description, but it is best in drafting the warrant to make this clear. Possibly, even if he did not "personally see," the detailed evidence he acquired will be sufficient to be the equivalent of personal knowledge.

Untested Informer. The usual rule is that information from an untested informer (one whose reliability has not been established) does not create probable cause. However, an untested informer's evidence can become probable cause if it is corroborated. Corroborating what the informer tells you involves securing additional evidence of a different character that will confirm and strengthen what the informer said. It is not the quantity of the information as much as the quality which evidences probable cause.

Disclosure of Informer. One of the perennial problems with informers concerns the ability to hold their identity in confidence. If an informer is a material witness on the issue of guilt, his identity must be disclosed. A material witness is an eyewitness or a participant in a crime or a person who could give evidence on the issue of guilt which might result in the defendant's acquittal. On the other hand, if the informer only supplied information for probable cause, it may be possible to keep his identity confidential. The problem with relying on this latter method is that the defendant only has to show a reasonable possibility that the informer would be a material witness on the issue of guilt. Recent statutes permit the judge to hold a hearing to decide this.

These rules make it difficult to preserve confidentiality. If disclosure is a problem, it is advisable to place reliance on other evidence of probable cause and to eliminate the use of the informer from the affidavit, at least when there is other ample noninformer probable cause.

Production of Informer. A related problem concerns how much information the prosecution must accumulate about the informer. Can officers fail to ask where the informer lives and what his full name is? If the informer is a material witness, the police should make such inquiries and arrangements as are reasonably necessary to enable the prosecution and defense to locate him. (It is not necessary, however, for the prosecution to produce the informer.) Failure to obtain such information may result in losing the case.

Citizen Informer. An average person who does not appear to be enmeshed in criminal activity usually need not be corroborated to be reliable. The citizen informer who, by calling the police acts openly in aid of law enforcement, is more than a mere informer. He is ordinarily per se reliable. However, it is helpful to describe the informer's place in the community and to specify, for example, if he is a clergyman or a principal of a school.

It is usually not difficult to distinquish the citizen informer who is ordinarily the victim or witness to a crime from a paid informer or one who has cooperated with officers for different motives.

Expert Opinion. An expert opinion may buttress the right to seize any property that would require identification by an expert. *Example:* "Your affiant states that the narcotic paraphernalia listed on page one of this affidavit are articles commonly associated with the use of narcotics." The officer's qualifications as an expert should be stated. If the officer is not qualified, he can talk to an expert, relate the expert's qualifications, and tell what the expert said.

Execution of the Warrant

The search warrant is obtained by presenting the affidavit and warrant to a judge, who then signs the warrant. Once the warrant is issued by the judge, the officer may serve it and make the search.

Time of Search. Some penal codes state that a search must be made within ten days after issuance of the warrant. However, the officer should be cautioned that the courts have construed any delay by the officer in the execution of the warrant which can not be justified by the court to be unreasonable. The mere terminology of the warrant itself, ordering the officer "to go forthwith," indicates that it is an order that the officer should obey at the earliest moment possible. The courts will look with a jaundiced eye upon any unreasonable delays in the execution of the warrant.

Secrecy. The affidavit and other papers related to the search warrant need not be made public until the end of ten days, or until the execution and return of the warrant. After that, the affidavit will be open to the public as a judicial record. There is no requirement that the affidavit be served.

Entry by Force. An officer should give notice of his authority and purpose and be refused admittance before he resorts to force unless he or others are in danger of physical harm or there is a danger of destruction of evidence. Failure to comply with these rules can result in exclusion of the evidence.

Entry at Night. If the warrant is to be served at night, after 10 P.M. or after sundown, a judge should specifically grant permission to do so on the face of the warrant. It generally will not suffice for the judge strictly to allow the following words to be typed on the warrant: *nighttime authorization*. Most printed search warrant forms have day or night service authorized on the face of the warrant, and an express act done by the judge such as underlining, initialing, or circling the word *nighttime* will not be valid. The basis for the nighttime search has to be set forth in the affidavit under a separate paragraph, or the search will never be justified, even if the judge has so authorized on the face of the warrant.

Items Not Listed in the Warrant. In the course of searching for the items listed in the warrant, an officer may find other items he will want to seize. Contraband may be taken, as well as stolen property or evidence that a crime is being committed in the presence of the police officer. If the officer seizes an unlisted item as evidence, or as an instrumentality of a crime, he should be prepared to explain the facts that caused him to believe the item was evidence or an instrumentality. Peace officers can seize items of this kind that fall unexpectedly into plain view when they are making a proper warrant search. However, if the police seize an item they anticipate will be there, but have not had it listed in the warrant, the seizure will be questionable. It is best to have the warrant list all of the things to be seized.

Server of the Warrant. Any officer mentioned in the directions of a search warrant, and no other person, except a person aiding the police officer upon that officer's request, may serve a warrant. A deputy sheriff can serve a warrant directed to the sheriff. A warrant is usually limited to the county of its origin.

The Receipt

The usual practice is to show a copy of the warrant to the person present and to leave a receipt for the items taken. If no person is available for service, a receipt should be left in a conspicuous place. A failure to leave a receipt will not invalidate the seizure, however. The property taken is held by the officer, subject to court order.

The Return

The return of a search warrant consists of filing with the court the original warrant and a verified inventory of what has been seized. This should be done within ten days from the date the warrant was issued. The following is an example of the return:

In the Municipal Court of _____ Judicial District
    County of _____,
    State of _____

or

In the Superior Court of the State of _____
    In and for the County of _____

RETURN TO SEARCH WARRANT

The following property was taken from the premises located at _____
_____
_____
by virtue of a Search Warrant, dated _____, 19____, and executed by Honorable _____, Judge of the Municipal Court of _____ Judicial District—Superior Court of the State of _____, for the County of _____:

    I, _____, by whom this Warrant was executed, do swear that the above inventory contains a true and detailed account of all the property taken by me under the Warrant.

All of the property taken by virtue of said Warrant will be retained in my custody subject to the order of this court or of any other court in which the offense(s) in respect to which the property or things taken is triable.

Subscribed and sworn to before me this _____ day of _____, 19 _____.

_____
Judge of the Municipal Court
Judge of the Superior Court

It is well that the officer should understand the law as it relates to property that has been seized with a valid search warrant. A search warrant is an order of the court to a peace officer telling him to go out, to find the property, and to bring it back before the court. Thus, the property becomes that of the issuing magistrate and does not belong to the individual law enforcement officer or agency which seized it. The law codes clearly define what an officer must do and, in fact, say that he must take the property before the judge. If the items are large or bulky and cannot be easily transported to the judge, the officer should take photographs and attach them to the return of the search warrant so that the judge may view the property. The officer must do with the property seized as he is directed by the court. If the court directs the officer to keep it in his evidence locker, then that is what he must do. If the officer desires to place it in the hands of someone, such as a criminalist, he must get a specific court order to do this.

A problem arises when the judge has ordered the return of the property to the rightful owner or when the case is finished. The officer should, on his own initiative, go back before the judge who handled the case and obtain a separate order from the court as to what to do with the property that was seized. The law states that an officer must maintain all property seized under a warrant in his possession until the court orders it to be disposed of. Thus, if an officer has seized 30 RCA color television consoles taken in a burglary, he cannot release any of those RCA consoles to the rightful owner without an order from the court. The officer should be cautioned to never take it upon himself to release property seized on a search warrant without an order from the issuing magistrate or from the magistrate before whom the offense is triable.

Lineups

In two important cases in 1967 (Gilbert v. California, 388 U.S. 263, and U.S. v. Wade, 388 U.S. 218), the U.S. Supreme Court held that a lineup was a critical stage of a case and was just as important as the trial itself, and that in certain cases the defendant was entitled to the presence of counsel. From 1967 to 1972, judges and prosecutors interpreted these two cases to mean that in all lineups the police officer must have in fact informed a defendant of his right to have a counsel present at said lineup. However, in 1972, the U.S. Supreme Court in Kirby v. Illinois (404 U.S. 1055) stated that this interpretation was erroneous. The Court held in the Kirby v. Illinois case that, in fact, in all preindictment lineups, a defendant has no such right. The Court went on to define a postindictment lineup as being a lineup conducted after one of the following has occurred: (1) issuance of a complaint or warrant; (2) an arraignment; (3) a preliminary hearing; (4) an indictment; (5) commencement of the trial.

If in fact none of the preceding has occurred, the officer need not advise the defendant of any rights as far as having an attorney present at a lineup is concerned. The following information is only to be used by law enforcement officers in a postindictment lineup proceeding.

The Lineup Admonition

An investigating officer who plans to include a suspect in a lineup must inform him of his right to counsel. The suspect must be advised that: (1) The officer intends to place him in a lineup, at which time several people will be present; (2) He has a right to have an attorney present at the lineup; and (3) If he is unable to employ counsel, an attorney will be provided at no cost. The following is a sample admonition to the suspect:

"Later on today we will have a lineup in which you will take part. Witnesses will observe you and determine whether you are responsible for the crime of _____ or if you are not involved. You have a right to have an attorney present at the lineup to observe the proceedings. If you do not have an attorney and are unable to afford one, we will obtain an attorney for you to be at the lineup at no cost to you. If you wish, you need not have an attorney present at the lineup. Do you understand what I have just told you? What do you want to do? Do you want to have an attorney present at the lineup?"

Note that this admonition is not the Miranda admonition. The Miranda admonition has nothing to do with the lineup admonition. Since the officer does not intend to question the suspect at that time, but rather intends to have him observed by witnesses, he should not be advised of his Miranda rights. Miranda only requires that you inform the defendant of his right to remain silent if you intend to question him.

A suspect may waive his right to an attorney at a lineup, and officers may solicit that waiver. The officer however should keep in mind that if a waiver is taken, defense counsel will probably attack the waiver at trial on the grounds that it was not voluntarily or intelligently made. He should consider this factor in deciding whether or not to solicit a waiver.

Rights of Defense Counsel

If an attorney is present at a lineup, his role is one of an observer. He may not interfere in the conduct of the lineup. At the conclusion of the lineup, he may consult with witnesses or victims, but they are not obliged to talk to him. Witnesses should be so informed.

A suspect is also entitled to the presence of counsel if an oral identification is made by a witness after the lineup. The lineup includes the viewing of possible suspects by witnesses and the questioning of the witnesses by police regarding identification. Many law enforcement agencies do not conduct such interviews and instead rely exclusively on information obtained from printed cards distributed to witnesses who are asked to mark down their identification or lack thereof. In such cases, there is no interview for counsel to attend. However, the cases (Gilbert v. California and U.S. v. Wade) suggest that counsel may be entitled to examine the identification cards.

The purpose of an attorney at a lineup is to enable him to meaningfully cross-examine witnesses at the time of trial. If in the attorney's opinion the lineup is prejudicial to his client, he may use this information in court. However, he has no right or authority to interfere with the conduct of the lineup. To minimize objections, the officer in charge should explain the lineup procedure to the attorney. If the attorney makes objections, such objections should be noted and transmitted to the investigating officer. If an attorney obstructs, interferes with, or disrupts the proceedings, he should be warned that failure to refrain from such conduct will result in his exclusion from the premises. To avoid conflicts between the investigator and defense counsel, many counties provide local law enforcement agencies with representatives from the district attorney's office. Since this practice varies, local law enforcement agencies need to be informed of the district attorney's resources to provide this service.

Right to Refuse

A suspect has no right to refuse to participate in a lineup. If he does refuse, he should be informed that his refusal can and will be used in evidence against him. If an attorney advises his client to refuse participation in the lineup, the procedure is the same. The suspect should, however, be asked whether it is true that he refuses to participate in the lineup and whether he is aware that he has no right to refuse to do so. The investigating officer should determine from the attorney the grounds on which such a refusal is predicated—perhaps the objection can be overcome.

Although lineups may be conducted over objections of counsel, investigating officers should remember that if at the trial the attorney's objections to the fairness of the lineup are sustained, the identification evidence at the lineup may be inadmissible. A suspect should not be physically forced to appear in a lineup, since the element of force would be obvious, and suggestive of guilt. The prosecutor may argue to the jury, however, that a suspect's refusal to participate is evidence of consciousness of guilt.

Requirements of Lineup Members

A suspect may be asked to speak, walk, turn, assume a stance or a gesture, or don clothing. A refusal to do any of these should be followed by a statement that such refusal will be used in evidence against the suspect. If a suspect refuses to speak, he should be informed that his constitutional right to remain silent does not include a right to refuse to speak for identification, and that his refusal to speak for identification purposes can and will be used as evidence against him.

Advice to Witnesses

It is quite common for witnesses to be extremely nervous when attending a lineup. It is good practice to hand them a printed summary of the oral instruction, in advance of reading an oral explanation of procedure, such as the following:

"Ladies and gentlemen, in a few moments, several men will appear on the stage. You will be able to see them, but they will not be able to see you. Each man will be assigned a number and will be referred to only by number. Each will be asked to do certain things, such as turning, speaking, etc. When the entire line has completed this process, I will ask whether any of you desires one or more of the suspects to repeat something. If you do, please raise your hand and an officer will talk with you. In the event one of the men is asked to repeat, we will ask the entire line to repeat. Please do not talk with each other at any time. During the lineup, please communicate only with the officer, and then do so in private. When the lineup is completed, please fill out the card we have given you and hand it to the officer, whether you have made an identification or not. If you cannot identify anyone, please so indicate. If you can identify a suspect, mark the card with his number in the line. You received an instruction sheet when you entered. Please read it carefully. At the end of the lineup, fill out the back side and return it to one of the officers conducting this lineup."

Procedure

When witnesses arrive, the investigating officers should space them as far apart as possible and explain the procedure of the lineup. (See the sample advice above.) Each witness should be furnished with a card on which to write his name and other data which the officers need. After the witnesses finish marking the cards, they should be collected. These cards should be retained for possible future use as evidence.

Written instructions for lineup witnesses (sample)

You are about to see and participate in a lineup conducted by the (name of law enforcement agency). The following information may be helpful to you in understanding the procedure to be used:

(1) The lineup will be conducted by _____

(2) The place of this lineup is _____
_____.
(3) Please use the seats closest to the stage, keeping one vacant seat between you and other persons.
(4) Do not discuss the case with other witnesses.
(5) There may be deputy district attorneys present who may wish to speak to you regarding your case. If so, they will identify themselves.
(6) There may be attorneys present for various prisoners. They may wish to speak to you regarding your case. You may or may not discuss the case with them, as you choose.
(7) Do not call out a suspect's number or do or say anything which might show you have identified someone in line.
(8) The individuals you will be shown will not be named; they will be assigned numbers. If the suspect or suspects in your case are in line, mark down the number on a card which will be given to you.
(9) If you identify anyone, please tell the investigating officer if he has changed his appearance in any way.
(10) If you wish to have a certain person in the line do certain things (speak, wear a hat, walk rapidly, etc.), make this request to the investigator or the officer conducting the lineup and all members of the line will be asked to do the same thing. No member of the line will be singled out to speak or perform a certain act.
(11) Do not hesitate in making an identification because you think a person can see you; he cannot see through the screen (omit if inapplicable).
(12) Remember, you are not obliged to identify anyone if you cannot do so.
(13) Please fill out the identification card provided and return it to the investigator in your particular case.

If a court determines that a lineup was improperly conducted, either because counsel was requested but did not appear, or the lineup itself was unfair, the identification evidence of the witness at trial may be excluded.

A lineup should be conducted with no less than six persons, all of comparable race, height, weight, and general description (including dress). Police officers should not be used, if at all possible. Each person in the lineup should be asked to do exactly the same as required of the others. If all members in the lineup are asked to repeat words for the purpose of voice identification, any nonincriminatory words may be repeated. They may be directed to utter words purportedly used during the commission of the crime under investigation (for example, "Freeze!" "Hold it! This is a stick-up!" etc.). If the investigating officers need to ask questions, they should be of a nonincriminatory nature. Suspects should not be asked questions which call for information which only the perpetrator of the crime would know, such as where they were arrested, or whether they had weapons on their persons at the time of the arrest. If a witness asks for repetition of a certain phrase at the lineup, all individuals in the lineup should repeat the phrase.

Record Keeping and Photographs

The investigating officers should maintain a record of all those who appear in the lineup, including names, addresses, booking numbers, and positions in the lineup. If facilities are available, the entire lineup should be photographed, preferably from the front and the sides, and the photographs should be printed for use in trial. Of course, if videotaping facilities are available, they should be used.

If a suspect, for whatever reason, refuses to cooperate in the lineup, his refusal may be used as evidence against him. His photograph may be shown to the witnesses in a manner similar to that used when a suspect is not in custody. Identification by photograph is permissible because a fair and impartial lineup is impossible unless a suspect cooperates. Before the identification by photograph procedure is used, the suspect (and his attorney, if he has one) should be advised as follows:

"There is no right to refuse to take part in a lineup. I have already said that refusal to take part in a lineup can and will be used as evidence against you (addressing the suspect). The legality of the lineup can be decided by a judge if the case goes to court, and any objections can be made to him. If you persist in refusing to take part in the lineup, we will show photographs to the witnesses. Do you still refuse to take part in the lineup? (To the attorney, if any) Do you withdraw your objection to your client's taking part in the lineup?)"

If a suspect persists in refusing to take part in a lineup, witnesses may be shown photographs of the suspect and others which have been fairly and impartially selected so that the risk of misidentification is minimized. Photographs should be selected using the guidelines similar to those involved in the selection of persons appearing in a formal lineup. Mug shots showing names, dates, or other "suggestive" matter should be modified, or not used, if possible. Any photographs shown to witnesses as part of the identification procedure should be retained for any subsequent criminal proceedings. Before the identification by photograph procedure is followed, the witnesses should be advised as follows:

"You were invited to be here to watch a lineup. This will not take place for reasons which I am not at liberty to discuss with you. However, each of you will be asked to look at several photographs. You will be alone with me (or an investigating officer) when you look at these photographs. The fact that photographs are shown to you should not influence your judgment. You should not conclude or guess that the photographs contain the picture of the person suspected of committing the crime. You are not obliged to identify anyone. It is just as important that innocent persons are freed from suspicion as that guilty parties are identified. Please do not discuss the case with other witnesses or indicate in any way that you have identified someone."

Each witness should view the photographs alone. The officer showing the photographs should be very careful in avoiding any suggestion that the photographs contain the picture of the suspect. When possible, the use of officers in lineups should be avoided. In appropriate cases, "blank" lineups, i.e., lineups in which the suspect is not included may be useful. Thereafter, the lineup should be conducted using the suspect. The witnesses should then be asked whether they can identify anyone from either lineup. This procedure requires extra members for the lineup, but it may be an effective method.

It is of the utmost importance to the prosecutor that complete and accurate notes be made and included in any report concerning the lineup. This is particularly true of communications with the suspect, his attorney, and the witnesses.

Field Showups

The Supreme Court has held under the Sixth Amendment to the U.S. Constitution that a suspect is entitled to counsel at all stages of the proceedings. The Supreme Court has further held that postindictment lineups are a critical stage in the proceedings, and, therefore, a suspect must be afforded a chance to obtain an attorney before a lineup. However, is a field showup (lineup in the field) within the scope of the Sixth Amendment? Generally, the courts have held that it is not if the showup is postindictment.

Can an officer ask a victim or a witness to a crime to go with him to view the arrestee, who is sitting in a police car two blocks or two miles away from the scene of the crime? Does the officer have to provide an attorney for the suspect before this viewing?

The General Rule

An officer may have a victim identify a suspect in the field when the arrestee is apprehended in close proximity in time and place to the occurrence of a serious crime. Counsel for the suspect is not required, because the emergency nature of the confrontation (i.e., the necessity of immediate identification of a suspect) does not allow time for contacting an attorney. There are no hard and fast rules as to how close the proximity of time and place of the field showup must be to the crime, or the degree of seriousness of the crime.

The following factors should be kept in mind when considering a field showup:

A legitimate need for immediate identification must be present. For example, if a suspect has been at-large for some time, the need for immediate identification has passed, even if he is arrested near the original scene of the crime.

Since the absence-of-counsel requirement is based in part on the impracticality of furnishing counsel in the field, if a suspect has been detained for any substantial period of time or has been moved to a place accessible to counsel, the reason for the exception fails, and a field showup cannot be held.

The courts have indicated that field showups of petty-crime suspects, who may raise less apprehension in the minds of the public and possibly tie up fewer police personnel, will be more closely scrutinized.

The courts will also scrutinize each case for any attempt by officers to circumvent the requirements of a formal lineup by conducting an unneeded field showup.

Procedure

The courts have held that although a suspect in a field showup is not entitled to all of the rights of a suspect in a formal lineup, the procedure used must be fair. While any confrontation between a suspect and a witness is to some degree inherently suggestive (since the witness may assume that the police would not have arrested the suspect unless they thought they had the right person, any suggestive comments or conduct by police officers may be a violation of due process—in this case, the right to be fairly identified. For this reason, the following suggestions are offered:

The victim's description of the suspect should be recorded in as much detail as possible before the field showup, when the victim will see the suspect again. This procedure increases the likelihood that the victim's identification evidence will not be excluded at trial should the court find the field showup defective. It also aids the prosecutor in examining the witness regarding his identification at trial.

If there are several witnesses, they should each view the suspect separately, and be requested not to discuss their identification with the other witnesses.

The witnesses should be advised that they are not obliged to identify anyone, and that it is just as important to free innocent persons from suspicion as to identify guilty parties.

The suspect may be asked to repeat any nonincriminatory words, such as words used during the crime under investigation (for example, "This is a stick-up," etc.). Suspects should not be asked questions which call for information which only the perpetrator of the crime would know, such as where they were arrested, whether they had weapons on their persons at the time of the arrest, or similar questions which call for incriminating statements.

Police officers must not present to the witnesses incriminating evidence obtained from the suspect, such as stolen property or weapons used in the crime, until after the witnesses have made an identification. Doing so before the identification would be suggestive, and could result in an accusation of priming.

Photographic Identification

In Simons v. U.S. (390 U.S. 377), the U.S. Supreme Court endorsed the photographic identification of suspects as a legitimate investigative tool. The Court indicated, however, that the procedure must be free from any suggestion by the investigating officer, verbal or pictorial, that a particular suspect's picture should be chosen by an identifying witness. The Court ruled that in evaluating the element of suggestiveness, each case must be considered on its own facts, but that a conviction would be set aside only if the photographic identification "was so impermissibly suggestive as to give rise to a very substantial likelihood of irreparable misidentification." This means that the defense has a formidable burden of proof in establishing prejudice in photographic identification cases. However, care should be taken in conducting such identifications since the appellate courts will examine and evaluate each case on its own facts.

Photographs of individuals of the same general appearance as the suspect should be selected. Some of the obvious characteristics that should be approximated are race, age, hair style (straight, natural or processed, short, medium, or long), hair color, facial hair (beards, mustaches, sideburns), features, and complexion. As a general rule, the photographs of at least five other individuals should be included with that of the suspect.

Some photographs bearing notations or attachments, or depicting unusual physical characteristics which cannot be duplicated, should be modified or not used. For example, photographs bearing names, dates, or suggestive matter such as "rap" or "make" sheets, fingerprint cards, or notations which suggest that law enforcement agencies have some special interest in a particular individual, should be modified by either removing or blocking out the suggestive material. The backs of mug photographs often have extraneous writing on them. The backs of the photographs should be covered, or the witnesses instructed not to turn them over while looking at them.

A photograph of a suspect depicting unusual physical characteristics should be modified or not used because of the difficulty of finding photographs of persons with similar characteristics. Only one photograph of the suspect should be included in each group unless there are also several photos of the other individuals. If an officer wishes, for example, to show the suspect with and without a toupee, he should place the two pictures in groups of persons of similar appearance, one with hair, the other without hair. Photographs should be displayed as soon after the crime as possible.

Advice to Witnesses

The following advice should be given to witnesses at photographic identifications:

"Each of you will be asked to look at several photographs. You will be alone with me (or an investigating officer) when you look at these photographs. The fact that the photographs are shown to you should not influence your judgment. You should not conclude nor guess that the photographs contain the picture of the person suspected of committing the crime. You are not obliged to identify anyone. It is just as important to free innocent people from suspicion as to identify guilty parties. Please do not discuss the case with other witnesses nor indicate in any way that you have identified someone."

Presence of Counsel

The suspect does not have a right to have counsel present at photographic identifications. There are several rationales for this rule. First, it would be impractical to have a lawyer appointed at this stage of the investigation, as the suspect is very often still at-large or is not yet a prime suspect. This factor, in conjunction with the considerations that the photographs can be examined at trial and the investigating officer cross-examined regarding the identification procedure, is said to outweigh the need for counsel at such an identification.

Procedure

Each witness should view the photographs alone. The officer showing the photographs to the witness should be scrupulously careful to avoid any suggestion that the photographs contain the picture of the suspect.

Care should be taken that all groups of photos from which the witnesses made identifications are available at trial. This is important for the following reasons: First, the trial and appellate courts may want to look at them, since the issue of suggestiveness is decided on a case-by-case basis. Second, failure to preserve the photographs could result in a reversal on the grounds that the defendant was deprived of his right of cross-examination. Third, upon loss or destruction of the photos, a strong defense argument could be made to the jury that the prosecutor has kept valuable evidence from the jury, even though that is not the case.

Other Uses of Photographs

A set of properly selected photographs may be shown to witnesses before lineups, and the suspect may appear in both the photographs and the lineup. A set of photographs may also be shown to witnesses before court proceedings to refresh their prior identifications. However, a photograph of the defendant must not be shown without the inclusion of the other photos originally shown to the witness, or photos of persons of similar appearance. In addition, if defense counsel cannot be located after diligent efforts to procure his presence at a lineup, or if after reasonable notice counsel fails to appear at a lineup, or refuses to be present, or fails to attend, a photograph of the lineup may be taken, from which an identification may be made by the witnesses. This method of showing photographs of a simulated lineup is permissible as long as the photographs are preserved and made available at trial so that the defense may use them in preparing its cross-examination. However, a photograph of a simulated lineup may not be used as evidence if it was taken simply to obviate contacting defense counsel. As many law enforcement agencies have discovered, a lineup conducted without consideration of the proper legal procedures can foreclose the testimony of identification witnesses at a trial.

SPINELLI v. UNITED STATES
Supreme Court of the United States, 1969.
393 U.S. 410, 89 S.Ct. 584, 21 L.Ed.2d 637.

MR. JUSTICE HARLAN delivered the opinion of the Court. William Spinelli was convicted under 18 U.S.C. § 1952 of traveling to St. Louis, Missouri, from a nearby Illinois suburb with the intention of conducting gambling activities proscribed by Missouri law. See Mo. Rev.Stat. § 563.360 (1959), V.A.M.S. At every appropriate stage in the proceedings in the lower courts, the petitioner challenged the constitutionality of the warrant which authorized the FBI search that uncovered the evidence necessary for his conviction. At each stage, Spinelli's challenge was treated in a different way. At a pretrial suppression hearing, the United States District Court for the Eastern District of Missouri held that Spinelli lacked standing to raise a Fourth Amendment objection. A unanimous panel of the Court of Appeals for the Eighth Circuit rejected the District Court's ground, a majority holding further that the warrant was issued without probable cause. After an *en banc* rehearing, the Court of Appeals sustained the warrant and affirmed the conviction by a vote of six to two, 382 F.2d 871. Both the majority and dissenting *en banc* opinions reflect a most conscientious effort to apply the principles we announced in Aguilar v. Texas, 378 U.S. 108, 84 S.Ct. 1509, 12 L.Ed. 2d 723 (1964), to a factual situation whose basic characteristics have not been at all uncommon in recent search warrant cases. Believing it desirable that the principle of *Aguilar* should be further explicated, we granted certiorari, 390 U.S. 942, 88 S.Ct. 1025, 19 L.Ed.2d 1130, our writ being later limited to the question of the constitutional validity of the search and seizure. 391 U.S. 933, 88 S.Ct. 1834, 20 L.Ed.2d 853. For reasons that follow we reverse.

In *Aguilar,* a search warrant had issued upon an affidavit of police officers who swore only that they had "received reliable information from a credible person and do believe" that narcotics were being illegally stored on the described premises. While recognizing that the constitutional requirement of probable cause can be satisfied by hearsay information, this Court held the affidavit inadequate for two reasons. First, the application failed to set forth any of the "underlying circumstances" necessary to enable the magistrate independently to judge of the validity of the informant's conclusion that the narcotics were where he said they were. Second, the affiant-officers did not attempt to support their claim that their informant was " 'credible' or his informaion 'reliable.' " The Government is, however, quite right in saying that the FBI affidavit in the present case is more ample than that in *Aguilar.* Not only does it contain a report from an anonymous informant, but it also contains a report of an independent FBI investigation which is said to corroborate the informant's tip. We are then required to delineate the manner in which *Aguilar's* two-pronged test should be applied in these circumstances.

In essence, the affidavit, reproduced in full in the Appendix to this opinion, contained the following allegations:

1. The FBI had kept track of Spinelli's movements on five days during the month of August 1965. On four of these occasions, Spinelli was seen crossing one of two bridges leading from Illinois into St. Louis, Missouri, between 11 a. m. and 12:15 p.m. On four of the five days, Spinelli was also seen parking his car in a lot used by residents of an apartment house at 1108 Indian Circle Drive in St. Louis, between 3:30 p. m. and 4:45 p. m. On one day, Spinelli was followed further and seen to enter a particular apartment in the building.

2. An FBI check with the telephone company revealed that this apartment contained two telephones listed under the name of Grace P. Hagen, and carrying the numbers WYdown 4–0029 and WYdown 4–0136.

3. The application stated that "William Spinelli is known to this affiant and to federal law enforcement agents and local law enforcement agents as a bookmaker, an associate of bookmakers, a gambler, and an associate of gamblers."

4. Finally it was stated that the FBI "has been informed by a confidential reliable informant that William Spinelli is operating a handbook and accepting wagers and disseminating wagering information by means of the telephones which have been assigned the num-

bers WYdown 4–0029 and WYdown 4–0136."

There can be no question that the last item mentioned, detailing the informant's tip, has a fundamental place in this warrant application. Without it, probable cause could not be established. The first two items reflect only innocent-seeming activity and data. Spinelli's travels to and from the apartment building and his entry into a particular apartment on one occasion could hardly be taken as bespeaking gambling activity; and there is surely nothing unusual about an apartment containing two separate telephones. Many a householder indulges himself in this petty luxury. Finally the allegation that Spinelli was "known" to the affiant and to other federal and local law enforcement officers as a gambler and an associate of gamblers is but a bald and unilluminating assertion of suspicion that is entitled to no weight in appraising the magistrate's decision. Nathanson v. United States, 290 U.S. 41, 46, 54 S.Ct. 11, 12, 78 L.Ed. 159 (1933).

So much indeed the Government does not deny. Rather, following the reasoning of the Court of Appeals, the Government claims that the informant's tip gives a suspicious color to the FBI's reports detailing Spinelli's innocent-seeming conduct and that, conversely, the FBI's surveillance corroborates the informant's tip, thereby entitling it to more weight. It is true, of course, that the magistrate is obligated to render a judgment based upon a common-sense reading of the entire affidavit. United States v. Ventresca, 380 U.S. 102, 108, 85 S.Ct. 741, 745, 13 L.Ed.2d 684 (1965). We believe, however, that the "totality of circumstances" approach taken by the Court of Appeals paints with too broad a brush. Where, as here, the informer's tip is a necessary element in a finding of probable cause, its proper weight must be determined by a more precise analysis.

The informer's report must first be measured against *Aguilar's* standards so that its probative value can be assessed. If the tip is found inadequate under *Aguilar*, the other allegations which corroborate the information contained in the hearsay report should then be considered. At this stage as well, however, the standards enunciated in *Aguilar* must inform the magistrate's decision. He must ask: Can it fairly be said that the tip, even when certain parts of it have been corroborated by independent sources, is as trustworthy as a tip which would pass *Aguilar's* tests without independent corroboration? *Aguilar* is relevant at this stage of the inquiry as well because the tests it establishes were designed to implement the long-standing principle that probable cause must be determined by a "neutral and detached magistrate," and not by "the officer engaged in the often competitive enterprise of ferreting out crime." Johnson v. United States, 333 U.S. 10, 14, 68 S.Ct. 367, 369, 92 L.Ed. 436 (1948). A magistrate cannot be said to have properly discharged his constitutional duty if he relies on an informer's tip which — even when partially corroborated — is not as reliable as one which passes *Aguilar's* requirements when standing alone.

Applying these principles to the present case, we first consider the weight to be given the informer's tip when it is considered apart from the rest of the affidavit. It is clear that a Commissioner could not credit it without abdicating his constitutional function. Though the affiant swore that his confidant was "reliable," he offered the magistrate no reason in support of this conclusion. Perhaps even more important is the fact that *Aguilar's* other test has not been satisfied. The tip does not contain a sufficient statement of the underlying circumstances from which the informer concluded that Spinelli was running a book-making operation. We are not told how the FBI's source received his information — it is not alleged that the informant personally observed Spinelli at work or that he had ever placed a bet with him. Moreover, if the informant came by the information indirectly, he did not explain why his sources were reliable. Cf. Jaben v. United States, 381 U.S. 214, 85 S.Ct. 1365, 14 L.Ed.2d 345 (1965). In the absence of a statement detailing the manner in which the information was gathered, it is especially important that the tip describe the accused's criminal activity in sufficient detail that the magistrate may know that he is relying on something more substantial than a casual rumor circulating in the underworld or an accusation based merely on an individual's general reputation.

The detail provided by the informant in Draper v United States, 358 U.S. 307, 79 S.Ct. 329, 3 L.Ed.2d 327 (1959), provides a suitable benchmark. While Hereford, the Government's informer in that case did not state the way in which he had obtained his information, he reported that Draper had gone to Chicago the day before by train and that he would return to Denver by train with three ounces of heroin, on one of two specified mornings. Moreover, Hereford went on to describe, with minute particularity, the clothes that Draper would be wearing upon his arrival at the Denver station. A magistrate, when confronted with such detail, could reasonably infer that the informant had gained his information in a reliable way. Such an inference cannot be made in the present case. Here, the only facts supplied were that Spinelli was using two specified telephones and that these phones were being used in gambling operations. This meager report could easily have been obtained from an offhand remark heard at a neighborhood bar.

Nor do we believe that the patent doubts *Aguilar* raises as to the report's reliability are adequately resolved by a consideration of the allegations detailing the FBI's independent investigative efforts. At most, these allegations indicated that Spinelli could have used the telephones specified by the informant for some purpose. This cannot by itself be said to support both the inference that the informer was generally trustworthy and that he had made his charge against Spinelli on the basis of information obtained in a reliable way. Once again, *Draper* provides a relevant comparison. Independent police work in that case corroborated much more than one small detail that had been provided by the informant. There, the police, upon meeting the inbound Denver train on the second morning specified by informer Hereford, saw a man whose dress corresponded precisely to Hereford's detailed description. It was then apparent that the informant had not been fabricating his report out of whole cloth; since the report was of the sort which in common experience may be recognized as having been obtained in a reliable way, it was perfectly clear that probable cause had been established.

We conclude, then, that in the present case the informant's tip — even when corroborated to the extent indicated — was not sufficient to provide the basis for a finding of probable cause. This is not to say that the tip was so insubstantial that it could not properly have counted in the magistrate's determination. Rather, it needed some further support. When we look to the other parts of the application, however, we find nothing alleged which would permit the suspicions engendered by the informant's report to ripen into a judgment that a crime was probably being committed. As we have already seen, the allegations detailing the FBI's surveillance of Spinelli and its investigation of the telephone company records contain no suggestion of criminal conduct when taken by themselves—and they are not endowed with an aura of suspicion by virtue of the informer's tip. Nor do we find that the FBI's reports take on a sinister color when read in light of common knowledge that bookmaking is often carried on over the telephone and from premises ostensibly used by others for perfectly normal purposes. Such an argument would carry weight in a situation in which the premises contain an unusual number of telephones or abnormal activity is observed, cf. McCray v. Illinois, 386 U.S. 300, 302, 87 S.Ct. 1056, 1057, 18 L.Ed.2d 62 (1967), but it does not fit the case where neither of these factors is present. All that remains to be considered is the flat statement that Spinelli was "known" to the FBI and others as a gambler. But just as a simple assertion of police suspicion is not itself a sufficient basis for a magistrate's finding of probable cause, we do not believe it may be used to give additional weight to allegations that would otherwise be insufficient.

The affidavit, then, falls short of the standards set forth in *Aguilar, Draper,* and our other decisions that give content to the notion of probable cause. In holding as we have done, we do not retreat from the established propositions that only the probability, and not a prima facie showing, of criminal acivity is the standard of probable cause, Beck v. Ohio, 379 U.S. 89, 96, 85 S.Ct. 223, 228, 13 L.Ed.2d 142 (1964); that affidavits of probable cause are tested by much less rigorous standards than those governing the admissibility of evidence at trial, McCray v. Illinois, 386 U.S. 300, 311, 87 S.Ct. 1056, 1062 (1967); that in judging probable cause issuing magistrates are not to be confined by niggardly limitations or by restrictions on the use of their common sense, United States v. Ventresca, 380 U.S.

102, 108, 85 S.Ct. 741, 745 (1965); and that their determination of probable cause should be paid great deference by reviewing courts, Jones v. United States, 362 U.S. 257, 270–271, 80 S.Ct. 725, 735–736 (1960). But we cannot sustain this warrant without diluting important safeguards that assure that the judgment of a disinterested judicial officer will interpose itself between the police and the citizenry.

The judgment of the Court of Appeals is reversed and the case is remanded to that court for further proceedings consistent with this opinion.

It is so ordered.

Reversed and remanded.

MR. JUSTICE MARSHALL took no part in the consideration or decision of this case. . . .

MR. JUSTICE WHITE, concurring.

An investigator's affidavit that he has seen gambling equipment being moved into a house at a specified address will support the issuance of a search warrant. The oath affirms the honesty of the statement and negatives the lie or imagination. Personal observation attests to the facts asserted — that there is gambling equipment on the premises at the named address.

But, if the officer simply avers, without more, that there is gambling paraphernalia on certain premises, the warrant should not issue, even though the belief of the officer is an honest one, as evidenced by his oath, and even though the magistrate knows him to be an experienced, intelligent officer who has been reliable in the past. This much was settled in Nathanson v. United States, 290 U.S. 41, 54 S.Ct. 11, 78 L.Ed. 159 (1933), where the Court held insufficient an officer's affidavit swearing he had cause to believe that there was illegal liquor on the premises for which the warrant was sought. The unsupported assertion or belief of the officer does not satisfy the requirement of probable cause. Jones v. United States, 362 U.S. 257, 269, 80 S.Ct. 725, 735, 4 L.Ed.2d 697 (1960); Grau v. United States, 287 U.S. 124, 53 S.Ct. 38, 77 L.Ed. 212 (1932); Byars v. United States, 273 U.S. 28, 29, 47 S.Ct. 248, 71 L.Ed. 520 (1927).

What is missing in *Nathanson* and like cases is a statement of the basis for the affiant's believing the facts contained in the affidavit—the good "cause" which the officer in *Nathanson* said he had. If an officer swears that there is gambling equipment at a certain address, the possibilities are (1) that he has seen the equipment; (2) that he has observed or perceived facts from which the presence of the equipment may reasonably be inferred; and (3) that he has obtained the information from someone else. If (1) is true, the affidavit is good. But in (2), the affidavit is insufficient unless the perceived facts are given, for it is the magistrate, not the officer, who is to judge the existence of probable cause. Aguilar v. Texas, 378 U.S. 108, 84 S.Ct. 1509, 12 L.Ed.2d 723 (1964); Giordenello v. United States, 357 U.S. 480, 486, 78 S.Ct. 1245, 1250, 2 L.Ed.2d 1503 (1958); Johnson v. United States, 333 U.S. 10, 14, 68 S.Ct. 367, 369, 92 L.Ed. 436 (1948). With respect to (3), where the officer's information is hearsay, no warrant should issue absent good cause for crediting that hearsay. Because an affidavit asserting, without more, the location of gambling equipment at a particular address does not claim personal observation of any of the facts by the officer, and because of the likelihood that the information came from an unidentified third party, affidavits of this type are unacceptable.

Neither should the warrant issue if the officer states that there is gambling equipment in a particular apartment and that his information comes from an informant, named or unnamed, since the honesty of the informant and the basis for his report are unknown. Nor would the missing elements be completely supplied by the officer's oath that the informant has often furnished reliable information in the past. This attests to the honesty of the informant, but Aguilar v. Texas, supra, requires something more—did the information come from observation, or did the informant in turn receive it from another? Absent additional facts for believing the informant's report, his assertion stands no better than the oath of the officer to the same effect. Indeed, if the affidavit of an officer, known by the magistrate to be honest and experienced, stating that gambling equipment is located in a certain building is unacceptable, it would be quixotic if a similar statement from an honest informant were found to furnish probable cause. A strong argument can be made that both should be acceptable under the Fourth Amendment, but under our cases neither is. The past reliability of the informant can no more furnish probable cause for believing his current report than can previous experience with the officer himself.

If the affidavit rests on hearsay—an informant's report—what is necessary under *Aguilar* is one of two things: the informant must declare either (1) that he has himself seen or perceived the fact or facts asserted; or (2) that his information is hearsay, but there is good reason for believing it—perhaps one of the usual grounds for crediting hearsay information. The first presents few problems: since the report, although hearsay, purports to be first-hand observation, remaining doubt centers on the honesty of the informant, and that worry is dissipated by the officer' previous experience with the informant. The other basis for accepting the informant's report is more complicated. But if, for example, the informer's hearsay comes from one of the actors in the crime in the nature of admission against interest, the affidavit giving this information should be held sufficient.

I am inclined to agree with the majority that there are limited special circumstances in which an "honest" informant's report, if sufficiently detailed, will in effect verify itself—that is, the magistrate when confronted with such detail could reasonably infer that the informant had gained his information in a reliable way. See ante, at 589. Detailed information may sometimes imply that the informant himself had observed the facts. Suppose an informant with whom an officer has had satisfactory experience states that there is gambling equipment in the living room of a specified apartment and describes in detail not only the equipment itself but also the appointments and furnishings in the apartment. Detail like this, if true at all must rest on personal observation either of the informant or of someone else. If the latter, we know nothing of the third person's honesty or sources; he may be making a wholly false report. But it is arguable that on these facts it was the informant himself who has perceived the facts, for the information reported is not usually the subject of casual day-to-day conversation. Because the informant is honest and it is probable that he has viewed the facts, there is probable cause for the issuance of a warning....

MR. JUSTICE BLACK, dissenting.

In my view, this Court's decision in Aguilar v. Texas, 378 U.S. 108, 84 S.Ct. 1509, 12 L.Ed.2d 723 (1964) was bad enough. That decision went very far toward elevating the magistrate's hearing for issuance of a search warrant to a full-fledged trial, where witnesses must be brought forward to attest personally to all the facts alleged. But not content with this, the Court today expands *Aguilar* to almost unbelievable proportions. Of course, it would strengthen the probable-cause presentation if eyewitnesses could testify that they saw the defendant commit the crime. It would be stronger still if these witnesses could explain in detail the nature of the sensual perceptions on which they based their "conclusion" that the person they had seen was the defendant and that he was responsible for the events they observed. Nothing in our Constitution, however, requires that the facts be established with that degree of certainty and with such elaborate specificity before a policeman can be authorized by a distinterested magistrate to conduct a carefully limited search.

The Fourth Amendment provides that "no Warrants shall issue, but upon probable cause, supported by Oath or affirmation, and particularly describing the place to be searched, and the persons or things to be seized." In this case a search warrant was issued supported by an oath and particularly describing the place to be searched and the things to be seized....

I repeat my belief that the affidavit given the magistrate was more than ample to show probable cause of the petitioner's guilt. The affidavit meticulously set out facts sufficient to show the following:

1. The petitioner had been shown going to and coming from a room in an apartment which contained two telephones listed under the name of another person. Nothing in the record indicates that the apartment was of that large and luxurious type which could only be occupied by a person to whom it would be a "petty luxury" to have two separate telephones, with different numbers, both listed under the name of a person who did not live there.

2. The petitioner's car had been observed parked in the apartment's parking lot. This fact was, of course, highly relevant in show-

ing that the petitioner was extremely interested in some enterprise which was located in the apartment.

3. The FBI had been informed by a reliable informant that the petitioner was accepting wagering information by telephones—the particular telephones located in the apartment the defendant had been repeatedly visiting. Unless the Court, going beyond the requirements of the Fourth Amendment, wishes to require magistrates to hold trials before issuing warrants, it is not necessary—as the Court holds—to have the affiant explain "the underlying circumstances from which the informer concluded the Spinelli was running a bookmaking operation." Ante, at 589.

4. The petitioner was known by federal and local law enforcement agents as a bookmaker and an associate of gamblers. I cannot agree with the Court that this knowledge was only a "bald and unilluminating assertion of suspicion that is entitled to no weight in appraising the magistrate's decision." Ante, at 588. Although the statement is hearsay that might not be admissible in a regular trial, everyone knows, unless he shuts his eyes to the realities of life, that this is a relevant fact which, together with other circumstances, might indicate factual probability that gambling is taking place.

The foregoing facts should be enough to constitute probable cause for anyone who does not believe that the only way to obtain a search warrant is to prove beyond a reasonable doubt that a defendant is guilty. Even *Aguilar,* on which the court relies, cannot support the contrary result, at least as that decision was written before today's massive escalation of it. In *Aguilar* the Court dealt with an affidavit that stated only:

"Affiants have received reliable information from a credible person and do believe that heroin . . . and other narcotics and narcotic paraphernalia are being kept at the above described premises for the purpose of sale and use contrary to the provisions of the law." 378 U.S., at 109, 84 S.Ct., at 1511.

The Court held, over the dissent of Mr. Justice Clark, Mr. Justice Stewart, and myself, that this unsupported conclusion of an unidentified informant provided no basis for the magistrate to make an independent judgment as to the persuasiveness of the facts relied upon to show probable cause. Here, of course, we have much more, and the Court in *Aguilar* was careful to point out that additional information of the kind presented in the affidavit before us now would be highly relevant:

"If the fact and results of such a surveillance had been appropriately presented to the magistrate, this would, of course, present an entirely different case." 378 U.S., at 109, n. 1, 84 S.Ct., at 1511.

In the present case even the two-judge minority of the court below recognized, as this Court seems to recognize today, that this additional information took the case beyond the rule of *Aguilar.* Six of the other circuit judges disagreed with the two dissenting judges, finding that all the circumstances considered together could support a reasonable judgment that gambling probably was taking place. I fully agree with this carefully considered opinion of the court below. 382 F.2d 871.

I regret to say I consider today's decision an indefensible departure from the principles of our former cases. Less than four years ago we reaffirmed these principles in United States v. Ventresca, 380 U.S. 102, 108, 85 S.Ct. 741, 746, 13 L.Ed.2d 684 (1965):

"If the teachings of the Court's cases are to be followed and the constitutional policy served, affidavits for search warrants . . . must be tested and interpreted by magistrates and courts in a commonsense and realistic fashion. . . . Technical requirements of elaborate specificity once exacted under common law pleadings have no proper place in this area."

See also Husty v. United States, 282 U.S. 694, 700–701, 51 S.Ct. 240, 241–242, 75 L.Ed. 629 (1931).

Departures of this kind are responsible for considerable uneasiness in our lower courts, and I must say I am deeply troubled by the statements of Judge Gibson in the court below:

"I am, indeed, disturbed by decision after decision of our courts which place increasingly technical burdens upon law enforcement officials. I am disturbed by these decisions that appear to relentlessly chip away at the ever narrowing area of effective police operation. I believe the holdings in *Aguilar,* and Rugendorf v. United States, 376 U.S. 528 [84 S.Ct. 825, 11 L.Ed.2d 887] (1964) are sufficient to protect the privacy of individuals from hastily conceived intrusions, and I do not think the limitations and requirements on the issuance of search warrants should be expanded by setting up over-technical requirements approaching the now discarded pitfalls of common law pleadings. Moreover, if we become increasingly technical and rigid in our demands upon police officers, I fear we make it increasingly easy for criminals to operate, detected but unpunished. I feel the significant movement of the law beyond its present state is unwarranted, unneeded, and dangerous to law enforcement efficiency." (Dissenting from panel opinion.)

The Court of Appeals in this case took a sensible view of the Fourth Amendment, and I would wholeheartedly affirm its decision.

Mapp v. Ohio, 367 U.S. 643, 81 S.Ct. 1684, 6 L.Ed.2d 1081 decided in 1961, held for the first time that the Fourth Amendment and the exclusionary rule of Weeks v. United States, 232 U.S. 383, 34 S.Ct. 341, 58 L.Ed. 652 (1914) are now applicable to the States. That Amendment provides that search warrants shall not be issued without probable cause. The existence of probable cause is a factual matter that calls for the determination of a factual question. While no statistics are immediately available, questions of probable cause to issue search warrants and to make arrests are doubtless involved in many thousands of cases in state courts. All of those probable-cause state cases are now potentially reviewable by this Court. It is, of course, physically impossible for this Court to review the evidence in all or even a substantial percentage of those cases. Consequently, whether desirable or not, we must inevitably accept most of the fact findings of the state courts, particularly when, as here in a federal case, both the trial and appellate courts have decided the facts the same way. It cannot be said that the trial judge and six members of the Court of Appeals committed flagrant error in finding from evidence that the magistrate had probable cause to issue the search warrant here. It seems to me that this Court would best serve itself and the administration of justice by accepting the judgment of the two courts below. After all, they too are lawyers and judges, and much closer to the practical, everyday affairs of life than we are.

Notwithstanding the Court's belief to the contrary, I think that in holding as it does, the Court does:

"retreat from the established propositions that only the probability, and not a prima facie showing, of criminal activity is the standard of probable cause, Beck v. Ohio, 379 U.S. 89, 96, 85 S.Ct. 223, 228, 13 L.Ed.2d 142 (1964); that affidavits of probable cause are tested by much less rigorous standards than those governing the admissibility of evidence at trial, McCray v. Illinois, 386 U.S. 300, 311, 87 S.Ct. 1056, 1062 (1967); that in judging probable cause issuing magistrates are not to be confined by niggardly limitations or by restrictions on the use of their common sense, United States v. Ventresca, 380 U.S. 102, 108, 85 S.Ct. 741, 745 (1965); and that their determination of probable cause should be paid great deference by reviewing courts, Jones v. United States, 362 U.S. 257, 270–271, 80 S.Ct. 725, 735–736 (1960)." Ante, at 590.

In fact, I believe the Court is moving rapidly, through complex analyses and obfuscatory language, toward the holding that no magistrate can issue a warrant unless according to some unknown standard of proof he can be persuaded that the suspect defendant is actually guilty of a crime. I would affirm this conviction.

Mr. Justice Fortas, dissenting. . . .

Today's decision deals, not with the necessity of obtaining a warrant prior to search, but with the difficult problem of the nature of the showing that must be made before the magistrate to justify his issuance of a search warrant. While I do not subscribe to the criticism of the majority expressed by my Brother Black in dissent, I believe—with all respect—that the majority is in error in holding that the affidavit supporting the warrant in this case is constitutionally inadequate. . . .

Mr. Justice Stewart, dissenting.

CHIMEL v. CALIFORNIA
Supreme Court of the United States, 1969.
395 U.S. 752, 89 S.Ct. 2034, 23 L.Ed.2d 685. Noted, 15 Howard L.J. 715,
10 Am.U.L. Rev. 575.

MR. JUSTICE STEWART delivered the opinion of the Court. This case raises basic questions concerning the permissible scope under the Fourth Amendment of a search incident to a lawful arrest.

The relevant facts are essentially undisputed. Late in the afternoon of September 13, 1965, three police officers arrived at the Santa Ana, California, home of the petitioner with a warrant authorizing his arrest for the burglary of a coin shop. The officers knocked on the door, identified themselves to the petitioner's wife, and asked if they might come inside. She ushered them into the house, where they waited 10 or 15 minutes until the petitioner returned home from work. When the petitioner entered the house, one of the officers handed him the arrest warrant and asked for permission to "look around." The petitioner objected, but was advised that "on the basis of the lawful arrest," the officers would nonetheless conduct a search. No search warrant had been issued.

Accompanied by the petitioner's wife, the officers then looked through the entire three-bedroom house, including the attic, the garage, and a small workshop. In some rooms the search was relatively cursory. In the master bedroom and sewing room, however, the officers directed the petitioner's wife to open drawers and "to physically move contents of the drawers from side to side so that [they] might view any items that would have come from [the] burglary." After completing the search, they seized numerous items—primarily coins, but also several medals, tokens, and a few other objects. The entire search took between 45 minutes and an hour.

At the petitioner's subsequent state trial on two charges of burglary, the items taken from his house were admitted into evidence against him, over his objection that they had been unconstitutionally seized. He was convicted, and the judgments of conviction were affirmed by both the California Court of Appeal, 61 Cal.Rptr. 714, and the California Supreme Court, 68 Cal.2d 436, 67 Cal.Rptr. 421, 439 P. 2d 333. Both courts accepted the petitioner's contention that the arrest warrant was invalid because the supporting affidavit was set out in conclusory terms, but held that since the arresting officers had procured the warrant "in good faith," and since in any event they had had sufficient information to constitute probable cause for the petitioner's arrest, that arrest had been lawful. From this conclusion the appellate courts went on to hold that the search of the petitioner's home had been justified, despite the absence of a search warrant, on the ground that it had been incident to a valid arrest. We granted certiorari in order to consider the petitioner's substantial constitutional claims, 393 U.S. 958, 89 S.Ct. 404, 21 L.Ed.2d 372.

Without deciding the question, we proceed on the hypothesis that the California courts were correct in holding that the arrest of the petitioner was valid under the Constitution. This brings us directly to the question whether the warrantless search of the petitioner's entire house can be constitutionally justified as incident to that arrest. The decisions of this Court bearing upon that question have been far from consistent, as even the most cursory review makes evident.

Approval of a warrantless search incident to a lawful arrest seems first to have been articulated by the Court in 1914 as dictum in Weeks v. United States, 232 U.S. 383, 34 S.Ct. 341, 58 L.Ed. 652, in which the Court stated:

"What then is the present case? Before answering that inquiry specifically, it may be well by a process of exclusion to state what it is not. It is not an assertion of the right on the part of the Government, always recognized under English and American law, to search the person of the accused when legally arrested to discover and seize the fruits or evidences of crime." Id., at 392, 34 S.Ct., at 344.

That statement made no reference to any right to search the *place* where an arrest occurs, but was limited to a right to search the "person." Eleven years later the case of Carroll v. United States, 267 U.S. 132, 45 S.Ct.

280, 69 L.Ed. 543, brought the following embellishment of the *Weeks* statement:

"When a man is legally arrested for an offense, whatever is found upon his person *or in his control* which it is unlawful for him to have and which may be used to prove the offense may be seized and held as evidence in the prosecution." *Id.*, at 158, 45 S.Ct., at 287. (Emphasis added.)

Still, that assertion too was far from a claim that the "place" where one is arrested may be searched so long as the arrest is valid. Without explanation, however, the principle emerged in expanded form a few months later in Agnello v. United States, 269 U.S. 20, 46 S.Ct. 4, 70 L.Ed. 145—although still by way of dictum:

"The right without a search warrant contemporaneously to search persons lawfully arrested while committing crime and to search the place where the arrest is made in order to find and seize things connected with the crime as its fruits or as the means by which it was committed, as well as weapons and other things to effect an escape from custody, is not to be doubted. See Carroll v. United States, 267 U.S. 132, 158, 45 S.Ct. 280, 69 L.Ed. 543; Weeks v. United States, 232 U.S. 383, 392, 34 S.Ct. 341, 58 L.Ed. 652." 269 U.S., at 30, 46 S.Ct., at 5.

And in Marron v. United States, 275 U.S. 192, 48 S.Ct. 74, 72 L.Ed. 231, two years later, the dictum of *Agnello* appeared to be the foundation of the Court's decision. In that case federal agents had secured a search warrant authorizing the seizure of liquor and certain articles used in its manufacture. When they arrived at the premises to be searched, they saw "that the place was used for retailing and drinking intoxicating liquors." *Id.*, at 194, 48 S.Ct., at 75. They proceeded to arrest the person in charge and to execute the warrant. In searching a closet for the items listed in the warrant they came across an incriminating ledger, concededly not covered by the warrant, which they also seized. The Court upheld the seizure of the ledger by holding that since the agents had made a lawful arrest, "[t]hey had a right without a warrant contemporaneously to search the place in order to find and seize the things used to carry on the criminal enterprise." *Id.*, at 199, 48 S.Ct., at 77.

That the *Marron* opinion did not mean all that it seemed to say became evident, however, a few years later in Go-Bart Importing Co. v. United States, 282 U.S. 344, 51 S.Ct. 153, 75 L.Ed. 374, and United States v. Lefkowitz, 285 U.S. 452, 52 S.Ct. 420, 76 L.Ed. 877. In each of those cases the opinion of the Court was written by Mr. Justice Butler, the author of the opinion in *Marron*. In *Go-Bart*, agents had searched the office of persons whom they had lawfully arrested, and had taken several papers from a desk, a safe, and other parts of the office. The Court noted that no crime had been committed in the agents' presence, and that although the agent in charge "had an abundance of information and time to swear out a valid [search] warrant, he failed to do so." 282 U.S., at 358, 51 S.Ct., at 158. In holding the search and seizure unlawful, the Court stated:

"Plainly the case before us is essentially different from Marron v. United States, 275 U.S. 192, 48 S.Ct. 74, 72 L.Ed. 231. There, officers executing a valid search warrant for intoxicating liquors found and arrested one Birdsall who in pursuance of a conspiracy was actually engaged in running a saloon. As an incident to the arrest they seized a ledger in a closet where the liquor or some of it was kept and some bills beside the cash register. These things were visible and accessible and in the offender's immediate custody. There was no threat of force or general search or rummaging of the place." 282 U.S., at 358, 51 S.Ct., at 158.

This limited characterization of *Marron* was reiterated in *Lefkowitz*, a case in which the Court held unlawful a search of desk drawers and a cabinet despite the fact that the search had accompanied a lawful arrest. 285 U.S., at 465, 52 S.Ct., at 423.

The limiting views expressed in *Go-Bart* and *Lefkowitz* were thrown to the winds, however, in Harris v. United States, 331 U.S. 145, 67 S.Ct. 1098, 91 L.Ed. 1399, decided in 1947. In that case, officers had obtained a warrant for Harris' arrest on the basis of his alleged involvement with the cashing and interstate transportation of a forged check.

He was arrested in the living room of his four-room apartment, and in an attempt to recover two canceled checks thought to have been used in effecting the forgery, the officers undertook a thorough search of the entire apartment. Inside a desk drawer they found a sealed envelope marked "George Harris, personal papers." The envelope, which was then torn open, was found to contain altered Selective Service documents, and those documents were used to secure Harris' conviction for violating the Selective Training and Service Act of 1940. The Court rejected Harris' Fourth Amendment claim, sustaining the search as "incident to arrest." *Id.*, at 151, 67 S.Ct., at 1101.

Only a year after *Harris*, however, the pendulum swung again. In Trupiano v. United States, 334 U.S. 699, 68 S.Ct. 1229, 92 L.Ed. 1663, agents raided the site of an illicit distillery, saw one of several conspirators operating the still, and arrested him, contemporaneously "seiz[ing] the illicit distillery." *Id.*, at 702, 68 S.Ct. at 1231. The Court held that the arrest and others made subsequently had been valid, but that the unexplained failure of the agents to procure a search warrant—in spite of the fact that they had had more than enough time before the raid to do so—rendered the search unlawful. The opinion stated:

"It is a cardinal rule that, in seizing goods and articles, law enforcement agents must secure and use search warrants wherever reasonably practicable. . . . This rule rests upon the desirability of having magistrates rather than police officers determine when searches and seizures are permissible and what limitations should be placed upon such activities. . . . To provide the necessary security against unreasonable intrusions upon the private lives of individuals, the framers of the Fourth Amendment required adherence to judicial processes wherever possible. And subsequent history has confirmed the wisdom of that requirement. . . .

"A search or seizure without a warrant as an incident to a lawful arrest has always been considered to be a strictly limited right. It grows out of the inherent necessities of the situation at the time of the arrest. But there must be something more in the way of necessity than merely a lawful arrest." *Id.*, at 705, 708, 68 S.Ct., at 1232, 1234.

In 1950, two years after *Trupiano*, came United States v. Rabinowitz, 339 U.S. 56, 70 S.Ct. 430, 94 L.Ed. 653, the decision upon which California primarily relies in the case now before us. In *Rabinowitz*, federal authorities had been informed that the defendant was dealing in stamps bearing forged overprints. On the basis of that information they secured a warrant for his arrest, which they executed at his one-room business office. At the time of the arrest, the officers "searched the desk, safe, and file cabinets in the office for about an hour and a half," *id.*, at 59, 70 S.Ct., at 432, and seized 573 stamps with forged overprints. The stamps were admitted into evidence at the defendant's trial, and this Court affirmed his conviction, rejecting the contention that the warrantless search had been unlawful. The Court held that the search in its entirety fell within the principle giving law enforcement authorities "[t]he right 'to search the place where the arrest is made in order to find and seize things connected with the crime. . . .'" *Id.*, at 61, 70 S.Ct., at 433. *Harris* was regarded as "ample authority" for that conclusion. *Id.*, at 63, 70 S.Ct., at 434. The opinion rejected the rule of *Trupiano* that "in seizing goods and articles, law enforcement agents must secure and use search warrants wherever reasonably practicable." The test, said the Court, "is not whether it is reasonable to procure a search warrant, but whether the search was reasonable." *Id.*, at 66, 70 S.Ct., at 435.

Rabinowitz has come to stand for the proposition, *inter alia*, that a warrantless search "incident to a lawful arrest" may generally extend to the area that is considered to be in the "possession" or under the "control" of the person arrested. And it was on the basis of that proposition that the California courts upheld the search of the petitioner's entire house in this case. That doctrine, however, at least in the broad sense in which it was applied by the California courts in this case, can withstand neither historical nor rational analysis.

Even limited to its own facts, the *Rabinowitz* decision was, as we have seen, hardly founded on an unimpeachable line of authority. As Mr. Justice Frankfurter commented in dissent in that case, the "hint" contained in

Weeks was, without persuasive justification, "loosely turned into dictum and finally elevated to a decision." 339 U.S., at 75, 70 S.Ct., at 439. And the approach taken in cases such as *Go-Bart, Lefkowitz,* and *Trupiano* was essentially disregarded by the *Rabinowitz* Court.

Nor is the rationale by which the State seeks here to sustain the search of the petitioner's house supported by a reasoned view of the background and purpose of the Fourth Amendment. Mr. Justice Frankfurter wisely pointed out in his *Rabinowitz* dissent that the Amendment's proscription of "unreasonable searches and seizures" must be read in light of "the history that gave rise to the words"— a history of "abuses so deeply felt by the Colonies as to be one of the potent causes of the Revolution. . . ." 339 U.S., at 69, 70 S.Ct., at 436. The Amendment was in large part a reaction to the general warrants and warrantless searches that had so alienated the colonists and had helped speed the movement for independence. In the scheme of the Amendment, therefore, the requirement that "no Warrants shall issue, but upon probable cause," plays a crucial part. As the Court put it in McDonald v. United States, 335 U.S. 451, 69 S.Ct. 191, 93 L.Ed. 153:

"We are not dealing with formalities. The presence of a search warrant serves a high function. Absent some grave emergency, the Fourth Amendment has interposed a magistrate between the citizen and the police. This was done not to shield criminals nor to make the home a safe haven for illegal activities. It was done so that an objective mind might weigh the need to invade that privacy in order to enforce the law. The right of privacy was deemed too precious to entrust to the discretion of those whose job is the detection of crime and the arrest of criminals. . . . And so the Constitution requires a magistrate to pass on the desires of the police before they violate the privacy of the home. We cannot be true to that constitutional requirement and excuse the absence of a search warrant without a showing by those who seek exemption from the constitutional mandate that the exigencies of the situation made that course imperative." *Id.*, at 455–456, 69 S.Ct., at 193.

Even in the *Agnello* case the Court relied upon the rule that "[b]elief, however well founded, that an article sought is concealed in a dwelling house, furnishes no justification for a search of that place without a warrant. And such searches are held unlawful notwithstanding facts unquestionably showing probable cause." 269 U.S., at 33, 46 S.Ct., at 6. Clearly, the general requirement that a search warrant be obtained is not lightly to be dispensed with, and "the burden is on those seeking [an] exemption [from the requirement] to show the need for it. . . ." United States v. Jeffers, 342 U.S. 48, 51, 72 S.Ct. 93, 95, 96 L.Ed. 59.

Only last Term in Terry v. Ohio, 392 U.S. 1, 88 S.Ct. 1868, 20 L.Ed.2d 889, we emphasized that "the police must, whenever practicable, obtain advance judicial approval of searches and seizures through the warrant procedure," *id.*, at 20, 88 S.Ct. at 1879, and that "[t]he scope of [a] search must be 'strictly tied to and justified by' the circumstances which rendered its initiation permissible." *Id.*, at 19, 88 S.Ct., at 1878. The search undertaken by the officer in that "stop and frisk" case was sustained under that test, because it was no more than a "protective . . . search for weapons." *Id.*, at 29, 88 S.Ct., at 1884. But in a companion case, Sibron v. New York, 392 U.S. 40, 88 S.Ct. 1889, 20 L.Ed.2d 917, we applied the same standard to another set of facts and reached a contrary result, holding that a policeman's action in thrusting his hand into a suspect's pocket had been neither motivated by nor limited to the objective of protection. Rather, the search had been made in order to find narcotics, which were in fact found.

A similar analysis underlies the "search incident to arrest" principle, and marks its proper extent. When an arrest is made, it is reasonable for the arresting officer to search the person arrested in order to remove any weapons that the latter might seek to use in order to resist arrest or effect his escape. Otherwise, the officer's safety might well be endangered, and the arrest itself frustrated. In addition, it is entirely reasonable for the arresting officer to search for and seize any evidence on the arrestee's person in order to prevent its concealment or destruction. And the area into which an arrestee might reach in order to grab a weapon or evidentiary items must, of course, be governed by a like rule. A gun on a table or in a drawer in front of one who is arrested can be as dangerous to the arresting officer as one concealed in the clothing of the person arrested. There is ample justification, therefore, for a search of the arrestee's person and the area "within his immediate control"—construing that phrase to mean the area from within which he might gain possession of a weapon or destructible evidence.

There is no comparable justification, however, for routinely searching any room other than that in which an arrest occurs—or, for that matter, for searching through all the desk drawers or other closed or concealed areas in that room itself. Such searches, in the absence of well-recognized exceptions, may be made only under the authority of a search warrant. The "adherence to judicial processes" mandated by the Fourth Amendment requires no less.

This is the principle that underlay our decision in Preston v. United States, 376 U.S. 364, 84 S.Ct. 881, 11 L.Ed.2d 777. In that case three men had been arrested in a parked car, which had later been towed to a garage and searched by police. We held the search to have been unlawful under the Fourth Amendment, despite the contention that it had been incidental to a valid arrest. Our reasoning was straightforward:

"The rule allowing contemporaneous searches is justified, for example, by the need to seize weapons and other things which might be used to assault an officer or effect an escape, as well as by the need to prevent the destruction of evidence of the crime—things which might easily happen where the weapon or evidence is on the accused's person or under his immediate control. But these justifications are absent where a search is remote in time or place from the arrest." Id., at 367, 84 S.Ct., at 883.

The same basic principle was reflected in our opinion last Term in *Sibron*. That opinion dealt with Peters v. New York, No. 74, as well as with Sibron's case, and *Peters* involved a search that we upheld as incident to a proper arrest. We sustained the search, however, only because its scope had been "reasonably limited" by the "need to seize weapons" and "to prevent the destruction of evidence," to which *Preston* had referred. We emphasized that the arresting officer "did not engage in an unrestrained and thorough going examination of Peters and his personal effects. He seized him to cut short his flight, and he searched him primarily for weapons." 392 U.S., at 67, 88 S.Ct., at 1905.

It is argued in the present case that it is "reasonable" to search a man's house when he is arrested in it. But that argument is founded on little more than a subjective view regarding the acceptability of certain sorts of police conduct, and not on considerations relevant to Fourth Amendment interests. Under such an unconfined analysis, Fourth Amendment protection in this area would approach the evaporation point. It is not easy to explain why, for instance, it is less subjectively "reasonable" to search a man's house when he is arrested on his front lawn—or just down the street—than it is when he happens to be in the house at the time of arrest. As Mr. Justice Frankfurter put it:

"To say that the search must be reasonable is to require some criterion of reason. It is no guide at all either for a jury or for district judges or the police to say that an 'unreasonable search' is forbidden—that the search must be reasonable. What is the test of reason which makes a search reasonable? The test is the reason underlying and expressed by the Fourth Amendment: the history and experience which it embodies and the safeguards afforded by it against the evils to which it was a response." United States v. Rabinowitz, 339 U.S., at 83, 70 S.Ct., at 443 (dissenting opinion).

Thus, although "[t]he recurring questions of the reasonableness of searches" depend upon "the facts and circumstances—the total atmosphere of the case," *id.*, at 63, 66, 70 S.Ct., at 434, 435 (opinion of the Court), those facts and circumstances must be viewed in the light of established Fourth Amendment principles.

It would be possible, of course, to draw a line between *Rabinowitz* and *Harris* on the one hand, and this case on the other. For *Rabinowitz* involved a single room, and *Harris* a four-room apartment, while in the case before us an entire house was searched. But such a distinction would be highly artificial. The rationale that allowed the searches and seizures in *Rabinowitz* and *Harris* would allow the searches and seizures in this case. No consideration relevant to the Fourth Amendment suggests any point of rational limitation, once the search is allowed to go beyond the area from which the person arrested might obtain weapons or evidentiary items. The only reasoned distinction is one between a search of the person arrested and the area within his reach on the one hand, and more extensive searches on the other.

The petitioner correctly points out that one result of decisions such as *Rabinowitz* and *Harris* is to give law enforcement officials the opportunity to engage in searches not justified by probable cause, by the simple expedient of arranging to arrest suspects at home rather than elsewhere. We do not suggest that the petitioner is necessarily correct in his assertion that such a strategy was utilized here, but the fact remains that had he been arrested earlier in the day, at his place of employment rather than at home, no search of his house could have been made without a search warrant. In any event, even apart from the possibility of such police tactics, the general point so forcefully made by Judge Learned Hand in United States v. Kirschenblatt, 2 Cir., 16 F.2d202, 51 A.L.R. 416 remains:

"After arresting a man in his house, to rummage at will among his papers in search of whatever will convict him, appears to us to be indistinguishable from what might be done under a general warrant; indeed, the warrant would give more protection, for presumably it must be issued by a magistrate. True, by hypothesis the power would not exist, if the supposed offender were not found on the premises; but it is small consolation to know that one's papers are safe only so long as one is not at home." Id., at 203.

Rabinowitz and *Harris* have been the subject of critical commentary for many years, and have been relied upon less and less in our own decisions. It is time, for the reasons we have stated, to hold that on their own facts, and insofar as the principles they stand for are inconsistent with those that we have endorsed today, they are no longer to be followed.

Application of sound Fourth Amendment principles to the facts of this case produces a clear result. The search here went far beyond the petitioner's person and the area from within which he might have obtained either a weapon or something that could have been used as evidence against him. There was no constitutional justification, in the absence of a search warrant, for extending the search beyond that area. The scope of the search was, therefore, "unreasonable" under the Fourth and Fourteenth Amendments and the petitioner's conviction cannot stand.

Reversed.

Mr. Justice Harlan, concurring. . . .

Mr. Justice White, with whom Mr. Justice Black joins, dissenting. . . .

TERRY v. OHIO
Supreme Court of the United States, 1968.
392 U.S. 1, 88 S.Ct. 1868, 20 L.Ed.2d 889.

Mr. Chief Justice Warren delivered the opinion of the Court. This case presents serious questions concerning the role of the Fourth Amendment in the confrontation on the street between the citizen and the policeman investigating suspicious circumstances.

Petitioner Terry was convicted of carrying a concealed weapon and sentenced to the statutorily prescribed term of one to three years in the penitentiary. Following the denial of a pretrial motion to suppress, the prosecution introduced in evidence two revolvers and a number of bullets seized from Terry and a codefendant, Richard Chilton, by Cleveland Police Detective Martin McFadden. At the hearing on the motion to suppress this evidence, Officer McFadden testified that while he was patrolling in plain clothes in downtown Cleveland at approximately 2:30 in the afternoon of October 31, 1963, his attention was attracted by two men, Chilton and Terry, standing on the corner of Huron Road and Euclid Avenue. He had never seen the two men before, and he was unable to say precisely what first drew his eye to them. However, he testified that he had been a policeman for 39 years and a detective for 35 and that he had been assigned to patrol this vicinity of downtown Cleveland for shoplifters and pickpockets for 30 years. He explained that he had developed routine habits of observation over the years and that he would "stand and watch people or walk and watch people at many intervals of the day." He added: "Now, in this case when I looked over they didn't look right to me at the time."

His interest aroused, Officer McFadden took up a post of observation in the entrance to a store 300 to 400 feet away from the two men. "I get more purpose to watch them when I seen their movements," he testified. He saw one of the men leave the other one and walk southwest on Huron Road, past some stores. The man paused for a moment and looked in a store window, then walked on a short distance, turned around and walked back toward the corner, pausing once again to look in the same store window. He rejoined his companion at the corner, and the two conferred briefly. Then the second man went through the same series of motions, strolling down Huron Road, looking in the same window, walking on a short distance, turning back, peering in the store window again, and returning to confer with the first man at the corner. The two men repeated this ritual alternately between five and six times apiece—in all, roughly a dozen trips. At one point, while the two were standing together on the corner, a third man approached them and engaged them briefly in conversation. This man then left the two others and walked west on Euclid Avenue. Chilton and Terry resumed their measured pacing, peering and conferring. After this had gone on for 10 to 12 minutes, the two men walked off together, heading west on Euclid Avenue, following the path taken earlier by the third man.

By this time Officer McFadden had become thoroughly suspicious. He testified that after observing their elaborately casual and oft-repeated reconnaissance of the store window on Huron Road, he suspected the two men of "casing a job, a stick-up," and that he considered it his duty as a police officer to investigate further. He added that he feared "they may have a gun." Thus, Officer McFadden followed Chilton and Terry and saw them stop in front of Zucker's store to talk to the same man who had conferred with them earlier on the street corner. Deciding that the situation was ripe for direct action, Officer McFadden approached the three men, identified himself as a police officer and asked for their names. At this point his knowledge was confined to what he had observed. He was not acquainted with any of the three men by name or by sight, and he had received no information concerning them from any other source. When the men "mumbled something" in response to his inquiries, Officer McFadden grabbed petitioner Terry, spun him around so that they were facing the other two, with Terry between McFadden and the others, and patted down the outside of his clothing. In the left breast pocket of Terry's overcoat Officer McFadden felt a pistol. He reached inside the overcoat pocket, but was unable to remove the gun. At this point, keeping Terry between himself and the others, the officer ordered all three men to enter Zucker's store. As they went in, he removed Terry's overcoat completely, removed a .38-caliber revolver from the pocket and ordered all three men to face the wall with their hands raised. Officer McFadden proceeded to pat down the outer clothing of Chilton and the third man, Katz. He discovered another revolver in the outer pocket of Chilton's overcoat, but no weapons were found on Katz. The officer testified that he only patted the men down to see whether they had weapons, and that he did not put his hands beneath the outer garments of either Terry or Chilton until he felt their guns. So far as appears from the record, he never placed his hands beneath Katz' outer garments. Officer McFadden seized Chilton's gun, asked the proprietor of the store to call a police wagon, and took all three men to the station, where Chilton and Terry were formally charged with carrying concealed weapons.

On the motion to suppress the guns the prosecution took the position that they had been seized following a search incident to a lawful arrest. The trial court rejected this theory, stating that it "would be stretching the facts beyond reasonable comprehension" to find that Officer McFadden had had probable cause to arrest the men before he patted them down for weapons. However, the court denied the defendants' motion on the ground that Officer McFadden, on the basis of his experience, "had reasonable cause to believe . . . that the defendants were conducting themselves suspiciously, and some interrogation should be made of their action." Purely for his own protection, the court held, the officer had the right to pat down the outer clothing of these men, who he had reasonable cause to believe might be armed. The court distinguished between an investigatory "stop" and an arrest, and between a "frisk" of the outer clothing for weapons and a full-blown search for evidence of crime. The frisk, it held, was essential to the proper performance of the officer's investigatory duties, for without it "the answer to the police officer may be a bullet, and a loaded pistol discovered during the frisk is admissible."

After the court denied their motion to suppress, Chilton and Terry waived jury trial and pleaded not guilty. The court adjudged them guilty, and the Court of Appeals for the Eighth Judicial District, Cuyahoga County, affirmed. State v. Terry, 5 Ohio App.2d 122, 214 N.E.2d 114 (1966). The Supreme Court of Ohio dismissed their appeal on the ground that no "substantial constitutional question" was involved. We granted certiorari, 387 U.S. 929, 87 S.Ct. 2050, 18 L.Ed.2d 989 (1967), to determine whether the admission of the revolvers in evidence violated petitioner's rights under the Fourth Amendment, made applicable to the States by the Fourteenth. Mapp v. Ohio, 367 U.S. 643, 81 S.Ct. 1684, 6 L.Ed.2d 1081 (1961). We affirm the conviction.

I. The Fourth Amendment provides that "the right of the people to be secure in their persons, houses, papers, and effects, against unreasonable searches and seizures, shall not be violated. . . ." This inestimable right of personal security belongs as much to the citizen on the streets of our cities as to the homeowner closeted in his study to dispose of his secret affairs. For, as this Court has always recognized,

"No right is held more sacred, or is more carefully guarded, by the common law, than the right of every individual to the possession and control of his own person, free from all restraint or interference of others, unless by clear and unquestionable authority of law." Union Pac. R. Co. v. Botsford, 141 U.S. 250, 251, 11 S.Ct. 1000, 1001, 35 L.Ed. 734 (1891).

We have recently held that "the Fourth Amendment protects people, not places," Katz v. United States, 389 U.S. 347, 351, 88 S.Ct. 507, 511, 19 L.Ed.2d 576 (1967), and wherever an individual may harbor a reasonable "expectation of privacy," id., at 361, 88 S.Ct. at 507, (Mr. Justice Harlan, concurring), he is titled to be free from unreasonable governmental intrusion. Of course, the specific content and incidents of this right must be shaped by the context in which it is asserted. For "what the Constitution forbids is not all searches and seizures, but unreasonable searches and seizures." Elkins v. United States, 364 U.S. 206, 222, 80 S.Ct. 1437, 1446, 4 L.Ed.2d 1669 (1960). Unquestionably petitioner was entitled to the protection of the Fourth Amendment as he walked down the street in Cleveland. . . . The question is whether in all the circumstances of this on-the-street encounter, his right to personal security was violated by an unreasonable search and seizure.

We would be less than candid if we did not acknowledge that this question thrusts to the fore difficult and troublesome issues regarding a sensitive area of police activity—issues which have never before been squarely presented to this Court. Reflective of the tensions involved are the practical and constitutional arguments pressed with great vigor on both sides of the public debate over the power of the police to "stop and frisk"—as it is sometimes euphemistically termed—suspicious persons.

On the one hand, it is frequently argued that in dealing with the rapidly unfolding and often dangerous situations on city streets the police are in need of an escalating set of flexible responses, graduated in relation to the amount of information they possess. For this purpose it is urged that distinctions should be made between a "stop" and an "arrest" (or a "seizure" of a person), and between a "frisk" and a "search." Thus, it is argued, the police should be allowed to "stop" a person and detain him briefly for questioning upon suspicion that he may be connected with criminal activity. Upon suspicion that the person may be armed, the police should have the power to "frisk" him for weapons. If the "stop" and the "frisk" give rise to probable cause to believe that the suspect has committed a crime, then the police should be empowered to make a formal "arrest," and a full incident "search" of the person. This scheme is justified in part upon the notion that a "stop" and a "frisk" amount to a mere "minor inconvenience and petty indignity," which can properly be imposed upon the citizen in the interest of effective law enforcement on the basis of a police officer's suspicion.

On the other side the argument is made that the authority of the police must be strictly circumscribed by the law of arrest and search as it has developed to date in the traditional jurisprudence of the Fourth Amendment. It is contended with some force that there is not—and cannot be—a variety of police activity which does not depend solely upon the voluntary cooperation of the citizen and yet which stops short of an arrest based upon probable cause to make such an arrest. The heart of the Fourth Amendment, the argument runs, is a severe requirement of specific justification for any intrusion upon protected personal security, coupled with a highly developed system of judicial controls to enforce upon the agents of the State the commands of the Constitution. Acquiescence by the courts in the compulsion inherent in the field interrogation practices at issue here, it is urged, would constitute an abdication of judicial control over, and indeed an encouragement of, substantial interference with liberty and personal security by police officers whose judgment is necessarily colored by their primary involvement in "the often competitive enterprise of ferreting out crime." Johnson v. United States, 333 U.S. 10, 14, 68 S.Ct. 367, 369, 92 L.Ed. 436 (1948). This, it is argued, can only serve to exacerbate police-community tensions in the crowded centers of our Nation's cities.

In this context we approach the issues in this case mindful of the limitations of the judicial function in controlling the myriad daily situations in which policemen and citizens confront each other on the street. The State has characterized the issue here as "the right of a police officer . . . to make an on-the-street stop, interrogate and pat down for weapons (known in street vernacular as 'stop and frisk')." But this is only partly accurate. For the issue is not the abstract propriety of the police conduct, but the admissibility against petitioner of the evidence uncovered by the search and seizure. Ever since its inception, the rule excluding evidence seized in violation of the Fourth Amendment has been recognized as a principal mode of discouraging lawless police conduct. See Weeks v. United States, 232 U.S. 383, 391–393, 34 S.Ct. 341, 344, 58 L.Ed. 652 (1914). Thus its major thrust is a deterrent one, see Linkletter v. Walker, 381 U.S. 618, 629–635, 85 S.Ct. 1731, 1741, 14 L.Ed.2d 601 (1965), and experience has taught that it is the only effective deterrent to police misconduct in the criminal context, and that without it the constitutional guarantee against unreasonable searches and seizures would be a mere "form of words." Mapp v. Ohio, 367 U.S. 643, 655, 81 S.Ct. 1684, 1692, 6 L.Ed.2d 1081 (1961). The rule also serves another vital function—"the imperative of judicial integrity." Elkins v. United States, 364 U.S. 206, 222, 80 S.Ct. 1437, 1447, 4 L.Ed.2d 1669 (1960). Courts which sit under our Constitution cannot and will not be made party to lawless invasions of the constitutional rights of citizens by permitting unhindered governmental use of the fruits of such invasions. Thus in our system evidentiary rulings provide the context in which the judicial process of inclusion and exclusion approves some conduct as comporting with constitutional guarantees and disapproves other actions by state agents. A ruling admitting evidence in a criminal trial, we recognize, has the necessary effect of legitimizing the conduct which produced the evidence, while an application of the exclusionary rule withholds the constitutional imprimatur.

The exclusionary rule has its limitations, however, as a tool of judicial control. It cannot properly be invoked to exclude the products of legitimate police investigative techniques on the ground that much conduct which is closely similar involves unwarranted intrusions upon constitutional protections. Moreover, in some contexts the rule is ineffective as a deterrent. Street encounters between citizens and police officers are incredibly rich in diversity. They range from wholly friendly exchanges of pleasantries or mutually useful information to hostile confrontations of armed men involving arrests, or injuries, or loss of life. Moreover, hostile confrontations are not all of a piece. Some of them begin in a friendly enough manner, only to take a different turn upon the injection of some unexpected element into the conversation. Encounters are initiated by the police for a wide variety of purposes, some of which are wholly unrelated to a desire to prosecute for crime. Doubtless some police "field interrogation" conduct violates the Fourth Amendment. But a stern refusal by this Court to condone such activity does not necessarily render it responsive to the exclusionary rule. Regardless of how effective the rule may be where obtaining convictions is an important objective of the police, it is powerless to deter invasions of constitutionally guaranteed rights where the police either have no interest in prosecuting or are willing to forego successful prosecution in the interest of serving some other goal.

Proper adjudication of cases in which the exclusionary rule is invoked demands a constant awareness of these limitations. The wholesale harassment by certain elements of the police community, of which minority groups, particularly Negroes, frequently complain, will not be stopped by the exclusion of any evidence from any criminal trial. Yet a rigid and unthinking application of the exclusionary rule, in futile protest against practices which it can never be used effectively to control, may exact a high toll in human injury and frustration of efforts to prevent crime. No judicial opinion can comprehend the protean variety of the street encounter, and we can only judge the facts of the case before us. Nothing we say today is to be taken as indicating approval of police conduct outside the legitimate investigative sphere. Under our decision, courts still retain their traditional responsibility to guard against police conduct which is overbearing or harassing, or which trenches upon personal security without the objective evidentiary justification which the Constitution requires. When such conduct is identified, it must be condemned by the judiciary and its fruits must be excluded from evidence in criminal trials. And, of course, our approval of legitimate and restrained investigative conduct undertaken on the basis of ample factual justification should in no way discourage the employment of other remedies than the exclusionary rule to curtail abuses for which that sanction may prove inappropriate.

Having thus roughly sketched the perimeters of the constitutional debate over the limits on police investigative conduct in general and the background against which this case presents itself, we turn our attention to the quite narrow question posed by the facts before us: wheher it is always unreasonable for a policeman to seize a person and subject him to a limited search for weapons unless there is probable cause for an arrest. Given the narrowness of this question, we have no occasion to canvass in detail the constitutional limitations upon the scope of a policeman's power when he confronts a citizen without probable cause to arrest him.

II. Our first task is to establish at what point in this encounter the Fourth Amendment becomes relevant. That is, we must decide whether and when Officer McFadden "seized" Terry and whether and when he conducted a "search." There is some suggestion in the use of such terms as "stop" and "frisk" that such police conduct is outside the purview of the Fourth Amendment because neither action rises to the level of a "search"" or "seizure" within the meaning of the Constitution. We emphatically reject this notion. It is quite plain that the Fourth Amendment governs "seizures" of the person which do not eventuate in a trip to the station house and prosecution for crime — "arrests" in traditional terminology. It must be recognized that whenever a police officer accosts an individual and restrains his freedom to walk away, he has "seized" that person. And it is nothing less than sheer torture of the English language to suggest that a careful exploration of the outer surfaces of a person's clothing all over his or her body in an attempt to find weapons is not a "search." Moreover, it is simply fantastic to urge that such a procedure performed in public by a policeman while the citizen stands helpless, perhaps facing a wall with his hands raised, is a "petty indignity." It is a serious intrusion uopn the sanctity of the person which may inflict great indignity and arouse strong resentment, and it is not to be undertaken lightly.

The danger in the logic which proceeds upon distinctions between a "stop" and an "arrest," or "seizure" of the person, and between a "frisk" and a "search" is twofold. It seeks to isolate from constitutional scrutiny the initial stages of the contact between the policeman and the citizen. And by suggesting a rigid all-or-nothing model of justification and regulation under the Amendment, it obscures the utility of limitations upon the scope, as well as the initiation, of police action as a means of constitutional regulation. This Court has held in the past that a search which is reasonable at its inception may violate the Fourth Amendment by virtue of its intolerable intensity and scope. Kremen v. United States, 353 U.S. 346, 77 S.Ct. 828, 1 L.Ed.2d 876 (1957); Go-Bart Importing Co. v. United States, 282 U.S. 344, 356–358, 51 S.Ct. 153, 158, 75 L.Ed. 374 (1931); see United States v. Di Re, 332 U.S. 581, 586–587, 68 S.Ct. 222, 225, 92 L.Ed. 210 (1948). The scope of the search must be "strictly tied to and justified by" the circumstances which rendered its initiation permissible. Warden v. Hayden, 387 U.S. 294, 310, 87 S.Ct. 1642, 1652 (1967) (Mr. Justice Fortas, concurring); see, e.g., Preston v. United States, 376 U.S. 364, 367–368, 84 S.Ct. 881, 884, 11 L.Ed.2d 777 (1964); Agnello v. United States, 269 U.S. 20, 30–31, 46 S.Ct. 4, 6, 70 L.Ed. 145 (1925).

The distinctions of classical "stop-and-frisk" theory thus serve to divert attention from the central inquiry under the Fourth Amendment —the reasonableness in all the circumstances of the particular governmental invasion of a citizen's personal security. "Search" and "seizure" are not talismans. We therefore reject the notions that the Fourth Amendment does not come into play at all as a limitation upon police conduct if the officers stop short of something called a "technical arrest" or a "full-blown search."

In this case there can be no question, then, that Officer McFadden "seized" petitioner and subjected him to a "search" when he took hold of him and patted down the outer surfaces of his clothing. We must decide whether at that point it was reasonable for Officer McFadden to have interfered with petitioner's personal security as he did. And in determining whether the seizure and search were "unreasonable" our inquiry is a dual one—whether the officer's action was justified at its inception, and whether it was reasonably related in scope to the circumstances which justified the interference in the first place.

III. If this case involved police conduct subject to the Fourth Amendment, we would have to ascertain whether "probable cause" existed to justify the search and seizure which took place. However, that is not the case. We do not retreat from our holdings that the police must, whenever practicable, obtain advance judicial approval of searches and seizures through the warrant procedure, see e. g., Katz v. United States, 389 U.S. 347, 88 S.Ct. 507, 19 L.Ed.2d 576 (1967); Beck v. State of Ohio, 379 U.S. 89, 96, 85 S.Ct. 223, 228, 13 L.Ed.2d 142 (1964); Chapman v. United States, 365 U.S. 610, 81 S.Ct. 776, 5 L.Ed.2d 828 (1961), or that in most instances failure to comply with the warrant requirement can only be excused by exigent circumstances, see e. g., Warden v. Hayden, 387 U.S. 294, 87 S.Ct. 1642, 18 L.Ed.2d 782 (1967) (hot pursuit); cf. Preston v. United States, 376 U.S. 364, 367–368, 84 S.Ct. 881, 884, 11 L.Ed.2d 777 (1964). But we deal here with an entire rubric of police conduct—necessarily swift action predicated upon the on-the-spot observations of the officer on the beat—which historically has not been, and as a practical matter could not be, subjected to the warrant procedure. Instead, the conduct involved in this case must be tested by the Fourth Amendment's general proscription against unreasonable searches and seizures.

Nonetheless, the notions which underlie both the warrant procedure and the requirement of probable cause remain fully relevant in this context. In order to assess the reasonableness of Officer McFadden's conduct as a general proposition, it is necessary "first to focus upon the governmental interest which allegedly justifies official intrusion upon the constitutionally protected interests of the private citizen," for there is "no ready test for determining reasonableness other than by balancing the need to search [or seize] against the invasion which the search [or seizure] entails." Camara v. Municipal Court, 387 U.S. 523, 534–535, 536–537, 87 S.Ct. 1727, 1735, 18 L.Ed.2d 930 (1967). And in justifying the particular intrusion the police officer must be able to point to specific and articulable facts which, taken together with rational inferences from those facts, reasonably warrant that intrusion. The scheme of the Fourth Amendment becomes meaningful only when it is assured that at some point the conduct of those charged with enforcing the laws can be subjected to the more detached, neutral scrutiny of a judge who must evaluate the reasonableness of a particular search or seizure in light of the particular circumstances. And in making that assessment it is imperative that the facts be judged against an objective standard: would the facts available to the officer at the moment of the seizure or the search "warrant a man of reasonable caution in the belief" that the action taken was appropriate? Cf. Carroll v. United States, 267 U.S. 132, 45 S.Ct. 280, 69 L.Ed. 543 (1925); Beck v. State of Ohio, 379 U.S. 89, 96–97, 85 S.Ct. 223, 229, 13 L.Ed.2d 142 (1964). Anything less would invite intrusions upon constitutionally guaranteed rights based on nothing more substantial than inarticulate hunches, a result this Court has consistently refused to sanction. See e. g., Beck v. Ohio, supra; Rios v. United States, 364 U.S. 253, 80 S.Ct. 1431, 4 L.Ed.2d 1688 (1960); Henry v. United States, 361 U.S. 98, 80 S.Ct. 168, 4 L.Ed.2d 134 (1959). And simple " 'good faith on the part of the arresting officer is not enough.' . . . If subjective good faith alone were the test, the protections of the Fourth Amendment would evaporate, and the people would be 'secure in their persons, houses, papers and effects,' only in the discretion of the police." Beck v. Ohio, supra, at 97, 85 S.Ct. at 229.

Applying these principles to this case, we consider first the nature and extent of the governmental interests involved. One general interest is of course that of effective crime prevention and detection; it is this interest which underlies the recognition that a police officer may in appropriate circumstances and in an appropriate manner approach a person for purposes of investigating possibly criminal behavior even though there is no probable cause to make an arrest. It was this legitimate investigative function Officer McFadden was discharging when he decided to approach petitioner and his companions. He had observed Terry, Chilton, and Katz go through a series of acts, each of them perhaps innocent in itself, but which taken together warranted further investigation. There is nothing unusual in two men standing together on a street corner, perhaps waiting for someone. Nor is there anything suspicious about people in such circumstances strolling up and down the street, singly or in pairs. Store windows, moreover are made to be looked in. But the story is quite different where, as here, two men hover about a street corner for an extended period of time, at the end of which it becomes apparent that they are not waiting for anyone or anything; where these men pace alternately along an identical route, pausing to stare in the same store window roughly 24 times; where each completion of this route is followed immediately by a conference between the two men on the corner; where they are joined in one of these conferences by a third man who leaves swiftly; and where the two men finally follow the third and rejoin him a couple of blocks away. It would have been poor police work indeed for an officer of 30 years' experience in the detection of thievery from stores in this same neighborhood to have failed to investigate this behavior further.

The crux of this case, however, is not the propriety of Officer McFadden's taking steps to investigate petitioner's suspicious behavior, but rather, whether there was justification for McFadden's invasion of Terry's personal security by searching him for weapons in the course of that investigation. We are now concerned with more than the governmental interest in investigating crime; in addition, there is the more immediate interest of the police officer in taking steps to assure himself that the person with whom he is dealing is not armed with a weapon that could unexpectedly and fatally be used against him. Certainly it would be unreasonable to require that police officers take unnecessary risks in the performance of their duties. American criminals have a long tradition of armed violence, and every year in this country many law enforcement officers are killed in the line of duty, and thousands more are wounded. Virtually all of these deaths and a substantial portion of the injuries are inflicted with guns and knives.

In view of these facts, we cannot blind ourselves to the need for law enforcement officers to protect themselves and other prospective victims of violence in situations where they may lack probable cause for an arrest. When an officer is justified in believing that the individual whose suspicious behavior he is investigating at close range is armed and presently dangerous to the officer or to others, it would appear to be clearly unreasonable to deny the officer the power to take necessary measures to determine whether the person is in fact carrying a weapon and to neutralize the threat of physical harm.

We must still consider, however, the nature and quality of the intrusion on individual rights which must be accepted if police officers are to be conceded the right to search for weapons in situations where probable cause to arrest for crime is lacking. Even a limited search of the outer clothing for weapons constitutes a severe, though brief, intrusion upon cherished personal security, and it must surely be an annoying, frightening, and perhaps humiliating experience. Petitioner contends that such an intrusion is permissible only incident to a lawful arrest, either for a crime involving the possession of weapons or for a crime the commission of which led the officer to investigate in the first place. However, this argument must be closely examined.

Petitioner does not argue that a police officer should refrain from making any investigation of suspicious circumstances until such time as he has probable cause to make an arrest; nor does he deny that police officers in properly discharging their investigative function may find themselves confronting persons who might well be armed and dangerous. Moreover, he does not say that an officer is always unjustified in searching a suspect to discover weapons. Rather, he says it is unreasonable for the policeman to take that step until such time as the situation evolves to a point where there is probable cause to make an arrest. When that point has been reached, petitioner would concede the officer's right to conduct a search of the suspect for weapons, fruits or instrumentalities of the crime, or "mere" evidence, incident to the arrest.

There are two weaknesses in this line of reasoning however. First, it fails to take account of traditional limitations upon the scope of searches, and thus recognizes no distinction in purpose, character, and extent between a search incident to an arrest and a limited search for weapons. The former, although justified in part by the acknowledged necessity to protect the arresting officer from assault with a concealed weapon, Preston v. United States, 376 U.S. 364, 367, 84 S.Ct. 881, 883, 11 L.Ed.2d 777 (1964), is also justified on other grounds, ibid., and can therefore involve a relatively extensive exploration of the person. A search for weapons in the absence of probable cause to arrest, however, must, like any other search, be strictly circumscribed by the exigencies which justify its initiation. Warden v. Hayden, 387 U.S. 294, 310, 87 S.Ct. 1642, 1652, 18 L.Ed.2d 782 (1967) (Mr. Justice Fortas, concurring). Thus it must be limited to that which is necessary for the discovery of weapons which might be used to harm the officer or others nearby, and may realistically be characterized as something less than a "full" search, even though it remains a serious intrusion.

A second, and related, objection to petitioner's argument is that it assumes that the law of arrest has already worked out the balance between the particular interests involved here — the neutralization of danger to the policeman in the investigative circumstance and the sanctity of the individual. But this is not so. An arrest is a wholly different kind of intrusion upon individual freedom from a limited search for weapons, and the interests each is designed to serve are likewise quite different. An arrest is the initial stage of a criminal prosecution. It is intended to vindicate society's interest in having its laws obeyed, and it is inevitably accompanied by future interference with the individual's freedom of movement whether or not trial or conviction ultimately follows. The protective search for weapons, on the other hand, constitutes a brief, though far from inconsiderable, intrusion upon the sanctity of the person. It does not follow that because an officer may lawfully arrest a person only when he is apprised of facts sufficient to warrant a belief that the person has committed or is committing a crime, the officer is equally unjustified, absent that kind of evidence, in making any intrusion short of an arrest. Moreover, a perfectly reasonable apprehension of danger may arise long before the officer is possessed of adequate information to justify taking a person into custody for the purpose of prosecuting him for a crime. Petitioner's reliance on cases which have worked out standards of reasonableness with regard to "seizures" constituting arrests and searches incident thereto is thus misplaced. It assumes that the interests sought to be vindicated and the invasions of personal security may be equated in the two cases, and thereby ignores a vital aspect of the analysis of the reasonableness of particular types of conduct under the Fourth Amendment. See Camara v. Municipal Court, supra.

Our evaluation of the proper balance that has to be struck in this type of case leads us to conclude that there must be a narrowly drawn authority to permit a reasonable search for weapons for the protection of the police officer, where he has reason to believe that he is dealing with an armed and dangerous individual, regardless of whether he has probable cause to arrest the individual for a crime. The officer need not be absolutely certain that the individual is armed; the issue is whether a reasonably prudent man in the circumstances would be warranted in the belief that his safety or that of others was in danger. Cf. Beck v. State of Ohio, 379 U.S. 89, 91, 85 S.Ct. 223, 226, 13 L.Ed.2d 142 (1964); Brinegar v. United States, 338 U.S. 160, 174–176, 69 S.Ct. 1302, 1311, 93 L.Ed. 1879 (1949); Stacey v. Emery, 97 U.S. 642, 645, 24 L.Ed. 1035 (1878). And in determining whether the officer acted reasonably in such circumstances, due weight must be given, not to his inchoate and unparticularized suspicion or "hunch," but to the specific reasonable inferences which he is entitled to draw from the facts in light of his experience. Cf. Brinegar v. United States, supra.

IV. We must now examine the conduct of Officer McFadden in this case to determine whether his search and seizure of petitioner were reasonable, both at their inception and as conducted. He had observed Terry, together with Chilton and another man, acting in a manner he took to be preface to a "stick-up."

We think on the facts and circumstances Officer McFadden detailed before the trial judge a reasonably prudent man would have been warranted in believing petitioner was armed and thus presented a threat to the officer's safety while he was investigating his suspicious behavior. The actions of Terry and Chilton were consistent with McFadden's hypothesis that these men were contemplating a daylight robbery — which, it is reasonable to assume, would be likely to involve the use of weapons — and nothing in their conduct from the time he first noticed them until the time he confronted them and identified himself as a police officer gave him sufficient reason to negate that hypothesis. Although the trio had departed the original scene, there was nothing to indicate abandonment of an intent to commit a robbery at some point. Thus, when Officer McFadden approached the three men gathered before the display window at Zucker's store he had observed enough to make it quite reasonable to fear that they were armed; and nothing in their response to his hailing them, identifying himself as a police officer, and asking their names served to dispel that reasonable belief. We cannot say his decision at that point to seize Terry and pat his clothing for weapons was the product of a volatile or inventive imagination, or was undertaken simply as an act of harassment; the record evidences the tempered act of a policeman who in the course of an investigation had to make a quick decision as to how to protect himself and others from possible danger, and took limited steps to do so.

The manner in which seizure and search were conducted is, of course, as vital a part of the inquiry as whether they were warranted at all. The Fourth Amendment proceeds as much by limitations upon the scope of governmental action as by imposing preconditions upon its initiation. Compare Katz v. United States, 389 U.S. 347, 354–356, 88 S.Ct. 507, 514, 19 L.Ed.2d 576 (1967). The entire deterrent purpose of the rule excluding evidence seized in violation of the Fourth Amendment rests on the assumption that "limitations upon the fruit to be gathered tend to limit the quest itself." United States v. Poller, 43 F.2d 911, 914, 74 A.L.R. 1382 (C.A.2d Cir. 1930). . . . Thus, evidence may not be introduced if it was discovered by means of a seizure and search which were not reasonably related in scope to the justification of their initiation. Warden v. Hayden, 387 U.S. 294, 310, 87 S.Ct. 1642, 1652, 18 L.Ed.2d 782 (1967) (Mr. Justice Fortas, concurring).

We need not develop at length in this case, however, the limitations which the Fourth Amendment places upon a protective seizure and search for weapons. These limitations will have to be developed in the concrete factual circumstances of individual cases. See Sibron v. New York, 392 U.S. 40, 88 S.Ct. 1889, 1912, 20 L.Ed.2d 917 decided today. Suffice it to note that such a search, unlike a search without a warrant incident to a lawful arrest, is not justified by any need to prevent the disappearance or destruction of evidence of crime. See Preston v. United States, 376 U.S. 364, 367, 84 S.Ct. 1642, 1652, 18 L.Ed.2d 782 (1964). The sole justification of the search in the present situation is the protection of the police officer and others nearby, and it must therefore be confined in scope to an intrusion reasonably designed to discover guns, knives, clubs, or other hidden instruments for the assault of the police officer.

The scope of the search in this case presents no serious problem in light of these standards. Officer McFadden patted down the outer clothing of petitioner and his two companions. He did not place his hands in their pockets or under the outer surface of their garments until he had felt weapons, and then he merely reached for and removed the guns. He never did invade Katz' person beyond the outer surfaces of his clothes, since he discovered nothing in his patdown which might have been a weapon. Officer McFadden confined his search strictly to what was minimally necessary to learn whether the men were armed and to disarm them once he discovered the weapons. He did not conduct a general exploratory search for whatever evidence of criminal activity he might find.

V. We conclude that the revolver seized from Terry was properly admitted in evidence against him. At the time he seized petitioner and searched him for weapons, Officer McFadden had reasonable grounds to believe that petitioner was armed and dangerous, and it was necessary for the protection of himself and others to take swift measures to discover the true facts and neutralize the threat of harm if it materialized. The policeman carefully restricted his search to what was appropriate to the discovery of the particular items which he sought. Each case of this sort will, of course, have to be decided on its own facts. We merely hold today that where a police officer observes unusual conduct which leads him reasonably to conclude in light of his experience that criminal activity may be afoot and that the persons with whom he is dealing may be armed and presently dangerous, where in the course of investigating this behavior he identifies himself as a policeman and makes reasonable inquiries, and where nothing in the initial stages of the encounter serves to dispel his reasonable fear for his own or others' safety, he is entitled for the protection of himself and others in the area to conduct a carefully limited search of the outer clothing of such persons in an attempt to discover weapons which might be used to assault him. Such a search is a reasonable search under the Fourth Amendment, and any weapons seized may properly be introduced in evidence against the person from whom they were taken.

Affirmed.

MR. JUSTICE BLACK concurs. . . .
MR. JUSTICE HARLAN, concurring. . . .
MR. JUSTICE WHITE, concurring. . . .
MR. JUSTICE DOUGLAS, dissenting. . . .

KATZ v. UNITED STATES
Supreme Court of the United States, 1967.
389 U.S. 347, 88 S.Ct. 507, 19 L.Ed.2d 576.

MR. JUSTICE STEWART delivered the opinion of the Court. The petitioner was convicted in the District Court for the Southern District of California under an eight-count indictment charging him with transmitting wagering information by telephone from Los Angeles to Miami and Boston in violation of a federal statute. At trial the Government was permitted, over the petitioner's objection, to introduce evidence of the petitioner's end of telephone conversations, overheard by FBI agents who had attached an electronic listening and recording device to the outside of the public telephone booth from which he had placed his calls. In affirming his conviction, the Court of Appeals rejected the contention that the recordings had been obtained in violation of the Fourth Amendment, because "[t]here was no physical entrance into the area occupied by, [the petitioner]." We granted certiorari in order to consider the constitutional questions thus presented.

The petitioner has phrased those questions as follows:

"A. Whether a public telephone booth is a constitutionally protected area so that evidence obtained by attaching an electronic listening recording device to the top of such a booth is obtained in violation of the right to privacy of the user of the booth.

"B. Whether physical penetration of a constitutionally protected area is necessary before a search and seizure can be said to be violative of the Fourth Amendment to the United States Constitution.

We decline to adopt this formulation of the issues. In the first place the correct solution of Fourth Amendment problems is not necessarily promoted by incantation of the phrase "constitutionally protected area." Secondly, the Fourth Amendment cannot be translated into a general constitutional "right to privacy." That Amendment protects individual privacy against certain kinds of governmental intrusion, but its protections go further, and often have nothing to do with privacy at all. Other provisions of the Constitution protect personal privacy from other forms of govermental invasion. But the protection of a person's *general* right to privacy — his right to be let alone by other pepole — is, like the protection of his property and of his very life, left largely to the law of the individual States.

Because of the misleading way the issues have been formulated, the parties have attached great significance to the characterization of the telephone booth from which the petitioner placed his calls. The petitioner has strenuously argued that the booth was a "constitutionally protected area." The Government has maintained with equal vigor that it was not. But this effort to decide whether or not a given "area," viewed in the abstract, is "constitutionally protected" deflects attention from the problem presented by this case. For the Fourth Amendment protects people, not places. What a person knowingly exposes to the public, even in his own home or office, is not a subject of Fourth Amendment protection. See Lewis v. United States, 385 U.S. 206, 210, 87 S.Ct. 424, 427. 17 L.Ed.2d 312; United States v. Lee, 274 U.S. 559, 563, 47 S.Ct. 746, 748, 71 L.Ed. 1202. But what he seeks to preserve as private, even in an area accessible to the public, may be constitutionally protected. See Rios v. United States, 364 U.C. 253, 80 S.Ct. 1431, 4 L.Ed.2d 1688; Ex parte Jackson, 96 U.S. 727, 733, 24 L.Ed. 877.

The Government stresses the fact that the telephone booth from which the petitioner made his calls was constructed partly of glass, so that he was as visible after he entered it as he would have been if he had remained outside. But what he sought to exclude when he entered the booth was not the intruding eye — it was the uninvited ear. He did not shed his right to do so simply because he made his calls from a place where he might be seen. No less than an individual in a business office, in a friend's apartment, or in a taxicab, a person in a telephone booth may rely upon the protection of the Fourth Amendment. One who occupies it, shuts the door behind him, and pays the toll that permits him to place a call is surely entitled to assume that the words he utters into the mouthpiece will not be broadcast to the world. To read the Constitution more narrowly is to ignore the vital role that the public telephone has come to play in private communication.

The Government contends, however, that the activities of its agents in this case should not be tested by Fourth Amendment requirements, for the surveillance technique they employed involved no physical penetration of the telephone booth from which the petitioner placed his calls. It is true that the absence of such penetration was at one time thought to foreclose further Fourth Amendment inquiry, Olmstead v. United States, 277 U.S. 438, 457, 464, 466, 48 S.Ct. 564, 565, 567, 568, 72

L.Ed. 944; Goldman v. United States, 316 U.S. 129, 134–136, 62 S.Ct. 993, 995–997, 86 L.Ed. 1322, for that Amendment was thought to limit only searches and seizures of tangible property. But "[t]he premise that property interests control the right of the Government to search and seize has been discredited." Warden, Md. Penitentiary v. Hayden, 387 U.S. 294, 304, 87 S.Ct. 1642, 1648, 18 L.Ed.2d 782. Thus, although a closely divided Court supposed in *Olmstead* that surveillance without any trespass and without the seizure of any material fell outside the ambit of the Constitution we have since departed from the narrow view on which that decision rested. Indeed, we have expressly held that the Fourth Amendment governs not only the seizure of tangible items, but extends as well to the recording of oral statements overheard without any "technical trespass under . . . local property law." Silverman v. United States, 365 U.S. 505, 511, 81 S.Ct. 679, 682, 5 L.Ed.2d 734. Once this much is acknowledged, and once it is recognized that the Fourth Amendment protects people—and not simply "areas"—against unreasonable searches and seizures it becomes clear that the reach of that Amendment cannot turn upon the presence or absence of a physical intrusion into any given enclosure.

We conclude that the underpinnings of *Olmstead* and *Goldman* have been so eroded by our subsequent decisions that the "trespass" doctrine there enunciated can no longer be regarded as controlling. The Government's activities in electronically listening to and recording the petitioner's words violated the privacy upon which he justifiably relied while using the telephone booth and thus constituted a "search and seizure" within the meaning of the Fourth Amendment. The fact that the electronic device employed to achieve that end did not happen to penetrate the wall of the booth can have no constitutional significance.

The question remaining for decision, then, is whether the search and seizure conducted in this case complied with constitutional standards. In that regard, the Government's position is that its agents acted in an entirely defensible manner: They did not begin their electronic surveillance until investigation of the petitioner's activities had established a strong probability that he was using the telephone in question to transmit gambling information to persons in other States, in violation of federal law. Moreover, the surveillance was limited, both in scope and duration, to the specific purpose of establishing the contents of the petitioner's unlawful telephonic communications. The agents confined their surveillance to the brief periods during which he used the telephone booth and they took great care to overhear only the conversations of the petitioner himself.

Accepting this account of the Government's actions as accurate, it is clear that this surveillance was so narrowly circumscribed that a duly authorized magistrate, properly notified of the need for such investigation, specifically informed of the basis on which it was to proceed, and clearly apprised of the precise intrusion it would entail, could constitutionally have authorized, with appropriate safeguards, the very limited search and seizure that the Government asserts in fact took place. Only last Term we sustained the validity of such an authorization, holding that, under sufficiently "precise and discriminate circumstances," a federal court may empower government agents to employ a concealed electronic device "for the narrow and particularized purpose of ascertaining the truth of the . . . allegations" of a "detailed factual affidavit alleging the commission of a specific criminal offense." Osborn v. United States 385 U.S. 323, 329–330, 87 S.Ct. 429, 433, 17 L.Ed.2d 394. Discussing that holding, the Court in Berger v. State of New York, 388 U.S. 41, 87 S.Ct. 1873, 18 L.Ed.2d 1040, said that "the order authorizing the use of the electronic device" in *Osborn* "afforded similar protections to those . . . of conventional warrants authorizing the seizure of tangible evidence." Through those protections, "no greater invasion of privacy was permitted than was necessary under the circumstances." Id., at 57, 87 S.Ct. at 1882. Here, too, a similar judicial order could have accommodated "the legitimate needs of law enforcement" by authorizing the carefully limited use of electronic surveillance.

The Government urges that, because its agents relied upon the decisions in *Olmstead* and *Goldman,* and because they did no more here than they might properly have done with prior judicial sanction, we should retroactively validate their conduct. That we cannot do. It is apparent that the agents in this case acted with restraint. Yet the inescapable fact is that this restraint was imposed by the agents themselves, not by a judicial officer. They were not required, before commencing the search, to present their estimate of probable cause for detached scrutiny by a neutral magistrate. They were not compelled, during the conduct of the search itself, to observe precise limits established in advance by a specific court order. Nor were they directed, after the search had been completed, to notify the authorizing magistrate in detail of all that had been seized. In the absence of such safeguards, this Court has never sustained a search upon the sole ground that officers reasonably expected to find evidence of a particular crime and voluntarily confined their activities to the least intrusive means consistent with that end. Searches conducted without warrants have been held unlawful "notwithstanding facts unquestionably showing probable cause," Agnello v. United States, 269 U.S. 20, 33, 46 S.Ct. 4, 6, 70 L.Ed. 145, for the Constitution requires "that the deliberate, impartial judgment of a judicial officer . . . be interposed between the citizen and the police. . . ." Wong Sun v. United States, 371 U.S. 471, 481–482, 83 S.Ct. 407, 414, 9 L.Ed.2d 441. "Over and again this Court has emphasized that the mandate of the [Fourth] Amendment requires adherence to judicial processes," United States v. Jeffers, 342 U.S. 48, 51, 72 S.Ct. 93, 95, 96 L.Ed. 59, and that searches conducted outside the judicial process, without prior approval by judge or magistrate, are *per se* unreasonable under the Fourth Amendment — subject only to a few specifically established and well-delineated exceptions.

It is difficult to imagine how any of those exceptions could ever apply to the sort of search and seizure involved in this case. Even electronic surveillance substantially contemporaneous with an individual's arrest could hardly be deemed an "incident" of that arrest. Nor could the use of electronic surveillance without prior authorization be justified on grounds of "hot pursuit." And, of course, the very nature of electronic surveillance precludes its use pursuant to the suspect's consent.

The Government does not question these basic principles. Rather, it urges the creation of a new exception to cover this case. It argues that surveillance of a telephone booth should be exempted from the usual requirement of advance authorization by a magistrate upon a showing of probable cause. We cannot agree. Omission of such authorization "bypasses the safeguards provided by an objective predetermination of probable cause, and substitutes instead the far less reliable procedure of an after-the-event justification for the . . . search, too likely to be subtly influenced by the familiar shortcomings of hindsight judgment." Beck v. State of Ohio, 379 U.S. 89, 96, 85 S.Ct. 223, 228, 13 L.Ed.2d 142.

And bypassing a neutral predetermination of the scope of a search leaves individuals secure from Fourth Amendment violations "only in the discretion of the police." Id., at 97, 85 S.Ct. at 229.

These considerations do not vanish when the search in question is transferred from the setting of a home, an office, or a hotel room to that of a telephone booth. Wherever a man may be, he is entitled to know that he will remain free from unreasonable searches and seizures. The government agents here ignored "the procedure of antecedent justification . . . that is central to the Fourth Amendment," a procedure that we hold to be a constitutional precondition of the kind of electronic surveillance involved in this case. Because the surveillance here failed to meet that condition, and because it led to the petitioner's conviction, the judgment must be reversed.

It is so ordered.

Judgment reversed.

MR. JUSTICE MARSHALL took no part in the consideration or decision of this case.

MR. JUSTICE DOUGLAS, with whom MR. JUSTICE BRENNAN joins, concurring.

While I join the opinion of the Court, I feel compelled to reply to the separate concurring opinion of my Brother WHITE, which I view as a wholly unwarranted green light for the Executive Branch to resort to electronic eavesdropping without a warrant in cases which the Executive Branch itself labels "national security" matters.

Neither the President nor the Attorney General is a magistrate. In matters where they believe national security may be involved they are not detached, disinterested, and neutral as a court or magistrate must be. Under the separation of powers created by the Constitution, the Executive Branch is not supposed to be neutral and disinterested. Rather it should vigorously investigate and prevent breaches of national security and prosecute those who violate the pertinent federal laws. The President and Attorney General are properly interested parties, cast in the role of adversary, in national security cases. They may even be the intended victims of subversive action. Since spies and saboteurs are as entitled to the protection of the Fourth Amendment as suspected gamblers like petitioner, I cannot agree that where spies and saboteurs are involved adequate protection of Fourth Amendment rights is assured when the President and Attorney General assume both the position of adversary-and-prosecutor and disinterested, neutral magistrate. . . .

MR. JUSTICE HARLAN, concurring. . . .

As the Court's opinion states, "the Fourth Amendment protects people, not places." The question, however, is what protection it affords to those people. Generally, as here, the answer to that question requires reference to a "place." My understanding of the rule that has emerged from prior decisions is that there is a twofold requirement, first that a person have exhibited an actual (subjective) expectation of privacy and, second, that the expectation be one that society is prepared to recognize as "reasonable." Thus a man's home is, for most purposes, a place where he expects privacy, but objects, activities, or statements that he exposes to the "plain view" of outsiders are not "protected" because no intention to keep them to himself has been exhibited. On the other hand, conversations in the open would not be protected against being overheard, for the expectation of privacy under the circumstances would be unreasonable. Cf. Hester v. United States, supra.

The critical fact in this case is that "[o]ne who occupies it, [a telephone booth] shuts the door behind him, and pays the toll that permits him to place a call is surely entitled to assume" that his conversation is not being intercepted. Ante, at 511. The point is not that the booth is "accessible to the public" at other times, ante, at 511, but that it is a temporarily private place whose momentary occupants' expectations of freedom from intrusion are recognized as reasonable. Cf. Rios v. United States, 364 U.S. 253, 80 S.Ct. 1431, 4 L.Ed.2d 1688. . . .

MR. JUSTICE WHITE, concurring.

I agree that the official surveillance of petitioner's telephone conversations in a public booth must be subjected to the test of reasonableness under the Fourth Amendment and that on the record now before us the particular surveillance undertaken was unreasonable absent a warrant properly authorizing it. This application of the Fourth Amendment need not interfere with legitimate needs of law enforcement.

In joining the Court's opinion, I note the Court's acknowledgment that there are circumstances in which it is reasonable to search without a warrant. In this connection, in footnote [51] the Court points out that today's decision does not reach national security cases. Wiretapping to protect the security of the Nation has been authorized by successive Presidents. The present Administration would apparently save national security cases from restrictions against wiretapping. See Berger v. State of New York, 388 U.S. 41, 112–118, 87 S.Ct. 1873, 1911–1914, 18 L.Ed.2d 1040 (1967) (White, J., dissenting). We should not require the warrant procedure and the magistrate's judgment if the President of the United States or his chief legal officer, the Attorney General, has considered the requirements of national security and authorized electronic surveillance as reasonable.

MR. JUSTICE BLACK, dissenting.

If I could agree with the Court that eavesdropping carried on by electronic means (equivalent to wiretapping) constitutes a "search" or "seizure," I would be happy to join the Court's opinion. For on that premise my Brother STEWART sets out methods in accord with the Fourth Amendment to guide States in the enactment and enforcement of laws passed to regulate wiretapping by government. In this respect today's opinion differs sharply from Berger v. State of New York, 388 U.S. 41, 87 S.Ct. 1873, 18 L.Ed.2d 1040, decided last Term, which held void on its face a New York statute authorizing wiretapping on warrants issued by magistrates on showings of probable cause. The *Berger* case also set up what appeared to be insuperable obstacles to the valid passage of such wiretapping laws by

States. The Court's opinion in this case, however, removes the doubts about state power in this field and abates to a large extent the confusion and near-paralyzing effect of the *Berger* holding. Notwithstanding these good efforts of the Court, I am still unable to agree with its interpretation of the Fourth Amendment.

My basic objection is twofold: (1) I do not believe that the words of the Amendment will bear the meaning given them by today's decision, and (2) I do not believe that it is the proper role of this Court to rewrite the Amendment in order "to bring it into harmony with the times" and thus reach a result that many people believe to be desirable. . . .

GILBERT v. CALIFORNIA
Supreme Court of the United States, 1967.
388 U.S. 263, 87 S.Ct. 1951, 18 L.Ed.2d 1178.

MR. JUSTICE BRENNAN delivered the opinion of the Court. This case was argued with United States v. Wade, 388 U.S. 218, 87 S.Ct. 1926, 18 L.Ed.2d 1149, and presents the same alleged constitutional error in the admission in evidence of in-court identifications there considered. In addition petitioner alleges constitutional errors in the admission in evidence of testimony of some of the witnesses that they also identified him at the lineup. . . .

Petitioner was convicted in the Superior Court of California of the armed robbery of the Mutual Savings and Loan Association of Alhambra and the murder of a police officer who entered during the course of the robbery. These were separate guilt and penalty stages of the trial before the same jury, which rendered a guilty verdict and imposed the death penalty. The California Supreme Court affirmed, 63 Cal.2d 690, 47 Cal.Rptr. 909, 408 P.2d 365. . . .

Three eyewitnesses to the Alhambra crimes who identified Gilbert at the guilt stage of the trial had observed him at a lineup conducted without notice to his counsel in a Los Angeles auditorium 16 days after his indictment and after appointment of counsel. The manager of the apartment house in which incriminating evidence was found, and in which Gilbert allegedly resided, identified Gilbert in the courtroom and also testified, in substance, to her prior lineup identification on examination by the State. Eight witnesses who identified him in the courtroom at the penalty stage were not eyewitnesses to the Alhambra crimes but to other robberies allegedly committed by him. In addition to their in-court identifications, these witnesses also testified that they identified Gilbert at the same lineup.

The line-up was on a stage behind bright lights which prevented those in the line from seeing the audience. Upward of 100 persons were in the audience, each an eyewitness to one of the several robberies charged to Gilbert. The record is otherwise virtually silent as to what occurred at the lineup.

At the guilt stage, after the first witness, a cashier of the savings and loan association, identified Gilbert in the courtroom, defense counsel moved, out of the presence of the jury, to strike her testimony on the ground that she identified Gilbert at the pretrial lineup conducted in the absence of counsel in violation of the Sixth Amendment made applicable to the States by the Fourteenth Amendment. Gideon v. Wainwright, 372 U.S. 335, 83 S.Ct. 792 9 L.Ed.2d 799. He requested a hearing outside the presence of the jury to present evidence supporting his claim that her in-court identification was, and others to be elicited by the State from other eyewitnesses would be "predicated at least in large part upon their identification or purported identification of Mr. Gilbert at the showup. . . ." The trial judge denied the motion as premature. Defense counsel then elicited the fact of the cashier's lineup identification on cross-examination and again moved to strike her identification testimony. Without passing on the merits of the Sixth Amendment claim, the trial judge denied the motion on the ground that, assuming a violation, it would not in any event entitle Gilbert to suppression of the in-court identification. Defense counsel thereafter elicited the fact of lineup identifications from two other eyewitnesses who on direct examination identified Gilbert in the courtroom. Defense counsel unsuccessfully objected at the penalty stage, to the testimony of the eight witnesses to the other robberies that they identified Gilbert at the lineup.

The admission of the in-court identifications without first determining that they were not tainted by the illegal lineup but were of independent origin was constitutional error. United States v. Wade, supra. We there held that a post-indictment pretrial lineup at which the accused is exhibited to identifying witnesses is a critical stage of the criminal prosecution; that police conduct of such a lineup without notice to and in the absence of his counsel denies the accused his Sixth Amendment right to counsel and calls in question the admissibility at trial of the in-court identifications of the accused by witnesses who attended the lineup. However, as in *Wade,* the record does not permit an informed judgment whether the in-court identifications at the two stages of the trial had an independent source. Gilbert is therefore entitled only to a vacation of his conviction pending the holding of such proceedings as the California Supreme Court may deem appropriate to afford the State the opportunity to establish that the in-court identifications had an independent source, or that their introduction in evidence was in any event harmless error.

Quite different considerations are involved as to the admission of the testimony of the manager of the apartment house at the guilt phase and of the eight witnesses at the penalty stage that they identified Gilbert at the lineup. That testimony is the direct result of the illegal lineup "come at by exploitation of [the primary] illegality." Wong Sun v. United States, 371 U.S. 471, 488, 83 S.Ct. 407, 417, 9 L.Ed.2d 441. The State is therefore not entitled to an opportunity to show that that testimony had an independent source. Only a *per se* exclusionary rule as to such testimony can be an effective sanction to assure that law enforcement authorities will respect the accused's constitutional right to the presence of his counsel at the critical lineup. In the absence of legislative regulations adequate to avoid the hazards to a fair trial which inhere in lineups as presently conducted, the desirability of deterring the constitutionally objectionable practice must prevail over the undesirability of excluding relevant evidence. Cf. Mapp v. Ohio, 367 U.S. 643, 81 S.Ct. 1684, 6 L.Ed.2d 1081. That conclusion is buttressed by the consideration that the witness' testimony of his lineup identification will enhance the impact of his in-court identification on the jury and seriously aggravate whatever derogation exists of the accused's right to a fair trial. Therefore, unless the California Supreme Court is "able to declare a belief that it was harmless beyond a reasonable doubt," Chapman v. State of California, 386 U.S. 18, 24, 87 S.Ct. 824, 828, 17 L.Ed.2d 705, Gilbert will be entitled on remand to a new trial or, if no prejudicial error is found on the guilt stage but only in the penalty stage, to whatever relief California law affords where the penalty stage must be set aside.

The judgment of the California Supreme Court and the conviction are vacated, and the case is remanded to that court for further proceedings not inconsistent with this opinion. It is so ordered.

Judgment and conviction vacated and case remanded with directions.

MR. JUSTICE WHITE, whom MR. JUSTICE HARLAN and MR. JUSTICE STEWART join, . . . dissenting.

7

Documentary Evidence

The evidentiary rules previously discussed in this book (e.g., relevancy, privileges, etc.) are as applicable to documents as they are to any other type of evidence. However, there are certain additional rules of evidence and principles which apply to writings that must be considered in connection with all the other rules of evidence.

Before any writing may be received into evidence, it must be authenticated. Authentication merely means that a foundation must be laid with evidence sufficient to support a finding that the document is genuine and is what it purports to be. The rule on authentication as to any writing also refers to any secondary evidence of the contents of that writing. *(Example of secondary evidence:* A police officer takes notes at the scene of a crime. His notes are the best evidence of what he did and saw. He then dictates a report from his notebook. The report is secondary evidence.) The exception to this rule occurs when the genuineness of the document has been admitted either in the pleadings or in open court by both parties, who have entered into a stipulation that the document is genuine, thus avoiding any evidence being introduced as to the authenticity of the document. The rule on authentication only requires evidence to establish a prima facie showing that the document is genuine. If the authenticity is disputed, then it is up to the jury to decide by a preponderance of the evidence whether the document is genuine.

The Best Evidence Rule

The Best Evidence Rule is a rule of law which upholds the strong public policy that when there are different types of evidence, the best possible evidence should be presented in a court of law. In seeking to admit a writing into evidence, the public policy has been codified in the Federal Rules and in most states, and holds that in order to prove the contents of a private writing, the original document itself must be produced unless it can be proven that it is unavailable. This rule, the Best Evidence Rule, only applies to private writings, and in no way limits law enforcement officials or other governmental entities which are seeking to introduce copies of official documents that they have in their possession.

Also, in any jurisdiction where a writing is prepared and executed in duplicate or triplicate, each copy of that writing is held to be an original even though it may be a carbon copy thereof. Thus, the carbon may be introduced and will not be excluded by the Best Evidence Rule.

The Best Evidence Rule applies to printed and written documents of any type. The student should again acquaint himself with the statutes defining evidence in his jurisdiction. The Federal Rules and some jurisdictions hold that a writing includes photographs, X rays, motion picture films, and recordings of any type. In these jurisdictions, a photograph deemed a writing must be properly authenticated, and the Best Evidence Rule stipulates that the original photograph must be introduced into the trial.

There is an exception to the Best Evidence Rule when the original document has been lost or destroyed without fault of the person seeking to introduce secondary types of evidence to prove the document. The Federal Rules and the general rule in the majority of the jurisdictions require that the party who is seeking to introduce a duplicate must be free from fault in having lost or destroyed that document and is not trying to perpetrate a fraud upon the court or upon the opponent in the case.

Another exception is when the original document cannot be brought in because it is in the possession of a person who is outside the subpoena power of the court. In this fact situation, the Best Evidence Rule does not apply, and secondary items of evidence may be introduced to prove the contents of the document. Some jurisdictions hold that if the document is outside the subpoena power of the court and the original document is not available, the party should use "letters rogatory" to the foreign jurisdictions, having them take testimony as to the contents of the original, or having them obtain the properly authenticated copy of the original to be introduced into the trial in the requesting state. Under the new Federal Rules, a writing is unobtainable only when it cannot be obtained by any available judicial process or procedure.

A third exception to the Best Evidence Rule occurs when the original writing is too voluminous and would thus be impractical to present in its entirety in court. *Example:* In the case of computer printouts on the bills sent by the Pacific Telephone and Telegraph Company for the month of June, 1974, the trial court would hold the Best Evidence Rule not applicable and allow a summary or a specific statement from that computer printout to be introduced.

The Parol Evidence Rule

Another rule concerning documentary evidence which comes into play in civil trials is the Parol Evidence Rule, which basically prohibits the introduction of any parol (oral evidence) to contradict the contents of a writing. Since this rule is not used in criminal procedures, the student need only know the statement of the rule.

Authentication of Official Records

The general rule requiring authentication of private writings is equally applicable to official records. Most jurisdictions will allow certified copies of official records into a court in place of the originals. A certified copy is "self-authenticating" if it is shown that: (1) the original record is a document required or authorized by law to be recorded and was recorded in the public office; (2) the certified copy is a true copy of the original; and (3) a certificate is made by the custodian of the original document and bears his signature and seal of office. A law enforcement officer who is required to make a report of a crime which he has investigated may have a photocopy made of that report, have a certificate attached thereto by the custodian of the original document, and may introduce that copy into a court of law.

Authentication of Private Writings

Before any private document may be introduced into evidence, it must be properly authenticated. Generally, documents may be authenticated by the testimony of a witness to the original document, by testimony of witnesses who saw the execution of that document or heard the parties who acknowledged that document, or by opinion testimony as to the handwriting of the person who signed that document. If testimony as to handwriting identification is being used, a lay person who is familiar with the handwriting of the supposed writer or an expert in the field of handwriting comparison should testify to authenticate the document. If the document is a recording, any person who is familiar with the voice on the recording may properly authenticate the recording by stating his opinion.

If a document has been notarized or has been properly recorded in a public office, there is a presumption of authenticity. A document which has been notarized need only be presented to the court showing a seal by the notary. No evidence needs to be offered unless the authenticity is questioned by the opponent to the introduction of the item of evidence.

Most jurisdictions have what is commonly referred to as the Ancient Document Doctrine. In a jurisdiction which has this statute in effect, any document which is at least 20 years old (in some jurisdictions, at least 30 years old), bears the date thereon, and has been acted upon as true during the time in question is authenticated merely because it is so old. No other evidence need be offered to prove its authenticity.

Procedures for Authenticating Private Documents

To authenticate a private document, the attorney for the plaintiff seeking to introduce a document would show it to the court clerk, have it numbered, take the document to the opposing counsel for his review, and then hand it to the witness. At this time, the attorney would then ask the witness if he has ever seen this document before. The procedure would be as follows:

Question: (attorney) "Have you ever seen this document before?"

Answer: (witness) "Yes, I have."

Question: "When was that?"

Answer: "On January 1, 1971."

Question: "Where?"

Answer: "At 111 West First Street, Washington, D.C."

Question: "What is it that you are looking at?"

Answer: "A contract I signed."

Question: "How do you know?"

Answer: "That's my signature on the document."

The attorney then would address the court and make a motion that this document be entered as the plaintiff's exhibit number one.

In a criminal case in which a person is on trial for burglary and the state is seeking to introduce a prior criminal conviction, the format would be as follows:

Question: (attorney) "What is your occupation?"

Answer: (witness) "County Clerk, County of Madison."

Question: "I show you a document entitled 'Judgment of Conviction of John Doe.' Have you ever seen it before?"

Answer: "Yes, it is a true copy of an original court document that I have in my possession and control at the courthouse."

Question: "Do you recognize the signature and seal on the document?"

Answer: "Yes, it is my signature and the seal of my office."

At this time, a motion would be made to admit the document into evidence.

Summary

The Best Evidence Rule states that only the original document may be introduced into evidence unless it has been lost, destroyed, or is beyond the subpoena power of the court. The Best Evidence Rule, however, only applies to private writings and not to any official documents of any sort. The term *writing* as used in the given jurisdiction will determine whether or not the document falls within the Best Evidence Rule. The student should remember that some jurisdictions hold that a writing is a document, tape recording, motion picture, film, or photograph. In order for any document to be introduced into any court, it must be properly authenticated, i.e., the genuineness of the document must be proven to the court.

DISCUSSION QUESTIONS

1. Discuss the theory of authentication.
2. Distinguish the requirements under the Best Evidence Rule between private documents and governmental documents.
3. Discuss what are considered original documents under the Best Evidence Rule.
4. Discuss the person in a law enforcement agency who normally could authenticate records of that department.
5. What is the rationale behind the Ancient Document Doctrine?

STATE v. SHUMAKER
Supreme Court of North Carolina, 1960.
251 N.C. 678, 111 S.E.2d 878.

Criminal prosecution upon a bill of indictment charging the defendant with the crime of embezzlement. Upon the trial the State introduced evidence tending to show the following: The defendant was employed by Automatic Lathe Cutterhead Company, Inc., in the capacity of bookkeeper. She kept the records of sales and accounts, received payments by cash and check, prepared deposit slips, endorsed the checks by use of a company stamp, "Payable to the order of Wachovia Bank & Trust Company, High Point, N.C." It was her duty to deposit company checks and cash in the company's bank account. She was not authorized to sign or to cash checks or endorse them except by use of the stamp, and then only for deposit. Items of cash and checks for deposit were entered on deposit slips by typewriter. The originals were kept in the office under the control of the defendant. According to the testimony of Clarice Snipes, another employee, "Frances Shumaker made them out. Mrs. Shumaker took those deposits to the bank. On occasions when Mrs. Shumaker did not actually make out the deposit slips, she had help when she was rushed and trying to get to the bank before the bank closed. Someone in the office would at her request help her list the checks. . . . On those occasions, after someone assisted her in making out a list of checks, she took the deposit slip to the bank. When someone assisted her, it was done under her supervision and control."

The defendant kept the books showing charges and credits to the accounts of the various customers. These records were in her own handwriting. The bank made microfilms of the deposit slips listing the checks and cash credited to the account of Automatic Lathe Cutterhead Company, Inc.

The State introduced (1) the deposit slips kept in the office under the defendant's control; (2) the microfilms of deposit slips left at the bank with the deposits; (3) microfilms of checks endorsed by defendant; and (4) the books of account kept by and in the handwriting of the defendant.

The State introduced evidence that on numerous occasions the defendant endorsed company checks, received the amount in cash. On one occasion the company received two checks for $600 each and $300 in cash to reimburse the company for payments it had made on certain stock transactions. These items were delivered to the defendant for deposit in the company's bank account. The checks were deposited but the cash was not deposited and not accounted for. The photostats of the deposit slips in the bank showed discrepancies between them and the copies which the defendant kept under her control in the company records.

The accountant who analyzed the office copies of the deposit slips and the microfilm copies kept by the bank, and the account books kept by the defendant, testified that checks in the amount of $3,346.29 were endorsed by the defendant. "When I say there was a total of $3,346.29 in checks cashed by Frances Shumaker, all I know is the checks have her signature on the back." During the period September 15, 1957, to March 31, 1958, a total amount of $1,950.82 cash was entered on the receipt journal but not on deposit slips.

At the close of the State's evidence the defendant moved to dismiss. The motion was denied and the defendant rested without offering evidence and renewed the motion, which was likewise denied. The jury returned a verdict of guilty as charged. From the judgment of imprisonment of not less than two years nor more than five years, the defendant appealed. . . .

HIGGINS, JUSTICE. The exceptive assignments argued in defendant's brief involve these questions: (1) Did the court commit error by admitting in evidence, over defendant's objection, the bank deposit slips retained by the depositor? (2) By admitting in evidence, over defendant's objection, the microfilm copies of endorsements on checks and deposit slips delivered to the bank? (3) Did the court, in its charge, give undue emphasis to the State's evidence and contentions?

The defendant's objections to the admissibility of the retained deposit slips is unsound. These slips were introduced as originals or duplicate originals. They were typewritten by the defendant or by someone under her direction. It was the defendant's duty to make and file them. She was the authorized custodian. They were in the files when she left. Clearly they were admissible. The duplicates of the deposit slips were filed with the bank at the time the deposits were made. The bank made photostats of these slips and of the checks. Dorothy Bowling testified: "I am employed in the main office of Wachovia Bank & Trust Company. . . . The various papers marked for the purpose of identification (here the numbers are given) are photostatic copies of original slips on deposit with the Wachovia Bank & Trust Company for Automatic Lathe Cutterhead Company for the period of time from September 23, 1957 to March 1, 1958. I personally made these photostats."

The defendant objected to the use of photostats on the ground the State did not "first account satisfactorily for nonproduction of the originals," citing among others the leading case of People v. Wells, 380 Ill. 347, 44 N.E.2d 32, 142 A.L.R. 1262. Under the North Carolina Uniform Photographic Copies of Business and Public Records Act (G.S. § 8-45.1 et seq.), any photographic, photostatic, or microfilm is as admissible in evidence as the original itself. The statute makes the photostat or microfilm reproduction primary evidence. Whether the original is in existence is immaterial. Of course, use of the reproduction does not render the original inadmissible.

Our statute making the reproduction competent evidence is modeled on the Act of Congress relating to the same subject. See 28 U.S.C.A. § 1732. More than 30 states have similar statutes. At the time People v. Wells, supra, was decided, Illinois did not have any statutory provision for the use of photostats. The opinion in the Wells case is based on the lack of statutory authority for such evidence.

One of the leading cases on the subject of reproductions is United States v. Manton, 2 Cir., 107 F.2d 834, 844, certiorari denied 309 U.S. 664, 60 S.Ct. 590, 84 L.Ed. 1012: "It is argued that the original checks themselves were the best evidence and that their absence should have been accounted for as a prerequisite to the admission of the recordaks. With this contention we cannot agree. These recordaks are made and kept among the records of many banks in due course of business and are within the words of 28 U.S.C.A. § 695 (now 1732). Their accuracy is not questioned. They represent, in the course of a year, perhaps millions of transactions. No one at all familiar with bank routine would hesitate to accept them as practically conclusive evidence. As proof of payment they constitute not secondary but primary evidence." See also, United States v. Kushner, 2 Cir., 135 F.2d 668; Beard v. United States, 4 Cir., 222 F.2d 84.

Enough appears in the evidence in this case to show a regular employee of the Wachovia Bank & Trust Company in the usual course of business made the photostats. She identified them. From this showing they were admissible in evidence. The deposit slips kept by the defendant, the microfilms of those at the bank, and the books and records kept by the defendant in her own handwriting showed discrepancies analyzed and summarized by the accountant. All were properly identified and received in evidence. . . .

In the trial below, we find no error.

RANDOLPH v. COMMONWEALTH
Supreme Court of Appeals of Virginia, 1926.
145 Va. 883, 134 S.E. 544, 47 A.L.R. 1084.

William Randolph was convicted of an assault with intent to kill, and he brings error. . . .

CAMPBELL, J. . . . The jury found the accused guilty and fixed his punishment at a fine of $100. The motion of the accused to set aside the verdict was overruled, and judgment was pronounced by the court in accordance with the verdict. Whereupon the accused appied for and obtained a writ of error from this court.

On the night of the alleged occurrence, the accused, who was a visitor in the home of his aunt, Mrs. Samuel Smith, accompanied by four young ladies and two young men, attended a service at the church situated near the Smith home. The accused, a short time after his departure from the Smith home, returned thereto and informed his aunt that he had become involved in a little trouble at the church, but that it would not amount to anything. Though 21 witnesses testified upon the trial of the accused, it is a remarkable fact that the record fails to disclose the nature of the trouble which occurred at the church. The nearest approach to any information upon the subject is the statement of a commonwealth's witness, named Johnson, who was a magistrate, that he issued a warrant for the arrest of the accused which charged a felony, and that he deputized Howard Carter and Rhea Miller to execute the warrant. Neither Howard Carter nor Rhea Miller testified in the case, so it is only to be inferred that some one armed with a warrant of arrest was present when the alleged crime was attempted.

It appears from the record that there were 13 people in the home of Samuel Smith at the time it is charged that the accused attempted to murder J. K. Carter. Among the people present were several ladies. While the record fails to show the number of persons engaged in the effort to arrest the accused, it is shown that there were at least 8 persons who were armed with pistols and a shotgun. Two witnesses testified that the "crowd" acted as if they were drinking; that they smelt liquor upon them.

Upon an examination of the Smith home after the difficulty, it was ascertained that in addition to the shotgun holes there were 27 bullet holes in the house, 24 of which were fired by the arresting party. The only person wounded was the accused, who was shot in the back.

The first assignment of error calls in question the action of the trial court in permitting the commonwealth's witness, Johnson, to testify that he issued a warrant of arrest for the accused which charged a felony. When this evidence was offered, counsel for the accused objected to its introduction on the ground that the warrant was the best evidence of what it charged; that, in order for secondary evidence of its contents to be admissible, it must be first shown that diligent search had been made for the warrant and that the same was either lost or destroyed.

We are of opinion that this assignment of error is well founded. It was incumbent upon the commonwealth to produce the warrant or account for its nonproduction. The commonwealth attempted to account for the nonproduction of the warrant by showing the connection of Johnson with the same. He testified as follows:

"The warrant issued for the defendant and placed in the hands of Howard Carter was brought back to me later on, and the return on it was in the handwriting of Sheriff C. C. Palmer. It was not in the handwriting of

Howard Carter nor Rhea Miller. I did not keep the warrant and do not know what was done with it. I authorized Howard Carter to execute the warrant."

This account is not sufficient to show that the warrant was lost. It was the duty of Howard Carter to return the warrant to either the issuing magistrate, Johnson, or to some other magistrate, whose duty, in turn, was to deliver the same to the clerk of the circuit court, the custodian delegated by law to receive it. Neither Carter nor the clerk were introduced to show that they did not possess the warrant.

In Marshall v. Commonwealth, 140 Va. 541, 125 S.E. 329, it is said:

"If the basis upon which the secondary evidence is sought to be introduced is that the instrument is lost . . . there must be proof that a diligent search has been made in the place where it is most likely to be found and that the search has been unsuccessful."

In Judson v. Eslava, Minor, Ala., 71, 12 Am.Dec. 32, it is said:

"The testimony of the last custodian of the paper or record should be produced." . . .

Reversed.

STATE v. FRESHWATER
Supreme Court of Utah, 1906.
30 Utah 442, 85 P. 447, 116 Am.St.Rep. 853.

McCARTY, J. The defendant was convicted of the crime of adultery alleged to have been committed on June 18, 1904, at Provo, Utah, with one Delia Nance, an unmarried woman, and was sentenced therefor to a term in the penitentiary. . . .

Delia Nance, the woman with whom it is alleged defendant committed the crime of which he stands convicted, was called as a witness and testified that defendant was criminally intimate with her on June 18, 1904, at Provo, Utah, and that, as a result of their criminal conduct, she became pregnant; that defendant, after he was arrested for the crime, prevailed upon her to go to her home in Colorado in order to avoid testifying against him; that on the night of September 5, 1904, the defendant took her to Springville in a buggy, at which point he gave her money, and she took the train for Colorado; that it was understood before they parted that defendant would ship her trunk to her later on. [The court admitted the further testimony of the witness as to the contents of letters written by her to the defendant, about the shipment of her trunk, and concerning the date of the trial of the criminal proceedings against defendant. Some of the letters received by her in reply were typewritten and these she produced in evidence, but one of the letters was written, and as to this she testified that she recognized it as being in the handwriting of the defendant.]

It is now urged that the court erred in permitting Delia Nance, who claimed to have seen the defendant write but once, to testify that the letter written by hand which she claimed was received by her, and the address on the envelope in which it came, was in the defendant's handwriting. The rule is well settled that writing may be proved by evidence of a witness who has seen the person write. . . . In 2 Jones on Ev. § 559, the author says: "But whatever degree of weight his testimony may deserve, which is a question exclusively for the jury, it is an established rule that if one has seen the person write, he will be competent to speak as to his handwriting; and this is true, although the impression on the witness may be faint and inaccurate. Thus, the testimony has been admitted although the witness has not seen the person write for many years before the trial and although he has only seen the person write on a single occasion, and even though he only saw the person write his name, or even his surname." And again: "It is not necessary that the witness should be an expert. These are matters affecting not the admissibility but the weight of such testimony." . . . Hammond v. Varian, 54 N.Y. 398; McNair v. Commonwealth, 26 Pa. 388; Rideout v. Newton, 17 N.H. 71; Pepper v. Barnett, 22 Grat., Va., 405; Keith v. Lothrop, 10 Cush., Mass., 453; Hopkins v. Megquire, 35 Me. 78; Edelen v. Gough, 8 Gill, Md., 87; 17 Cyc. 157. . . .

We find no reversible error in the record. The judgment is therefore affirmed.

BARTCH, C. J., and STRAUP, J., concur.

8

Judicial Notice

A police officer can save himself many hours of investigation if he has a proper understanding of what judicial notice is and how it is used. Judicial notice is nothing more than a legal function designed to save the court time. Although legal scholars define judicial notice as a substitute for evidence, its primary purpose is judicial economy.

Judicial notice consists of two classes, mandatory judicial notice (e.g., state statutes) and optional judicial notice (e.g., community facts). In the case of mandatory judicial notice, the judge is required to take notice of certain facts, whereas in optional judicial notice, he may or may not take notice of a fact. In both cases, notice is taken without the introduction of any evidence on the matter involved. The police officer, however, must distinguish from the judge's own knowledge and judicial notice. If the judge has personal knowledge of a fact that does not normally fall within one of the two classes, then he is not permitted to take judicial notice of the fact.

Mandatory Judicial Notice

In the majority of states, the judge is required to take notice of his own state's statutes as well as those of the federal government; e.g., if a person is attempting to establish the corpus delicti of the crime of burglary, it would be necessary for him to first show that his state had a law defining burglary and prescribing the penalty for it. Thus, the judge must take mandatory judicial notice that the state has a burglary statute and what it says. If it were not for this type of notice, it would be necessary to introduce an official of the state who could authenticate that this certain bill did in fact pass the House and Senate and was still in effect at the time of the crime.

The federal laws have preempted the state law in some areas, and, as the Constitution of the United States is the supreme law of the land, the state court is required to take judicial notice of the federal laws as they exist. Again, keep in mind that judicial notice is taken in the interest of judicial economy.

Most states require that their courts take mandatory notice of each city and county charter which exists within its borders. Thus, a city police officer or county deputy sheriff is not required before testifying to establish that the jurisdiction which employs him is in fact a legal entity.

Decisional Law

In the interest of judicial economy, the majority of states require that their courts take mandatory judicial notice of the case decisions of the higher courts within that state as well as those of the federal courts having appellate power. Just imagine the time that would be wasted if each time the prosecutor wanted to argue a point of law and referred to a U.S. Supreme Court decision, he had to bring in a clerk of the Supreme Court to authenticate a digest report of that decision before it could be introduced into evidence, keeping in mind the Best Evidence Rule that only the original writing may be introduced unless there is an exception to that rule and that there must be an exception to the Hearsay Rule.

Governmental Regulations

Each state has certain powers delegated to agencies created under its laws. Most of these agencies have certain quasi-legal powers to enact regulations and enforce them. However, in the majority of states, the regulations must be filed with the secretary of state before they can be introduced as judicial notice.

This rule also allows the judge to take judicial notice of federal agencies and their regulations, such as Presidential Proclamations and Executive Orders, Security and Exchange Commission regulations, Food and Drug Administration regulations, and so forth.

Rules of Court

Most state court rules are established by a judicial council. In the interest of judicial economy, the courts must take mandatory judicial notice of these rules of practice and procedure in existence within their borders. However, in the area of federal rules of practice and procedure, the state court is only required to take judicial notice of those rules which have been prescribed by the U.S. Supreme Court.

Facts of Universal Knowledge

If any fact is universally known to exist, and no one can reasonably dispute it, and it has been relied on, then the judge must take judicial notice of this fact. The test to determine if it is a fact on which the judge should take judicial notice is the reasonable man test, which states that if a reasonable man of ordinary intelligence would know that this fact existed, then it is a fact which must be judicially noticed (e.g., A.M. means the morning hours to the average reasonable man). Again, we save many hours and dollars by not having to introduce any evidence on these subjects.

English Words and Common English Phrases

The true meaning of all English words and common phrases must be recognized by the judge, as it would be a waste of time if two or three experts were allowed to come before the court to give the jury their interpretation of the simplest word or phrase. For instance, reasonable men of average intelligence know that the phrase *to get busted* is today accepted among the police profession and criminals as meaning "to be arrested." Thus, it is a phrase of which the judge would be required to take judicial notice.

Optional Judicial Notice

Optional judicial notice differs from mandatory judicial notice in that the judge has discretion of whether he will take judicial notice of a fact or will allow the introduction of evidence to the jury through the normal means.

Laws of Other States

Generally speaking, most attorneys will stipulate as to a law in effect in a sister state which is in the present trial; e.g., you have arrested an armed robber and learned that he has served time for two other felonies in another state. Your state has a habitual criminal statute for third offenders. It would be necessary for you to produce an expert of the law of the foreign state to establish that the suspect had in fact been tried and convicted of two felonies in that state before you could have him sentenced as an habitual criminal in your state.

If the attorneys in the case will stipulate (agree) to the foreign law (law of another state), then the problem is solved. However, a defense attorney would not want to do this, so the prosecutor is allowed to notify the court that he desires to take judicial notice of certain foreign laws and also gives notice to the defense. Here, through a pretrial hearing, the judge can determine what he will take optional notice of, allowing both sides the opportunity to be heard and to prepare for the trial based on his decision.

Judicial Records of Other Courts

Generally, the court will not take judicial notice of the record of another court now being sought to be introduced in the present case. [This will be covered at length in the chapter on hearsay (Chapter 9).] If the record is official, there is no question that if it complies with all the other rules of evidence it will in most instances be introduced into evidence, but it will not be judicially noticed. The judge will require that evidence be introduced to authenticate the record and establish its validity before the jury can consider it in the present matter.

Common Knowledge within the Jurisdiction of the Court

The concept of matters of common knowledge within the court's jurisdiction is similar to that of universal knowledge, but on a smaller scale. At a trial in a local court of limited jurisdiction, such as a county court, the court has the option of taking judicial notice of facts of common knowledge within its own jurisdiction. *Example:* A county court is hearing a case in which it becomes important to establish that the intersection of Fifth and Main Street is in fact in a commercial area in the downtown section. If everyone of reasonable intelligence in that county knew that Fifth and Main Street was in fact a downtown intersection, then the judge could take judicial notice of that fact so that numerous witnesses would not have to come before the court to establish what everyone in the community already knew.

Easily Ascertainable Facts

The Uniform Rules of Evidence state that "easily ascertainable facts" are "facts and propositions that are not reasonably subject to dispute and are capable of immediate and accurate determination by resort to sources of reasonable indisputable accuracy." *Example:* In a given case, it is necessary to establish that sundown was at a certain time on a certain date. This could be established not only by expert testimony, but also by going to an almanac. Thus, the fact is easily ascertainable, and the court may take judicial notice of that fact.

General Knowledge within the United States

The judge may take notice of matters that are not universally known, but that instead are limited to the United States. For instance, it is a matter of general knowledge that a person who drinks an intoxicating beverage may become intoxicated at some point in time. This does not mean that this person was intoxicated, but only that if he drinks enough, there exists a chance that he might become intoxicated. It also is general knowledge that certain types of criminals work during certain hours. A safe burglar generally works during hours of darkness, a dope pusher likes to work at night, a streetwalker generally works late afternoons and evenings, etc.

The court is also permitted to take notice that certain geographical and historical facts existed, e.g., a certain area was within the city limits of a town, or a river flowed between two cities.

Medical and Scientific Facts

Recently, the courts have been allowing expert testimony instead of judicial notice of medical and scientific facts. However, the court could take notice of certain medical and scientific facts that are indisputable;

e.g., certain organs of the body are located in certain places, and certain results will occur if a person incurs a certain disease, the sun sets at a certain time, etc. *Example:* The state law says that a search warrant is only valid during daylight, unless otherwise ordered by the court. A police officer executes the warrant during the winter at 6:30 P.M. Is that daytime or nighttime? This is a scientific fact, as well as one of general knowledge, which could be verified by an almanac. If the medical or scientific fact is not conclusive, then the judge will not take notice of it, but will allow the parties to introduce evidence concerning it.

The end result of the court taking judicial notice is that in the interest of judicial economy, they will save time and money for all parties.

If the judge has in fact decided to take optional notice or a fact comes in as mandatory notice, then the judge must so instruct the trier of fact that he has taken notice of certain fact and they must consider it as a proven fact without the introduction of any evidence before them.

Summary

The purpose of judicial notice is to save time and money for all parties. When the judge takes optional judicial notice, or must take mandatory judicial notice, of a fact, he presents that fact to the jury, and the jury must consider it as a proven fact without the introduction of any evidence. Thus, judicial notice is a substitute for evidence.

DISCUSSION QUESTIONS

1. What is the rationale for the judicial notice rules?
2. Distinguish between mandatory judicial notice and optional judicial notice.
3. Of what normally must the judge in your jurisdiction take mandatory notice?
4. What would generally be considered matters of common knowledge within the court's jurisdiction? Do these fall within optional or mandatory notice in your jurisdiction?
5. What is the rationale behind the courts generally not taking judicial notice of medical and scientific facts?

STATE v. MAIN
Supreme Court of Errors of Connecticut, 1897.
69 Conn. 123, 37 A. 80.

[Amasa M. Main was convicted of violating Pub.Acts 1893, C. 216, providing for the destruction of trees diseased with the "peach yellows". He appeals.]

BALDWIN, J. . . : The superior court was also right in refusing to instruct the jury, as requested, that if they should "find that the 'yellows' is not a contagious disease, and the existence of the disease in one tree does not cause it to spread from that tree to other trees, and thus endanger other trees, the property of others, and that a tree so diseased is not a public nuisance, then this statute is an improper and unwarrantable invasion of the rights and property of citizens, the right to care for his property, and plant and cultivate his trees as he desires, without interference, and is unconstitutional and void." Whether the "yellows" was such a disease as to justify the general assembly in enacting the statute under which the prosecution was brought depended on the existence and nature of the disease, and also on the apprehension of danger from it commonly entertained by the public at large.

That such a disease existed, and was one of a serious character, ordinarily resulting in the premature death of the tree affected, is a matter of common knowledge, of which the court had a right to take judicial notice. Cent.Dict. "Peach Yellows," and "Yellows"; Webst.Int. Dict. "Yellows." Such a disease it was proper for the general assembly, in the exercise of its police power, to endeavor to suppress, even by the destruction of the trees attacked by it, if there was a reasonable apprehension of substantial danger, from allowing them to live, to those who might eat their fruit, or to other peach orchards. Unless the courts can see that these could by no possibility be such danger, the propriety of such legislation as that now in question is to be determined solely by the discretion of the legislative department. The description of this disease given in standard works and government publications, and the legislation in regard to it to be found in the statute books of Delaware, Maryland, Michigan, New York, Pennsylvania, Virginia, and the province of Ontario, are amply sufficient to establish as a matter of judicial notice, the possibility, if not the probability, that it is a contagious disease. Grimes v. Eddy, 126 Mo. 168, 28 S.W. 756.

The destruction of a tree affected by a disease of that character, without compensation to the owner, and against his will, is as fully within the police power of a state as the destruction of a house threatened by a spreading conflagration, or the clothes of a person who had fallen a victim to smallpox. Such property is not taken for public use. It is destroyed because, in the judgment of those to whom the law has confided the power of decision, it is of no use, and is a source of public danger.

Judicial notice takes the place of proof, and is of equal force. As a means of establishing facts, it is therefore superior to evidence. In its appropriate field, it displaces, evidence, since, as it stands for proof, it fulfills the object which evidence is designed to fulfill, and makes evidence unnecessary. Brown v. Piper, 91 U.S. 37, 43; Com. v. Marzynski, 149 Mass. 68, 21 N.E. 228. "The true conception of what is judicially known is that of something which is not, or rather need not, unless the tribunal wishes it, be the subject of either evidence or argument,—something which is already in the court's possession, or, at any rate, is so accessible that there is no occasion to use any means to make the court aware of it." Thayer, Cas. Ev. 20. If, in regard to any subject of judicial notice, the court should permit documents to be referred to or testimony introduced, it would not be, in any proper sense, the admission of evidence, but simply a resort to a convenient means of refreshing the memory, or making the trier aware of that of which everybody ought to be aware. State v. Morris, 47 Conn. 179, 180. The defendant therefore had no right to have the jury pass upon the danger of contagion from trees affected by the yellows, as a means of determining the constitutionality of the statute, by such verdict as they might render under the instructions of the court. It was for the court to take notice that it was a disease which might be contagious. Norwalk Gaslight Co. v. Borough of Norwalk, 63 Conn. 495, 525, 527, 28 A. 32.

This being established, the validity of the statute became a matter of pure law. Police legislation for the extirpation of a disease of such a nature, which the legislative department deems dangerous to the public welfare, cannot be pronounced invalid by the judicial department by reason of any difference of opinion, should one exist, between these two agencies of government, as to the probability of such danger. If the law may be an appropriate means of protecting the public health and the agricultural interests of the state, it is for the legislature alone to determine as to its adoption. It may have been the opinion of the general assembly that peach growers in general would abandon their business from dread of contagion from orchards infected by the yellows. In such a case whether their apprehensions were well founded or ill founded would be immaterial, unless it also appeared that there could be no reasonable grounds for them.

Affirmed.

VARCOE v. LEE
Supreme Court of California, 1919.
180 Cal. 338, 181 P. 223.

OLNEY, J. This is an action by a father to recover damages suffered through the death of his child, resulting from her being run over by an automobile of the defendant Lee, driven at the time by the other defendant, Nichols, the chauffeur of Lee. The automobile was going south on Mission street in San Francisco, and was approaching the crossing of Twenty-First street, when the child, in an endeavor to cross the street, was run over and killed. The cause was tried before a jury, which returned a verdict of $5,000 for the plaintiff. From the judgment upon this verdict, the defendants appeal.

The alleged negligence, upon which plaintiff's right to recover is predicated, consisted in the speed at which it is claimed the automobile was proceeding. . . .

When he came to charge the jury, the trial judge instructed them that, if they found that the defendant Nichols was running the automobile along Mission street at the time of the accident at a greater speed than 15 miles an hour, he was violating the city ordinance, and also the state Motor Vehicle Act, and that such speed was negligence in itself. The trial judge then read to the jury the portion of subdivision "b" of section 22 of the Motor Vehicle Act (St.1913, p. 639), which provides that it shall be unlawful to operate a motor "in the business district" of any incorporated city or town at a greater speed than 15 miles an hour, and defines (see section 1) a business district as "territory . . . contiguous to a public highway, which is at that point mainly built up with structures devoted to business." Having read this definition, the court proceeded with its charge as follows:

"That is the situation on Mission street between Twentieth and Twenty-Second streets, where this accident happened, so that is a business district and the maximum legal rate of speed on that street at the time of the happening of this accident was 15 miles an hour." . . .

So far as the record itself goes, there is little to show what the character of Mission street between Twentieth and Twenty-Second streets is. The defendant Nichols himself refers to it in his testimony as part of the "downtown district," undoubtedly meaning thereby part of the business district of the city. The evidence shows incidentally that at the scene of the accident there was a drug store, a barber shop, a haberdashery, and a saloon. If there had been any issue or question as to the character of the district, the record in this meager condition would not justify the taking of the question from the jury, as was undoubtedly done by the instruction complained of.

The actual fact of the matter is, however, that Mission street, between Twentieth and Twenty-Second streets, is a business district, within the definition of the Motor Vehicle Act, beyond any possibility of question. It has been such for years. Not only this, but its character is known as a matter of common knowledge by any one at all familiar with San Francisco. Mission street, from its downtown beginning at the water front to and beyond the district of the city known as the Mission, is second in importance and prominence as a business street only to Market street. The probabilities are that every person in the courtroom at the trial, including judge, jury, counsel, witnesses, parties and officers of the court, knew perfectly well what the character of the location was. It was not a matter about which there could be any dispute or question. If the court had left the matter to the determination of the jury, and they for some inconceivable reason had found that it was not a business district, it would have been the duty of the court to set aside the verdict. We are asked now to reverse the judgment, because the court assumed, without submitting to the jury, what could not be disputed and what he and practically every resident in the county for which the court was sitting knew to be a fact. If error there was, it is clear that, upon the actual fact, there was no prejudice to the defendants.

It would have been much better if counsel for the plaintiff or the trial judge himself had inquired of defendants' counsel, before the case went to the jury, whether there was any dispute as to the locality being a business district within the meaning of the state law. There could have been but one reasonable answer, and, if any other were given, the matter could have been easily settled beyond any possibility of question. But this was not done, and we are now confronted by the question whether either this court or the trial court can take judicial notice of the real fact.

An appellate court can properly take judicial notice of any matter of which the court of original jurisdiction may properly take notice. Pennington v. Gibson, 16 How. 65, 14 L.Ed. 817; Salt Lake City v. Robinson, 39 Utah 260, 116 P. 442, 35 L.R.A.,N.S., 610, Ann.Cas. 1913E, 61; 15 Ruling Case Law, 1063.

In fact, a particularly salutary use of the principle of judicial notice is to sustain on appeal, a judgment clearly in favor of the right party, but as to which there is in the evidence an omission of some necessary fact which is yet indisputable and a matter of common knowledge, and was probably assumed without strict proof for that very reason. Campbell v. Wood, 116 Mo. 196, 22 S.W. 796.

The question, therefore, is: Was the superior court for the city and county of San Francisco, whose judge and talesman were necessarily residents of the city, entitled to take judicial notice of the character of one of the most important and best-known streets in the city? If it were, the court was authorized to charge the jury as it did. Section 2102, Code Civ.Proc.

It should perhaps be noted that the fact that the trial judge knew what the actual fact was, and that it was indisputable would not of itself justify him in recognizing it. Nor would the fact that the character of the street was a matter of common knowledge and notoriety justify him in taking the question from the jury, if there were any possibility of dispute as to whether or not that character was such as to constitute it a business district within the definition of the statute applicable. If such question could exist, the fact involved — whether the well-known character of the street was sufficient to make it a business district — was one for determination by the jury. But we have in this case a combination of the two circumstances. In the first place, the fact is indisputable and beyond question. In the second place, it is a matter of common knowledge throughout the jurisdiction in and for which the court is sitting. . . .

It is truly said that the power of judicial notice is, as to matters claimed to be matters of general knowledge, one to be used with caution. If there is any doubt whatever, either as to the fact itself or as to its being a matter of common knowledge, evidence should be required; but, if the court is of the certain opinion that these requirements exist, there can properly be no hesitation. In such a case there is, on the one hand, no danger of a wrong conclusion as to the fact — and such danger is the reason for the caution in dispensing with the evidence — and, on the other hand, purely formal and useless proceedings will be avoided.

Little assistance can be had by a search of the authorities for exactly similar cases. The one perhaps nearest to it that we have found is State v. Ruth, 14 Mo.App. 226. What may be a proper subject of judicial notice at one time or place may not be at another. It would be wholly unreasonable to require proof, if the fact became material, as to the general location in the city of San Francisco of its city hall before a judge and jury made up of residents of that city and actually sitting in the building. But before a judge and jury in another county proof should be made. The difference lies in the fact being one of common knowledge in one jurisdiction and not in the other. Similarly it has been held repeatedly that courts will judicially notice the general doctrines of any religious denomination prevalent within its jurisdiction, and yet it was held by an Ohio court, and properly held, in the early days of Christian Science, that notice would not be taken of the doctrines of that sect. Evans v. State, 9 Ohio St.C.Pl.Dec. 222, 6 Ohio N.P. 129. Now that the sect has grown to large numbers, and its general doctrines are a matter of common knowledge, it is as proper to notice them as to notice those of older denominations. As is well said by Wigmore, 4 Wigmore on Ev. § 2580:

"Applying the general principle (ante, section 2565), especially in regard to the element of notoriousness, courts are found noticing, from time to time, a varied array of unquestionable facts, ranging throughout the data of commerce, industry, history, and natural science. It is unprofitable, as well as impracticable, to seek to connect them by generalities and distinctions; for the notoriousness of a truth varies much with differences of period and of place. It is even erroneous, in many, if not in most instances, to regard them as precedents. It is the spirit and example of the rulings, rather than their precise tenor, that is to be useful in guidance."

The test, therefore, in any particular case where it is sought to avoid or excuse the production of evidence because the fact to be proven is one of general knowledge and notoriety, is: (1) Is the fact one of common, everyday knowledge in that jurisdiction, which every one of average intelligence and knowledge of things about him can be presumed to know? and (2) is it certain and indisputable? If it is, it is a proper case for dispensing with evidence, for its production cannot add or aid. On the other hand, we may well repeat, if there is any reasonable question whatever as to either point, proof should be required. Only so can the danger involved in dispensing with proof be avoided. Even if the matter be one of judicial cognizance, there is still no error or impropriety in requiring evidence.

Applying this test to the facts of the case, the matter is not in doubt. The character of Mission street is as well known to San Franciscans as the character of Spring street to residents of Los Angeles, or of State street to residents of Chicago, or of Forty-Second street to residents of New York, or of F street to residents of Washington. It is a matter of their everyday common information and experience, and one about which there can be no dispute.

The conclusion follows that the charge of the trial court that Mission street, between Twentieth and Twenty-Second streets, was a business district, was not error. That judgment is therefore affirmed.

9

The Hearsay Rule and Its Exceptions

The General Hearsay Rule

Basically, hearsay is an out-of-court act, statement, or writing which is now being offered in court in an attempt to prove that that which took place or which was outside the courtroom is in fact true. Hearsay is not admissible in any court. The Hearsay Rule is designed to keep out of evidence all out-of-court acts, statements, or writings which tend to be untrustworthy. However, this rule is not easy to apply because state legislature and the U.S. Congress have created numerous exceptions over the years. The student should keep in mind that each jurisdiction has different exceptions to the Hearsay Rule and that the different jurisdictions may call the exceptions to this rule by different names than used in this book. This chapter will only cover the more commonly used exceptions to the Hearsay Rule applicable to criminal procedures.

There are two main definitions of hearsay used in the United States today. The orthodox definition of hearsay, as enunciated by Professor Wigmore, defines hearsay as "oral testimony or documentary evidence as to somebody's words or conduct outside of court, where offered to prove the very thing asserted, thus resting its value upon the credibility of the person who made the assertion out of court." More modern statutes, including the new Federal Rules, adopt Professor Wigmore's definition and state that, "hearsay is a statement other than one made by the declarant while testifying at the hearing offered in evidence to prove the truth of the matter asserted." The jurisdictions following this definition of hearsay hold that such a statement may consist of any of the following as long as it is being offered to prove the truth: (1) assertive conduct; (2) a writing; (3) an oral statement. Assertive conduct is conduct intended by the actor to be a substitute for words. *Example:* A person is waving at another person. The question is, Does the person who is waving intend the wave of his arm to take the place of spoken words such as *goodbye* or *hello*? Here, a writing would be any item defined as a writing that is made outside of the courtroom, such as a police report, tape recording, motion picture, videotape, etc. An oral statement is made when the witness testifies to statements made by someone else or himself outside of court. Assertive conduct, writings, and oral statements as defined here are hearsay. Exceptions must be found before any may be admissible.

Other jurisdictions adopt Morgan's definition of hearsay: "Hearsay is evidence of words or conduct outside of court, assertive or nonassertive, which is offered to prove the truth of the facts therein, or that the declarant believed in them to be true." The main distinction between Professor Wigmore's definition and Morgan's definition is that under the Morgan definition, nonassertive conduct, that is, conduct which is not intended as a substitute for words, is also defined as hearsay. Only a minority of the jurisdictions today accept the Morgan view.

No jurisdiction in the United States bars the introduction into evidence of out-of-court conduct, words, or writings that are being offered to prove that certain things were done, words spoken, or a writing made, and not to prove the truth of them. If something is offered which is generally defined as hearsay, but an argument is made to the court that it is not being offered to prove the truth of the matter, but only to prove that certain things occurred, then the objection based upon the Hearsay Rule is overcome. *Example:* A police officer is dispatched by radio to the scene of an armed robbery at Fifth and Main Streets in Suburbia. The officer is then called to testify in court and is asked how he learned of the robbery. An objection is made, based on the Hearsay Rule, that the officer will not be testifying from personal knowledge, but that he received a radio transmission and does not know how the information was originally received; that is, that he is relying upon the dispatcher's knowledge to cause him to respond to a certain location, and thus the information he heard is hearsay and should be barred by the Hearsay Rule. The prosecuting attorney, however, would be correct in stating that even though the officer will testify as to another person's statement, the information is not being offered to prove the truth of the matter (that there was a robbery in progress), but is being offered only to show why the officer went to that location.

Assertive Conduct

Any assertive conduct, which is conduct intended as a substitute for words, is hearsay when it is being offered to prove the truth of what was intended to be asserted. *Example 1:* An officer arrives at the scene of a crime and asks who did it. At this time, one person points his finger at another person. The question is, Was the pointing of the finger at the other person intended to act as a substitute for words which could have been, "He did it."? *Example 2:* An officer is questioning an individual concerning his involvement in a crime and the person shakes his head either yes or no in response to questions put forth to him.

Nonassertive conduct generally only falls under an exclusion of the Hearsay Rule in a jurisdiction that follows Morgan's definition. *Example 1:* An officer responds to the scene of a robbery and sees the fleeing suspect, who is later arrested. Was the suspect's flight from the scene of the crime an act of conduct on his part which can be introduced against him, i.e., was he conscious of guilt and therefore ran from the scene of the crime? *Example 2:* Another instance of nonassertive behavior, which is now constitutionally barred due to the Fifth Amendment privilege, but was used for some years in the United States, was when an officer made a direct accusation to a defendant, who remained silent and did not respond to it. In jurisdictions following Morgan's views, either of the two preceding examples could be introduced into evidence if an exception was found in the Hearsay Rule.

Purpose

The main reason that hearsay has been frowned upon by the courts is that it lacks trustworthiness. If a witness is testifying in court, the judge or jury is able to determine or form an opinion based on its observations as to whether the witness is telling the truth. But when the statement or writing is done outside of court, neither is able to make this determination. More modernly, certain constitutional questions are raised when out-of-court statements, writings, or assertive or nonassertive conduct are being offered into evidence. In a criminal proceeding, the defendant or the prosecutor, depending on who is offering the declaration, is not afforded an opportunity to cross-examine the declarant, as the declarant is not testifying. Instead, someone else is testifying as to what the declarant did, said, or wrote out of court. Another constitutional issue is raised whenever hearsay is offered, because the defendant is denied his right to confront the witness against him. The defendant certainly has the right to confront the witness on the stand, but cannot confront the out-of-court declarant whose testimony is technically now being offered in the trial. Another major problem with hearsay is that at the time the declarant made the statement, writing, assertive act, or nonassertive act, he was not under oath and, thus, was under no obligation to tell the truth.

Admissions

An admission is an out-of-court statement or conduct by one of the parties to the action which is inconsistent with his present stand in court. *Example:* A defendant in a robbery trial told a friend of his that he robbed the victim and has now pled "not guilty" and is being tried. His present stand in court of pleading "not guilty" is not consistent with his previous statement to his friend. Thus, he has made an admission. The jurisdictions are divided on whether or not admissions are even hearsay. The Federal Rules state that admissions are not hearsay because their admissibility is the result of the adversary system rather than satisfaction of the conditions of the Hearsay Rule. Other jurisdictions hold that admissions are hearsay because they are being offered to prove the truth of the statement made by the declarant. Most jurisdictions hold that if an admission was freely and voluntarily given, it may be introduced as an exception to the Hearsay Rule.

An admission in criminal law differs from a confession in that an admission made by the declarant does not involve his acknowledgement of all elements of the corpus delicti of the crime but only certain aspects of his involvement. The student must remember that an admission obtained by a law enforcement officer must comply with the constitutional safeguards. Thus, if an officer uses any duress or force to obtain that admission, it will be excluded from court. *Example:* The police officer has arrested a suspect on a murder charge and is transporting the suspect to the police station. While enroute, the suspect is heard to state, "I'm so sorry I did it." This admission would be admitted into evidence in court, since it was freely and voluntarily given and not compelled by the law enforcement agent in any way.

The law enforcement officer should, by habit, record in writing all statements made to him by any person involved in any criminal activity, whether he thinks it is important or not, and even if he is not attempting to elicit information from the person who is making the statement. *Example:* A person is being booked into a jail and mumbles to himself, "I'm sorry I did it." Even though he has not been given a Miranda warning (discussed under the confession exception), this statement, if heard by any other person, is an admission and, if recorded, the prosecuting attorney will become aware of it and will be able to introduce it as evidence in the trial.

The officer is confronted more frequently with an admission which has been made in court, i.e., a plea of guilty. Under many of the state statutes, prior pleas in criminal cases will be admissible for the purposes of establishing that the person should be convicted under a habitual criminal statute, which allows for increased penalties for repeaters, or to show prior modus operandi. This prior plea is an admission made before a competent court outside of the present courtroom that it is being offered into evidence and, thus, is hearsay. A prior plea of guilty is generally admissible in subsequent criminal procedures, and in some civil actions as well. A withdrawn guilty plea or an offer to plead guilty, however, is not admissible and will be excluded.

An admission by silence is not now constitutionally permitted to be introduced into evidence in a criminal procedure. *Example:* A woman reports to the police department that she has been raped and names a suspect. The investigating officer confronts the suspect and accuses him of the rape. The suspect stands silently and does not respond. Under the old rules, his silence could be introduced against him as an admission, under the assumption that a normal, reasonable man, when being accused of this heinous crime, would not have stood silent, but would have denied it if in fact it was not true. Due to the Fifth Amendment of the U.S. Constitution, however, the defendant has a right to remain silent. This type of admission can no longer be used in criminal proceedings.

Admission of Coconspirator Exception

A statement made by one party to a conspiracy is generally admissible against the other parties to the conspiracy if the following elements are shown: (1) the conspiracy is established by independent evidence (evidence other than the statement); (2) the statement was made during the conspiracy; (3) the statement is related to some matters in furtherance of the conspiracy. Thus, a long-standing rule of public abhorence of conspiracies is furthered by stating that any member of a conspiracy may make incriminating admissions which can be utilized against all other coconspirators as a penalty for that person joining the conspiracy.

However, if in fact a statement is made by a coconspirator after one party has withdrawn from the conspiracy or after the conspirators have achieved their illegal objective, then the statement would be inadmissible, even though the declarant could be called as a witness as to what he observed or as to his personal knowledge of the crime. *Example:* Three suspects agree to rob the First City National Bank and proceed to plan and execute the robbery. After the robbery takes place and the three suspects divide the stolen property, they each go their separate ways, agreeing not to see each other again. After the separation, one coconspirator makes an admission concerning all three's participation in the robbery. This admission was made after the conspiracy had terminated and thus would not be admissible under this exception to the Hearsay Rule.

Confession Exception

A confession is a complete acknowledgement of guilt by a person accused of a crime in which he admits all elements of the crime. *Example:* "I confess that I entered that house with the intent to steal the television set and permanently deprive the owner thereof." This statement would be a perfect confession in that the person has admitted all elements of the crime. Although the Federal Rules state that confessions are not hearsay, most jurisdictions hold that they are hearsay. Therefore, an exception to the Hearsay Rule usually must be found before a confession can be admitted into court.

Before a confession can be admitted into court in any jurisdiction, the prosecution must prove the corpus delicti of the crime by other evidence. In other words, a confession cannot be utilized to prove any element of the crime; it may only be introduced after the elements have been proven with other means or types of evidence.

The constitutional standards imposed upon law enforcement officers strictly prohibit the introduction of any confession which has been obtained without benefit of the safeguards afforded the defendant under the U.S. Constitution. A confession must be freely and voluntarily obtained in order to be admissible. Before a law enforcement officer can question the accused, he must inform that accused of his Miranda rights, which state that: (1) the accused has the right to remain silent; (2) anything he says can and will be used against him in a court of law; (3) he has the right to consult with an attorney prior to the time of answering any questions or at any time during the questioning; and (4) if the accused cannot afford an attorney, one will be provided by the court, free of charge, to represent him. The law enforcement officer must be able to prove in court that he has advised the defendant in custody of all four of these rights and that the defendant freely and voluntarily waived these rights and acknowledged that he understood them.

Under the Miranda rule, before the officer is required to advise the defendant of his rights, the defendant must be in custody, and the officer must be attempting to illicit incriminating statements or information from the defendant. In custody basically means that the person is significantly deprived of his freedom or movement (even though he might not be in handcuffs) in the police station, or even sitting in the squad car. He also may be in custody if he does not feel that he is free to leave at any time or if the officer has predetermined that the suspect is not free to leave and will be arrested if he attempts to leave. It is not required, nor has it ever been required, under any of the U.S. Supreme Court decisions, that merely because a person is stopped, detained, or arrested he be advised of any constitutional rights. The advisement is not required unless he is in custody and the officer is attempting to interrogate the defendant. If both elements have occurred, then the law enforcement official must precede the obtaining of any statements by a Miranda warning and a full free and voluntary waiver of the accused's constitutional rights.

If all of the constitutional safeguards are met, then any confession will fall within the purview of the Hearsay Rule, and in the majority of the jurisdictions will be admissible as an exception to the Hearsay Rule.

Dying Declaration Exception

Most jurisdictions have an exception to the Hearsay Rule which allows a dying declaration made by a victim of a crime to be introduced into evidence. Under the general view, such dying declarations are admissible only in homicide cases. The more modern trend, however, is to admit dying declarations in all types of proceedings, civil and criminal. Noted scholars feel that a dying declaration may be made in many instances other than in criminal homicide cases and that any party should not be denied the benefit of the declarant's statement made prior to his death.

There are certain requirements that must be fulfilled before the court will allow a dying declaration to be introduced into evidence. For one thing, the declaration must be made by the victim upon whom the injury has been inflicted, and not by some third person. *Example:* An officer is obtaining a statement from a person who is dying, and the following is said: "John Smith was the one who killed Mary Doe." This statement would not be admissible as a dying declaration, since it was Mary Doe, not the person who is now the declarant, that was injured by John Smith.

Another element required to make a dying declaration admissible is that the declarant must fear that death is imminent. This means that the declarant must have a reasonable expectation based upon his present existing injuries that there is no hope for recovery and that he will in fact die from this injury. *Example:* A woman has been shot by her husband and tells the police officer, "My husband shot me and I can't wait to see him led away to jail after the trial." Even though the woman dies prior to trial, that statement will not be admissible as a dying declaration because the statement itself shows that she did not fear that death was imminent from the injury inflicted upon her by her husband (as she stated, she could not wait to see him be led away to jail). There may be another exception under which this statement may come, such as the spontaneous declarations rule (excited utterance), but it may not be admitted under the dying declaration exception.

It is also required under the general view that the person who made the dying declaration was a percipient witness, i.e., was capable of perceiving through any of his senses and telling someone what he had perceived. The statement being given by the declarant who is about to die must be added to facts related to his impending death. *Example:* John Doe is lying on the street suffering from a bullet wound. A police officer rushes up to him and John says, "My partner Dan and I just robbed the bank, and Dan shot me, and we also robbed another bank yesterday." Assuming that the man dies from the bullet wound inflicted by Dan, the statements relating to Dan shooting him are admissible under the dying declaration exception, provided the other elements are satisfied, but the statements concerning the prior crime are not admissible under this exception, as they do not relate directly to the cause of death.

Furthermore, it is required that the declarant die before the dying declaration exception applies. If a person makes what satisfies all elements required for admissibility of a dying declaration but does not die, that declaration may be introduced under another exception of the Hearsay Rule, but would be barred from being introduced as evidence as an exception based upon the dying declaration rule.

Reported Testimony Exception

The law enforcement officer is generally only confronted with the reported testimony exception to the Hearsay Rule when there has been a hearing in the same case which transpired prior to the trial, such as a preliminary hearing or even an arraignment. In civil actions, reported testimony is used more frequently when the parties have taken depositions or interrogatories (written questions required to be answered under the direction of a court) out of court. Before evidence may be introduced as prior reported testimony, it must be established that there was identity of parties at the prior proceeding, that there was an identity of issue at the prior proceeding, and that the witness is unavailable at the present time. The first two requirements simply mean that at the prior hearing the same parties as are now involved in the present trial must have had an interest in the action, and that both parties were attempting to litigate issues which are the same or similar to those in the present case. *Example:* A preliminary hearing has been held on a charge of armed robbery. A trial is now being conducted in which the defendant is being charged with armed robbery. In this example, there is an identity of issues and an identity of parties. The third requirement, that there be sufficient unavailability of the witness who testified in the first hearing, is defined differently from jurisdiction to jurisdiction. The common law view was that the witness was only unavailable if it could be shown that he was dead. The more modern view contained in the Federal Rules states that unavailability of a witness includes but is not limited to the following instances: (1) the witness has a privilege which he is asserting to bar his testimony in the present action; (2) the witness is dead; (3) the whereabouts of the witness are unknown, and the parties after a diligent search cannot locate him; (4) the witness has a physical or mental illness; (5) the witness is beyond the subpoena power of the court; (6) the witness refuses to testify or lacks memory of the subject matter.

The argument has been raised in many cases that by using reported testimony in a criminal matter the defendant's constitutional right to confront witnesses and to cross-examine witnesses is being violated. The U.S. Supreme Court, however, has rejected this argument and holds that the accused's rights are not violated as long as the defendant and his attorney were present and had the opportunity to cross-examine at the time the original testimony was given and as long as the witness whose testimony was recorded is now unavailable.

Official Records Exception

Any document or statement that has been prepared by a public official during the course and scope of his duties is admissible under various exceptions to the Hearsay Rule. The official record exception to the Hearsay Rule has been formulated to assist public officers in performing their jobs and to save them time by not having to appear in court to testify regularly to acts which they have done during the course and scope of their official duties. Another reason for the official record exception is that in most instances a public officer is under a duty to record correctly certain documents and reports, and due to this duty, the records are generally trustworthy.

In order for an official record to be admitted under the official record exception, it is necessary that the following foundational requirements be present: (1) The record that the attorneys are attempting to introduce into evidence must have been prepared by a public officer or employee acting within the scope and course of his official duties. This means that the officer or employee had a duty to record the facts involved. It is immaterial that the recorded document was of a private nature, such as a deed or mortgage, as long as the person who recorded it was under a duty to record that document; (2) The record must be based on the public officer's or employee's personal knowledge of the facts recorded. *Example:*

An officer who has investigated a scene of a burglary puts in his report that "suspects entered by forcing a window open." This part of his report would not be based on personal knowledge, since he was not there to see that the suspects entered by this method. If the report indicated his findings of an investigation as to what he personally observed, e.g., there was a broken window glass or fingerprints found on the windowsill or footprints found in the dust in front of the window, such information would be admissible, as he has first-hand knowledge of what he recorded. Most modern jurisdictions, however, have relaxed this personal knowledge requirement in the area of official vital statistics records, when the person recording the birth certificate, death certificate, or marriage license does not really have personal knowledge, but merely has the say so of some other person, such as a doctor who was present at the time of birth. Those jurisdictions which have relaxed the rules will admit vital statistics records as an exception to the Hearsay Rule even though there is no personal knowledge present on the part of the public officer who recorded the document.

Most police reports are generally held to be inadmissible because they are not based on the personal knowledge of the recording officer. They are merely reports which the officer has received from another person, a situation which is hearsay on top of hearsay. A new federal rule authorizes the admittance into court of factual findings which result from an investigation made pursuant to authority granted by law in a civil case, but in a criminal case, this type of information may only be admitted if it is being offered against the federal government. *Example:* The Alcohol, Tobacco and Firearms Bureau makes an investigation report concerning the defendant in a criminal case. They seek to admit the report into evidence at the trial. It could not be introduced by the federal government, but the defense could introduce the investigative report to be used against the government.

A question that often arises is, What effect would a public record have as evidence in court to show that no entry had been made or no report had been made to a public officer? The federal rule in the modern trend is to allow an affidavit from the custodian of the public record to the effect that there are no records on file concerning the matter, which in fact means it has not been recorded or even reported. *Example:* A state statute makes it mandatory that all police departments make a written record of any traffic accident reported to them. During the course of a criminal prosecution for failure to report an accident which resulted in the death of another, the defendant asserts that he did make a report in the jurisdiction where the accident occurred. The custodian of records at the police department files an affidavit with the court attesting to the fact that there was no such record or report made to his agency. This affidavit is admissible to prove that no record or report had been made.

A certified copy of a court order or judgment is always admissible proof that the judgment has been entered, and it comes under the official record exception to the Hearsay Rule. Most of the rules concerning judgments deal with civil actions; only occasionally can a criminal conviction be admitted in a subsequent criminal trial. For instance, it may be important in attempting to establish that a person comes within a habitual criminal act to admit a prior record of conviction. Also, as discussed in the chapter on witnesses, the officer may want to have a prior criminal conviction introduced for impeachment purposes.

Past Recollection Exception

Some of the jurisdictions, including the new Federal Rules, have an exception to the Hearsay Rule for allowing past recollection of the witnesses to be introduced into the trial. This exception can be used if the witness is testifying and has no present recollection of the events that transpired and a foundaton is laid establishing that (1) the witness made a writing at a time when the fact recorded in the writing actually occurred or was fresh in his memory; (2) the writing was made by the witness himself or under his direction or by some other person for the purpose of recording the witness' statement at the time it was made; (3) the writing is offered after the witness testifies that the statement he made is a statement of true fact; and (4) the witness has authenticated the writing as an accurate record of the statement. *Example:* An officer is called to testify concerning an armed robbery which he personally witnessed. The officer, upon taking the stand and being sworn in, testifies that he has no present recollection of what he had observed during the robbery. The prosecutor shows him a written statement allegedly signed by the officer and asks him if he has ever seen this writing. The officer testifies that it is a statement which he wrote himself and signed as soon as the robbers had fled from the store. The officer further states that the statement is true. At this point, the writing has been authenticated and may be read into evidence either by the witness, the court clerk, or one of the attorneys, and the writing itself will be received into evidence.

The objection most frequently raised by attorneys concerning the offering of past recollection into evidence in a criminal trial is that it violates the confrontation clause of the Sixth Amendment of the U.S. Constitution. The person who actually made the writing, however, is on the witness stand testifying and may be cross-examined. Thus, the confrontation clause is not violated, as that witness is now in court and the attorney has the right to confront him.

The past recollection rule differs somewhat from the present memory revived rule, which states that a witness who is testifying and presently has no recollection of an event may use items such as newspaper clippings, reports that he personally made, or reports made by another person to refresh his memory. If upon reading the material he has now revived his memory, he may testify without the aid of the recording.

Res Gestae Exception

The term *res gestae* is defined as acts or words through which a main event speaks. The term has further been defined as acts and words which are spontaneous and so related to the transaction or occurrence in question as reasonably to appear to be evoked and prompted by it. This exception has been in the Hearsay Rule for a long time and has been upheld due to the spontaneity of the statement being made satisfying the "trustworthy" rationale behind the exceptions to the Hearsay Rule. *Example:* Mr. Jones and Ms. Smith are standing on a cliff overlooking the ocean and Mr. Jones observes a man throw a woman over the cliff. He immediately states, "He threw her over the cliff." The words should be in the confines of the res gestae rule.

Modern jurisdictions now recognize that the res gestae exception actually consists of three exceptions, each having its own characteristics and different requirements for admissibility. The three are as follows: (1) spontaneous statements, (2) declarations of present sense impressions, (3) declarations of physical condition and state of mind.

Spontaneous Statements

Spontaneous statements of any person made at the time of an exciting event and under the stimuli of the excitement of the event may be admissible under both jurisdictions of the Rules of Evidence and under the new Federal Rules. In order for the spontaneous statement to be admissible, however, there first must be an occurrence which is startling enough to produce some shock or excitement to the person who has observed it. *Example:* A person is standing on the street corner when a man runs out of the store firing a pistol. This is a startling event or an exciting event to say the least.

The second requirement is that the spontaneous statement be made while the person observing the event is under the excitement of the event, meaning that the statement must be spontaneous and that there has been no appreciable time for that person to pause and deliberate or to intentionally make a false statement. *Example:* The person who sees the man run from the store firing a pistol also hears someone yell, "Halt him, he's a robber!" In this situation, there has not been enough time for any person to pause and reflect upon the statement during the course of the startling or exciting event. Thus, the courts would deem the statement trustworthy and admit it into evidence.

The third requirement is that the spontaneous declaration narrate, describe, or explain an act or condition perceived by the declarant. Some of the courts require further that the statement must have been from the declarant's personal observation of the facts. (However, it is not required that the declarant who made the declaration be available, or that his identity even be known.) *Example:* A bystander is standing at an intersection and observes a vehicle run a red light and strike another vehicle in the intersection. During this exciting event, the bystander makes this declaration: "Oh, he ran the red light and I saw him do it last week too." The statement pertaining to the exciting event that he has just witnessed will be admissible, but his declaration as to past conduct of the driver will not fall under this exception to the Hearsay Rule, as it does not pertain to the exciting event which he is now perceiving.

Under the spontaneous statement exception to the Hearsay Rule, it is not required that the declarant be shown to have been competent, or to show that he is unavailable, or even to identify the declarant. It is only required that the existence of the declarant and the observations of the facts be shown by inferences from the circumstances surrounding the exciting event. *Example:* An officer on the witness stand testifies, "I heard someone yell, 'Stop, he's a robber.'" The fact that the officer does not know who made the statement does not bar its admissibility. If the identity of the declarant is now known, however, that fact adds to the weight of the declaration.

Declarations of Present Sense Impressions

A spontaneous declaration made by a person who is engaged in an act or witnessing an event, even if it is not exciting, as long as it describes or explains the observation, is admissible under the exception of declarations of present sense impressions. Again, as under spontaneous declarations, the untrustworthy element which usually bars hearsay is overcome, again because the statement is being made spontaneously and the words themselves are regarded as the best evidence of what the person is perceiving and experiencing. *Example:* A man is driving down the highway and utters, "I can't seem to turn the wheel." This may be offered in court to show his conduct in driving the car and that he presently sensed that he could not turn the wheel.

This exception, similar to the spontaneous declaration exception, also generally holds that the declaration must have been made while the person is perceiving the event or engaged in the conduct about which he is explaining, so as to insure the spontaneity and accuracy of the first impression. The new Federal Rules expand on this doctrine, however, and will admit statements made either while the declarant was perceiving an event or condition or immediately thereafter. *Example:* Under the Federal Rules, a witness who is making a report of a crime to a law enforcement officer after it has been committed and after the excitement has died down could have a statement admitted under this exception, where as it could not be a spontaneous declaration exception due to the time elapsed since the exciting event. As in the case of a spontaneous declaration, a person who is making a declaration of a present sense impression need not be shown to be unavailable or even be identified at court.

Most modern rules hold as admissible evidence the fact that a witness to a crime has made an out-of-court identification of the suspect after perceiving him at a police lineup. As long as the witness is present at the trial, he may be examined concerning that lineup. The rationale behind this rule is strictly the fact that the testimony that the victim was able to identify the suspect shortly after the incident is probably more reliable than a later courtroom identification. The accused is not denied his rights of cross-examination or confrontation under the U.S. Constitution, as the witness is now in court and can be subjected to cross-examination. Most jurisdictions that allow this type of identification in evidence hold that the evidence is not hearsay. On the other hand, there are still some jurisdictions that hold that it is hearsay but admissible as an exception. In addition, a number of jurisdictions hold that this type of prior identification is hearsay and will be treated as a prior consistent statement by the witness who is testifying. It will not be admitted unless the witness' credibility has been impeached, in which case the prior identification may be used to rehabilitate that witness.

Declarations of Physical Condition and State of Mind

Whenever a person's physical condition at a certain time is an issue, his spontaneous statements made at that time are admissible to prove the condition. In a battery trial, one of the issues is whether or not the victim was touched, and in some jurisdictions, whether it was a harmful or offensive touching. Any statements that the victim made at or right after the battery will be helpful to prove the crime. The statement made by the victim may be merely a moan or groan or an exclamation of present pain. Again, as with other exceptions to the Hearsay Rule, if the statement is being made concerning a now existing condition, then it is trustworthy, as there has not been time to pause and reflect or to fabricate a story. There are some jurisdictions, however, that will only allow under this exception declarations of state of mind and not other types of exclamations. However, the majority rule is to allow any statement concerning any bodily condition to come into evidence if it is to show an existing present condition.

A statement made by a person concerning a past bodily condition will not be admissible as evidence in the majority of the courts. The rationale, of course, is that the person has had time to pause and reflect upon his statements and to fabricate a story. In most cases, even statements made by a person who has been taken to a hospital or a doctor as to how he previously felt or where he hurt are not admissible, whereas if he was experiencing present body pains, they would be.

Family History Exception

The rationale underlying the family history exception is that most declarations made by a member of a family regarding matters of family history are usually trustworthy. Also, in most cases, other types of evidence are unavailable on these matters. The general rule allows hearsay evidence to establish a birth, a death, or a marriage if the event has been entered in a family bible or other type of ancient writing, or if the person making the declaration has been closely associated with the other person's family and is aware of the reputation of that family. Most courts will require that the declarant be related by blood or marriage to the person to whose history he is testifying. More modernly, however, any other person closely associated with that family will be allowed to testify concerning that declaration. The rules concerning unavailability must be followed, i.e., the common law rule, that the declarant be dead; the modern rules that the declarant deceased, be beyond the subpoena power of the court, has a privilege to exert, be seriously ill, or be insane. This exception is rarely applied in the jurisdictions which today have extensive recordation systems concerning births, deaths, and marriages as well as statutes making it mandatory that these family activities be so recorded (refer to the official records exception).

Ancient Document Exception

Most jurisdictions have an ancient document exception to the Hearsay Rule. Some jurisdictions hold that any document which is at least 30 years old and that appears to be fair on its face and has been in the proper custody and accepted as true by persons having an interest in a piece of property may be admitted as an exception to the Hearsay Rule. The new Federal Rules provide that a statement made in any document that is related to the purpose of the document and which has been in existence for 20 years or more and whose authenticity has been established may be admitted under this exception.

Learned Treatise Exception

Learned treatises are generally inadmissible as evidence even though they are written by recognized authorities in a specific field such as a medicine. The reason that the courts generally exclude learned treatises (in addition to the other hearsay objections) is the possibility that the present trial might be reduced to a conflict between textbook authors. The one exception generally recognized here is when an expert witness is giving his opinion has relied on an accepted textbook or treatise in his field. If the expert does so rely, he may then be cross-examined to point out that his opinion differs from that in the learned treatise upon which he stated he relied. A minority of states have liberalized the rules on learned treatises and recognize a hearsay exception for "historical works, books of science or art, and published maps or charts made by persons indifferent between the parties to the action." In the jurisdictions having these liberalized rules, the statutes have been very narrowly construed so as to exclude any controversial works, in particular, medical textbooks.

Affidavit Exception

As noted previously, an affidavit is an out-of-court statement made by a person who affirms, under the penalty of perjury, that the contents thereof are true. A few jurisdictions will permit the use of an affidavit in lieu of testimony. In those jurisdictions, an affidavit is generally only authorized to prove service of process, such as subpoena, or in a motion on a judgment being sought by the moving party.

Deposition Exception

As discussed, a deposition is a sworn statement given before a certified court reporter under oath, when both parties and their attorneys are present. The modern trend is to allow depositions which are utilized in the discovery process to be admitted as substantive evidence against the declarant.

THE HEARSAY RULE AND ITS EXCEPTIONS

The Hearsay Rule has as many as 42 exceptions in some jurisdictions in the United States. The student should acquaint himself with the evidence code or rules of evidence in his particular jurisdiction. This chapter only discusses the major exceptions that are more commonly used in the field of criminal investigation in the United States.

Summary

The Hearsay Rule, being so complex and having so many exceptions, is one of the most confusing rules in the field of evidence. The student should remember a simplified definition of hearsay: an out-of-court act, statement, or writing which is now being offered in court in an attempt to prove that what took place outside the courtroom is in fact true. The person who made the out-of-court declaration is not generally present in court or not generally able to testify in court. Therefore, another person is trying to testify as to the act, words, or writing which were prepared or done outside the courtroom.

Hearsay is generally not allowed in court due to its basic untrustworthiness in that the person was not under oath at the time he made the declaration or the writing, the judge and jury were unable to observe the person at the time he was making the writing, and in that the hearsay in a criminal prosecution does not afford the defendant his constitutional rights to confront and/or to cross-examine the actual person who made the writing or statement. If the out-of-court declaration or writing appears to have been made under circumstances that would lead a reasonable man to believe that it is a truthful statement, then most likely there will be an exception to the Hearsay Rule which would allow it to be admitted into evidence at a trial.

DISCUSSION QUESTIONS

1. What is the rationale behind the Hearsay Rule and the general rule on hearsay?
2. Distinguish between assertive conduct and nonassertive conduct?
3. What are the general reasons that hearsay is not allowed into court?
4. Distinguish between admissions and confessions and define the rules on admissibility under the exception in your jurisdiction.
5. State the rationale behind the dying declaration exception to the Hearsay Rule and the requirements for admitting a dying declaration.
6. What is a spontaneous declaration? What are the requirements for its admissibility in your jurisdiction?
7. Discuss the most commonly used exceptions to the Hearsay Rule in your jurisdiction.
8. Distinguish between the past recollection recorded exception to the Hearsay Rule and past memory revived rules.
9. What is the difference between the introduction of a business document record and a governmental agency record?
10. Explain when a confession of a coconspirator may be introduced against another member of the conspiracy.

BRIDGES v. STATE
Supreme Court of Wisconsin, 1945.
247 Wis. 350, 19 N.W.2d 529.

[The defendant was convicted of taking indecent liberties with Sharon Schunk, a child of seven. The identification of the defendant as the man who committed the crime depended largely upon whether the house and room to which Sharon was taken by the man who assaulted her was the house and room at 125 East Johnson Street in which the defendant resided.]

FRITZ, JUSTICE. . . . Defendant contends the court erred also in admitting testimony by police officers as to matters stated by Sharon in defendant's absence. He claims these statements were hearsay evidence and therefore were not admissible. . . .

There is testimony by police officers and also Mrs. Schunk as to statements which were made to them by Sharon on February 26 and 27, 1945, and also during the course of their subsequent investigations to ascertain the identity of the man who committed the offense and of the house and room in which it was committed. In those statements she spoke, as hereinbefore stated, of various matters and features which she remembered and which were descriptive of the exterior and surroundings of the house; and of the room and various articles and the location thereof therein. It is true that testimony as to such statements was hearsay and as such, inadmissible if the purpose for which it was received had been to establish thereby that there were in fact the stated articles in the room, or that they were located as stated, or that the exterior features or surroundings of the house were as Sharon stated. That, however, was not in this case the purpose for which the evidence as to those statements was admitted. It was admissible in so far as the fact that she had made the statements can be deemed to tend to show that at the time those statements were made—which was a month prior to the subsequent discovery of the room and house at 125 East Johnson Street—she had knowledge as to articles and descriptive features which, as was proven by other evidence, were in fact in or about that room and house. If in relation thereto Sharon made the statements as to which the officers and her mother testified, then those statements, although they were extra judicial utterances, constituted at least circumstantial evidence that she then had such knowledge; and that such state of mind on her part was acquired by reason of her having been in that room and house prior to making the statements. . . .

Judgement affirmed.

UNITED STATES v. BARBATI
United States District Court, E. D. New York, 1968.
284 F.Supp. 409.

WEINSTEIN, DISTRICT JUDGE. Having been convicted of passing a Ten Dollar counterfeit bill (18 U.S.C. § 472), defendant moves for a new trial on the ground that the verdict rested upon inadmissible hearsay evidence. See Fed.R.Crim.Proc. 33.

A barmaid and a policeman were the chief witnesses for the prosecution. Two counterfeit Ten Dollar bills had been given to the barmaid in payment for drinks by two men sitting together at the bar. She showed the bills to the manager who hailed a passing police car. Within a few minutes of the time the bills were passed, the policeman had arrested the defendant and his companion in the bar.

At the trial the notes were identified by the policeman as those the barmaid had turned over to him. She also identified the notes, relying upon the signature she had affixed at the time of the arrest.

While the barmaid testified that two men had given her the bills and that she had pointed out the men who gave them to her, she could not, at the time of the trial, recognize the defendant or his companion. Testimony by the policeman, however, established that the defendant was the one pointed out to him as soon as he was called into the bar and that, following identification and arrest, the defendant was taken to the stationhouse where he was fingerprinted and booked.

The critical testimony of the barmaid was as follows:

"A: ... they [the police] came and they asked me where I got the money, I showed them.
"Q: Did you point out the two men?
"A: Yes, I did.
"Q: What if anything happened after that?
"A: Well, they searched the men.
"Q: Did they search the two men that you pointed out?
"A: Yes.
"Q: Do you see any of them here now?
"A: I can't remember them.
"Q: You wouldn't remember what the men looked like now?
"A: No, it was so long ago.
"Q: What if anything did you do with the $10 notes you got from these men, after the police came?
"A: I was taken in the back with the money and the police and I signed those notes at that time. . . .
"Q: Those were the two notes that were given to you in the bar by the two men?
"A: Yes.
"Q: What if anything did the police do with the two men that you pointed out in your presence?
"A: They put their hands on the walls and they searched them for weapons, I guess and after that I don't know what happened to the two men, I suppose they took them away."

The policeman had no doubt that the defendant was the person identified in the bar by the barmaid. The barmaid had no doubt that the man she pointed out and who was arrested was the person who gave her one of the notes. It is not disputed that the person so identified was physically in police custody until after he was fingerprinted. No one suggests that the person fingerprinted is not the defendant who was tried in this case.

The evidence was highly probative and reliable. No more satisfactory proof was available. The apparatus for testing the credibility of these two key witnesses was available—the oath, cross-examination and presence at the trial where the jury could observe demeanor. . . .

There is more force to defendant's contention that the testimony with respect to the identification by the barmaid at the scene of the crime constituted hearsay. Whether made orally, or by pointing him out, the barmaid was then, the argument goes, making an extra-judicial testimonial statement. This out-of-court statement was being relied upon at the trial to prove its truth, namely, that the man she pointed out was the one who passed a counterfeit bill to her. Since its use required reliance upon all elements of her credibility—observation power, memory, truthfulness and ability to communicate—the barmaid's testimony, defendant concludes, involved serious hearsay dangers.

This analysis is not conclusive. Much that might be classified as hearsay is held not to be hearsay. Much that is hearsay is, nonetheless, admissible.

Courts have not hesitated to characterize as non-hearsay evidence whose use involves hearsay dangers when it is highly probative and necessary. Typical are those criminal cases involving conversations received over the telephone at suspected betting parlors. Use of the statements of the assumed betters requires reliance on the callers' credibility to conclude that they intended to place bets and had some reason to believe that they were calling a bookie. Despite the existence of hearsay dangers this evidence is admitted as non-hearsay. See, e. g., State v. Tolisano, 136 Conn. 210, 70 A.2d 118 (1949); Annot., 13 A.L.R.2d 1405 (1950).

The evidence in the case before us can be classified as non-hearsay without doing violence to theory by analogizing it to proof of identification of objects. In a sense the barmaid turned both the bills and the defendant over to the police. She signed the bills but not the defendant. He, however, was taken in hand and the chain of custody continued until he was brought to the police station where he was fingerprinted—the equivalent of being signed. Defendant's subsequent release on his own recognizance does not break the chain of identification-authentication since there is no doubt that he was the one fingerprinted. Analytically, the barmaid now testifies from present memory, "I was given a counterfeit bill by a man, X, and I saw the police arrest X." The policeman testifies from present memory, "the man we arrested, X, was the defendant." Neither of these statements is hearsay.

The analogy will become clearer by assuming the case of a blind man who feels a pickpocket taking his wallet. Assume he seizes the thief, holds him, and calls for help and that a policeman comes by immediately and arrests the man being held. No one would apply the hearsay rule to prevent the identification even though the blind man would not be able to recognize the defendant at the trial. His testimony plus that of the arresting officer would suffice.

Despite the fact that a respectable argument can be made that no hearsay is involved in the instant case, the Court prefers to proceed on the more realistic assumption that hearsay was relied upon by the prosecution. Both the policeman and the barmaid were permitted to buttress each other's testimony by testifying, in effect, that the barmaid said, at the time of arrest, "This is the man who gave me these bills."

The current clear tendency is for federal courts to ask whether admissibility will tend to aid in the search of truth. Hearsay is admitted when it is highly reliable, highly probative, and where the opponent has an adequate opportunity to attack it. See, e. g., United States v. Castellana, 349 F.2d 264, 276 (2d Cir. 1965), cert. denied, 383 U.S. 928, 86 S.Ct. 935, 15 L.Ed.2d 847 (1966) ("We are loath to reduce the corpus of hearsay rules to a straitjacketing, hypertechnical body of semantical slogans to be mechanically invoked regardless of the reliability of the proffered evidence"); Dallas County v. Commercial Union Assurance Co., 286 F.2d 388, 398 (5th Cir. 1961) (hearsay "admissible because it is necssary and trustworthy"); United States v. Schwartz, 252 F. Supp. 866 (E.D.Pa.1966). Cf. United States v. Nuccio, 373 F.2d 168, 174 (2d Cir.), cert. denied, 387 U.S. 906, 87 S.Ct. 1688, 18 L.Ed.2d 623 (1967) ("the notion that evidentiary use of anything emerging from the mouth is banned unless it comes within an exception to the hearsay rule is as fallacious as it is durable"). Use of necessary and trustworthy hearsay in a criminal case is typified by the *Schwartz* case where the court found that the prior writing of a witness who was "evasive, unresponsive and contradictory" and "apparently a very sick man," was more satisfactory than his testimony on the witness stand; his prior written statement was admitted even though it was hearsay. 252 F.Supp. at 868. The Court pointed out that there was a necessity for his testimony, that the "jurors had the opportunity to observe the witness' demeanor," and that there was a guarantee of trustworthiness in the way that the statement had been prepared. 252 F.Supp. at 868–869.

The matter before us is quite unlike those in the typical common law line of exclusionary cases where identification takes place sometime after the event. See, e. g., Leeper v. United States, 117 U.S. App.D.C. 310, 329 F.2d 878, cert. denied, 377 U.S. 959, 84 S.Ct. 1641, 12 L.Ed.2d 502 (1964) (concurrence) (identification in stationhouse without lineup); Poole v. United States, 97 F.2d 423 (9th Cir. 1938) (same); People v. Caserta, 19 N.Y.2d 18, 277 N.Y.S.2d 647, 224 N.E.2d 82 (1966) (identification of defendant from photograph to buttress credibility); People v. Jung Hing, 212 N.Y. 393, 106 N.E. 105 (1914) (identification at lineup to buttress credibility). The exclusion is warranted in these cases because the reliability of such identifications is uncertain. See generally P. Wall, Eye-Witness Identification in Criminal Cases (1965). Admitting evidence with such questionable probative force, when added to the hearsay dangers, substantially increases the possibility that it will be overvalued by the jury.

Hearsay evidence introduced against a defendant in criminal cases should, of course, be closely scrutinized and controlled by the court. The defendant does not have the same discovery opportunities in federal criminal cases as in civil cases; and we recognize the need to afford the criminal defendant the greatest possible protection against false convictions.

Nonetheless, hearsay should be admitted where, as here, there is no more satisfactory evidence available, probative force is high, and availability of the hearsay declarant for cross-examination makes the possibility of prejudice slight. The statement of the barmaid identifying defendant was spontaneously made within a few moments of the time the bill was passed and while defendant was still in his place at the bar. It is unlikely that her observation of the man who gave her the bill was mistaken—he was awaiting her return with his change. There was no time for lapse of memory. No reason for her to lie was suggested; in any event, any motive she might have had to falsify, would not have been substantially different at the trial than it was at the time of the event. The process of pointing out the defendant was so simple that an error in communication was improbable. The barmaid was unlikely to have remained silent if the police had collared an innocent bystander rather than the man she intended to point out.

Danger of the jury's overvaluing the hearsay was reduced by giving specific warning. The court pointed out that the patrolman's statement with respect to the barmaid's identification of the defendant was hearsay, that it was dangerous to rely upon it, and that the jury should evaluate it carefully. No inference with respect to the correctness of the identification arose from defendant's constitutionally protected silence. Cf. Di Carlo v. United States, 6 F.2d 364, 366 (2d Cir. 1925).

In view of the admissibility of the identification evidence pursuant to general principle, it is not necessary to decide whether it falls within a specific recognized hearsay exception. See, e. g., United States v. Nuccio, 373 F.2d 168, 172 (2d Cir. 1967), cert. denied, 387 U.S. 906, 87 S.Ct. 1688, 18 L.Ed.2d 623 (1967) ("When a witness specifically reaffirms the truth of something he has said elsewhere, the earlier statement constitutes evidence as fully as what he says on the stand"); United States v. Borelli, 336 F.2d 376, 391, n. 11 (2d Cir. 1964), cert. denied sub nom. Cinquegrano v. United States, 379 U.S. 960, 85 S.Ct. 647, 13 L.Ed.2d 555 (1965) (where a witness affirms truth of a prior statement it is evidence in chief); United States v. De Sisto, 329 F.2d 929 (2d Cir.), cert. denied, 377 U.S. 979, 84 S.Ct. 1885, 12 L.Ed.2d 747 (1964) (prior identification testimony by a witness before grand jury admissible); Uniform Rules of Evidence 1, 4(b); Morgan, A Suggested Classification of Utterances Admissible as Res Gestae, 31 Yale L.J. 229 (1922); III Wigmore, Evidence § 1018 at pp. 687–688 (3d ed. 1940) (no reason to classify as hearsay extrajudicial statement by person present at trial and subject to cross-examination).

We should not blind ourselves to what the law has learned by bitter experience—identification in court is frequently an almost worthless formality. See, e.g., authorities collected in United States v. Wade, 388 U.S. 218, 228–229, nn. 6–7, 87 S.Ct. 1926, 18 L.Ed.2d 1149 (1967), particularly P. Wall, Eye-Witness Identification in Criminal Cases, 26–27 (1965). By the time of trial positions have often become so fixed and memory so attenuated and distorted by subsequent events that witnesses seldom make identifications on the basis of their raw recollection of the original event. Their apparent certitude is often misleading and not infrequently less reliable than earlier reactions. We cannot permit the mechanical and unreasoned application of the hearsay rule to deny evidence vital to our search for the truth.

The motion is denied.

So ordered.

CALIFORNIA v. GREEN
Supreme Court of the United States, 1970.
399 U.S. 149, 90 S.Ct. 1930, 26 L.Ed.2d 489.

Mr. Justice White delivered the opinion of the Court. Section 1235 of the California Evidence Code, effective as of January 1, 1967, provides that "evidence of a statement made by a witness is not made inadmissible by the hearsay rule if the statement is inconsistent with his testimony at the hearing and is offered in compliance with Section 770." In People v. Johnson, 68 Cal.2d 646, 68 Cal. Rptr. 599, 441 P.2d 111 (1968), cert. denied,

393 U.S. 1051, 89 S.Ct. 679, 21 L.Ed.2d 693 (1969), the California Supreme Court held that prior statements of a witness which were not subject to cross-examination when originally made, could not be introduced under this section to prove the charges against a defendant without violating the defendant's right of confrontation guaranteed by the Sixth Amendment and made applicable to the States by the Fourteenth Amendment. In the case now before us the California Supreme Court applied the same ban to a prior statement of a witness made at a preliminary hearing, under oath and subject to full cross-examination by an adequately counseled defendant. We cannot agree with the California court for two reasons, one of which involves rejection of the holding in People v. Johnson.

I. In January 1967, one Melvin Porter, a 16-year-old minor, was arrested for selling marihuana to an undercover police officer. Four days after his arrest, while in the custody of juvenile authorities, Porter named respondent Green as his supplier. As recounted later by one Officer Wade, Porter claimed that Green had called him earlier that month, had asked him to sell some "stuff" or "grass," and had that same afternoon personally delivered a shopping bag containing 29 "baggies" of marihuana. It was from this supply that Porter had made his sale to the undercover officer. A week later, Porter testified at respondent's preliminary hearing. He again named respondent as his supplier, although he now claimed that instead of personally delivering the marihuana, Green had showed him where to pick up the shopping bag, hidden in the bushes at Green's parents' house. Porter's story at the preliminary hearing was subjected to extensive cross-examination by respondent's counsel— the same counsel who represented respondent at his subsequent trial. At the conclusion of the hearing, respondent was charged with furnishing marihuana to a minor in violation of California law.

Respondent's trial took place some two months later before a court sitting without a jury. The State's chief witness was again young Porter. But this time Porter, in the words of the California Supreme Court, proved to be "markedly evasive and uncooperative on the stand." People v. Green, 70 Cal.2d 654, 657, 75 Cal.Rptr. 782, 783, 451 P.2d 422, 423 (1969). He testified that respondent had called him in January 1967, and asked him to sell some unidentified "stuff." He admitted obtaining shortly thereafter 29 plastic "baggies" of marihuana, some of which he sold. But when pressed as to whether respondent had been his supplier, Porter claimed that he was uncertain how he obtained the marihuana, primarily because he was at the time on "acid" (LSD), which he had taken 20 minutes before respondent phoned. Porter claimed that he was unable to remember the events which followed the phone call, and that the drugs he had taken prevented his distinguishing fact from fantasy. . . .

At various points during Porter's direct examination, the prosecutor read excerpts from Porter's preliminary hearing testimony. This evidence was admitted under § 1235 for the truth of the matter contained therein. With his memory "refreshed" by his preliminary hearing testimony, Porter "guessed" that he had indeed obtained the marihuana from the backyard of respondent's parents' home, and had given the money from its sale to respondent. On cross-examination, however, Porter indicated that it was his memory of the preliminary testimony which was "mostly" refreshed, rather than his memory of the events themselves, and he was still unsure of the actual episode. . . . Later in the trial, Officer Wade testified, relating Porter's earlier statement that respondent had personally delivered the marihuana. This statement was also admitted as substantive evidence. Porter admitted making the statement, . . . and insisted that he had been telling the truth as he then believed it both to Officer Wade and at the preliminary hearing; but he insisted that he was also telling the truth now in claiming inability to remember the actual events.

Respondent was convicted. The District Court of Appeal reversed, holding that the use of Porter's prior statements for the truth of the matter asserted therein, denied respondent his right of confrontation under the California Supreme Court's recent decision in People v. Johnson, supra. The California Supreme Court affirmed, finding itself "impelled" by recent decisions of this Court to hold § 1235 unconstitutional insofar as it permitted the substantive use of prior inconsistent statements of a witness, even though the statements were cross-examined at a prior hearing. We granted the State's petition for certiorari, 396 U.S. 1001, 90 S.Ct. 547, 24 L.Ed.2d 492 (1970).

II. The California Supreme Court construed the Confrontation Clause of the Sixth Amendment to require the exclusion of Porter's prior testimony offered in evidence to prove the State's case against Green because in the court's view, neither the right to cross-examine Porter at the trial concerning his current and prior testimony, nor the opportunity to cross-examine Porter at the preliminary hearing satisfied the commands of the Confrontation Clause. We think the California court was wrong on both counts.

Positing that this case posed an instance of a witness who gave trial testimony inconsistent with his prior, out-of-court statements, the California court, on the authority of its decision in People v. Johnson, supra, held that belated cross-examination before the trial court, "is not an adequate substitute for the right to cross-examination contemporaneous with the original testimony before a different tribunal." People v. Green, supra, 70 Cal.2d at 659, 75 Cal.Rptr., at 785, 451 P.2d, at 425. We disagree.

Section 1235 of the California Evidence Code represents a considered choice by the California legislature between two opposing positions concerning the extent to which a witness' prior statements may be introduced at trial without violating hearsay rules of evidence. The orthodox view, adopted in most jurisdictions, has been that the out-of-court statements are inadmissible for the usual reasons that have led to the exclusion of hearsay statements: the statement may not have been made under oath; the declarant may not have been subjected to cross-examination when he made the statement; and the jury cannot observe the declarant's demeanor at the time he made the statement. Accordingly, under this view, the statement may not be offered to show the truth of the matters asserted herein, but can be introduced under appropriate limiting instructions to impeach the credibility of the witness who has changed his story at trial.

In contrast, the minority view adopted in some jurisdictions and supported by most legal commentators and by recent proposals to codify the law of evidence would permit the substantive use of prior inconsistent statements on the theory that the usual dangers of hearsay are largely nonexistent where the witness testifies at trial. "The whole purpose of the Hearsay rule has been already satisfied [because] the witness is present and subject to cross-examination [and] [t]here is ample opportunity to test him as to the basis for his former statement."

Our task in this case is not to decide which of these positions purely as a matter of the law of evidence, is the sounder. The issue before us is the considerably narrower one of whether a defendant's constitutional right "to be confronted with the witnesses against him" is necessarily inconsistent with a State's decision to change its hearsay rules to reflect the minority view described above. While it may readily be conceded that hearsay rules and the Confrontation Clause are generally designed to protect similar values, it is quite a different thing to suggest that the overlap is complete and that the Confrontation Clause is nothing more nor less than a codification of the rules of hearsay and their exceptions as they existed historically at common law. Our decisions have never established such a congruence; indeed, we have more than once found a violation of confrontation values even though the statements in issue were admitted under an arguably recognized hearsay exception. See Barber v. Page, 390 U.S. 719, 88 S.Ct. 1318, 20 L.Ed.2d 255 (1968); Pointer v. Texas, 380 U.S. 400, 85 S.Ct. 1065, 13 L.Ed.2d 923 (1965). The converse is equally true; merely because evidence is admitted in violation of a long-established hearsay rule does not lead to the automatic conclusion that confrontation rights have been denied.

Given the similarity of the values protected, however, the modification of a State's hearsay rules to create new exceptions for the admission of evidence against a defendant, will often raise questions of compatibility with the defendant's constitutional right to confrontation. Such questions require attention to the reasons for, and the basic scope of, the protections offered by the Confrontation Clause.

The origin and development of the hearsay rules and of the Confrontation Clause have been traced by others and need not be recounted in detail here. It is sufficient to note that the particular vice which gave impetus to the confrontation claim was the practice of trying defendants on "evidence" which consisted solely of *ex parte* affidavits or depositions secured by the examining magistrates, thus denying the defendant the opportunity to challenge his accuser in a face-to-face encounter in front of the trier of fact. Prosecuting attorneys "would frequently allege matters which the prisoner denied and called upon them to prove. The proof was usually given by reading depositions, confessions of accomplices, letters, and the like; and this occasioned frequent demands by the prisoner to have his 'accusers,' *i. e.,* the witnesses against him, brought before him face to face. . . .

But objections occasioned by this practice appear primarily to have been aimed at the failure to call the witness to confront personally the defendant at his trial. So far as appears, in claiming confrontation rights no objection was made against receiving a witness' out-of-court depositions or statements, so long as the witness was present at trial to repeat his story and to explain or repudiate any conflicting prior stories before the trier of fact.

Our own decisions seem to have recognized at an early date that it is the literal right to "confront" the witness at the time of trial which forms the core of the values furthered by the Confrontation Clause:

"The primary object of the constitutional provision in question was to prevent depositions or *ex parte* affidavits, such as were sometimes admitted in civil cases, being used against the prisoner in lieu of a personal examination and cross-examination of the witness, in which the accused has an opportunity, not only of testing the recollection and sifting the conscience of the witness, but of compelling him to stand face to face with the jury in order that they may look at him, and judge by his demeanor upon the stand and the manner in which he gives his testimony whether he is worthy of belief." Mattox v. United States, 156 U.S. 237, 242–243, 15 S.Ct. 337, 339, 39 L.Ed. 409 (1895).

Viewed historically, then, there is good reason to conclude that the Confrontation Clause is not violated by admitting a declarant's out-of-court statements, as long the declarant is testifying as a witness and subject to full and effective cross-examination.

This conclusion is supported by comparing the purposes of confrontation with the alleged dangers in admitting an out-of-court statement. Confrontation: (1) insures that the witness will give his statements under oath — thus impressing him with the seriousness of the matter and guarding against the lie by the possibility of a penalty for perjury; (2) forces the witness to submit to cross-examination, the "greatest legal engine ever invented for the discovery of truth"; (3) permits the jury that is to decide the defendant's fate to observe the demeanor of the witness in making his statement, thus aiding the jury in assessing his credibility.

It is, of course, true that the out-of-court statement may have been made under circumstances subject to none of these protections. But if the declarant is present and testifying at trial, the out-of-court statement for all practical purposes regains most of the lost protections. If the witness admits the prior statement is his, or if there is other evidence to show the statement is his, the danger of faulty reproduction is negligible and the jury can be confident that it has before it two conflicting statements by the same witness. Thus, as far as the oath is concerned, the witness must now affirm, deny, or qualify the truth of the prior statement under the penalty of perjury; indeed, the very fact that the prior statement was not given under a similar circumstance may become the witness' explanation for its inaccuracy—an explantion a jury may be expected to understand and take into account in deciding which, if either, of the statements represents the truth.

Second, the inability to cross-examine the witness at the time he made his prior statement cannot easily be shown to be of crucial significance as long as the defendant is assured of full and effective cross-examination at the time of trial. The most successful cross-examination at the time the prior statement was made could hardly hope to accomplish more than has already been accomplished by the fact that the witness is now telling a different, inconsistent story, and—in this case—one that is favorable to the defendant. We cannot share the California Supreme Court's view that belated cross-examination can never serve as a constitutionally adequate substitute for cross-examination contemporaneous with the original statement. The main danger in substituting subsequent for timely cross-examination seems to lie in the possibility that the witness' "[f]alse testimony is apt to harden and become unyielding to the blows of truth in proportion as the witness has opportunity for reconsideration and influence by the suggestions of others, whose interest may be, and often is, to maintain falsehood rather than truth." State v. Saporen, 205 Minn. 358, 362, 285 N.W. 898, 901 (1939). That danger, however, disappears when the witness has changed his testimony so that, far from "hardening," his prior statement has softened to the point where he now repudiates it.

The defendant's task in cross-examination is, of course, no longer identical to the task that he would have faced if the witness had not changed his story and hence had to be examined as a "hostile" witness giving evidence for the prosecution. This difference, however, far from lessening, may actually enhance the defendant's ability to attack the prior statement. For the witness, favorable to the defendant, should be more than willing to give the usual suggested explanations for the inaccuracy of his prior statement, such as faulty perception or undue haste in recounting the event. Under such circumstances, the defendant is not likely to be hampered in effectively attacking the prior statement, solely because his attack comes later in time.

Similar reasons lead us to discount as a constitutional matter the fact that the jury at trial is foreclosed from viewing the declarant's demeanor when he first made his out-of-court statement. The witness who now relates a different story about the events in question must necessarily assume a position as to the truth value of his prior statement, thus giving the jury a chance to observe and evaluate his demeanor as he either disavows or qualifies his earlier statement. The jury is alerted by the inconsistency in the stories, and its attention is sharply focused on determining either that one of the stories reflects the truth or that the witness who has apparently lied once, is simply too lacking in credibility to warrant believing either story. The defendant's confrontation rights are not violated, even though some demeanor evidence that would have been relevant in resolving this credibility issue is forever lost.

It may be true that a jury would be in a better position to evaluate the truth of the prior statement if it could somehow be whisked magically back in time to witness a gruelling cross-examination of the declarant as he first gives his statement. But the question as we see it must be not whether one can somehow imagine the jury in "a better position," but whether subsequent cross-examination at the defendant's trial will still afford the trier of fact a satisfactory basis for evaluating the truth of the prior statement. On that issue, neither evidence nor reason convinces us that contemporaneous cross-examination before the ultimate trier of fact is so much more effective than subsequent examination that it must be made the touchstone of the Confrontation Clause.

Finally, we note that none of our decisions interpreting the Confrontation Clause requires excluding the out-of-court statements of a witness who is available and testifying at trial. The concern of most of our cases has been focused on precisely the opposite situation — situations where statements have been admitted in the absence of the declarant and without any chance to cross-examine him at trial. These situations have arisen through application of a number of traditional "exceptions" to the hearsay rule, which permit the introduction of evidence despite the absence of the declarant usually on the theory that the evidence possesses other indicia of "reliability" and is incapable of being admitted, despite good-faith efforts of the State, in any way that will secure confrontation with the declarant.

Such exceptions, dispensing altogether with the literal right to "confrontation" and cross-examination, have been subjected on several occasions to careful scrutiny by this Court. In Pointer v. Texas, 380 U.S. 400, 85 S.Ct. 1065 (1965), for example, the State introduced at defendant's trial the transcript of a crucial witness' testimony from a prior preliminary hearing. The witness himself, one Phillips, had left the jurisdiction and did not appear at trial. "Because the transcript of Phillips' statement offered against petitioner at his trial had not been taken at a time and under circumstances affording petitioner through counsel an adequate opportunity to cross-examine Phillips," 380 U.S., at 407, 85 S.Ct., at 1070, we held that its introduction violated the defendant's confrontation rights. Similarly, in Barber v. Page, 390 U.S. 719 88 S.Ct. 1318, the State introduced the preliminary hearing testimony of an absent witness, incarcerated in a federal prison, under an "unavailability" exception to its hearsay rules. We held that that exception would not justify the denial of confrontation where the State had not made a good-faith effort to obtain the presence of the allegedly "unavailable" witness.

We have no occasion in the present case to map out a theory of the Confrontation Clause that would determine the validity of all such hearsay "exceptions" permitting the introduction of an absent declarant's statements. For where the declarant is not absent, but is present to testify and to submit to cross-examination, our cases, if anything, support the conclusion that the admission of his out-of-court statements does not create a confrontation problem. Thus, in Douglas v. Alabama, 380 U.S. 415, 85 S.Ct. 1074, 13 L.Ed.2d 934 (1965), decided on the same day as *Pointer*, we reversed a conviction in which the prosecution read into the record an alleged confession of the defendant's supposed accomplice, Loyd, who refused to testify on self-incrimination grounds. The confrontation problem arose precisely because Loyd could not be cross-examined as to his prior statement; had such cross-examination taken place, the opinion strongly suggests that the confrontation problem would have been nonexistent:

"In the circumstances of this case, petitioner's inability to cross-examine Loyd as to the alleged confession plainly denied him the right of cross-examination secured by the Confrontation Clause. . . . Loyd could not be cross-examined on a statement imputed to but not admitted by him. . . . [S]ince [the State's] evidence tended to show only that Loyd made the confession, cross-examination . . . as to its genuineness could not substitute for cross-examination of Loyd to test the truth of the statement itself. . . .

"Hence, effective confrontation of Loyd was possible only if Loyd affirmed the statement as his." 380 U.S., at 419–420, 85 S.Ct., at 1077.

Again, in Bruton v. United States, 391 U.S. 123, 88 S.Ct. 1620, 20 L.Ed.2d 476 (1968), the Court found a violation of confrontation rights in the admission of a codefendant's confession, implicating Bruton, where the co-defendant did not take the stand. The Court again emphasized that the error arose because the declarant "does not testify and cannot be tested by cross-examination," 391 U.S., at 136, 88 S.Ct., at 1628, suggesting that no confrontation problem would have existed if Bruton had been able to cross-examine his co-defendant. Cf. Harrington v. California, 395 U.S. 250, 252–253, 89 S.Ct. 1726, 1727–1728, 23 L.Ed.2d 284 (1969). Indeed, Bruton's refusal to regard limiting instructions as capable of curing the error, suggests that there is little difference as far as the Constitution is concerned between permitting prior inconsistent statements to be used only for impeachment purposes, and permitting them to be used for substantive purposes as well.

We find nothing, then, in either the history or the purposes of the Confrontation Clause, or in the prior decisions of this Court, that compels the conclusion reached by the California Supreme Court concerning the validity of California's § 1235. Contrary to the judgment of that court, the Confrontation Clause does not require excluding from evidence the prior statements of a witness who concedes making the statements, and who may be asked to defend or otherwise explain the inconsistency between his prior and his present version of the events in question, thus opening himself to full cross-examination at trial as to both stories.

III. We also think that Porter's preliminary hearing testimony was admissible as far as the Constitution is concerned wholly apart from the question of whether respondent had an effective opportunity for confrontation at the subsequent trial. For Porter's statement at the preliminary hearing had already been given under circumstances closely approximating those that surround the typical trial. Porter was under oath; respondent was represented by counsel — the same counsel in fact who later represented him at the trial; respondent had every opportunity to cross-examine Porter as to his statement; and the proceedings were conducted before a judicial tribunal, equipped to provide a judicial record of the hearings. Under these circumstances, Porter's statement would, we think, have been admissible at trial even in Porter's absence if Porter had been actually unavailable, despite good-faith efforts of the State to produce him. That being the case, we do not think a different result should follow where the witness is actually produced.

This Court long ago held that admitting the prior testimony of an unavailable witness does not violate the Confrontation Clause. Mattox v. United States, 156 U.S. 237, 15 S.Ct. 337, 39 L.Ed. 409 (1895). That case involved testimony given at the defendant's first trial by a witness who had died by the time of the second trial, but we do not find the instant preliminary hearing significantly different from an actual trial to warrant distinguishing the two cases for purposes of the Confrontation Clause. Indeed, we indicated as much in Pointer v. Texas, 380 U.S. 400, 407, 85 S.Ct. 1065, 1069 (1965), where we noted that "the case before us would be quite a different one had Phillips' statement been taken at a full-fledged hearing at which petitioner had been represented by counsel who had been given a complete and adequate opportunity to cross examine." And in Barber v. Page, 390 U.S. 719, 725–726, 88 S.Ct. 1318, 1322 (1968), although noting that the preliminary hearing is ordinarily a less searching exploration into the merits of a case than a trial, we recognized that "there may be some justification for holding that the opportunity for cross-examination of a witness at a preliminary hearing satisfies demand of the confrontation clause where the witness is shown to be actually unavailable. . . ." In the present case respondent's counsel does not appear to have been significantly limited in any way in the scope or nature of his cross-examination of the witness Porter at the preliminary hearing. If Porter had died or was otherwise unavailable, the Confrontation Clause would have been violated by admitting his testimony given at the preliminary hearing — the right of cross-examination then afforded provides substantial compliance with the purposes behind the confrontation requirement, as long as the declarant's inability to give live testimony is in no way the fault of the State. Compare Barber v. Page, supra, with Motes v. United States, 178 U.S. 458, 20 S.Ct. 993, 44 L.Ed. 1150 (1900).

But nothing in Barber v. Page or in other cases in this Court indicates that a different result must follow where the State produces the declarant and swears him as a witness at the trial. It may be that the rules of evidence applicable in state or federal courts would restrict resort to prior sworn testimony where the declarant is present at the trial. But as a constitutional matter, it is untenable to construe the Confrontation Clause to permit the use of prior testimony to prove the State's case where the declarant never appears, but to bar that testimony where the declarant is present at the trial, exposed to the defendant and the trier of fact, and subject to cross-examination. As in the case where the witness is physically unproducible, the State here has made every effort to introduce its evidence through the live testimony of the witness; it produced Porter at trial, swore him as a witness, and tendered him for cross-examination. Whether Porter then testified in a manner consistent or inconsistent with his preliminary hearing testimony, claimed a loss of memory, claimed his privilege against compulsory self-incrimination, or simply refused to answer, nothing in the Confrontation Clause prohibited the State from also relying on his prior testimony to prove its case against Green.

IV. There is a narrow question lurking in this case concerning the admissibility of Porter's statements to Officer Wade. In the typical case to which the California court addressed itself, the witness at trial gives a version of the ultimate events different from that given on a prior occasion. In such a case, as our holding in Part II makes clear, we find little reason to distinguish among prior inconsistent statements on the basis of the circumstances under which the prior statements were given. The subsequent opportunity for cross-examination at trial with respect to both present and past versions of the event, is adequate to make equally admissible, as far as the Confrontation Clause is concerned, both the casual, off-hand remark to a stranger, and the carefully recorded testimony at a prior hearing. Here, however, Porter claimed at trial he could not remember the events which occurred after respondent telephoned him and hence failed to give any current version of the more important events described in his earlier statement.

Whether Porter's apparent lapse of memory so affected Green's right to cross-examine as to make a critical difference in the application of the Confrontation Clause in this case is an issue which is not ripe for decision at this juncture. The state court did not focus on this precise question, which was irrelevant given its broader and erroneous premise that an out-of-court statement of a witness is inadmissible as substantive evidence, whatever the nature of the opportunity to cross-examine at the trial. Nor has either party addressed itself to the question. Its resolution depends much upon the unique facts in this record, and we are reluctant to proceed without the state court's views of what the record actually discloses relevant to this particular issue. What is more, since we hold that the admission of Porter's preliminary hearing testimony is not barred by the Sixth Amendment despite his apparent lapse of memory, the reception into evidence of the Porter statement to Officer Wade may pose a harmless-error question which is more appropriately resolved by the California courts in the first instance. Similarly, faced on remand with our decision that § 1235 is not invalid on its face, the California Supreme Court may choose to dispose of the case on other grounds raised by Green but not passed upon by that court; for example, because of its ruling on § 1235, the California court deliberately put aside the issue of the sufficiency of the evidence to sustain conviction.

We therefore vacate the judgment of the California Supreme Court and remand the case to that court for further proceedings not inconsistent with this opinion. It is so ordered.

Judgment of California Supreme Court vacated and case remanded.

MR. JUSTICE BLACKMUN took no part in the consideration or decision of this case.

MR. CHIEF JUSTICE BURGER, concurring.

I join fully in MR. JUSTICE WHITE'S opinion for the Court. I add this comment only to emphasize the importance of allowing the States to experiment and innovate, especially in the area of criminal justice. If new standards and procedures are tried in one State their success or failure will be a guide to others and to the Congress.

Here, California, by statute, recently adopted a rule of evidence that, as MR. JUSTICE WHITE observes, has long been advocated by leading commentators. Two other States, Kentucky and Wisconsin, have within the past year embraced similar doctrines by judicial decisions. None of these States have yet had sufficient experience with their innovations to determine whether or not the modification is sound, wise, and workable. The California Supreme Court, in striking down the California statute, seems to have done so in the mistaken belief that this Court, though the Confrontation Clause, has imposed rigid limits on the States in this area. As the Court's opinion indicates, that conclusion is erroneous. The California statute meets the tests of the Sixth and Fourteenth Amendments, and accordingly, the wisdom of the statute is properly left to the State of California; other jurisdictions will undoubtedly watch the experiment with interest. The circumstances of this case demonstrate again that neither the Constitution as originally drafted, nor any amendment, nor indeed any need, dictates that we must have absolute uniformity in the criminal law in all the States. Federal authority was never intended to be a "ramrod" to compel conformity to nonconstitutional standards.

MR. JUSTICE HARLAN, concurring.

The precise holding of the Court today is that the Confrontation Clause of the Sixth Amendment does not preclude the introduction of an out-of-court declaration, taken under oath and subject to cross-examination, to prove the truth of the matters asserted therein, when the declarant is available for being a witness at trial. With this I agree.

The California decision that we today reverse demonstrates, however, the need to approach this case more broadly than the Court has seen fit to do, and to confront squarely the Confrontation Clause because the holding of the California Supreme Court is the result of an understandable misconception, as I see things, of numerous decisions of this Court, old and recent, that have indiscriminately equated "confrontation" with "cross-examination."...

If "confrontation" is to be equated with the right to cross-examine, it would transplant the ganglia of hearsay rules and their exceptions into the body of constitutional protections. The stultifying effect of such a course upon this aspect of the law of evidence in both state and federal systems need hardly be labored, and it is good that the Court today, as I read its opinion, firmly eschews that course.

Since, in my opinion, this state decision imperatively demonstrates the need for taking a fresh look at the constitutional concept of "confrontation," I do not think that *stare decisis* should be allowed to stand in the way, albeit that the presently controlling cases are of recent vintage. As the Court's opinion suggests, the Confrontation Clause comes to us on faded parchment. History seems to give us very little insight into the intended scope of the Sixth Amendment Confrontation Clause. Commentators have been prone to slide too easily from confrontation to cross-examination.

Against this amorphous backdrop I reach two conclusions. First, the Confrontation Clause of the Sixth Amendment reaches no farther than to require the prosecution to *produce* any *available* witness whose declarations it seeks to use in a criminal trial. Second, even were this conclusion deemed untenable as a matter of Sixth Amendment law, it is surely agreeable to Fourteenth Amendment "due process," which, in my view, is the constitutional framework in which state cases of this kind should be judged. For it could scarcely be suggested that the Fourteenth Amendment takes under its umbrella all common-law hearsay rules and their exceptions....

Mr. Justice Brennan, dissenting.

... the facts of this case present two questions regarding the application of California Evidence Code, § 1235: first, whether the Confrontation Clause permits a witness' extra-judicial statement to be admitted at trial as substantive evidence when the witness claims to be unable to remember the events with which his prior statement dealt, and, second, whether the clause permits a witness' preliminary hearing statement, made under oath and subject to cross-examination, to be introduced at trial as substantive evidence when the witness claims to be unable to remember the events with which the statement dealt. In my view, neither statement can be introduced without unconstitutionally restricting the right of the accused to challenge incriminating evidence in the presence of the fact-finder who will determine his guilt or innocence....

BARBER v. PAGE
Supreme Court of the United States, 1968.
390 U.S. 719, S.Ct. 1318, 20 L.Ed.2d 255.

Mr. Justice Marshall delivered the opinion of the Court. The question presented is whether petitioner was deprived of his Sixth and Fourteenth Amendment right to be confronted with the witnesses against him at his trial in Oklahoma for armed robbery, at which the principal evidence against him consisted of the reading of a transcript of the preliminary hearing testimony of a witness who at the time of trial was incarcerated in a federal prison in Texas.

Petitioner and one Woods were jointly charged with the robbery, and at the preliminary hearing were represented by the same retained counsel, a Mr. Parks. During the course of the hearing, Woods agreed to waive his privilege against self-incrimination. Parks then withdrew as Woods' attorney but continued to represent petitioner. Thereupon Woods proceeded to give testimony that incriminated petitioner. Parks did not cross-examine Woods, although an attorney for another codefendant did.

By the time petitioner was brought to trial some seven months later, Woods was incarcerated in a federal penitentiary in Texarkana, Texas, about 225 miles from the trial court in Oklahoma. The State proposed to introduce against petitioner the transcript of Woods' testimony at the preliminary hearing on the ground that Woods was unavailable to testify because he was outside the jurisdiction. Petitioner objected to that course on the ground that it would deprive him of his right to be confronted with the witnesses against him. His objection was overruled and the transcript was admitted and read to the jury, which found him guilty. On appeal the Oklahoma Court of Criminal Appeals affirmed his conviction. Barber v. State, 388 P.2d 320 (Okl.Cr.App.1963).

Petitioner then sought federal habeas corpus, claiming that the use of the transcript of Woods' testimony in his state trial deprived him of his federal constitutional right to confrontation in violaion of the Sixth and Fourteenth Amendments. His contention was rejected by the District Court and on appeal the Court of Appeals for the Tenth Circuit, one judge dissenting, affirmed. 381 F.2d 479 (1966). We granted certiorari, 389 U.S. 819, 88 S.Ct. 115, 19 L.Ed.2d 69 (1967), to consider petitioner's denial of confrontation claim, and we reverse.

Many years ago this Court stated that "[t]he primary object of the [Confrontation Clause of the Sixth Amendment] ... was to prevent depositions or *ex parte* affidavits ... being used against the prisoner in lieu of a personal examination and cross-examination of the witness in which the accused has an opportunity, not only of testing the recollection and sifting the conscience of the witness, but of compelling him to stand face to face with the jury in order that they may look at him, and judge by his demeanor upon the stand and the manner in which he gives his testimony whether he is worthy of belief." Mattox v. United States, 156 U.S. 237, 242–243, 15 S.Ct. 337, 339, 39 L.Ed. 409 (1895). More recently, in holding the Sixth Amendment right of confrontation applicable to the States through the Fourteenth Amendment, this Court said, "There are few subjects, perhaps, upon which this Court and other courts have been more nearly unanimous than in their expressions of belief that the right of confrontation and cross-examination is an essential and fundamental requirement for the kind of fair trial which is this country's constitutional goal." Pointer v. State of Texas, 380 U.S. 400, 405, 85 S.Ct. 1065, 1068, 13 L.Ed.2d 923 (1965). See also Douglas v. State of Alabama, 380 U.S. 415, 85 S.Ct. 1074, 13 L.Ed.2d 934 (1965).

It is true that there has traditionally been an exception to the confrontation requirement where a witness is unavailable and has given testimony at previous judicial proceedings against the same defendant which was subject to cross-examination by that defendant. E. g., Mattox v. United States, supra (witnesses who testified in original trial died prior to the second trial). This exception has been explained as arising from necessity and has been justified on the ground that the right of cross-examination initially afforded provides substantial compliance with the purposes behind the confrontation requirement. See 5 Wigmore Evidence § § 1395–1396, 1402 (3d ed. 1940); C. McCormick, Evidence § § 231, 234 (1954).

Here the State argues that the introduction of the transcript is within that exception on the grounds that Woods was outside the jurisdiction and therefore "unavailable" at the time of trial, and that the right of cross-examination was afforded petitioner at the preliminary hearing, although not utilized then by him. For the purpose of this decision we shall assume that petitioner made a valid waiver of his right to cross-examine Woods at the preliminary hearing, although such an assumption seems open to considerable question under the circumstances.

We start with the fact that the State made absolutely no effort to obtain the presence of Woods at trial other than to ascertain that he was in a federal prison outside Oklahoma. It must be acknowledged that various courts and commentators have therefore assumed that the mere absence of a witness from the jurisdiction was sufficient ground for dispensing with confrontation on the theory that "it is impossible to compel his attendance, because the process of the trial Court is of no force without the jurisdiction, and the party desiring his testimony is therefore helpless." 5 Wigmore, Evidence § 1404 (3d ed. 1940)).

Whatever may have been the accuracy of that theory at one time, it is clear that at the present time increased cooperation between the States themselves and between the States and the Federal Government has largely deprived it of any continuing validity in the criminal law.

For example, in the case of a prospective witness currently in federal custody, 28 U.S.C. § 2241 (c) (5) gives federal courts the power to issue writs of habeas corpus *ad testificandum* at the request of state prosecutorial authorities. See Gilmore v. United States, 129 F. 2d 199, 202 (C.A. 10th Cir. 1942); United States v. McGaha, 205 F. Supp. 949 (D.C.E.D.Tenn.1962). In addition, it is the policy of the United States Bureau of Prisons to permit federal prisoners to testify in state court criminal proceedings pursuant to writs of habeas corpus *ad testificandum* issued out of state courts. Cf. Lawrence v. Willingham, 373 F.2d 731 (C.A. 10th Cir. 1967) (habeas corpus *ad prosequendum*).

In this case the state authorities made no effort to avail themselves of either of the above alternative means of seeking to secure Woods' presence at petitioner's trial. The Court of Appeals majority appears to have reasoned that because the State would have had to request an exercise of discretion on the part of federal authorities, it was under no obligation to make any such request. Yet as Judge Aldrich, sitting by designation, pointed out in dissent below, "the possibility of a refusal is not the equivalent of asking and receiving a rebuff." 381 F.2d, at 481. In short, a witness is not "unavailable" for purposes of the foregoing exception to the confrontation requirement unless the prosecutorial authorities have made a good-faith effort to obain his presence at trial. The State made no such effort here, and, so far as this record reveals, the sole reason why Woods was not present to testify in person was because the State did not attempt to seek his presence. The right of confrontation may not be dispensed with so lightly.

The State argues that petitioner waived his right to confront Woods at trial by not cross-examining him at the preliminary hearing. That contention is untenable. Not only was petitioner unaware that Woods would be in a federal prison at the time of his trial, but he was also unaware that, even assuming Woods' incarceration, the State would make no effort to produce Woods at trial. To suggest that failure to cross-examine in such circumstances constitutes a waiver of the right of confrontation at a subsequent trial hardly comports with this Court's definition of a waiver as "an intentional relinquishment or abandonment of a known right or privilege." Johnson v. Zerbst, 304 U.S. 458, 464, 58 S.Ct. 1019, 1023, 82 L.Ed. 1461 (1938); Brookhart v. Janis, 384 U.S. 1, 4, 86 S.Ct. 1245, 1246, 16 L. Ed.2d 314 (1966).

Moreover, we would reach the same result on the facts of this case had petitioner's counsel actually cross-examined Woods at the preliminary hearing. See Motes v. United States, 178 U.S. 458, 20 S.Ct. 993, 44 L.Ed. 1150 (1900). The right to confrontation is basically a trial right. It includes both the opportunity to cross-examine and the occasion for the jury to weigh the demeanor of the witness. A preliminary hearing is ordinarily a much less searching exploration into the merits of a case than a trial, simply because its function is the more limited one of determining whether probable cause exists to hold the accused for trial. While there may be some justification for holding that the opportunity for cross-examination of a witness at a preliminary hearing satisfies the demand of the confrontation clause where the witness is shown to be actually unavailable, this is not, as we have pointed out, such a case.

The judgment of the Court of Appeals for the Tenth Circuit is reversed and the case is remanded for further proceedings consistent with this opinion.

It is so ordered.

Reversed and remanded.

UNITED STATES v. ALLEN
United States Court of Appeals, Tenth Circuit, 1969.
409 F.2d 611.

BREITENSTEIN, CIRCUIT JUDGE. On trial to the court without a jury, the defendant-appellant was found guilty of violating the Mann Act, 18 U.S.C. § 2421. He appeals from the judgment imposing sentence.

Defendant was charged in a seven-count indictment. Four of the counts related to a woman named Davis and the other three to a woman named Whitehurst. On motion of the defendant, the Davis counts were severed from the Whitehurst counts. Later, a jury was waived and the government dismissed all but Count III pertaining to Davis and Count VI pertaining to Whitehurst.

The defendant was arrested on February 7, 1968. A preliminary hearing was held before a United States Commissioner on February 13. The defendant was present with counsel who has continued to represent him at the trials and on this appeal. No continuance was requested. The charge was a violation of 18 U.S.C. § 2421 by the separate interstate transportation of Davis and Whitehurst for purposes of prostitution. Davis and Whitehurst each testified and each was cross-examined by defense counsel. The opportunity for cross-examination was full, complete, and unrestricted.

At the trials, Davis and Whitehurst invoked the Fifth Amendment protection against self-incrimination and refused to testify. Over objections of the defendant, the district court received in evidence the transcripts of their testimony at the preliminary hearing. Without such testimony, the evidence was insufficient to sustain the conviction on either count.

The use at trial of testimony received in a preliminary hearing has been considered in several cases. In Motes v. United States, 178 U.S. 458, 471, 20 S.Ct. 993, 998, 44 L.Ed. 1150, the Court held that it was error to receive in evidence a statement made at the "examining trial" when the absence of the witness was not procured by the defendant but was "manifestly due to the negligence of the officers of the government." Pointer v. Texas, 380 U.S. 400, 85 S.Ct. 1065, 13 L.Ed.2d 923, holds that the Sixth Amendment right of confrontation applies to the States under the Fourteenth Amendment. The Court pointed out, 380 U.S. 407, 85 S.C. 1069, that a major reason for the confrontation rule is "to give a defendant charged with crime an opportunity to cross-examine the witnesses against him," and held that the preliminary hearing transcript was improperly received at the trial because at that hearing the defendant was not represented by counsel and had no opportunity for cross-examination. The Court said: (Id.)

"The case before us would be quite a different one had Phillips' [the witness] statement been taken at a full-fledged hearing at which petitioner had been represented by counsel who had been given a complete and adequate opportunity to cross-examine."

Douglas v. Alabama, 380 U.S. 415, 85 S.Ct. 1074, 13 L.Ed.2d 934, is not in point. There the witness who invoked the Fifth Amendment was subjected to cross-examination as a hostile witness and interrogated about a confession implicating the defendant. The witness refused to answer any questions in regard thereto. In that situation the witness could not be cross-examined on a statement "imputed to but not admitted by him." Accordingly, there was a denial of the adequate opportunity for cross-examination.

The Courts of Appeals have held that, in proper circumstances, statements made at a preliminary hearing may be received in evidence at a subsequent trial. See Government of the Virgin Islands v. Aquino, 3 Cir., 378 F.2d 540, 549; Smith v. United States, 4 Cir., 106 F.2d 726, 728; and Baldwin v. United States, 6 Cir., 5 F.2d 133, 134.

In Barber v. Page, 390 U.S. 719, 88 S.Ct. 1318, 20 L.Ed.2d 255, the Court held that a transcript of testimony received at a preliminary hearing was improperly received in a state trial when the witness was confined in a federal institution and the state made no effort to obtain his presence for the trial. Although Barber v. Page mentions demeanor evidence and the difference between a preliminary hearing and a trial, we read that opinion as deciding only that the transcript was improperly received because unavailability had not been established.

The case before us presents three points. The first is whether the requirement of unavailability is satisfied when the witness is physically present but the testimony is unavailable because of the invocation of the Fifth Amendment privilege. This point was resolved by our recent decision in Mason v. United States, 10 Cir., 408 F.2d 903. In that case witnesses who testified at the first trial claimed the Fifth Amendment privilege and refused to testify at the second trial. The government then used the transcript of their testimony at the first trial. In rejecting the contention that the transcripts were not properly received because of the physical presence of the witnesses, we said that "the important element is whether the *testimony* of the witness is sought and is available and not whether the witness's body is available." Here, like in Mason, the testimony was unavailable because of the invocation of the Fifth Amendment.

The second point goes to the difference between a preliminary hearing and a trial. At a preliminary hearing, the issue is whether there is probable cause to believe that the accused has committed the offense charged. At a trial, the issue is the guilt or innocence of the defendant. The argument is that because of this fundamental difference the cross-examination of a prosecution witness at a preliminary hearing is less searching into the merits and hence does not satisfy the demands of the confrontation clause. We believe that the test is the opportunity for full and complete cross-examination rather than the use which is made of that opportunity. At the hearing before the United States Commissioner, the defendant and his counsel were confronted by the witnesses who testified under oath and were subjected, without limitation, to extensive cross-examination. The extent of cross-examination, whether at a preliminary hearing or at a trial, is a trial tactic. The manner of use of that trial tactic does not create a constitutional right. To paraphrase Pointer the statements of the witnesses were made "at a full-fledged hearing" with accused present and represented by counsel who was given "a complete and adequate opportunity to cross-examine."

The third point is that the use of the transcripts does not disclose the demeanor of the witnesses and thus deprives the trier of the fact of an important indication of credibility. If opportunity to observe demeanor is the controlling factor, then transcripts of testimony at a former trial may not be received. The demeanor problem is the same there as it is with the use of transcripts taken at a preliminary hearing.

In Mattox v. United States, 156 U.S. 237, 240–244, 15 S.Ct. 337, 39 L.Ed. 409, the Court considered the use of transcripts, taken at a former trial, of testimony of witnesses who had died before the retrial. The Court discussed the confrontation problem and demeanor evidence. It concluded that public policy permitted the use of the transcripts. On the basis of Mattox, the Third Circuit has held that demeanor evidence is not an essential ingredient of the confrontation privilege. We agree. In the case at bar the right of confrontation has been satisfied. The defendant and the witnesses were brought face to face in a judicial proceeding. The witnesses were sworn and the opportunity for cross-examination was complete and adequate. In our opinion the transcripts were properly received.

Affirmed.

COMMONWEALTH v. DRAVECZ
Supreme Court of Pennsylvania, 1967.
424 Pa. 582, 227 A.2d 904.

MUSMANNO, JUSTICE. Joseph J. Dravecz was employed as a laborer by the Caisson Corporation which owned a trailer in which were stored many items of equipment being used on a construction job near Airport Exit No. 22 in Lehigh County. Some of this equipment disappeared and part or all of it was found on a farm owned by the parents of Dravecz. A couple of days later State Police questioned a Eugene Stockley, labor foreman for the Caisson Co. who gave the police a signed, notarized statement in which he said that Dravecz had appeared on a certain day at Stockley's residence with some of the missing Caisson equipment and asked Stockley to sell the equipment for him. When Dravecz learned of the visit to his parental home by the police, he voluntarily appeared at State Police headquarters and submitted himself to questioning by Corporal Poluka. He denied that he had taken the tools or was in any way criminally connected with them.

Corporal Poluka then brought Stockley before Dravecz and read to Dravecz the written statement which had been made by Stockley. Dravecz made no comment at the end of the reading of the statement. He was indicted on charges of burglary, larceny and receiving stolen goods, and found guilty on the three counts. He appealed to the Superior Court which affirmed the conviction and we allowed allocatur.

At the trial the statement made by Stockley was read to the jury. The defendant contends this was error and deprived him of his constitutional rights against self-incrimination under the Fifth Amendment to the Constitution of the United States.

The Supreme Court of the United States declared in Malloy v. Hogan, 378 U.S. 1, 84 S.Ct. 1489, 12 L.Ed.2d 653, that:

"The Fourteenth Amendment secures against state invasion . . . the right of a person to remain silent unless he chooses to speak in the unfettered exercise of his own will, and to suffer no penalty . . . for such silence."

Thus, in speaking of the right of a defendant against self-incrimination in Pennsylvania, it is no longer necessary to distinguish between States and Federal cases. The protection against self-incrimination because of the 14th amendment which guarantees to all United States citizens, no matter where located, the immunities proclaimed to them in Federal territory, applies as effectively in Pennsylvania and the other States as it does in territory actually under the jurisdiction of the United States government.

It accordingly follows that all cases which were decided in Pennsylvania prior to the *Malloy* decision are no longer authoritative if they conflict with the Fifth Amendment to the Constitution of the United States, which declares that no person "shall be compelled in any criminal case to be a witness against himself."

The Superior Court, in affirming the conviction of the defendant, declared that it was bound by Commonwealth v. Vallone, 347 Pa. 419, 32 A.2d 889, which pronounced the proposition:

"The rule of evidence is well established that, when a statement made in the presence and hearing of a person is incriminating in character and naturally calls for a denial but is not challenged or contradicted by the accused although he has opportunity and liberty to speak, the statement and the fact of his failure to deny it are admissible in evidence as an implied admission of the truth of the charges thus made."

This rule, which has become known as the tacit admission rule, is too broad, wide-sweeping, and elusive for precise interpretation, particularly where a man's liberty and his good name are at stake. Who determines whether a statement is one which "naturally" calls for a denial? What is natural for one person may not be natural for another. There are persons possessed of such dignity and pride that they would treat with silent contempt a dishonest accusation. Are they to be punished for refusing to dignify with a denial what they regard as wholly false and reprehensible?

The untenability of the tacit admission rule is illustrated in the following startling proposition. A defendant is not required to deny any accusation levelled at him in a trial no matter how inculpatory. He may be charged with the most serious of offenses, including murder and high treason. A cloud of witnesses may testify to circumstances, events, episodes which wrap him in a serpent's embrace of incrimination, but no inference of guilt may be drawn from his failure to reply or to take the witness stand. Indeed, and properly so, if the prosecuting attorney or the judge makes the slightest reference to the fact that the accused failed to reply to the accusations ringing against him, and a verdict of guilt follows, a new trial is imperative. And yet, under the *Vallone* holding, an accusatory statement made in any place chosen by the accuser, whether on the street, in the fields, in an alley or a dive, if unreplied to, may be used as an engine in court to send the defendant to prison or to the electric chair.

How so incongruous a doctrine ever gained solemn authoritativeness might well be a subject for a long article in a law review. Especially when one reflects on the fact that the rule is founded on a wholly false premise. One can understand how a principle of law built on solid rock might incline to slant from the perpendicular because of over-heavily superstructure piled on it as it rises higher and higher into the realm of hypothesis, but the tacit admission rule has no solid foundation whatsoever. It rests on the spongy maxim, so many times proved unrealistic, that silence gives consent. Maxims, proverbs and axioms, despite the attractive verbal packages in which they are presented to the public, do not necessarily represent universal truth.

Indeed, there are proverbs which contradict one another flatly, as, for instance, *a rolling stone gathers no moss*, as against *the traveling bee gathers the honey*; or *look before you leap*, as against, *he who hesitates is lost*.

The very proverb *Silence gives consent* has a number of vigorous opponents in *Silence is Golden; Closed lips hurt no one, speaking may; Speech is of time, silence is of eternity; For words divide and rend, but silence is most noble till the end; And silence like a poultice comes to heal the blows of sound; Be silent and safe, silence never betrays you.*

It may be desirable and dramatic for the wrongly accused person to shout: "I am innocent!" but not everybody responds spontaneously to stimuli. The accusation may be so startling that the accused is benumbered into speechlessness. There are persons so sensitive and hurt so easily, that they swallow their tongue in the face of overwhelming injustice.

In Alberty v. United States, 162 U.S. 499, 16 S.Ct. 864, 40 L.Ed. 1051, the Supreme Court said:

"It is not universally true that a man who is conscious that he had done a wrong 'will pursue a certain course not in harmony with the conduct of a man who is conscious of having done an act which is innocent, right and proper,' since it is a matter of common knowledge that men who are entirely innocent do sometimes fly from the scene of a crime through fear of being apprehended as the guilty parties, or from an unwillingness to appear as witnesses."

Under common law and, or course, this was doubly true in medieval continental Europe, forced confessions were as common as they were cruel and inhuman. The framers of our Bill of Rights were too aware of the excesses possible in all governments, even a representative government, to permit the possibility that any person under the protection of the United States flag could be forced to admit to having committed a crime. In order to make the protection hazard-proof, the framers went beyond coercion of confessions. They used the all-embracive language that no one could be compelled "to be a witness against himself". What did the Trial Court in this case do but compel Dravecz to be a witness against himself? Dravecz had said nothing, yet because something was read to him, to which he made no comment, the prosecution insisted that Dravecz admitted guilt. If Dravecz could not be made a self-accusing witness by coerced answers, he should not be made a witness against himself by unspoken assumed answers.

A direct confession unwillingly given is a coerced confession. A tacit admission is still an unwilling performance. It is more gentle because it is silent, but it is as insidious as monoxide gas which does not proclaim its presence through sound or smell. A forced confession is a steam-chugging locomotive moving down the track, blowing its whistle and clanging its bell with the victim tied to the rails. A tacit admission is a diesel locomotive silently but relentlessly moving forward without audible signals and striking the victim unawares. The approach is different, the effect is the same.

If the police prepare a statement reciting facts, which precisely and physically point to the defendant as the author of a certain crime, and read it to him and he remains silent during the reading, the statement may not be introduced in evidence against him. Yet, under the *Vallone* doctrine, a third person may utter anything he pleases, charging the defendant with any crime at all, and if the defendant fails to answer, then that third person's unmonitored, unauthenticated declaration may doom him. No system of law should countenance so blatant an illogicality, so untrustworthy a procedure, and so unsportsmanlike and unfair a practice.

Under the tacit admission rule, if a suspect is taken to the scene of the crime where people have gathered, mouthing all sorts of rumors and suppositions against him, it becomes his duty to single out every scandalmonger, every irresponsible gossip bearer, every loose-tongued hanger-on and reply to their accusations. Otherwise, their inflammatory, unsworn reproaches and denouncements may become formal swords of indictment. This is not rule by reason but by unrestrained babblement.

A confession is defined by Wigmore as "one species of admission, namely, an admission consisting of a direct assertion, by the accused in a criminal case, of the main fact charged against him or of some fact essential to the charge." (Wigmore Evidence, 1050, p. 7 (3rd ed. 1940). A tacit admission, according to *Vallone,* is an "implied admission of the truth of the charges thus made." It is more or less admitted that, without the tacit admission presented in the *Vallone* case, there could have been no conviction. The same could be true in the case at bar. As above stated, Dravecz voluntarily went to the police to be questioned, but he did not ask to be confronted by Stockley, nor to have any Stockley statement read to him. Springing a statement on him in this fashion suggests artifice. Requiring him to answer to it under pain of penalty spells illegality and injustice.

There is not the slightest suggestion in the record which would justify the intellectual conclusion that Dravecz knew that if he said nothing when Stockley's statement was read, his silence would be interpreted as an admission of guilt. Dravecz was a laborer, presumably with a minimum of formal education. Assuming that he might know, although there is no evidence even of this, that he was not required to answer questions put to him by the police, it is unrealistic, to say nothing of unjust, to assume that he knew that if he did not make some comment on Stockley's comments, this would prove he had committed a crime. Stockley's statement was a long one. It could have contained averments with which Dravecz agreed, and averments with which he disagreed as not being the truth. Was he sufficiently educated and trained in expression to analyze the wordy paper and specify what he regarded right and what he regarded wrong? The Supreme Court of the United States said in the monumental Escobedo case—

". . . No system of criminal justice can, or should, survive if it comes to depend for its continued effectiveness on the citizens' abdication through unawareness of their constitutional rights." (378 U.S. 478, 84 S.Ct. 1758, 12 L.Ed.2d 977)

Another infirmity in the tacit admission rule is that it invests hearsay with evidentiary authority which is not recognized in any of the exceptions to the hearsay rule.

The Courts and the Judges have not been silent in registering disapproval of the tacit admission rule. In the *Vallone* case itself, Chief Justice Maxey filed a 20-page Dissenting Opinion bristling with authority, precedent and logic devastating to the rule. He called attention to the case of Moore v. Smith, 14 Serg. & R. 388, where this Court said anent tacit admissions:

"That presupposes a declaration or proposition made to him, which he is bound either to deny or to admit. . . . Nothing can be more dangerous than this kind of evidence; it should always be received with caution, and never ought to be, unless the evidence is of direct declarations of that kind, which naturally calls for contradiction. . . . Of all evidence, loose, hasty conversation is entitled to the last weight."

In Commonwealth v. Zorambo, 205 Pa. 109, 54 A. 716, the prosecution introduced in evidence against the defendant a statement made by a co-defendant at a magistrate's hearing when, according to the Judge and the District Attorney, the hearing had ended. Justice Brown, speaking for this Court, said that the statement—

"cannot be regarded as any, not even the slightest, evidence of his guilt. . . . That he kept silent was his right as at the time he must have understood it, and the manifest error was committed in submitting his silence to the jury as circumstantial evidence against him."

In Hersey v. Barton, 23 Vt. 685, the Supreme Court of Vermont said:

"To hold that a person is bound, upon all occasions when his adversary, in his presence, is making statements to others and not addressed to him, but which are adverse to his interest, to repudiate the same, or that his silence should be taken as an admission of the truth of those statements, would in our judgment be unsound in principle and unwarranted by authority."

In State v. Kissinger, 343 Mo. 781, 123 S.W.2d 81, it was held that defendant's silence to a statement made by his wife in response to the inquiry of officers in his presence was inadmissible.

The New York Court of Appeals observed in People v. Page, 162 N.Y. 272, 56 N.E. 750:

"It cannot be that there is any such anomaly in the criminal law as is involved in the proposition that an accused person, when charged with the offense in open court by indictment, may stand mute without prejudice to his innocence, while the same person is bound to deny neighborhood gossip with respect to his guilt at the peril of furnishing by silence evidence against himself when on trial upon the charge."

The decisions of the Supreme Court of the United States in Malloy v. Hogan, 378 U.S. 1, 84 S.Ct. 1489, 12 L.Ed.2d 653; Gideon v. Wainwright, 372 U.S. 335, 83 S.Ct. 792, 9 L.Ed.2d 799; Escobedo v. State of Illinois, 378 U.S. 478, 84 S.Ct. 1758, 12 L.Ed.2d 977; Massiah v. United States, 377 U.S. 201, 84 S.Ct. 1199, 12 L.Ed.2d 246, and Miranda v. State of Arizona, 384 U.S. 436, 86 S.Ct. 1602, 16 L.Ed.2d 694, have, in effect, shattered the tacit admission rule as pronounced in *Vallone*. Whatever may be left of the rule after the enfilading fire of the Supreme Court is here overruled.

We accordingly decide that it was improper for the Trial Court to have allowed the Stockley statement in evidence against the defendant Dravecz. The order of the Superior Court is reversed, the verdict of the jury set aside and the record remanded for a venire facias de novo.

EAGEN, J., files a concurring opinion in which JONES, COHEN and O'BRIEN, J.J., join.

RORERTS, J., files a separate concurring opinion. . . .

BELL, CHIEF JUSTICE (dissenting). This defendant was tried and convicted of burglary, larceny and receiving stolen goods. For approximately a century *the silence of a defendant* (or an accused) *when accused of a crime* or of participation in a crime amounted to a "tacit admission," and such testimony was admissible in evidence as proof of an implied acquiescence on the part of the defendant (or the accused) in the truth of the criminal charges or accusations made against him.

The Supreme Court of the United States, merely by a footnote in Miranda v. State of Arizona, 384 U.S. 436, 468, 86 S.Ct. 1602 (June 13, 1966) has apparently overruled this important and long established law. However, Johnson v. State of New Jersey, 384 U.S. 719, 86 S.Ct. 1772, 16 L.Ed.2d 882, specifically decided that Miranda v. State of Arizona *was not to be applied retroactively*, and this Court so held in Commonwealth ex rel. Shadd v. Myers, 423 Pa. 82, 85, 223 A.2d 296, 298.

If the Supreme Court intends to overrule a law which has been established for approximately one hundred years, it would remove all doubt if the Court specifically overruled in the body of its Opinion all its prior contrary Opinions.

FILESI v. UNITED STATES
United States Court of Appeals, Fourth Circuit, 1965.
352 F.2d 339.

BOREMAN, CIRCUIT JUDGE. The Commissioner of Internal Revenue, asserting that the Jolly Tavern located at Glen Burnie, Maryland, had been operated as a cabaret because dancing had been permitted to the music of a juke box, assessed deficiencies in cabaret excise taxes, penalties and interest in the amount of $46,567.28 against the taxpayer, Alfred Filesi, based on the receipts from the operation of the tavern. . . .

In the District Court Filesi readily admitted that no excise tax returns had been filed for the periods covered by the assessments. He contended, however, that no excise tax was due and no returns were required because the Jolly Tavern had not been operated as a cabaret within the meaning of Section 4232(b) of the 1954 Code at any time as dancing had not been permitted, tolerated or regularly engaged in. . . .

The principal errors assigned on appeal relate to rulings of the court: . . . second, that it was error to permit Harvey Gold, an Internal Revenue Agent who was called as a witness by the Government, to testify as to statements made by Henry Muller to Gold during an interview in 1960. . . .

At trial the dancing issue was a highly controverted one which the jury resolved in the Government's favor. On this issue the trial court permitted Gold, a witness called by the Government, to testify as follows:

"Q: Would you tell the Court and jury the statements made by Mr. Muller concerning dancing?

"A: Mr. Muller stated that throughout this period of time, he was operating the Jolly Tavern and that during this period of time, there was juke box dancing as a general mode of business or operation of the business throughout the period. Insofar as the dancing was concerned, it was to the juke box.

"Q: Did he mention anything about dancing signs, 'No dancing' signs?

"A: Yes, he did. He mentioned that at times, there were 'No dancing' signs that were posted but there was never anything done as far as to stop the dancing was concerned, but this was just the mode of operation. There was dancing as the entertainment.

"Q: Did he make any statements regarding the frequency of dancing?

"A: Yes, he did. He stated that the dancing occurred most every time a crowd congregated at the Jolly Inn and that normally, the crowd would congregate on the weekends, which would be Friday, Saturday and Sunday and after your supper hours, which would be approximately 6:00 p.m. on until the close of business."

Filesi objected to this testimony on the ground that it was hearsay because Muller was not a party to the action and the statements were made in March of 1960, approximately three years after the partnership between him and Muller had been dissolved. The Government contends, however, that Muller's statements were admissible either as admissions against the partnership or as declarations against Muller's pecuniary interest. We conclude that these statements were inadmissible under either of these theories. . . .

Although declarations made by a person against his pecuniary or proprietary interest are admissible whenever relevant no matter what the relationship is between the declarant and the party against whom the statements are offered, we do not think Muller's statements to Gold were admissible under this exception to the hearsay rule. The basis for the declaration against interest exception is that a statement made by an individual against his interest would not be made unless truth compelled it and it is this element of trustworthiness which compensates for the absence of the oath and the opportunity for cross-examination. 3 Wigmore on Evidence §§ 1457 and 1475 (2d ed. 1923). It is implicit in the exception that for the declaration to be trustworthy the declarant must have known it was against his interest at the time he made the statement. As stated by Jefferson in 58 Harv.L.Rev. 1, 17 (1944):

". . . (I)t is not the fact that the declaration is against interest but the awareness of that fact by the declarant which gives the statement significance. . . ."

The rule is stated in 31A C.J.S. Evidence § 222 as follows:

"In order for a declaration to be admissible as a declaration against interest, it must clearly appear that the statement of declarant was actually against his interest, *and known or believed to be so*, at the time it was made; otherwise the statement will not be admitted." (Emphasis added.)

Although Muller's statements that dancing was permitted at the Jolly Tavern were against his pecuniary interest, there is nothing to indicate he was aware of this fact at the time the statements were made. The witness Gold stated that he spoke with Mr. Muller on two occasions at his office in March of 1960. According to Gold he informed Muller of his rights. The following is Gold's testimony on this point:

"Q: (The Court) What was the nature of the statements which you made?

"A: (Gold) The nature of the statements was to explain to Mr. Muller that he was a partner with Mr. Filesi in the Jolly Tavern and that we were after the—actually the facts insofar as the operation was concerned, *and that any development as such would be used in developing* the cabaret tax liability against him, as well as Mr. Filesi." (Emphasis added.)

There is nothing in Gold's testimony or in the testimony of any other witness to clearly indicate that Muller was made aware of or realized the possible serious financial consequences to him which could arise from his admission that dancing was permitted at the tavern. There is no showing that Muller knew that dancing at the tavern would transform it into a "cabaret" and create a liability for excise taxes where no such liability would otherwise exist. These damaging statements by Muller could have been made during a general conversation with Gold about some other phase of the business operation and without the realization that his statements concerning dancing might create a personal liability for the payment of excise taxes.

We are of the opinion that the effect of this inadmissible evidence on a hotly contested issue was clearly prejudicial and that Filesi is entitled to a new trial. Gold's testimony went to the heart of the case and for the Government to argue that it was not prejudicial is to ignore reality. . . .

Reversed and remanded for a new trial.

PEOPLE v. SPRIGGS
Supreme Court of California, 1964.
60 Cal.2d 868, 36 Cal.Rptr. 841, 389 P.2d 377, noted, 64 Colum.L.Rev. 1347; 37 S.Cal.L.Rev. 621; 12 U.C.L.A.L.Rev. 638.

TRAYNOR, JUSTICE. The trial court sitting without a jury convicted defendant of possessing heroin in violation of Health and Safety Code, section 11500. He appeals from the judgment of conviction, contending that the trial court erred in refusing to admit certain evidence.

The evidence is conflicting. Officer Cochran testified that from a darkened doorway he and two other police officers observed defendant and Mrs. Albertina Roland together on the street on the evening of February 17, 1962. When defendant was about 40 feet from the officers, he bent over and placed his hand under a hedge. He withdrew his hand with a piece of paper in it, looked around, again placed his hand under the hedge, and then stood up and began walking with his companion toward the officers. When they reached the doorway, Officer Cochran stepped out and shouted "Police Officer." Defendant jumped back and threw a balloon and a piece of paper to the ground. Officer Cochran picked up the balloon and paper, and observed a white powder in the balloon. The officers then arrested defendant and Mrs. Roland. At the trial the parties stipulated that the powder was heroin.

Defendant had just been released from prison in the afternoon of the day of the arrest. He testified that he did not purchase or receive narcotics from Mrs. Roland or any other person on that day and that he did not bend over or place his hand under any hedge, but did stop momentarily while Mrs. Roland bent over to fix her stockings. When the officers accosted him they poked him as if trying to make him gag, and continued to beat him for about 10 minutes until an officer said that he found something on the sidewalk. Defendant testified that he did not throw anything to the ground and that when he and Mrs. Roland were in the police car, an officer stated "One of you had this narcotics, and you are going to tell us which one of you had it." Officer Cochran testified that Mrs. Roland was known by the police as a user of narcotics. Defendant's counsel cross-examined Officer Cochran regarding Mrs. Roland's arrest as follows: "Q: Did you talk to her at the time you arrested her? A: Yes. Q: Did you ask her if the narcotics that you allegedly found were hers? A: Yes, I did. Q: What did she say?" The prosecutor objected on the grounds of immateriality and hearsay, and the trial court sustained the objection. Defendant did not rephrase the question or make an offer of proof of what the expected answer might be. Defendant contends that the witness should have been allowed to answer the question on the ground that the hearsay rule does not preclude admission of a declaration against penal interest.

In 1892 this court held that a hearsay declaration against penal interest was not admissible.... Although still the law in a majority of jurisdictions, this rule has been vigorously criticized by the scholars. (5 Wigmore, Evidence (3d ed.) §§ 1476, 1477; McCormick, Evidence, 549–553; McBaine, California Evidence Manual, § 813; Model Code of Evidence, Rule 509; Uniform Rules of Evidence, Rule 63(10); Holmes, J., dissenting in Donnelly v. United States, 228 U.S. 243, 277, 33 S.Ct. 449, 57 L.Ed. 820). The traditional rule excluding hearsay declarations against penal interest was first established by the House of Lords in 1844 in the Sussex Peerage case, 11 Clark & F. 85. Dean Wigmore points out that the Sussex case was a backward step from earlier English cases admitting declarations against interest. (5 Wigmore, supra, § 1476). Exclusion of declarations against penal interest now rests only on the historical accident of the Sussex case. (See McBaine, supra, § 813; 5 Wigmore, supra, § 1477.) A minority of courts, however, have departed from the Sussex case and admit hearsay declarations against penal interest. (Hines v. Com., 136 Va. 728, 117 S.E. 843, 846–850, 35 A.L.R. 431[hearsay testimony of decedent's confession admitted in behalf of defendant]; Newberry v. Com., 191 Va. 445, 61 S.E.2d 318, 325–326 [third person's written confession admitted although he refused to testify claiming right against self-incrimination]; Sutter v. Easterly, 354 Mo. 282, 189 S.W.2d 284, 289–290, 162 A.L.R. 437 [third person's affidavit making statements against penal interest admitted although he refused to testify claiming right against self-incrimination; hearsay declaration not admissible against the defendant in a criminal prosecution, State v. Gorden, 356 Mo. 1010, 204 S.W.2d 713, 715; but cf. Osborne v. Purdome, Mo., 250 S.W.2d 159, 163]; Blocker v. State, 55 Tex.Cr.R. 30, 114 S.W. 814, 815 [hearsay declaration admissible if prosecution's evidence solely circumstantial, and it is shown that declarant might have committed the crime]; People v. Lettrich, 413 Ill. 172, 108 N.E.2d 488, 492 [third person's confession admissible where prosecution's sole evidence was defendant's repudiated confession]; Brennan v. State, 151 Md. 265, 134 A. 148, 150–151, 48 A.L.R. 342 [hearsay declaration of paternity admitted in behalf of defendant prosecuted for bastardy]; Thomas v. State, 186 Md. 446, 47 A.2d 43, 45–46, 167 A.L.R. 390 [hearsay declaration admissible because declarant available as a witness]; see also McClain v. Anderson Free Press, 232 S.C. 448, 102 S.E.2d 750, 760–762 [approving rule admitting declarations against penal interest, but holding evidence inadmissible under facts of case]; United States v. Annunziato, 293 F.2d 373, 378 (2d Cir.) [admitting evidence on other grounds, but criticizing rule regarding penal interest]; In re Forsythe's Estate, 221 Minn. 303, 22 N.W.2d 19, 25 n. 3, 167 A.L.R. [dictum indicating admissibility of declarations against penal interest]; In re Winineger's Petition, Okl. Cr., 337 P.2d 445, 452–454 [dissenting opinion].)

In 1872 the California Legislature codified many of the common law rules of evidence, including some of the traditional rules governing admissibility of hearsay evidence. (Code Civ.Proc., § 1825.) The codification of the hearsay rule has remained largely unaltered, although in some instances the Legislature has added to its original enactment (e. g., Uniform Business Records as Evidence Act, Code Civ.Proc., §§ 1953e–1953h). The Legislature, however, did not freeze the law of evidence to the rules set forth in the Code of Civil Procedure or other statutes.... Numerous questions arise on which the Legislature has been silent or inexplicit. The Courts must answer these questions and develop judicially the law of evidence ... in the light of common-law principles and the basic objectives of the statutes....

The statutes do not exclude hearsay declarations against penal interest. Their admissibility must therefore be determined in the light of the principle that "the purpose of all rules of evidence is to aid in arriving at the truth, [and] if it shall appear that any rule tends rather to hinder than to facilitate this result ... it should be abrogated without hesitation." (Williams v. Kidd, 170 Cal. 631, 649, 151 P. 1, 8.)

When hearsay evidence is admitted it is usually because it has a high degree of trustworthiness.... Thus, declarations against pecuniary or proprietary interest are admitted because they are unikely to be false. (5 Wigmore, supra, §§ 1457–1475.) A declaration against penal interest is no less trustworthy. As we pointed out in People v. One 1948 Chevrolet Conv. Coupe, 45 Cal.2d 613, 622, 290 P.2d 538, 55 A.L.R.2d 1272, a person's interest against being criminally implicated gives reasonable assurance of the veracity of his statement made against that interest. Moreover, since the conviction of a crime ordinarily entails economic loss, the traditional concept of a "pecuniary interest" could logically include one's "penal interest." (Compare the theory that admits a third person's confession of a crime on the ground that the crime was also a tort, thus subjecting the declarant to civil liability for damages, a pecuniary interest. E. g., Weber v. Chicago, R. I. & P. Ry. Co., 175 Iowa 358, 151 N.W. 852, 864, L.R.A.-1918A, 626; McCormick, supra, § 255, p. 549). We have concluded, therefore, that the ruling of the trial court was erroneous insofar as it excludes hearsay declarations against penal interest. . . .

The question remains whether the admissibility of hearsay declarations against interest depends on the unavailability of the declarant to testify at the trial. If Mrs. Roland was deceased, insane, suffering from severe illness, absent from the jurisdiction, or otherwise unavailable as a witness, such unavailiability provided a necessity for the evidence, thus affording a basis for its admissibility in addition to the trustworthy character of the declaration. (See 5 Wigmore, supra, §§ 1420, 1421, 1456; McCormick, supra, 546, 554.) If she was available, however, the credibility of her extrajudicial statements would not be lessened by that fact. Furthermore, the opportunity for cross-examination would eliminate the basic objection to the hearsay character of the evidence. (See People v. Gould, 54 Cal.2d 621, 626–627, 7 Cal. Rptr. 273, 354 P.2d 865; McCormick, supra, § 39, p. 74; 5 Wigmore, supra, § 1362; Morgan, Hearsay Dangers and the Application of the Hearsay Concept, 62 Harv.L.Rev. 177, 192–193.) Thus if Mrs. Roland had taken the witness stand and denied possession of the narcotics, her out-of-court declaration against interest would have been admissible to prove the truth of the matter stated (see . . . McCormick, supra, 554; Uniform Rules of Evidence, Rule 63(10); Model Code of Evidence, Rule 509; . . .) as well as to impeach her by a prior inconsistent statement (Code Civ.Proc., §§ 2049, 2052). Thus, in the event of a retrial, defense counsel should be allowed to ask Officer Cochran the question objected to, whether or not the unavailability of Mrs. Roland is established.

There is no merit to the contention that regardless of the hearsay issue the question was properly objected to for immateriality. The Attorney General contends that the question sought to establish ownership of the narcotics, and not possession, which is all that is needed for a violation of the statute. The question was whether Mrs. Roland stated that the narcotics "were hers." If she answered "yes," such evidence, although not conclusive, would clearly be material to the issue of possession. Had the officer been allowed to answer the question, further questions might have brought out that she meant that it was she who had possession. The hearsay objection, however, blocked further inquiry. Since the trial judge correctly applied the then existing law on the hearsay issue, rephrasing the question of making an offer of proof would have been fruitless. Defendant is therefore not precluded from raising the hearsay issue on appeal. (See People v. Kitchens, 46 Cal.2d 260, 262–263, 294 P.2d 17.) . . .

The judgment is reversed.

CONNOR v. STATE
Court of Appeals of Maryland, 1961.
225 Md. 543, 171 A.2d 699, 86, A.L.R.2d 892.
Cert. denied, 368 U.S. 906. Noted, 22 Md.L.Rev. 42.

HORNEY, JUDGE. Aggrieved by his conviction of second degree murder as a result of his having run over his former wife in an automobile, the defendant, Edward Richard Connor, appealed and has assigned numerous errors with respect to the method of examining jurors on *voir dire* and in rulings on the evidence (some of which are subdivided into several parts) and in the instructions to the jury.

The defendant and the deceased had been married for many years. They had had five children, but had been divorced. At the time of the homicide — October 25, 1959 — she resided in Baltimore as did the children. He resided in Camden. On the day before in a telephone conversation between them it was agreed that the defendant would come to Baltimore to attend a birthday party for one of the older daughters, that he should stay with that daughter and that he would bring $25 to his former wife. The defendant came to Baltimore in his automobile.

Upon his arrival, he and his former wife talked together on friendly terms. Thereafter, she left the house and the defendant, with several of the minor children, watched television until he went to bed in an upper room. When the former wife returned to the house about 2:00 a.m. and found him sleeping upstairs she smacked him on the face and informed him that downstairs was good enough for him. The defendant arose immediately, dressed hurriedly, went down the back stairs, grabbed a few other things and left the house.

After the defendant had opened the door of his automobile, parked in front of the house, and had started the motor and turned on the parking lights, he saw his former wife standing at the left hand door. She demanded the $25 he had promised her and when he responded that he had no intention of giving it to her then or later, an altercation ensued as he attempted to drive slowly off while she followed alongside of the automobile and got in front of it. At this point he idled the motor long enough to tell her that he would give her the money on the next day and then, putting the automobile in gear, he again "started to move slowly" while she "insisted on staying in the same spot," but he continued to move forward about ten feet with her moving backward and still yelling for the money until there came a time when he did not "see her any more." Then he "gave it [the automobile] the gas" and moved away rapidly for about a hundred feet. In so doing—though he claimed he was not aware of it—the defendant drove over his former wife, crushed her chest and pelvis and dragged her body for at least a part of the distance he had traveled. She died at 5:40 p.m. on the same day. There was other evidence that the deceased was a heavy drinker at times, and the defendant, claiming that he was afraid of her, related the details of numerous other affrays between them in former years. But since it was not claimed that the evidence was insufficient to sustain the verdict of the jury, it is not necessary to relate more at this point. Such parts of the evidence and of the proceedings as may seem necessary to understand a question then under consideration will be set forth when and as required.

On the appeal it is claimed...; (ii) that it was prejudicial error to admit the dying declaration of the deceased as evidence....

Early in the trial of the case, the court over objection admitted into evidence as a dying declaration (but not as a part of the res gestae) a statement made by the deceased to a police officer (Horace Erwin) while she was lying in the street awaiting arrival of an ambulance. In pertinent parts the statement was as follows:

"Q: What, if anything, did Mrs. Connor, the person lying in the street say to you or to anyone in your presence? A: ...With the information I had received [from passers by], I asked Mrs. Connor certain questions at that time.

"Q: Was she conscious at the time? A: Yes, sir.

"Q: What did you ask her and what did she answer? A: I asked Mrs. Connor: 'Did your husband do this to you?'

"Q: What did she answer?

[At this point, after counsel for the defendant had stated that the answer would be hearsay, a colloquy ensued between the prosecutor, the defense counsel and the court as to whether the statement was a part of the res gestae or a dying declaration. Thereafter, the reporter read back the answer of the witness to the penultimate question: "I asked Mrs. Connor: 'Did your husband do this to you?' "]

"(The Witness). She answered yes. I asked her at that time 'Was this an accident?' This was acting on information I had received from passers by. I asked: 'Was this an accident or was it deliberate?' She answered: 'It was no accident.' "

Prior to this testimony there had been testimony by another witness (Erwin Behlert) that he had heard the injured woman say "get a priest." There was also prior testimony by another officer (Sanford Trojan) to the effect that the woman kept saying "take care of my baby."

The claim is that the statement was neither a dying declaration nor a part of the res gestae and that the admission of the statement was prejudicial. The defendant has stated eight reasons why the declaration was inadmissible. All are without merit.

First: The deceased was fully aware of her impending death. Her anguished entreaty that someone take care of the baby plus the fact that she had called for a priest before making the declaration was strong evidence that she was aware of her condition. "It is not necessary to prove expressions implying apprehension of death, if it is clear that the person does not expect to survive the injury. This expectation may be indicated by the circumstances of [her] condition, or by [her] own acts, such as sending for a priest of [her] church, before making the declaration." 1 Wharton, Criminal Evidence, § 306. . . . Nor was it necessary for the victim to state that she expected to die. It is sufficient if her condition is such (and she is aware of it) as to warrant an inference of impending death. . . . See also Wharton, op. cit., § 306, supra; 2 Jones, Evidence, § 301; McCormick, Evidence, § 259.

Second: Even if the statement was an opinion, and not a collective fact as the State suggests, the declaration was admissible. The majority rule—that "statements which amount merely to an expression of the declarant's mental impressions, estimates, opinions, and conclusions are not admissible in evidence as dying declarations if a witness could not testify in that manner in court," as stated in Wharton, op. cit., § 309—is not supported by the better reasoning, and we decline to follow it. We agree with the minority and with Professor Wigmore that the majority rule against the admission of an opinion as evidence ought not to apply to dying declarations. In 5 Wigmore, Evidence, § 1447, it is said:

"The opinion rule has no application to dying declarations. The theory of that rule . . . is that, wherever the witness can state specifically the detailed facts observed by him, the inferences to be drawn from them can equally well be drawn by the jury, so that the witness' inferences become superfluous. Now, since the declarant is here deceased, it is no longer possible to obtain from him by questions any more detailed data than his statement may contain, and hence his inferences are not in this instance superfluous, but are indispensable."

Both Virginia and Pennsylvania have accepted the Wigmore view. In Pendleton v. Commonwealth, 1921, 131 Va. 676, 109 S.E. 201, 209, it was said that a "dying declaration is not inadmissible in evidence merely because it states a conclusion of fact." And in Conmonwealth v. Knable, 1952, 369 Pa. 171, 85 A.2d 114, 117, there is an unequivocal statement that "the opinion rule has no application to dying declarations.". . .

Third: The dying declaration was complete and it was not improper for the court to exclude what the declarant had said with respect to the residence of her former husband and as to her continued concern over the welfare of her children. The record shows that Officer Erwin attempted to question her further as to what had actually occurred, but "she went off on a different subject." On the contrary, instead of her statement being only a part of the whole, it was all she had to say about the injury she had sustained and, as such, was all the court was required to admit as evidence. Dying declarations "are admissible only insofar as they relate to the circumstances of the killing and to the events . . . leading up to it." McCormick, op. cit., § 260. See also Wigmore, op. cit., § 1448.

Fourth: Instead of reflecting her mental state when she declared that the homicidal act of the defendant "was no accident," the record is clear that the declarant was merely answering a direct question as to causation. Moreover, the only evidence of her state of mind is that she was conscious when Officer Erwin was questioning her.

Fifth: Like the preceding claim, there is no evidence at all to indicate or even suggest that the declarant was not sane and rational at the time the dying declaration was made. On the contrary, since there was evidence that she was aware of her plight, it would have been improper to have excluded the declaration. The question of whether the declarant had sufficient understanding was for the jury. . . .

Sixth: The statement by the declarant that her injuries had not been accidentally inflicted was certainly not vague or indefinite. Instead, though the statement may not have been as specific as might be desired, it was, for all its brevity, direct and to the point in response to a specific question. It was for that reason clearly admissible as evidence. . . .

Seventh: Even if the statement was in response to a leading question, it was clearly admissible . . . [A] dying declaration may be made in answer to a leading question or even urgent solicitation. . . . The text writers also agree that a leading question will not vitiate a dying declaration. Jones, op. cit., § 306; Wharton, op. cit. § 322.

Eighth: The claim that the dying declaration was inadmissible because it invaded the province of the jury not only lacks merit but ignores the very reason why such declarations are held to be admissible in homicide cases. Since, as is pointed out in Wigmore, op. cit., § 1447, supra, it is no longer possible to obtain from a deceased declarant the detailed facts observed by him or her, the inferences contained in the dying declaration — instead of being improper for superfluousness as the defendant in effect claims — are in fact indispensable. Moreover, since by definition a declaration made *in extremis* is admissible as evidence because the law considers that such a situation creates an obligation as solemn as that of a positive oath to tell the truth, a dying declaration if and when it is admitted becomes as much a part of the evidence to be considered by the jury as any other admitted testimony bearing on the innocence or guilt of a defendant. Clearly, the admission of the dying declaration did not impinge upon the province of the jury to decide the issue of whether the killing of the declarant was deliberate or accidental.

We agree with the trial court that the statement of the declarant was a dying declaration and that it was properly admitted as evidence. With this holding it is unnecessary to consider whether the statement was also a part of the res gestae. . . .

Judgment affirmed.

PEOPLE v. ALCALDE
Supreme Court of California, 1944.
24 Cal.2d 177, 148 P.2d 627.

SHENK, JUSTICE. The defendant, Florencio "Frank" Alcalde, was convicted of first degree murder and sentenced to suffer the penalty of death. His motion for a new trial was denied. He appealed from the judgment and from an order denying his motion for a new trial.

On Monday morning, November 23, 1942, the body of Bernice Curtis was found in a plowed field adjacent to Alma Road between Palo Alto and Mountain View in Santa Clara County. Death had been caused by a basal fracture of the skull resulting from the application of some blunt instrument or substance. . . . The circumstances under which the body was discovered indicated unmistakably that Bernice Curtis had been killed with premeditated design. . . .

The deceased was a divorced woman of about thirty years of age. She was described as a "blond" her hair having been bleached. About four months prior to her death she had gone to San Francisco from Chicago to be with and to assist her married sister and the latter's husband, who were about to become parents. She stayed with them in their home on Sacramento Street until after the event. She then moved to a rooming house on San Jose Avenue where other young women resided and with one of whom she shared a room. She accepted employment at a cigar store located at Powell and Market Streets in San Francisco.

The defendant worked as a welder at the shipyards of the Western Pipe and Steel Company in South San Francisco. He was married and had been residing with his wife and five-year-old daughter in the nearby town of San Bruno on premises owned and also occupied by his father. About November 9, 1942, because of a misunderstanding with his wife, he moved to a hotel in South San Francisco under the assumed name of Frank Galarda....

On November 22d Bernice Curtis stated to two persons, her brother-in-law and her roommate, that she was going to dinner that night with "Frank." She spent a portion of the day riding horseback wth one of the other young women who lived at the rooming house on San Jose Avenue. Her riding companion saw Bernice board a homeward bound streetcar about 4:30 in the afternoon. That evening at 6:00 her roommate saw Bernice dressing, and it was then that the latter expressed her intention of going out with Frank....

The defendant contends that prejudicial error was committed by admitting in evidence over the defendant's objection the declarations of the decedent made on November 22d that she was going out with "Frank" that evening. In overruling the objection the court took the precaution to state in the presence of the jury that the evidence was admitted for the limited purpose of showing the decedent's intention. It is argued by the defendant that declarations not under oath, made when the declarant is not confronted by the adverse party, are admissible to prove physical or mental condition and only when either condition is a matter in issue. The admission of such utterances, due precaution having been taken by the court as here, is not so limited.

This is not a case such as People v. Wright, 167 Cal. 1, 138 P. 349, or People v. Thomas, 51 Cal.App. 731, 197 P. 677, where the defendant was charged with homicide resulting from criminal abortion and the physical condition of the decedent was a matter in issue. Nor is it a case such as Estate of Snowball, 157 Cal. 301, 107 P. 598, or Bridge v. Ruggles, 202 Cal. 326, 260 P. 553, where the mental state of the declarants was material on issues of duress and undue influence. In those cases the declarants' utterances were received in evidence not to prove their truth, but to indicate the mental condition of the declarants. See, also, Adkins v. Brett, 184 Cal. 252, 193 P. 251; Estate of Carson, 184 Cal. 437, 194 P. 5, 17 A.L.R. 239. In the present case the decedent's mental condition at the time of her declaration was not an issue, and her utterance could not be offered as proof thereof. Her utterance was hearsay. It was made extrajudicially and offered as proof of the truth of its content. It was a declaration of intent to do an act in the future, offered as evidence that the deceased had the intent she declared and that the intent was probably carried out, namely, that she intended to and did go out that night with a man named "Frank."

From the declared intent to do a particular thing an inference that the thing was done may fairly be drawn. Such declarations have been deemed admissible where they possessed a high degree of trustworthiness. Where they are relevant to an issue in the case and the declarant is dead or otherwise unavailable the necessity for their admission has been recognized. Mutual Life Insurance Co. v. Hillmon, 145 U.S. 285, 12 S.Ct. 909, 36 L.Ed. 706, appears to be the leading case on the admissibility of declarations of intent to do an act as proof that the act thereafter was accomplished. The courts of this state have followed what is deemed to be the weight of authority (see Wigmore, Evidence, 2d Ed. 1923 § 1725; 19 Cal.L.Rev. 231 and 367; 35 Harv.L.Rev. 302, 444) to the effect that declarations of present intent are admissible to prove a future act. In cases of homicide the admissibility of uncommunicated threats of the deceased against the defendant has been upheld to show that the declarant was the aggressor. People v. Arnold, 15 Cal. 476; People v. Scoggins, 37 Cal. 676; People v. Alivtre, 55 Cal. 263; People v. Thomson, 92 Cal. 506; 28 P. 589; People v. McGann, 194 Cal. 688, 230 P. 169; People v. Speraic, 87 Cal.App. 724, 262 P. 795. Declarations by the deceased of an intent to commit suicide have been held admissible. Rogers v. Manhattan Life Insurance Co., 138 Cal. 285, 71 P. 348; Benjamin v. District Grand Lodge, 171 Cal. 260, 152 P. 731; People v. Tugwell, 28 Cal. App. 348, 152 P. 740; see, also, Wilbur v. Emergency Hospital Ass'n, 27 Cal.App. 751, 151 P. 155.

In Estate of McNamara, 181 Cal. 82, 183 P. 552, 7 A.L.R. 313, involving the issue of paternity, a declaration of intention of the husband to leave his home and go to a distant city was held admissible to show that the declarant actually went where he said he was going. The court said, in reliance on Mutual Life Insurance Co. v. Hillmon, supra, that it was well established that declarations of intention were admissible under such circumstances. In Union Oil Co. v. Stewart, 158 Cal. 149, 110 P. 313, Ann.Cas.1912A, 567, an action to quiet title, a husband's declaration of intent to desert his wife was admitted as bearing upon the fact of desertion.

In People v. Thomas, supra, a declaration of intent to go to the defendant's office for an operation was admitted as proof that the intention was carried out. Admissibility of a declaration of intent to go to a certain place was upheld in the case of People v. Fong Sing, 38 Cal.App. 253, 175 P. 911, where the defendant sought to rely on his own declaration to establish an alibi. See, also, People v. Burke, 18 Cal.App. 72, 122 P. 435.

In other jurisdictions cases are found which recognize the admissibility of declarations of intent to go to a certain place or with a certain person in the future. Hunter v. State, 40 N.J.L. 495; State v. Hayward, 62 Minn. 474, 65 N.W. 63; State v. Mortensen, 26 Utah 312, 73 P. 562, 633.

In some of the cases the declaration of an intent to do a certain act in the future has been admitted as a part of the res gestae. But such declarations are not, strictly speaking, part of the transaction. They are not encompassed within section 1850 of the Code of Civil Procedure. They more properly fall within section 1870, subdivision 15, as one of "Any other facts from which the facts in issue are presumed or are logically inferable." Greenleaf on Evidence, vol. 1, 16th ed., § 162, points out that the existence of a person's design or plan to do a certain thing is relevant circumstantially to show that he did it, and may be evidenced by his assertion of present intent when made in a natural way and not under circumstances of suspicion; that the declaration is admissible not properly as part of the res gestae, but merely as an exception to the general rule excluding hearsay evidence; that where such declarations have been excluded it has usually been due to a misapplication of the res gestae doctrine. Some courts have expressly rejected any necessity for concluding that they were part of the res gestae. Commonwealth v. Trefethen, 157 Mass. 180, 31 N.E. 961, 24 L.R.A. 235; State v. Mortensen, supra.

No attempt need be made here to define or summarize all the limitations or restrictions upon the admissibility of declarations of intent to do an act in the future or to indicate what degree of unavailability or corroboration should exist in every case. Elements essential to admissibility are that the declaration must tend to prove the declarant's intention at the time it was made; it must have been made under circumstances which naturally give verity to the utterance; it must be relevant to an issue in the case. Those qualifications are here present. The declaration of the decedent made on November 22d that she was going out with Frank that evening stated a present intention to do an act in the future. Certainly it was a natural utterance made under circumstances which could create no suspicion of untruth in the statement of her intent. It did not necessarily refer to the defendant as the person named. But the defendant was called "Frank" as a nickname and he registered as Frank at the hotel where he lived. The defendant admittedly had been entertaining the decedent. Manifestly that fact, together with other corroborating circumstances, bore directly on the question of the relevancy of the declaration. Unquestionably the deceased's statement of her intent and the logical inference to be drawn therefrom, namely, that she was with the defendant that night, were relevant to the issue of the guilt of the defendant. But the declaration was not the only fact from which an inference could be drawn that the deceased was with the defendant that night. Other facts were in evidence from which the inference could reasonably be drawn. The cumulation of facts corroborative of the guilt of the defendant was sufficient to indicate that the trial court did not err in admitting the declaration. . . .

The judgment and the order are affirmed.

GIBSON, C. J., and CURTIS, CARTER, and SCHAUER, JJ., concurred.

TRAYNOR, JUSTICE (dissenting). It is my opinion that the trial court erred in admitting the testimony that the deceased said on November 22d that she was going out with "Frank" that evening. A declaration of intention is admissible to show that the *declarant* did the intended act, if there are corroborating circumstances and if the declarant is dead or unavailable and hence cannot be put on the witness stand. See McBaine, Admissibility in California of Declarations of Physical or

Mental Condition, 19 Cal.L.Rev. 231, 371, 378. A declaration as to what one person intended to do, however, cannot safely be accepted as evidence of what another probably did. See Maguire, The Hillmon Case — Thirty Three Years After, 38 Harv.L.Rev. 709, 717, 719. The declaration of the deceased in this case that she was going out with Frank is also a declaration that he was going out with her, and it could not be admitted for the limited purpose of showing that she went out with him at the time in question without necessarily showing that he went with her. In the words of Mr. Justice Cardozo, "Discrimination so subtle is a feat beyond the compass of ordinary minds. The reverberating clang of those accusatory words would drown all weaker sounds. It is for ordinary minds, and not for psychoanalysts, that our rules of evidence are framed." Shepard v. United States, 290 U.S. 96, 104, 54 S.Ct. 22, 25, 78 L.Ed. 196. Such a declaration could not be admitted without the risk that the jury would conclude that it tended to prove the acts of the defendant as well as of the declarant, and it is clear that the prosecution used the declaration to that end. There is no dispute as to the identity of the deceased or as to where she was at the time of her death. Since the evidence is overwhelming as to who the deceased was and where she was when she met her death, no legitimate purpose could be served by admitting her declarations of what she intended to do on the evening of November 22d. The only purpose that could be served by admitting such declarations would be to induce the belief that the defendant went out with the deceased, took her to the scene of the crime and there murdered her. Her declarations cannot be admitted for that purpose without setting aside the rule against hearsay.

The evidence in question was so damaging to the defendant that it cannot reasonably be said that it probably had no effect on the jury's verdict. People v Putnam, 20 Cal.2d 885, 892, 893, 129 P.2d 367.

EDMONDS J., concurred.

UNITED STATES v. ANNUNZIATO
United States Court of Appeals, Second Circuit, 1961.
293 F.2d 373, cert. den. 368 U.S. 919, 7 L.Ed.2d 134.

FRIENDLY, CIRCUIT JUDGE. The trial of this seemingly simple criminal case, involving an alleged violation of 29 U.S.C.A. § 186(b), which at the time made it unlawful "for any representative of any employees who are employed in an industry affecting commerce to receive or accept, or to agree to receive or accept, from the employer of such employees any money or other thing of value," has raised a host of problems, to the proper solution of which the Government's seven page brief, filed, in violation of our Rule 15(a), 28 U.S.C.A. on the eve of the argument, has rendered almost no assistance.

In 1957 the Terry Contracting Company, Inc., a New York City concern, was engaged in constructing the Connecticut Turnpike in Bridgeport, using materials from outside the state. Annuziato was business agent for the International Union of Operating Engineers, members of which were engaged in work on the site. The indictment alleged two violations of 29 U.S.C.A. § 186(b) by Annunziato — the receipt of $300 on or about July 3, 1957, and the receipt of $50 on or about December 24, 1957. Prior to trial the Government filed and information charging him with the same offense stated in the second count; without objection on his part, Count 2 of the indictment was nolled and Count 1 and the information were tried together. The jury brought in a verdict of guilty on the former, of not guilty on the latter. The court gave Annunziato the maximum prison sentence, one year, and imposed a fine of $2,500 plus costs of prosecution, 29 U.S.C.A. § 186(d).

The Government's proof on Count 1 was presented primarily through five employees of the Terry company, hereafter Terry, whose testimony can be summarized as follows. . . .

(3) *William ("Bill") Mayhew* was in general charge of all Terry construction projects. In June, 1957, the president of Terry was Harry Terker, deceased at the time of trial.

Mayhew was permitted to testify over objection that in the summer of 1957, on a day before he was scheduled to make a trip to New Haven, Harry Terker gave him a small manila envelope to deliver to the business agent for the operating engineers at Bridgeport. Mayhew asked the purpose; Harry Terker replied "It's for a commitment that I have made." When Mayhew demurred, Terker said, "Well, I have made the commitment, and I would like to keep up with it, and I would like you to do it, to take it with you, since you are going to New Haven." Arriving at Bridgeport, Mayhew and Wolf entered the trailer office. Annunziato came in and identified himself; Mayhew sought to introduce him to Wolf and proposed going out for a cup of coffee. Annunziato "said that he had not come for a social call; he was not interested in going for coffee." Mayhew handed the small envelope to Annunziato, who put it in his pocket. The envelope was about half an inch thick and flexible.

(4) *Ralph Cohen* was comptroller of Terry. He identified a Cash Voucher dated June 28, 1957, for $300, bearing the name "B. Mayhew" at the top and reading "Job #719, Sundries." It also bore the legend "Receipt of above is hereby acknowledged," with Cohen's initials. If in fact Cohen had given the money to Mayhew, he would have made Mayhew sign the receipt; instead Cohen had put it in an envelope and given it to Harry Terker. Cohen was allowed to testify, over objection, that Harry Terker had told him to draw the petty cash "for Mr. Mayhew's use to pay somebody" on the job.

(5) *Richard Terker,* son of Harry Terker, had been secretary and treasurer of Terry; after his father's death he became president. He was allowed, over objection, to testify to a luncheon conversation with his father late in June or early in July, 1957. The father informed the son "that he had received a call from Mr. Annunziato" and "that he had been requested by Mr. Annunziato for some money on the particular project in question, the Bridgeport Harbor Bridge. I asked him what he intended to do, and he had agreed to send some up to Connecticut for him." Cross-examination developed that the sum of money mentioned was $250....

Our statement of the evidence has surely presaged another and more serious set of attacks — alleged violations of the hearsay rule. Appellant asserts this with respect to Mayhew's testimony that Harry Terker asked him to take the money to Bridgeport in order to keep a commitment that Terker had made to Annunziato, to Cohen's testimony that Harry Terker told him to draw $300 "For Mr. Mayhew's use to pay somebody" on the Bridgeport job, and, most importantly, to Richard Terker's account of his luncheon talk with his father.

We need not tarry long over the first two statements. These fall so clearly within Professor Morgan's sixth class, "Cases in which the utterance is contemporaneous with a non-verbal act, independently admissible, relating to that act and throwing some light upon it," A Suggested Classification of Utterances Admissible as Res Gestae, 31 Yale L.J. 229, 236 (1922), see Beaver v. Taylor, 1863, 1 Wall. 637, 642, 17 L.Ed. 601; Lewis v Burns, 1895, 106 Cal. 381, 39 P. 778; Shapiro v. United States, 2 Cir., 1948, 166 F.2d 240, 242, certiorari denied 1948, 334 U.S. 859, 68 S.Ct. 1533, 92 L.Ed. 1779; McCormick, Evidence (1954), pp. 586–587, that we do not need here to consider other possible grounds of admissibility.

Richard Terker's account seems to have been admitted on the basis that his father's luncheon statement was a declaration of a co-conspirator; the Government now seeks to sustain admissibility both on that ground and as a declaration of the father's intention. We think it was admissible on both grounds.

If the manila envelope had popped out of Harry Terker's wallet as he was settling the luncheon check and Harry had told Richard "This is money I'm sending up to Annunziato," admissibility would clearly follow from the combination, logically unassailable although practically debatable, of two principles, "that the existence of a *design* or *plan to do* a specific act is relevant to show that the act was probably done as planned" and that the plan or design may be evidenced, under an exception to the hearsay rule, "by the *person's own statements* as to its existence." 6 Wigmore, Evidence (3d ed.), pp. 79–80; Mutual Life Ins. Co. of New York v. Hillmon, 1892, 145 U.S. 285, 295, 12 S.Ct. 909, 36 L.Ed. 706. The question is whether a different result is demanded because here the declarant accompanied his statement of future plan with an altogether natural explanation of the reason, in the very recent past, that had prompted it.

We do not think such nicety is demanded either by good sense or by authority. State v. Farnam, 1916, 82 Or. 211, 161 P. 417; People v. Alcalde, 1944, 24 Cal.2d 177, 148 P.2d 627. As Professor Morgan has pointed out, Basic Problems of Evidence (1954), p. 293, the famous letter from Walters, oral evidence of which was held admissible in the Hillmon case, was actually a declaration of Walters' intention not simply to travel to Colorado but to travel with Hillmon, and the inference the jury would almost certainly draw was that this represented a previous arrangement between them. Shepard v. United States, 1933, 290 U.S. 96, 103–106, 54 S.Ct. 22, 23, 78 L.Ed. 196, does not hold that a declaration of design is rendered inadmissible because it embodies a statement why the design was conceived. In that case there was no relevant declaration of design; the statement, "Dr. Shepard has poisoned me", was wholly of past fact and was offered and received as a dying declaration, erroneously as the Supreme Court held. In Mr. Justice Cardozo's words, the Government "did not use the declarations by Mrs. Shepard to prove her present thoughts and feelings, or even her thoughts and feelings in times past ... The testimony ... faced backward and not forward ... at least ... in its most obvious implications." Here the "most obvious implications" of Harry Terker's statement looked forward — he was going to send money to Bridgeport. To say that this portion of his statement is sufficiently trustworthy for the jury to consider without confrontation, but that his reference to the telephone call from Annunziato which produced the decision to send the money is not, would truly be swallowing the camel and straining at the gnat. The "vigorous leap" with respect to the hearsay exception for declarations of state of mind was taken when this was extended from cases where "it is material to prove the state of a person's mind, or what was passing in it, and what were his intentions," Sugden v. St. Leonards, L.R. 1 P.D. 154, 251 (1876), as to which the declaration may well be the most reliable evidence attainable, to cases where the state of mind is relevant only to prove other action, where it surely is not. See Maguire, The Hillmon case — Thirty-Three Years After, 38 Harv.L.Rev. 709, 714 (1925); Hutchins and Slesinger, State of Mind to Prove an Act, 38 Yale L.J. 283, 284–288 (1929). True, inclusion of a past event motivating the plan adds the hazards of defective perception and memory to that of prevarication; but this does not demand exclusion or even excision, at least when, as here, the event is recent, is within the personal knowledge of the declarant and is so integrally included in the declaration of design as to make it unlikely in the last degree that the latter would be true and the former false. True also, the statement of the past event would not be admitted if it stood alone, as the Shepard case holds; but this would not be the only hearsay exception where the pure metal may carry some alloy along with it. See 5 Wigmore Evidence (3d ed.) § 1465, and cases cited, and American Law Institute, Model Code of Evidence, Rule 509(2), for the application of such a principle under the hearsay exception for statements of fact against interest—an exception that would itself be applicable here but for the rather indefensible limitation that it does not relate to statements only against penal interest, see Wigmore, § 1476, American Law Institute, Model Code of Evidence, Rule 509(1)....

Affirmed.

PRESTON v. COMMONWEALTH
Court of Appeals of Kentucky, 1966.
406 S.W.2d 398.

PALMORE, JUDGE. Britton Preston and Melvin Caldwell were jointly indicted, tried and convicted of armed robbery and sentenced to life imprisonment. KRS 433.140. They appealed.

According to the evidence presented in support of the indictment, one George B. Blanton and two friends, William C. Powers and Smith Kelly, Jr., were drinking beer in the kitchen of Blanton's home in the Green Rock neighborhood of Johnson County, Kentucky, during the late hours of Saturday night, June 6, 1964, and until shortly after midnight, when someone knocked at the front door, which was located in an adjoining room. Kelly went to the door and in a moment returned and said to Powers, "Let's get out of here." As Powers made his way to the front door he met and passed a man coming in. At the trial he expressed the belief that this man was the appellant Caldwell, though he would not positively swear to it. Powers got into his automobile with Kelly and undertook to leave the premises, but in backing out he accidentally "let the wheel drop back over the hill." When this happened he said to Kelly, "Get the jack and jack the car up," to which Kelly replied, "Let's get out of here, they are robbing George B." Powers then said, "Well, give me the gun out of the glove compartment," but at that point a man standing at the corner of Blanton's house, whom Powers could not identify, said, "Buddy, you stay out of it," and fired a shot, whereupon Powers "fell over the fence and laid in the creek until they brought George B. out of the back of the house, and was pushing him up the road and telling him to run," etc. The two robbers then got into their car and drove away.

Blanton testified that the first man to enter the house walked into the kitchen and struck him over the head with a pistol, got him down on the floor and took some $500 in money out of his pockets, after which he forced him to go into the other room and lie down on a bed, face down, threw a quilt over his head and told him if he moved he would be killed. Then the second man entered, and Blanton, who says he "could see out from under the cover," recognized him at once at the appellant Melvin Caldwell, whom he had known "ever since he was a baby." The two intruders proceeded to ransack the house and at length got Blanton up, took him out the back door, and at gun point forced him to walk about 100 yards up the road. According to Blanton, the two men returned to the inside of the house before leaving, though Powers says they drove away without again entering the house. Blanton then came back, ran down the road to his son's home a mile or so away, and telephoned the police.

Blanton said he never had seen or known the appellant Preston before the robbery, but that when he returned to the house immediately after his assailants had driven away, and before he ran on to his son's home, Kelly and Powers told him who he was. At the trial Blanton positively identified Britton Preston as the man who had struck him in the head with a pistol.

Smith Kelly, Jr., did not appear to testify at the trial. His identification of Preston right after the commission of the robbery was related to the jury only through Blanton's testimony, which we have already recited. The first question to arise is whether Blanton should have been permitted to relate what was told him by either Kelly or Powers. The answer is not entirely easy, as the facts make this a close case. It therefore may be well to approach it from the fundamentals.

According to Wigmore, and it is demonstrably so, courts in general have reduced the term "res gestae" to a useless and misleading shibboleth by embracing within it two separate and distinct categories of verbal statements, one of which is truly an exception to the hearsay rule and the other of which is not, the two being admissible in evidence under different principles. Wigmore on Evidence § 1767 (Vol. VI, p. 182). When the utterance of certain words constitutes or is part of the details of an act, occurrence or transaction which in itself is relevant and provable, the utterance may be proved as a verbal act, just as may be a visual observation of an event. This is not hearsay evidence; it is not admitted for the purpose of proving the truth of what was said, but for the purpose of describing the relevant details of what took place. One of the several qualifications for admissibility of this type of statement is that "the words must be contemporaneous with the conduct, or, in the usual phrase, must accompany the act." Id., § 1776 (Vol. VI, p. 197).

The character of utterance that is admissible as a genuine exception to the hearsay rule, also under the customary label of "res gestae," is a spontaneous exclamation, which may or may not be exactly contemporaneous with the provable act or event. Id., § 1745 et seq. (Vol. VI, pp. 131 et seq.). See Norton's Adm'r v. Winstead, 218 Ky. 488, 291 S.W. 723 (1927). See also note, Res Gestae in Kentucky, by H. E. Edmonds, 39 Ky.L.J. 200 (1950–51). "The typical case presented is a *statement or exclamation, by a participant, immediately after an injury, declaring the circumstances of the injury,* or *by a person present* at an affray, a railroad collision, or *other exciting occasion,* asserting the circumstances of it as observed by him." Wigmore on Evidence, § 1746 (Vol. VI, p. 134). This type of statement is received in a testimonial capacity as evidence of the truth of the fact asserted. Ibid.

"It will be seen that these two classes of statements or exclamations are based on very different principles, and that the question of their admissiblity must be determined by the principles applicable to the class within which they fall.... The true test in spontaneous exclamations is not when the exclamation was made, but whether under all the circumstances of the particular exclamation the speaker may be considered as speaking under the stress of nervous excitement and shock produced by the act in issue, or whether that nervous excitement has died away," etc. Keefe v. State, 50 Ariz. 293, 72 P.2d 425, 427 (1937).

"This general principle is based on the experience that, under certain external circumstances of physical shock, a stress of nervous excitement may be produced which stills the reflective faculties and removes their control, so that the utterance which then occurs is a spontaneous and sincere response to the actual sensations and perceptions already produced by the external shock. Since this utterance is made under the immediate and uncontrolled domination of the senses, and during the brief period when considerations of self-interest could not have been brought fully to bear by reasoned reflection, the utterance may be taken as particularly trustworthy (or, at least, as lacking the usual grounds of untrustworthiness), and thus as expressing the real tenor of the speaker's belief as to the facts just observed by him; and may therefore be received as testimony to those facts." Wigmore on Evidence, § 1747 (Vol. VI, p. 135).

Under the genuine "verbal act" doctrine the conduct and the verbal utterances must be by the same person, but under the spontaneous exclamation exception to the hearsay rule, "that nervous excitement which renders an utterance admissible may exist equally for a mere *bystander* as well as for the injured or injuring person, and therefore the utterances of either, concerning what they observed, are equally admissible." Id., § 1755 (Vol. VI, pp. 159–160), citing Kentucky decisions at footnote 2. The admissibility of what Powers and Kelly, or either of them, said to Blanton immediately following the robbery must, of course, be determined under the spontaneous exclamation exception to the hearsay rule. Thus it is unnecessary to consider whether they were participants or bystanders. See, however, Hemphill v. Commonwealth, Ky., 379 S.W.2d 223, 228 (1964).

The facts are not far different from those in Daws v. Commonwealth, 314 Ky. 265, 234 S.W.2d 953 (1950), in which the defendant was on trial for shooting at one Daulton with intent to kill. The incident occurred at a place 100 to 125 yards from a church. Daulton drove his truck on to the church and told several persons the defendant had shot at him. According to the opinion reversing a judgment of conviction, Daulton's statement was made "after he had driven slowly in his truck 100 to 125 yards from the place of the shooting to the Church *and after he had been at the church for three minutes."* (Emphasis added.) Hence it was held inadmissible, being neither spontaneous nor contemporaneous with the shooting. The case was distinguished from Norton's Adm'r v. Winstead, 218 Ky. 488, 291 S.W. 723 (1927), which involved about the same time lapse, on the ground that in the latter case the statement was made at the place of the shooting. On that basis, this case is more like the *Norton* case, in that the statement or statements identifying the appellants were made at the scene of the crime.

In Barton v. Commonwealth, 238 Ky. 356, 38 S.W.2d 218 (1913), on which the court relied in the *Daws* opinion, a statement made by the victim of an assault within three minutes after he had been beaten, and only 39 steps away from the place where the offense had been committed, was held inadmissible. As in *Daws,* the statement was not made right at the scene of the crime, but the court today is unwilling to draw such a tenuous distinction. Actually the *Norton* and *Barton* opinions appear to be in substantial conflict, *Daws* notwithstanding. And see Louisville & N. R. Co. v. Molloy's Adm'x, 122 Ky. 219, 91 S.W. 685,

688, 28 Ky. Law Rep. 1113 (1906), which also appears inconsistent with *Barton.*

The length of time between the event and the statement, and the distance between the scene of the event and the place where the statement was uttered, can have significance only insofar as they bear on the question of spontaneity. It is our conclusion that although the *Daws* opinion may have been justified on the theory that Daulton's statement was not spontaneous (because it was not made immediately upon his arrival at the church), the *Barton* decision was too restrictive and is unsound. Accordingly, we are of the view in the case now before us that whatever statements Powers or Kelly made to Blanton when he returned to the house following the departure of his assailants came so closely after the event that the possibility of their being fabrications, and not genuine observations, is most unlikely. The evidence does not disclose precisely how many minutes or seconds elapsed, but that kind of an estimate often is inaccurate anyway. He did return immediately, and as soon as the coast was clear. It could not have been many minutes. We hold the evidence admissible.

Appellants contend also that Powers should not have been allowed to relate (a) what was said to him by Kelly when they came out of the house and got in the car and (b) what was said and done by the unidentified man standing at the corner of the house. The first of these items of evidence clearly was admissible under the principles we have already discussed, and just as obviously the second was admissible as being merely descriptive of a part of the main event itself, the robbery (the man at the corner of the house being one of the participating actors)....

The judgment is affirmed.

KINSEY v. STATE
Supreme Court of Arizona, 1937.
49 Ariz. 201, 65 P.2d 1141, 125 A.L.R. 3.

[Appeal from conviction of second degree murder by abortion. The state offered in evidence a statement made by the defendant, by introducing the testimony of two official stenographers, each of whom took down a part of the statement in shorthand. Both testified that they took down correctly what the defendant said and were allowed, over objection, to read from typewritten transcripts of their shorthand notes. Each testified that his memory was not so refreshed that he could testify independently of the transcript.]

LOCKWOOD, JUDGE. . . . The fundamental question before us is the extent to which a written record of a statement made or act done, which was reduced to writing at the time by or under the direction of a person who actually heard the statement or saw the act, may be used in evidence. . . . In the early English cases, the distinction between the use of the memorandum as an aid to recollection and its use as evidence of past recollection was hardly appreciated, but by the middle of the eighteenth century, these courts generally permitted the use of the memorandum itself as a direct evidence of past recollection recorded. As was said in Starkie on Evidence, 176: "The law goes further, and in some instances, permits a witness to give evidence as to a fact although he has no present recollection of the fact itself. This happens, in the first place, where the witness, having no longer any recollection of the fact itself, is yet enabled to state that at some former time, and whilst he had a perfect recollection of a fact, he committed it to writing. If the witness be correct in that which he positively states from a present recollection, viz. that at a prior time he had a perfect recollection, and having that recollection, truly stated it in the document produced, the writing, though its contents are thus but mediately proved, must be true." Notwithstanding this, for a long time many members of the bar did not seem to appreciate the difference between a present recollection revived and a past recollection recorded. This was probably due to the fact that the loose term of "refreshing the memory" was applied both to the renewal of a present actual memory and to the adoption of a past recorded memory. The impropriety of the use of the term to "refresh the memory of the witness," when a past recorded recollection was in question, was well pointed out in the case of Talbot v. Cusack, 17 Ir.C.L. 213: ". . . that is a very inaccurate expression; because in nine cases out of ten the witness' memory is not at all refreshed; he looks at it again and again, and he recollects nothing of the transaction; but, seeing that it is in his own handwriting, he gives credit to the truth and accuracy of his habits, and, though his memory is a perfect blank, he nevertheless undertakes to swear to the accuracy of his notes."

The question arose early in the American courts, and the legitimacy of the use of the third method was promptly adopted in regard to certain types of events, such as the subscribing witness to a will, a protest by a notary public, and similar matters. Pearson v. Wightman, 1 Mill Const. (S.C.) 336, 344, 12 Am.Dec. 636; Haig v. Newton, 1 Mill Const. (S.C.) 423; Shove v. Wiley, 18 Pick. (Mass.) 558. The difference between present recollection revived and past recollection recorded is well set forth in the case of Davis v. Field, 56 Vt. 426: "Nor was it necessary that the witnesses should have had an independent recollection. . . . The old notion that the witness must be able to swear from memory is pretty much exploded. All that is required, is, that he be able to swear that the memorandum is correct. . . . There seems to be two classes of cases on this subject: 1. Where the witness, by referring to the memorandum, has his memory quickened and refreshed thereby, so that he is enabled to swear to an actual recollection; 2. Where the witness, after referring to the memorandum, undertakes to swear to the fact, yet not because he remembers it, but because of his confidence in the correctness of the memorandum. In both cases the oath of the witness is the primary, substantive evidence relied upon; in the former, the oath being grounded on actual recollection, and in the latter, on the faith reposed in the verity of the memorandum." . . .

Notwithstanding this very forceful and logical reasoning, the American authorities are in hopeless conflict upon the question whether a past recorded recollection of events in general is admissible, but a majority, and we think the better considered, opinions, in civil cases at least, uphold the rule of the admissibility of such memoranda of past recollection recorded when the witness who made them or under whose direction they were made testifies (a) that he at one time had personal knowledge of the facts, (b) that the writing was, when made, an accurate record of the event, and (c) that after seeing the writing, he has not sufficient present independent recollection of the facts to testify accurately in regard thereto. 70 C.J. 595–598, and notes. This rule has been applied more sparingly in criminal cases, but even there, we think the better considered cases uphold it. . . .

Regardless of the weight of the authority on the question, it seems to us that upon every principle of logic and common sense, evidence of this class should be admissible. It is an undisputed and undisputable fact that the human memory weakens with the passage of time, more with some individuals, less with others, but to some extent with all, and that a written record, unless changed by extrinsic forces, remains the same for all time. It would seem, then, that such a record, made contemporaneously with the event by a witness who was honest and capable of observing accurately what happened, would be far better proof of the true facts than the present recollection of that same witness six months later, whether unrefreshed or refreshed by some extrinsic aid, but still in the last resort presumably independent in its nature.

There are but two objections to the use of evidence which have been seriously urged. The first is that it is hearsay in its nature, and the second, that the witness who vouches for the record cannot be properly cross-examined. We think both of these objections are without foundation. The recorded memory of the witness is just as much the statement of that witness as to what he personally saw or heard as is his present independent recollection of the same fact. We think the confusion as to hearsay has arisen from cases where it was endeavored to prove the authenticity of the memorandum which was offered in evidence by some person other than the one who made it or under whose direction it was made. In such a case, of course, the memorandum would be hearsay just as much as if there were an attempt to prove by a third person an oral statement of the person who made the memorandum, in regard to the facts in issue. But when the person who witnessed the event testifies to the accuracy of the memorandum as made, that memorandum is just as much direct and not hearsay evidence as the language of the witness when he testifies to his independent recollection of what he saw. The objection in regard to cross-examination, on its face, might seem to have some weight, but we think a careful analysis of the question will show that it also is unfounded. What is the purpose of cross-examination? Obviously it is to convince the triers of fact, in some manner, that the testimony of the witness is untrue, for if the cross-examiner accepts it as true, there will be no need nor desire for cross-examination. How, then, may the truthfulness of the evidence of a witness be attacked through cross-examination? It seems to us that all attacks thereon must be reduced to one of three classes: (a) Upon the honesty and integrity of the witness; (b) upon his ability to observe accurately at the time the incident occurred; and (c) upon his accuracy of recollection of the past events. When a witness testifies as to his present recollection, independent or revived, he may, of course, be cross-examined fully on all three of these points. When he testifies as to his past recollection recorded, he can be examined to the same extent and in the same manner as to the first and second of these matters. He cannot well be cross-examined on the third point, but this is unnecessary, for he has already stated that he has no independent recollection of the event, which is all that could be brought out by the most rigid cross-examination on this point when the witness testifies from his present recollection, independent or revived. . . .

We hold, therefore, that memoranda of statements made and acts done, when such memoranda are made at the time by witnesses to the statements or acts, and such witnesses testify to the accuracy of the memoranda, are admissible to prove such statements or acts to the same extent as the oral testimony of such witnesses, based on their independent recollection thereof. It was therefore permissible to admit the transcript of the reporter's notes itself in evidence, and if such was the case, certainly there was no reversible error in permitting the witness who made the notes to read them to the jury. In all such circumstances, however, the procedure followed, in this case, of permitting opposite counsel to examine the transcript fully before it was read to the jury, must be followed and, of course, cross-examination permitted in the usual manner. It is contended that the original shorthand notes themselves should have been produced and offered in evidence. They might have been used on cross-examination for the purpose of testing the accuracy of the transcript, but, in view of the fact that the original notes would be figuratively, if not literally, "so much Greek" to the average jury, and even counsel, we can see no reason why it was essential to offer the originals themselves in evidence, if the witness testified that the transcript was a true and accurate transcript of the original notes. . . .

Affirmed.

STATE v. SUTTON
Supreme Court of Oregon, 1969.
450 P.2d 748.

HOLMAN, JUSTICE. Defendant was convicted of drunken driving and appealed.

His sole assignment of error was the receipt into evidence of a checklist used by a police officer in the operation of a breath analysis machine when he conducted a test upon defendant's breath. The checklist was one furnished by the State Board of Health for the use of police officers to assure the machine's correct operation. Proper operation of the machine requires certain steps to be taken in sequence and the officer checks each step off the list as he performs it. The officer testified to the successive steps he took in the machine's operation and that he used the checklist introduced in evidence in doing so. He said that he checked off each step as he performed it and then signed the checklist when the test was completed. He also testified that he used the list in aid of his testimony for the purpose of refreshing his present recollection.

Defendant contends the admission into evidence of the checklist was error because, in effect, it put into evidence twice the testimony of the witness. He also contends that a writing used to refresh present recollection is not admissible in evidence and that a writing is not admissible as past recollection recorded unless the witness has no present recollection of its subject matter.

The use of a writing to refresh present recollection does not make it admissible in evidence. Hall v. Brown, 102 Or. 389, 393, 202 P. 719 (1921); Manchester Assur. Co. v. Oregon R. R. Co., 46 Or. 162, 166–167, 79 P. 60, 69 L.R.A. 475 (1905); Friendly v. Lee, 20 Or. 202, 205, 25 P. 396 (1890). The witness's independent recollection is the evidence—not the writing which aided in refreshing that recollection.

The writing in question met all but one of the qualifications of past recollection recorded. The witness identified the written memorandum, recalled the making of it at the time of the event when his recollection was fresh, and testified as to its accuracy. He did not say "it was accurate" but he testified to the actual performance of each step reflected in the memorandum. This testimony would qualify the writing to be received in evidence except for a rule, adopted in Oregon and many other states that, before a memorandum of past recollection recorded may be received in evidence, the witness must have no present recollection of the subject matter of which the memorandum is a record. . . .

We have come to the conclusion that the above and similar cases are in error which held that the absence of a present recollection by the writer is a prerequisite to the receiving in evidence of a past recollection recorded. Professor Wigmore has put his finger upon the fallacy in our present rule. In disapproving such a rule he states:

". . . Is the use of past recollection necessary (1) because in the case in hand there is not available a present actual recollection in the specific witness, or (2) because in the usual case a faithful record of past recollection, if it exists, is more trustworthy and desirable than a present recollection of greater or less vividness?

"The latter view, it would seem, is more in harmony with general experience, as well as with the attitude of the judges who early vindicated the use of past recollection. A faithful memorandum is acceptable, not conditionally on the total or partial absence of a present remnant of actual recollection in the particular witness, but *unconditionally*; because, for every moment of time which elapses between the act of recording and the occasion of testifying, the actual recollection must be inferior in vividness to the recollection perpetuated in the record." (Emphasis theirs.) Wigmore Evidence (3d ed.) 76 § 738.

In footnote 1 under the same section Wigmore states as follows:

"Thus even though the witness has testified from present recollection, he may *also introduce a book or memorandum* which satisfies the ensuing rules [rules concerning past recollection recorded]. This record serves to corroborate his present testimony; common sense dictates this. . . ." (Emphasis theirs.)

Also see Jordan v. People, 151 Colo. 133, 376 P.2d 699, 702–703 (1962); Hull v. State, 223 Md. 158, 162 A.2d 751, 759–760 (1960).

We are satisfied that the checklist was admissible and that no error was committed.

The judgment of the trial court is affirmed.

PEOPLE v. ZALIMAS
Supreme Court of Illinois, 1925.
319 Ill. 186, 149 N.E. 759.

DUNN, C. J. Bernice Zalimas was convicted in the criminal court of Cook county of the murder of her husband, Dominick Zalimas, by poison, was sentenced to 14 years' imprisonment in the penitentiary, and has sued out a writ of error. . . .

Charles Ruben testified that he had a drug store a few blocks from 4804 Lincoln street, and on November 8, 1924, sold some arsenic to a woman. He had no recollection of the woman, but he made a memorandum at the time of the sale of the name of the woman, the amount of arsenic, and the purpose for which it was sold. He identified the memorandum, but said he did not recall the date; that he only saw what the memorandum said; that looking at it he did not recall the name that was given him, though he did recall the purpose, which was to kill rats. He had seen Mrs. Zalimas for 3 or 4 years a great many times, but did not know her name until this case came up in court. He did not identify her as the person to whom he sold the arsenic, but testified that he could not say that he delivered the package to her and could not say whether she was the person to whom it was delivered or not. The memorandum about which he testified was admitted in evidence over the plaintiff in error's objection, and is as follows:

"November 8th, 1924.

"Bernice Zalimas, 4804 S. Lincoln Street.

"I # arsenic, to poison rats. Paid 75 cents." . . .

It is contended that the court error in admitting in evidence, over the plaintiff in error's objection, the memorandum of the witness Ruben of a sale of arsenic on November 8. Ruben had no recollection of the person to whom he sold the poison except that it was a woman. He testified that he knew the plaintiff in error by sight, had seen her a great many times for 3 or 4 years, but did not know her name, until this case came up in court, when he was told her name. When he sold the poison he did not know the name of the person to whom he sold it, and when he testified he did not recognize the plaintiff in error as the woman to whom he sold it but stated that he could not say whether she was or was not the person. After he stated that he had no independent recollection of the woman to whom he sold the poison, he was handed the memorandum and asked if, on looking at it, he recalled the day on which the arsenic was sold, and he answered that was just what he did not recall—he only saw what the memorandum said. The memorandum was not admissible as original evidence, but it was proper for the witness to use it to refresh his memory, and, after doing so, to testify to such facts as he was then able to remember. He did so testify, but his memory did not enable him to recall the purchaser either as the plaintiff in error or Bernice Zalimas. The memorandum itself was then offered in evidence, but it was not admissible. If admissible in any case, such a memorandum can be received only where the witness testifies that the facts were correctly stated in it at the time it was made. People v. Krauser, 315 Ill. 485, 146 N.E. 593; Diamond Glue Co. v. Wietzychowski, 227 Ill. 338, 81 N.E. 392. The witness did not and could not so testify. He did not know the name of the purchaser, but inserted in the memorandum the name which the unknown purchaser chose to give him. It was error to admit the memorandum in evidence, and there was no evidence connecting the plaintiff in error with the purchase of arsenic.

Reversed and remanded.

GLOSSARY

ACQUIT   To judicially determine that a person is not guilty of a crime.

ADMISSIBLE EVIDENCE   Evidence that may properly be received into a trial and considered by the jury.

ADMISSION   A statement made by a person who is suspected of committing a crime that falls short of being a confession in that the person only admits a portion of the act and not the entire act.

ADMONITION   Advice given orally to the jury respecting their duty. A warning given usually by the judge to any party.

AFFIANT   The person (usually a peace officer) who is swearing to an affidavit for a search warrant.

AFFIDAVIT   A written declaration confirmed by an oath.

AFFIRM   To establish a judgment or decree of a lower court.

ANCIENT DOCUMENT DOCTRINE   A rule that allows into a court trial an ancient writing, which is defined as a writing that is 20–30 years of age and has been geneally relied upon by the parties to the writings. (See your local rules as to how old the document must be.)

APPEAL   The method by which either side that legally can takes a final determination made by a trial judge to a higher court.

APPELLANT   The person who requests an appeal of a case.

ARGUMENTATIVE QUESTION   A question asked by an attorney of a witness that appears to be stated as if the attorney is arguing with the witness.

ARRAIGNMENT   The first appearance in court of a person who has been formally charged with a crime. At this appearance, the defendant is asked to plead to the charge.

ASSERTIVE CONDUCT   An act of conduct which is intended to take the place of verbal communication.

AUTHENTICATE   To prove that an item is real or true. Usually done in attempting to introduce a writing. A witness will testify that he made it or saw it made and that the writing being used in the trial is the same one.

BALLISTICS   The science of studying projectiles (bullets) to determine if they were fired from a certain weapon.

BEST EVIDENCE RULE   The rule that only the original writing may be introduced into court. This rule only applies to private writings.

BREATHALYZER   A machine that measures the amount of alcohol consumed by a person.

BURDEN OF GOING FORWARD   When the prosecutor has proven the corpus delicti of a crime, the burden of going forward then shifts to the defense to attempt to prove the defendant did not commit the crime.

BURDEN OF PROOF (PERSUASION)   The prosecutor must prove the crime was committed by the defendant. Therefore the burden of proof as to guilt is with the prosecution. The prosecution must prove the entire corpus delicti of the crime. Who has met his burden of proof is not known until the decision is rendered, either by the judge or the jury.

CERTIORARI, WRIT OF   An order issued by a higher court to a lower court directing the lower court to cease any further proceedings in a certain case and send all the records pertaining to that case to the higher court for review. Only issued after one of the parties has filed for this writ in the higher court.

CHARACTER EVIDENCE   Testimony relating to the general reputation of a witness or defendant in either the community where that person lives or the community where he works.

CIRCUMSTANTIAL EVIDENCE   Facts from which the jury may infer other facts that reasonably follow.

COMPETENT WITNESS   A witness who is legally qualified to give testimony in court. One who understands his duty to tell the truth and has some knowledge of relevant material and can communicate that to the court.

COMPOUND QUESTION   A question asked of a witness that is really two questions.

CONCLUSIVE EVIDENCE   Facts in evidence which, as a matter of law, determine an issue.

CONCLUSIVE PRESUMPTION   A presumption drawn from specific facts that the law will not permit to be rebutted by other evidence.

CONFESSION   Either out of court (extrajudicial) or in court. A statement given by an accused to a crime in which he admits all elements of the crime.

CONTEMPORANEOUS SEARCH   A search made at or near the scene of the arrest and at or near the time of the arrest.

CONTRABAND   Items which some law prohibits a person from possessing under any conditions.

CORPUS DELICTI   The elements of a crime that must be proven to establish guilt.

CORROBORATIVE EVIDENCE   Evidence which bolsters other evidence already introduced into a trial.

CRIMINALIST   A person who has studied criminalistics and analyzes evidence in a crime lab.

CRIMINALISTICS   The science of comparing items to determine if they are the same or from the same source or to determine the source.

CROSS-EXAMINATION   Questions asked of a witness after the witness has answered questions from the attorney that called him to the witness stand. Questions on cross-examination are always put to the witness by the attorney who did not call the witness.

CUMULATIVE EVIDENCE   Evidence that does not add to nor deduct from evidence that has already been introduced.

DECISIONAL LAW   Case law that previously has been decided by a higher court.

DEFENSE   The case presented by the defendant to answer the charges placed against him by the prosecutor.

DEGREE OF PROOF   The amount of evidence necessary to establish the truth of an element to a crime or to defend a person of a crime. In a criminal case, the degree of proof must be beyond a reasonable doubt.

DEMONSTRATIVE EVIDENCE   Evidence that serves as a visual aid to the jury. Usually the same as real evidence.

DEPOSITION   Written testimony of a witness given under oath before the trial. All parties except the judge are present.

DIRECTED VERDICT   Situation in which the judge directs the jury to come in with a given verdict, since the evidence could not support any other finding as a matter of law.

DIRECT EVIDENCE   Evidence that proves a point without need for other evidence from which to draw inferences.

DIRECT EXAMINATION   Questioning of a witness by the attorney who called that witness to testify.

DOCUMENTARY EVIDENCE   Usually a writing, tape recording, videotape, X-ray film, or photograph.

DYING DECLARATION   An exception to the Hearsay Rule. Made by a person who is dying from a wound caused by a person committing a crime. The dying person makes a statement concerning that crime.

EVIDENCE   The means by which any fact may be established or disproved.

EVIDENTIARY RULES   Rules established by each state for the orderly collection and introduction of evidence into a trial.

EXCLUSIONARY RULES   Rules developed by each state for keeping certain items from being used in a trial. Some of the rules have been developed by court decisions and are not statutory.

EXONERATE   To find one not guilty of a wrong.

EXPERT TESTIMONY   Testimony by a person who has some special knowledge, experience, or training in a field that is unknown to the ordinary reasonable man. If the person is established as an expert due to his special education, training, or experience, he may give an opinion on a matter within his speciality.

FELONY   A serious crime, usually one that will result in a person going to a state prison if found guilty.

FIELD SHOWUP   Situation in which the police find a person in the vicinity of a criminal act shortly after the crime has been committed and that person is returned to the scene of the crime for identification or a victim or witness is brought to his location for viewing.

FOREIGN LAW   Law of another state or country.

FRISK   The running of the officer's hands over the outer clothing of a person stopped in the field on probable cause in an attempt to insure that that person does not have a weapon on his person.

"FRUIT OF THE POISONOUS TREE"   An item of evidence acquired by a law enforcement officer which is only acquired due to a prior illegal search or confession.

FRUITS OF THE CRIME   The item or items taken or acquired by a person committing a crime, such as money, a TV set, and so forth.

GAS CHROMATOGRAPH   A machine used to determine the alcohol content in a person's system.

HABITUAL CRIMINAL STATUTE   A state law which allows for increased punishment for a person who has previously been convicted of a certain number of felony crimes.

HANDWRITING EXEMPLAR   A sample of a person's handwriting obtained by a peace officer for the purpose of comparison.

HEARSAY   An out-of-court statement or act that is now being offered into a court trial for the purpose of proving that what was said or written out of court is true.

HEARSAY RULE   A general rule that hearsay is not admissible unless an exception is written into the evidence rules.

IMMATERIAL   Not essential or important.

IMPEACHMENT OF A WITNESS The discrediting of a witness's testimony by other testimony or evidence that tends to show that the first witness was not telling the truth or does not know what occurred.

IN CAMERA HEARING A hearing held to determine if a privilege exists in which a peace officer may refuse to identify an informant or any other issue involving a state secret. This hearing is held in the judge's chambers without the defense attorney or defendant being present.

INCOMPETENT Evidence which is not admissible under the evidence rules or a person who is not physically or mentally competent as a witness.

INFERENCE A deduction which the law allows the jury to make based upon other evidence being introduced into the trial. A reasonable assumption of a fact deducted from another fact.

INSTRUMENTALITIES OF THE CRIME The items or tools used by a person to commit a crime.

INTERROGATION The process of questioning a person suspected of committing a crime in an attempt to elicit incriminating answers.

INTERROGATORY A set of written questions sent to a party to a court action which the party must answer under penalty of perjury and return to the other party and the court. An interrogatory may be used against a party in the trial.

IRRELEVANT Does not tend to prove or disprove any material issue in the trial.

JUDICIAL NOTICE A substitute for evidence. A method by which the judge will take mandatory or optional notice of certain well-proven and/or established facts and not allow any evidence to be introduced to prove those facts.

JURISDICTION The power of a court to try a case.

LAY WITNESS A person who is testifying from personal knowledge of a fact that is relevant to the case.

LEADING QUESTION A question asked of a witness which in itself tells the witness the desired answer.

LEARNED TREATISE A book of science, law, or other educational writings generally relied upon in a certain profession.

LETTERS ROGATORY A written request from one court to another court in another jurisdiction asking the other court to call in a person and obtain answers under oath to questions submitted by the requesting court.

MANDATORY JUDICIAL NOTICE A substitute for evidence to save the court time. A statute that holds that the judge is required to take notice of certain facts and cannot allow any evidence to be introduced to prove those facts.

MATERIALITY A word that is interchangeable with *relevancy*. Evidence that will aid the jury in arriving at the truth.

MATERIAL OBJECT An object having substance that is offered into evidence.

MISDEMEANOR A petty or minor crime, one that usually results in a person paying a fine or going to a county jail for not longer than one year.

MISTRIAL In effect, that no trial has taken place. Due to prejudicial error being committed during the first trial.

MODUS OPERANDI The method that a criminal uses to commit a crime.

MOTION Either an oral or written communication to the judge requesting a ruling on a certain point.

MOTION TO STRIKE A request by an attorney to the action to have a portion or all of a witness's testimony or an item of evidence disregarded by the jury. If granted, the jury is instructed not to consider the striken item or testimony.

NIHYDRANT PROCESS TEST   A chemical test used by a criminalist to bring out writing on an object that cannot be seen with the naked eye.

NONASSERTIVE CONDUCT   An act of a person not intended to take the place of spoken words.

OBJECTION   Made by an attorney during the course of a hearing or trial in an attempt to keep out certain items of evidence or testimony. The objection must be timely and specific or it will not be allowed. If the objection is sustained, the item or testimony will not be allowed into evidence.

OFFER OF PROOF   Presenting to the judge facts to show that an item or testimony that has been objected to is relevant or admissible.

OPINION RULE   A lay person may only testify to certain limited things as to his own opinion. An expert may only give an opinion in his special field. Generally, opinions are frowned upon by the court, and a person is only allowed to testify to facts which he has personal knowledge of.

OPTIONAL JUDICIAL NOTICE   A substitute for evidence used to save the court time. A statute that leaves it to the discretion of the judge to not allow evidence on a fact which he may take optional notice of.

PAROL EVIDENCE   Oral testimony of a witness.

PAROL EVIDENCE RULE   Rule that excludes oral evidence or agreements made at or before a written contract was entered into by the parties.

PREJUDICIAL ERROR   An error made during the course of a trial in which the rights of one of the parties has been so seriously injured that a miscarriage of justice has occurred.

PREPONDERANCE OF THE EVIDENCE   The weight of the evidence. The amount of evidence which results in the jury's decision of guilt or innocence. The value of the evidence introduced.

PRESUMPTION   An inference drawn by the process of reasoning which is a rule of law established due to the probable answer based on the reasoning of ordinary men to the fact. Presumptions are either rebuttable or conclusive. A rebuttable presumption is one that must be accepted as the truth unless overcome by other evidence. A conclusive presumption is an irrebuttable conclusion of a fact established by law. Contrary evidence may not be introduced in an attempt to overcome a conclusive presumption.

PRIVILEGE   A statutory right which allows a person not to testify.

PRIVILEGED COMMUNICATION   An oral or written communication made between persons holding a privilege. This communication must be made in confidence.

PROBABLE CAUSE   The same as *reasonable cause*. That set of facts which would lead an ordinary reasonable man to believe in the existence or nonexistence of the right of an officer to make an arrest or to conduct a search.

PROBATIVE VALUE   That evidence that tends to prove an issue or does, in fact, prove an issue.

QUANTUM   The amount or quantity of evidence.

QUASI-JUDICIAL ACT   An act by the clerk of the court. A hearing or determination done under a law by a person who is not a judge but who is given power to determine certain things.

REAL EVIDENCE   An item presented to the court which is tangible in nature. Also known as *material objects*.

REASONABLE MAN TEST   A test to determine if a peace officer had probable cause to make an arrest or conduct a search; i.e., would any reasonable man in the same or similar circumstances have acted in the same manner as did the officer?

RECROSS-EXAMINATION   Examination of a witness after redirect examination has taken place.

REDIRECT EXAMINATION   Examination of a witness after cross-examination has taken place.

REHABILITATION OF A WITNESS   An attempt to impress on the jury that a witness whose credibility has been attacked by the other side is in fact telling the truth.

RELEVANT EVIDENCE   Evidence which logically tends to prove or disprove an issue in a trial. Synonymous with *materiality*.

RELIABLE INFORMANT   An informant who has previously given to a law enforcement officer reliable information which has been used and proven reliable.

REMAND   In the ordinary sense, when a case is sent back to a lower court by a higher court with instructions to consider certain additional facts.

REPORTED TESTIMONY   A exception to the Hearsay Rule. Testimony that was given prior to the present trial in a court and that was recorded or reported and transcribed.

RES GESTAE   Acts or words through which a main event speaks. Things done. Usualy used in regard to the excited utterance doctrine, which is an exception to the Hearsay Rule. Acts or words made shortly after or during an exciting event.

SEARCH WARRANT   A warrant issued by a magistrate to a peace officer to go forth and search a person and/or place for certain items and to bring those items before the court.

SECONDARY EVIDENCE   Usually a copy of a writing which cannot be found or which has been destroyed and which is being introduced to prove what the original document contained.

SELF-INCRIMINATION   Situation in which a person gives testimony or evidence to be used against himself after waving his Fifth Amendment right against having to give this evidence or testimony.

SELF-SERVING STATEMENT   A statement made by a person which tends to serve his own best interest.

SOBRIETY TEST   A test given by a peace officer to determine if a person is under the influence of alcohol or drugs.

SPONTANEOUS DECLARATION   The same as an *excited utterance*. A statement made at or near the time of an exciting event before the person making it has had time to pause and reflect upon what he is going to say. This is an exception to the Hearsay Rule.

STANDING   The right of a person to maintain that he has an interest in an item of evidence or cause of action so that he may attempt to suppress illegally seized evidence or evidence he thinks has been illegally seized.

STATUTE   A written law or rule created by a public entity having the power to make said law or rule.

STIPULATE   To agree. Usually done by the attorneys in a trial as to facts that are not disputed.

STOP-AND-FRISK When a peace officer stops a person on the street and conducts a frisk for weapons based on probable cause to believe that the person has committed or is about to commit a crime.

SUBSTANTIVE RULES Laws which define and regulate rights, such as penal statutes, as opposed to procedural rules, which regulate procedures in court.

SUGGESTIVE QUESTION A question asked of a witness which infers the desired answer. The same as a *leading question*.

TESTIMONIAL EVIDENCE Oral testimony given under oath in a court of law.

TIMELY OBJECTION An objection that is made before an item is introduced or an answer is given to a question by a witness.

TRIER OF FACT The jury.

TRIER OF LAW The judge in a trial.

UNIFORM RULES OF EVIDENCE Suggested rules written by the American Law Institute in hopes that most states will follow them for the sake of uniformity.

UNTESTED INFORMANT A person giving information to a law enforcement officer for the first time.

VOLUNTEERED STATEMENT A statement made to a peace officer by a suspect when he is not being questioned by the officer.

WAIVER The giving up of a known right.

WEIGHT OF EVIDENCE The effect and value of evidence introduced into a trial which tends to prove to the jury which verdict it should render.

WRITINGS Documents, tape recordings, videotapes, X rays, photographs, or anything which has an impression made in or on it and which can be introduced into evidence.

INDEX

Abandoned property, search of, 214–15
Admission
 adoptive, defined, 131
 coconspirators and, 295
 defined, 116, 293
 probable cause, as, 209
 by silence, 294–95, 321–25
Affiant, defined, 188
Affidavit, defined, 229, 304
Aguilar's test, 188, 245–52
Air-tight case, defined, 126
Alcohol
 confessions and, 119
 tests for determining presence of, 60–61, 75–77, 77–81 (cases)
Alibi, as conflicting evidence, 8–9
Ancient document
 defined, 304
 family history and, 303
Ancient Document Doctrine, defined, 275
Animals, trained, admissibility of evidence gained through use of, 59–60, 81–84
Appellate court, requirements for reversing a verdict, 46–47
Appliances, description of in search warrant, 228
Arraignment, delay in and confession, 120
Arrest
 defined, 207
 illegal, and confession, 120
 as pretext to search, 212
 search for confederates and, 212
 search incident to, 212
 search of person and, 212
 search of vehicles and, 216–17
 search related to, 213
Assumption, improper, 46
Attenuation, defined, 221
Authentication
 defined, 273
 handwriting, 275, 280
 official records, 275
 private records, by testimony, 275
Authority, apparent, defined, 199

Best Evidence Rule
 carbon copy and, 274
 cases, 279–80
 decisional law and, 282
 defined, 46, 273–74
 description of, 2

Best Evidence Rule (cont.)
 exceptions to, 274
 objection and, 46
 official documents and, 274
 photostatic copy and, 46
Blood tests
 for alcohol, 60–61
 for identification, 61, 86–89
 for paternity, 10, 61
Bookmaking items, description of in search warrant, 228
Burden of persuasion. *See* Burden of proof
Burden of proof
 cases, 12–13, 19–23
 character evidence and, 56
 defined, 7
Burglary, common law definition of, 8
Business machines, description of in search warrant, 228
Business record, confession as, 131

Certification, of official document, 275
Children, as witnesses, 95–96
Citizen, private, policeman as, 219
Citizen search, legality of, 219
Clothing
 inner, search of, 215–16
 outer, search of, 215
Codefendant, confession and, 132
Competence of witness, defined, 95
Conclusion, objection and, 46
Conduct
 assertive
  case, 306–9
  defined, 292
 nonassertive, defined, 292
Confession
 codefendant and, 132
 coercion in obtaining, 178–79
 corpus delicti and, 295
 defined, 116, 295
 due process clause and, 117
 involuntary, 179–82
 Miranda rights and, 295
 oral, admissibility of, 130
 restrictions on admitting, 117–21
 translation of, 131–32
 written, admissibility of, 130
Consent, valid, parties to, 213–14
Consent search
 conditions required for, 213

INDEX

Consent search (cont.)
  cotenant and, 200
  defined, 197
  minor child and, 199–200
  parolee and, 200–201
  probationer and, 201
  scope of, 200
  valid consent, 198–99
Consent to search, withdrawal of, 214
Constitution, U.S.
  Fifth Amendment, and nonassertive conduct, 293
  Fourteenth Amendment, and self-incrimination, 116
  Fourth Amendment
    defined, 186, 206
    emergency exception to, 195–96
  Sixth Amendment
    confrontation clause, case, 317–19
    described, 241
    past recollection and, 300
Contemporaneity, defined, 194
Contemporaneous, defined, 217
Corpus delicti
  confession and, 295
  defined, 7
  materiality and, 54
  objection and, 46
  prosecution and, 8–9
Corroboration
  defined, 211
  as source of probable cause, 211
Criminal record, as probable cause, 208
Cross-examination
  argumentative questions and, 103
  common law rule of, 104
  counsel's presence at lineup and, 237
  cumulative evidence and, 103
  inconsistent statements and, 108–9
  leading questions and, 103
  oral confession and, 130–31
  purpose of, 103
  right of, case, 148–51, 153–54
  scope of, 103–4
Custody, defined, 121, 296

Death
  husband-wife privilege and, 113
  privilege and, 110
Defense counsel
  presence of at photographic identification, 244
  purpose of at lineup, 237
  rights of at lineup, 236–37

Deposition
  defined, 2, 304
  as testimonial evidence, 4
Detention, illegal, and confession, 120
Direct examination
  cumulative evidence and, 103
  leading questions and, 102
  questions permissible and, 101
  repetitive questions and, 102
Directed verdict, defined, 8
Dismissal due to lack of evidence, defined, 8
Doctrine of privacy, defined, 206
Document
  defined, 4
  notarized, authenticity of, 275
Due process
  confession and, 117
  violation of in field showup, 242
Dying declaration, Hearsay Rule and, 296

Eavesdropper, and privileged communication, 111
Emergency conditions, search in, 215
Evasiveness, as probable cause, 209
Evidence
  admissibility of, defined, 1
  arrest, types of, for making, 208–10
  corroborative, defined, 5
  defined, 1
  direct, defined, 4
  hearsay, defined, 45
  immaterial, defined, 45
  introduction of, 8–9, 47–48
  irrelevant, defined, 45
  judicial notice and, 4, 281
  material objects as, 2
  past recollection, cases, 340–43
  self-serving, defined, 45
  striking from record, 44
  testimony as, 2
  things presented to the senses, 2–3
  writings as, 2
Evidence, character
  criminal prosecution and, 64–65
  cross-examination and, 73–75
  defined, 55
  impeachment of witness and, 106–8
  restrictions on, 70–73
  types of, 55
Evidence, circumstantial
  case, 23–25
  defined, 5
Evidence, cumulative
  cross-examination and, 103

Evidence, cumulative (cont.)
   defined, 5, 45
   exclusion of, 5, 102
   direct examination and, 103
Evidence, documentary
   admissibility of, 3-4
   defined, 3
   to promote recollection, case, 145-48
Evidence, inadmissible
   examples, 44
   appeal and, 46
Evidence, real
   admissibility of, 3
   attorney-client privilege and, 113
   defined, 3, 57
   identification of, 3
   testimony to authenticate, 57-58
Evidence, secondary, defined, 46, 273
Evidence, testimonial
   admissibility of, 4
   defined, 4
   lay person's opinion and, 97-99
Evidence Code, defined, 104
Exclusion, and probative value or danger, 54
Exclusionary rule
   husband-wife privilege and, 111
   relevancy rule as, 53
Expert opinion
   defined, 99
   restrictions on, 99-100
   seizure and, 232
   weight of, to jury, 100
Expert witness, impeachment of, 100
Express authority, defined, 199

Facts, easily ascertainable, defined, 284
Federal Rules of Criminal Procedure, 190
Federal Rules of Evidence
   admissions and, 294
   Best Evidence Rule and, 274
   cross-examination and, 100, 103
   exclusion of witness, 101
   factual findings of investigations and, 299
   felony conviction and impeachment, 106
   hearsay and, 101, 291
   impeachment of witness, 105
   interrogation of witnesses, 101
   juvenile convictions and impeachment, 107
   lay person's opinion rule and, 97
   materiality and, 54
   newsman privilege and, 116
   pardon, in impeachment, 106
   priest-penitent privilege and, 114

Federal Rules of Evidence (cont.)
   rehabilitation of witness and, 109
   relevancy and, 53
   search and seizure rules and, 186
   unavailability of witness and, 298
   writing, defined, 274
Field showup
   defined, 241
   requirements for, 241-42
Fingerprints, Miranda warnings and, 125
Flight, as probable cause, 209
Forcible entry
   residence search and, 218
   search warrant and, 233
Foreign language, confessions and, 131
Foreign law, defined, 283
Frisk, defined, 222
Frisking, considerations in, 223
"Fruits of the poisonous tree," 120, 186, 220-21
Furtive conduct
   as probable cause, 208-9
   search of vehicle and, 217

Garage, description of, in search warrant, 229
Governmental regulations, defined, 282

Handwriting, authentication of, 275, 280
Handwriting exemplars, 125
Handwriting identification, lay person's opinion and, 98
Hearsay
   admissibility of, 291
   declaration against interest, cases, 325-27, 327-29
   declaration of coconspirator, case, 335-37
   declaration of intent, case, 332-35
   defined, 45, 291
   dying declaration, 296, 329-32 (case)
   as evidence, 1
   oral statement, 130, 306
   prior statement and, cases, 309-17, 319-21
   search warrant and, 187
Hearsay Rule
   coconspirator admission, 295
   decisional law, 282
   defined, 44
   and dying declaration, 296
   police broadcasts and, 292
   texts and treatises and, 101
High crime area
   cause for detention, 222

INDEX

High crime area (cont.)
    as probable cause, 209
House, description of in search warrant, 227
Hypnosis, evidence reliability and, 60

Identification
    lay person's opinion and, 97
    of police informers, privilege and, 115–16
Impeachment
    by another witness' opinion, 107
    credibility, lack of, 107
    defined, 96, 105, 133
    effect of on jury, 105
    exclusion of testimony in, 106–7
    of expert witness, 100
    felony conviction and, 106
    general rule of, 105
    improper, defined, 45
    juvenile convictions and, 107
    kinship and, 107–8
    methods of, 105–8
    misconduct and, 107
    through illegally seized evidence, 186
    misdemeanor conviction and, 106
    pardon and, 106
    perceptory ability, lack of, 108
    statements in violation of Miranda, 130
Implied authority, defined, 199
In camera, defined, 115
Incompetence
    husband-wife privilege and, 111
    of witness, 45, 48–51
Inference
    defined, 9, 11
    statutory, case, 34–41
    witness, inadmissibility of, case, 137–38
Informer
    citizen
        defined, 188–89, 211
        reliability of, 232
        as source of probable cause, 211
    disclosure of, 232
    production of, 232
    reliable
        in affidavit for search warrant, 229
        defined, 188
        as source of probable cause, 211
    untested
        and affidavit for search warrant, 231
        defined, 231
        source for probable cause, 211
    Innkeepers, rights of, to consent to search, 214

Insanity
    competence as witness, case, 136–37
    confessions, 119–20
Insanity plea, character evidence and, 56
Instrumentalities, defined, 190
Interrogatories, defined, 297
Irrelevancy of evidence, defined, 45
Judicial notice
    common knowledge, case, 287–89
    defined, 281
    easily ascertainable facts, case, 285–86
    as evidence, 4
    mandatory, defined, 281
    optional, defined, 281
    scientific tests and, 59
Kinship, as grounds for impeachment, 107–8
"Knock and announce" requirements
    parolee and, 201
    residence search and, 218–19
    search warrant and, 191
Landlord, rights of, to consent to search, 214
Lay person's opinion
    rule, defined, 97
    weight of, to jury, 100
Legitimacy of issue, as conclusive presumption, 9–10
Lineup
    admonition, described, 236
    defined, 237
    and Miranda warning, 125, 236
    postindictment, defined, 236
    presence of counsel at, 235–36
    record keeping, 239
    requirements, 237, 271–72 (case)
    right to refuse to participate, 237
Mann Act, 112
Materiality
    defined, 54
    Federal Rules of Evidence and, 54
Material objects, defined, 2
Mathematical probability, admissibility of as evidence, case, 89–94
Mental condition, lay person's opinion and, 98–99
Mental incapacity and competence as witness, 96
Mercy rule, 56
Minor person, confession and, 120
Miranda rights
    case, 182–83
    confession, 295
    defined, 295–96
    waiver of, and confession, 120

Miranda rule, conditions of, 296
Miranda warning
  admission and, 294
  confession and, 119, 295
  fingerprints and, 125
  lineup and, 125, 236
  listed, 127
  repetition of, 127–28
  in search procedures, 198, 214
  voice identification and, 125
  volunteered statements and, 125
Modus operandi
  character evidence and, 55, 66 (case)
  defined, 54
  expert testimony regarding, 99
Motion to strike, defined, 44
Motor vehicle law violation, as cause for detention, 222
Multi-residence dwellings, description of in search warrant, 227

Nalline tests, 125
Narcotics
  description of in search warrant, 228
  usage as probable cause, 209
Nighttime
  as cause for detention, 221
  definition, 191, 228, 233
  search, authorization for, 228, 233

Oath, defined, 2
Objection
  general, defined, 44–45
  purpose of in court, 43
  right of discovery and, 55
  specific
    defined, 44
    waiver of privilege, 110
  timely
    defined, 44, 48
  waiver of right to, 43–44
Offer of proof, defined, 47
Official records, Hearsay Rule and, 298–300
Opinions
  admissibility of, 96–97
  defined, 96–97

Parol, defined, 275
Parole, termination of, 130
Parolee
  defined, 200
  search of, 219–20
Parol Evidence Rule, 275
Pat search
  case, 257–66
  defined, 215

Perceptory ability, impeachment and, 108
Personal knowledge of informer, defined, 231
Photographic identification
  admissibility of, 243
  at lineup, 239
  precautions in using, 243
  presence of counsel at, 244
Physical abuse and confessions, 118
Physical condition, lay person's opinion and, 98–99
"Plain error" doctrine, defined, 45
Police broadcasts
  Hearsay Rule and, 292
  as probable cause, 210–11
Police informers, 115–16
Police officers, use of in lineup, 238, 241
Polygraph test, admissibility of, 60, 84–86 (case)
Presence (in the officer's), defined, 208
Presence of other known felons, as probable cause, 210
Presumption
  conclusive
    defined, 11
    and rules of evidence, 9
  defined, 9
  rebuttable
    case, 25–34
    defined, 10, 11
    examples of common, 10–11
Previous conviction, as cause for detention, 222
Privacy, reasonable expectation of, 206, 207
Privilege
  against self-incrimination
    case, 166–69, 169–74
    defined, 116
  attorney-client
    cases, 157–63
    defined, 113
    proposed crimes and, 113–14
    real evidence and, 113
  claiming, 110
  defined, 109–10
  doctor-patient
    defined, 114
    restrictions on, 114
    waiver of, 114
  governmental official
    case, 163–66
    defined, 115
    state secrets and, 115

INDEX

Privilege (cont.)
  husband-wife
    case, 155–56
      communication and, 112–13
      death and, 113
      reasons for, 111
      restrictions on, 112
  newsman, defined, 116
  priest-penitent, defined, 114
  stipulated by statute, 110
  waiver of, 110–11
Privileged communication
  case, 133–36
  defined, 44, 45
Probable cause
  defined, 187, 205, 208
  sources of, 231
Probation, revocation of, 130
Probative danger
  defined, 59
  exclusion and, 54
Probative value
  of character evidence, 55
  defined, 53
  exclusion and, 54
  of impeachment testimony, 106
Promises, confessions and, 118
Proof
  defined, 11
  degrees of, 8
  offer of, defined, 47
Prosecution, in criminal case, defined, 8
Public offense, defined, 192

Questions
  argumentative
    cross-examination and, 103
    defined, 45, 103
  calling for conclusion, 102
  compound
    cross-examination and, 103
    defined, 45, 103
  leading
    cross-examination and, 103
    defined, 45, 102
    direct examination and, 102
  "lifesaving"
    defined, 127
    Miranda warnings and, 127
  narrative, use of, 101–2
  permissible during judicial examination
    of witness, 104–5
  prolonged, and confessions, 119

Questions (cont.)
  repetitive
    defined, 45
    use of, 102
    routine, and Miranda warnings, 124
  suggestive, defined, 45

Reasonable cause, defined, 192, 205
Reasonable man test, defined, 283
Reasonable search, 193
Receipt for seized property, 191–92
Recent neighborhood crime
  cause for detention, 221
  probable cause, 209
Recording statement, after Miranda
    waiver, 128
Recross-examination, defined, 104
Redirect examination
  defined, 104
  rehabilitation and, 109
Rehabilitation of witness
  defined, 105, 109, 133
  permissibility of, 109
  redirect examination and, 109
Relevancy
  admissibility of evidence, case, 62–65
  defined, 53
  real evidence and, 57
Relevancy rule, as exclusionary rule, 53
Remuneration, discrediting witnesses,
    100, 107
Reputation of premises, 209
Resemblance of suspect, as probable
    cause, 208
Res gestae, defined, 300
Right of discovery, 55
Rules, court, establishment of, 282
Scientific tests
  alcohol, presence of, cases, 75–81
  restrictions on admissibility of,
    case, 174–78
Search
  border, 219
  defined, 206
  exploratory
    arrest and, 213
    illegality of, 194
  of garages, 207
  illegal, and confession, 120
  incident to arrest, 212, 213, 252–57 (case)
  open fields, 207
  scope of, 214
  time of, 233
  vehicles, 216–17

Search and seizure
  emergency provisions for, 201–2
  illegal evidence and, 186
Search warrant
  affidavit and, 187, 229
  categories of property, 190
  defined, 187, 191, 225, 235
  execution of, 232–35
  forcible entry and, 233
  receipt for items, 234
  return, 234
  secrecy of, 233
  seizing unlisted items, 233
  server of, 233–34
  telephonic, legality of, 192
  uses of, 225
Search warrant law, defined, 225
Seizure, defined, 207
Self-incrimination
  Fifth Amendment and, 116
  laws against, case, 151–53
  rule, 45
Sex crimes, character evidence and, 57, 67–70 (case)
Siblings, rights of, to consent to search, 214
"Silver platter doctrine," defined, 186–87
Sobriety tests, Miranda warning and, 125
Spontaneous declarations
  case, 337–40
  defined, 297
  as evidence, 301
Statement, inconsistent
  cross-examination and, 108
  effect of, 109
State secrets, defined, 115
Stipulate, defined, 283
Stolen property, and search warrant, 228
Stopping a citizen, 221
Surprise, and exclusion, 55
Surveillance
  and Fourth Amendment, case, 266–71
  of public restrooms, 206–7
Testimony
  authenticating documentary evidence, 3
  as evidence, 2
  exclusion of, by privilege, 110
  to identify real evidence, 3
Things presented to the senses, defined, 2–3
Threats, and confessions, 118
"Totality of the circumstances," and confessions, 117
Traffic stop, regulations for, 216–17
Translation of confession, 131–32

Trial judge
  calling of witness by, case, 144–45
  dismissal and, 8
  examination of witness, 104–5
  excluding impeachment testimony, 106–7
  questioning witness, 143–44
Truth serum
  confession and, 119
  evidence reliability and, 60
Uniform Rules of Evidence
  easily ascertainable facts and, 284
  restrictions under, 2
Unusual behavior, detention and, 222
Unusual hour as probable cause, 209
Vehicle
  description
    as reasonable cause, 208
    in search warrant, 227–28
  search of, 216–17
Voice identification, Miranda warnings and, 125
Voice prints, admissibility of, 60
Voice recording, authentication of, 275
Volunteered statements
  defined, 125
  Miranda warnings and, 125
Weapons, deadly, search warrant and, 228
Witness
  admonition to
    in field showup, 242
    in lineup, 238
    in photographic identification, 243–44
  competence of, defined, 95
  expert
    admissibility of testimony of, case, 140–42
    competency of, case, 138–40
  impeachment of, defined, 96
  incompetent
    case, 50–51
    defined, 45
  judicial examination of, 104–5
  material
    defined, 211
    informer as, 232
  percipient, defined, 297
  unavailable, Federal Rules of Evidence and, 298
Writings
  defined, 2
  refreshing memory, case, 343–44